AN EGYPTIAN HIEROGLYPHIC READING BOOK

FOR BEGINNERS

AN EGYPTIAN HIEROGLYPHIC READING BOOK FOR BEGINNERS

E. A. Wallis Budge

DOVER PUBLICATIONS, INC.
New York

Published in Canada by General Publishing Company, Ltd., 30 Lesmill Road, Don Mills, Toronto, Ontario.

Published in the United Kingdom by Constable and Company, Ltd., 3 The Lanchesters, 162–164 Fulham Palace Road, London W6 9ER.

This Dover edition, first published in 1993, is an unabridged, unaltered republication of the work originally published by Kegan Paul, Trench, Trübner & Co., Ltd., London, 1896, under the title *An Egyptian Reading Book for Beginners: Being a Series of Historical, Funereal, Moral, Religious and Mythological Texts Printed in Hieroglyphic Characters Together with a Transliteration and a Complete Vocabulary*. The author credit on the original title page reads "E. A. Wallis Budge, Litt. D. (Cantab.), Keeper of the Egyptian and Assyrian Antiquities in the British Museum."

Manufactured in the United States of America
Dover Publications, Inc., 31 East 2nd Street, Mineola, N.Y. 11501

Library of Congress Cataloging in Publication Data

Egyptian reading book for beginners. English & Egyptian.
An Egyptian hieroglyphic reading book for beginners / [edited by] E. A. Wallis Budge.
p. cm.
Egyptian texts in hieroglyphs, transliteration, and English translation, with notes.
Originally published: An Egyptian reading book for beginners. London : Kegan Paul, Trench, Trübner & Co., 1896.
Includes bibliographical references.
ISBN 0-486-27486-1
1. Egyptian language—Readers. I. Budge, E. A. Wallis (Ernest Alfred Wallis), Sir, 1857–1934. II. Title.
PJ1141.E3513 1993
493′.1—dc20 92-39418
CIP

PREFACE.

OF the twenty Egyptian texts printed in the following pages, nine are taken from monuments inscribed in the hieroglyphic character, and eleven are transcripts into hieroglyphics from hieratic texts; the most ancient belongs to the period of the VIth dynasty, about B. C. 3500, and the most modern to the Ptolemaïc period, about B. C. 250. The "Inscription of Unȧ" is a fine example of the biographical texts of the VIth dynasty; the "Inscription of Khnemu-ḥetep" is a good type of a similar document of the XIIth dynasty; the inscriptions of Ḥātshepset and Rameses II. are short but excellent specimens of the historical inscriptions of the XVIIIth and XIXth dynasties; the extracts from the great Harris Papyrus illustrate the historical and religious writings of the XXth dynasty; the "Inscription of Pi-ạ̄nkhi-meri-Ȧmen" is a fine piece of narrative of the XXIVth dynasty; and the Decree of Canopus illustrates the literary composition of the Ptolemaïc period. Thus we have good and complete examples of the historical writings of the best periods of Egyptian history. Religious texts are represented by the "Hymn to Amen-Rā", a work belonging probably to the period of the XXth or XXIInd dynasty; and moral texts by the works of Kaqemna and Ptaḥ-ḥetep, both of which were written before the VIth dynasty; and funereal texts by the Stelae of Nekht-Ȧmsu, of the XVIIIth dynasty, by the "Festival Songs of Isis and Nephthys", by the "Litanies of Seker", and by the "Lamentations of Isis and Nephthys"; legal literature is illustrated by the account of the legal proceedings taken against certain robbers of royal tombs by the Egyptian Government in the time of the XXth dynasty; and of works of fiction better examples than the "Tale of the Two Brothers", and the story of the "Possessed Princess of Bekhten", and the "Travels of an Egyptian" could hardly be found. Each text is complete in itself.

This series of texts was given in my *Egyptian Reading Book,* which appeared in 1888, and although they were printed without transliterations, and without notes or explanations, they seemed to fill a want. Several friends who used the book, however, pointed out that its usefulness would have been greater if the lines of Egyptian had been broken up into words, and if a complete transliteration and vocabulary had been added. With the view of making the work as useful as possible I recopied the texts, dividing them into words, and I wrote transliterations of them and made a complete vocabulary; the result is the book now before the reader. In dividing the words I have been guided solely by the wish to make them easily distinguishable, and in transliterating them I have followed the old system sanctioned by Birch, Lepsius and others, for in spite of its defects it is, in my opinion, as good as any which has been suggested. Where possible, I have added a number of references to each word in the Vocabulary, so that the student may compare their use in several passages, for this, after all, is frequently the only way in which the true meaning of a word can be ascertained. The exact meanings of many of the words which occur in works like the "Precepts of Ptaḥ-ḥetep" can only be guessed at, and the explanations of many of them given in the vocabulary must be understood to be little more than suggestions as to their meanings; to illustrate the use of verb or noun I have erred on the side of giving too many references rather than too few. No pains have been spared to make the vocabulary complete. With the view of helping the beginner English versions of a few of the texts have been added, and it is hoped that these may smooth his way and lead him to the perusal of the others in the volume.

London, August 29th, 1896.

E. A. WALLIS BUDGE.

CONTENTS.

A transcript into hieroglyphics from the hieratic text of the D'Orbiney Papyrus, Brit. Mus. No. 10,183. The hieratic text has been published by Birch, *Select Papyri*, II, plates IX—XIX; by Moldenke, *The Tale of the Two Brothers*; and by Reinisch, *Aegyptische Chrestomathie*, Taff. 22—40. For discussions on the text and translations see *Revue Archéologique*, tom. IX, p. 385 (1st Series); *Atlantis*, vol. IV, pp. 23—57; Goodwin, *Cambridge Essays*, pp. 232—239; Brugsch, *Ein altägyptisches Märchen*,[1] p. 7 ff.; *Revue Archéologique*, N. S., t. XXXV, pp. 164—179; *Records of the Past*, Old Series, vol. II, p. 133 ff.; Groff, *Étude sur le Papyrus d'Orbiney*, Paris, 1888; Maspero, *Contes Égyptiens*, pp. 5—42.

1. This work is bound up as the second part of *Aus dem Orient*, Berlin, 1864, but it is really a separate publication, and it has its own distinct pagination.

TRANSLATIONS

The Tale of the Two Brothers.

(See pp. 1—40.)

I. Now there were once two brethren, [the children] of the same father and mother; Anpu was the name of the elder, and Bata was the name of the younger. Now Anpu had a house and a wife, and his young brother lived with him in the condition of a menial, for it was he who made clothes for him, and he used to follow and tend his cattle in the fields; it was he who did the ploughing, it was he who laboured, and it was he who carried out all the works concerning the fields. And behold, his young brother was a good farmer whose like existed not in all the land of Egypt. . . . . And for many days afterwards, his young brother used to go out after his cattle according to his daily wont, and he came back each evening to his house laden with all kinds of vegetables of the fields, which when he had returned from the meadows he placed before his great brother, who was sitting with his wife; and when he had drunk and eaten he went to bed in the cow-byre with his cattle. And at daybreak on the morrow after the bread-cakes were baked he laid them before his elder brother, and having provided himself with bread for [his need] in the fields, he drove out his cattle to let them feed in the fields. And as he tended his cattle they said to him, "In such and such a place the herbage is good," and he hearkened unto everything which they said, and he led them to the place where **II.** the herbage which they loved grew abundantly; and the cattle which were before him grew exceedingly fine, and they increased and multiplied exceedingly.

And when the season for ploughing had come, then Anpu said to Bata, "Come, let us take our teams and plough, for the land hath again appeared, and it is in good condition for ploughing; do thou then go into the fields with the grain [to-day], for we will begin to plough at daybreak to-morrow;" this was what he said to him, and his young brother did everything even as his elder brother had commanded him. And it came to pass at daybreak on the following day that they went forth into the fields with their teams, and they ploughed, and their heart was exceedingly glad by reason of their work..... And some time afterwards while they were in the fields [working] the elder brother sent the younger, saying, "Run quickly and bring wheat from the homestead;" and the younger brother found the wife of his elder brother sitting [doing] her hair, and he said to her, "Rise up and give me wheat, **III.** that I may run back to the fields, for in sending me my elder brother [wished] that no delay should be caused." And she said, "Go and open the granary, and do thou thyself carry away that which thy heart desireth, lest [if I rise up] my hair fall in going." Then the young man went into his byre and brought out a large jar, for his desire was to carry away much grain, and he filled it with wheat and barley, and as he was coming out with them she said to him, "How much hast thou on thy shoulder?" And he said to her, "Of barley three measures, and of wheat two; in all, five measures; that is what I have on my shoulder;" that is what he said to her. Then she spake unto him, saying, "There is great strength in thee, for I have watched it daily;" and her heart knew him with the desire of love, and she rose up being filled with him, and she said to him, "Prithee let us lie together for a season, and if thou wilt consent verily I will make for thee fine raiment." Then the young man became like a raging wild beast of the south with fury by reason of the shameful words which she had spoken to him; and she feared exceedingly. And the young man spake with her, saying, "Verily thou hast been in my sight as a mother, and thy husband as a father, for he is older than I, and he hath made me to live. How **IV.** shameful are the words which thou hast spoken to me! do not repeat them. I myself will not speak of them to any one, and I will not allow them to escape from my mouth to any living person;" [and thus saying] he took up his load and went into the fields, and he came to his elder brother, and they continued their toil unbrokenly.

And towards the evening the elder brother returned to his house, and the younger brother [followed] after his cattle, and he loaded himself with all the produce of the field, and drove his cattle before him to put them to bed in their byres in the homestead; and behold the wife of the elder brother was afraid by reason of the words which she had spoken, and she took rancid (?) fat, and she made herself to appear like one who hath been evilly entreated by a ravisher, wishing to say to her husband when he should return according to his daily wont at eventide, "It is thy young brother who hath treated me thus violently." And when Anpu came into his house he found his wife lying prostrate and ill like unto one on whom violence had been committed; she poured no water upon his hands, according to her daily wont, she lit no fire before him, his house was in darkness, and she was lying prostrate and sick and ill. Her husband said to her, "Who hath had converse with thee?" and she said to him, "None hath had converse with me except thy **V.** young brother. When he came to fetch corn for thee, he found me sitting by myself, and he said to me, 'Prithee let us lie together for a season; tie up thy hair.' That was what he said to me, but I did not hearken unto him. [And I said], Behold, am I not thy mother? and is not thy elder brother in thy sight as a father? That was what I said to him. And he was afraid, and he entreated me evilly that I might not tell thee of it. If thou lettest him live, I shall die, and behold, moreover, when he cometh home at eventide, inasmuch as I have told thee of his shameful words, what he will do [to me] is manifest."

And the elder brother became like a raging wild animal of the south, and having sharpened his dagger he took it in his hand,

and stood behind the door of his byre to slay his young brother when he came in there at eventide to put to bed his cattle in their stalls. And at sunset the younger brother loaded himself with field produce of all kinds according to his daily wont, and when he had come home and the leader of the herd was going into her byre, she said to her keeper, "Verily thy elder brother is standing in front of thee with his dagger [in his hand] to slay thee; flee from before him." And having heard the speech of the cow which went first, as **VI.** the second went into the byre she spake unto him in like manner, and looking under the door of his byre he saw the feet and legs of his elder brother who stood behind the door with his dagger in his hand; and setting down his load upon the ground he betook himself to flight with all speed, and his elder brother pursued him with his dagger [in his hand]. And the younger brother appealed to Rā-Harmachis, saying, "O my fair lord, it is thou who judgest wrong from right;" and Rā listened to all his words. And Rā caused a great stream filled with crocodiles to come between the young man and his elder brother, and thus one stood upon one side, and the other upon the other; and the elder brother smote his hand twice because he had not been able to slay him. That was what he did. And the younger brother called out to him from one side, saying, "Wait until daybreak, and when Aten riseth **VII.** I will plead with thee before him, for it is he that setteth the crooked straight. And as for me I shall nevermore live with thee, and I shall nevermore abide in any place wherein thou art; and I shall go to the Valley of the Cedar."

Now when it was daybreak on the morrow, and Rā-Harmachis had risen, each one looked upon the other, and the young man spake again to his elder brother, saying, "How couldst thou pursue me to slay me basely without having heard what my mouth had to say? But I am indeed thy young brother, and thou thyself hast been to me like a father, and thy wife hath been to me as a mother. And behold, when thou didst send me to bring wheat for us, did not thy wife say to me, 'Prithee let us lie together awhile?' but see, she hath turned the matter into something quite different." Then he made him to understand everything which had taken place between his wife and himself, and he took an oath by Rā-Harmachis, saying, "Verily thy lying in wait for me craftily in secret behind the door (?) with thy dagger [in thy hand] was a foul and abominable thing [to do]!" and taking a flint knife he mutilated himself and threw the piece into the water where a *nār* fish swallowed it; and **VIII.** he became weak and fainted from exhaustion. And the heart of the elder brother was smitten with exceeding great grief, and he wept loudly because he did not know how to cross over to where his young brother was by reason of the crocodiles. Then his young brother cried out to him, saying, "Behold, thou wouldst keep in remembrance one evil act, and yet thou wouldst not keep in mind either one good deed, or even one thing of all those which I have done for thee. And now, go thou to thy house and tend thine own cattle, because I will never abide in the place where thou art; I am going to the Valley of the Cedar. And as concerning that which thou shalt do for me when thou comest to minister unto me, give heed unto the account of the things which shall happen unto me. I shall enchant my heart, and I shall place it upon the top of the flower of the cedar. Now the cedar will be cut down and my heart will fall to the ground, and thou shalt come to seek for it, even though thou pass seven years in seeking it, but when thou hast found it put it in a vase of cold water, and in very truth I shall live, and make answer to him that would attack me. And thou shalt know when these things have happened unto me [by this sign]; when one putteth a vessel of beer in thy hand, and it frotheth over, tarry not when this hath actually happened to thee." And he went to the Valley of the Cedar, and his elder brother went to his house with his hand laid upon his head which was covered with dust and ashes; and when he had come into his house he slew his wife and threw her to the dogs, and he sat down in grief for his younger brother.

And it came to pass some time afterwards that the younger brother was living in the Valley of the Cedar, and that no one was with him, and he used to pass his time in hunting the beasts of the mountain, and at eventide he came to sleep under the cedar upon the top of the flowers of which was his heart. And some time **IX.** afterwards he built himself with his own hands, in the Valley of the Cedar, a house which was filled with all kinds of beautiful things, for he wished to found a house for himself. And it came to pass that as he came out from his house he met the cycle of the gods who were going forth to do their will in all the earth, and they spake to one of their number who said to Bata, "O Bata, bull of the cycle of the gods, dost thou dwell alone having fled from thy native town before the wife of Anpu, thy elder brother? Behold, he hath slain his wife, and thus hast thou returned answer to him to all the attacks [which he made] upon thee;" and their hearts grieved for him exceedingly. Then Rā-Harmachis said to the god Khnemu, "Do thou fashion a wife for Bata, that thou mayest not dwell alone"; and Khnemu fashioned a help-meet to dwell with him. Now she was more beautiful in her person than any other woman in all the earth, for every god was contained in her. And the seven Hathors came to look upon her, and they spake with one voice, saying, "Her death will be caused by the knife;" and Bata loved her with an exceeding great love, and she dwelt in his house while he passed his time in **X.** hunting the beasts of the mountain and in bringing them to lay before her. And he said to her, "Go not forth from thy house lest the stream seize thee, and I know not how to deliver thee therefrom because I myself am a woman like unto thee; for my heart is placed upon the top of the flowers of the cedar, but if another man cometh I will do battle with him therefor." And he revealed to her his whole and entire mind.

And some days after when Bata had gone out to hunt according to his daily wont, the young woman went out to walk under the cedar tree which was near unto her house, and she saw the water of the stream pursuing her, and she fled from before it into her own house; and the stream cried to the cedar, saying, "Verily I long for her." And the cedar brought [to it] a lock of her hair, and the stream carried it to Egypt and laid it upon the place of the washermen of Pharaoh, may he live, and be strong and in good health! Now the smell of the lock of hair clung to the garments of Pharaoh, and there arose strife among the washermen of Pharaoh [because] one said, "There is a smell of scent in the garments of Pharaoh:" so there arose strife among them daily, and **XI.** they knew not what they were doing, and the overseer of the washermen of Pharaoh went to the stream's side with an exceedingly sore heart on account of the strife which they made with him daily, and he placed himself there. Now he stood on the bank opposite to the lock of hair which was in the water, and he made a man go down and bring it to him, and he found the smell exceedingly pleasant, and he took it unto Pharaoh. Then the scribes and learned men of Pharaoh were brought unto him, and they said to him, "Verily this lock of hair belongeth to a daughter of Rā-Harmachis, and the essence of every god is in her; . . . . send envoys into every land to seek her, but with the envoy who is going to the Valley of the Cedar thou must send many men to bring her;" and his Majesty said, "That which ye have spoken to us is exceedingly good," and the king caused envoys to set out with all speed.

And it came to pass some time afterwards that the men who had been sent into foreign lands came to report to His Majesty, but those who had gone to the Valley of the Cedar came not with them, for Bata had slain them all except one to tell the tale to His Majesty. Then His Majesty caused men and picked soldiers and cavalry likewise to fetch [the daughter of Rā-Harmachis] and to bring her there, and there was **XII.** with them a woman who gave into her hands all kinds of beautiful trinkets for women, and this woman came to Egypt with [the daughter of Rā-Harmachis]; and there were rejoicings for her throughout the whole land. And His Majesty loved her exceedingly and made her the "Great Sacred Lady", and when one spake with her to make her tell concerning the condition of her husband, she said to His Majesty, "Prithee cut down the cedar, and thou wilt slay him;" and he caused men and soldiers to go with their axes to cut down the cedar, and they went forth to the cedar and cut off the flowers upon which was the heart of Bata, and he fell down dead at that moment.

And it came to pass at daybreak on the morrow after the cedar had been cut down, that Anpu the elder brother of Bata went into his house and sat down, and when he had washed his hands one put into them a vessel of beer which frothed over, and one gave him another vessel of wine, and it also was thick and clouded (?). Then he took his **XIII.** staff, and his sandals, and garments, together with his tools for work, and he betook himself straightway to the Valley of the Cedar, and going into his brother's house he found his young brother lying dead upon his bed. And as he looked upon his young brother lying in death, he wept, and he went to search for the heart of his young brother under the cedar where he used to lie in the evening; and he passed three years in seeking for it, but he found it not, and when the fourth year came on his heart desired to go to Egypt, and he said, "I will depart to-morrow." That was what his heart said. And it came to pass at daybreak on the following day that he walked under the cedar and passed his time in seeking it, and he returned in the evening, and again he devoted time to seeking it; and he found a fruit, and having turned it over and sought beneath it, behold the heart of his young brother. Then he brought a vessel of cold water, and placed it therein, and he sat down according to his daily wont. And it came to pass that when the night was come **XIV.** the heart had absorbed the water, and Bata trembled in all his members, and he looked at his elder brother, and his heart was helpless. Then Anpu his elder brother took the vessel of cold water in which was the heart of his young brother, [and behold], it had drunk it up, and his heart was in its proper place, and it had become to him as it had ever been; and each embraced the other, and each spake with his fellow. And Bata said to his elder brother, "Behold, I am going to turn into a great bull wholly [covered] with beautiful hair, but whose methods (?) are unknown. Sit thou upon [my] back when the Sun riseth, and when we are in the place where my wife is, I will return [to her] an answer [to all the attacks which she made upon me]. Then shalt thou take me where the King is, for all manner of good things will be done for thee, and thou shalt be laden with gold and silver because thou hast brought me to Pharaoh, for I am going to become a very marvellous thing, and there will be rejoicings on my account throughout the whole earth; then shalt thou return to thine own city."

And it came to pass **XV.** on the morrow that Bata took the form of which he had spoken to his elder brother. Then Anpu his elder brother mounted on his back at daybreak, and he came to the place where the king was, and one showed the bull to His Majesty, and he looked upon him and rejoiced in him exceedingly, and he celebrated a great festival in his honour, saying, "This which has happened is a most marvellous thing;" and rejoicings were made for him throughout the whole earth. And one loaded his elder brother with silver and gold, and he dwelt in his own city, and one gave him many men and many things, and Pharaoh loved him exceedingly, more than any one else in all the earth. And it came to pass that some time afterwards the bull went into the place of purification and stood where the sacred lady [his wife] was, and he spake with her saying, "Behold, I live in very truth;" and she said to him, "Who then art thou?" and he said to her, "I am Bata. Thou hast understood how to make Pharaoh cut down the cedar together with my dwelling-place, and hast not even allowed me to live, but behold **XVI.** I live in very truth in the form of a bull;" and the sacred lady feared exceedingly at the words which her husband had spoken unto her. And when she had come forth from the place of purification His Majesty sat with her and passed a happy day with her, and she was at His

Majesty's table, and he was exceedingly gracious unto her. And she spake unto His Majesty, saying, "Swear an oath to me in God's name, saying, 'Whatsoever thou sayest, to that will I listen';" and he listened unto everything which she spake, saying, "Give me, I pray, the liver of this bull to eat, for he will never be of any use;" this was what she said to him. And His Majesty grieved exceedingly at that which she had said to him, and the heart of Pharaoh was very sad indeed. And it came to pass at the dawn of the morrow that the [priests] proclaimed a great festival with offerings in honour of the bull, and His Majesty caused one of his first royal workmen to go and slay the bull; and it fell out that, after one had killed him, and he was [being carried] upon the shoulders of the men, he shook his neck, and cast two drops of blood near the two great portals of His Majesty, and one fell upon one side of Pharaoh's door, and the other fell upon the other, and they grew up into two great trees, **XVII.** each one of which was very fine. And one went and told His Majesty, saying, "Two mighty trees have grown up for His Majesty in a most miraculous manner during the night near the great door of His Majesty;" and there were rejoicings for them throughout the whole land, and His Majesty made offerings unto them.

And it came to pass some time after this that His Majesty rose like the sun from the lapis-lazuli chamber, wearing wreaths made of all kinds of flowers around his neck, and he [sat] in his chariot of *smu* metal, and he came forth from the royal palace to see the two trees, and the sacred lady came forth [in a chariot drawn by] two horses by Pharaoh's side; and His Majesty sat under one of the trees, [and the sacred lady sat under the other. And the tree under which she sat, that is to say Bata], spake to his wife, saying, "Alas, thou faithless one! I am Bata, and I am alive . . . . . . It is thou who hast known how to make Pharaoh cut down the tree by which was my dwelling; then I took the form of a bull, and thou didst cause me to be slain." And it came to pass some time afterwards that the sacred lady was at His Majesty's table, and he was exceedingly gracious unto her, and she spake unto him, saying, "Swear an oath to me in God's name, saying, 'Whatsoever the sacred lady shall say unto me, I will listen unto; let her say on'." And he listened unto everything **XVIII.** which she spake, saying, "I pray thee let these two trees be cut down, and then they will make them into fine planks"; and His Majesty listened unto all that she spake. And some time afterwards His Majesty caused skilful workmen to go and to cut down Pharaoh's trees, and as the royal spouse, the sacred lady herself stood looking on, a splinter flew off and went into the sacred lady's mouth, and she swallowed it and conceived . . . . and His Majesty did for her everything which she desired. And it came to pass some time afterwards that she gave birth to a man-child, and one went and told His Majesty, saying, "A man-child is born unto thee;" and one brought the child to him, and one gave him a nurse and servants of the bed-chamber. And His Majesty made rejoicings throughout the whole land, and he sat down to pass a happy day, and one began to call the child after His Majesty, who loved him exceedingly, and homage was paid to him under the title, "Royal, sacred son of Kush." **XIX.** And it came to pass some time afterwards that His Majesty made him an *Erpāt* of the whole country, and after some time, when he had for many years ruled the whole country as *Erpāt*, His Majesty flew up to heaven. And Bata said, "Let the chiefs and nobles of His Majesty be brought to me that I may cause them to know all the things which have happened to me," and one brought to him his wife, and he entered into judgment with her before them, and one carried out their decree. And one brought to him his elder brother, and he made him *Erpāt* over all his country, and when he had reigned over Egypt for twenty years he departed this life, and his elder brother stood in his room [until] the day of his death.

Here happily endeth this book which hath been written by Qaḳabu the scribe of the treasūry, of the treasury of Pharaoh, the scribe Ḥeru-à, and the scribe Mer-em-àptu. It was composed by the scribe Ȧnnana, the master of books. Whosoever readeth in this book, may Thoth make himself his guardian.

The Possessed Princess of Bekhten.

(See pp. 40—49.)

Horus, the mighty Bull, crowned with crowns, stablished in royalty, like the god Temu, the golden Horus, who wieldeth the sword with might, the subduer of the hostile tribes, the King of the North and of the South, the lord of the double country, (User-Maāt-Rā-setep-en-Rā), the son of the Sun, and offspring of his body, (Rāmeses-meri-Amen, beloved of Amen and Amen-Rā) the lord of all the thrones in the world, and of the entire company of the gods, the lords of Thebes. The beloved of the beautiful god, the son of Amen, born of Horus, begotten by Horus of the two horizons, the glorious offspring of the lord of the universe, begotten by his mother's husband, the King of the country of black mud (*i. e.*, Egypt), the ruler of the ruddy deserts, the Prince who hath led all hostile tribes captive. As a newborn babe he set his forces in battle array and took command thereof, and scarcely was he born before, like a valiant bull, he drove [all] before him; the King is a Bull, and like the god Menthu doth he show himself on the day of battle, and he is great, and mighty, and strong, like the son of Nut (*i. e.*, Osiris).

Now, behold, according to his wont year by year, His Majesty the King was in Mesopotamia, and the chiefs of all the lands there came to pay homage unto him, and to entreat his goodwill and favour, and [the people of] the countries round about brought unto him their offerings of gold, lapis-lazuli, turquoise, and every kind of thing which that divine land produceth, upon their backs, and each chief sought to outdo his fellow. And it came to pass that when the Prince of the country of Bekhten was bringing his offerings and tribute, he placed his eldest daughter at the front thereof, to show his reverence for His Majesty, and to gain favour before him. Now she was a very beautiful girl, and His Majesty thought her more beautiful than any other girl he had ever seen before, and the title of "Royal spouse, mighty lady, Rā-neferu," was straightway given to her, and when His Majesty had arrived in Egypt she became in very truth the "Royal spouse".

And lo! it came to pass on the twenty-second day of the second month of the summer of the fifteenth year of His Majesty, that the King was in Thebes, the mighty city, the mistress of [all other] cities, performing the ceremonies of father Amen, the lord of the thrones of the world, during the beautiful festival in the Southern Apt, the place which he hath loved from times of old, when, behold, one came and told His Majesty, saying, "An ambassador of the Prince of Bekhten hath arrived, bringing with him a multitude of gifts for the Royal spouse."

And when he had been led into the presence of His Majesty together with his offerings, he spake words of fealty and homage to him, saying, "Glory and praise be to thee, O thou Sun of the Nations, grant that we may live before thee." And when he had given utterance to his words of homage, at the same time prostrating himself with his head down to the ground before His Majesty, he spake again, and said before him, "I have come unto thee, O my Sovereign and Lord, on behalf of the lady Bent-reshet, the younger sister of the Royal spouse Rā-neferu, for, behold, an evil disease hath laid hold on her body. I beseech thy Majesty to send a physician to see her."

And His Majesty said, "Let the men who are learned in the knowledge of books and the books of the learned ones be brought to me." And when they had been led in before him, His Majesty straightway said, "I have caused you to be summoned in order that ye may hear these words which I am about to say. Let there be brought in to me from out of your company a man wise of heart and cunning with his hands." And it came to pass, when the Royal scribe Teḥuti-em-Ḥeb had come into the presence of His Majesty, that he ordered him to set out on a journey to the land of Bekhten, together with the ambassador from that land. Now, when that physician had accomplished the journey into the land of Bekhten, he found the lady Bent-reshet in the state of a woman of whom a demon had taken possession, and he found himself utterly unable to contend against him successfully.

And it came to pass that the Prince of Bekhten sent an ambassador a second time unto His Majesty, saying, "O my Sovereign and Lord, I beseech thy Majesty to command that a god be brought [unto this country to heal my daughter]."

Now on the twenty-sixth day of the first month of the season of inundation, during the time of the celebration of the festival of Amen, His Majesty was in Thebes, and he went a second time into the presence of the god Khonsu Nefer-ḥetep in Thebes, and said, "O my fair Lord, I have come once again into thy presence [to entreat] thee on behalf of the daughter of the Prince of Bekhten." Then the god Khonsu Nefer-ḥetep in Thebes was brought in to Khonsu, who performeth mighty things and wonderful, the great god, the vanquisher of the hosts of darkness, and His Majesty spake in the presence of Khonsu Nefer-ḥetep in Thebes, saying, "O my fair Lord, turn then thy face upon Khonsu, who performeth mighty things and wonderful, the great god, the vanquisher of the hosts of darkness, and do thou most graciously grant that he may go into the country of Bekhten." And His Majesty spake yet again, saying, "Grant, then, that thy saving power may go with him, and let me send his divine Majesty unto Bekhten to deliver the daughter of the Prince of that land from the power of the demon."

And behold the god Khonsu Nefer-ḥetep in Thebes granted his request, and he bestowed upon Khonsu, who performeth mighty things and wonderful in Thebes, his saving power in a fourfold measure.

And His Majesty commanded them to send Khonsu, who performeth mighty things and wonderful in Thebes, on his journey in a boat, together with five other boats, and a multitude of chariots and horses accompanied them on the right hand and on the left; and the god arrived in Bekhten after travelling one year and five months.

And the Prince of Bekhten, together with his soldiers and his nobles, came forth to meet Khonsu, who performeth mighty things and wonderful in Thebes, and he threw himself upon his face, saying, "Thy coming unto us at the sending of the King of Northern and Southern Egypt, (User-Maāt-Rā-setep-en-Rā), is grateful unto us and welcome." And the god Khonsu went to the place wherein was the lady Bent-reshet, and he bestowed his saving power upon the daughter of the Prince of Bekhten, and she was healed straightway. And the demon which had possessed her spake before Khonsu, who performeth mighty things and wonderful in Thebes, "Grateful and welcome is thy coming unto us, O great god, the vanquisher of the hosts of darkness; Bekhten is thy city, the inhabitants thereof are thy slaves, and I am thy servant; and I will depart unto the place whence I came that I may gratify thee, for unto this end hast thou come hither. And I beseech thy Majesty to command that the Governor of Bekhten and myself may hold a festival together."

And the god Khonsu graciously granted this request, and spake to his priest, saying, "Let the Prince of Bekhten make a great festival in honour of the demon." Now, while the god Khonsu, who performeth mighty things and wonderful in Thebes, was arranging these things with the demon, the Prince of Bekhten and his army stood by in exceedingly great fear.

The Prince of Bekhten made a great festival in honour of Khonsu, who performeth mighty things and wonderful in Thebes, and of the demon of the Prince of Bekhten, and they passed a happy day together; and by the command of Khonsu, who performeth mighty things and wonderful in Thebes, that demon departed in peace unto the place which he loved.

And the Prince of Bekhten and all those who were in that country rejoiced exceedingly, and he conceived a design in his heart, saying, "The god Khonsu shall be made to abide in the country of Bekhten, and I will not allow him to depart into Egypt," and the god Khonsu tarried in Bekhten for three years, four months, and five days.

And it came to pass on a day that the Prince of Bekhten was sleeping upon his couch, and he saw in a dream the god Khonsu come out from his shrine: now he was like unto a hawk of gold, and he flew up into the air and departed to the land of Egypt. And when he woke up, he was stupefied with terror, and he spake unto the priest of Khonsu, who performeth mighty things and wonderful in Thebes, saying, "The god hath departed from us, and hath made his way into Egypt; we must now send his chariot back to Egypt."

And the Prince of Bekhten gave the command, and the god set out for Egypt, and he gave unto him multitudes of offerings and gifts of all kinds of precious things, and he went accompanied by many soldiers and horses. And when he had made the journey to Thebes in peace, Khonsu, who performeth mighty things and wonderful in Thebes, departed to the temple of Khonsu Nefer-ḥetep in Thebes, and he laid before him all the offerings and gifts of all kinds of precious things which the Prince of Bekhten had given him, and he did not devote to his own temple anything of it all.

And so Khonsu, who performeth mighty things and wonderful in Thebes, returned to his own temple happily on the nineteenth day of the second month of spring in the thirty-third year of the King of Northern and Southern Egypt, (User-Maāt-Rā-setep-en-Rā), the giver of life, like the Sun, for ever and ever.

The Litanies of Seker.

(See pp. 87—94.)

XVIII. (1) The Litanies of the bringing in of Seker; to be recited in addition to the mysteries already said. (2) Hail, prince, who comest forth from the womb. (3) Hail, eldest son of primeval matter. (4) Hail, lord of multitudes of aspects and evolutions. (5) Hail, golden Disk in the temples. (6) Hail, lord of time and bestower of years. (7) Hail, thou everlasting lord of life. (8) Hail, lord of myriads and millions. (9) Hail, thou who shinest in rising and in setting. (10) Hail, thou who makest beings to be joyful. (11) Hail, thou lord of terror, thou fearful one. (12) Hail, thou lord of multitudes of aspects and divinities. (13) Hail, thou who art crowned with the white crown; thou master of the *urerer* crown. (14) Hail, thou sacred babe of Horus, praise! (15) Hail, son of Rā, who sittest in the boat of millions of years. (16) Hail, restful leader, come to thy hidden place. (17) Hail, lord of terror self-produced. (18) Hail, Still-heart, come to thy town. (19) Hail, thou who causest acclamation to be made, come to thy town. (20) Hail, thou Darling of the gods and goddesses. (21) Hail, thou who dippest thyself in the water, come to thy temple. (22) Hail, thou who dwellest in the underworld, come to thy offerings. (23) Hail, thou protector, come to thy temple. (24) Hail, thou growing one, Moon god, illumining the Disk. (25) Hail, sacred flower of the great temple. (26) Hail, thou who bringest the sacred cordage of the *sekti* boat. (27) Hail, thou lord of the *ḥennu* boat, thou becomest young in the secret place. (28) Hail, thou perfect Soul who dwellest in the underworld. (29) Hail, thou sacred Visitor of the North and South. (30) Hail, thou hidden one, unknown to mankind. (31) Hail, thou who givest light to him that is in the underworld that he may see the Disk. **XIX.** (1) Hail, thou lord of the *atef* crown, thou great one in Ḥenensu (Heracleopolis). (2) Hail, thou mighty one of terror in the town of trees (Närt). (3) Hail, thou who art in Thebes, who flourishest for ever. (4) Hail, Amen-Rā, thou king of the gods, who makest thy limbs to grow in rising and setting. (5) Hail, [thou who receivest] oblations and offerings in Re-stau (*i. e.*, the passages of the tomb). (6) Hail, thou who placest the crown upon the head of its lord. (7) Hail, thou who stablishest the earth upon its foundations. (8) Hail, thou who openest the mouth of the four great gods who are in the underworld. (9) Hail, thou living soul of Osiris, diademed of the Moon. (10) Hail, thou who hidest thy body in the great coffin in Annu (Heliopolis). (11) Hail, mighty one, thou hidden one, Osiris in the underworld. (12) Hail, thou who unitest thy soul to heaven, thine enemy hath fallen. (13) The goddess Isis crying out saith, Hail from the river, (14) thou who separatest the *abṭu* fish from the front (15) of the boat of Rā, thou lord of the excretion which turneth into the rejoicing gods, (16) thou egg which turneth into the Lake of Hen. She cutteth off the heads (17) of the rebels in her name of "Lady of Ṭep-àḥet" (Aphroditopolis). (18) Lord of excretion, thou comest in front of the heads in her name of (19) "Hathor, lady of emerald, lady of Thebes". (20) Thou comest in peace in her name of "Hathor, lady of Thebes". (21) Thou comest in peace, O Tait, in her name of "Lady (22) of peace". Thou comest in front to overthrow her enemy (23) in her name of "Hathor, lady of Ḥenensu" (Heracleopolis). (24) O Golden one, thou comest in peace in her name of "Hathor, (25) lady of Memphis". Thou restest near Neb-er-tcher in her name of "Hathor, lady of the Red Water". The Golden one riseth near her father (26) in her name of "Bast", and advanceth over (27) the temples near the great double house in her name of "Sati". (28) Thou who makest the earth green, thou leadest the gods in her name of "Uatchit". (29) Hathor gaineth the mastery over the fiends in her name of "Sekhet". (30) Uatchit gaineth the mastery over the fire in her name of "Lady of Ammu". (31) She hath perfume upon her head and hair in her name of "Neith".

XX. (1) Hail, ye gods, by reason of his virtues. (2) Hail, Hathor, Lady of Thebes. (3) Hail, Hathor, Lady of Ḥenensu. (4) Hail, Lady of Ṭep-àḥet. (5) Hail, Hathor, Lady of Nehau. (6) Hail, Hathor, Lady of Reḥsau. (7) Hail, Hathor, Lady of Red Water. (8) Hail, Hathor, Lady of the turquoise land. (9) Hail, Hathor, lady of Memphis. (10) Hail, Hathor, Lady of Uaua. (11) Hail, Hathor, Lady of Ammu. (12) Hail, Hathor, Lady of Amem. (13) Hail, Hathor, Lady of the city of Sixteen (Lycopolis). (14) Hail, ye nine *smeri*, come ye bearing your father Osiris on your hands, (15) come ye with divine adorations (*or* amulets) (say four times). (16) Hail, crown of the festival, (say twice) thou prince. (17) Hail, thou rejoicest the nurses whom thou lovest. (18) Hail, thou livest, thou livest, for ever! (19) Hail, thou makest festival for ever. (20) Hail, thou adored one, thou passest over the ways. (21) Hail, thou who art established in the celestial Tattu. (22) Hail, thou god, who hearest songs of adoration (?), hail, thou who hearest songs of adoration (?) from the mouth of the divine nomes. (23) Hail, thou that comest forth from thy two eyes, thou divine son, thou prophet. (24) Hail, thou who art protected by amulets when thou speakest. (25) Hail, protect me, O great one, to do thy pleasure. (26) Hail, protect me, O great one, to do thy will. (27) Hail, the one who resteth, that is to say Still-heart, cometh to thee. (28) Hail, son of the prophet, the festal service is recited for thee. (29) Hail, thou whose name is established in the celestial Tattu. (30) Hail, thou who art sweet of smell in the celestial Tattu. (31) Hail, thou who comest to destroy the fiends. (32) Hail, thou who comest to praise the Babe.

XXI. (1) Hail, thou who strikest thy fear into the evil-hearted (2) . . . . . . (3) Hail, thou rebel, who hatest the temple, death is driven into thy throat. (4) Hail, the lord of the celestial Tattu cometh, he hath repulsed the rebel. (5) To be recited by players on tambourines sixteen times.

(6) Here endeth the book.

COLOPHON. May their names be established and be made permanent and never be destroyed before Osiris, Horus, Isis, Nephthys, and the gods and goddesses whose names are written in this book, in the presence of the gods and goddesses, whosoever they are, who are in the underworld and within the mighty and secret pylons which are there. May these names be made to come forth in the mighty underworld. Mayest thou be proclaimed by them in the boat of Rā; mayest thou have given to thee by them sepulchral meals upon the table of the great god in the course of every day; mayest thou have given to thee by them fresh water and incense such as are given to the mighty kings of the north and south who are in the underworld; may there be given to thee by them the power to come forth and to go forward among the favoured ones of Osiris at the head of those who are in the underworld; and may they grant to thee that the rays of the disk shall fall upon thy body daily.

COLOPHON.

(See pp. 94—96.)

If any person from any foreign land whatsoever, whether he be Negro, or Ethiopian, or Syrian, shall remove this book, or any thief shall carry it off, may his body never come into the Presence; may he never be placed in the cool region; may he never breathe the breezes of the north wind; may neither son nor daughter arise to him from his seed; may his name never be remembered on earth through his children; and may he never see the beams of the disk. But if any person shall look upon this book and shall so act that my name and my double be established among the favoured ones of Osiris, may this be done likewise for him after his death in return for what he hath done for me.

Stelae of Nekht-Ȧmsu.

(See pp. 126—134.)

I. (1) The first day of the fourth month of *shat* (*i. e.*, time of the inundation) of the fourth year of the reign of the majesty of Horus Rā, the mighty bull, the king diademed with saffron crowns, the king of the North and South, the most mighty ruler, the conqueror of the land of the Asiatics, the golden hawk, the just prince, the sustainer of the two lands [of Egypt], (2) the king of the North and South, the prince of the Nine bows (Rā-kheperu-ȧri-Maāt), the son of the Sun, the offspring of his body, the lord of diadems, (Ai "the divine father" and prince of Thebes), beloved of Osiris, the lord of Abydos, the giver of life. (3) [May all the gods of the] north and south and Anubis upon his hill give glory in heaven, and power upon earth, and triumph in the underworld! May they allow me to go in and come forth from my tomb; may my majesty (4) refresh its shade; may I drink water out of my cistern daily; may all my limbs germinate; may the Nile give me (5) bread and all manner of green things at its season; may [I] pass over the length of my land daily without ceasing; may my soul alight (6) upon the branches of the trees which I have planted; may I refresh myself under my sycamores; may I eat of the food which they give; (7) may I have my mouth wherewith I may speak even like the followers of Horus; may I come forth from heaven; and may I come down to earth. Let me not be shut out upon (8) the way; let there not be done unto me that which my *ka* hateth; and let not my soul be carried away captive. Let me rise up among the favoured ones and among the venerable ones; (9) let me plough my homestead in Sekhet-Aaru and let me attain to the "Fields of Peace"; let them come forth to me with vessels [of beer] and with cakes, (10) the cakes of the lords of eternity; let me receive my meat from the basket of flesh which is upon the altar of the great god. [Let these things be done] for the double of the first prophet of Amsu, Nekht-Amsu, who saith, (11) "I have done what was pleasing unto me and the will of the gods. For this reason I have given bread to the hungry; I have satisfied the needy with food; I have followed (12) the god in his house; my mouth hath not spoken haughtily against the noble ones; there hath been no undue extension in my stride, for I walked measuredly; I performed the right and truth which were beloved of the king; (13) I observed what commands he gave and I watched in my station ready to exalt his will; I stood up to praise him daily; I gave my attention to what (14) he said without ever hesitating at what he determined with reference to myself; I made myself master of uprightness and integrity, and I comprehended concerning which things I ought to preserve silence; (15) and my lord was gracious to me and favoured me for my good deeds, because he saw that my hands were vigorous through my heart, and he advanced my station greatly, and set me in [his] council chamber." [These things he did] for the (16) person of the overseer of the prophets of the lords of Apu (Panopolis), triumphant, who saith, "O [all] ye who live upon earth, who will live for eternity and for ever and for aye, O ye priests and (17) readers of Osiris, O every one learned in divine tradition, when ye enter my tomb and pass through it, recite ye sacred words by the side of [this] my sepulchral tablet, and make ye mention of my name, without fail, (18) in the presence of the lords of right and truth. And your God shall shew favour unto you, and ye shall hand on your dignities to your children after ye have lived to a ripe old age, provided that ye say :— (19) May Osiris grant a royal oblation to the overseer of works in the Temple of Ai; and may the tomb of Nekht-Amsu, the venerable one, the prince, the first prophet of Amsu and Isis, abide for ever in the abode of eternity."

II. (1) The first day of the fourth month of the season *shat* of the fourth year of the reign of the majesty of Horus-Rā, the mighty bull, the king diademed with saffron crowns, the king of the North and South, the most mighty ruler, the conqueror of the land of the Asiatics, the golden hawk, the just prince, the sustainer of the two lands [of Egypt], (2) the king of the North and South, the prince of the Nine bows, (Rā-kheperu-åri-Maāt), the son of the Sun, the offspring of his body, his beloved one, the lord of diadems (Ai, the "divine father" and prince of Thebes), beloved of Osiris, the lord of Ta-tchesert, the giver of life. (3) May Amen-Rā, the lord of the thrones of the two lands, and Ptah-Seker-Ausar Unnefer, lord of Re-stau, give a royal oblation. May they give sepulchral meals and oxen, and feathered fowl, and linen garments, and thousands of every kind of good and pure things, and thousands of every kind of (4) sweet and pleasant things, which heaven bestoweth, and which the earth produceth, and which the Nile bringeth forth from his source, [and may they grant me] to breathe the sweet breezes of the north wind, to eat bread (5), to gather flowers, and to enjoy meat and drink the produce of the Sekhet-Aaru in felicity. May I walk along (6) the road of eternity among the sainted doubles and spiritual beings of light; may I perform my transformations at will among the servants of Un-nefer, may I go in and come out from the underworld; (7) may my soul be turned not back when it willeth [to come forth]; may it come forth like a living soul; may I drink water from the depths of the stream; may I receive cakes (8) from the lord of eternity; may I come into the presence every day [as well as] on the festival of the new moon, on the festival of the month, on the festival of the sixth day, on the festival of the half month, on the festival of Uaka, on the festival of Thoth, (9) on the festival of the rising of Amsu, on the festival of the rising of Sothis, on the festival of the great heat, on the festival of the little heat, on the festival of the "things of the altar", and on all the festivals of the receiving of Nile water of Osiris [which are celebrated] at the beginning of the seasons of the (10) lord of the gods.

A hymn of praise to Rā when he riseth, a hymn of adoration to Rā when he setteth in life. May he (*i. e.*, Nekht-Amsu) breathe the wind which cometh forth from the horizon — the full blast of the north wind which cometh (*i. e.*, bloweth) (11) on both sides; may his name be proclaimed; may [his] hand be stretched out over oblations, and provisions, and sepulchral offerings when he is invoked; may he receive water at the two hands of the *ka* priest; (12) may he gain possession of bread and beer from the table at which his double is pleased [to appear]; may he eat meat at the table of the god Neb-er-tcher, at the table of the lords of eternity; (13) may pure meat and drink be given to him from the meat and drink of Un-nefer; may he travel along in the boat of the underworld to the lands of (14) the Sekhet-Aaru; may he open up the ways and pass along the roads; may he follow the god Seker in Re-stau; may he be not turned back at the (15) door of the Tuat; may he take his fill there of wine and milk and receive ointment, and unguent, and eye paint [which] rejoiceth the heart, and clothing and (16) linen garments — he the double of the overseer of the double storehouse of all the gods in Taqahti and of Amsu in Khenti, the first prophet of Amsu and Isis in Apu (Panopolis), Nekht-Amsu, triumphant, who offereth (17) divine offerings to the gods and sepulchral meals to the spiritual beings of light for the king of the North and South (Rā-kheperu-ari-Maāt) life, health and strength! May he be established, may he endure like heaven, may he renew himself like Amsu (?). And may prayers (18) be made for his salvation for millions of years to all the gods by the real royal relative who loveth him, Nekht-Amsu, who saith, "Hail ye gods who are in heaven! Hail ye gods who are on (19) earth! Hail ye gods who are in the Tuat, who transport Rā and who lead along the beautiful god to the western horizon of heaven, let my words come to you (20) like the entreaties of a servant before his lord, and be gracious unto me. I was favoured by [my] sovereign upon earth, grant ye that I may also rest in peace in my everlasting habitation, and grant that I may join . . . ."

The Battle of Kadesh.

(See pp. 134—141.)

The ninth day of the third month of the season *shemu* (*i. e.*, summer) of the fifth year of the reign of Horus-Rā (the mighty bull, beloved of Maāt), the king of the North and South, (Usr-maāt-Rā setep-en-Rā), the son of the Sun (Rāmeses, beloved of Amen), the giver of life for ever. Behold now, his Majesty was in the country of Tchah on his second expedition of victory. A good look-out [was kept] in life, strength and health in the camp of his Majesty on the southern side of Kadesh. His Majesty rose up like Rā and put on the ornaments of the god Menthu, and the lord continued on his journey and arrived at the southern border of the city of Shabtun. And two members of the Shasu people came and spake to his Majesty, saying, "Our brethren who are among the chiefs of the tribes who are in league with the abominable prince of Kheta have made us come to his Majesty to say, 'We are [ready] to render service to Pharaoh, (life, health and strength)!' and they have broken with the abominable prince of Kheta. Now the abominable prince of Kheta is encamped in the land of Aleppo, to the north of the country of Tunep, and he is afraid to advance because of Pharaoh, life, health, and strength." In this wise did the Shasu speak; but they spake to his Majesty lying words, for the abominable prince of the Kheta had made them come to spy out the place where his Majesty was, so that he might not be able to arrange his forces in a proper way to do battle with the abominable prince of the Kheta.

And behold, the abominable chief of the Kheta had come together with the chiefs of every district, and with the footmen, and with the horsemen whom he had brought with him in mighty numbers, and they stood ready to fight drawn up in ambush behind the abominable city of Kadesh, his Majesty having no knowledge whatever of their plans. So his Majesty marched on and arrived at the north-west side of the abominable city of Kadesh, and there he and his troops encamped. Now his Majesty was sitting on his *smu* metal throne when two of the spies who were in the service of his Majesty brought in two spies of the abominable chief of the Kheta. And when they had been led into his presence his Majesty said to them, "Who and what are ye?" And they replied, "We belong to the abominable prince of the Kheta who made us to come to see where his Majesty was." His Majesty said to them, "Where is this abominable chief of the Kheta? Verily I have heard that he is in the country of Aleppo." They replied, "Behold, the abominable chief of the Kheta standeth [ready] and multitudes [of the peoples] of the districts are with him; he hath brought them with him in vast numbers from all the provinces of the country of the Kheta, and from the country of Mesopotamia, and from the whole country of Qetti. They are provided with footmen and with cavalry fully equipped, and they are like the sand of the sea shore for multitude; and behold, they are drawn up in fighting order but are concealed behind the abominable city of Kadesh." Then his Majesty caused his chief officers to be called into his presence that he might make them to know every matter which the two spies of the abominable prince of the Kheta who had been before him had spoken. And his Majesty spake unto them, saying, "Enquire into the actions of the officers of the peoples and of the chiefs of the district where Pharaoh (life, health, and strength!) is [encamped]." They did so, and reported to Pharaoh (life, health, and strength!) that the abominable chief of the Kheta was in the land of Aleppo whither he had fled before his Majesty as soon as he had heard the report of him, and that, indeed, [the officers and chiefs] should have reported these things correctly to his Majesty. [And his Majesty replied], "See now what I have made you to know at this time through the two spies of the country of Kheta, namely that the abominable chief of the Kheta hath come together with [the peoples of] a multitude of countries, and with men and with horses, like the sand for multitude, and that they are standing behind the abominable city of Kadesh; is it possible that the officers of the districts and the princes of the country wherein Pharaoh (life, health and strength!) now is — under whose direction the district is — did not know this?" Now when these things had been said to them the officers who were in the presence of his Majesty admitted that the officers of the country and the princes of Pharaoh (life, health and strength!) had committed a gross breach of duty in not reporting to them the various places to which the abominable chief of the Kheta had marched.

And it came to pass that when they had spoken his Majesty issued an order for the officers who were in charge of the troops that were marching to the south of Shabtun to bring their troops as quickly as possible to the place where his Majesty was. Now whilst his sacred Majesty was sitting and talking with his officers, the abominable prince of the Kheta came together with his footmen, and cavalry, and the multitudes of people who were with him, and they crossed over the canal at the south of Kadesh and came upon the soldiers of his Majesty who were marching along in ignorance of what was happening. Then the footmen and cavalry of his Majesty lost their courage and rushed on headlong to where his Majesty was, and the troops of the abominable prince of the Kheta surrounded the servants who were round about his Majesty. When his Majesty saw them he raged at them like his father Menthu, the lord of Thebes, and, putting on his armour and seizing his spear, like the god Bāru in his moment, he mounted his horse and dashed forward alone among the troops of the abominable prince of Kheta and among the multitudes which he had with him. His Majesty, like the most mighty god Sutekh, made slaughter among them, and he cut them down dead into the waters of the Orontes. [He saith], "I conquered all countries, I was quite alone, my footmen and cavalry had forsaken me, and no man among them dared to come back [to save] my life. But Rā loved me, and my father Tmu had a favour for me, and every thing which my Majesty hath said I performed in very truth before my footmen and before my cavalry."

The Annals of Rameses III.

(See pp. 142—161.)

I. (1) The sixth day of the third month of the season *shemu* (*i. e.*, summer) of the thirty-second year of the reign of the king of the North and South, (User-Maāt-Rā-meri-Amen), L. H. S.[1]; the son of the Sun, (Rāmeses, prince of Annu), L. H. S.; beloved of all the gods and goddesses; (2) the king diademed with the white crown like Osiris; the prince rising in Aḳert (*i. e.*, the underworld) like Tum; . . . . great house within Ta-tchesert; traversing eternity and everlastingness as king of the underworld; the king of the North and South (User-Maāt-Rā-meri-Amen), the son of the Sun, (Rāmeses, prince of Annu), L. H. S.; the great god (3) who declareth with adoration, and praise, and thanksgiving the numerous glorious and mighty actions which he did as king and prince on earth for the temple of his sacred father Amen-Rā, the king of the gods (4), and Mut, and Khonsu, and all the gods of Thebes; and for the temple of his sacred father Tum, the lord of the two lands of Annu (Heliopolis), and Rā-Ḥeru-khuti, and Iusāaset, and Nebt-ḥetep, and all the gods of Annu; and for the temple of his sacred father (5) Ptah, the mighty one of the southern wall, lord of the life of the two lands, and Sekhet greatly beloved of Ptah, and Nefer-Tum protector of

1. *I. e.*, life, health, strength!

the two lands; and for all the gods of Memphis, the sacred fathers, and for all the gods and goddesses of the South and (6) North; and all the splendid and noble acts which he wrought for the people of all the land of Egypt; and how he gathered them all together at one time that he might make (7) the divine fathers, and all the gods and the goddesses of the South and North, and all men, and all the *pāt*, and all the *rekhit*, and all the *hememet* to see the many glorious and most splendid deeds (8) which he wrought on earth whilst he was the great prince of Egypt.

III. (1) The adoration, and praise, and mighty and splendid deeds which he wrought for the Temple of his sacred father Amen-Rā, the king of the gods, and for Mut and Khonsu, and for all the gods of Thebes. (2) Saith the king (User-Maāt-Rā-meri-Amen), L. H. S., the son of the Sun, (Rāmeses, prince of Annu), L. H. S., the great god, in making adoration to his father, this same sacred god Amen-Rā, the king of the gods, the matter which had already in the earliest times come into being, (3) the divine god who created himself, the god who lifteth the hand and who exalteth the *atef* crown, the maker of things which are, the creator of things which shall come into being, the god who is hidden both from men and from gods, lend me thine ears, O lord of the gods, (4) and hearken unto the words of praise which I speak unto thee. Grant thou to me that I may come unto thee to thy city Thebes the hidden, O thou who art god in the company of the gods who are under thy leadership, who restest in Neb-ānkh, thy holy place, (5) opposite to the sacred statue of thy court. Grant that I may be joined unto the gods, who are the lords of the underworld like my father Osiris, the lord of Ta-tchesert; grant that my soul may be like unto the souls of the company of the gods who rest near thee in the (6) everlasting horizon; give breath to my nostrils, and water to my soul, and let me eat of the substance and matter of the food of thy divine offerings; let my sacred Majesty abide continually in thy presence (7) like the great gods the lords of Aḳert; may I enter in and come forth from thee as do they; do thou direct my soul, even as thou dost direct theirs, against my enemies; and establish thou the offerings obligatory for my (8) double by an everlasting stablishing which shall endure for ever and for ever. I have become king upon earth and prince of living men and women, and thou hast established the divine diadem upon my head even as thou hast made thy way in peace to the sacred temple. (9) Thou hast taken thy seat upon thy double throne with joy of heart, and I am established upon the throne of my father, even as thou hast made Horus to sit upon the throne of Osiris. I have neither injured nor wronged (10) any in the matter of his throne; I have not transgressed that which thou didst command me [to do]; and thou hast given peace and rest unto my subjects, and every land praiseth thee. I consider the things which I have caused to be made [for thee], (11) which I have wrought as king and I will double [my] manifold great and glorious deeds [for thee]. I made for thee the sacred Temple of Millions of Years which is [situated] on the mountain of Neb-ānkhtet opposite to thee.

IV. (1) It is built of sandstone, and *bàait* stone, and black basalt, and it hath portals and doors made of fine chased copper; its pylons are built of stone and tower into heaven, (2) and they are inscribed and sculptured with the chisel in the mighty name of thy Majesty. I built a wall round about it, and I caused to be built therein staircases and inside chambers made of sandstone. (3) I dug a lake in front of the temple which I filled to overflowing with the water of heaven, and I planted [the sides thereof] with flowering trees and shrubs like unto [those of] the land of the North. I filled its treasuries with the products of the districts of Egypt, (4) and with gold, and silver, and precious stones of all kinds by hundreds of thousands. Its granaries were filled to overflowing with wheat and grain, and the cattle of its fields were as numerous as the sand of the furrows. I laid under contribution for it (5) the land of the South as well as the land of the North, the land of Phoenicia, and the land of Tchah, and it contained the results of their labours and was filled with the captives whom thou didst give to me from among the nine peoples of Pet, and with young men who amounted [in number] to tens of thousands. (6) I sculptured for thee thy mighty image, which was to rest within the temple and the sacred name of which was, "Amen comprising eternity," and I ornamented it with real jewels like the double horizon wherein he riseth; it is a joy to him that beholdeth it. (7) I made for it libation slabs, and vessels of pure gold, and countless instruments of silver and bronze. I multiplied the divine offerings which were obligatory before thee, cakes, wine, ale, fat feathered fowl, (8) oxen, calves, cattle of various kinds, antelopes, and gazelles which were due to its place of slaughter. I dragged along mighty monuments as large as mountains made of fine white marble and alabaster, (9) and I sculptured them and made them to be set at the right and left of the doorway of the temple, and they were inscribed with the great name of thy Majesty for ever. [And I made] other statues of *maa* and *bàait* stone (10) together with plinths of black basalt to be set therein. And I sculptured figures of Ptah-Seker, and of Nefer-Tum, and of the company of the gods, the lords of heaven and earth, to be set in its shrine, which was wrought with fine gold and (11) silver, and was inlaid with jewels and real precious stones, and was of the finest work possible. I made for thee a sacred chamber of the king within it, like unto the chamber of the god Tum which is in heaven above; the pillars and (12) folding-doors were made of fine copper, and the great opening for the coronation of the god was of fine gold. I made for the temple boats wherein to load corn and grain and wherein to carry it to

V. (1) its granary incessantly. I made for the temple a storehouse and huge barges to sail on the river laden with manifold things for the sacred storehouse. (2) I surrounded the temple with gardens and summerhouses and booths, the trees of which were laden with fruits and flowers for thy two faces; I built their cottages with (3) windows, and I dug a lake in front of them which was planted with lilies. (4) I made for thee a hidden horizon in thy city of Thebes which faced thy courtyard, and for the gods of the Temple of (Rāmeses, prince of Annu), L.

H. S., in the Temple of Amen, "Established in heaven with the disk" [is its name]. (5) I built and fashioned it with sandstone and it had great doors [made] of fine gold; I filled its storehouses with the things which both my hands brought to set before (6) thy face daily. I made the southern Apt to keep a [constant] feast by reason of the mighty monuments [which I placed therein]. I built for thee a temple therein like unto the double throne of Neb-er-tcher, namely, the Temple of (Rāmeses, prince of Annu), L. H. S., (7) uniting gladness in the Apts. I caused to be built again monuments to thee in Thebes, the mighty city, the place where thy heart reposeth, near to thyself, namely, the place of (Usr-Maāt-Rā-meri-Amen), L. H. S., in the House of Amen. (8) [I built] likewise the shrine of Neb-er-tcher of a marvellous kind of stone, and I ornamented it with works [to last] for ever; the posts of the doors were of *maa* stone and the folding-doors of gold, and I provided it with a staff of men, and I endowed it with property of every kind by hundreds of thousands. (10) I made for thee a hidden shrine cut out of one piece of beautiful *maat* stone, and the doors thereof were of bronze chased and inscribed with thy divine name; (11) inside it rested thy noble image, like that of Rā in his double horizon, established upon its throne for ever and for ever in thy great and sacred court. (12) I made for thee a great table for offerings of chased silver inlaid with fine gold, and with figures in gold, and with figures of the lord, L. H. S., in gold ornamented with divers designs, for the offerings and oblations which are to be made duly to thee.

VI. (1) I made for thee a great shrine in thy court wrought with figures in fine gold and with precious stones, and [I made] its vessels of gold for the wine and ale which are offered unto thee every morning. (2) I made for thee chambers wherein the festivals of the "shewing of the face" were to be celebrated, and I provided them with manservants and maidservants, together with cakes, and ale, and oxen, and feathered fowl, and wine, and incense, and fruits, and herbs, and flowers, for the holy offerings which are to be made before thee daily, for ever. (3) I made for thee holy amulets of gold and precious stones, and large collars, and chains of the finest gold wherewith to tie them to thy body at each time of thy majestic rising on thy great and sacred throne in the Apts. (4) I made for thee an image of the lord in worked and chased gold to rest in the place to which it belongeth in thy holy shrine. (5) I made for thee large tablets of gold inlaid and inscribed with the great name of thy Majesty and with [the account of] my thanksgivings. (6) I made for thee other tablets of silver inlaid and inscribed with the great name of thy Majesty and with the decree [for the foundation of] the temple. (7) I made for thee large tablets of silver inlaid and inscribed with the great name of thy Majesty; they were engraved by the chisel with the proclamations and with the decrees for the foundation and maintenance of the temples which I had built in Ta-mera (8) during my reign over the land to proclaim thy name for ever and for ever. O be thou their protector and their advocate! (9) I made for thee other tablets of worked bronze, they were made of a six-fold (?) composition and were of the colour of gold, and they were inscribed and engraved by the chisel with the great name of thy Majesty, and with the foundation decrees of the house and of the temples likewise, (10) and with the manifold praises and thanksgivings which were made to thee, whereat thou wert graciously pleased to listen, O lord of the gods. (11) I made for thee a huge laver of pure silver, the edge of which was made of gold inscribed with thy name, with a cover (?) beaten out of pure silver; [and I made] a huge bath (?) of gold having a cover and legs. (12) I made also the images of the deities Mut and Khonsu which I caused to be newly modelled in the gold foundry, they were made of fine gold chased and engraved, and they were set with jewels and inlaid with precious stones of the workmanship of Ptaḥ. They had collars before and behind, (13) and they were supplied with fine gold fittings, and [the gods] were graciously pleased with the noble things which I wrought for them.

VII. (1) I made for thee great tablets for thy storehouse inlaid with fine gold and with designs in choice gold; they had large edges with inlayings of silver and had golden figures which reached down to the ground. (2) I dedicated to thee ten times ten thousand measures of grain for the perpetual maintenance of thy divine offerings, which [I ordered] to be transported to Thebes every year to supply in abundance thy granaries with corn and grain. (3) I brought to thee captives from the Pet nations and tributes from native and foreign lands to thy court-yard; I made the Theban road to be like the leg which bore offerings in abundance to thee. (4) I added festal seasons to the yearly festivals whereon offerings were made to thee at each time of thy manifestation, and they were provided with cakes, and ale, and oxen, and feathered fowl, and wine, and incense, and fruits without number; for these I laid the princes and officers under a new contribution in addition to the benefits which I had already conferred upon thy double. (5) I hewed out for thee thy sacred boat [called] User-ḥāt, one hundred and thirty cubits long, to sail upon the water; it was made of cedar and acacia (?) wood of marvellous quality, and it was studded with fine gold. It rode upon the water like the bark of Rā when he proceedeth onwards to Mount Bakhat; at the sight thereof (6) all men lived. It had a great double cabin within it made of fine gold, set with jewels of every kind, which was like unto the Temple of the "God of the awful face"; of gold from front to back it was laden with uraei wearing the *atef* crown. (7) I brought Araby and Somali land to thee with their fragrant unguents to pervade thy Temple each morning, and I planted sycamores and incense-bearing trees in thy courts; the like of them had never before been seen. (8) I made for thee boats, and ships, and sailing craft [manned] by armed crews to sail upon the Mediterranean Sea, I appointed to them captains and officers of the crews together with countless mariners, and [commanded] them to bring the products of the land of Tchah and of the remote countries of the world to thy great treasuries in Thebes the mighty. (9) I dedicated to thee cattle from the South and North, and oxen, and feathered fowl, and beasts by hundreds of thousands, and inspectors, and scribes, and overseers, and officers, and numerous shepherds to give fodder unto the beasts which were to be offered to thy double during all thy festivals; and thereat was thy heart graciously pleased, O ruler of the company of the gods. (10) I made for thee vineyards in the Southern Oasis and in the Northern Oasis, and countless others likewise in the South, and in the land of the North they also existed by hundreds of thousands; and I provided them with gardeners taken from the captives from foreign lands. There was a lake . . . . . . (11) planted with lilies and provided with vessels and wine like a water-course to bring them as offerings to thee in Thebes the mighty. (12) I planted thy city Thebes with trees, and with flowering plants and shrubs, and with trees bearing sweet smelling blossoms for thy nostrils. (13) I built a house for thy son Khonsu in Thebes of fine sandstone, and of *bàait* stone and black basalt, and I inlaid its folding-doors with gold and with figures of fine copper like the horizon of heaven.

Hymn to Amen-Rā.

(See pp. 294—305.)

"A hymn of praise to Amen-Rā, the bull in Annu (Heliopolis), president of all the gods, beautiful god, beloved one, the giver of the life of all warmth to all beautiful cattle!

"Hail to thee, Amen-Rā, lord of the thrones of the two lands, at the head of the Apts (Karnak). The bull of his mother, at the head of his fields, the extender of footsteps, at the head of the "land of the South", lord of the Mātchau, prince of Araby, lord of the sky, eldest son of earth, lord of things which exist, establisher of things, establisher of all things.

"One in his times, as among the gods. Beautiful bull of the cycle of the gods, president of all the gods, lord of Law, father of the gods, maker of men, creator of beasts, lord of things which exist, creator of the staff of life, maker of the green food which makes cattle to live. Form made by Ptaḥ, beautiful child, beloved one. The gods make adorations to him, the maker of things which are below, and of things which are above. He shines on the two lands sailing through the sky in peace. King of the South and North, the SUN (Rā), whose word is law, prince of the world! The mighty of valour, the lord of terror, the chief who makes the earth like unto himself. How very many more are his forms than those of any (other) god! The gods rejoice in his beauties, and they make praises to him in the two great horizons, at (his) risings in the double horizon of flame. The gods love the smell of him when he, the eldest born of the dew, comes from Araby, when he traverses the land of the Mātchau, the beautiful face coming from Neter-ta (*i. e.*, Arabia and Somali land). The gods cast themselves down before his feet when they recognize their lord in his majesty, the lord of fear, the mighty one of victory, the mighty of Will, the master of diadems, the verdifier of offerings (?), the maker of *tchefau* food.

"Adorations to thee, O thou maker of the gods, who hast stretched out the heavens and founded the earth! The untiring watcher, Amsu-Amen, lord of eternity, maker of everlastingness, to whom adorations are made (literally, lord of adorations), at the head of the Apts, established with two horns, beautiful of aspects; the lord of the uræus crown, exalted of plumes, beautiful of tiara, exalted of the white crown; the serpent *meḥen* and the two uræi are the (ornaments) of his face; the double crown, helmet and cap are his decorations in (his) temple. Beautiful of face he receives the *atef* crown; beloved of the south and north is he, he is master of the *sekhti* crown. He receives the *amsu* sceptre, (and is) lord of the . . . . . . and of the whip. Beautiful prince, rising with the white crown, lord of rays, creator of light! The gods give acclamations to him, and he stretches out his hands to him that loves him. The flame makes his enemies fall, his eye overthrows the rebels, it thrusts its copper lance into the sky and makes the serpent Nak vomit what it has swallowed.

"Hail to thee, Rā, lord of Law, whose shrine is hidden, master of the gods, the god Khepera in his boat; by the sending forth of (his) word the gods spring into existence. Hail god Atmu, maker of mortals. However many are their forms he causes them to live, he makes different the colour of one man from another. He hears the prayer of him that is oppressed, he is kind of heart to him that calls unto him, he delivers him that is afraid from him that is strong of heart, he judges between the mighty and the weak.

"The lord of intelligence, knowledge (?) is the utterance of his mouth. The Nile cometh by his will, the greatly beloved lord of the palm tree comes to make mortals live. Making advance every work, acting in the sky, he makes to come into existence the sweet things of the daylight; the gods rejoice in his beauties, and their hearts live when they see him. O Rā, adored in the Apts, mighty one of risings in the shrine; O Ani (*i. e.*, a form of Rā), lord of the festival of the new moon, who makest the six days' festival and the festival of the last quarter of the moon; O prince, life, health, and strength! lord of all the gods, whose appearances are in the horizon, president of the ancestors of Auḳer (*i. e.*, the underworld); his name is hidden from his children in his name 'Amen'.

"Hail to thee, O thou who art in peace, lord of dilation of heart (*i. e.*, joy), crowned form, lord of the *ureret* crown, exalted of the plumes, beautiful of tiara, exalted of the white crown, the gods love to look upon thee; the double crown of Upper and Lower Egypt is established upon thy brow. Beloved art thou in passing through the two lands. Thou sendest forth rays in rising from thy two beautiful eyes. The *pāt* (*i. e.*, ancestors, *or* the dead) are in raptures of delight when thou shinest, the cattle become languid when thou shinest in full strength; thou art loved when thou art in the sky of the south, thou art esteemed pleasant in the sky of the north. Thy beauties seize and carry away all hearts, the love of thee makes the arms drop; thy beautiful creation makes the hands to tremble and (all) hearts to melt at the sight of thee.

"O Form, ONE, creator of all things, O ONE ONLY, maker of existences! Men came forth from his two eyes, the gods sprang into existence at the utterance of his mouth. He maketh the green herb to make cattle live, and the staff of life for the (use of) man. He maketh the fishes to live in the rivers, the winged fowl in the sky; he giveth the breath of life to (the germ) in the egg, he maketh birds of all kinds to live, and likewise the reptiles that creep and fly; he causeth the rats to live in their holes, and the birds that are on every green twig. Hail to thee, O maker of all these things, thou ONLY ONE.

"He is of many forms in his might! He watches all people who sleep, he seeks the good for his brute creation. O Amen, establisher of all things, Atmu and Harmachis, all people adore thee, saying, 'Praise to thee because of thy resting among us; homage to thee because thou hast created us.' All creatures say, 'Hail to thee', and all lands praise thee; from the height of the sky to the breadth of the earth, and to the depths of the sea art thou praised. The gods bow down before thy majesty to exalt the Will of their creator; they rejoice when they meet their begetter, and say to thee, Come in peace, O father of the fathers of all the gods, who hast spread out the sky and hast founded the earth, maker of things which are, creator of things which exist, prince, life, health, strength! president of the gods. We adore thy will, inasmuch as thou hast made us, thou hast made (us) and given us birth, and we give praises to thee by reason of thy resting with us.

"Hail to thee, maker of all things, lord of Law, father of the gods, maker of men, creator of animals, lord of grain, making to live the cattle of the hills! Hail Amen, bull, beautiful of face, beloved in the Apts, mighty of risings in the shrine, doubly crowned in Heliopolis, thou judge of Horus and Set in the great hall. President of the great cycle of the gods, ONLY ONE, without his second, at the head of the Apts, Ani at the head of the cycle of his gods, living in Law every day, the double horizoned Horus of the East! He has created the mountain (or earth), the silver, the gold, and genuine lapis-lazuli at his Will .... Incense and fresh *ānti* are prepared for thy nostrils, O beautiful face, coming from the land of the Mātchau, Amen-Rā, lord of the thrones of the two lands, at the head of the Apts, Ani at the head of his shrine. King, ONE among the gods, myriad are his names, how many are they is not known; shining in the eastern horizon and setting in the western horizon, overthrowing his enemies by his birth at dawn every day. Thoth exalts his two eyes, and makes him to set in his splendours; the gods rejoice in his beauties which those who are in his . . . . . . exalt. Lord of the *sekti* boat, and of the *ātet* boat, which travel over the sky for thee in peace, thy sailors rejoice when they see Nak overthrown, his limbs stabbed with the knife, the fire devouring him, his foul soul beaten out of his foul body, and his feet carried away. The gods rejoice, Rā is satisfied, Heliopolis is glad, the enemies of Atmu are overthrown, and the heart of Nebt-ānkh (*i. e.*, Isis) is happy because the enemies of her lord are overthrown. The gods of Kher-āba are rejoicing, those who dwell in the shrines are making obeisance when they see him mighty in his strength (?), Form (?) of the gods of law, lord of the Apts in thy name of 'maker of Law'. Lord of *tchefau* food, bull . . . . . . in thy name of 'Amen, bull of his mother'. Maker of mortals, making . . . . . become, maker of all things that are in thy name of Atmu Khepera. Mighty Law making the body festal, beautiful of face, making festal the breast. Form of attributes (?), lofty of diadem, the two uræi fly by his forehead. The hearts of the *pātu* go forth to him, and unborn generations turn to him; by his coming he maketh festal the two lands. Hail to thee, Amen-Rā, lord of the thrones of the two lands! his town loves his shining."

NOTE. On p. XXI, l. 26, after the words "seeking it" add "be not disheartened".

HIEROGLYPHIC TEXTS WITH TRANSLITERATION

THE TALE OF THE TWO BROTHERS.

I. 1. — *Àr ementuf χertu sen sen en uā muθet en uā àtef Ànpu ren* 1
pa āa àu Batau ren pa śeràu χer àr Ànpu su χeri pa χeri ḥemt 2. *àu* 2
paif sen śeràu emmā-f mà seχeru en śeràu àu ementuf à àritu-nef ḥebsu
àu-f ḥer śemi em-sa naif àaut er seχet 3. *àu ementuf à àritu seka ementuf* 3
āuait àu ementuf à àrit-nef àput neb enti em seχet àstu àu

4 *paif sen śerȧu* 4. *ḥenuti nefer ȧn un qeṭu-f em ta ṫer-f ȧs un . . . . en*
5 *. . . . . ȧm χer ȧr emχet hru qennu ḥer sa enen ȧu paif sen śerȧu* 5. *śemi*
em-sa naif ȧaut em paif seχeru enti hru neb ementuf ḥer āu er paif pa er
6 *tennu ruha ȧu-f atep* 6. *em semu neb en seχet ȧu ementuf ȧ ȧritu-nef em-*
7 *χet āu-nef em seχet emtuf uaḥ-u embaḥ paif sen āa ȧu-f er ḥems ḥenā* 7. *taif*
ḥemt emtuf surȧ emtuf ȧm emtuf . . . . . . pa . . . . paif ȧhait emtuf em-sa
naif ȧaut

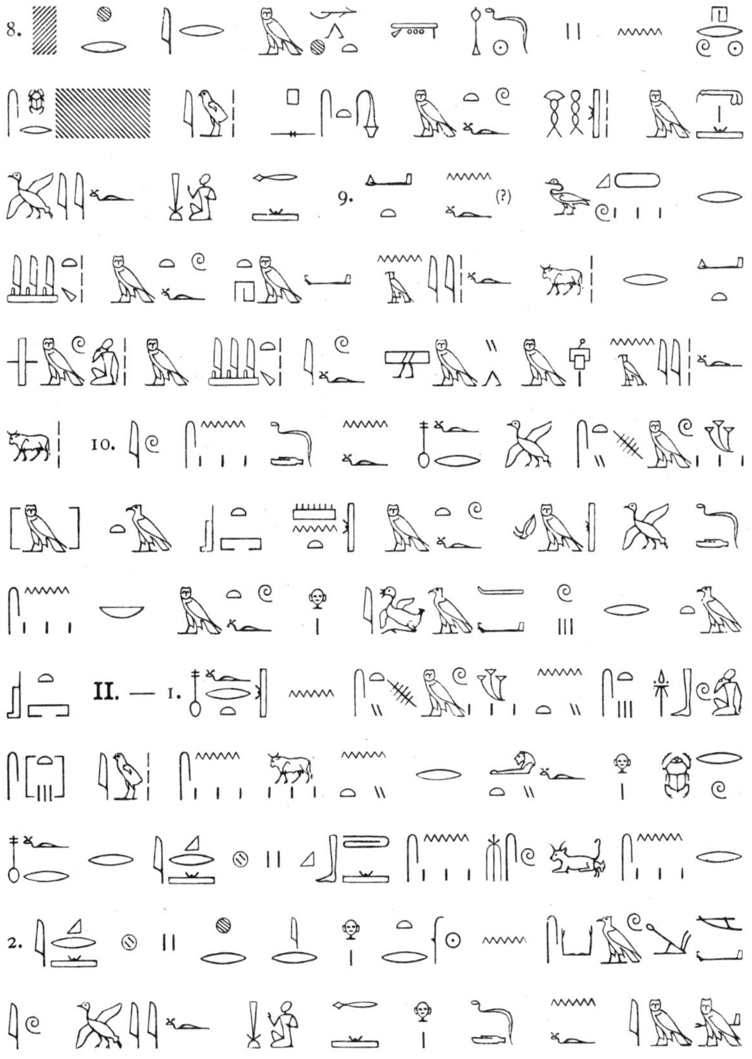

8. χer ȧr emχet ta ḥet' sen en hru seχeper . . . . . . ȧu pesset emtuf·uaḥ-u 8
embaḥ paif sen āa 9. ṭāt-nef āqu er seχet emtuf tehem naif ȧaut er ṭāt ȧmu 9
em seχet ȧu-f śemi em-sa naif ȧaut 10. ȧu-sen ťeṭ-nef nefer pa semu em ta ȧuset 10
ment emtuf setem pa ťeṭ-sen neb emtuf ḥer ȧťa-u er ta ȧuset **II.** — *1. nefert* 1
en semu enti set ȧbu set ȧu-sen ȧaut enti er ḥāti-f ḥer χeperu nefer er ȧqer
sep sen qeb-sen mesu-sen er 2. ȧqer sep sen χer ȧr ḥer trȧ en sekau ȧu paif 2
sen āa ḥer ťeṭ-nef ȧmmā

3 *ḳer en-n ḥetri-n* 3. *er sekau pa un ta aḥet perθȧ ȧu-set neferθȧ er sekau set*
4 *emmȧtet emtuk ī-nek er* 4. *seχet χeri pertu pa un ȧu-n er meḥ sekau em*
5 *ṭuau ȧ nef ťeṭ-nef un ȧn paif* 5. *sen śerȧu ḥer ȧrit seχeru neb ȧ ťeṭ-nef*
6 *paif sen āa er ťer-sen χer ȧr emχet ta ḥeť sen en* 6. *hru seχeperu ȧu-sen*
ḥer śemi er seχet χeri nai-sen ḥetri ȧu-sen meḥ sekau ȧu ḥāti-sen ḥer
7 7. *neťem er ȧqer sep sen ḥer pai-sen rā baku em . . . . aā baku χer*
ȧr emχet

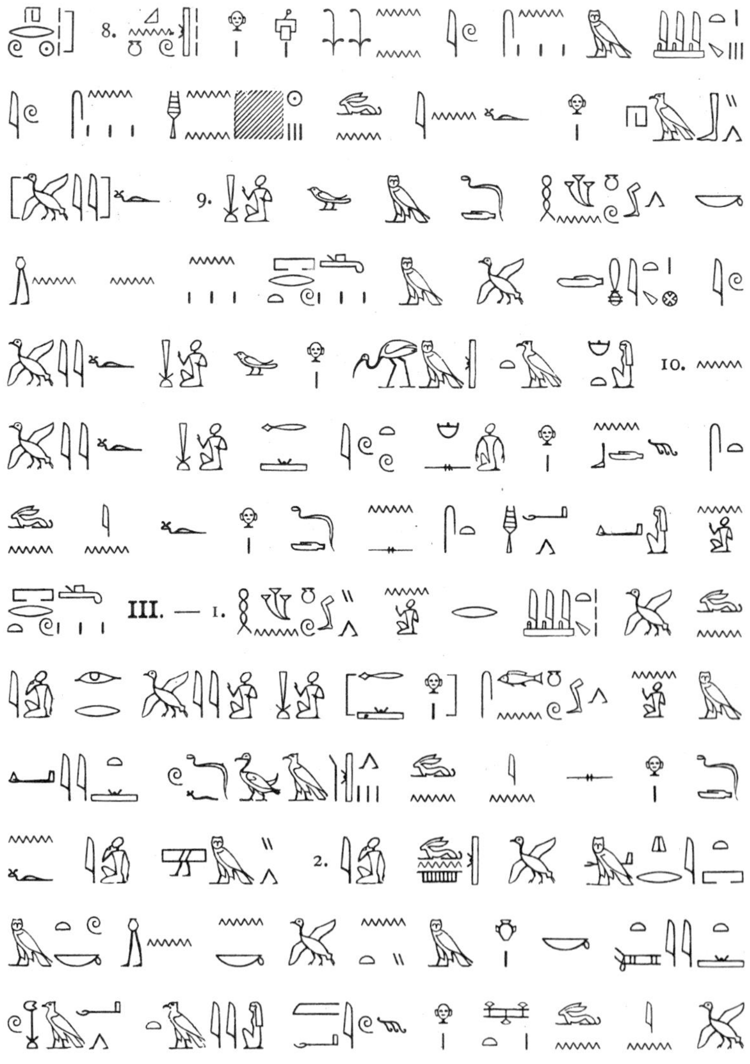

hru 8. *qennu ḥer sa enen ȧu-sen em seχet ȧu-sen āḥā* (?) *n n . . . . un* 8
ȧn-f ḥer habi paif 9. *sen śerȧu em ťeṭ ḥennu-k ȧn-en-n pertu em pa ṭemȧt* 9
ȧu paif sen śerȧu ḥer qem ta ḥemt 10. *en paif sen āa ȧutu ḥems ḥer nebṭ-* 10
set un ȧn-f ḥer ťeṭ-nes set āḥā ṭā-t-nȧ pertu **III.** — 1. *ḥennui-nȧ er seχet* 1
pa un ȧ ȧri paiȧ sen āa ḥer s-ȧnnu-nȧ em ṭāit uťefa un ȧn-s ḥer ťeṭ-nef
ȧ śemi 2. *ȧ un pa māχerȧt emtuk ȧn-nek pa enti em ȧb-k temit uχaā taiȧ* 2
māȧu ḥer uat un ȧn pa

3 *āťeṭu n ḥer* 3. *āq er paif ȧhait ȧu-f ȧn uā en ḥennu āa ȧu ȧb-f er ȧťa*
4 *pertu qennu ȧu-f ḥer atep-f* 4. *em pertu beti ȧu-f ḥer per χeri-sen un*
5 *ȧn-s set ťeṭ-nef ȧχ śau enti ḥer erment-k ȧu-f ḥer ťeṭ-nes set beti* 5. *ḥetep* (?)
χemt pertu ḥesb sen ḥetep ṭua ȧu enti ḥer erment-k (read *erment-ȧ*) *ȧ nef*
6 *ḥer ťeṭ-nes set un ȧn-s set ḥer . . . . . . em ťeṭ un peḥti* 6. *ȧm-k χer tuȧ*
ḥer petrȧ naik θenre emment ȧu ȧb-set reχ-f em reχ en mer [tu] . . . .
7 *un ȧn-s set ḥer* 7. *āḥā ȧu-set meḥ ȧm-f ȧu-set ťeṭ-f māȧi ȧri-n en-*

n unnut st'eru χu-nek paiȧ ka ȧri-ȧ 8. *nek ḥebsu neferu un ȧn pa āt'eṭu* 8
ḥer χeper mȧ ȧbu qemātu em qenṭtu . . . . en pa smȧ 9. *bȧn ȧ t'eṭ-* 9
nes set nef ȧu-set senṭu er ȧqer sep sen un ȧn-f ḥer t'eṭtu emmā-s set em t'eṭ
χer māk tu-t 10. *emmā-ȧ em seχeru en mut χer pait hai emmā-ȧ em seχeru* 10
en ȧtef χer pa āa er-ȧ ementuf seχeperu-ȧ ȧχ **IV.** — 1. *pai betau āa ȧ* 1
t'eṭ-net em ȧri t'eṭ-tuf-nȧ ān χer ȧn ȧu-ȧ ḥer t'eṭ-tuf en uā χer ben ȧu-ȧ
er ṭāt per-f em re-ȧ

2 *en reθ* 2. *nebt àu-f ḥer fa taif atep àu-f ḥer šemi-nef er seχet un àn-f ḥer*
3 *sper er paif sen āa àu-sen meḥ er* (?) *baku* 3. *pai sen rā baku χer àr*
emχet ḥer trà en ruha un àn paif sen āa āu er paif pa 4. *àu paif*
4 *sen šeràu emsa naif àaut àu-f ḥer atep-tuf em χet neb en seχet emtuf*
5 *àn naif àaut* 5. *er ḥāt-f er ṭāt sťer-u em pai sen àhait enti em pa*
6 *ṭemàit às ta ḥemt en paif sen āa senṭu-θà* 6. *pa smà à ťeṭ-nes set un*
àn-s set

ḥer ȧn āṭu qeṭeter ȧu-set ḥer χeperu mȧ enti qenqenθȧ en āťau ȧbu 7. *ťeṭ en* 7
paiset hai em paik sen śerȧu ȧ ȧri qenqen ȧu paiset hai ḥer āu em ruha
8. *em paif seχeru enti hru neb ȧu-f ḥer sper er paif pa ȧu-f ḥer qem taif* 8
ḥemt sťerθȧ merθa en āťau ȧu-set 9. *ḥer temt ṭāt mu ḥer ṭet-f em paif* 9
seχeru [enti hru neb] ȧu bu pui set setau er ḥāt-f ȧu paif pa em kekui
ȧu-set sťerθȧ 10. *beś ȧu paiset hai ḥer ťeṭ-nes set em nimā ťeṭet emmā-t* 10
āḥā ťeṭ-set nef

V. — 1.

2.

3.

4.

1 *bu pu uā ťeṭet emmā-ȧ ḥeru paik* **V.** — 1. *sen śerȧu ȧr n* (?) *ťertu īut-f*
ḥer ȧťa-nek pertu ȧu-f qem-ȧ ḥems-kuȧ uā-ȧ ȧu-f ḥer ťeṭ-nȧ māȧi-t ȧri-en-n
2 *unnut sťer-n* 2. *unχu paiȧ nebṭ ȧ nef ḥer ťeṭ-nȧ ȧuȧ ḥer tem setem nef ȧs*
3 *ben ȧnuk taik muθ χer paik sen āa emmā-k em seχeru en ȧtef* 3. *ȧ nȧ*
ḥer ťeṭ-nef ȧu-f ḥer senṭ ȧu-f ḥer qenqen er tem ṭāt ȧri-ȧ nek ȧput χer ȧr
4 *ṭā-k ānχ-f ȧu-ȧ er mit-nȧ petrȧ* 4. *un-nef ī em ruha pa un-tuȧ sennu pai*
smȧi

bȧn unu au-f er ȧri-f em sḥeť un ȧn paif sen āa ḥer χeperu 5. *mȧ ȧbu qemātu* 5
ȧu-f ḥer ṭāt ṭemtu paif nui ȧu-f ḥer ṭātu-f em ťeṭ-f un ȧn paif sen āa āḥā
en ḥa pa sebai 6. *paif ȧhait er χaṭbu paif sen s̀erȧu em paif ī em ruha er* 6
ṭāt āq naif ȧaut er pa 7. *ȧhait χer ȧr pa Śu ḥer ḥetep ȧu-f ḥer atep-f semu* 7
neb en seχet em paif seχeru enti hru neb ȧu-f ḥer 8. *ī ȧu ta ȧḥ ḥāuti ḥer* 8
āq er pa ȧhait ȧu-set ḥer ťeṭ en paiset sȧu māku-ȧ

9 *paik sen āa āḥā er* 9. *ḥāt-tuk χeri paif nui er χaṭbu-k ruȧ-k-tu er ḥāt-f*
1 *un ȧn-f ḥer setem pa ṭeṭ taif ȧḥ ḥāuti ȧu* **VI.** — 1. *ta ketθȧ ḥer āq ȧu-set*
2 *ḥer ṭeṭθȧ-f emmȧtet ȧu-f ḥer ennu χeri pa seba en paif ȧhait* 2. *ȧu-f ḥer*
3 *petrȧ reṭ en paif sen āa ȧu-f āḥā en ḥa pa seba ȧu paif nui em ṭet-f* 3. *ȧu-f*
4 *ḥer uaḥ taif atep er pa āuṭent ȧu-f ḥer fa-f er seχseχ θāu ȧu paif* 4. *sen*
āa ḥer śemi em-sa-f χeri paif nui-f un ȧn paif sen śerȧu

* In these places the text has been altered by a modern hand.

ḥer smaāt en pa Rā-Ḥeru-χuti 5. *er t̓eṭ paiȧ neb nefer entek en pa* 5
enti ḥer ȧput pa āt̓au er maāt āḥā pa Rā ḥer 6. *setem speru-f neb ȧu pa* 6
Rā ḥer ṭāt χeperu uā en mu āa er āuṭ-f er āuṭ paif sen āa ȧu-f 7. *meḥ em-* 7
seḥu ȧu pa uā ȧm-sen ḥer χeperu ḥer uā en reȧat ȧu pa ki ḥer ketθȧ
ȧu 8. *paif sen āa ḥer ȧrit sep sen ḥu ḥer ṭet-f en pa tem χaṭbu-f ȧ ȧri-f* 8
un ȧn paif 9. *sen śerȧu ḥer āś-nef ḥer ta reȧat em t̓eṭ āḥā ṭi er ḥet̓ ta un* 9
pa ȧten ḥer uben ȧu-ȧ

1 **VII.** — 1. *ḥer àput ḥenā-k embaḥ-f emtuf ḥer ṭāt pa àťau en pa maāt pa*
2 *un àn àu-à χeperu emmā-k . . . . . . er neḥeḥ* 2. *àn àu-à er χeperu em àuset*
àu-k àm-sen àu-à er śemi er ta ànt pa āś χer àr emχet ta ḥeť sen en hru
3 *χeperu àu pa* 3. *Rā-Ḥeru-χuti ḥer uben àu uā ḥer petrà uā àm-sen un àn*
4 *pa aťeṭu n* (?) *ḥer ťeṭu emmā paif sen āa em ťeṭ* 4. *àχ paik ī em-sa-à er*
χaṭbu em ḳer àu àn setem-k re-à ḥer ťeṭtu χer ànuk paik sen śeràu em rā
5 *χer* 5 *tuk emmā-à em seχeru en àtef χer*

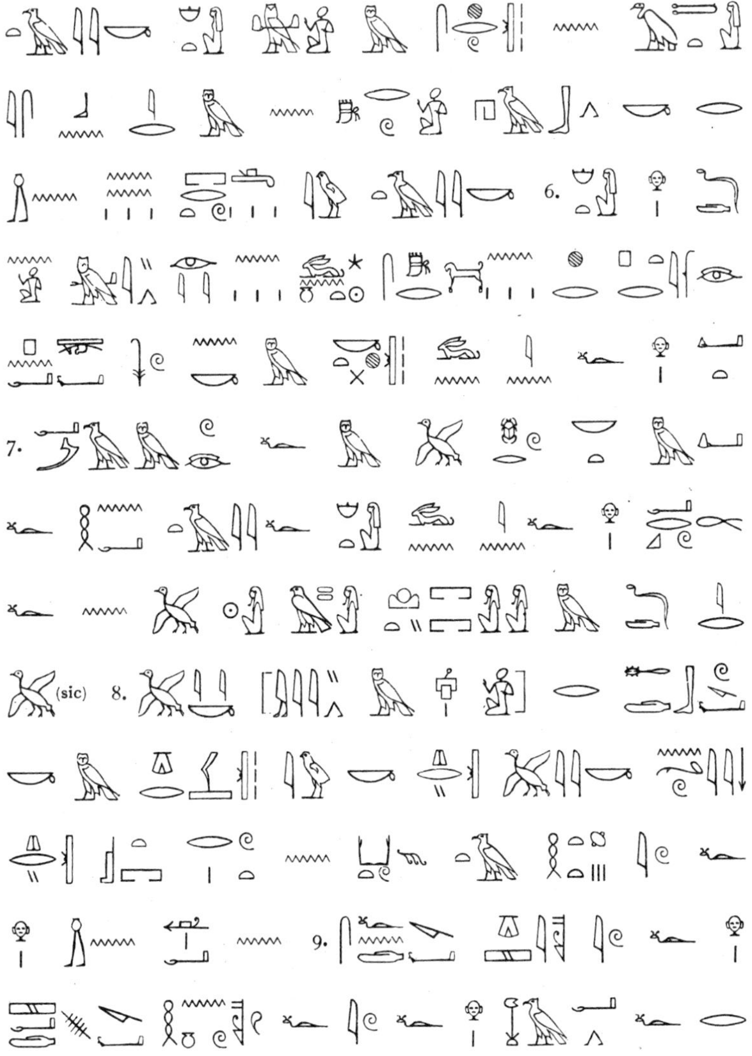

taik ḥemt emmā-ȧ em seχeru en muθet ȧs ben ȧr em n (?) *ťeru-ȧ hab-k er*
ȧn-en-n pertu ȧu taik 6. *ḥemt ḥer ťeṭ-nȧ māȧi ȧri-n unnut sťer-n χer petrȧ* 6
penā su nek em keteχ un ȧn-f ḥer ṭāt 7. *āmamu-f em pa χeperu nebt emmā-f* 7
ḥenā taif ḥemt un ȧn-f ḥer ārqu-f en pa Rā-Ḥeru-χ̣uti em ťeṭ ȧr pa (sic)
8. *paik ī em-sa-ȧ er χaṭbu-k em ḳer ȧu-k χeri paik nui χeri ȧuset re-tu en* 8
katu ta ḥetet ȧu-f ḥer ȧn uā en 9. *sfenṭ ḳešȧ ȧu-f ḥer šāṭ ḥennu-f ȧu-f ḥer* 9
χaā-f er

1 *pa mu àu pa nāru ḥer āmam àu-f* **VIII.** — 1. *ḥer ḳenen àu-f ḥer χeperu*
χas su àu pai-k (sic) *sen āa ḥer šennu ḥāti-f er àqer sep sen àu-f ḥer*
āḥā ḥer remit-nef qa-f àn reχ-f ṭai er pa enti paif sen šeràu àm em ṭer na
2 *en emseḥu* 2. *un àn paif sen šeràu ḥer āš-nef em ṭeṭ àstu àr sχai-k uā en*
bàn àstu bu àru-k sχai uā en nefer em re pu uā en neket àu àri-à su nek
3 *àχ ḥer šemi-k er paik pa emtuk* 3. *ennuit naik àaut pa un àn àu-à āḥā em*
àuset àu-k àm-set

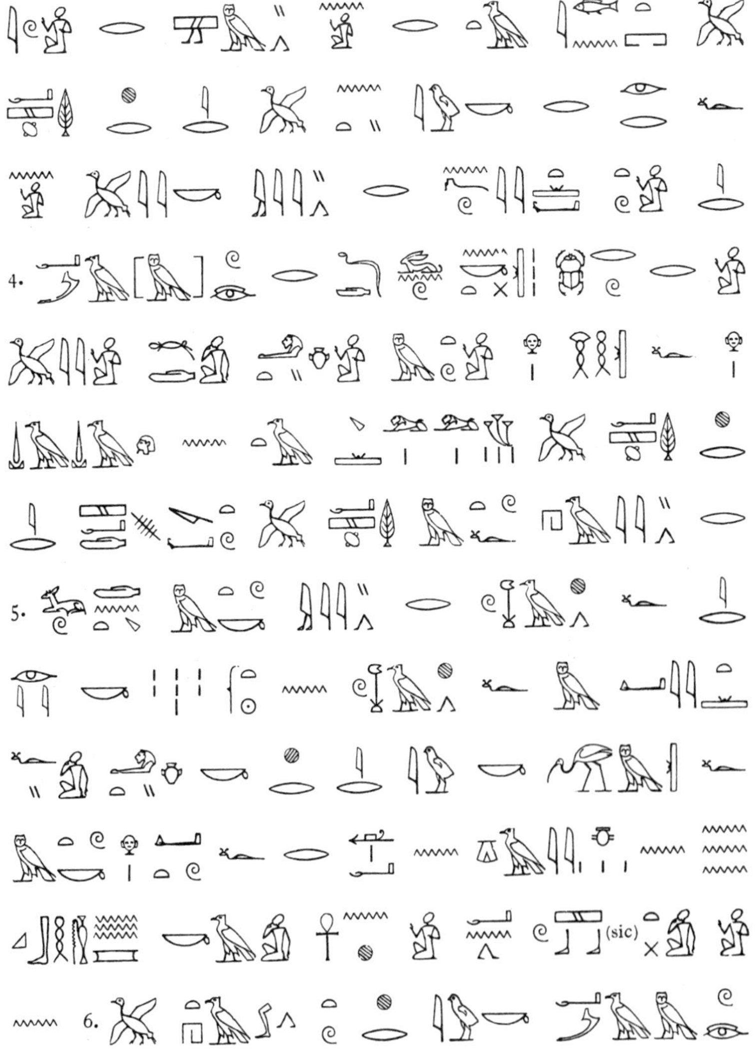

ȧu-ȧ er śemi-nȧ er ta ȧnt pa āś χer ȧr pa enti ȧu-k er ȧri-f-nȧ paik ī er
ennuit-tuȧ ȧr 4. *āmamu er ťeṭ unu neket χeperu er-ȧ paiȧ seśeṭ ḥāti-ȧ* 4
emtuȧ ḥer uaḥ-f ḥer ťaťa en ta ḥurere pa āś χer ȧr śāṭ-tu pa āś emtuf hai
er 5. *āuṭent emtuk ī er uχaχ-f ȧr ȧri-k seχef renput en uχaχ-f em ṭāit fi* 5
ḥāti-k χer ȧr ȧu-k qem-f emtuk ḥer ṭātu-f er uā en ḳai en mu qebḥ ka ānχ-ȧ
ān uśebt-ȧ en 6. *pa teha-tu χer ȧu-k āmamu* 6

er ťeṭ unu ṅeket er-ȧ emtutu ḥer ṭāt-nek uā en θebu en ḥeqt ḥer ṭet-k
emtuf ḥer ȧri setef em ȧri āḥā χer rā ȧu-f ḥer χeperu emmā-k un ȧn-f
7 *ḥer śemi- 7. nef er ta ȧnt pa āś ȧu paif sen āa ḥer śemi-nef er paif*
pa ȧu ṭet-f uaḥ ḥer ťaťa-f ȧu-f urḥu en āuṭent sper pu ȧri-nef er paif
8 *pa ȧu-f ḥer χaṭbu 8. taif ḥemt ȧu-f ḥer χaā-set na en āu ȧu-f ḥems*
em ḳasa en paif sen śerȧu χer ȧr emχet hru qennu ḥer sa enen ȧu paif sen
9 *śerȧu em ta ȧnt pa āś 9. ȧu ȧn*

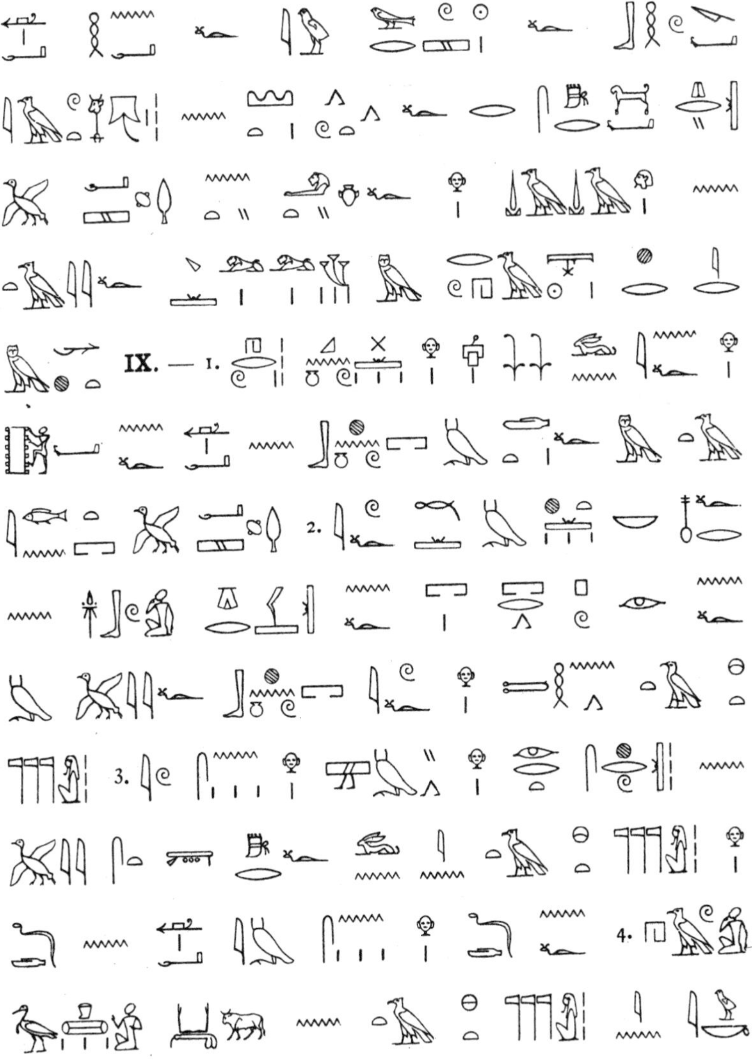

uā ḥenā-f ȧu uruś-f beḥu ȧaut en set ῑut-f er sťer χeri pa āś enti ḥāti-f
ḥer ťaťa en taif ḥurere em ruha χer ȧr emχet **IX.** — 1. *hru qennu ḥer-* 1
sa enen un ȧn-f ḥer qeṭ-nef uā en beχennu em ṭet-f em ta ȧnt pa āś 2. *ȧu-f* 2
meḥ em χet neb nefer en ȧbu ḳer-nef pa per pu ȧri-nef em paif beχennu
ȧu-f ḥer θeḥen ta paut neteru 3. *ȧu-sen ḥer śemi ḥer ȧrit seχeru en paiset* 3
ta ťer-f un ȧn ta paut neteru ḥer ťeṭ en uā ȧm sen ḥer ťeṭ-nef 4. *hau Bata* 4
ka en ta paut neteru ȧn ȧu-k

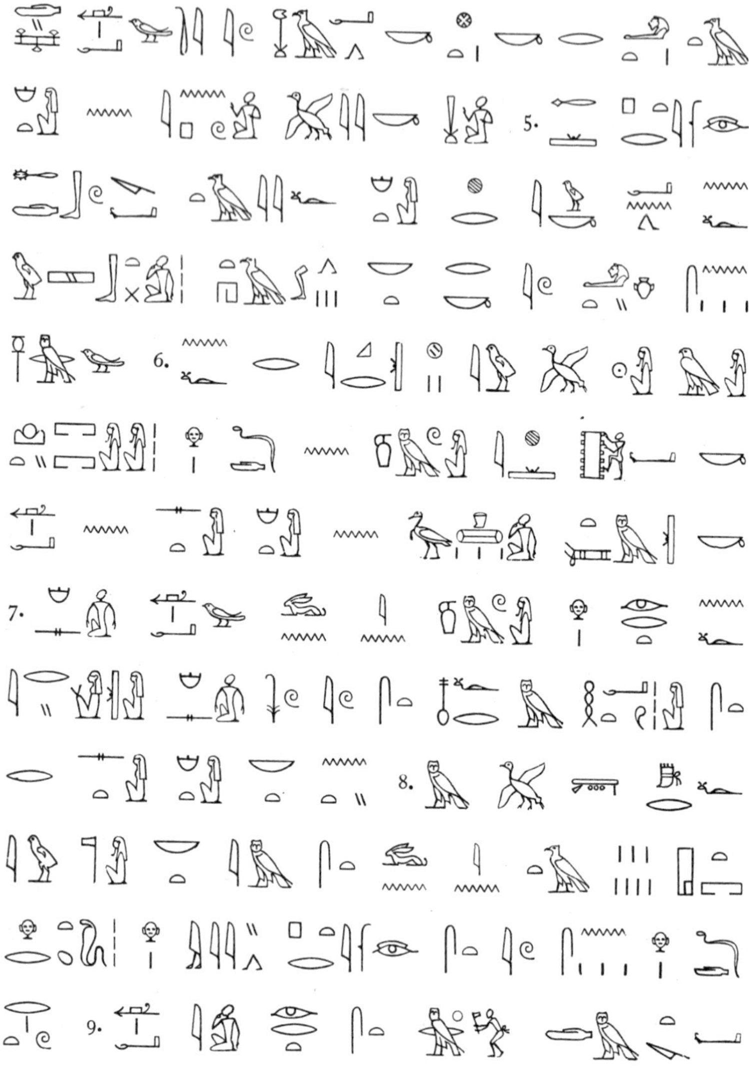

5 *ṭi uā-θȧ ȧu χaā-k nut-k er ḥāt ta ḥemt en Ȧnpu paik sen* 5. *āa petrȧ*
6 *χaṭbu taif ḥemt χer ȧu-k ān-nef uśebt teha nebt erek ȧu ḥāti-sen mer-* 6. *nef*
er ȧqer sep sen ȧu pa Rā-Ḥeru-χuti ḥer ťeṭ en Χnemu ȧχ qeṭ-k uā en set
7 *ḥemt en Bata tem-k* 7. *ḥems uā un ȧn Χnemu ḥer ȧrit-nef ȧri ḥems su*
8 *ȧu-set nefer em ḥāt-set er set ḥemt nebt enti* 8. *em pa ta ťer-f ȧu neter nebt*
9 *ȧm set un ȧn ta seχef Ḥet-ḥert ḥer ī petrȧ-set ȧu-sen ḥer ťeṭ re-ut* 9. *uā ȧ*
ȧrit-set mit ṭemt

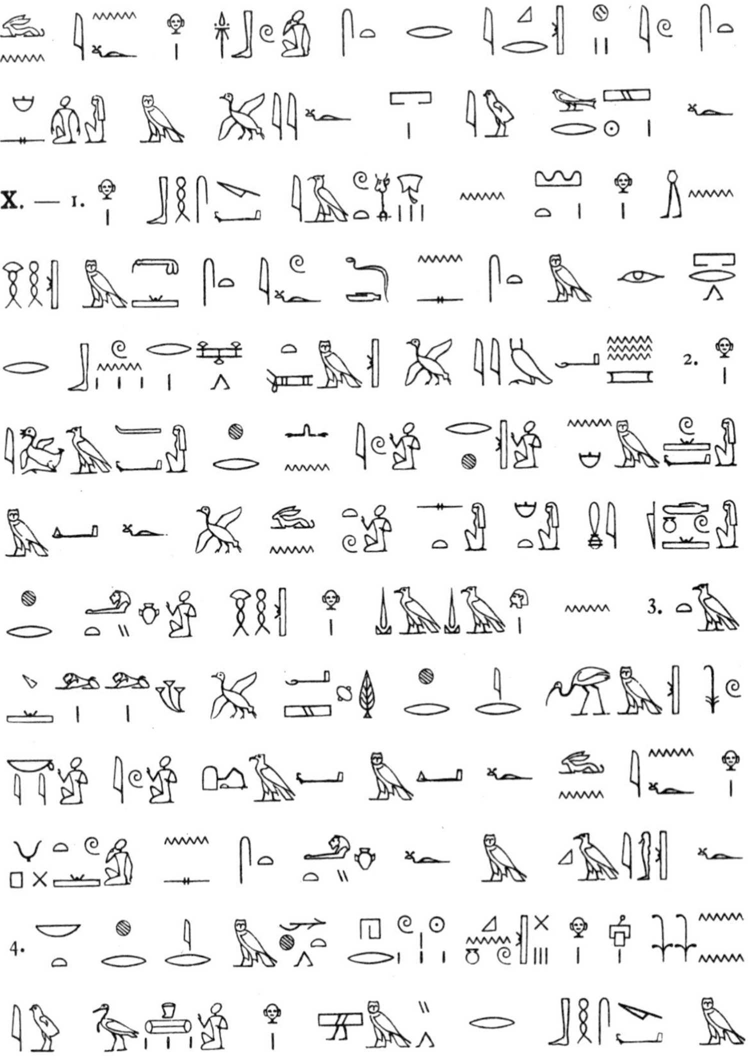

un ȧn-f ḥer ȧbu-set er ȧqer sep sen ȧu-set ḥems em paif pa ȧu urśu-f
X. — 1. *ḥer beḥes ȧaut en set ḥer ȧn uaḥ embaḥ set ȧu-f [ḥer] ťeṭ-nes set* 1
em ȧri per er bun-re tem pa imā 2. *ḥer ȧťa-t χer ȧn ȧu-ȧ reχ-ȧ neḥemu-t* 2
emmā-f pa un-tuȧ set ḥemt mȧ qeṭu-t χer ḥāti-ȧ uaḥ ḥer ťaťa en 3. *ta* 3
ḥureṛe pa āś χer ȧr qem-su ki ȧu-ȧ āba emmā-f un ȧn-f ḥer ȧput-nes set
ḥāti-f em qaȧ-f 4. *nebt χer ȧr emχet hru qeṇnu ḥer-sa enen ȧu Bata ḥer* 4
śemi er beḥes em

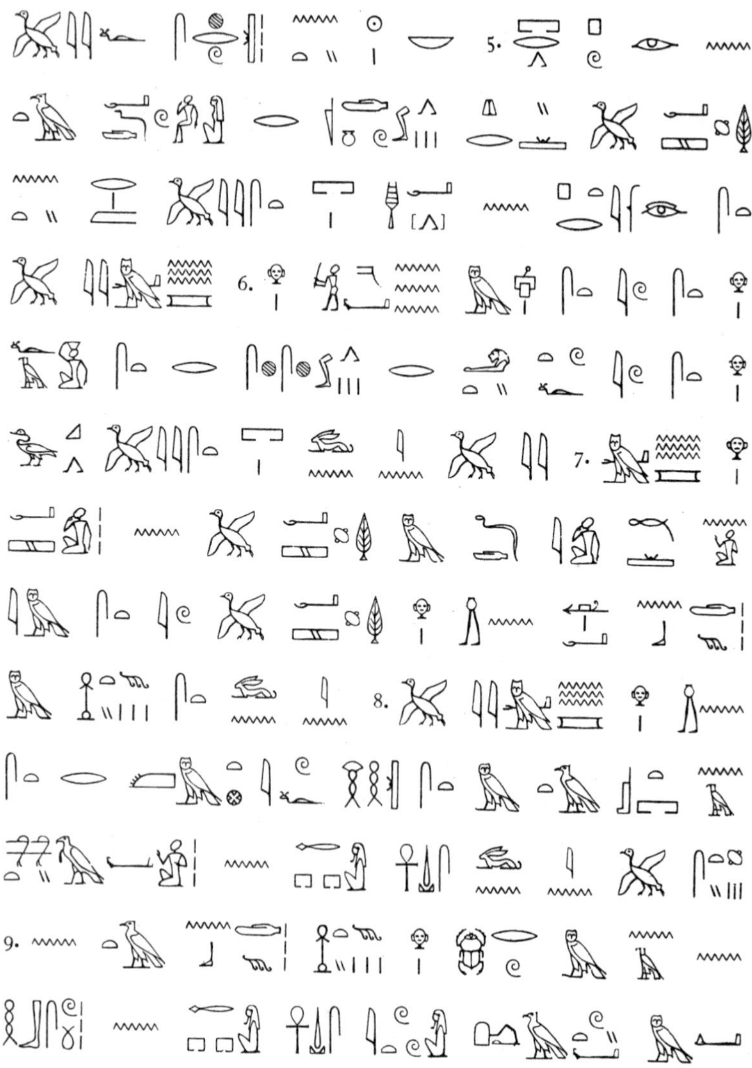

5 *paif seχeru enti hru neb* 5. *per pu ȧri en ta āťeṭu er qeṭenu χeri pa āś enti*
6 *erma paiset pa āḥā en petrȧ-set pa imā* 6. *ḥer ḥu mu em-sa set ȧu-set*
ḥer fa-set er seχseχ er ḥāti-tuf ȧu-set ḥer āq paiset pa un ȧn pa imā
7 7. *ḥer āś en pa āś em ťeṭ ȧ meḥ-nȧ ȧm-set ȧu pa āś ḥer ȧn uā nebṭ em*
8 *śenti-set un ȧn* 8. *pa imā ḥer ȧn-set er Qamt ȧu-f uaḥ-set em ta ȧuset na*
9 *reχti en Āa-perti ānχ uťa senb un ȧn pa sti* 9. *en ta nebṭ śenti ḥer χeperu*
em na en ḥebsu en Āa-perti ānχ uťa senb ȧu-tu ābauti emmā

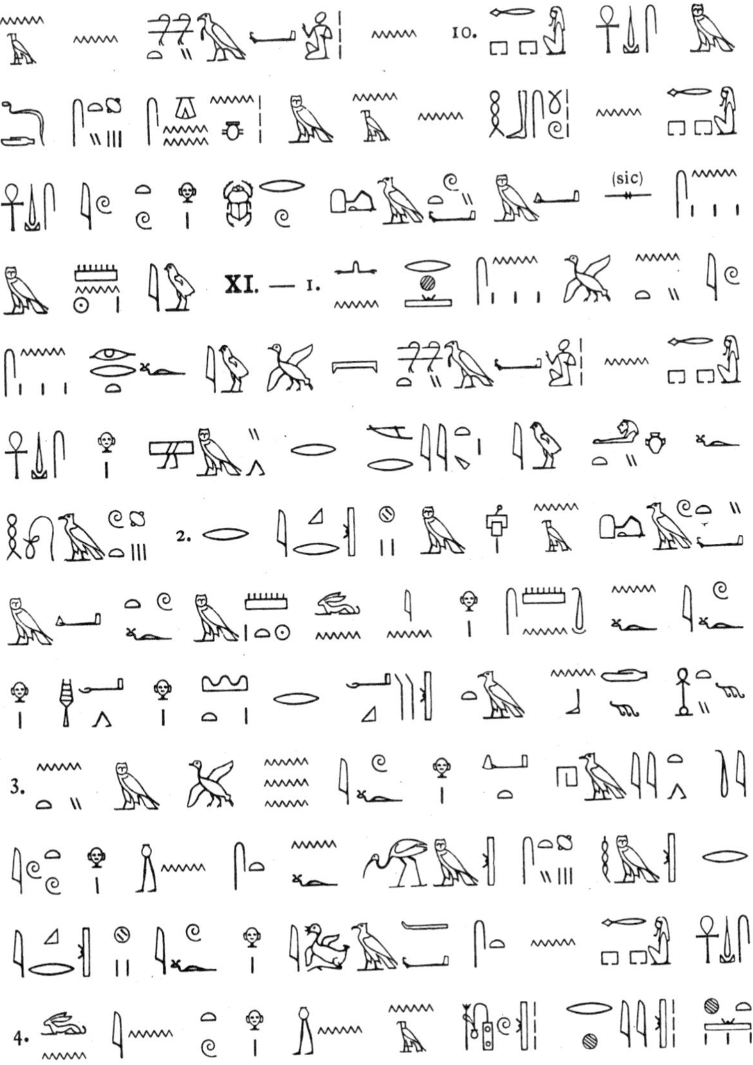

na en reχti en 10. *Āa-perti ānχ uťa senb em ťeṭ sti seḳenen em na en ḥebsu en Āa-* 10
perti ānχ uťa senb ȧu-tu ḥer χeperu ābauti emmā s sen em men ȧu **XI.** — 1. *ȧn* 1
reχ-sen pa enti ȧu-sen ȧrit-f ȧu pa ḥer reχti en Āa-perti ānχ uťa senb ḥer šemi
er merit ȧu ḥāti-f ḥuaut 2. *er ȧqer sep sen em-sa na ābauti emmā-tuf em* 2
ment un ȧn ḥer smen-nef ȧu-f ḥer āḥā ḥer set er āq ta nebṭ šenti 3. *enti em* 3
pa mu ȧu-f ḥer ṭāt hait-θȧ ȧu-tu ḥer ȧn-set nef qem sti neťem er ȧqer sep sen
ȧu-f ḥer ȧťa-set en Āa-perti ānχ uťa senb 4. *un ȧn tu ḥer ȧn na ānu reχi χet* 4

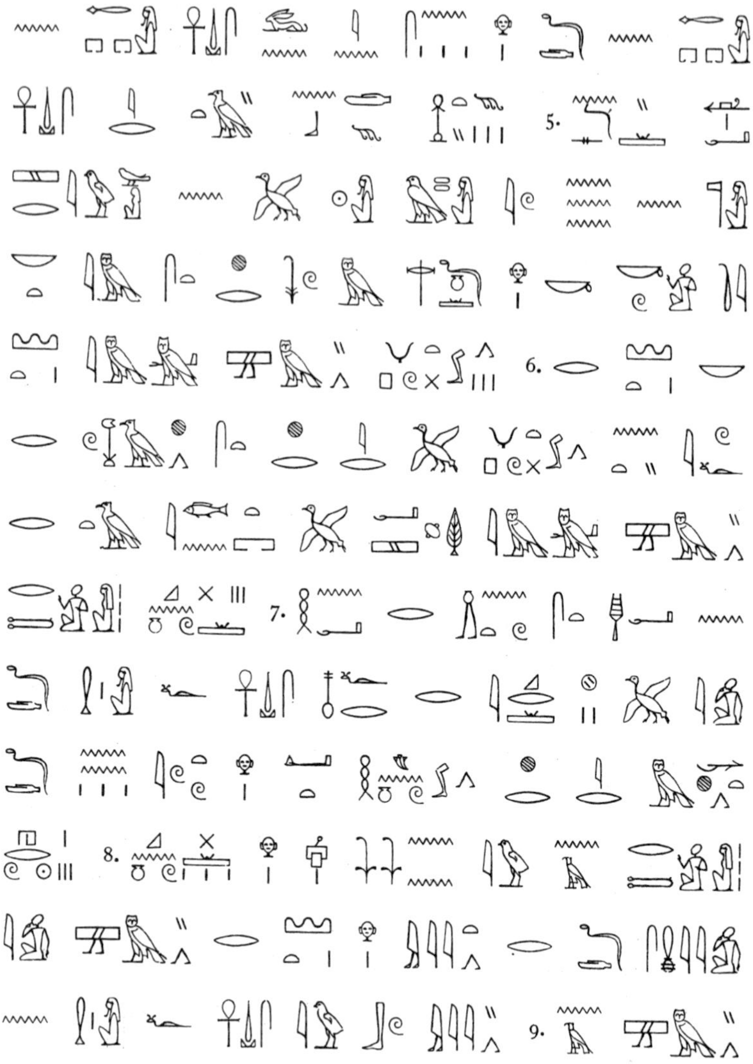

en Āa perti ānχ uťa senb un ȧn-sen ḥer ťeṭ en Āa-perti ānχ uťa senb ȧr tai
5 *nebṭ śenti* 5. *nesi uā śerȧu en pa Rā-Ḥeru-χuti ȧu mu en neter neḃt ȧm-set*
6 *χer su em neť ḥrȧ-k kuȧ-θȧ set ȧmmā śemi ȧput* 6. *er set neb er uχaχ-set*
7 *χer ȧr pa ȧput enti ȧu-f er ta ȧnt pa āś ȧmmā śemi reθ qennu* 7. *ḥenā er*
ȧntu-set āḥā en ťeṭ ḥen-f ānχ uťa senb nefer er ȧqer sep sen pa ȧ ťeṭ en-n
8 *ȧu-tu ḥer ṭāt ḥennu χer ȧr emχet hru* 8. *qennu ḥer sa enen ȧu na reθ ȧ*
śemi er seṭ ḥer īt er ťeṭ smȧi en ḥen-f ānχ uťa senb ȧu bu ī 9. *na śemi*

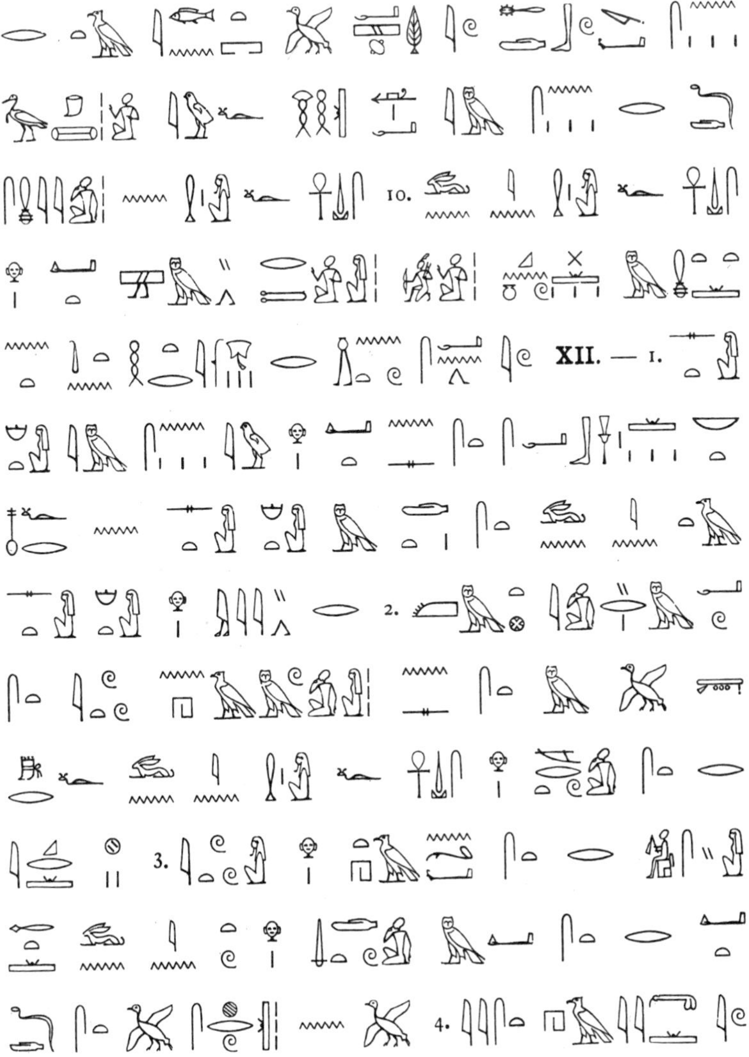

er ta ȧnt pa āś ȧu χaṭbu-sen Bata ȧu-f uaḥ uā ȧm-sen er ťeṭ smȧi en ḥen-f
ānχ uťa senb 10. *un ȧn ḥen-f ānχ uťa senb ḥer ṭāt śemi reθ māśā qennu em-* 10
mȧtet ent θent ḥetrȧ er ȧntu sān ȧu **XII.** — 1. *set ḥemt ȧm-sen ȧu ḥer ṭāt-* 1
nes set sāb nebt nefer en set ḥemt em ṭet-set un ȧn ta set ḥemt ḥer ī er 2. *Qamt* 2
ȧre-māu set ȧu-tu nehamu-nes set em pa ta ťer-f un ȧn ḥen-f ānχ uťa senb
ḥer mertu set er ȧqer sep sen 3. *ȧu-tu ḥer tehan-set er śepsi āat un ȧn tu* 3
ḥer ťeṭtu emmā-set er ṭāt ťeṭ-set pa seχeru en pai 4. *set hai ȧu-*

5 *set ḥer ťeṭ en ḥen-f ānχ uťa senb ȧmmā śāṭ pa āś emtutu seksek-f ȧu-tu* 5. *ḥer*
6 *ṭāt śemi reθ māśā χeri naisen nui er śāṭ pa āś ȧu-sen sper* 6. *er pa āś*
7 *ȧu-sen ḥer śāṭ ta ḥurere enti ḥāti en Bata ḥer-s set* 7. *ȧu-f hait mit em ta*
8 *unnut śerȧu χer ȧr emχet ta ḥeť sen en hru χeperu ȧu śāṭ* 8. *pa āś ȧu*
9 *Ȧnpu pa sen āa en Bata ḥer āq er paif pa ȧu-f* 9. *ḥer ḥems ȧā ṭet-f ȧu-tu*
10 *ḥer ṭāt-nef uā en θebu en ḥeqt ȧu-f ḥer ȧri setef* 10. *ȧu-tu ḥer ṭāt-nef ki en*
ȧrpu ȧu-f ḥer ȧri ḥuaut

XIII. — 1.

2.

3.

4.

5.

un ȧn-f ḥer ȧťa paif **XIII.** — 1. *ḥāu ḥenā naif θetu em-mȧtet naif ḥebsu* 1
ḥenā naif χāāu nu rā ȧu-f ḥer fa-tuf er māšā 2. *er ta ȧnt pa āš ȧu-f* 2
ḥer āq er pa beχennu en paif sen šerȧu ȧu-f ḥer qem paif sen šerȧu sťer
3. *ḥer paif ḥāθȧ ȧu-f miθ ȧu-f remi em ťerti petrȧ paif sen šerȧu sťer* 3
em rā miθ ȧu-f ḥer šemi 4. *er uχaχ ḥāti en paif sen šerȧu χeri pa āš* 4
enti paif sen šerȧu sťer χeri-f em ruha 5. *ȧu-f ȧri χemet renput en uχaχ-f* 5
ȧn qem-f

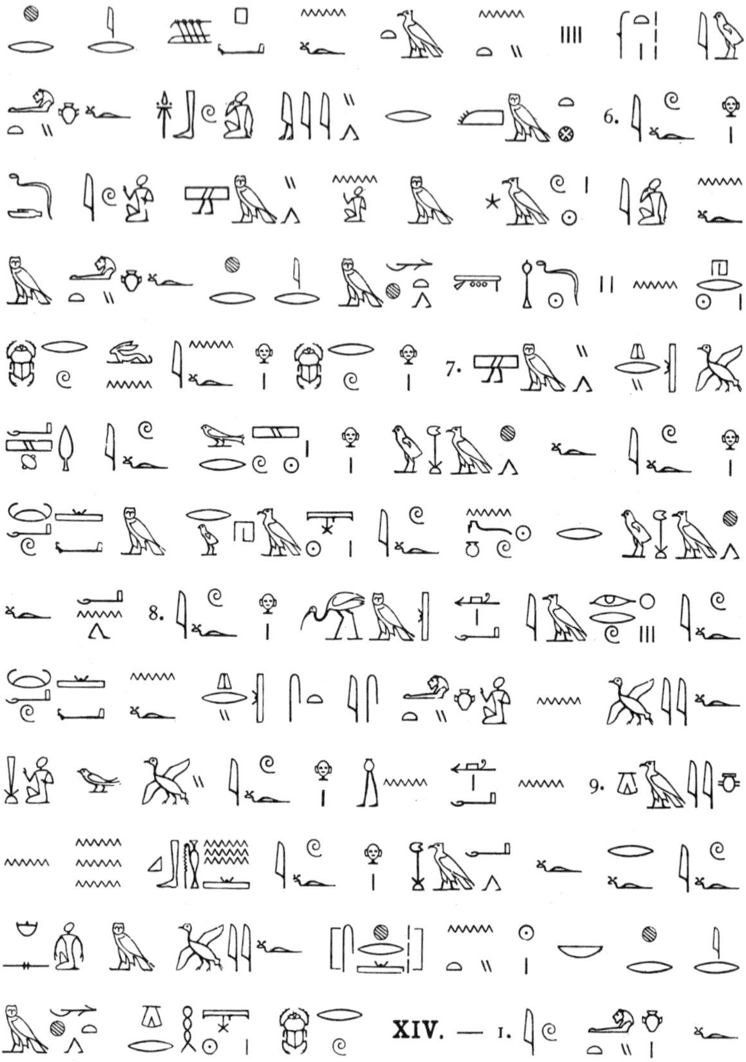

6 *χer ȧr seśep-nef ta enti fṭu renput ȧu ḥāti-f ȧbu ī er Qamt* 6. *ȧu-f ḥer t̓eṭ*
ȧu-ȧ śemi-nȧ em ṭuau ȧ nef em ḥāti-f χer ȧr emχet ta ḥet̓ sen en hru χeperu
7 *un ȧn-f ḥer χeperu ḥer* 7. *śemi χeri pa āś ȧu-f urśu ḥer uχaχ-f ȧu-f ḥer*
8 *āu em ruha ȧu-f ennu er uχaχ-f ān* 8. *ȧu-f ḥer qem uā ȧaru ȧu-f āu-*
nef χeri set ȧs ḥāti en paif sen śerȧu pai ȧu-f ḥer ȧn uā en 9. *ḳai en*
9 *mu qebḥ ȧu-f ḥer χaā-f eref ȧu-f ḥems em paif seχeru enti hru neb χer ȧr*
1 *emχet ḳerḥ χeperu* **XIV.** — 1. *ȧu ḥāti-f*

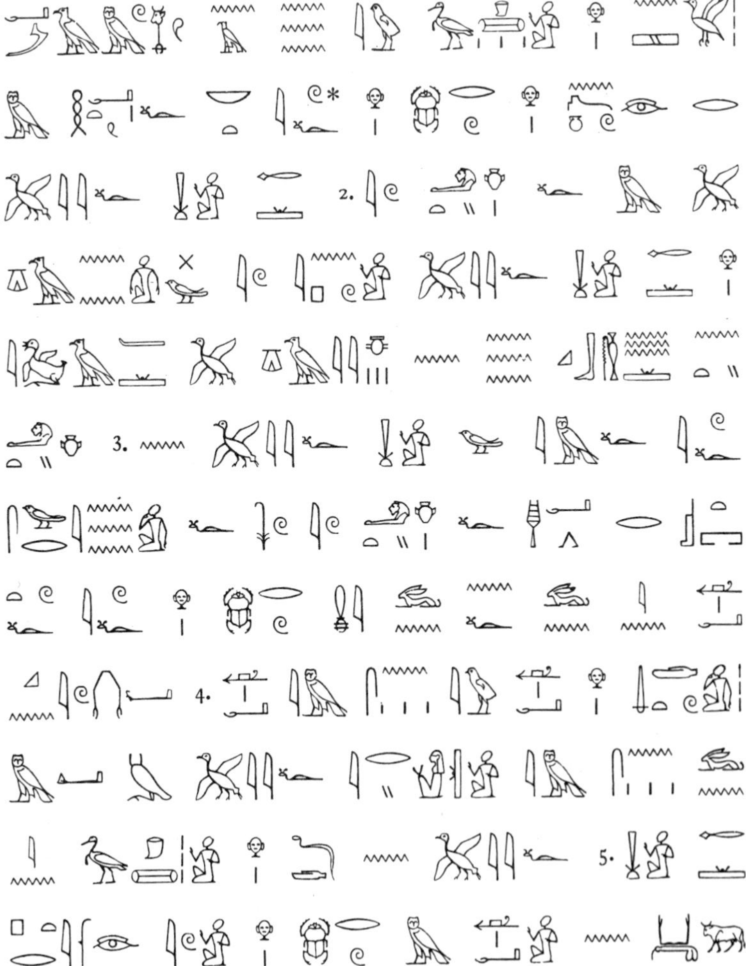

āmamu na mu ȧu Bata ḥer neś em ḥāt-f nebt ȧu-f ḥer χeperu ḥer ennu er paif sen āa 2. *ȧu ḥāti-f em pa ḳanen ȧu Ȧnpu paif sen āa* 2
ḥer ȧt'a pa ḳai en mu qebḥ enti ḥāti 3. *en paif sen śerȧu ȧm-f* 3
ȧu-f surȧ-f su ȧu ḥāti-f āḥā er ȧuset-tuf ȧu-f ḥer χeperu mȧ un-nef un ȧn uā qenȧu 4. *uā ȧm-sen ȧu uā ḥer t'eṭtu emmā em paif ȧri ȧm-* 4
sen un ȧn Bata ḥer t'eṭ en paif 5. *sen āa petrȧ ȧu-ȧ ḥer χeperu em uā* 5
en ka

* The papyrus has

6 *āa ȧu-f em ȧnnu nebt nefer ȧu ȧn reχ-tu paif seχeru* 6. *emtuk ḥems-kuȧ*
7 *ḥer pesṭ ȧ ȧrit pa Śu ḥer uben ȧu-n em pa enti taiȧ ḥemt ȧm ān-* 7. *nȧ*
uśebt emtuk ḥer ȧťa-ȧ er pa enti tutu ȧm pa un ȧu-tu ȧrit-nek neket nebt
8 *nefer χer ȧutu* 8. *ḥer fa-tuk em ḥeť nub ḥer paik ȧťa-ȧ en Āa-perti ānχ uťa*
9 *senb pa un ȧu-ȧ ḥer χeperu em bȧat āa emtutu* 9. *nehamu-nȧ em pa ta ťer-f*
1 *emtuk ḥer śemi-nek er paik ṭemȧt χer ȧr emχet ta ḥeť* **XV.** — 1. *sen en*
hru χeperu un ȧn Bata ḥer χeperu em pa χeperu ȧ

ťeṭ-f en paif sen āa un ȧn Ȧnpu 2. *paif sen āa ḥer ḥems ḥer pesṭ-f er ḥeť* 2
ta ȧu-f ḥer sper er pa enti tutu ȧm ȧu-tu ḥer ṭāt 3. *āmamu ḥen-f ānχ uťa* 3
senb em ȧm-f ȧu-f ḥer petrȧ-f ȧu-f ḥer χeperu reštu-nef er ȧqer sep sen
ȧu-f ḥer ȧrit-nef 4. *ābtu āat er ťeṭ buȧaitu āat tai χeperu-θa ȧu-tu nehamu-* 4
nef em pa ta ťer-f un ȧn tu 5. *fa-tuf em ḥeť nub en paif sen āa ȧu-f ḥems* 5
em paif ṭemȧt ȧu-tu ḥer ṭāt-nef reθ 6. *qennu χet qennu ȧu Āa-perti ānχ uťa* 6
senb ḥer mertu-f er ȧqer sep sen er reθ neb

7 *enti em pa ta er ťer-f* 7. *χer ȧr emχet hru qennu ḥer-sa enen ȧu-f ḥer āq*
8 *er ta ābet ȧu-f āḥā em pa enti* 8. *ta šepsi ȧm ȧu-f ḥer χeperu ḥer ťeṭtu*
9 *emmā-s set em ťeṭ petrȧ tuȧ ānχ-kuȧ em rā ȧu-set ḥer* 9. *ťeṭ-nef ementek n*
10 *nimā trȧ ȧu-f ḥer ťeṭ-nes set ȧnuk Bata tu-t ḥer āmamu em ťerti* 10. *ṭāt-t*
ȧritu seksek pa āš en Āa-perti ānχ uťa senb χeri ȧuset er-ȧ tem ṭāt ānχ-kuȧ
1 *petrȧ-* **XVI.** — 1. *tuȧ ānχ-kuȧ em rā ȧu-ȧ em ka un ȧn ta šepsi ḥer senṭu*
er ȧqer sep sen en pa smȧi ȧ ťeṭ-set en

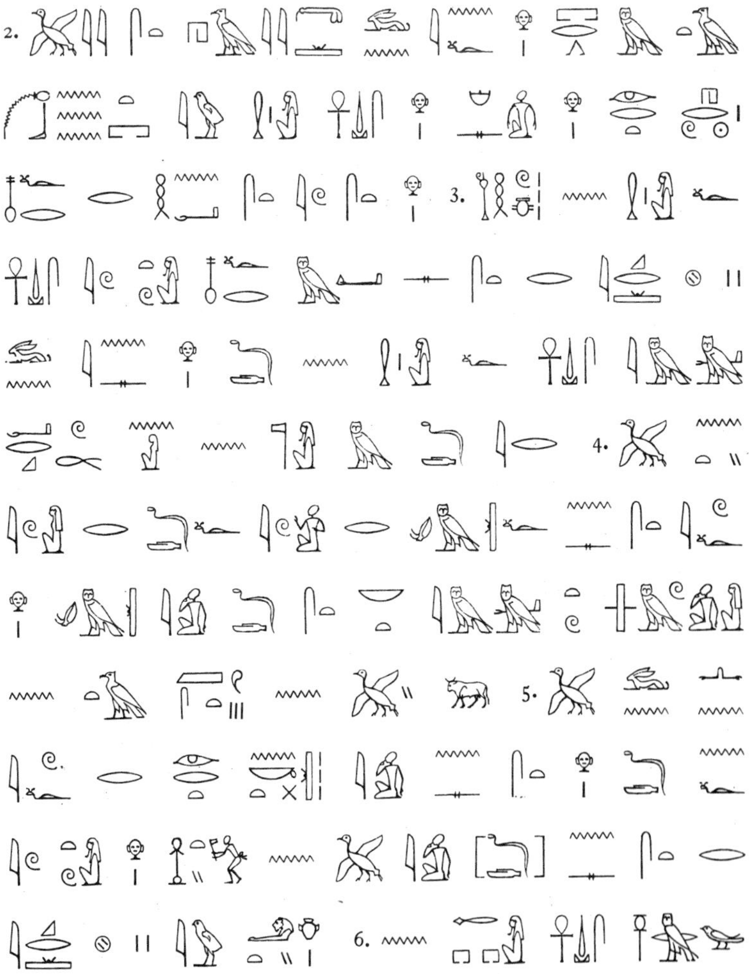

2. paiset hai un ȧn-f ḥer per em ta ābet ȧu ḥen-[f] ānχ uťa senb ḥer 2
ḥems ḥer ȧrit hru nefer er ḥenā set ȧu-set ḥer 3. uṭḥu en ḥen-f ānχ uťa 3
senb ȧu-tu nefer emmā-s-set er ȧqer sep sen un ȧn-s [set] ḥer ťeṭ en ḥen-f
ānχ uťa senb ȧmmā ārqu-nȧ en neter em ťeṭ ȧr 4. pa enti ȧu-t er ťeṭ-f 4
ȧu-ȧ er setem-f nes set ȧu-f ḥer setem ȧ ťeṭ-set nebt ȧmmā-tu ȧmu-ȧ en ta
maāset en pai ka 5. pa un ȧn ȧu-f er ȧrit neket ȧ nes set ḥer ťeṭ-nef ȧu-tu 5
ḥer śenti en pa ȧ ťeṭ-nes set er ȧqer sep sen ȧu ḥāti 6. en Āa-perti ānχ uťa 6
senb mer-

7. 8. 9. 10. **XVII.** — 1.

nef er ȧqer sep sen χer ȧr emχet ta seḥeṭ' sen en hru χeperu ȧu-tu ḥer na nȧs
7 *ābtu āat em* 7. *uṭennu en pa ka ȧu-tu ḥer ṭāt ṡem uā en suten ābu ṭep en*
8 *ḥen-f ānχ uṭa senb er ṭāt maā pa ka χer ȧr* 8. *ḥer-sa ȧu-tu ḥer ṭāt maāt-f*
χer ȧr su ḥer ermenui na en reθ ȧu-f ḥer ketket em neḥeb-f ȧu-f ḥer ṭāt
9 9. *χaā-nef ṭ'ef sen en senf er pa ur neṡu sen en ḥen-f ānχ uṭa senb ȧu ta*
10 *uā ḥer χeperu ta reȧai en* 10. *pa θȧireȧa āa en Āa-perti ānχ uṭa senb ȧu ta*
1 *ketθȧ ḥer ta ketθȧ reȧai ȧu-sen ḥer ruṭ em ṡauabu* **XVII.** — 1. *sen*

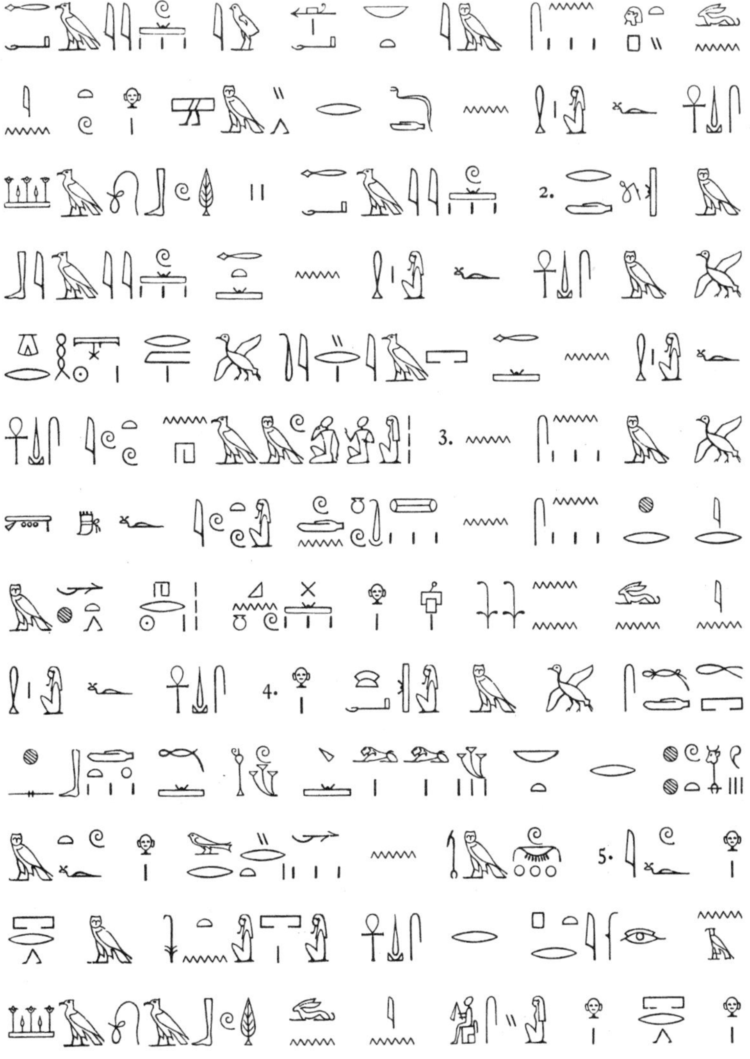

āāaiu ȧu uā nebt ȧm-sen ṭepti un ȧn-tu ḥer śemi er ťeṭ en ḥen-f ānχ uťa
senb śauabu āāaiu 2. *ruṭ em bȧaiu āat en ḥen-f ānχ uťa senb em pa ḳerḥ* 2
erma pa θȧireȧa āa en ḥen-f ānχ uťa senb ȧu-tu nehamu 3. *en sen em pa* 3
ta ťer-f ȧu-tu uṭennu en sen χer ȧr emχet hru qennu ḥer-sa enen un ȧn ḥen-f
ānχ uťa senb 4. *ḥer χāā em pa seśeṭ χesbeṭet meḥ utu ḥurere nebt er χeχut* 4
emtuf ḥer uriret en smu 5. *ȧu-f ḥer per em suten pa ānχ uťa senb er petrȧ* 5
na śauabu un ȧn śepsi ḥer per ḥer

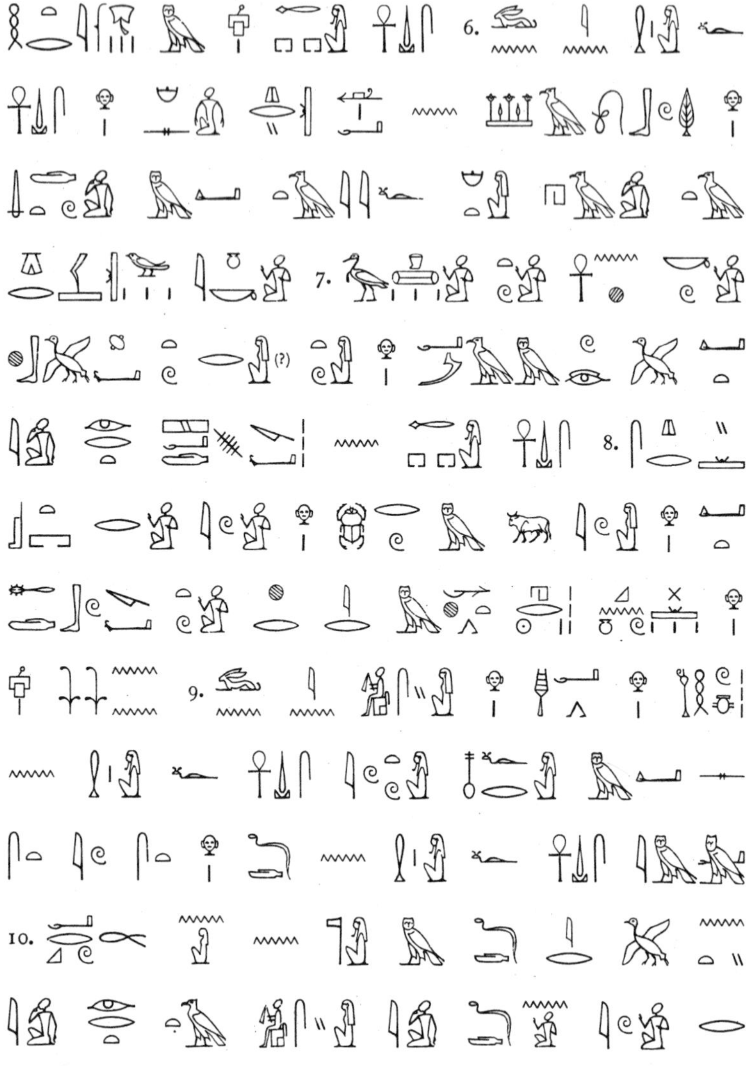

6 *ḥetrȧ em sa Āa-perti ānχ uťa senb* 6. *un ȧn ḥen-f ānχ uťa senb ḥer ḥems*
7 *χeri uā en šauabu ḥer ťeṭtu emmā taif ḥemt ha ta ḳer ȧnuk* 7. *Bata tuȧ*
ānχ-kuȧ χebba-tu er-t (?) *tu-t ḥer āmamu pa ṭāt ȧ ȧrit šāṭ en Āa-perti ānχ*
8 *uťa senb* 8. *s χeri ȧuset er-ȧ ȧu-ȧ ḥer χeperu em ka ȧu-t ḥer ṭāt χaṭbu-tuȧ*
9 *χer ȧr emχet hru qennu ḥer-sa enen* 9. *un ȧn šepsi ḥer āḥā ḥer utḥu en*
ḥen-f ānχ uťa senb ȧu-tu nefer emmās-set ȧu-set ḥer ťeṭ en ḥen-f ānχ uťa senb
10 *ȧmmā* 10. *ārqu-nȧ en neter em ťeṭ ȧr pa enti ȧ ȧrit ta šepsi ȧ ťeṭ-nȧ ȧu-ȧ er*

XVIII. — 1. 2. 3. 4. 5.

[2 in., in red, illegible to me] 6.

setem-f nes set ka-k àu-f ḥer setem **XVIII.** — 1. *à t'eṭ-set nebt àu-set t'eṭ* 1
àmmā śāṭ-tu pai śauabu sen emtutu à àritu em àpṭu neferu 2. *un àn-tu ḥer* 2
setem à t'eṭ-set nebt χer àr emχet hru qennu ḥer-sa enen un àn ḥen-f ānχ ut'a
senb ḥer ṭāt 3. *śemi ābuu reχi àu-tu ḥer śāṭ na en śauabu en Āa-perti ānχ* 3
ut'a senb ḥer āḥā petrà su 4. *suten ḥemt ta śepsi un àn uā en at'a ḥer pui* 4
àu-f ḥer āq em re en ta śepsi un àn set 5. *ḥer āmamu àu-set ḥer seśep āuur* 5
. . . . . . *àu-tu ḥer àrit* 6. *pa enti nebt em àb-set* 6

7 *àm-sen un àn emχet hru qennu ḥer-sa enen un àn set* 7. *ḥer mesi uā en se*
8 *t'ai àu-tu ḥer māšem er t'eṭ en ḥen-f ānχ ut'a senb mesi-tu* 8. *nek uā en se t'ai*
9 *un àntu ḥer àn-tuf àu-tu ḥer ṭāt-nef menāt χenemem àu-tu* 9. *ḥer nehamu*
10 *em pa ta t'er-f àu-tu ḥems ḥer àrit hru nefer àu-tu ḥer χeperu* 10. *em ren-nef*
àu ḥen-f ānχ ut'a senb ḥer mertu-nef er àqer sep sen em ta unnut àu-tu
1 *ḥer ṭehan-f* **XIX.** — 1. *suten se šeps en Kešt χer àr emχet hru qennu ḥer-sa*
enen un àn ḥen-f ānχ ut'a senb ḥer ṭā-tuf

* The papyrus has

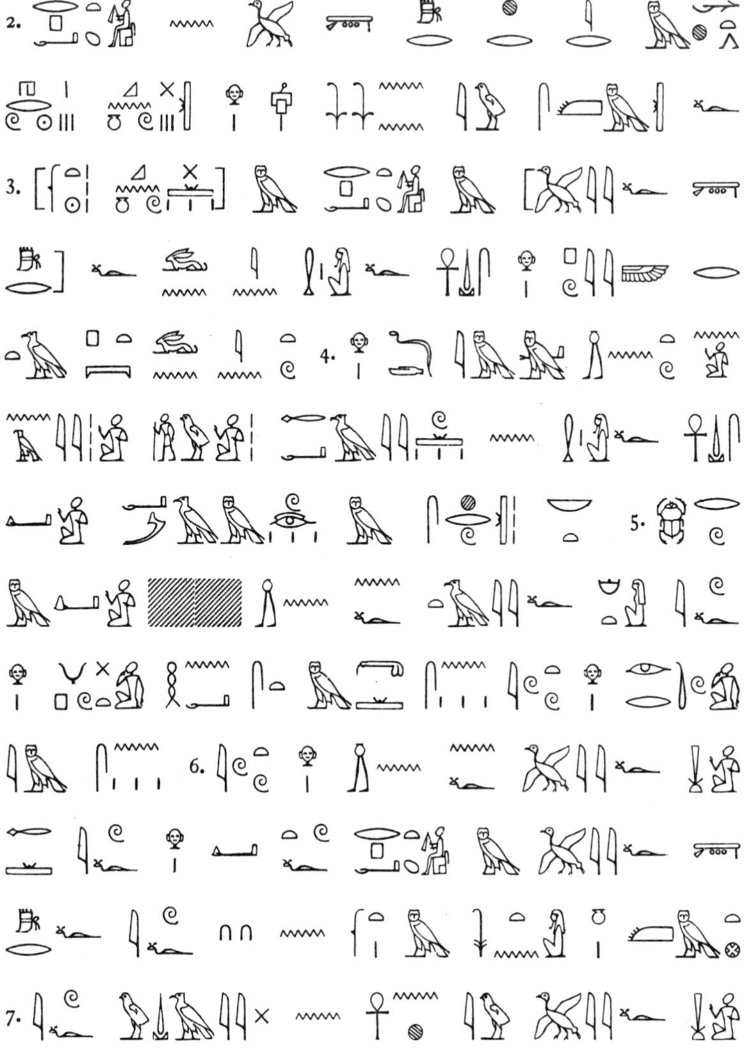

2. *erpāt en pa ta ťer χer ȧr emχet hru qennu ḥer-sa enen ȧu seqam-f* 3. *renput* 2 3
qennu em erpāt em paif ta ťer-f un ȧn ḥen-f ānχ uťa senb ḥer pui er ta pet
un ȧn tu 4. *ḥer ťeṭ ȧmmā ȧntu-nȧ naiȧ seru āāaiu en ḥen-f ānχ uťa senb ṭā-ȧ* 4
āmamu em seχeru nebt 5. *χeperu emmā-ȧ [un ȧn-tu ḥer] ȧn-nef taif ḥemt ȧu-f* 5
ḥer ȧput ḥenā-set embaḥ sen ȧu-tu ḥer ȧriθu ȧm-sen 6. *ȧu-tu ḥer ȧn-nef* 6
paif sen āa ȧu-f ḥer ṭā-tuf erpāt em paif ta ťer-f ȧu-f ťaut en renpit em
suten nu Qamt 7. *ȧu-f uťai en ānχ ȧu paif sen* 7

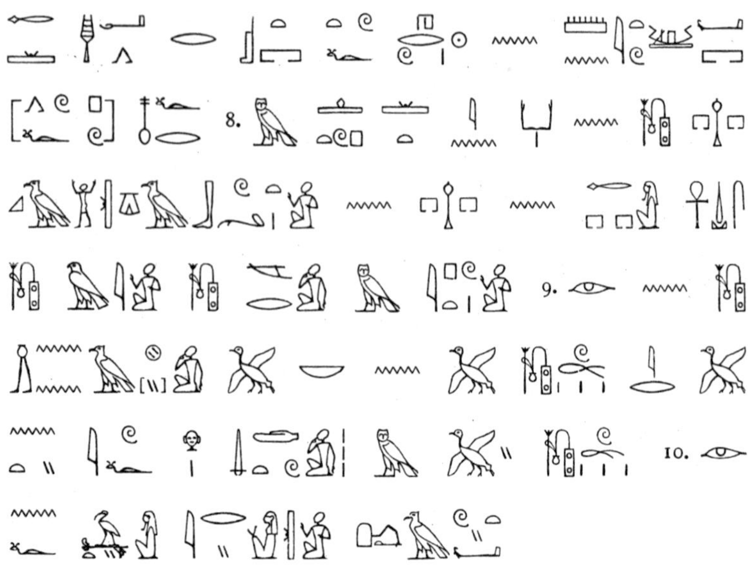

8 *āa āḥā er àuset-tuf hru en menàtu [īu-f pu] nefer* 8. *em ḥetepu śāt àn ka*
en ān per-ḥeť Qaḳabut en per ḥeť en Āa-perti ānχ uťa senb ān Ḥeruà ān
9 *Meremàptu* 9. *àri en ān Ànnana pa neb en pa ānu àr pa enti àu-f ḥer ťeṭtu*
10 *em pai ānu* 10. *àri-nef Teḥuti àri ābauti*

THE POSSESSED PRINCESS OF BEKHTEN.

1 1. *Ḥeru ka neχt tut χāāu ṭeṭṭeṭ suteniu mà Tmu Ḥeru nub usr χepeś ṭer*
pet paut suten net neb taiu *Usr-Maāt-Rā-setep-nu-Rā* *se Rā en χat-f*
2 *Àmen-meri Rā-meses* *Àmen-Rā* 2 *neb nest*

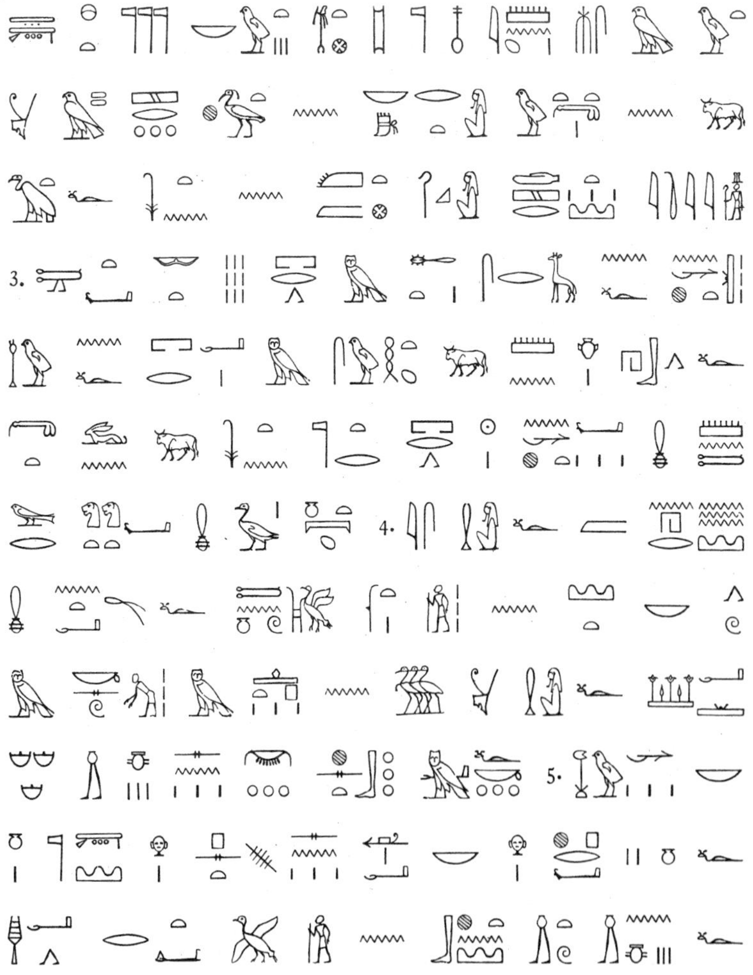

taiu paut neteru nebut Uast meri neter nefer Ȧmen se mes Ḥeru ut en
Ḥeru-χuti śer χut en Neb-er-ťert utet en ka mut-f suten en Qamt ḥeq ṭeśert
ȧθi 3. *θet pet paut per em χat ser-nef neχt utu-nef per ā em suḥt ka men ȧb* 3
hab-f met un ka suten neter per hru neχt mȧ Menθ ur peḥtpeḥt mȧ se
Nut 4. *ȧs ḥen-f em Neher mȧ entā-f θennu renpit seru en set neb iu em* 4
kesu em ḥetepu en baiu en ḥen-f śaā peḥu ȧntu ȧn-sen nub χesteb māfek
5. *χau neb nu Neter-ta ḥer pest-sen uā neb ḥer χerp sen-f āḥā erṭāt pa* 5
ser en Beχten ȧntu ȧn-f

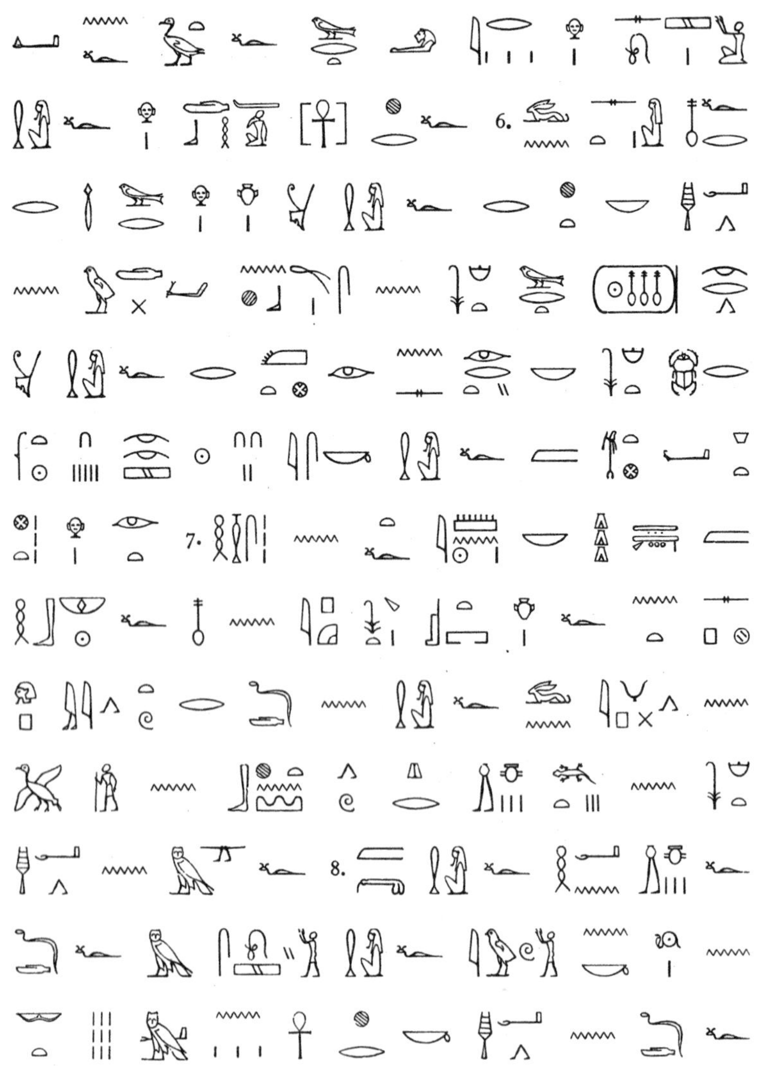

6 *ṭā-nef set-f urt ḥā āru ḥer suaś ḥen-f ḥer ṭebḥ ānχ χer-f* 6. *un-set nefer er āa ur*
ḥer-āb en ḥen-f er χet neb āḥā en uṭ neχeb-s en suten ḥemt urt (*Rā-neferu*) *sper*
en ḥen-f er Qamt āri-nes āriti neb suten ḥemt χeper renpit met ṭua ābeṭ sen śe hru
7 *t'aut sen ās-k ḥen-f em Uast neχt ḥent nut ḥer ārit* 7. *ḥesu en tef Āmen-Rā neb*
nest taiu em ḥeb-f nefer en Āpt resu āuset āb-f ent sep ṭep ī-tu er t'eṭ en ḥen-f un āp
8 *en pa ser en Beχten īu χer ān āśt en suten ḥemt āḥā en mes-f* 8. *embaḥ ḥen-f ḥān*
ān-f t'eṭ-f em seuaśi ḥen-f āuu-nek Rā en pet paut mā-n ānχ χer-k āḥā en t'eṭ-f

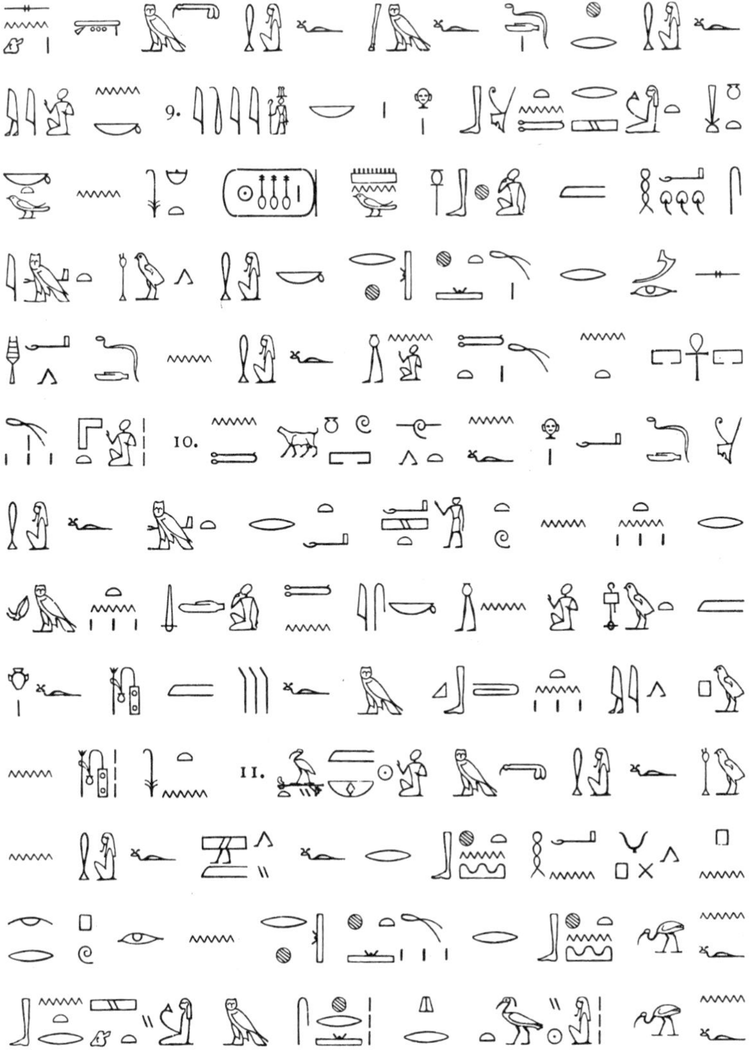

sen-ta embaḥ ḥen-f nem-f ṭ'eṭ χer ḥen-f ī-ȧ nek 9. *ȧθi neb-ȧ ḥer Bent-enθ-* 9
reŝt sennut ket en suten ḥemt (*Rā-neferu*) *men ābeχ em ḥāu-s ȧmāt utu ḥen-k*
reχ χet er ma-s āḥā ṭ'eṭ en ḥen-f ȧn-nȧ θet ent per ānχ ŝāt qenbet 10. *enθ χennu* 10
stat-nef ḥer-ā ṭ'eṭ en ḥen-f māt erṭāt āŝt-tu-en-ten er setem-ten ṭ'eṭ-θen ȧsk ȧn-
nȧ ābut em ȧb-f ān em ṭ'ebā-f em qeb-ten ī pu en ānu suten 11. *Teḥuti-* 11
em-ḥeb em-baḥ ḥen-f utu en ḥen-f māŝemi-f er Beχten ḥān ȧp pen sper pu
ȧri en reχ χet er Beχten qem-nef Bentreŝti em seχeru χer χuti qem-nef

12 12. *su śui en āba ḥenā-f un ser en Beχten nem .... em-baḥ ḥen-f em ťeṭ ȧθi neb-ȧ*
13 *ȧm utu ḥen-f erṭāt ȧntu neter ...* 13. *er ḥen-f en renpit ťaut sas ȧbeṭ uā śe χefṭ ḥeb*
Ȧmen ȧu ḥen-f em χennu Uast āḥā en nem en ḥen-f embaḥ Χensu em Uast Nefer-
14 *ḥetep em ťeṭ pa neb nefer ȧri-ȧ nem embaḥ-k ḥer set en pa ser en Beχten* 14. *āḥā*
en stat en Χensu em Uast Nefer-ḥetep er Χensu pa ȧri seχer neter āa seḥer śema āḥā
en ťeṭ en ḥen-f embaḥ Χensu em Uast Nefer-ḥetep pa neb nefer ȧu ȧr ṭā-k ḥrȧ-k er
15 *Χensu* 15. *p ȧri seχer neter āa seḥer śema erṭāt māśem-f er Beχten hen ur sep sen āḥā*

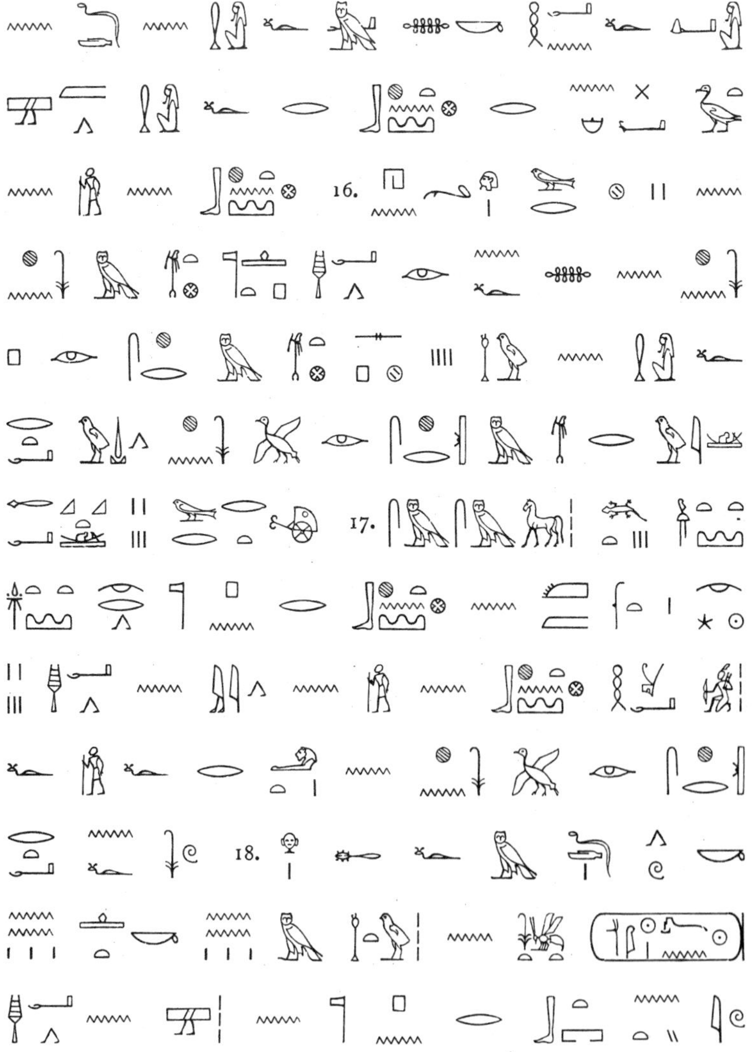

en t'eṭ en ḥen-f mā sa-k ḥān-f ṭā-ȧ māśem ḥen-f er Beχten er neḥem set en ser en
Beχten 16. *hen ṭep ur sep sen en Χensu em Uast Nefer-ḥetep āḥā ȧri-nef sa en* 16
Χensu p ȧri seχer em Uast sep fṭu utu en ḥen-f erṭāt ut'a Χensu pa ȧri seχer em
Uast er uȧ āā qeqet ṭua ureret 17. *semsem āśt unemtet semeḥi sper neter pen er Beχten* 17
en qam renpit uā ȧbeṭ ṭua āḥā en ī en ser en Beχten ḥenā māśā-f ser-f er ḥāt en
Χensu pa ȧri seχer erṭāt-nef su 18. *ḥer χat-f em t'eṭ īu-k en-n ḥetepet-k en-n em utut* 18
en suten net (*Usr-maāt-Rā setep-en-Rā*) *āḥā en śem en neter pen er bet enti ȧu*

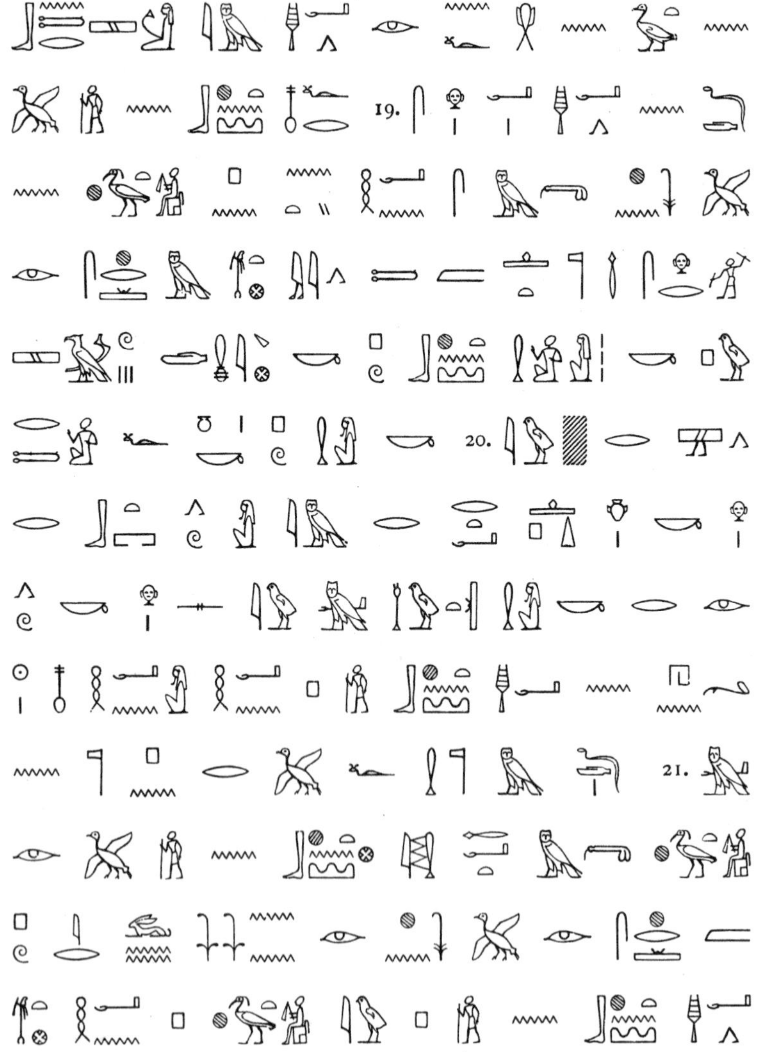

19 *Benθreš ȧm āḥā ȧri-nef sa en set en pa ser en Beχten nefer* 19. *-s ḥer ā āḥā en*
t'eṭ en χut pen enti ḥān-s embaḥ Χensu pa ȧri seχer em Uast ī-θ em ḥetepet
20 *neter āa seḥer šemau ṭemȧ-k pu Beχten ḥenu-k pu reθ-f nuk pu ḥen-k* 20. *ȧu-*
[ȧ] er māšem er bet īu-ȧ ȧm er erṭāt ḥetep ȧb-k ḥer īu-k ḥer-s ȧu mā utut ḥen-k
er ȧri hru nefer ḥān-ȧ ḥān p ser [en] Beχten āḥā en hen en neter pen er pa-f
21 *neter ḥen em t'eṭ* 21. *mā ȧri pa ser en Beχten āb āāt embaḥ χut pu ȧr unen*
enen ȧri Χensu pa ȧri seχer em Uast ḥān p χut ȧu p ser en Beχten āḥā

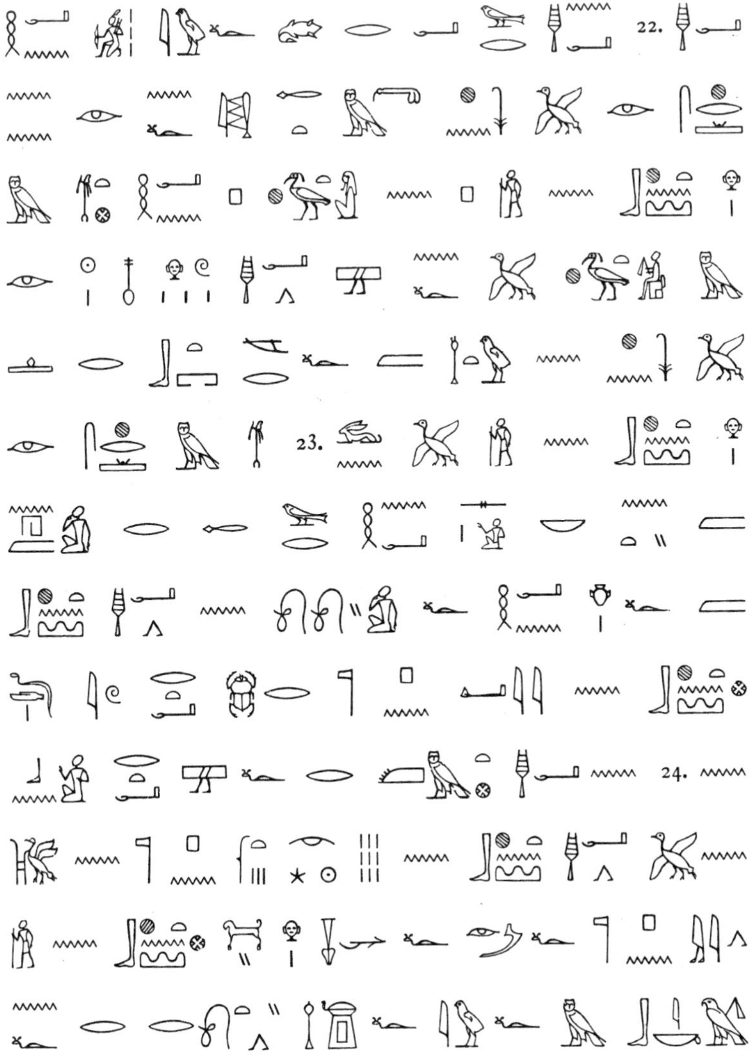

ḥān māšā ȧu-f senṭ er ā ur āḥān 22. *āḥān n ȧri-nef āb āat embaḥ Χensu pa* 22
ȧri seχer em Uast ḥān p χut en p ser en Beχten ḥer ȧri hru nefer ḥrȧu āḥā māšem-
nef pa χut em ḥetep er bet mer-f em utu en Χensu pa ȧri seχer em Uast 23. *un pa* 23
ser en Beχten ḥer nehem er āa ur ḥenā se neb enti em Beχten āḥā en uaua-f ḥān
ȧb-f em ťeṭ ȧu erṭāt χeper neter pen ṭāi en Beχten ben-ȧ erṭāt māšem-f er Qamt
āḥān 24. *en ten* (?) *en neter pen renpit χemt ȧbeṭ paut en Beχten āḥā pan ser* 24
en Beχten sťeri ḥer sam(?)*-f maa-f neter pen ī-nef er ruati ḥeť-f ȧu-f em bȧk*

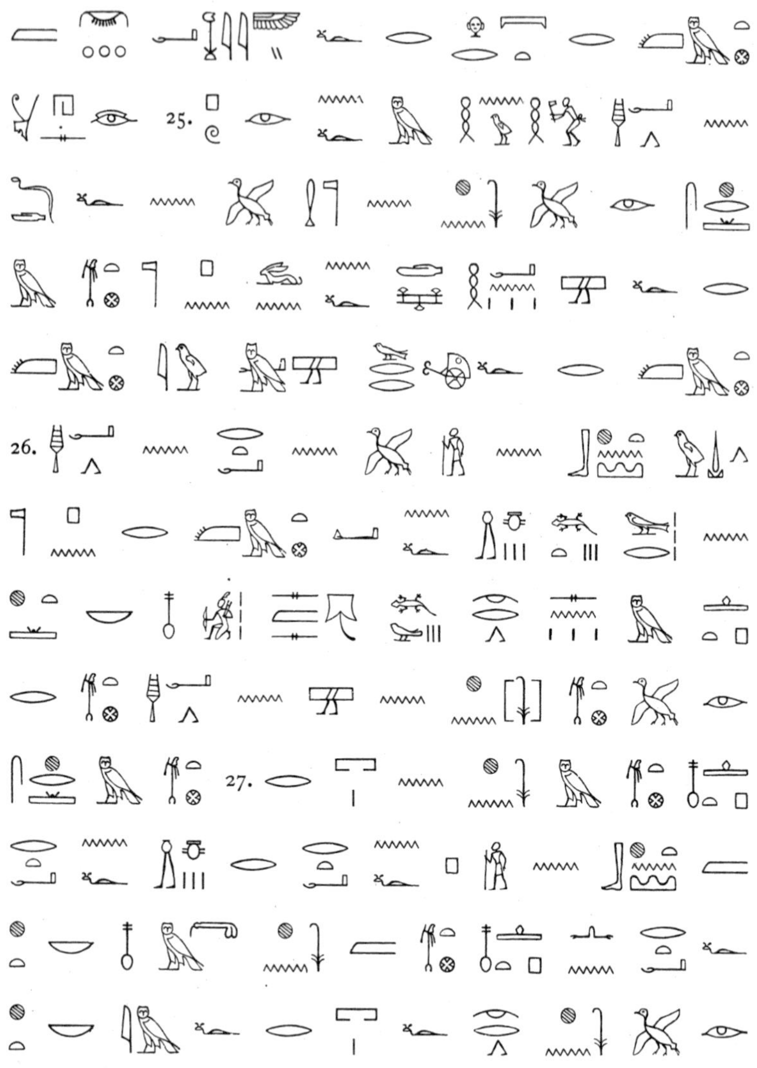

25 *em nub āχai-f er ḥert er Qamt nehes* 25. *pu ȧri-nef em ḥenuḥ āḥā en t̓eṭ-f en pa*
neter ḥen en Ꭓensu pa ȧri seχer em Uast neter pen un-nef ṭ ḥān māśem-f er Qamt ȧu
26 *māśem urer-f er Qamt* 26. *āḥā en erṭāt en pa ser en Beχten ut̓a neter pen er Qamt*
ṭā-nef ȧn āśt uru en χet neb nefer māśā semsu āśt uru sper-sen em ḥetep er Uast
27 *āḥā en māśem en Ꭓensu-[em] Uast pa ȧri seχer em Uast* 27. *er pa en Ꭓensu em Uast*
Nefer-ḥetep erṭāt-nef ȧn er erṭāt-nef p ser en Beχten em χet neb nefer embaḥ
Ꭓensu em Uast Nefer-ḥetep ȧn erṭāt-f χet neb ȧm-f er pa-f sper Ꭓensu pa ȧri

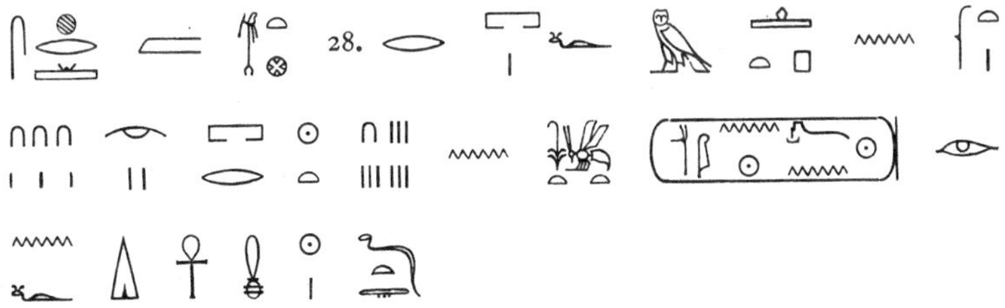

seχer em Uast 28. *er per-f em ḥetep en renpit māb χemt ȧbeṭ sen pert hru met-paut en suten net* (or *bȧt*) (*Usr-māt-en-Rā setep-en-Rā*) *ȧri-nef ṭā ānχ mȧ Rā t'etta*

THE FESTIVAL SONGS OF ISIS AND NEPHTHYS.

(British Museum, Egyptian Papyrus, No. 10188.)

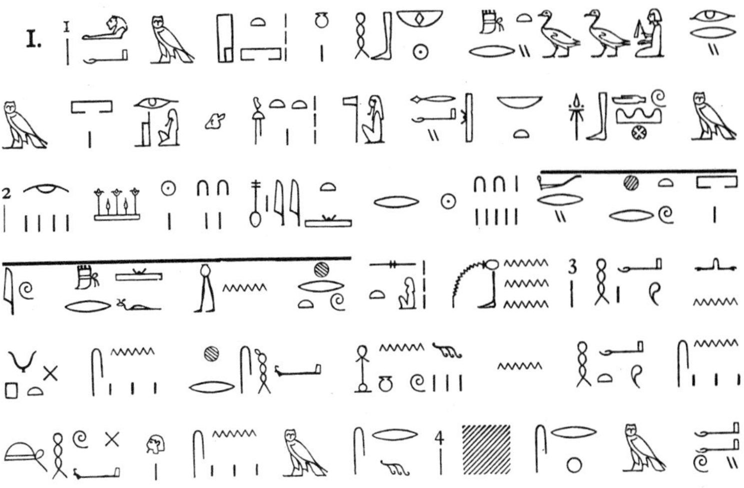

I. *Ḥā em ḥet nu ḥeb T'erti ȧri em per Ȧusȧr χent Ȧmentiu neter āāi nebt Ȧbṭu em ȧbeṭ fṭu ša hru t'aut-sen neferit er hru t'aut-sȧs seri χertu per ȧu t'er-f ȧn χertu set āb ḥāu ȧn ȧpt-sen χersek šennu en ḥāt-sen meḥu ṭep-sen em ser . . . . . ser em āāui-*

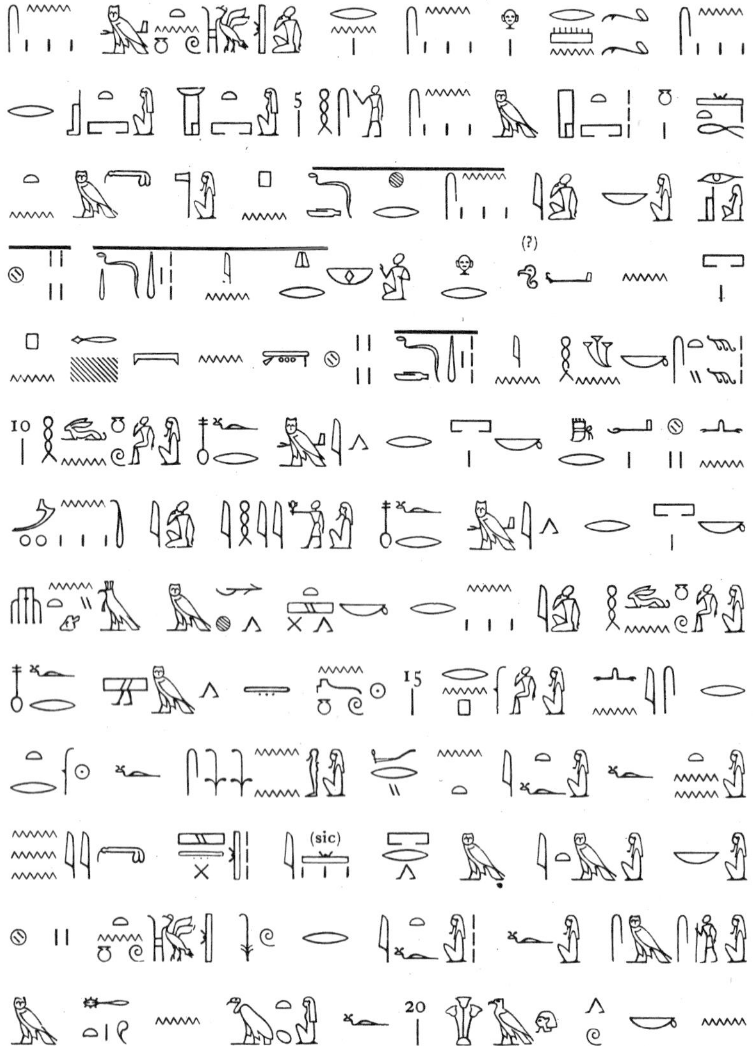

sen mātennu ren-sen ḥer ermen-sen er Áuset Nebt-ḥet ḥes-sen em ḥet nu šāt ten embaḥ neter pen t'eṭ χer sen á neb Áusár sep fṭu t'eṭ án χerḥeb ḥer . . . . . en per pen āa (?) . . . ḥer (?) en ta sep fṭu t'eṭ án ḥenksti ḥunnu nefer māá er per-k t'er ā sep sen án maa-n-θ á áḥi nefer māá er per-k χenti emχet teš-k er-n á ḥunnu nefer šem-ta ennu renp án-ás er trá-f senen seri ent átf-f Tenen mui šetaá per em Átm neb sep sen tennu su er átef-f sems em χat en mut-f ḥa īu-k en-

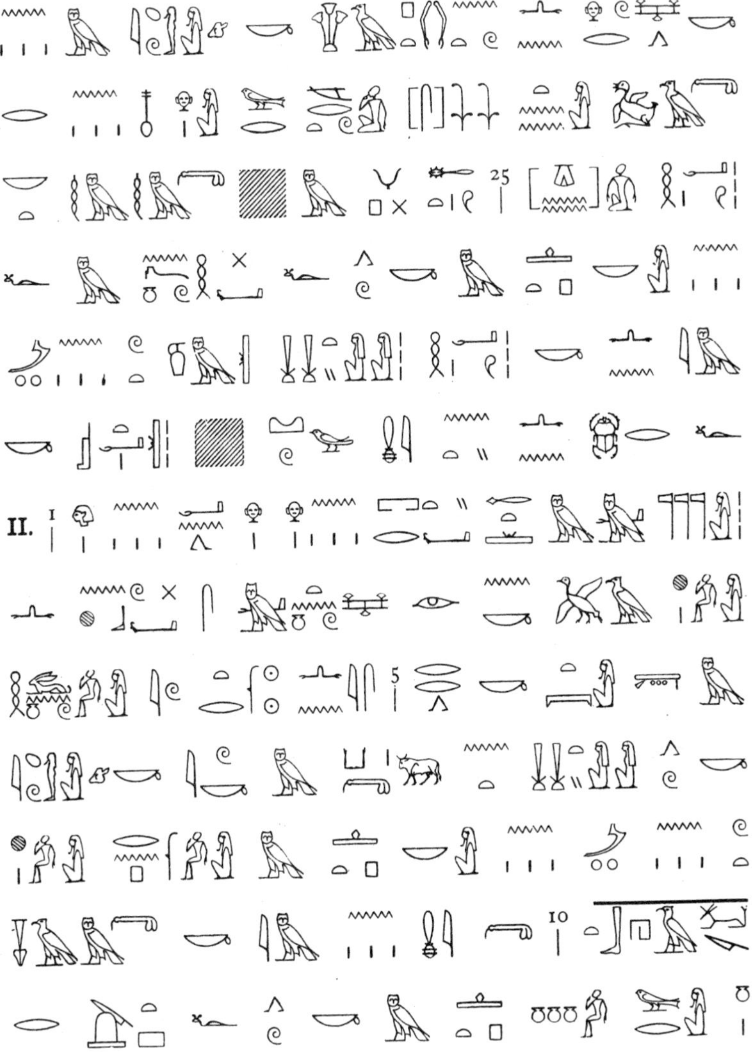

n em ȧru-k ḥapt-entu ȧn ḥeru-k er-n nefer ḥrȧ ur mertu senen Tenen ťa nebt neťemťem [sems] em ȧp χat ḳenen ḥāu-f em ennuḥ-f īu-k em ḥetep neb-n maa-n-tu χnem senti ḥāu-k ȧn ȧm-k ȧuset-ā . . . ṭu mȧ enti ȧn χeper-f

II. *ṭep-n ān ḥer ḥrȧu-n perti āat emmā neteru ȧn neχebu-s mātennu ȧri-nek pa χi ḥunnu ȧu trȧui ȧn-ȧs* (?) *rer-k pet ta em ȧru-k ȧu-k em ka ent senti īu-k χi renp em ḥetep neb-n maa-n-tu sam-k ȧm-n mȧ sam Tebha er nemmat-f īu-k em ḥetep nu ur nu*

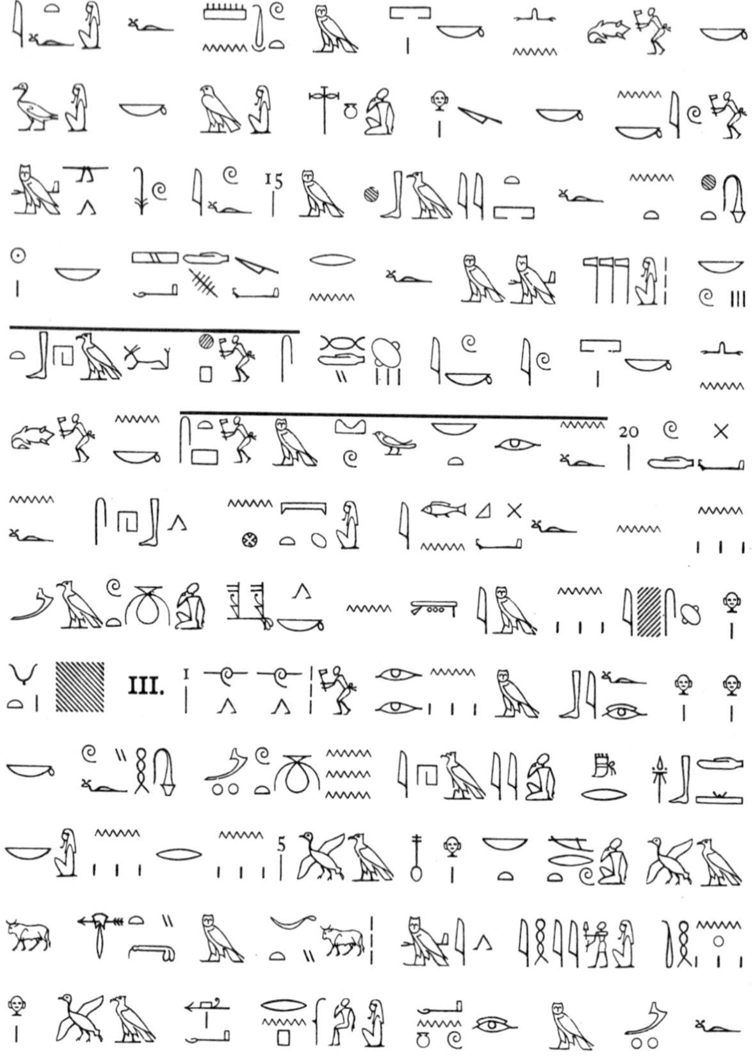

ȧtf-f men-tu em per-k ȧn senṭ-k se-k Ḥeru neť ḥrȧ-k Nekȧu mās su ȧu-f em χebait-f ent χet hru neb śāṭ ren-f emmā neteru nebu Tebha χep-s āṭi ȧu-k ȧu per-k ȧn senṭ-nek Sut em ṭu nebt ȧri-nef uṭ-nef sehab Nut ȧnq-f-en-n maut seḥ-k en ta ȧm-n ȧ . . . s ḥer ȧpt . . . . **III.** *stastau maa-n em bȧf ḥer ḥrȧ-k ufiḥ maut ȧhai ťer ȧbṭ neb-n er-n pa nefer ḥrȧ nebt mertu pa ka sati em kauti māȧ ȧḥi θeḥen ḥrȧ pa uā renp ānnu em maa-f*

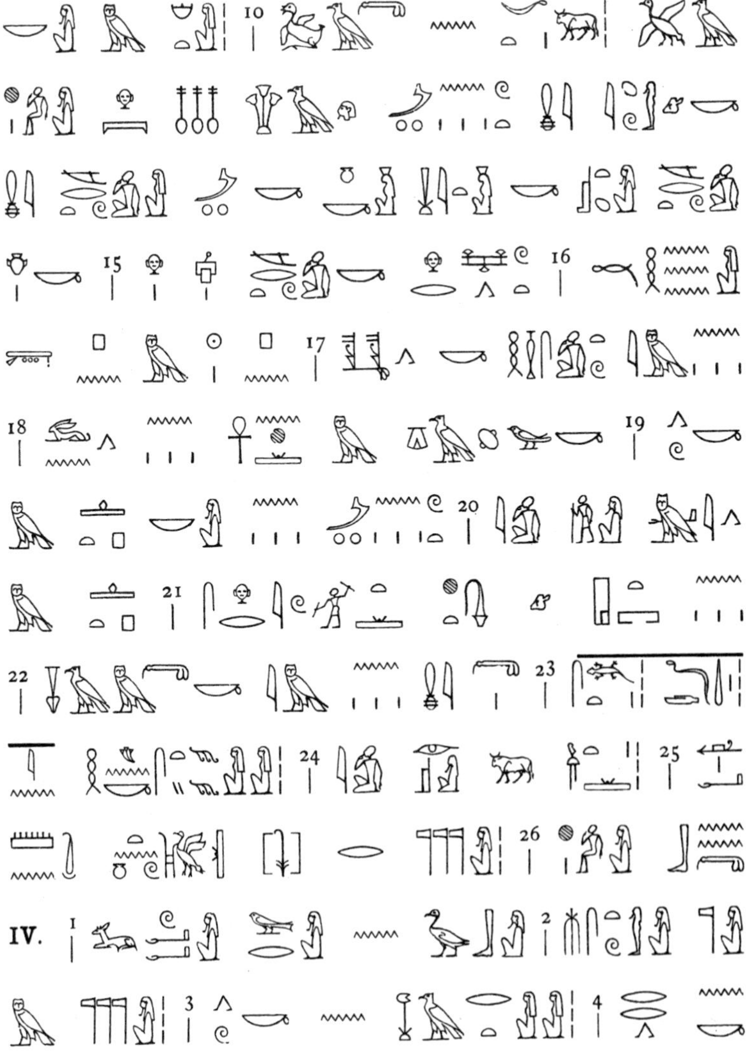

neb em ḥemt ťa en kauti pa χi ḥer neferu ḥa maa-n-tu mà àru-k mà mertu-à maa-k nuk senàt-k Àuset mertu àb-k ḥer-sa mertu-k ḥer-tu meḥ-à ta pen em hru pen seḥ-k ḥes-tu àm-n un-n ānχ em ḳa-k īu-k em ḥetep neb-n maa-n-tu à ser māā em ḥetep seḥeràut χet χent ḥet-n sam-k àm-n mà sam [Tebha] se-āšt ťeṭ àn ḥenksti à Àusàr ka Àmentiu uā men tennu [su] er neteru χi benen **IV.** *āuāā ur en Seb mestu neter em neteru īu-k en χart rer-nek*

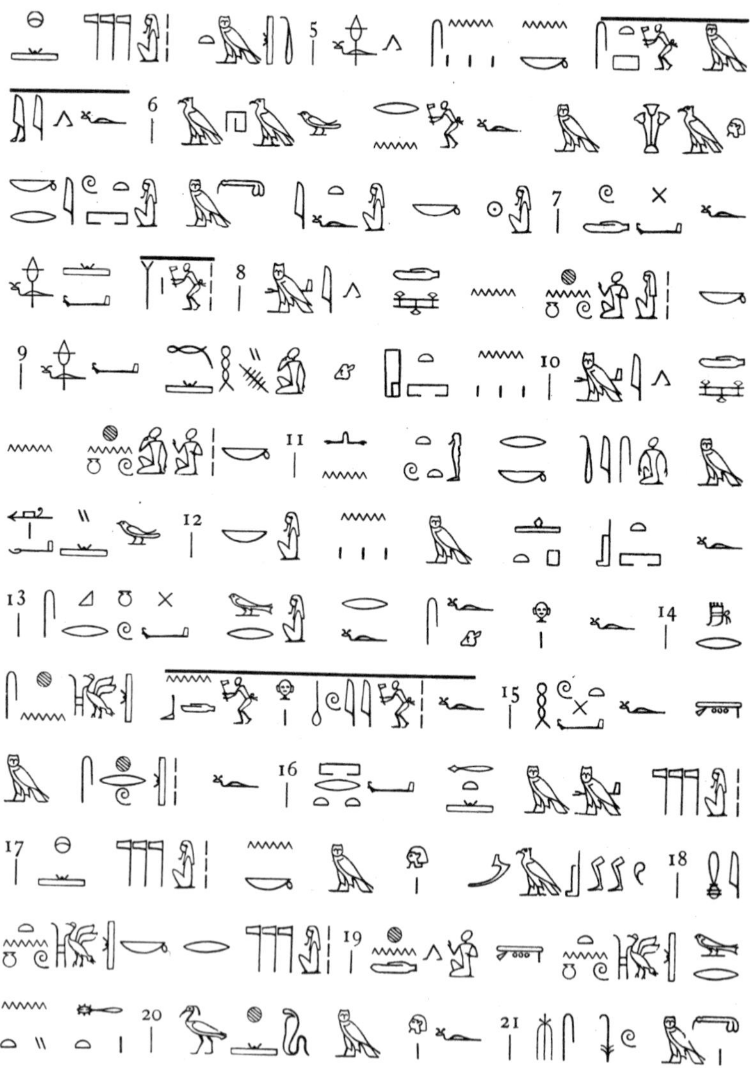

paut neteru temθ χesef-sen-nek Sut em ī-f aha ren-f em ḥa keràut embaḥ àtf-k Rā uṭ-f χesef Sebàu māā ṭi en χennu-k χesef meḥi χent ḥet-n māā ṭi en χennu-k àn tut erek θàs em uāi neb-n em ḥetep àuset-f seqernu ur eref sef ḥrà-f t'er seχen nebṭ ḥer χerui-f ḥut-f ta em seχeru-f pertet āat emmā neteru paut neteru nek em ṭep mast mà tennu-k er neteru χenṭ-à ta tennu ur enti χat χu em ṭep-f mes su embaḥ

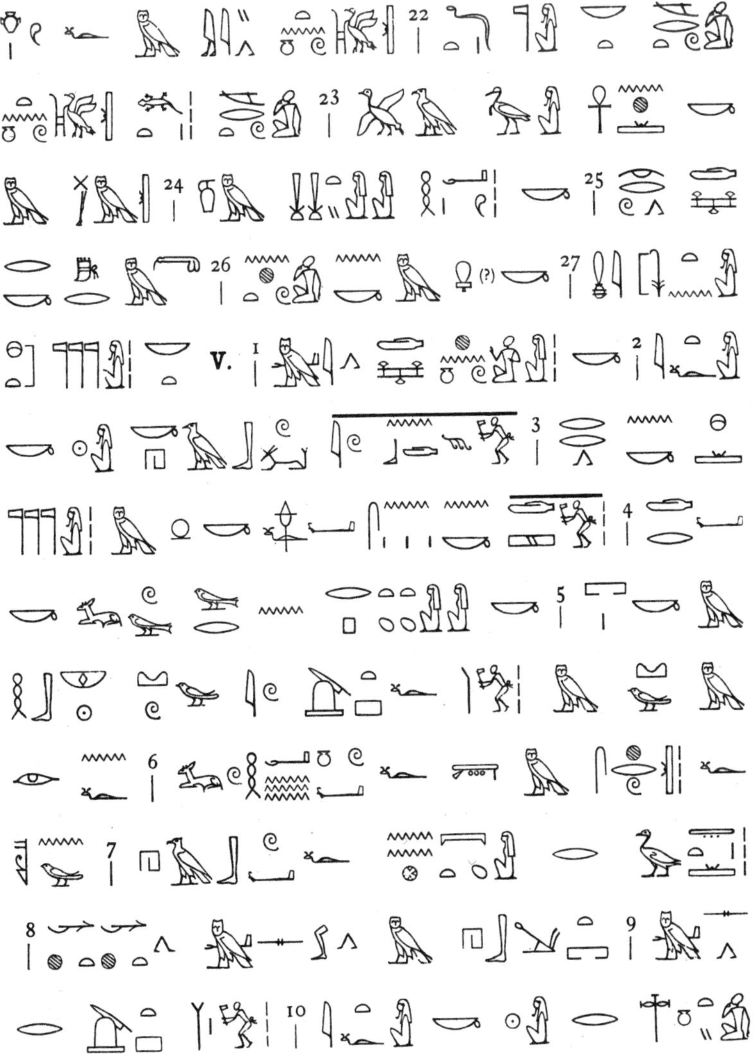

ȧb-f em ī tennu ťet neter nebt mertu tennu āšt mertu pa ba ānχ-k em nem χnem senti ḥāu-k speru ṭi erek ťer embaḥ neχtu (?) nek em sāḥ-k mȧ [suten paut] neteru nebt **V.** *māȧ ṭi χennu-k ȧtf-k Rā kehabu ȧu nebṭ rer-nek paut neteru em šen-k χesef-sen nek ṭeš ṭer-k āu ur en erpetet-k per-k em ḥeb ṭu ȧu nemmat-f sebȧu em ṭu em ȧri-nef āuḥānu-f ta em seχeru-f ḳesen habu-f Nut er setat χetχet mās em hebt mās er nemmat sebȧu ȧtf-k Rā er netťi*

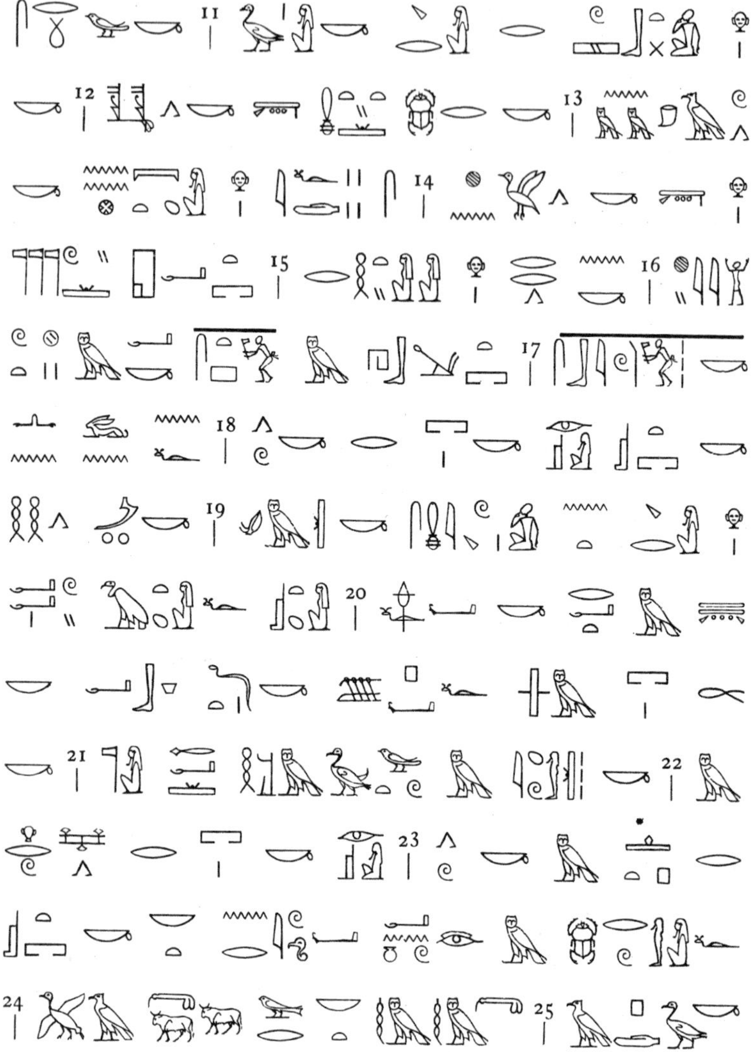

ser-k se-k Ḥeru er uśebt ḥrȧ-k seḥ-k ta mȧteti χeper-k nememtau-k Nut ḥer ȧfṭ-s χen-k ta ḥer neterui ḥetāt Reḥti ḥer rer-nek χi-tu sep sen māk Sut em hebt sebȧu-k ȧn un-nef īu-k er per-k Ȧusȧr ȧuset-k ḥeḥ maa-k setem-k smȧu ent Ḥeru ḥer āāui mut-f Ȧuset χesef-k erṭāt em taui neb āb t'et-k seśep-f ȧm per śāt-k neter āā ḥetem-tu em ȧru-k em ḥeru er per-k Ȧusȧr īu-k em ḥetep er ȧuset-k nebt nerȧu ānnu em χeperu-f pa ka ur nebt net'emt'em apṭ-k

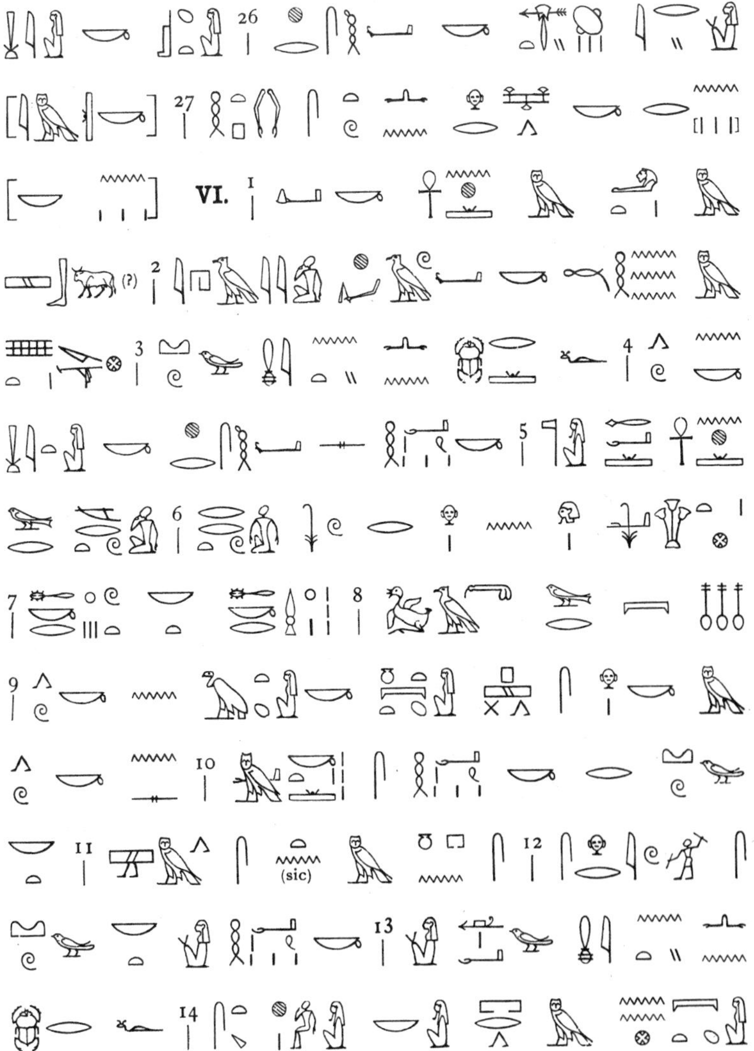

senȧ-k Ȧuset χersek-k sati ȧri ȧm-k ḥept-s-tu ȧn ḥer-k er-n neb-n **VI.** *ṭā-k ānχ em ḥāt em śeb ȧhai χau-k meḥ em sept Tes ṭu mȧ enti ȧn χeper-f īu-nek senȧt-k χersek-s ḥāu-k neter āā ānχ ur mertu rertu su er ḥer en ṭep Qemā-meḥt χaker-tu nebt χakeru t'a ur ḥer neferu īu-k en mut-k Nut peś-s ḥer-k em īu-k nes māket-s ḥāu-k er ṭu nebt māśem set en em χennu-nes seḥerȧu-s ṭu nebt ȧri ḥāu-k sau uā mȧ enti ȧn χeper-f set χi neb per em Nut*

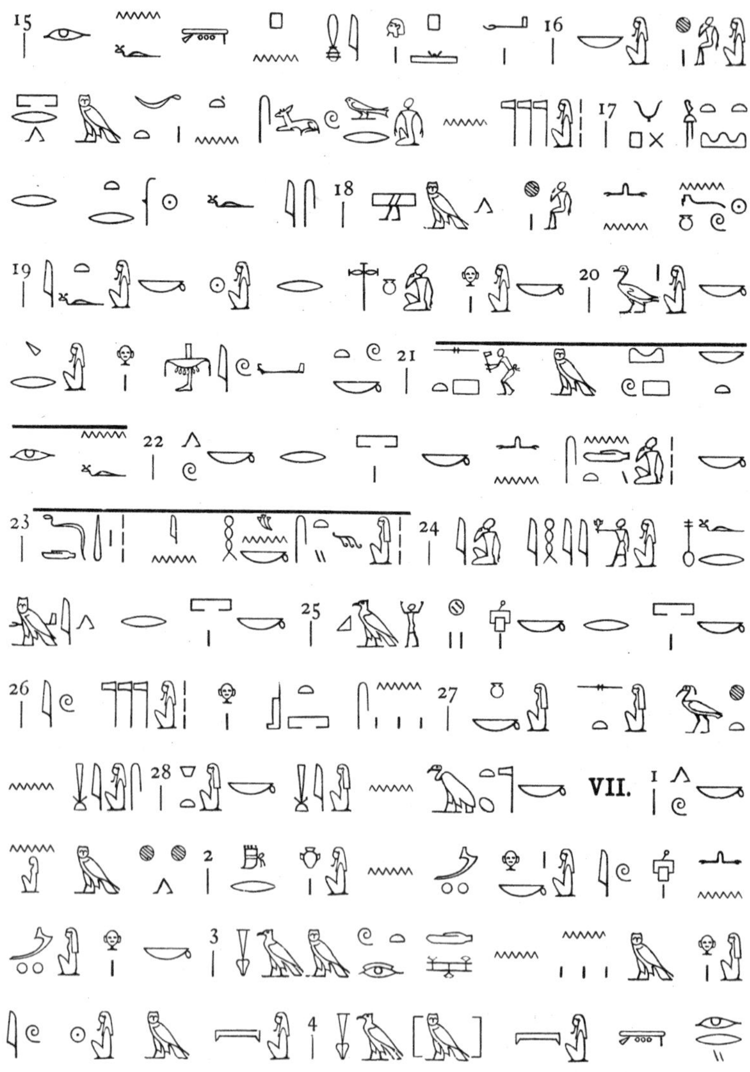

ȧri-nef ta pen mȧ ṭep-ā neb χi per em kaut ten seāuur en neteru ȧp Ȧmentet er trȧ-f ȧs māšem χi ȧn ennu ȧtf-k Rā er net' ḥrȧ-k se-k Ḥeru ḥer nubȧu-k-tu Sut em ṭu nebt ȧri-nef īu-k er per-k ȧn senṭetu-k t'eṭ ȧn ḥenksti ȧ ȧḥi nefer māȧ er per-k qa sep sen sa-k er per-k ȧu neteru ḥer ȧuset-sen nuk set χut en senȧ-s ḥent-k senȧ en mut-k **VII.** *īu-k-nȧ em χeχ t'er ȧb-ȧ en maa ḥrȧ-k ȧu sa ȧn maa-ȧ ḥrȧ-k sam-tu ṭi en-n em ḥrȧ-ȧ ȧu Rā em pet sam pet ta ȧri*

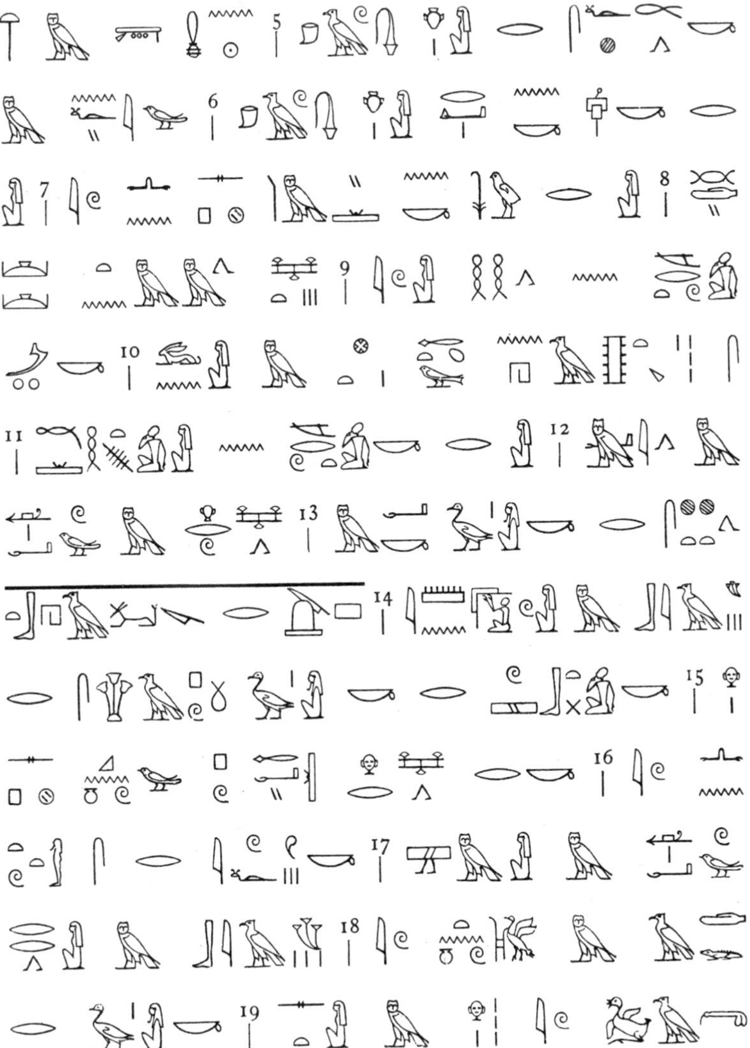

χaibit em ta mȧn tau ȧb-ȧ er sefeχ-k em nefiȧ tau ȧb-ȧ erṭā-nek sa-k er-ȧ ȧu ȧn sep qemi-nek su er-ȧ āṭi ȧatui tenemem uat ȧu-ȧ ḥeḥ en mertu maa-k un-ȧ em nut āat ur nehat-s meḥt-ȧ en mertu-k er-ȧ māȧ em uāu em ḥeru māk se-k er seχetχet Tebha er nemmat ȧmen-uȧ em bȧa er seḥapu se-k er uśebt-k ḥer sep qennu pu āāi ḥer erek ȧu ȧn tut-s er ȧuf-k māśem-ȧ em uāu rer-ȧ em bȧa ȧu tennu em aṭ er se-k set em ḥrȧu ȧu ta pu nuk ȧs reχ-kuȧ ḥenā Ȧp-uat (?) *rer-nȧ uat tenemem-nȧ ḥer senȧ beθet em nefi tau ȧbu en ḥefnu ḥrȧu maut āāi em neteru bef-n neb ȧn uśer en mertu-k ḥer ḥrȧ-n pa sam nebt neṭemṭem net* (or *bȧt*) *nebt ḥeḥ* **VIII.** *āχ em ānχ ḥeq ṭetta ḳu ȧn reχ suten net* (or *bȧt*) *neb uṭa er Tasertet ȧu ȧn sep-k meḥ-nȧ ȧb-ȧ ȧm-f senȧ neb uṭa er sept Ȧqertet īu-k-nȧ em ȧru-k māā em ḥetep sep sen net* (or *bȧt*) *ser māā em ḥetep ḥa maa-n ḥrȧ-k mȧ χent mȧ mertu-nȧ maa-k āāui-ȧ qa er χau-tu-k mertu-nȧ mertu-nȧ śenui* (?) *ȧatui*

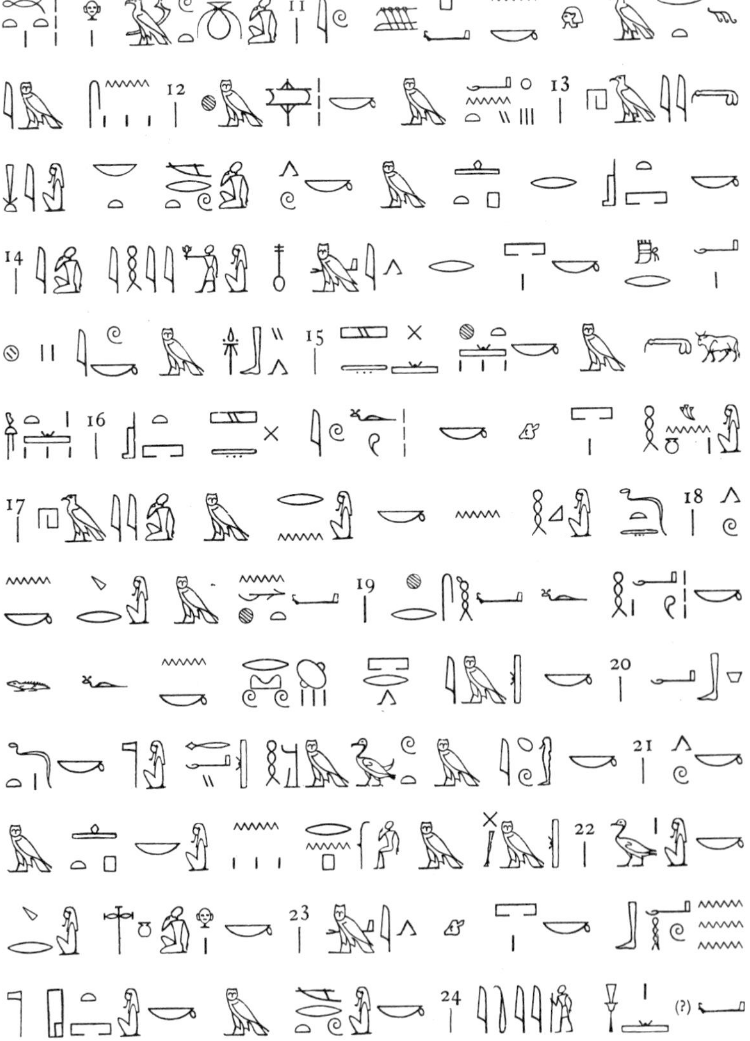

meḥtet ḥer maut ȧu seśep-nek ṭep art ȧm-sen χem-k em ānti hai senȧ nebt mertu īu-k em ḥetep er ȧuset-k ȧ ȧḥi nefer māȧ er per-k ťer-ā sep sen ȧu-k em ȧbi śeta χet-k em ka Ȧmentiu ȧuset śeta ȧuf-k χent per Ḥennu hai em ren-k en ḥeq ťetta īu-nek Ḥeru em neχt χersek-f ḥāu-k seqȧ-f-nek erṭuu per ȧm-k āb ťet-k neter āāi ḥetem-tu em ȧru-k īu-k em ḥetep neb-n renp em nem se-k Ḥeru neť ḥrȧ-k māȧ χent per-k bāḥu neter-ḥet-k em mertu-k ȧθi seχem seṭ-nes em suḥt uā user peḥti se ȧs pu ȧp χat seχem Seb ḥer mut-f **IX.** *χakeru āāi mertu ȧri er Ȧmentet qennu-f aṭi nebt ṭuaut ka Ȧmentet mestu en Rā-Ḥeru-χuti χi ānnu en maa-f īu-k en-n em ḥetep sep sen χer-sek-k neśeni-k seḥer-k at neb-n īu-k en-n em ḥetep sep sen hai renp māȧ em ḥetep hai senȧ māȧ maa-tu-ȧ net* (or *bȧt*) *ḥeq t'etta em urṭu em urṭu ȧb-k neb-n īu-k er per-k ȧn senṭeti-k pa seāśt āāi ȧn maa ȧn setem t'eṭ ȧn χerḥeb ȧ ȧḥi neferi māȧ er*

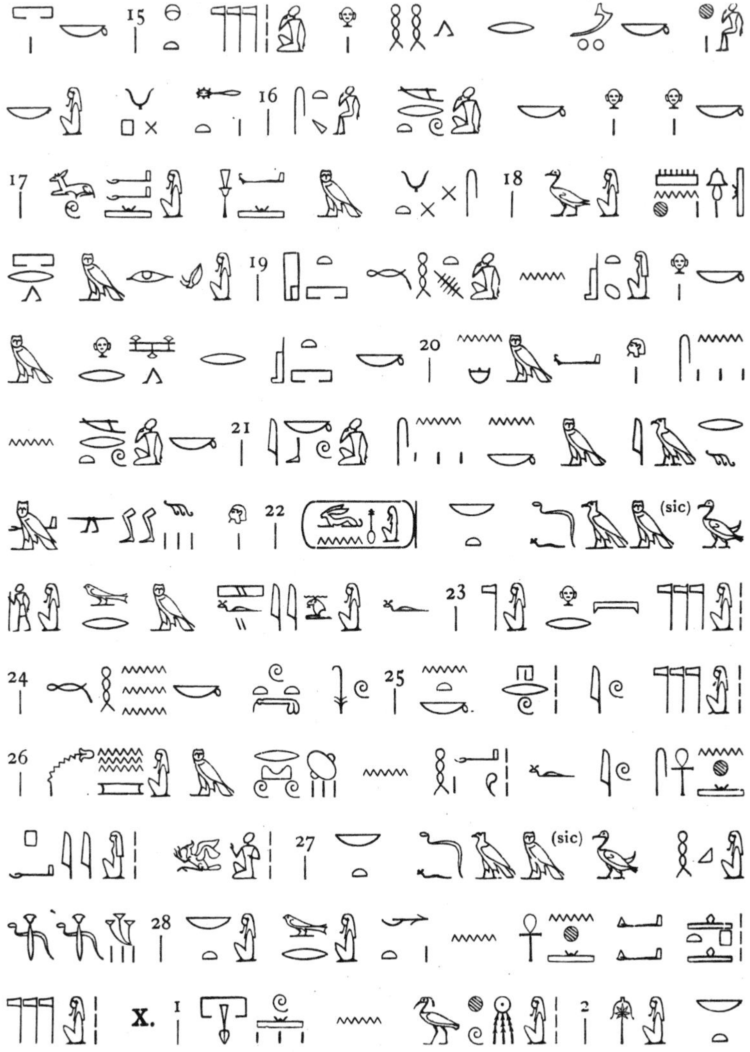

per-k paut neteru ḥer ḥeḥ er maa-k χi neb ȧp χat set mertu-k ḥer ḥrȧ-k āuāā seχem em ȧpt-s se menχ per em maa setem ḥet meḥt en Ȧuset ḥer-k em ḥer er ȧuset-k neḥem ṭep-sen en mertu ȧkebu-sen-nek em ȧar mās ṭep Un-nefer nebt ťefau ser ur em šefi-f neter ḥer neteru meḥ-k utet su enṭek heru ȧu neteru tef (?) *em erṭuu en ḥāu-f ȧu seānχ pāi reχi nebt ťefau ḥeq uaťuať nebt ur χet en ānχ ṭāṭā ḥetepu neteru* **X.** *perχeru en χu Sešeta* (?) *nebt* *nemmȧt nebt uťau seśeta em χut seśep er trȧ-f uben er ennu-f entek χu āperi mau seśep-k en ȧb en Ȧtmu maa-k em ȧuset Rā sam maut-f sāḥu-k āpi ba-k emχet Rā pesṭ-k em ṭuau ḥetep-k em māśer hru neb pu un-nek un-nek em ȧb en Ȧtm ḥeḥ ťetta χāā-k but nebṭ ḥetem embaḥ ȧpiut-f ḥer-baḥ qennu-f un χer-f ān Sebȧu neken tui ī er-ef Ȧmseḥti āuāā-f erek suaś-f neteru nebt ḥāā paut neteru em χesef-k urśu-k*

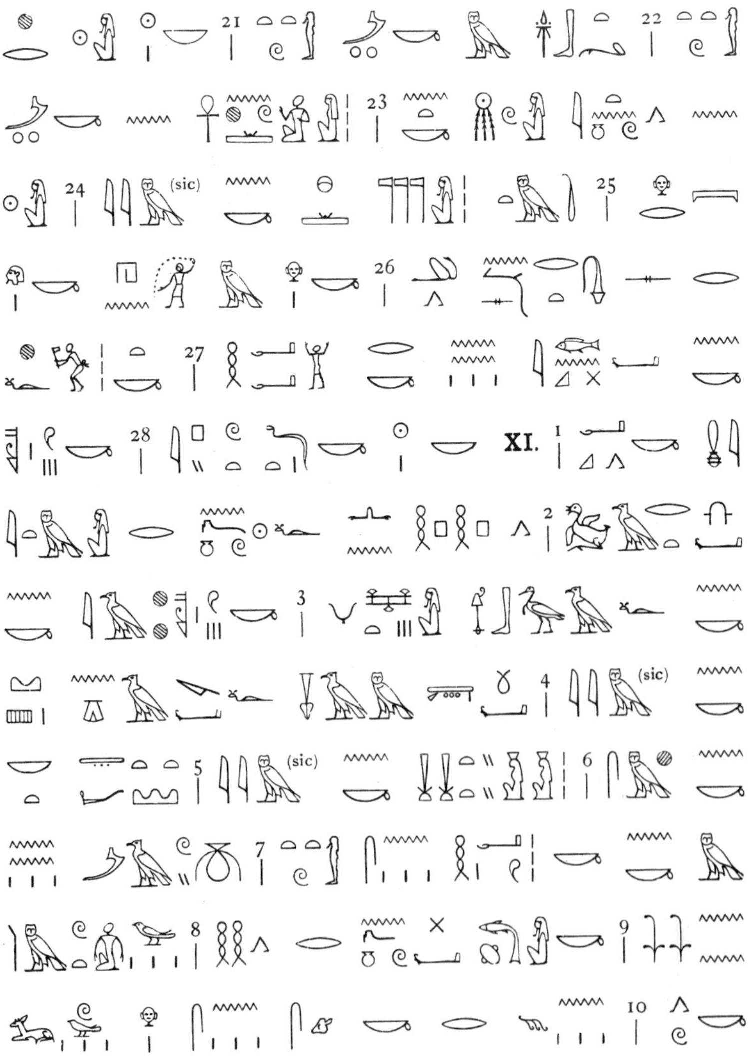

χer Rā hru neb tut maa-k em ȧbt tut maa-k en ānχiu entek χu ȧtennu en Rā īu-nek paut neteru temθ ḥer ṭep-k hen em ḥrȧ-k peḥ nesert-s er χeft-k ḥāā er-ek en-n ȧnq-nek qesu-k ȧpitu t'et-k hru neb **XI.** *āq-k mȧ Ȧtm er ennu-f ȧn ḥepḥep t'art-nek ȧaχeχ-k Ȧp-uat āba-f nek ṭu neḳa-f sam-ta īu-nek nebt Tat'esertet īu-nek sentiti seχem-nek-en-n maui tut-sen ḥāu-k nek em qemtu ḥeḥ er ennu χa-k enen āu ḥer sen seχent-k er šennu-n īu-k-*

en-n tem seχau-k īu-k em ȧru-k ḥer ṭep ta ruȧa tenten-k ḥetep-k-en-n nebt sešeṭu āuāā taiu neter uā menχet seχeru en neteru hen-nek neteru nebu īu-k ȧu per-k ȧn senṭ-k mertu-tu Rā mertu-tu erpetet-k ḥetep-tu em ȧuset-k t́etta t́eṭ meṭu ȧn ḥenksti ȧ ȧḥi nefert māȧ er per-k qa sep sen sa-k er per-k ȧu neteru ḥer ȧuset-sen hai māȧ em ḥetep net (or *bȧt*) *māȧ em ḥetep sa-k Ḥeru er net́ ḥrȧ-k ṭā-k āu ur er erpetet-k ḥai-n ḥer-k em χentȧ-k χi mȧ mertu maa-k*

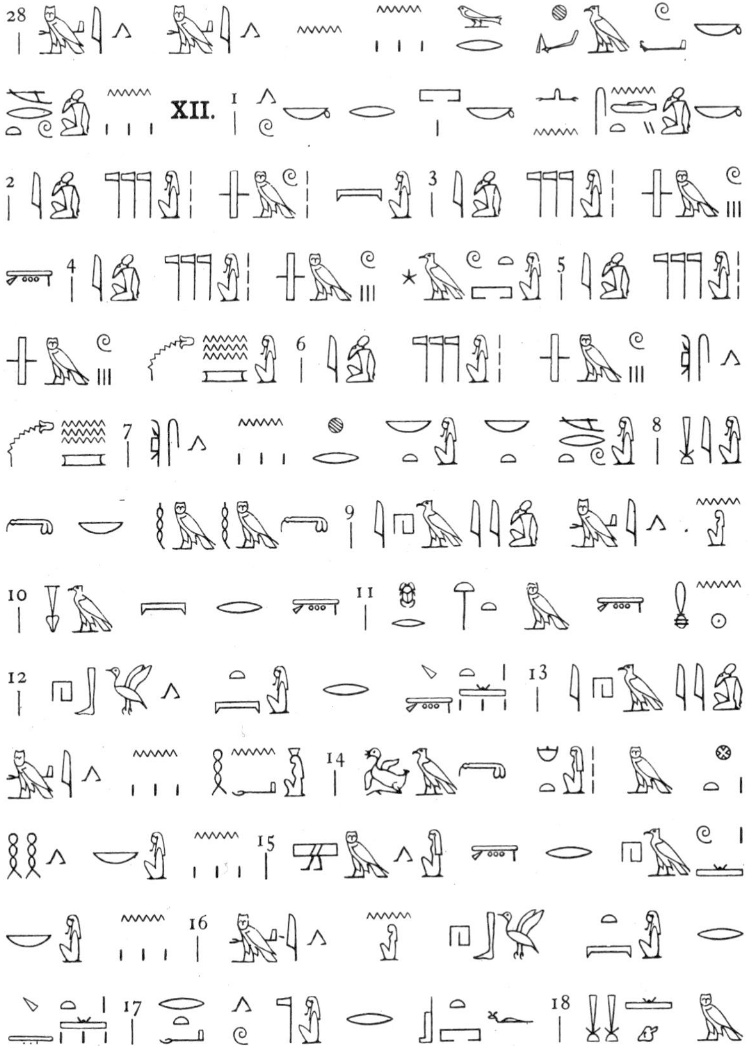

māā māā-en-n ur χau-k mertu-n **XII.** *īu-k er per-k ȧn sențeti-k ȧ neteru ȧmu pet ȧ neteru ȧmu ta ȧ neteru ȧmu țuaut ȧ neteru ȧmu tef* (?) *ȧ neteru ȧmu ś̌es tef* (?) *ś̌es-n χer nebt nebt mertu senȧ sam neb netemtem ȧhai māā-nȧ sam pet er ta χeper χaibet em ta mān hab pet er baḥeset ȧhai māā-n ḥnā-ȧ ťa ḥemt em nut ḥeḥ neb-n māśem-ȧ ta er hau neb-n māā-nȧ hab pet er baḥeset er țāt īu neter er ȧuset-f sensen em*

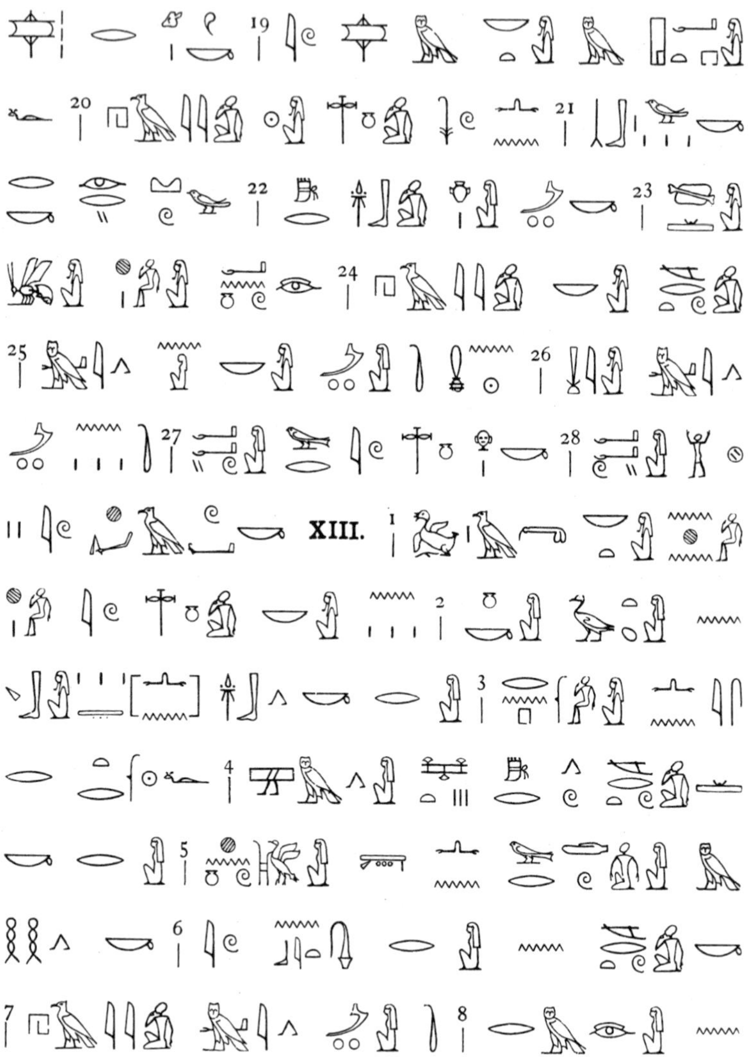

nifu er fenṭ-k àu nifu em nebt em ḥet-āt-f hai Rā neť su àn seťebu-k erek àri ṭu ťer àb àb-à maa-k āu net (or *bàt*) *χi ānnu hai neb mertu māà-nà neb maa-à-θ màn senà māà maa-n-θ āāui-à ur àu neť ḥrà-k āāui-à qa sep sen àu χau-k* **XIII.** *ťa nebt neχen χi àu neť neb-n nuk set en Seb àn àb-k er-à renp àn-às er trà-f māśem-à uat ťer īu mertu-k er-à χennu-à ta àn urṭu-à em ḥeḥ-k àu nebàt er-à en mertu-k hai māà maa-à-θ rem-à en*

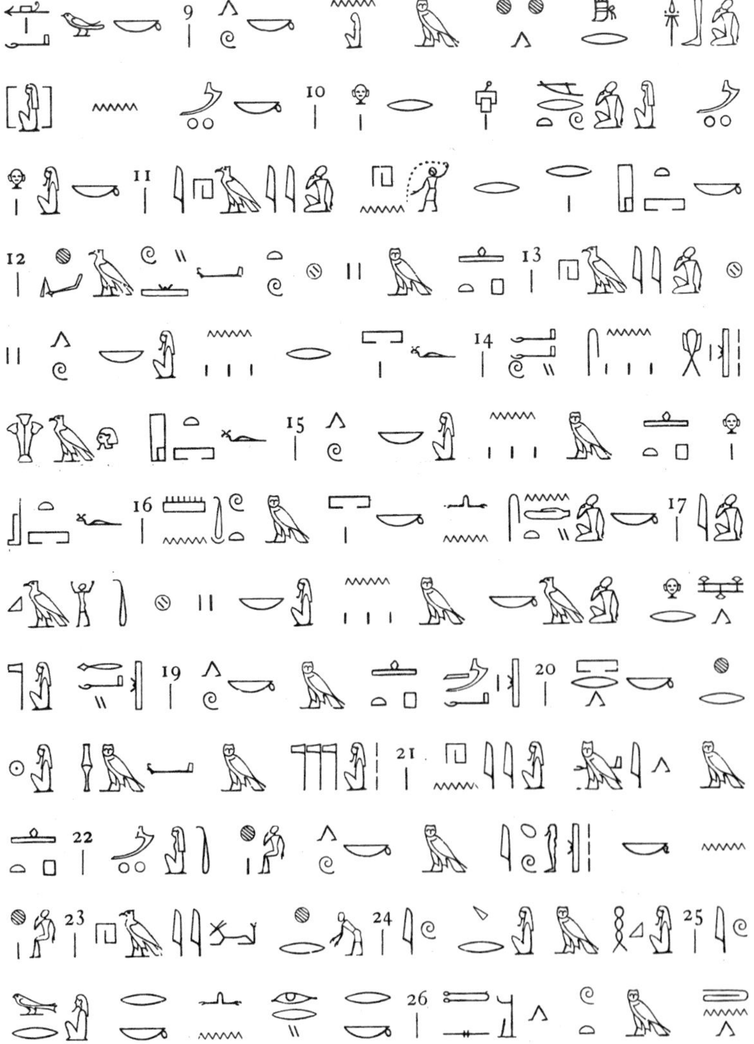

uā-k īu-k nȧ em χeχ t'er ȧb-[ȧ] en maa-k ḥer-sa mertu-ȧ maa ḥrȧ-k ȧhai hen er re ḥet-k χaui-tu sep sen em ḥetep hai sep sen īu neb-n er per-f āāui-sen sau ḥa ḥet-f īu neb-n em ḥetep ḥer ȧuset-f men-tu em per-k ȧn sențti-k ȧ qa-θ sep sen neb-n em ka ḥer neter āāi īu-k em ḥetep maā per-k χer Rā seχem em neteru Heni māā em ḥetep maa-ȧ-θ χi īu-k em ȧru-k en χi Hai χer ȧu Ḥeru em ḥeq ȧu ur erek ȧn ȧri erek θes-tu em țeben īui senti pa mertu ȧtef-f nebt θeθeḥḥut śa-nek ȧbu paut neteru ȧpeś neter ḥet-k em neferu-k nerȧu paut neteru em śefi-k **XIV.** *ta setet en ḥeri-k nuk ḥemt-k ȧri īu-k senȧt χut en senȧ-s māȧ maa-ȧ-tu nebt mertu-ȧ qa sep sen āā ȧru māȧ maa-ȧ-tu nu māśem χi māȧ maa-ȧ-tu rerem nek ȧṭebiu taiu ḥeteb-nek ȧat mȧ entek Seśeta (?) rerem-nek pet ta mȧ ur-k er neteru ȧn un śu em ṭuau ka-k māȧ er per-k ȧn senṭti-k sa-k Ḥeru ȧḥi śen (?) en pet Bebi (?) em sepeḥu ȧn*

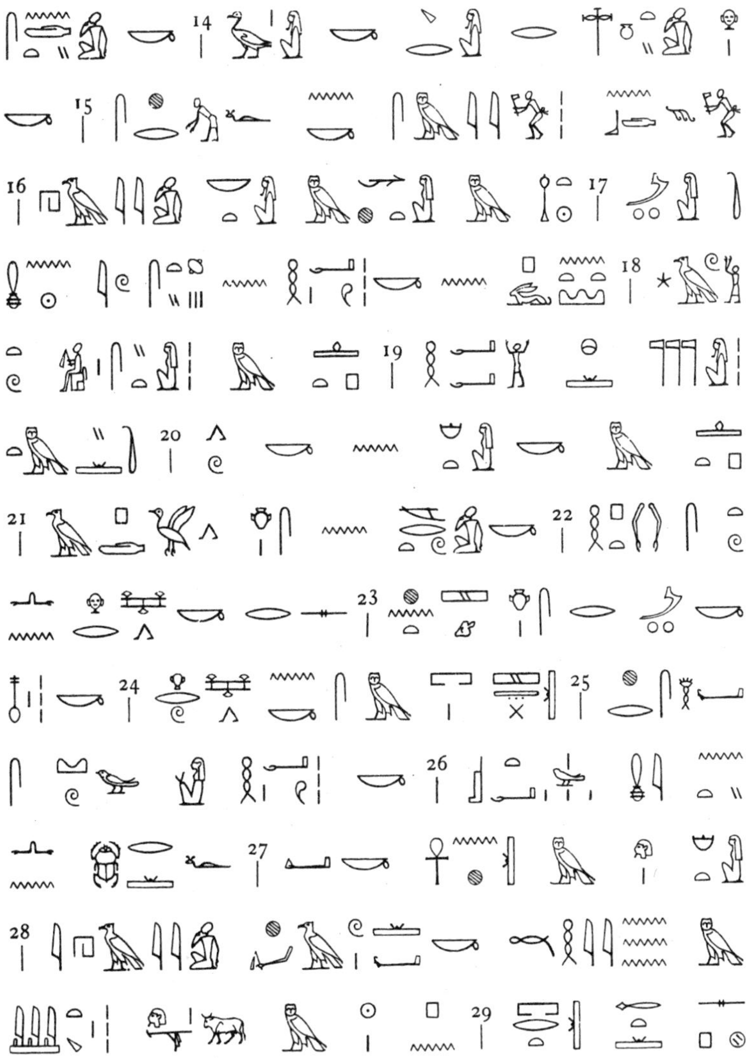

senṭti-k sa-k Ḥeru er netʻti ḥrȧ-k seχer-f nek semi Nebṭ hai nebt emχet-ȧ em ḥetʻet maa-ȧ-θ mȧn ȧu sti en ḥāu-k en Puntet ṭuau-tu śepsit em ḥetep ḥāā paut neteru temi-θ īu-k en ḥemt-k em ḥetep apṭ ȧb-s en mertu-k ḥept-s-tu ȧn ḥer-k er-es χenteś ȧb-s er maa-k neferu-k ḥeru-nek-s em per śeta χersek-s ṭu ȧri ḥāu-k ȧuset-ā mȧ enti ȧn χeper-f ṭā-k ānχ em ṭep ḥemt ȧhai χau-k meḥi em seχet Ṭepȧḥet em hru pen pert āat sep

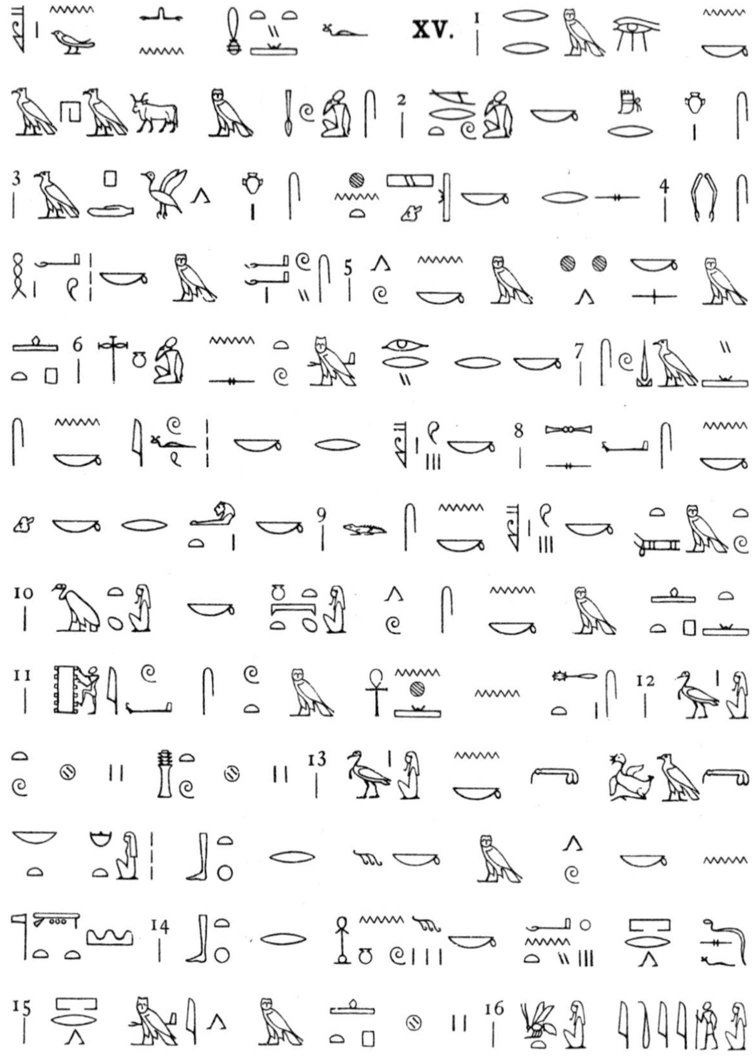

qesen ȧn mȧteti-f **XV.** *rerem-nek aha em χeru-s mertu-k ťer ȧb-s apṭ ȧb-s χenteś-k eres ḥept-s ḥāu-k em āāui-s īu-nek em χeχ ki ṭeṭ em ḥetep neť-nes-tu mā ȧri erek suťai-s-nek ȧuf-k er qesu-k θes-s nek fenṭ-k er ḥāt-k seqa-s-nek qesu-k temtu mut-k Nut īu-s nek em ḥetepet qeṭȧu-s-tu em ānχ en χat-s ba-tu sep sen ṭeṭ-tu sep sen ba nek sam ťa nebt ḥemt bet er śennu-k em īu-k en neter tatet bet er śennu-k ānti per ťesef per māā em ḥetep sep sen net* (or *bȧt*) *ȧθi*

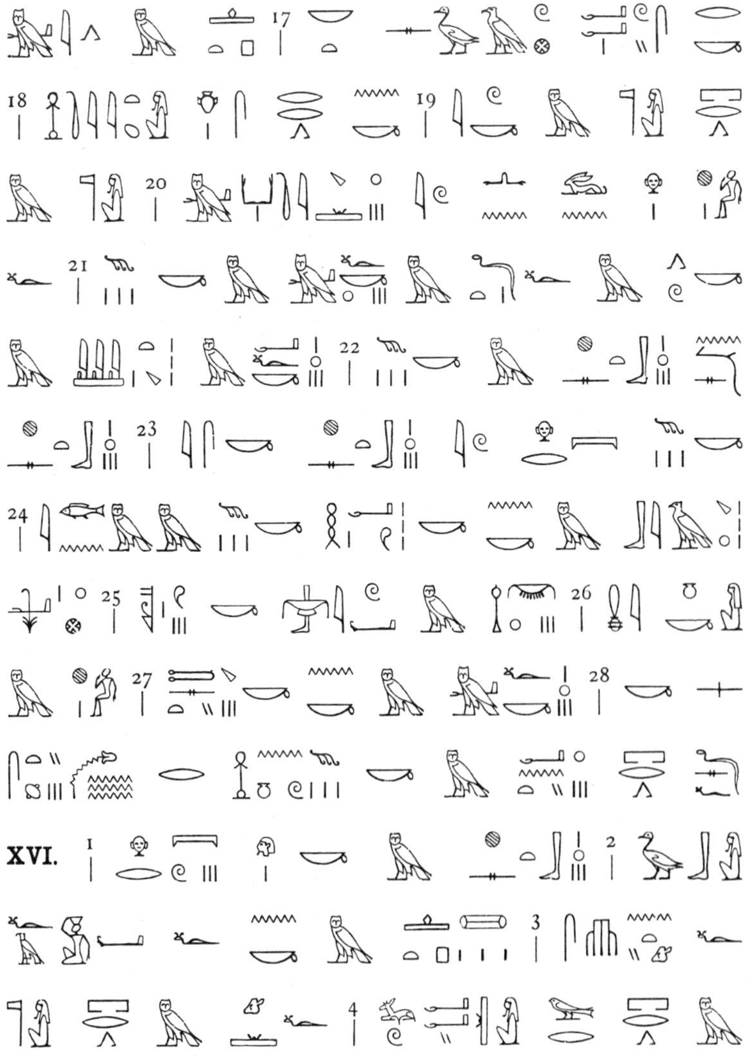

māȧ em ḥetep nebt Sau āāui-s erek Śenθit ȧb-s rer-nek ȧu-k em neter per em neter mākaθȧ ȧu ȧn un ḥer χi-f śennu-k em māfek em t̔et-f em īu-k em seχet māfek śennu-k em χesteb nes χesteb ȧs-k χesteb ȧu ḥer śennu-k ȧnemem-k ḥāu-k nek em bȧa qemā qesu-k nubȧu em ḥet̔ mȧ nuk em χi θesti-k nek em māfek ki t̔eṭ sti . . . . . er śennu-k em ānti per t̔esef **XVI.** *ḥeru ṭep-k em χesteb Seb fa-f nek em ḥetepu seχenti-f neter per em fenṭ-f āuāā ur per em*

Rā sems seru nefer ḥrȧ ba ānχ enti Ȧstennu χi per em Maa-setem sems seru ȧturti āu en Seb ṭā-f nek śen nebt en ȧten māā er per-k Ȧusȧr ȧp neteru un-nek maa-k maa-k ȧm-sen χersek-k ḥaθȧtu ṭā-k ḥet'et'a-k en ta em sati ḳerḥ māā er per-k Ȧusȧr χent Ȧmentet māā er per-k per em χat ārāt em ṭep-f seḥet' maa-f taui neteru θestu sep sen seru neb-n sebȧu-k er nemmat ȧn un-nef ṭeṭṭeṭ sep sen em ren-k Ṭeṭ ḥāu-k nek (Un-nefer) ānχ ut'a senb ȧuf-k-nek urṭu ȧb Ȧusȧr nefertu per ȧm-k

Ḥu pu ṭep re-k Tatenen àtf-k ḥer uθes pet er χenṭ-k ḥer fṭu-s āpi ba-k em àbt un-nek em senen en Rā seśep-tu àmu ṭuaut em ḥāā neḳa-nek Seb àm-f īu-sen nek em ḥetep nāi-nek em ḥetep er Ṭeṭṭu
XVII. *θes-tu erek Àusàr θes-tu sep sen em ḥetep īu-nek Àuset nebt χut mà utet-s uā semi neteru àu-s àu neťi ḥrà-k àu-s àu neť ḥrà-k neťi-s ḥrà en Ḥeru set àri ťa en àtef-s Neb-er-ťer àri per em maa Ḥeru śepset but em Rā per em ťefeť em maat*

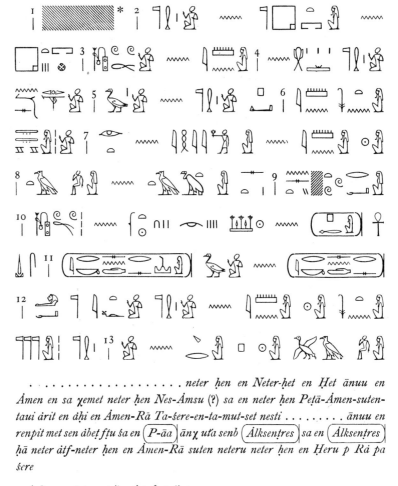

Ȧtm t'er uben Rā em sep ṭepi

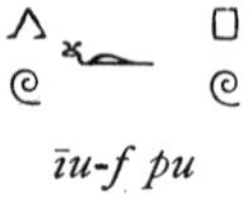

īu-f pu

COLOPHON.

. . . . *neter ḥen en Neter-ḥet en Ḥet ānuu en Ȧmen en sa χemet neter ḥen Nes-Ȧmsu* (?) *sa en neter ḥen Peṭā-Ȧmen-suten-taui ȧrit en ȧḥi en Ȧmen-Rā Ta-śere-en-ta-mut-set nesti* . . . . *ānuu en renpit met sen ȧbeṭ fṭu śa en* (*P-āa*) *ānχ uťa senb* (*Ȧlksenṭres*) *sa en* (*Ȧlksenṭres*) *ḥā neter ȧtf-neter ḥen en Ȧmen-Rā suten neteru neter ḥen en Ḥeru p Rā pa śere*

* I cannot transcribe the first line.

āā ur ṭep en Ȧmen neter ḥen en Ȧmen sepṭ ābui neter ḥen en Χensu ḥer ȧb ben[b]ent neter ḥen en Ȧusȧr ur pa ȧšta neter ḥen en Ȧusȧr ḥer ȧb Ȧšer neter ḥen en Ȧmen qa ȧuset ḥer ȧb Ȧpi āb en p Rā ṭep ḥet en per Ȧmen ḥer sa sen ānuu neter netu (?) *en Ȧmen ḥer sa sen ȧtennu en Ȧmen en sa sen sa fṭu neter ḥen en Nefer-ḥetep pa neter āā neter ḥen en Nefer-ḥetep pa šere neter ḥen en Ȧusȧr Ḥeru Ȧuset Nebt-ḥet neter ḥen en neter ḥet en Ḥet neter ḥen en Ȧmsu neter ḥen en Ḥet-ḥert nebt Ḥet-seχem neter ḥen en Meḥit neter ḥen en Ȧtmu neb Ḥet-*

seχem ȧtennu en Nefer-ḥetep en pa sa fṭu neter ḥen en ṭep en Nefer-ḥetep neter ḥen en na neteru

---

THE LAMENTATIONS OF ISIS AND NEPHTHYS.

(Berlin papyrus No. 1425.)

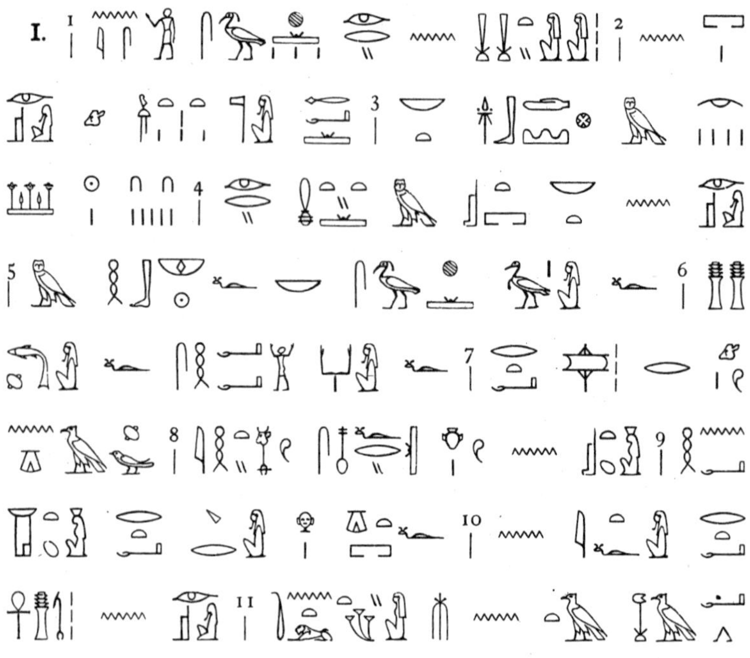

1, 2 **I.** 1. — *Nȧs seχu ȧri en senti* 2. *en per Ȧusȧr χent Ȧmentiu neter āā*
3, 4 3. *nebt Ȧbṭ em ȧbeṭ fṭu ŝa hru met ṭua* 4. *ȧri mȧteti em ȧuset nebt en Ȧusȧr*
5, 6, 7 5. *em ḥeb-f neb seχu ba-f* 6. *ṭeṭṭeṭ χa-f seḥāā ka-f* 7. *erṭāt nifu er fenṭ*
8, 9 *neḳa* 8. *ȧḥti seneferi ȧb en Ȧuset* 9. *ḥnā Nebt-ḥet erṭāt Ḥeru ḥer nest-f*
10, 11 10. *en ȧtf erṭāt ānχ ṭeṭ usr en Ȧusȧr* 11. *θent-reti mes en Ta-χaā-*

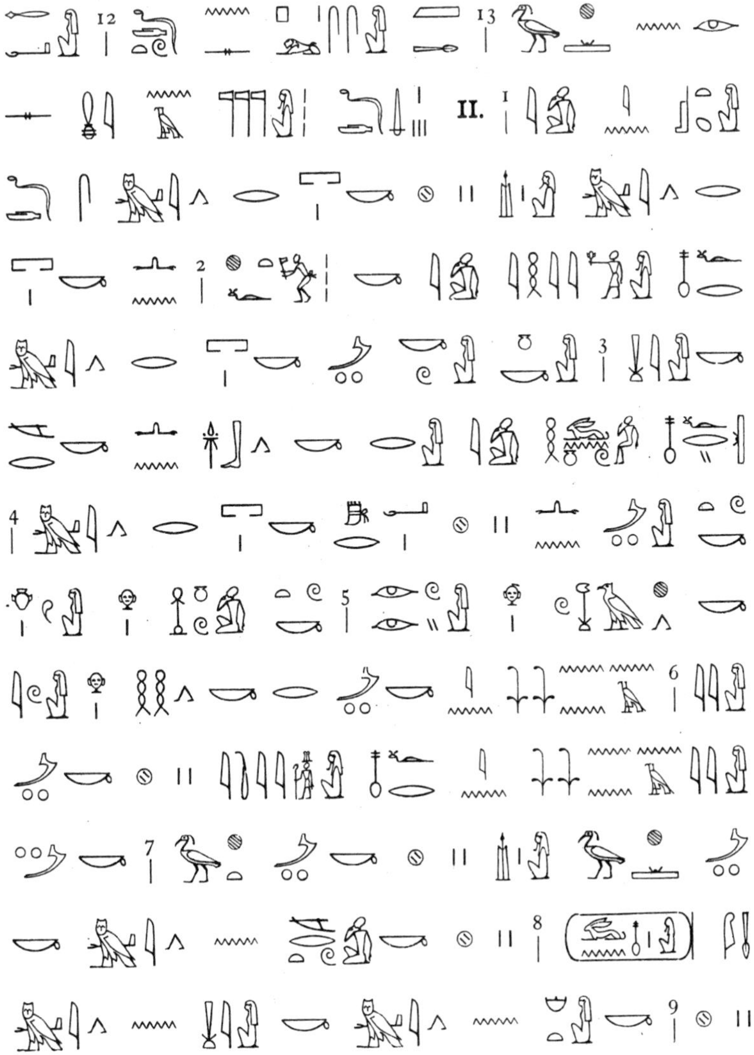

āā 12. *ťeṭtu-nes P-r-ses maāt-χeru* 13. *χu en ȧri-s mȧ na neteru ťeṭ meṭu* 12, 13
II. 1. — *Ȧ ȧn Ȧuset ťeṭ-s māȧ er per-k sep sen Ȧn māȧ er per-k ȧn* 2. *χeft-k* 1, 2
ȧ ȧḥi nefer māȧ er per-k maa-kuȧ nuk 3. *senȧ-k mer-k ȧn ȧb-k er-ȧ ȧ ḥunnu* 3
neferi 4. *māȧ er per-k ťer-ā sep sen ȧn maa-ȧ-tuk ȧb-ȧ ḥer śennu-tuk* 5. *maa-* 4, 5
ui-ȧ ḥer uχaχ-k ȧu-ȧ ḥer ḥeḥ-k er maa-k ȧn enenna 6. *i-ȧ maa-k sep sen ȧθi* 6
nefer ȧn enennai-ȧ maa-k 7. *χut maa-k sep sen Ȧn χut maa-k māȧ en mertu-k* 7
sep sen 8. (*Un-nefer*) *maātχeru māȧ en senȧ-k māȧ en ḥemt-k* 9. *sep sen* 8, 9

10 *urṭu ȧb māȧ en nebt per-k nuk senȧti-k en mut-k* 10. *ȧn ḥeru-k er-ȧ neteru*
11 *ret ḥrȧ-sen-nek ḥer rem-* 11. *tuk em sep uā t'er maa-ȧ ȧu-ȧ ḥer nȧs-nek*
12, 13 12. *em rerem er qa en pet ȧu ȧn setem-* 13. *k χeru-ȧ ȧu nuk senȧ-k mer-k*
1 *ḥer ṭep ta ȧn mer-k kert senȧ sep sen* **III.** 1. — *Ȧ ȧn Nebt-ḥet t'eṭ-s ȧ ȧθi*
2, 3 2. *nefer māȧ er per-k s-net'em s-net'em ȧb-k ȧn χeft-k nebu* 3. *sensenti-k*
4 *er ḳes-k em sa nemmȧt-k* 4. *ḥer nȧs-nek em rerem penā-tuk ḥer nemm*
5 5. *it-k maa-k neferu t'eṭtu ḥnā-n* 6. *ȧθi neb-n ṭer-k aha*

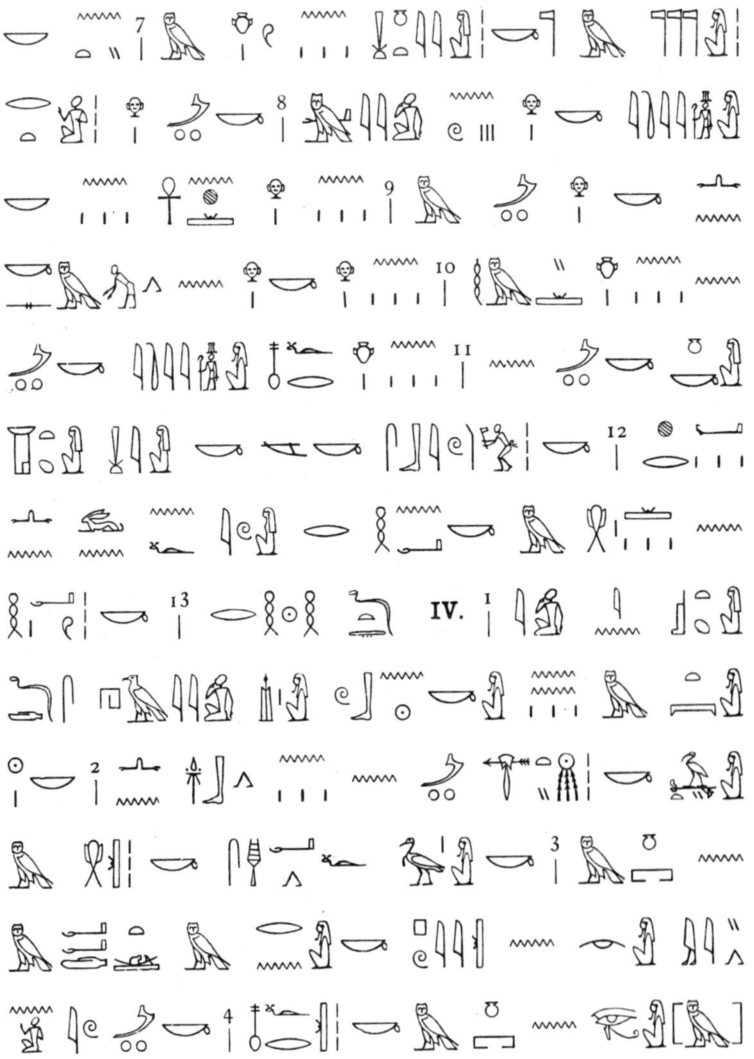

neb enti 7. *em ȧb-n senti-k em neteru ret ḥer maa-k* 8. *māi-nu ḥrȧ-k* 7, 8
ȧθi neb-n ānχ ḥrȧ-n 9. *em maa ḥrȧ-k ȧn kesem en ḥrȧ-k ḥer-n* 10. *neṫem* 9, 10
neṫem ȧb-n en maa-k ȧθi nefer ȧb-n 11. *en maa-k nuk Nebt-ḥet senȧ-k mer-k* 11
sebȧu-k 12. *χer ȧn un-nef ȧu-ȧ er ḥnā-k em sa en ḥāu-k* 13. *er ḥeḥ ṫetta* 12, 13
IV. — 1. *Ȧ ȧn Ȧuset ṫeṭ-s hai Ȧn uben-k en-n em pet hru neb* 2. *ȧn ȧb-n* 1, 2
en maa sati-k Teḥuti em sa-k s-āḥā-f ba-k 3. *em χennu en māāṭet em ren-k* 3
pui en Ȧāḥ ī-nȧ ȧu maa-k 4. *neferu-k em χennu en Uṫat [em]* 4

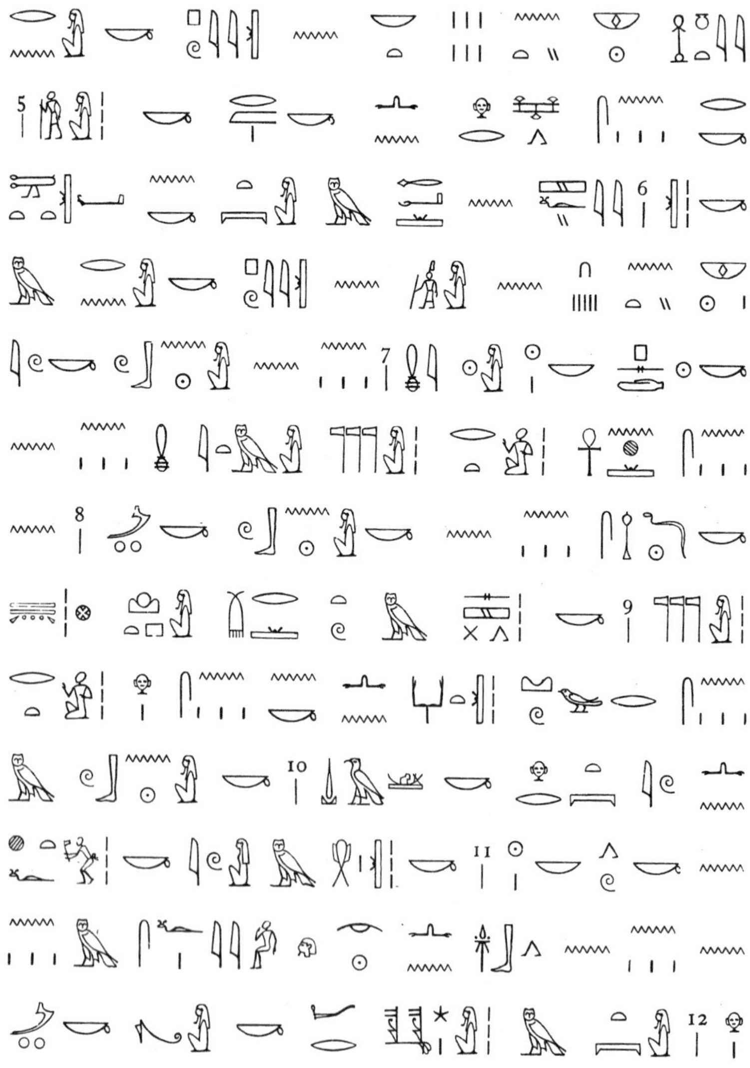

5 *ren-k pui en nebt sȧs enti ḥeb śenit-* 5. *k er ḳes-k ȧn ḥer-sen erek θetet nek pet*
6 *em āā en śefi-* 6. *k em ren-k pui en ser en met ṭua enti ḥeb ȧuk uben-en-n*
7, 8 7. *mȧ Rā hru neb pesṭ-k-en-n mȧ Ȧtem neteru ret ānχ-sen en* 8. *maa-k*
9 *uben-k-en-n s-ḥeť-k ṭaui χut āper-tu em seś-k* 9. *neteru ret ḥrȧ-sen nek ȧn*
10, 11 *kat ṭu er-sen em uben-k* 10. *ťa-k ḥert ȧu ȧn χeft-k ȧu-ȧ em sau-k* 11. *hru*
neb īu-k-en-n em sefi ṭep ȧāḥ ȧn ȧb-en-n en maa-k tȧa-k ťeser saḥu em pet
12 12. *ḥer*

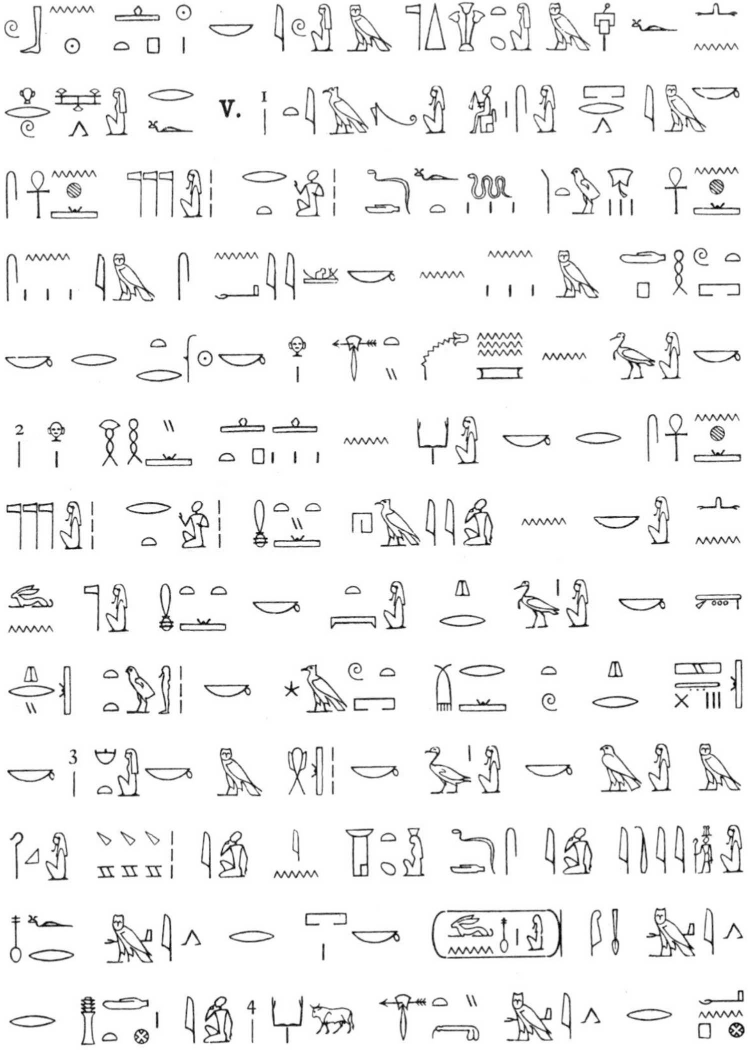

uben ḥetep hru neb ȧu-ȧ em neter sept ḥat em sa-f ȧn ḥeru-ȧ er-f **V.** — 1. *tȧa* 1
śeps per ȧm-k s-ānχ neteru ret ťeṭfet āutu ānχ-sen ȧm-s nāi-k-en-n em ṭepḥut-k
er trȧ-k ḥer sati tef (?) *en ba-k* 2. *ḥer uaḥi ḥetepu en ka-k er s-ānχ neteru* 2
ret mȧteti hai en neb ȧn un neter mȧtet-k pet χer ba-k ta χeri tetu-k ṭuaut
āper-tu χer śeta-k 3. *ḥemt-k em sa-k sa-k Ḥeru em ḥeq taiu Ȧ ȧn Nebt-ḥet* 3
ťeṭ-s ȧ ȧθi nefer māȧ er per-k (*Un-nefer*) *maātχeru māȧ er Ṭeṭet ȧ* 4. *ka* 4
sati māȧ er Ānep

mertu χenȧ māȧ er Ꭓar māȧ er Ṭeṭṭeṭ ȧuset mertu ba-k baiu nu ȧtfu-k
5 *sen erek* 5. *sa-k āṭ' Ḥeru mes en senti er χeft ḥrȧ-k ȧu-ȧ em ḥeṭ'et em sa-k*
6 *hru neb ȧn ḥer-ȧ erek ṭ'etta ȧ Ȧn māȧ er Sau Sau pu ren-k* 6. *māȧ*
er Āper (?) *maa-k mut-k Nut χi nefer ȧn ȧb-k er-es māȧ en menṭ-s bāḥu*
7 *ȧm-f senȧ nefer ȧn ȧb-k eres ȧ sa māȧ* 7. *er Sau Ȧusȧr Taruṭ ṭ'eṭtu-nes*
Ni sep sen mes en Perses maāṭχeru māȧ er Āper (?) *nut-k ȧuset-k Ḥet-ṭeb*
ȧuk ḥetep-tu er ḳes mut-

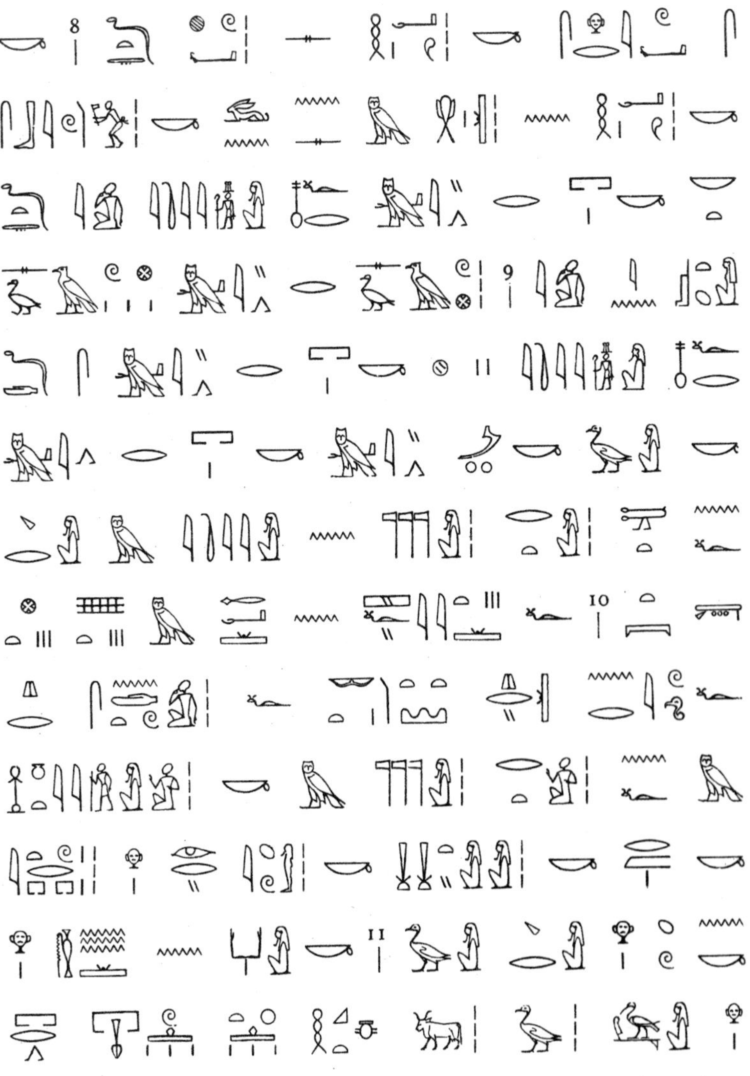

k 8. *ťetta χu-s ḥāu-k seḥerȧu-s sebȧu-k un-nes em sa en ḥāu-k ťetta Ȧ ȧθi*
nefer māāi er per-k nebt Sau māāi er Sau 9. *Ȧ ȧn Ȧuset ťeṭ-s māāi er* 9
per-k sep sen ȧθi nefer māā er per-k māāi maa-k sa-k Ḥeru em ȧθi en neteru
ret θet-nef nut sept em āā en śefit-f 10. *pet ta χer senṭetu-f Pettet χeri* 10
nerȧu-f śennit-k em neteru ret nef em ȧtur ḥer ȧri ȧru-k senti-k er ḳes-k
ḥer qebḥ en ka-k 11. *sa-k Ḥeru ḥer ȧru-nek per per-χeru ta ḥeqt ȧḥ apt* 11
Teḥuti ḥer

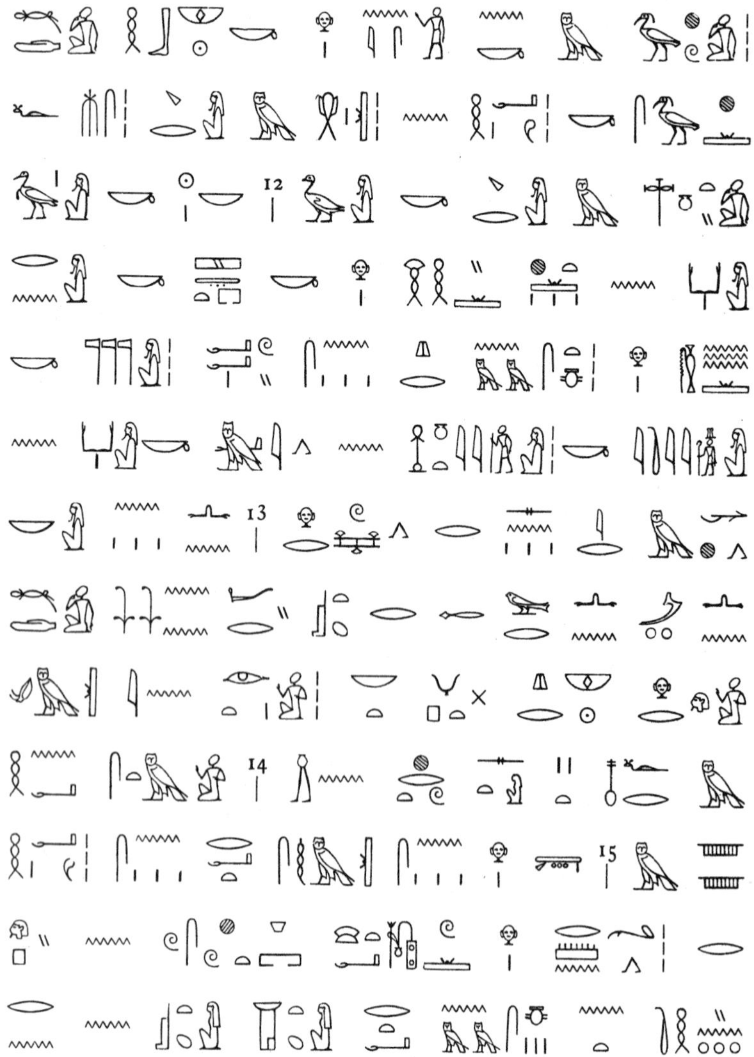

sešeṭ ḥeb-k ḥer nȧs-nek em χu-f mesu Ḥeru em sa en ḥāu-k s-χu ba-k hru neb
12 12. *sa-k Ḥeru em neťťi ren-k šetat-k ḥer uaḥi χet en ka-k neteru āāui-sen*
13 *χer nemmeset ḥer qebḥ en ka-k māā en šenit-k ȧθi neb-n ȧn* 13. *ḥeru er sen*
ȧr emχet sešeṭ enen ťeseri Ȧuset er āa ur ȧn maa ȧn setem ȧn maat nebt ȧpt
14 *χer-ḥeb ḥer ḥnā setem* 14. *ȧn χertu set sent nefer em ḥāu-sen erṭāt s-neťem-*
15 *sen ḥer ta* 15. *em āā ṭepi en useχut χāātu ḥer ermen er ren en Ȧuset Nebt-*
ḥet erṭāt nemmes ent θeḥin

meḥ em mu em āāui-sen unemi pau ȧri em Ȧneb-ḥeṭ'et em āāui-sen ȧb erṭāt ḥrȧ-sen em χert ȧri ḥeṭ'eṭ χemt ent hru mȧteti ḥeṭ'et χemennu ent hru ȧn urṭu-k en seśeṭ śāt ten em ḥeṭ'et ent ḥeb

īu-f pu

THE LITANIES OF SEKER.

I. — 1. *Entāu en ȧn Seker er ḥer śetai Ṭeṭ meṭu* 2. *ȧ seṭennu per em χat* 3. *ȧ sa semsu nu paut ṭepi* 4. *ȧ nebt ḥrȧu āśt χeperu* 5. *ȧ rer en nub em er peru* 6. *ȧ nebt āḥā ṭāt renpit* 7. *ȧ nebt ānχ*

er neḥeḥ 8. *ȧ nebt ḥeḥ āšt ḥefen* 9. *ȧ pesṭ ḥer uben ḥetep* 10. *ȧ seneťemi nef ȧḥetit* 11. *ȧ pa nebt senṭet āāi setet* 12. *ȧ nebt ḥrȧu āšt ārāt* 13. *ȧ χāā em ḥeť nebt urerer* 14. *ȧ pa sefi šeps nu Ḥeru ḥekennu* 15. *ȧ ba en Rā em uȧa ḥeḥ* 16. *ȧ semi ḳaḥu māȧ er šetatet-k* 17. *ȧ pa nebt senṭeti χeper ťesef* 18. *ȧ urṭu ȧb māȧi er nut-k* 19. *ȧ ȧri hai māȧi er nut-k* 20. *ȧ pa meriti en na neteru neterit* 21. *ȧ semeḥ-f māȧi er ḥet-k* 22. *ȧ ȧm ṭuaut māȧi er ābtu-k*

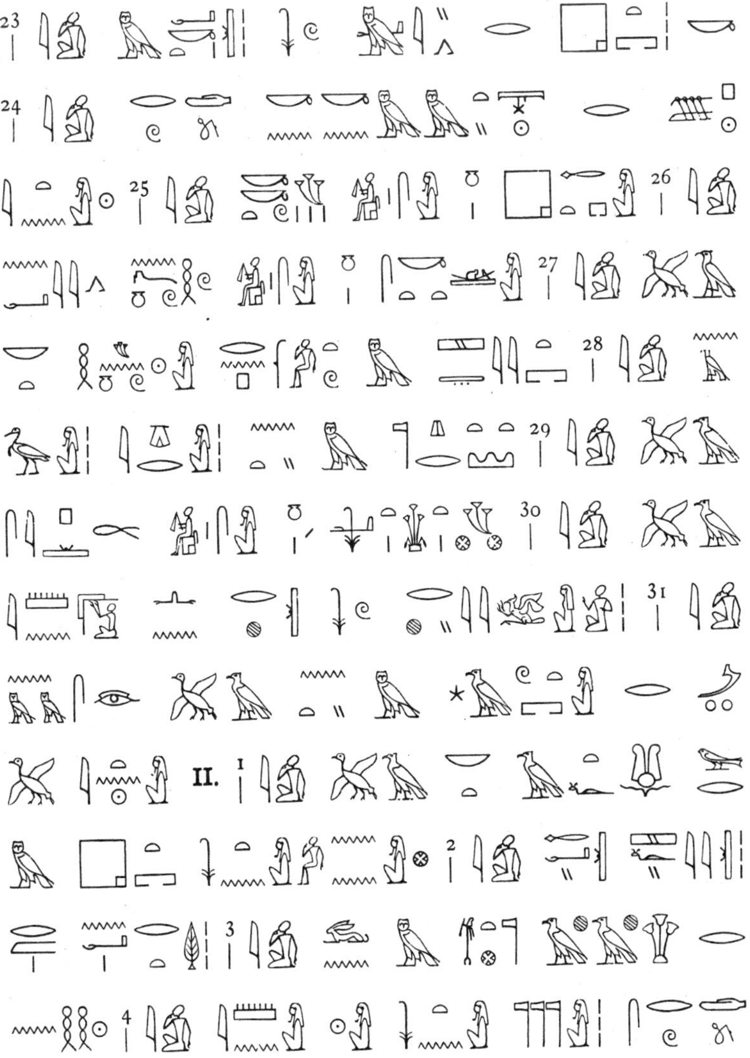

23. *ȧ māket su māȧi er ḥet-k* 24. *ȧ ruṭ kenkenememti er seśep ȧten* 25. *ȧ kektu śeps nu ḥet-āat* 26. *ȧ nāi ennuḥu śeps nu sektet* 27. *ȧ pa nebt ḥennu renp-tu em śetait* 28. *ȧ na baiu ȧḳer enti em Neter-χertet* 29. *ȧ pa sȧp śeps nu qemāt meḥit* 30. *ȧ pa ȧmen ȧn reχ su reχi* 31. *ȧ nemmes pa enti em ṭuaut er maa pa ȧten* **II.** — 1. *ȧ pa nebt atef ur em ḥet Suten-ḥenen* 2. *ȧ āāi śefi er ḳes Nārt* 3. *ȧ un em Uast aχaχ er neḥeḥ* 4. *ȧ Ȧmen Rā suten neteru seruṭ*

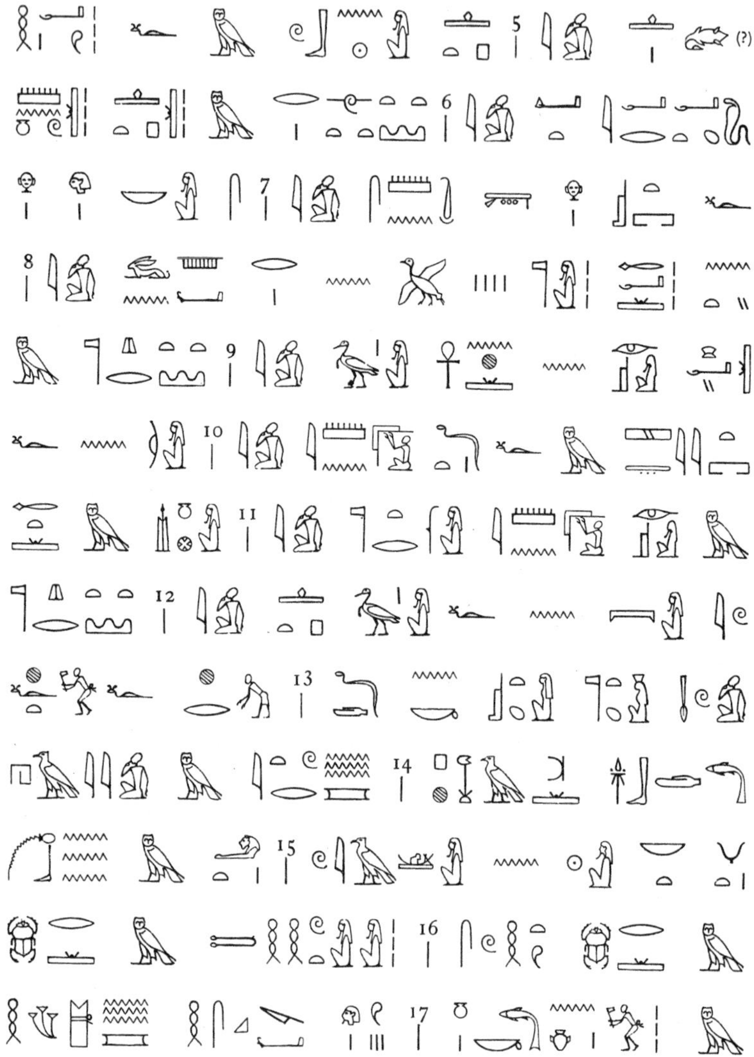

ḥāu-f em uben ḥetep 5. *à* . . . . . . *mennu ḥetepu em Re-statet* 6. *à ṭāt àārāt ḥer ṭep neb-s* 7. *à smen ta ḥer àuset-f* 8. *à un re en pa fṭu neteru āāiu enti em Neter-χertet* 9. *à ba ānχ en Àusàr χāāi-f en àāḥ* 10. *à àmen ṭet-f em šetait āat em Ànnu* 11. *à neter àmen Àusàr em Neter-χertet* 12. *à ḥetep ba-f en pet àu χeft-f χer* 13. *ṭeṭ-nek Àuset neterit χeru hai em àtur* 14. *peχa àbṭ āb em ḥāt* 15. *uàa en Rā nebt àpt* (?) *χeper em θeḥḥut* (?) 16. *suḥt χeper em ḥen ḥeseq ṭepu* 17. *nu χak-en-àbu em*

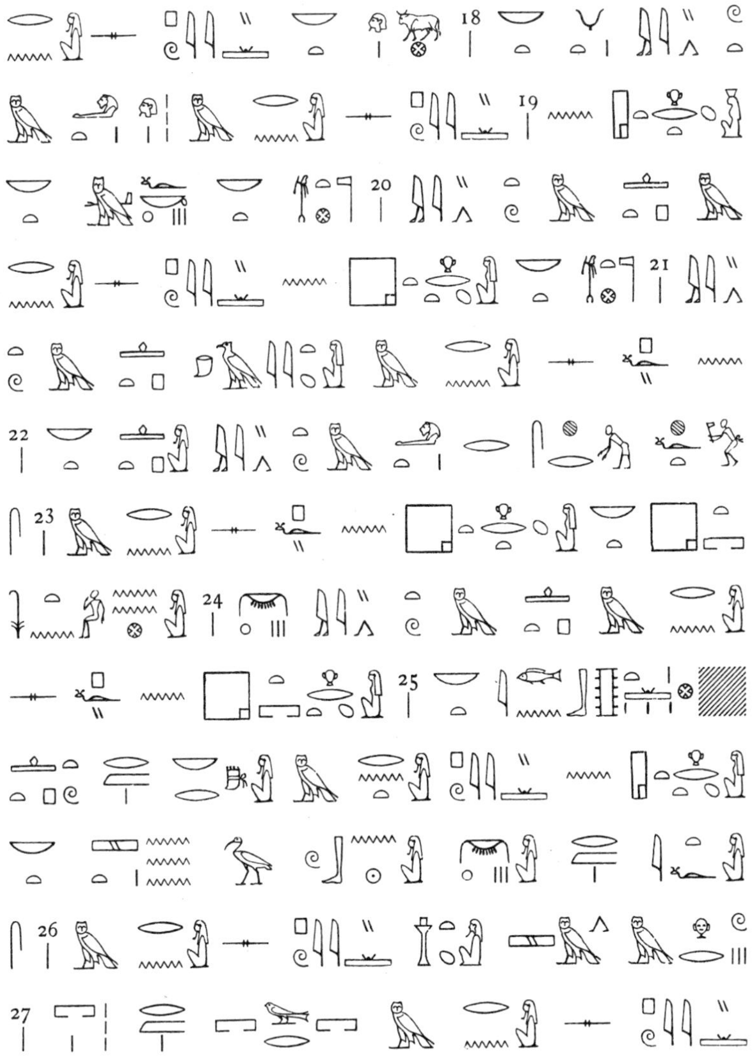

ren-s pui nebt Ṭep-āḥet 18. *nebt āpt ī-tu em ḥāt ṭepu em ren-s pui* 19. *en Ḥet-ḥert nebt māfek nebt Uast* 20. *ī-tu em ḥetep em ren-s pui en Ḥet-ḥert nebt Uast* 21. *ī-tu em ḥetep Taït em ren-s pfi en* 22. *Nebt ḥetep ī-tu em ḥāt er seχer χeft-s* 23. *em ren-s pfi en Ḥet-ḥert nebt Ḥet-suten-ḥenen* 24. *nub ī-tu em ḥetep em ren-s pfi en Ḥet-ḥert* 25. *nebt Ānebet . . . . . . ḥetep-tu er ḳes Neb-er-ṫer em ren-t pui en Ḥet-ḥert nebt Śet ṭeśer uben nub er ḳes ātf-s* 26. *em ren-s pui Bast māśem em ḥeru* 27. *peru er ḳes peru ur em ren-s pui*

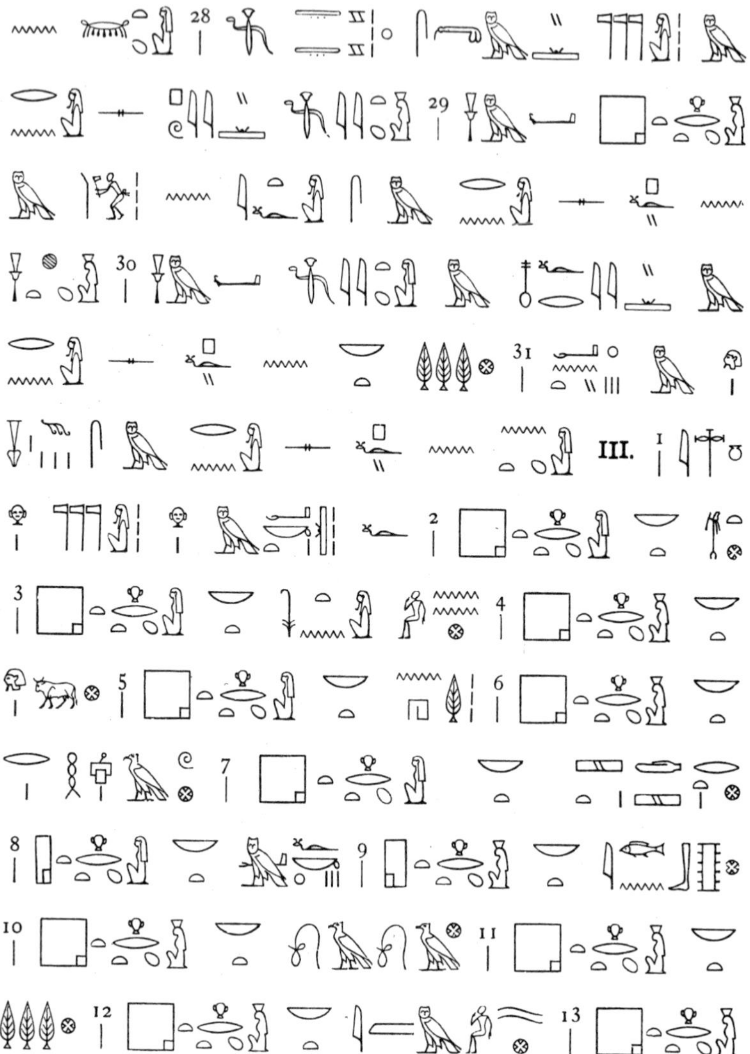

en Satet 28. *uaṭ' taui semi neteru em ren-s pui Uaṭit* 29. *seχem Ḥet-ḥert em Sebȧu en ȧtf-s em ren-s pfi en Seχet* 30. *seχem Uaṭit em neferi em ren-s pfi en nebt Ȧmmu* 31. *ānti em ṭep sam-s em ren-s pfi en Net* **III.** — 1. *ȧneṭ' ḥrȧ neteru ḥer māket-f* 2. *Ḥet-ḥert nebt Uast* 6. *Ḥet-ḥert nebt Suten-ḥenen* 4. *Ḥet-ḥert nebt Ṭep-ȧḥet* 5. *Ḥet-ḥert nebt Nehet* 6. *Ḥet-ḥert nebt Reḥesau* 7. *Ḥet-ḥert nebt Śet-ṭeśert* 8. *Ḥet-ḥert nebt māfek* 9. *Ḥet-ḥert nebt Ȧneb* 10. *Ḥet-ḥert nebt Uaua* 11. *Ḥet-ḥert nebt Ȧmmu* 12. *Ḥet-ḥert nebt Ȧmem* 13. *Ḥet-ḥert* *ḥenut Met-sȧs* (?) 14. *pa paut Smeri māi-ten āāui-ten χer ȧtef-ten Ȧusȧr* 15. *ī neter sa-ta sep fṭu* 16. *ȧ seχet ḥeb sep sen ȧθi* 17. *ȧ neťemitu χenemem mer-k* 18. *ȧ ānχ-tu sep sen er neḥeḥ* 19. *ȧ ḥeb-k en ťetta* 20. *ȧ senȧ ta ābaa uat* 21. *a ṭeṭṭeṭ-θ em Ṭeṭṭeṭ ḥert* 22. *ȧ neter setem-k sa-ta hai setem-k sa-ta em re en neter sept* 23. *ȧ bes em maatu-f sa neter ḥen* 24. *ȧ setep sa χeft ťeṭ-k* 25. *ȧ māku-ȧ* (*P-āa*) *ḥer ȧri mer-k* 26. *ȧ māku-ȧ* (*P-āa*) *ḥer ȧri ḥesu-k* 27. *ȧ ḥems māȧi er-ek urṭu ȧb pu* 28. *ȧ sa neter ḥen seśeṭ-nef ḥeb* 29. *ȧ ṭeṭṭeṭ ren*

em Ṭeṭṭeṭ ḥert 30. *ȧ neťemi sti em Ṭeṭṭet ḥert* 31. *ȧ māȧi ṭer sebȧu* 32. *ȧ māȧi ṭuau neχen* **IV.** — 1. *ȧ ṭāt senṭet-f em χakȧbu* 2. *ȧ ȧr bakȧu ŝes neb-f ȧn neter ḥen Bast ȧm-f* 3. *ȧ χakȧbu mesṭ neter ḥet ḥu menȧnȧu er χeχ-f* 4. *ȧ ī en nebt Ṭeṭṭeṭ ḥert ḥu-nef χakȧbu* 5. *ťeṭ meṭu sep met-sȧs seŝep ṭeχen*

6. *īu-f pu*

Colophon.

Ȧu ren-sen men uaḥi ȧn sek-k er neḥeḥ embaḥ Ȧusȧr Ḥeru Ȧuset Nebt-ḥet neteru

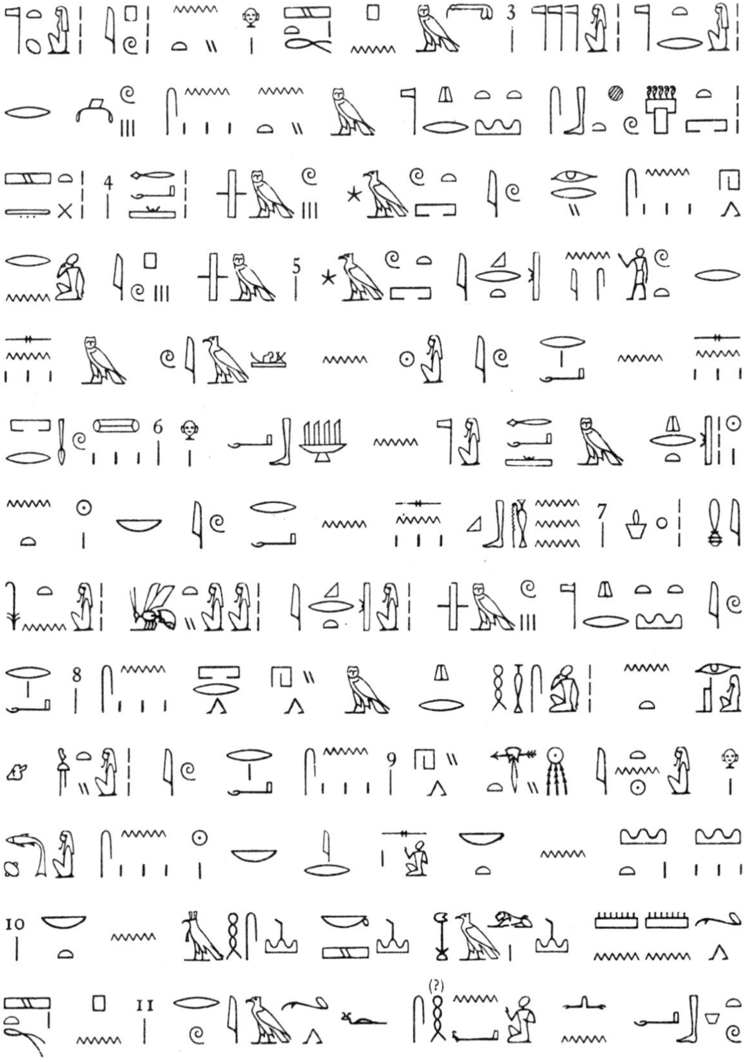

neterit àpu enti ḥer šāt pen embaḥ neteru neterit er āu-sen enti em Neter-χertet sebeχtut šetat āā àmu ṭuaut àu àri-sen h ren àpu àm ṭuaut àqert nàs-tu er sen em uàa en Rā àu erṭā-en-sen per-χeru ḥer āb en neter āā em χert ent hru neb àu erṭā-en-sen qebḥ sentrà mà suteniu-net (or *bàti*) *àqert àmu Neter-χertet àu erṭā-sen per hi em χer ḥesiu ent Àusàr χent Àmentiu àu erṭā-sen hi sati àten ḥer χa-sen hru neb àr sa nebt en set set nebt Neḥes Keš Χaru menmen šāt pen ruàa-f seḥn* (?) *àn ābtu*

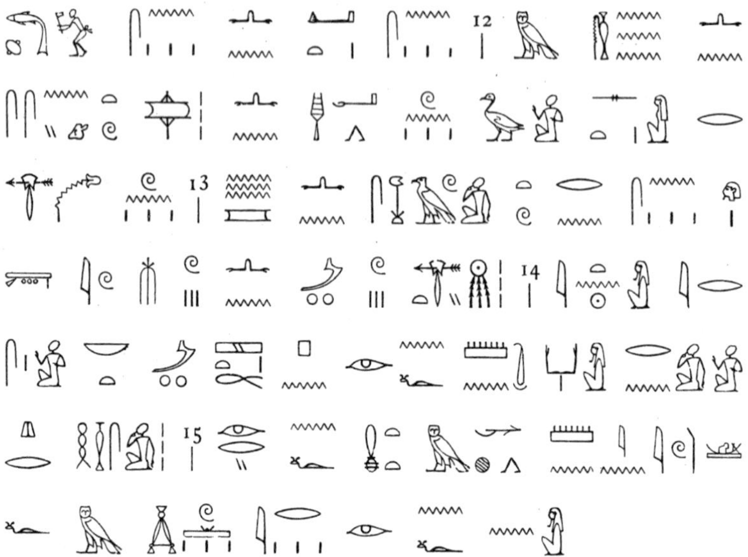

χa-sen ȧn ṭāt-sen em qebḥ ȧn seseni-tu nifu ȧn āḥā-un sa set er sati-un ȧn seχau-tu ren-sen ṭep ta ȧu mesu ȧn maa-u sati ȧten ȧr se nebt maa šāt pen ȧri-nef men ka-ȧ ren-ȧ χer ḥesiu ȧri-nef mȧtet emχet menȧnȧu-f em ṭebu ȧru ȧri-nef-nȧ

THE INSCRIPTION OF UNȦ.

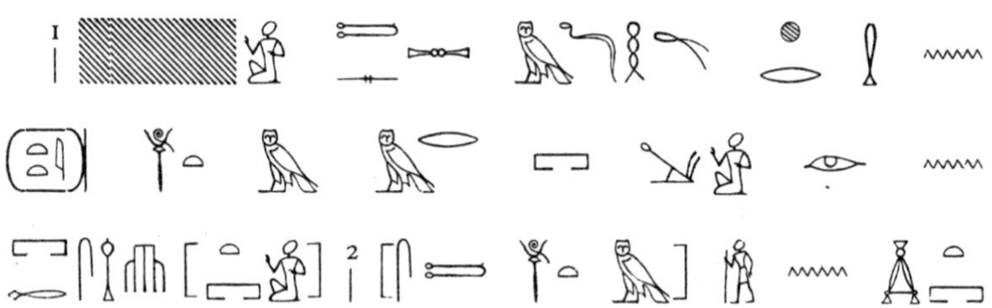

1\. . . . . . *θes met'eḥ χer ḥen en* (*Tetȧ*) *ȧaut-[ȧ] em mer per ār ȧri-nȧ Per-āa seḥet' χent* 2. *[ȧsθ ȧaut-ȧ em] ser en t'ebt*

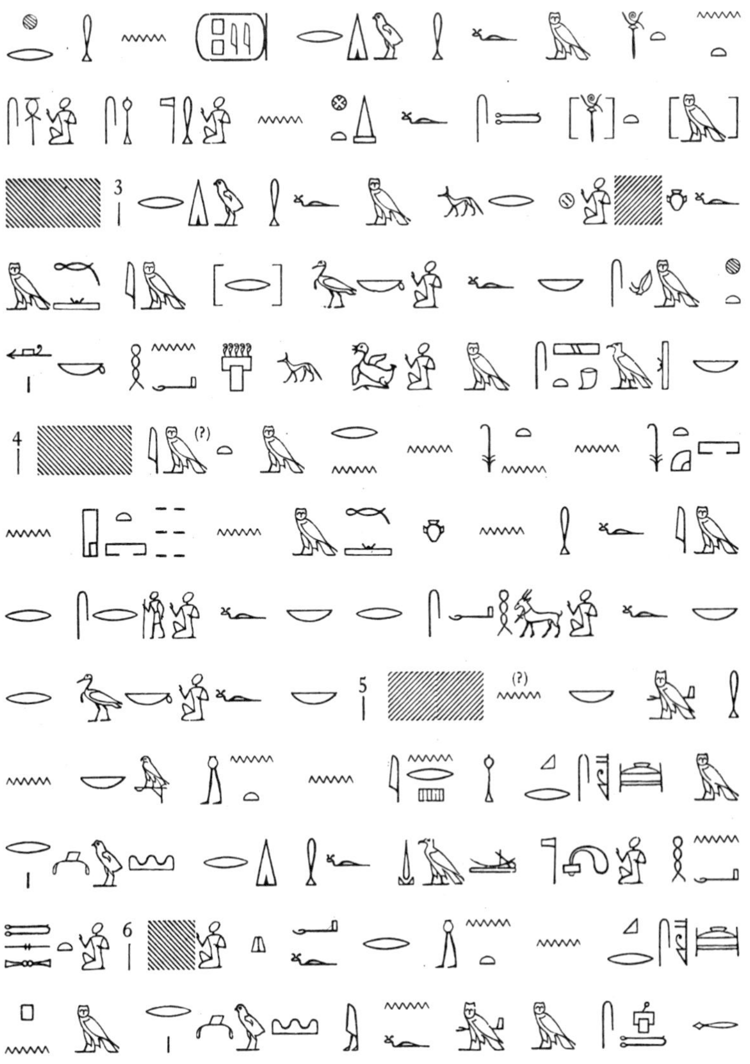

χer ḥen en Pepi erṭāu-[ȧ] ḥen-f em ȧaut ent smer seḥetʹ neter ḥen en nut-f
. . ȧsθ ȧaut-[ȧ em] . . . . 3. *erṭāu-[ȧ] ḥen-f em sab ȧr Neχen . . . ȧb-f meḥ* 3
ȧm-[ȧ er] bak-f neb setem-[ȧ] χet uā-k[uȧ] ḥnā ta sab ťa em seśeta neb
4\. . . . . . . *em ren en suten en sutėn ȧpt en ḥet sȧs en meḥ ȧb en ḥen-f* 4
ȧm [ȧ] er ser-f neb er sāḥ-f neb er bak-f neb 5. . . . . . . *neb mā ḥen en* 5
neb-[ȧ] ȧnt-nȧ ȧner ḥetʹ qeres em Reāu erṭā ḥen-f ťa neter net (or *bȧt*) *ḥnā*
θest 6. . . . . . . *χer ā-f er ȧnt en qeres pen em Reāu ī-nef mā em saθ āa* 6

7 *en χennu ḥnā āa-f* 7. *āret reuit ḳemḥu sen seθ uā ȧn sep pat ȧrit mȧtet en bak*
8 *neb ȧχer ȧqer-[ȧ] ḥer ȧb en ḥen-f* 8. *ȧχer uab-[ȧ] ḥer ȧb en ḥen-f ȧχer meḥ ȧb*
en ḥen-f ȧm-[ȧ] ȧsθu-[ȧ] em sab ȧr Neχen erṭāu-[ȧ] ḥen-f em smer uāt Per-āa
9 *mer χent* 9. *en . . . . en Per-āa mer χent unu ȧm ȧri-k[uȧ] er ḥeset ḥen-f*
10 *em ȧrit setep sa em ȧrit uat suten em erṭā āḥā seru ȧri-k[uȧ] mȧqeṭ* 10. *er*
ḥesetu-[ȧ] ḥen-f ḥer-s er χet neb šent χet em suten ȧpt er suten ḥemt urt Ȧmts
11 *em sešeta erṭā ḥen-f hai-[ȧ] er setem uā-k[uȧ] ȧn unt . . . .* 11. *ta sab ṫa neb*

ser neb ȧm ȧper-[ȧ] uā-k[uȧ] en ȧqer-[ȧ] en uab-[ȧ] ḥer ȧb en ḥen-f en meḥ
ḥen-f ȧb-f ȧm-[ȧ] nuk ȧri em ān uā-k[uȧ] 12. *ḥnā sab ȧr Neχen uā ȧsθ* 12
ȧaut-ȧ em Per-āa mer χent ȧn sep pa mȧtu-[ȧ] setem seśeta en suten ȧpt ťer
baḥ ȧper [ȧ] erṭāt ḥen-f 13. *setem-[ȧ] en ȧqer-[ȧ] ḥer ȧb en ḥen-f er ser-f* 13
neb er sāḥ-f neb er bak-f neb χesef en ḥen-f χet en Ām-ḥru-śā 14. *ȧri en* 14
ḥen-f maśā en ťebā āśu em res mȧqeṭ-f χent em Ābu meḥt em . . . . . . em ta
meḥ em ḳesui mȧqeṭ-sen 15. *em sťer em χen sťeru em Ȧrθet neḥes* 15

16 *em Ṭam neḥes em Ȧmam neḥes* 16. *em Uauat neḥes em Kaau neḥes em*
17 *Taθām neḥes habu-[ȧ] ḥen-f χer ḥāt maśā pen* 17. *ȧsθ ḥāu ȧsθ net* (or *bȧt*)
ȧsθ ḥet-āat smer uāt ȧsθ ḥrȧu ḥer ṭep ḥequ ḥet nu res ta meḥ smeru nub
18 18. *mer neter ḥenu nu res ta meḥ meru ḳes χer ḥāt θeset ent res ta meḥ ḥet*
19 *nut ḥeqt-sen neḥes nu set peten* 19. *nuk un ȧri en sen seχer ȧsθ ȧaut-[ȧ]*
em Per-āa mer χent en met en ȧuset er nefer en ṭeṭ uā ȧm em senu-f neb (?)
20 20. *er nefer en neḥem uā ȧm*

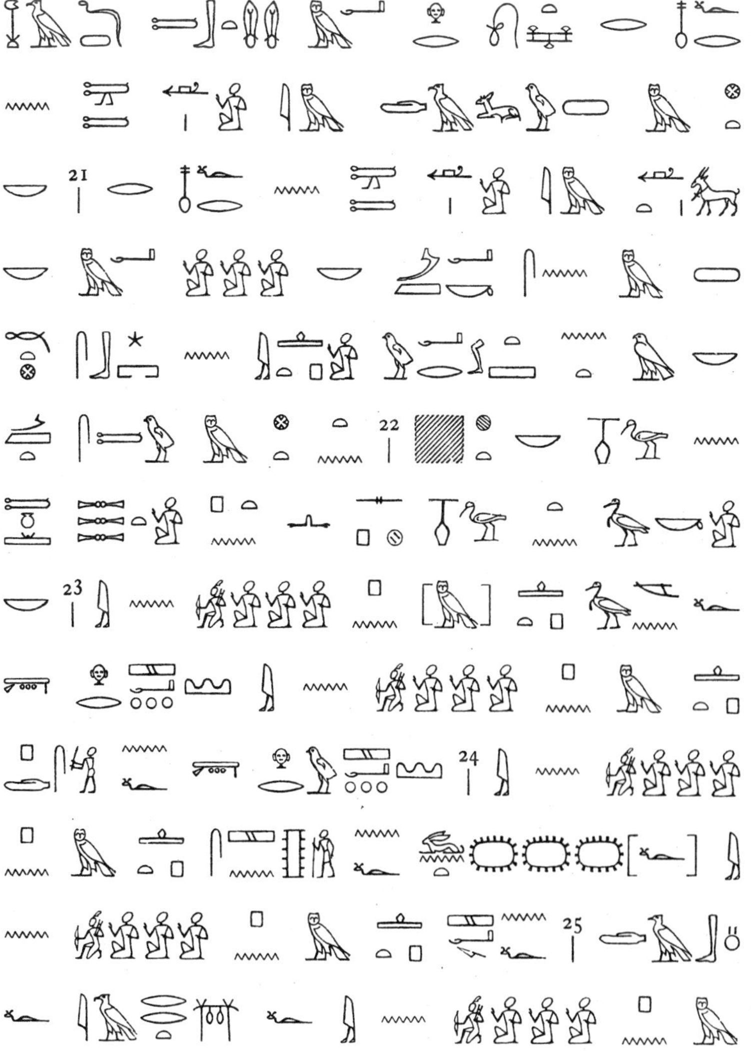

χat' θebt mā ḥer uat er nefer en θeθ uā àm ṭaāu em nut neb 21. *er nefer* 21
en θeθ uā àm uāt neb mā reθ neb maā-k[uà] sen em àa meḥt sba en Ī-ḥetep
uārt ent Ḥeru neb maāt àsθu em nut ten 22. . . . . . *χet neb* . . . . . . *en θenu* 22
θest peten àn sep . . . . . *ten bak neb* 23. *ī en maśā pen em ḥetep ban-f ta* 23
Ḥeru-śā ī en maśā pen em ḥetep peṭes-nef ta Ḥeru-śā 24. *ī en maśā pen em* 24
ḥetep seśen-nef unt-f ī en maśā pen em ḥetep śā-nef 25. *ṭab-f àareret-f ī en* 25
maśā pen em

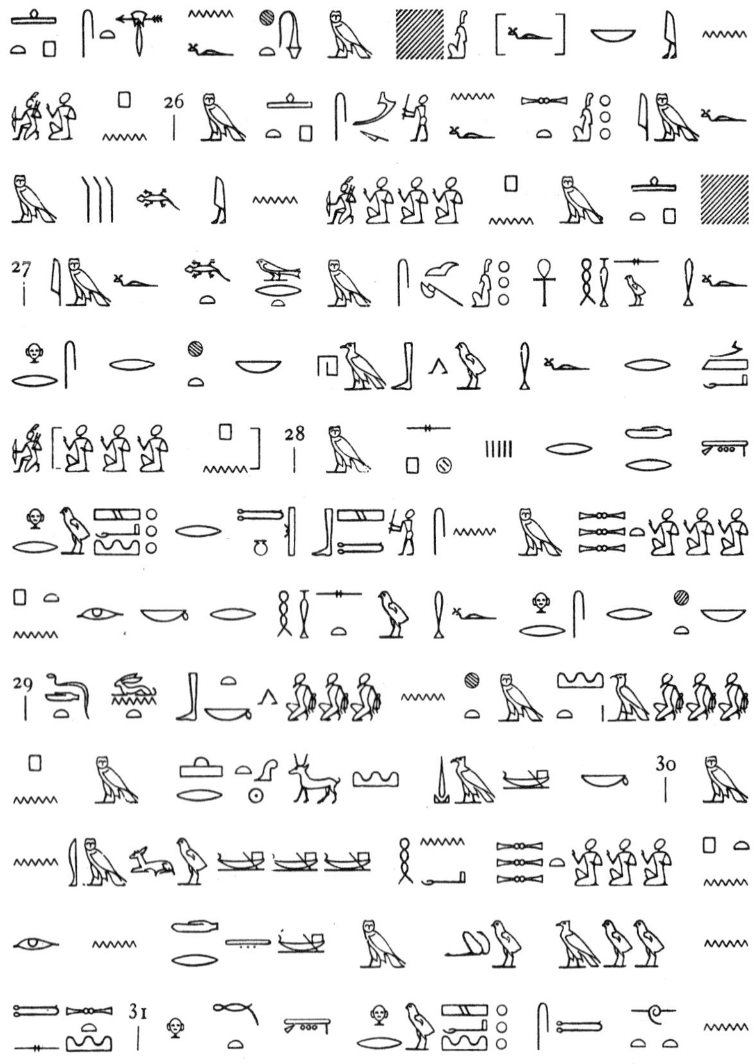

26 *ḥetep set-nef χet em . . . . . . f neb ī en mašā pen* 26. *em ḥetep sma-nef*
27 *θest åm-f em ťebā āš ī en mašā pen em ḥetep . . . . .* 27. *åm-f āšt urt*
em seqer ānχ ḥesu-å ḥen-f ḥer-s er χet neb habu-[å] ḥen-f ermaā mašā pen
28 28. *em sep ṭua er ṭer ta Ḥeru-šā er θenu bešθ-sen em θest peten åri-ku[å]*
29 *er ḥesetu-å ḥen-f ḥer-s er χet neb* 29. *ťeṭet unt betek en χet em seta pen em*
30 *. . . . rt . . . . ťa-ku[å]* 30. *em nemāu-[å] ḥnā θest peten åri-n[å] ṭer ta*
31 *em peḥu auu en θest* 31. *ḥer meḥt ta Ḥeru-šā åsθ statet en*

mašā pen em ḥert ī-n[ȧ] neťer-n[ȧ]-sen mȧqeṭ-sen sma-n[ȧ] 32. *betek neb* 32
ȧm-sen un-[ȧ] em ḥet āat aθu χer θebt erṭāu-[ȧ] ḥer . . . . suten net (or *bȧt*)
(*Mer-en-Rā*) *neb ānχ . . . . . .* 33. *em ḥā mer res χent em Ābu meḥt em . . . . t en* 33
ȧqer-[ȧ] ḥer ȧb en ḥen-f en uab-[ȧ] ḥer ȧb en ḥen-f en meḥ ȧb en ḥen-f [ȧm-ȧ]
34. *un-[ȧ] em aθet χer θebut ḥesu-[ȧ] ḥen-f ḥer res* (?)*-u-[ȧ] ḥer setep sa ȧri-* 34
n[ȧ] em ȧuset āḥā er ser-f neb er sāḥ-[f neb] 35. *er bak-f neb ȧn sep ȧrit* 35
ȧaut ten en bak neb ťer baḥ ȧri-k[uȧ] nef mer res er hert er nefer en ṭeṭ-ȧ

ȧm-f em senu-[f] neb 36. *er kat neb ȧp-[ȧ] χet neb ȧpt en χennu em res*
37 *pen em sep sen unnut neb ȧpt en χennu em res pen em sep sen ȧri sert* 37. *ȧrit*
qeṭ em res pen ȧn sep pat ȧrit mȧtet em res pen ťer baḥ ȧri-k[uȧ] mȧqeṭ er
38 *ḥestu[ȧ] ḥen-f ḥer-s habu[ȧ] ḥen-f* 38. *er Ȧbhat er ȧnt neb ānχ hen en ānχu*
39 *ḥnā āa-f ḥnā benbenet net* (?) *šepset en* (*Mer-en-Rā*) *χā nefer ḥenut* 39. *ha-*
40 *bu[ȧ] ḥen-f er Ābu er ȧnt maθ ārretu ḥnā seθ-s maθ . . . . ruit* 40. *er*
ȧnt maθ sebau seθu nu sešepet ḥert ent (*Mer-en-Rā*) *χā nefer ḥenut χeṭ-*

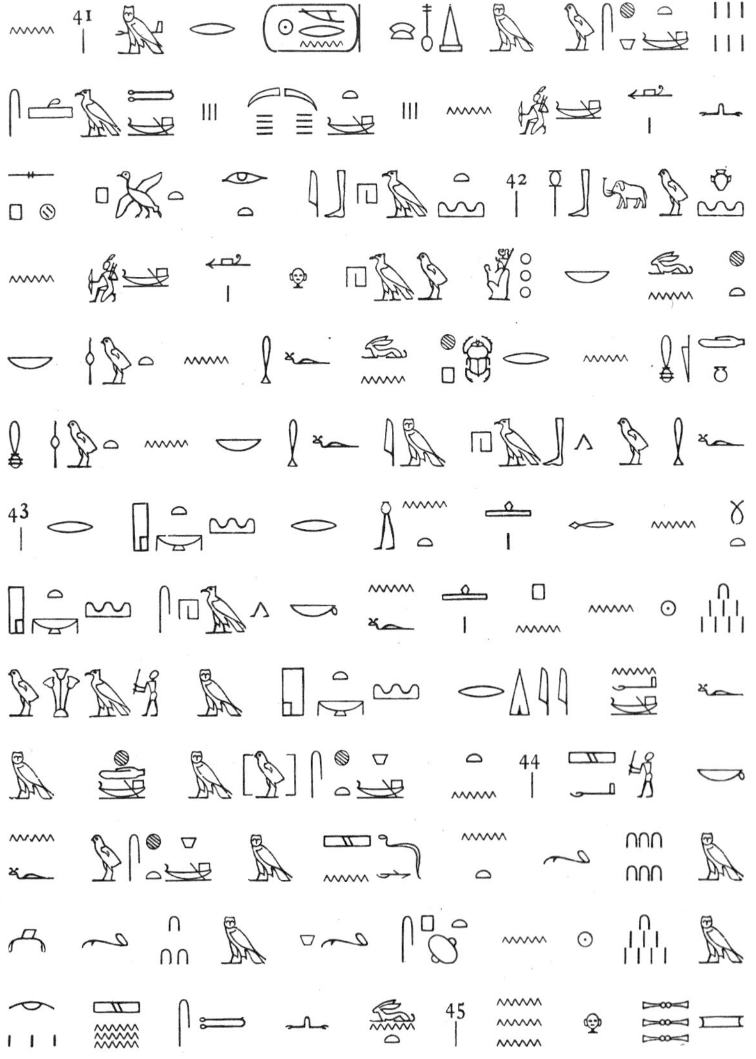

n[ȧ] 41. *mā er* (*Mer-en-Rā*) *χā nefer em useχt sȧs saθ χemet χemennut χemet* 41
en . . . . . uā ȧn sep pat ȧrit Ȧbhat 42. *Ābu en . . . . uā ḥer hau suteniu neb* 42
un χet neb uťut-n[ȧ] ḥen-f un χeper-n[ȧ] mȧqeṭ mȧ uťut-n[ȧ] neb ḥen-f
ȧm hab-u[ȧ] ḥen-f 43. *er Ḥet-nub er ȧnt ḥetep āa en śeset Ḥet-nub seha-* 43
k[uȧ] nef ḥetep pen en hru met seχef uḥa[ȧ] em Ḥet-nub erṭāi-[ȧ] nā-f em
χeṭ em useχt ten 44. *śā-k[uȧ] nef useχt em śeneť ent meḥ* 60 *em āu meḥ māb* 44
em useχt sept-[ȧ] en hru met seχef em ȧbeṭ χemt śe ȧsθ ȧn unt 45. *mu ḥer θesu* 45

menȧ-[ȧ] er (*Mer-en-Rā*) *χā nefer em ḥetep χeper-n[ȧ] mā mȧqeṭ χeft ḥu uťu-*
46 *n[ȧ] ḥen neb-[ȧ] hab-[uȧ] ḥen-f er śaṭ χenta* (?) *ṭua* 46. *em reset er ȧrit useχt χemt*
47 *saθ fṭu em śeneť en Uauat ȧsθ ḥequ set nu Ȧrθet Uauat Ȧam Meťa* 47. *ḥer saθ*
χet eres ȧu ȧri-n[ȧ] mȧqeṭ en renpet uāt meḥ-[ȧ] aθep-[ȧ] em maθ āā urt er
48 (*Mer-en-Rā*) *χā nefer ȧu ḳer ȧri-[ȧ] seneťes* 48. *en āḥā em χenta ṭua pen*
mȧqeṭ-sen en śepses-[ȧ] en θettaa-[ȧ] en uaś-[ȧ] baiu suten net (or *bȧt*) (*Mer-*
49 *en-Rā*) *ānχ ťetta er neteru neb en unn-[ȧ] χeper χet neb* 49. *χeft ḥu uťu ka-f nuk*

unenet merit en tef-f ḥesi en mut-f ser 50. *am en senu-f ḥā mer res maā åmaχu χer Åusår Unȧ*

THE INSCRIPTION OF KHNEMU-ḤETEP.

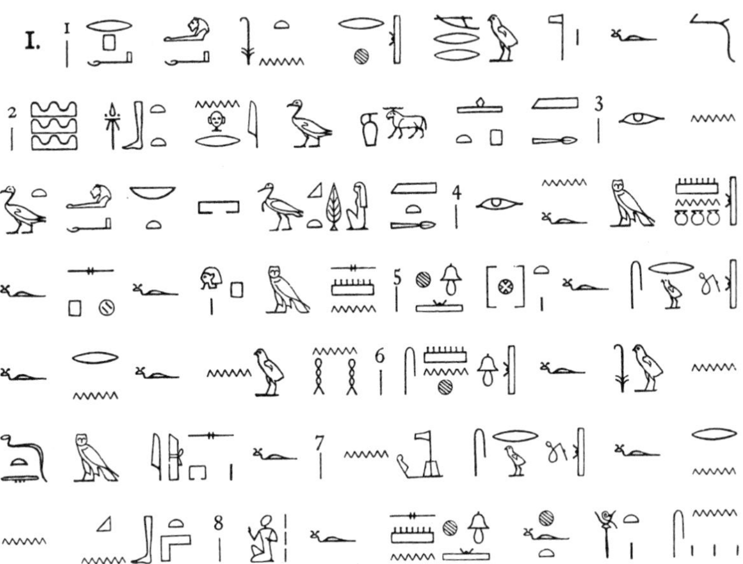

I. — 1. *erpā ḥā suten reχ merru neter-f mer* 2. *set åbtet Neḥrå sa Χnemu-ḥetep maāχeru* 3. *åri en sat ḥā nebt per Baqet maātχeru* 4. *åri-nef em men-f sep-f ṭep em* 5. *semenχ nut-f seruṭ-f ren-f nu neḥeḥ* 6. *semenχ-f su en ṭetta em ås-f* 7. *en neter-χert seruṭ-f ren en qenbet-* 8. *f semenχ χeft åaut-sen*

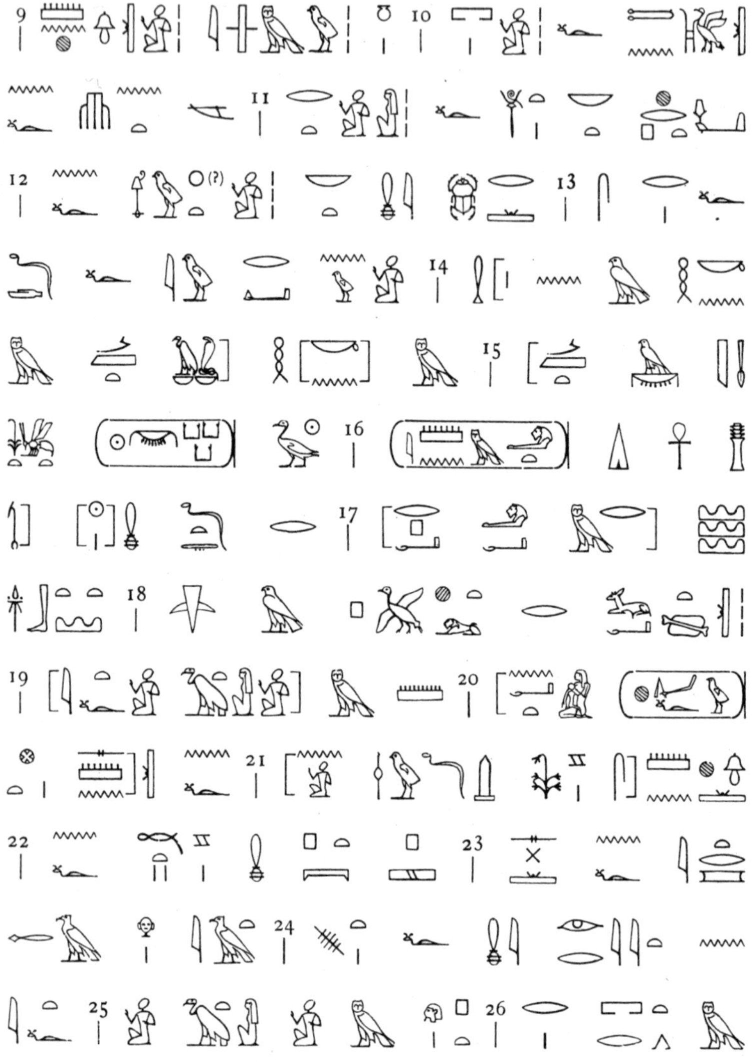

9. *menχu ȧmmu-χenu-* 10. *f θen-nef χent mert-f* 11. *ȧaut nebt χerpt-* 12. *nef ḥemut nebt mȧ χeper-* 13. *s re-f ťeṭ-f ȧu erṭā-nuȧ* 14. *ḥen en Ḥeru ḥeken em maāt neb śeta neb ārā* (or *smauti*) *ḥeken em* 15. *maāt Ḥeru nub maāχeru suten net* (or *bȧt*) (*Nub-kau-Rā*)| *sa Rā* 16. (*Ȧmen-em-ḥāt*)| *ṭā ānχ ṭeṭ us mȧ Rā ťetta er* 17. *erpā ḥā mer set ȧbtet* 18. *uťeb Ḥeru Paχet er āuāt* 19. *ȧtf mut-ȧ em Menāt-* 20. (*Χufu*)| *semen-nef* 21. *nȧ uť resu semenχ-* 22. *nef meḥti mȧ pet* 23. *peśes-nef ȧter āa ḥer ȧatet-* 24. *f mȧ ȧrit en ȧtf* 25. *mut-ȧ em ṭept* 26. *re pert em*

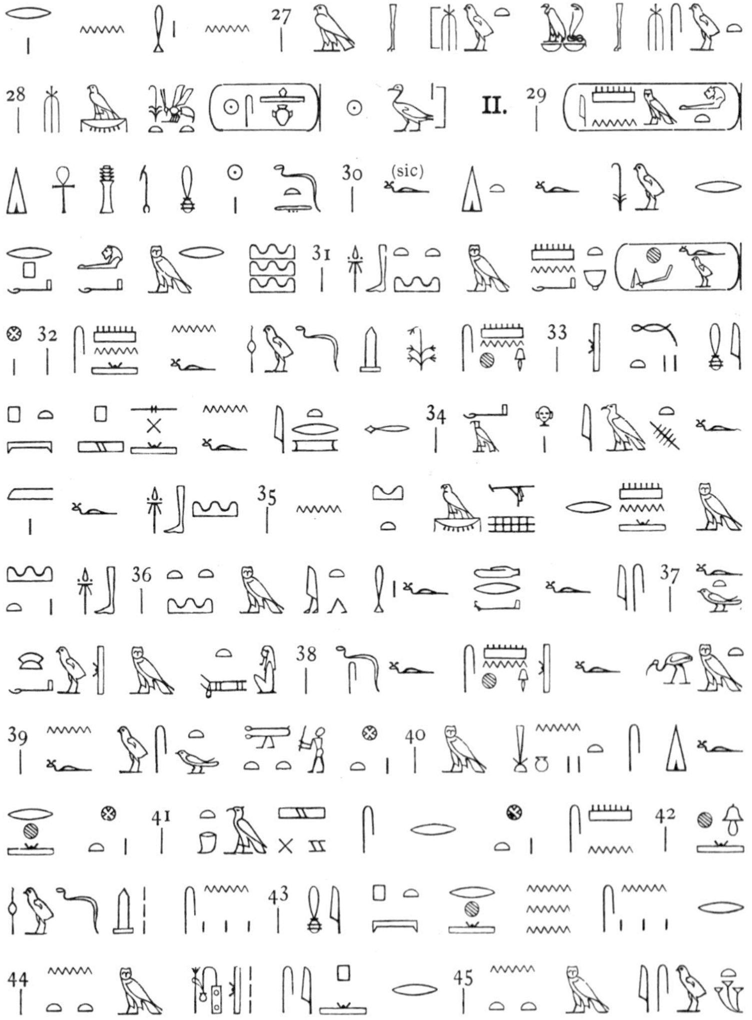

re en ḥen en 27. *Ḥeru uḥem mesut neb śeta neb ārā* (or *smauti*) *uḥem mesut* 28. *mes Ḥeru nub suten net* (or *bāt*) (*Seḥetep-āb-Rā*) *sa Rā* **II.**—29. (*Ȧmen-em-ḥāt*) *ṭā ānχ ṭeṭ us mȧ Rā t̔etta* 30. *f* (sic) *ṭāt-f su er erpā ḥā mer set* 31. *ābtet em Menāt-*(*χufu*) 32. *semen-nef uťu resu semenχ* 33. *meḥti mȧ pet peśes-nef ȧter āāa* 34. *ḥer ȧat-f ḳes-f ȧb* 35. *en Ṭut-Ḥeru nub er-men em set* 36. *ȧbtet em it ḥen-f ṭer-f* 37. *ȧsfet χāāu em Tem* 38. *t̔esef semenχ-f qemt-* 39. *nef ust θetet nut* 40. *em sent-s ṭā-f reχ nut* 41. *taś-s er nut semenχ* 42. *uťu-sen* 43. *mȧ pet reχ mu-sen er* 44. *entet em ān sȧp er* 45. *entet em ȧsut*

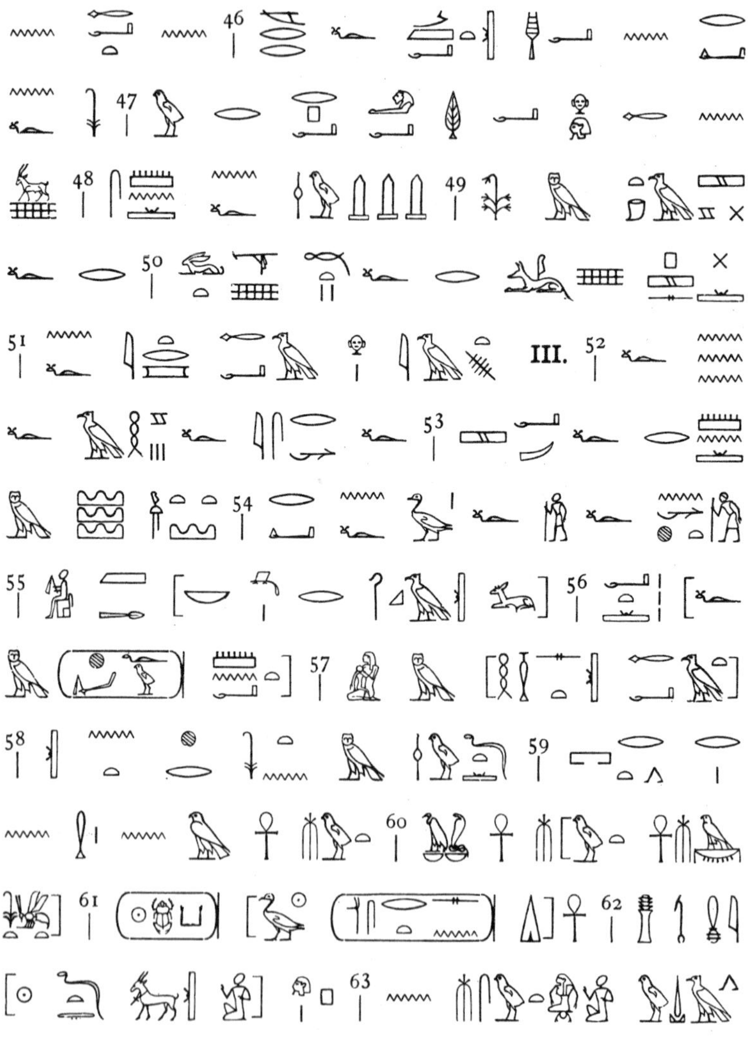

en āāt en 46. *merer-f maāt āḥā en erṭā-nef su* 47. *er erpā ḥā am ā ḥer ṭep āa en Maḥet'* 48. *smen-nef ut'u* 49. *resu em taš-f er* 50. *Unt meḥti-f er Ȧnpu pešes-* 51. *nef ȧter āāa ḥer ȧat-* **III.** — 52. *f mu-f aḥ-f ȧser-f* 53. *šā-f er-men em set ȧmentet* 54. *erṭā-nef sa-f ur-f Neχt* 55. *maāχeru neb ȧmaχ er ḥeqa* 56. *āuāt-f em Menāt* (*χufu*) 57. *em ḥeset āāat* 58. *ent χer suten em ut'et* 59. *pert re en ḥen en Ḥeru ānχ mesut* 60. *neb šeta neb ārā* (or *smauti*) *ānχ mesut ānχ mes Ḥeru nub suten net* (or *bȧt*) 61. (*χeper-ka-Rā*) *sa Rā* (*Usertsen*) *ṭā ānχ* 62. *ṭeṭ us mȧ Rā t'etta sāḥ-ȧ ṭep* 63. *en mesut-ȧ ut'a*

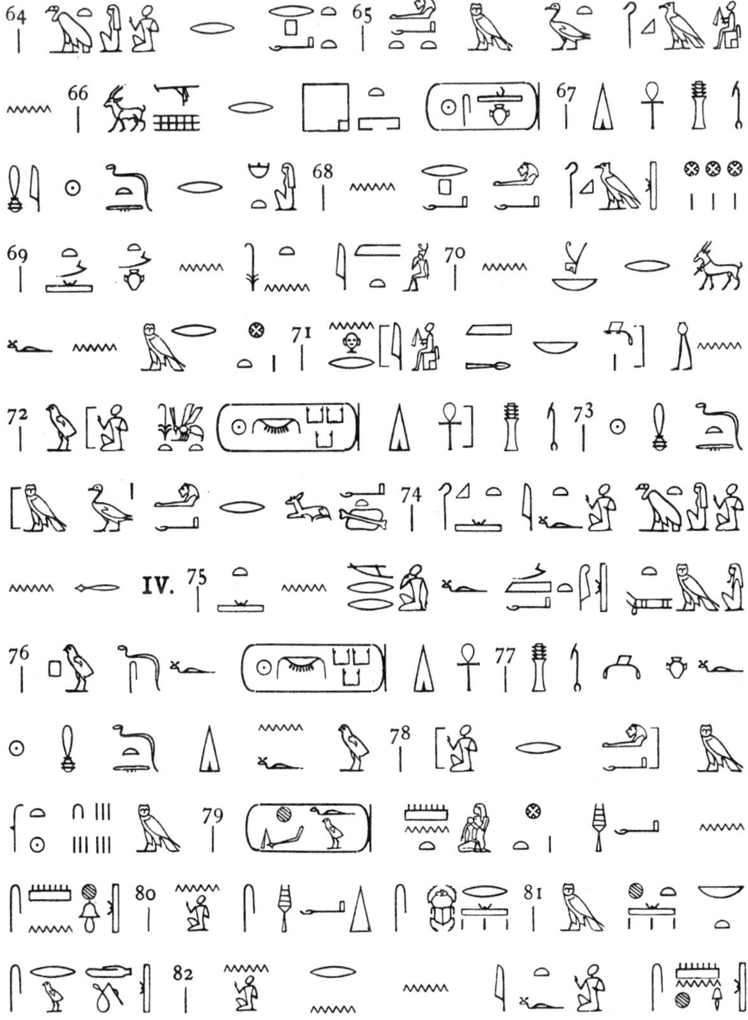

64. *mut-ȧ er erpātet* 65. *ḥātet em sat ḥeqa en* 66. *Maḥeṭ' er ḥet* (*Seḥetep-ȧb-Rā*) 67. *ṭā ānχ ṭeṭ us mȧ Rā t'etta er ḥemt* 68. *en erpā ḥā ḥeqa nut* 69. *mat mat en suten ȧmt* 70. *en net* (or *bȧt*) *er sāḥ-f en mer nut* 71. *Neḥrȧ maāχeru neb ȧmaχ ȧn-* 72. *uȧ suten net* (or *bȧt*) (*Nub-kau-Rā*) *ṭā ānχ ṭeṭ us* 73. *Rā mȧ t'etta em sa ḥā er āuāt* 74. *ḥeqt ȧtf mut-ȧ en* **IV.**—75. *āat en merer-f maāt Tem* 76. *pu t'esef* (*Nub-kau-Rā*) *ṭā ānχ* 77. *ṭeṭ us āu ȧb-f Rā mȧ t'etta ṭā-nef-uȧ* 78. *er ḥā em renpet met paut em* 79. *Menāt-* (*Χufu*) *āḥā en semenχ-* 80. *nȧ-s āḥā-sχeperu* 81. *em χet nebt seruṭ-* 82. *nȧ ren en ȧtf-ȧ semenχ-*

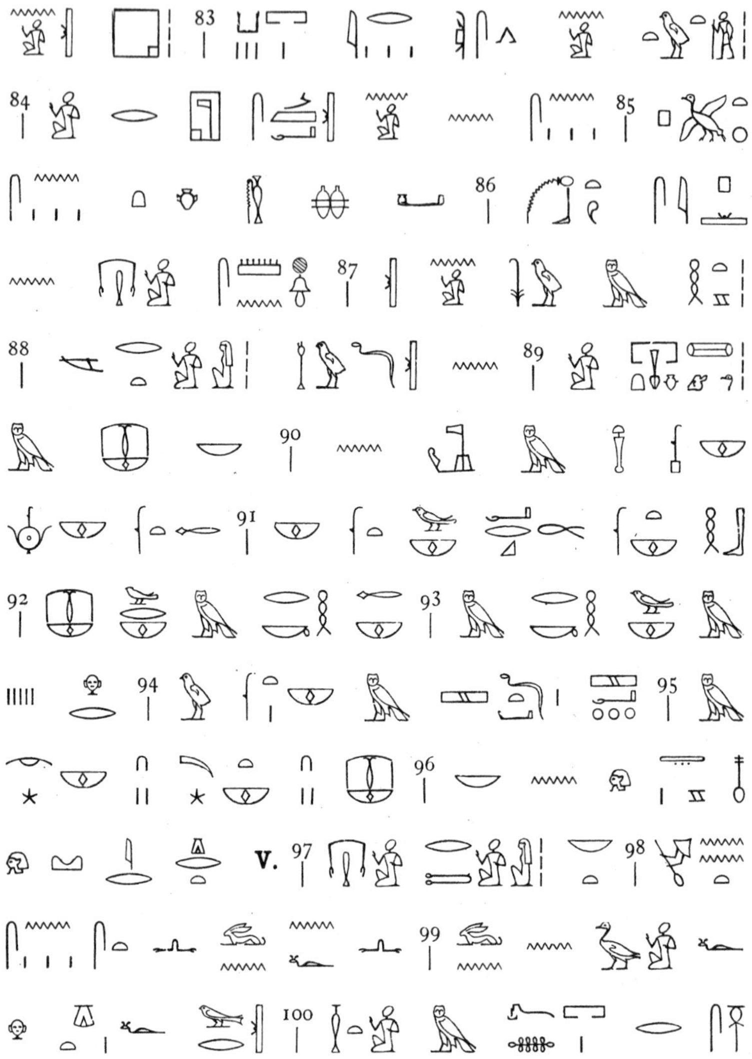

nȧ ḥet 83. *kau ȧru šes-nȧ tut-ȧ* 84. *er ḥet neter semaā-nȧ en-sen* 85. *pat-sen ta ḥeq qebḥ ȧrp sentrȧ* 86. *ābt sȧp-n[ȧ] ḥen ka semenχ-* 87. *nȧ su em ḥet* 88. *mert uť-nȧ* 89. *per χeru em ḥeb neb* 90. *en neter-χert em ṭep renpet ȧp renpet āa* 91. *renpet šerȧt ārq renpet ḥeb* 92. *ur em rekeḥ āa* 93. *em rekeḥ šerȧ em ṭua ḥeru* 94. *renpet em šeťet šā* 95. *em ȧbeṭ met sen smat met sen ḥeb* 96. *neb en ṭep ta nefer ṭep ṭu ȧr ḳert* **V.** — 97. *ḥen ka reθ nebt* 98. *χenenet-sen set ȧn un-nef ȧn* 99. *un en sa-f ḥer nest-f ur* 100. *ḥeset em setep sa er smer*

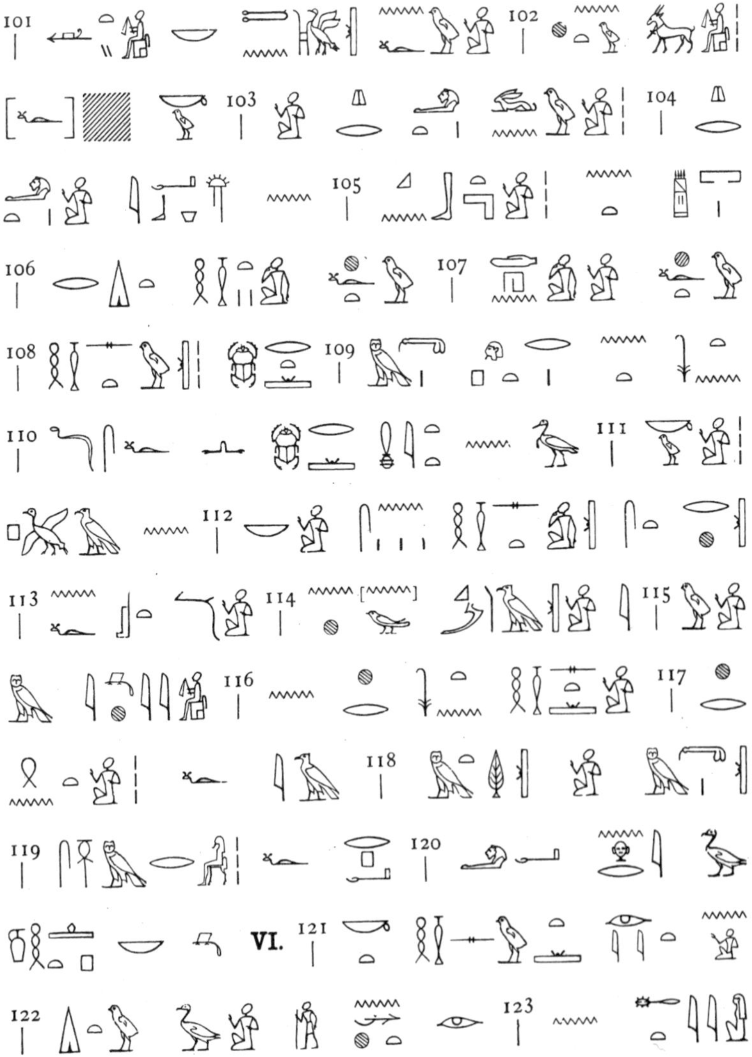

101. *uāti neb θen-nef-uȧ* 102. *χentu sāḥu-f . . . . kuȧ* 103. *χer ḥāt unu* 104. *χer ḥāt-ȧ ȧāb en* 105. *qenbet ent āḥāt* 106. *erṭāt ḥesti χeftu* 107. *ṭehen-ȧ χeftu* 108. *ḥestu χepert* 109. *embaḥ ṭept re ent suten* 110. *ťesef ȧn χeper mȧtet en* 111. *baku pa en* 112. *neb-sen ḥest-set reχ-* 113. *nef ȧuset nes-ȧ* 114. *neχen qema-ȧ* 115. *ȧu-ȧ em ȧmaχi* 116. *en χer suten ḥest-ȧ* 117. *χer šent-f* 118. *ȧamet-ȧ em-baḥ* 119. *smeru-f erpā* 120. *ḥā Neḥrȧ sa Χnemu-ḥetep neb ȧmaχ* **VI.** — 121. *ket ḥesut ȧrit-nȧ* 122. *ṭātu sa-ȧ ur Neχt ȧri* 123. *en Χati*

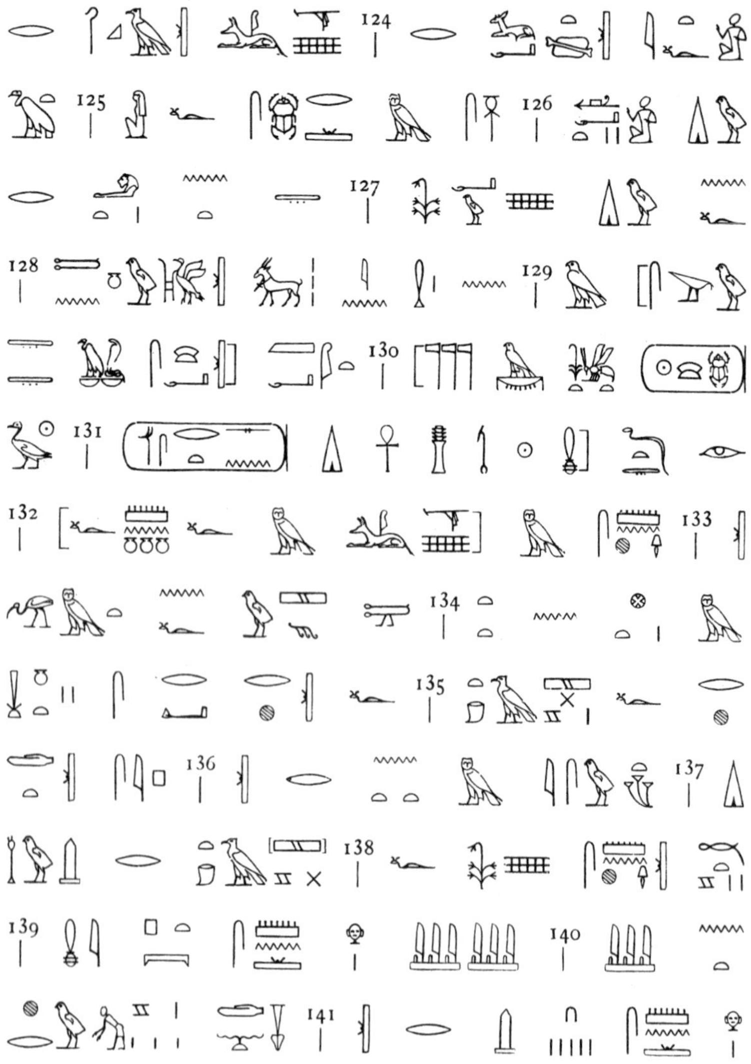

er ḥeqa Ȧnpu 124. *er āuāt ȧtf mut-f* 125. *seχeper em smer* 126. *uāti ṭāu er ḥāt ent ta* 127. *qemāu ṭāu-nef* 128. *θennu sāḥu ȧn ḥen en* 129. *Ḥeru semu taui neb śeta neb ārā seχāā maāt* 130. *neteru Ḥeru nub suten net* (or *bȧt*) (*χeper-χā-Rā*) *sa Rā* 131. (*Usertsen*) *ṭā ānχ ṭeṭ us Rā mȧ t̄etta ȧri-* 132. *f menu-f em Ȧnpu em semenχ* 133. *qemt-nef uś θetet* 134. *en nut em sent-s erṭā reχ-f* 135. *taś-f reχ ṭet sȧp* 136. *er entet em ȧsut* 137. *ṭā ut̄u er taś-* 138. *f qemā semenχ meḥti* 139. *mȧ pet smen ḥer seχet* 140. *ent χeru ṭemṭ* 141. *er ut̄ met ṭua smen ḥer*

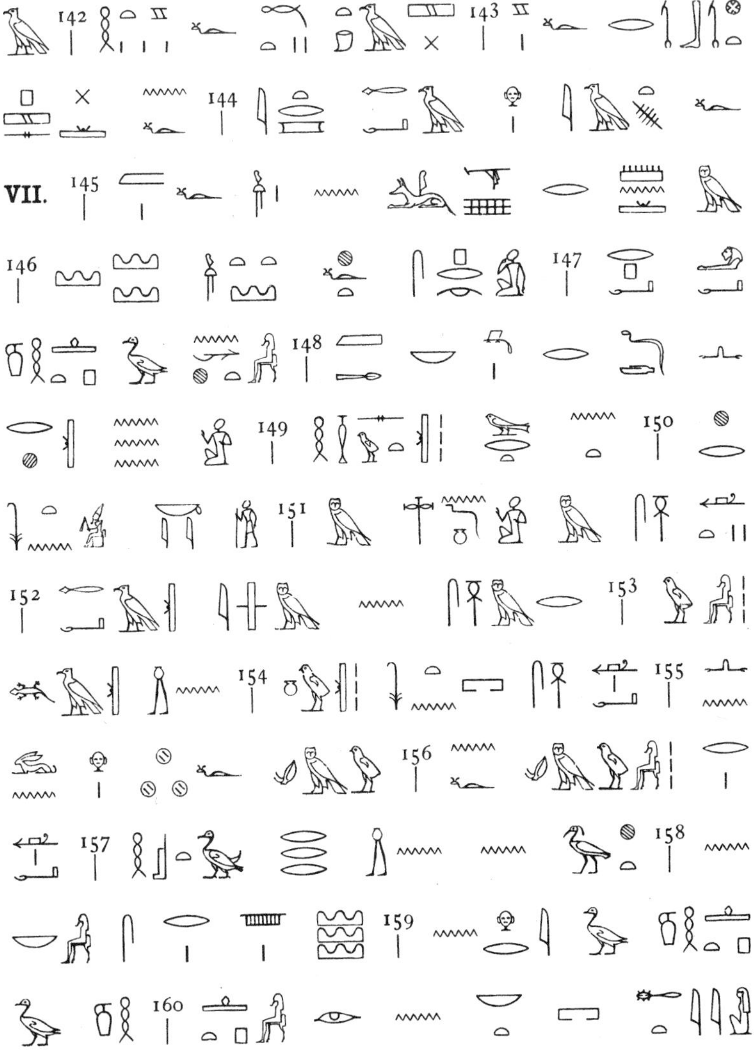

aḥet- 142. *f meḥti taś-* 143. *f er Uabet peśes-nef* 144. *ȧter āāa ḥer ȧat-f*
VII. — 145. *ḳes-f ȧment en Ȧnpu er men em* 146. *set ȧmentet χeft sper*
147. *erpā ḥā Χnemu-ḥetep sa Neχt* 148. *maāχeru neb ȧmaχ er t̓eṭ ȧn reχ mu-ȧ*
149. *ḥestu urt ent* 150. *χer suten ki ur* 151. *em net̓-ȧ em smer uāti* 152. *āāa ȧm en smeru* 153. *āśa* 154. *ȧnnu suten per smer uā* 155. *ȧn un ḥer sepu-f setemu-*
156. *nef setemu re uā* 157. *ḥetemet reu ȧn en χut* 158. *en neb-s re āa set*
159. *Neḥrȧ sa Χnemu-ḥetep sa Χnemu-* 160. *ḥetep ȧri en nebt per Χati*

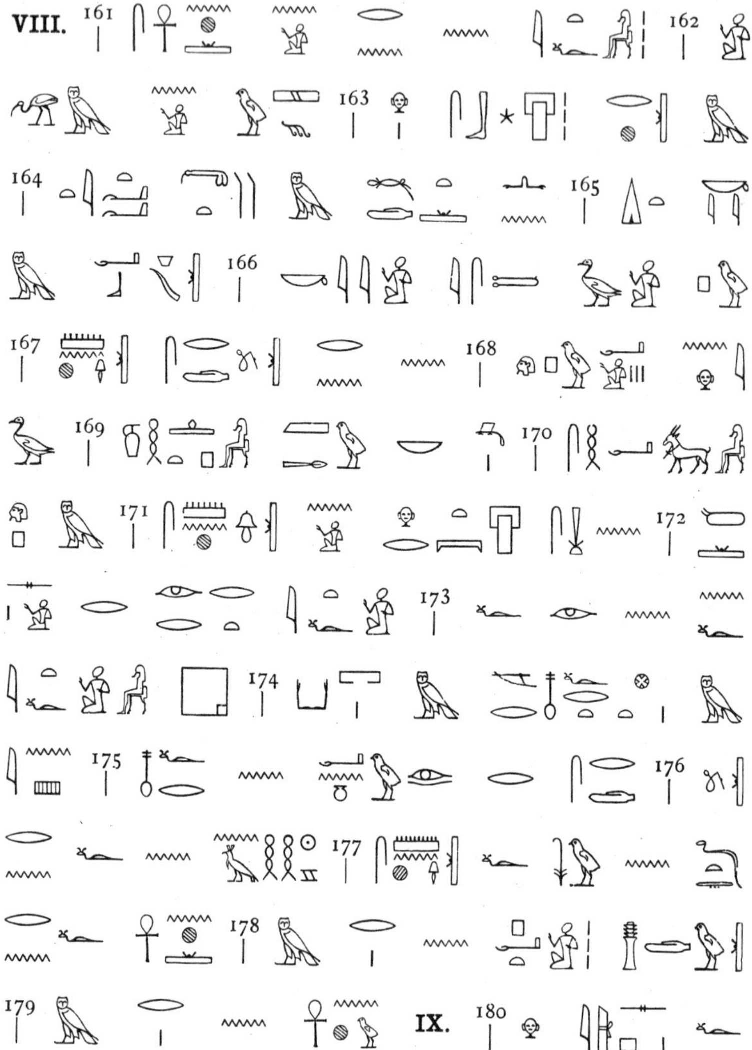

VIII. — 161. *seānχ-nȧ ren en ȧtfu-* 162. *ȧ qem-nȧ uś* 163. *ḥer sebau reχ em* 164. *tȧt met em seśeṭet ȧn* 165. *ṭāt ki em āb* 166. *ki ȧsθ sa pu* 167. *menχ seruṭ ren en* 168. *ṭepu-ā Neḥrȧ sa* 169. *Χnemu-ḥetep maāχeru neb ȧmaχ* 170. *sāḥ ṭep em* 171. *semenχ-nȧ ḥert sen* 172. *sa er ȧrret ȧtf-* 173. *f ȧri-n nef ȧtf-ȧ ḥet* 174. *ka em Mer-nefert em ȧner* 175. *nefer en ānnu er seruṭ* 176. *ren-f en neḥeḥ* 177. *semenχ-f su en t̄etta ren-f ānχ* 178. *em re en pāt ṭeṭu* 179. *em re en ānχu* **IX.** — 180. *ḥer ȧs-f*

en Neter-χert em per-f 181. *menχ en neḥeḥ àuset-* 182. *f ent ťetta χeft ḥest en χer* 183. *suten mertu-f em* 184. *setep sa ḥeq-nef nut-f em seťet* 185. *en feχt-f em ťam* 186. *àri-nef àpt suten šuti-f* 187. *àba-sen em χennu* 188. *en qebat-f em suten reχ* 189. *àuset nes-f neχen qa-f Sebek-* 190. *ānχ sa Neḥrà maāχeru neb àmaχ* 191. *θen-nef χent sàḥ-f* 192. *er ḥeq nut-f χepert ḥā Χnemu-ḥetep* 193. *àri en men χen en nut-à qeṭ-* 194. *nà uχχa qem-* 195. *n em aa sāḥā-nà* 196. *su em uχ en mat* 197. *ān em ren-à ťes-à*

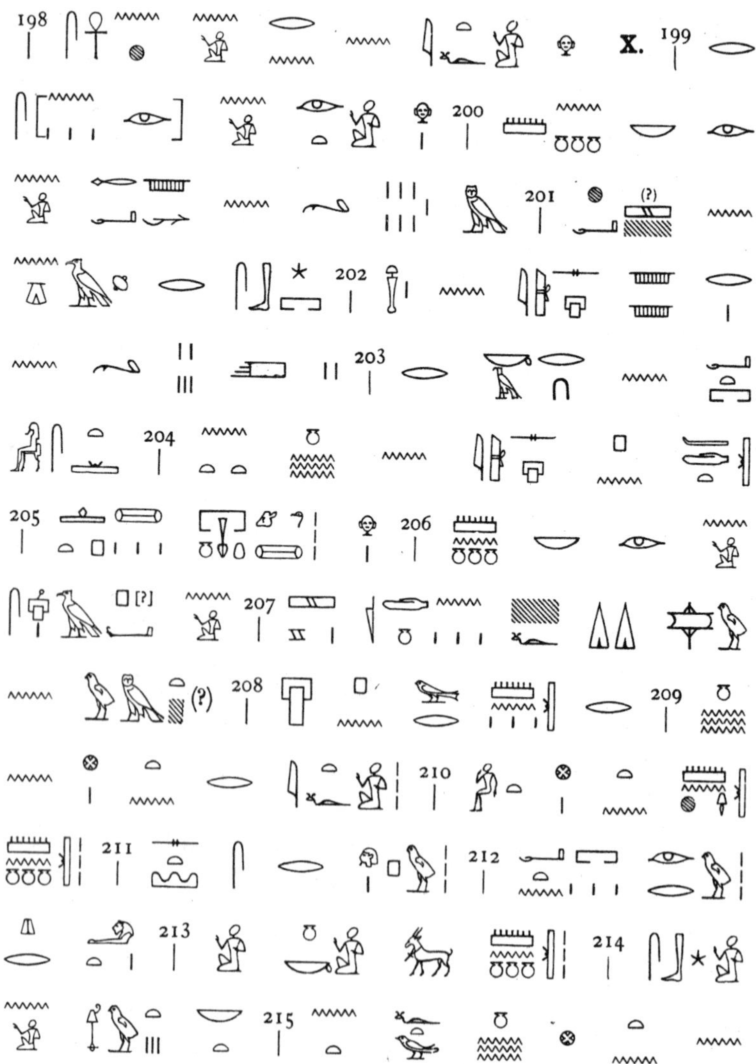

198. *seānχ-nȧ ren en ȧtf-ȧ ḥer* **X.** — 199. *sen ȧri-nȧ ȧrit-ȧ ḥer* 200. *menu neb ȧri-nȧ āā en meḥ seχef em* 201. *χā . . . . en neḳa er seba* 202. *ṭep en ȧs āāui re en meḥ ṭua šep sen* 203. *er kar en āt šepset* 204. *entet χen en ȧs pen ṭebḥeṭet* 205. *ḥetepu per χeru ḥer* 206. *menu neb ȧri-nȧ sap-nȧ* 207. *še qeṭ . . . . . f ṭāṭā nifu en umet* 208. *pen ur men er* 209. *χen en nut ten er ȧtefu* 210. *χrat nut ten menχ menu* 211. *set-s er ṭepu* 212. *ā ten ȧru χer ḥāt-ȧ* 213. *ȧ nuk sāḥ menu* 214. *seba-nȧ ubut nebt* 215. *ent fet χen nut ten en*

216. *meru menχ ren-ȧ ḥer* 217. *menu neb ȧri-nȧ ḳerḳ ḥert* 218. *ȧn ment-s ȧm seha-* 219. *nȧ ȧmmu-k ḥeť* 220. *ȧtf[-ȧ] erpā ḥā Neḥrȧ sa Χnemu-* 221. *ḥetep ȧri en Baqet maāχeru neb ȧmaχ* 222. *χerp ȧs mer net Baqet*

INSCRIPTION ON THE BASE OF THE OBELISK OF ḤĀTSHEPSET.

I. — 1. *Ānχet Ḥeru usert kau neb śeta neb ārā uaťet renput Ḥeru nub neteret χāu suten net* (*Maāt-ka-Rā*) *sat Rā* (*Ḥātshepset χnem Ȧmen*) *ānχ ťetta ḥeḥ Ȧmen-Rā sat ȧmt ȧb-f* 2. *uātet-f χepert χer-f tȧt χut ent Neb-er-ťer*

qemat en baiu Ȧnnu nefer seθet taiu mȧ ȧri su seχeper-nef er uθes χāu-f
3 *3. χeperet χeperu mȧ Χeperȧ χāāt χāu mȧ χuti suḥt ābt pert χuθ renenet Urt-*
4 *ḥekau neb śeta neb ārā seχāāt en Ȧmen ťesef* 4. *ḥer nest-f em Ȧnnu-resu setep-nef*
5 *er sau Qemt er nerit pāt reχit Ḥert neťet ȧtf-s urt ent ka mut-f* 5. *Ȧmsu utet en*
Rā er ȧrit-nef pert χu ṭep ta er uťau en hamemet χent-f ānχ suten net (*Maāt-*
6 *ka-Rā*) *smu en sutenit* 6. *ȧri-nes menu en tef-s Ȧmen neb nest taiu χent Ȧpt*
7 *ȧrit-nef teχenui urui em mat ruṭet ent qemā ḳes sen ḥer em smu* 7. *en ṭepu set nebt*

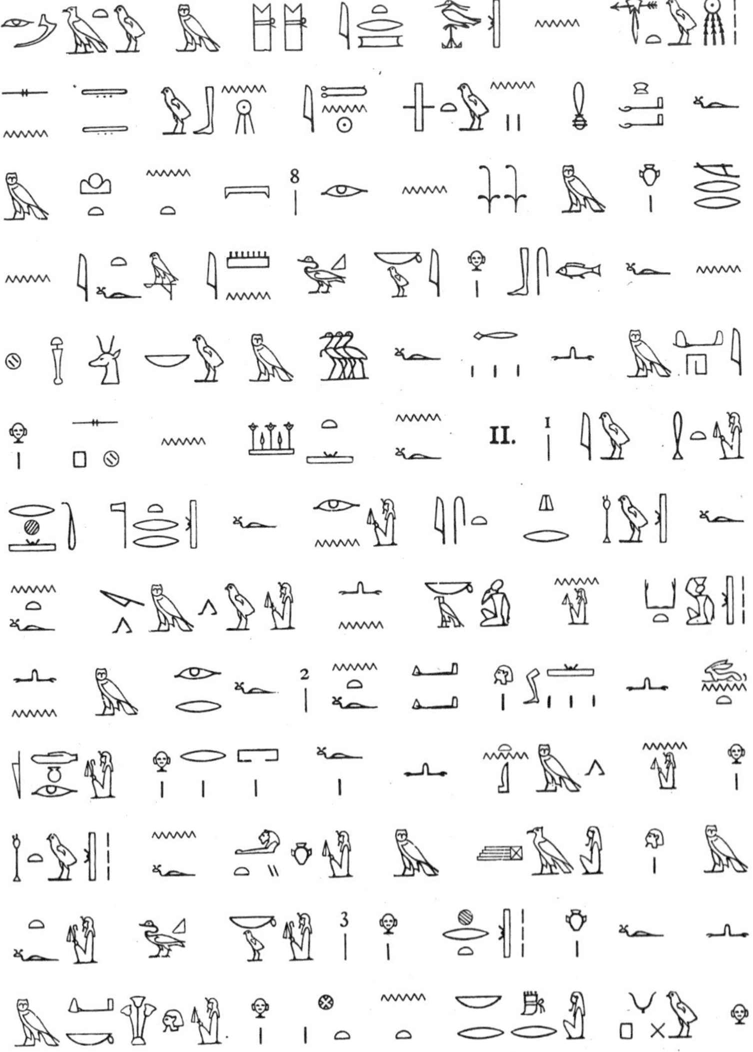

maatu em ḥenui ȧter bāḥ en satu-sen taiu uben ȧθen ȧm-tun mȧ χāā-f em
χut ent pet 8. *ȧri-nȧ enen em ȧb merer en ȧtf-[ȧ] Ȧmen āq-kuȧ ḥer bes-f* 8
en sep ṭep qen (?) *nebu em baiu-f āaiu ȧn māh-ȧ ḥer sep en śat-nef* **II.** — 1. *ȧu* 1
ḥent ȧ reχ-θ neterer-f ȧri-nȧ ȧst χer utu-f entef sem-uȧ ȧn ka-nȧ kat ȧn
em ȧri-f 2. *entef ṭāṭā ṭep-reṭ ȧn unt qeṭ-ȧ ḥer erpa-f ȧn tenemem-nȧ ḥer* 2
utu-nef ḥāti-ȧ em Sa ṭep em tef-ȧ āq-kuȧ 3. *ḥer χert ȧb-f ȧn mākḥa-ȧ ḥer nut* 3
ent Neb-er-ťer ȧpu ḥer

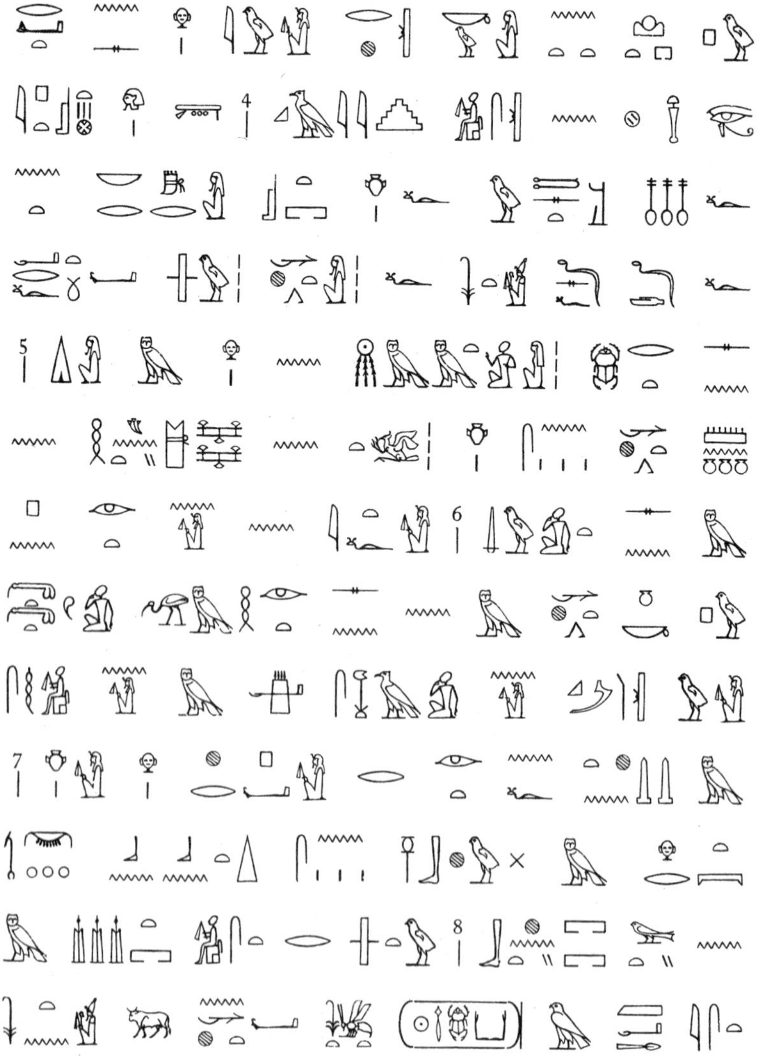

4 *erṭāt-nes ḥer ȧu-ȧ reχ-kuȧ entet χut pu Ȧptet ṭep ta* 4. *qai śeps en sep ṭep uťat*
ent Neb-er-ťer ȧuset ȧb-f uθeset neferu-f ārfet ȧmu-χet-f sutenet ťesef ťeṭ-f
5 5. *ṭā-ȧ em ḥrȧ en hamemet χepert-sen en ḥenti en reχit ȧbu-sen χet menu pen*
6 *ȧrit-nȧ en ȧtf-ȧ* 6. *meṭu-t sen em metmet qemḥet-sen en em χet nuk pu seneťem-*
7 *nȧ em āḥāt seχa-nȧ qema-uȧ* 7. *ȧb-ȧ ḥer χerp-ȧ er ȧrit-nef teχenui em smu*
8 *benbenet-sen ābeχu em ḥert em āāuit śepset er ȧmtu* 8. *beχenti urti en suten*
ka neχt suten net (Āa-χeper-ka-Rā) Ḥeru maātχeru ȧst

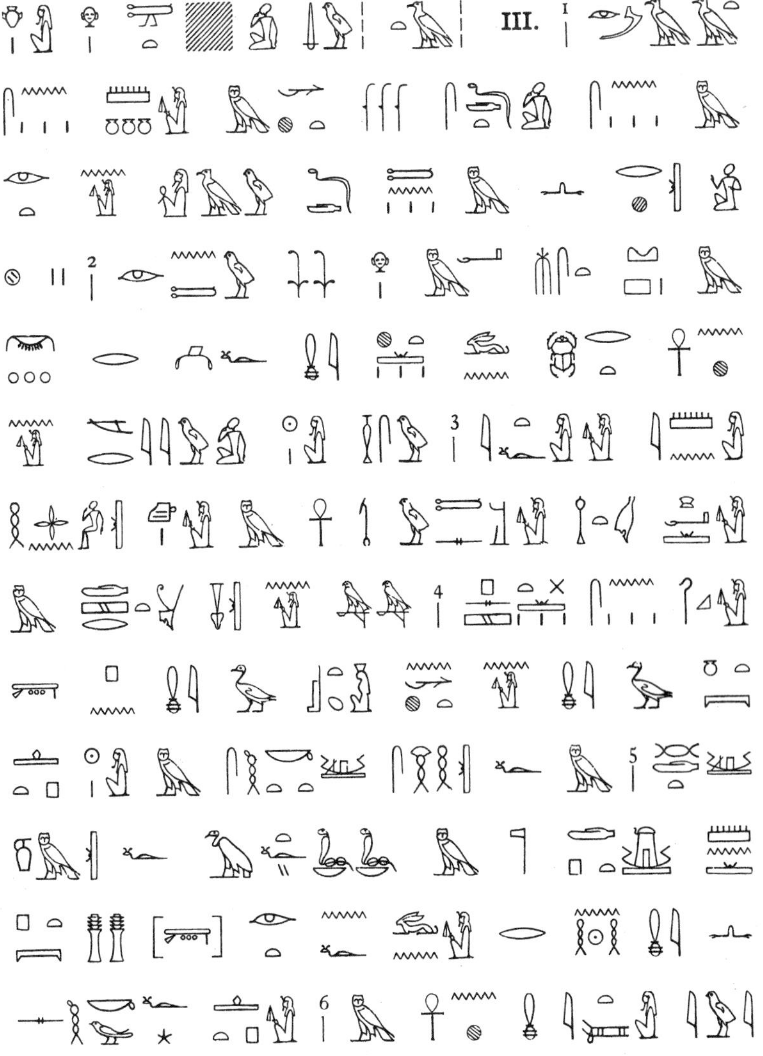

ȧb-ȧ ḥer θet . . . . . . meṭu reχit **III.** — 1. *maat-sen menu-ȧ emχet renput* 1
seṫeṭet-sen em ȧrit-nȧ sau ṫeṭ-θen em ȧn reχ-ȧ sep sen 2. *ȧri enθu enen ḥer* 2
mā meset ṭu em nub er āu-f mȧ χet un χepert ānχ-nȧ meriu Rā ḥesu 3. *ȧtf-ȧ* 3
Ȧmen ḥunen fenṭ-ȧ em ānχ us uθes-ȧ ḥeṫet χāā-ȧ em ṭešert sam-nȧ Ḥerui
4. *pesešet-sen ḥeq-ȧ ta pen mȧ sa Ȧuset neχt-nȧ mȧ sa Nut ḥetep Rā em* 4
sektet seuaḥ-f em 5. *āṭet χnem-f mutui-f em neter ṭept men pet ṭeṭṭeṭ [ta]* 5
ȧrit-nef un-ȧ er neḥeḥ mȧ ȧn sek-f ḥetep-ȧ 6. *em ānχ mȧ Ȧtmu ȧu-ȧ* 6

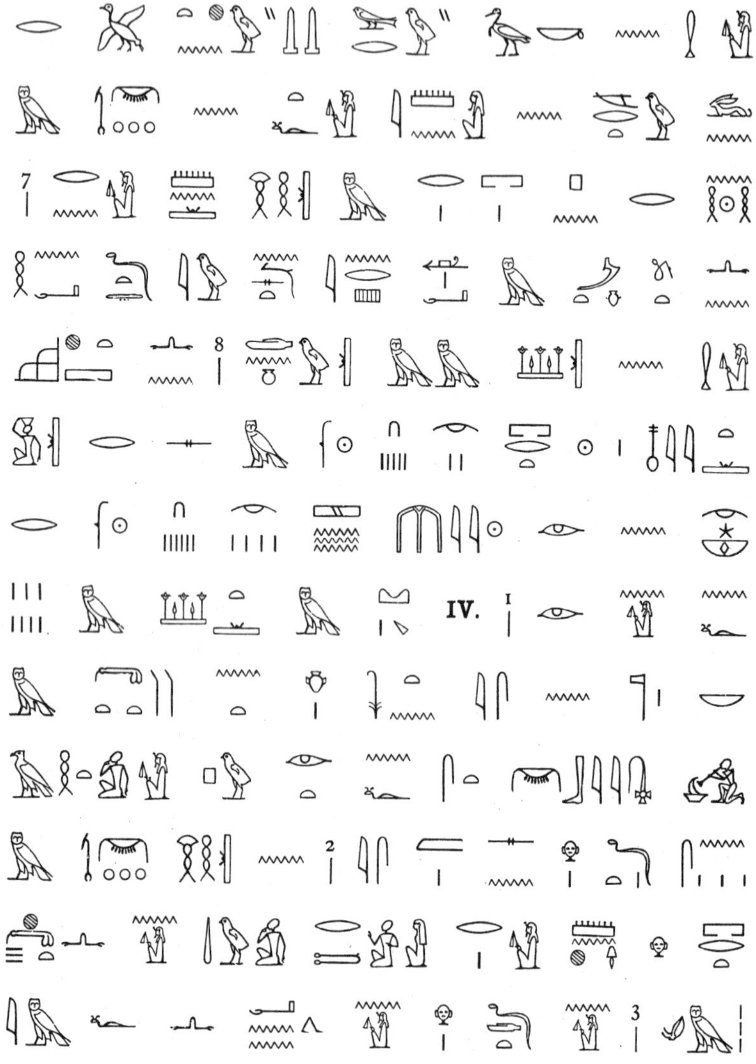

7 *er pa teχenui urui bak en ḥen-ȧ em smu en tef-ȧ Ȧmen en mertu un* 7. *ren-ȧ*
men uaḥ em erpa pen er neḥeḥ ḥnā t'etta ȧu nest ȧner uā em mat ruṭet ȧn seχet
8 *ȧn* 8. *ṭennu emma ša en ḥen-ȧ fa er-es em renpet met ṭua ȧbeṭ sen pert hru*
uā neferit er renpet met sȧs ȧbeṭ fṭu še ārqi ȧri en ȧbeṭ seχef em šat em ṭu
1 **IV.** — 1. *ȧri-nȧ nef em metet ent ȧb suten ȧs en neter neb aḥet-ȧ pu ȧrit-nef*
2 *set nubi em smu uaḥ-nȧ* 2. *ȧs ḳes-sen ḥer t'et-sen χemet-nȧ meṭu reθ re-ȧ*
3 *menχ ḥer pert ȧm-f ȧn ānen-nȧ ḥer t'eṭet-nȧ* 3. *setemu*

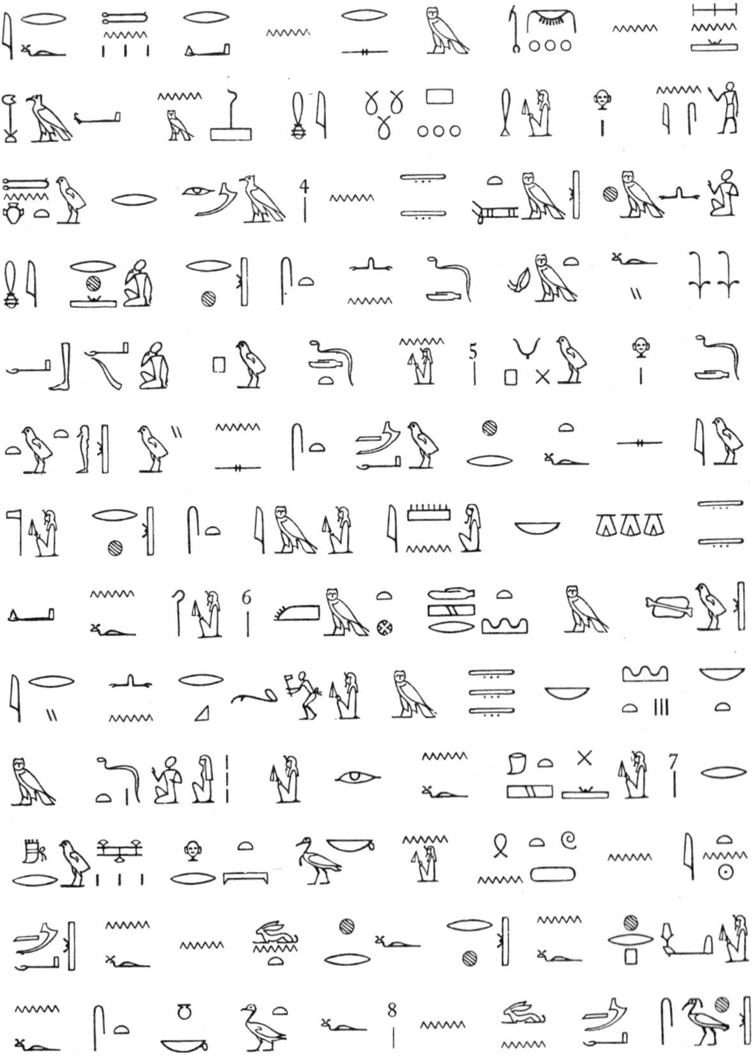

ȧref-θen erṭā-nȧ er-es em smu en qen χa nem mȧ śes ḥen-ȧ ḥer nȧs θentu er
maa 4. *en taiu tem χem mȧ reχ reχ-set ȧn ťeṭ setemet-f enen ābā pu ťeṭet-nȧ* 4
5. *ȧpu ḥer ťeṭ tut-ui nes set maāu χer tef-s ȧu neter-ȧ reχ-set ȧm-ȧ* 5
Ȧmen neb nest taiu ṭā-nef ḥeq-ȧ 6. *Qemt ṭeśert em āu ȧri ȧn req-ȧ em* 6
taiu neb set nebt em ťet-ȧ ȧri-nef taś-ȧ 7. *er ťeru ḥert bak-nȧ śentu en* 7
ȧten maā-nef en unt χer-f reχ-nef χerp-ȧ nef set nuk sat-f 8. *en un* 8
maā seχu

su śat-nef met-ȧ pu χer ȧtf-ȧ ānχ ṭeṭ usr ḥer ȧuset Ḥeru ent ānχiu nebu Rā mȧ t'etta

---

STELAE OF NEKHT-ȦMSU.

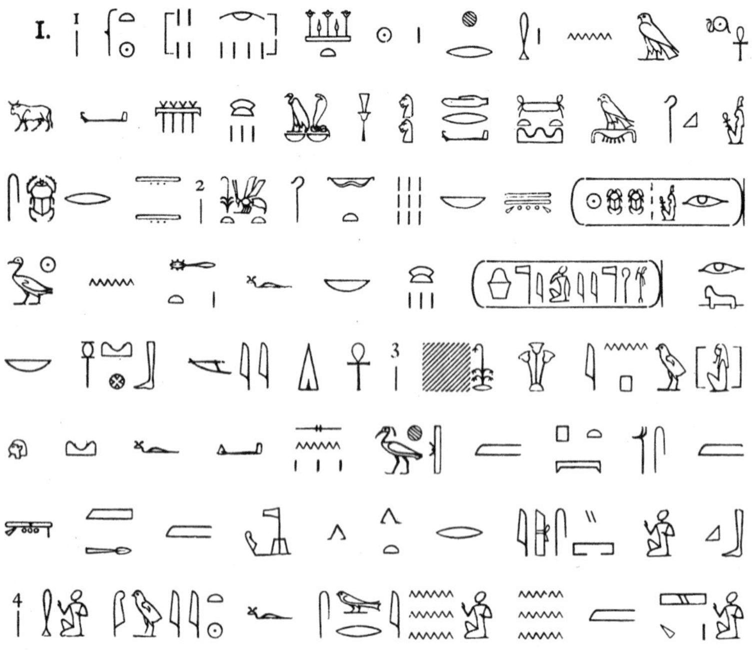

1 **I.** — 1. *Renpet [fṭu ȧbeṭ fṭu] śat hru uā χer ḥen en Ḥeru Rā ānχ ka*
neχt θeḥent χāu neb śeta neb ārā χerp peḥpeḥ ṭer Satet Ḥeru nub ḥeq maāt
2 *s-χeper taui* 2. *suten net ḥeq pet paut neb taui* (*Rā-χeperu-ȧri-maāt*) *sa Rā*
en χat-f neb χāu (*ȧtf neter Ȧi neter ḥeq Uast*) *Ȧusȧr neb Ȧbṭu meri ṭā ānχ*
3 3. *[suten ṭā ḥetep] res meḥ Ȧnpu ḥer ṭu-f ṭā-sen χu em pet usr em ta maāt-*
4 *χeru em neter χert pert āq er ȧsi-ȧ qeb* 4. *ḥen-ȧ śuit-f surȧ-ȧ mu em śe-ȧ*

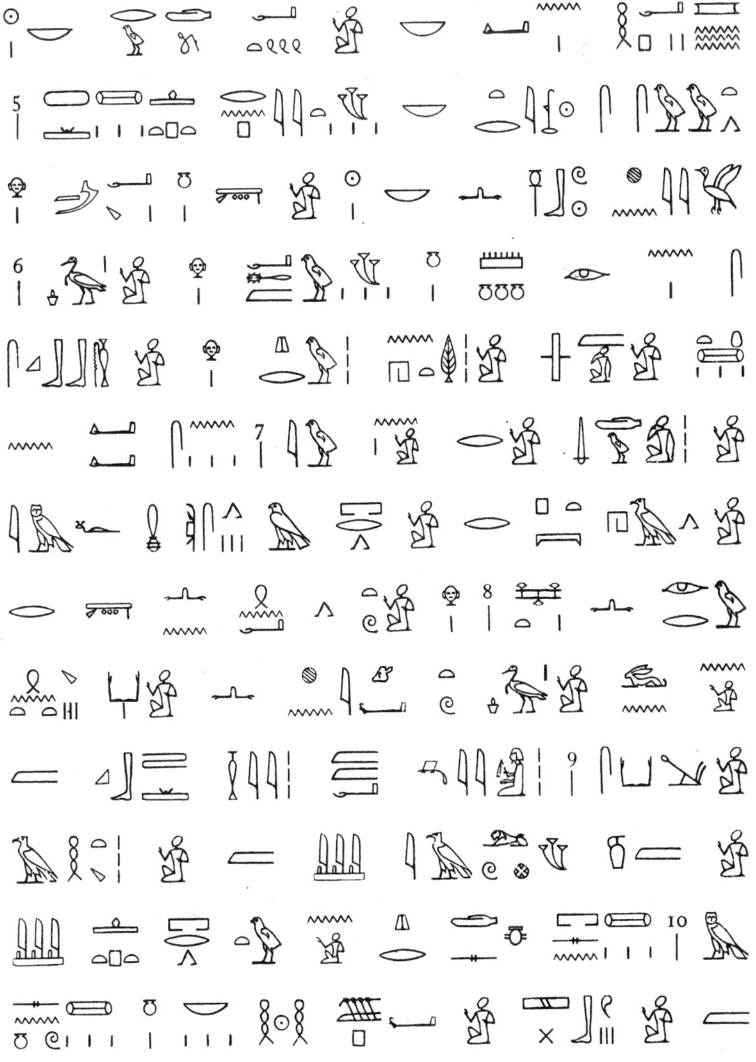

hru neb ruṭ āt-ȧ neb ṭā-nȧ Ḥāpi 5. *ta ḥetepet renpit neb trȧ sesuut ḥer maā* 5
nu ta-ȧ hru neb ȧn ābu χeni 6. *ba-ȧ ḥer āχamu nu menu ȧri-nȧ-s seqebeb-ȧ* 6
ḥrȧ-ȧ χeru nehet-ȧ ȧm-ȧ ta en ṭāṭā-sen 7. *ȧu-nȧ re-ȧ meṭu-ȧ ȧm-f mȧ šesu* 7
Ḥeru per-ȧ er pet ha-ȧ er ta ȧn šenā-tu-ȧ ḥer 8. *uat ȧn ȧru šentet ka-ȧ* 8
ȧn χenȧ-tu ba-ȧ un-nȧ em qeb ḥesiu emmā ȧmaχiu 9. *seka-ȧ aḥet-ȧ em* 9
Seχet-ȧaru χnem-ȧ seχet ḥetepet pertu-nȧ χer ṭes pasen 10. *em sennu nu* 10
nebu ḥeḥ sešep-ȧ šebu-ȧ em

ur en ȧuf ḥer χaut ent neter āa en ka en neter ḥen ṭep en Ȧmsu Neχt-
11 *Ȧmsu* 11. *ťeṭ-f ȧu ȧri-nȧ ḥeseset ret hereret neteru ḥer-s ȧu ṭā-nȧ ta en*
12 *ḥeqer sesa-nȧ ȧti ȧu śes-nȧ* 12. *neter em per-f ȧn āā re-ȧ em śenit ȧn peṭ*
13 *em nemt-ȧ māśem-ȧ ḥer-sa χenṭ ȧri-nȧ em maāt mer en suten* 13. *reχ-kuȧ*
entet utu-nef-set res-nȧ ḥer ȧuset-ȧ er seqa baiu-f ṭua-nȧ er ṭua-f hru neb
14 *erṭā-nȧ ȧb-ȧ χenti* 14. *ťeṭet-f ȧn māhi ḥer śa-nef χer-ȧ θet-nȧ metrit ḥnā*
15 *metit peḥ-nȧ enen ḥer ḳer* 15. *qebeb ḥes-nuȧ neb-ȧ ḥer menχ-ȧ*

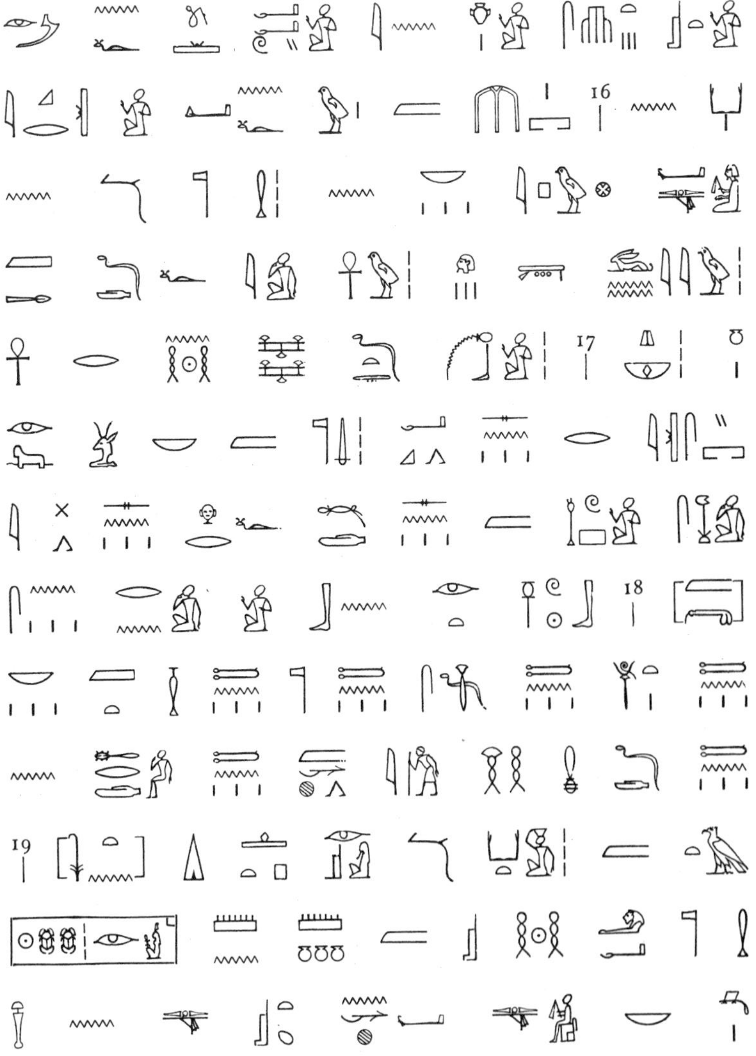

maa-nef ruṭ āāui-ȧ ȧn ȧb-ȧ se-χenti ȧuset-ȧ ȧqer-ȧ ṭā-nef-uȧ em seḥ 16. *en* 16
ka en mer neter ḥenu en nebu Ȧpu Neχt-Ȧmsu maāχeru ṫeṭ-f ȧ ānχu ṭepu ta
unniu ānχ er neḥeḥ ḥentui ṫetta ābu 17. *χer ḥebu nu Ȧusȧr seśa neb em neter* 17
meṭu āq-sen er ȧsi-ȧ seś-sen ḥer-f seśeṭ-sen em utu-ȧ seχa-sen ren-ȧ ben ȧrit ābu
18. *embaḥ nebu maāt ḥes-θen neter-θen suat'-θen aȧut-θen en χarṭ-θen emχet ȧau* 18
uaḥ mȧ ṫeṭ-θen 19. *suten ṭā ḥetep Ȧusȧr mer kat em ta ḥet* (*Rā-χeperu-ȧri-maāt*) 19
men men em ȧuset ḥeḥ ḥā neter ḥen ṭep en Ȧmsu Ȧuset Neχt-Ȧmsu neb ȧmaχ

1 **II.** — 1. *Renpet fṭu ȧbeṭ fṭu śat hru uā χer ḥen en Ḥeru Rā ka neχt θeḥent χāu*
neb śat neb ārā (or *sma taui*) *χerp peḥpeḥ ṭer Satet Ḥeru nub ḥeq maāt se-*
2 *χeper taui* 2. *suten net ḥeq pet paut neb taui* (*Rā-χeperu-ȧri-maāt*) *sa Rā*
en χat-f meri-f neb χāu (*Ȧtf-neter Ȧi neter ḥeq Uast*) *Ȧusȧr neb Ta-ser*
3 *meri ṭā ānχ* 3. *suten ṭā ḥetep Ȧmen-Rā neb nest taiu Ptaḥ-Sekeri-Ȧusȧr*
Un-nefer neb Re-stau ṭā-sen perχeru ȧḥ apt menχ χa em χet nebt nefert
4 *ābt χa em χet nebt* 4. *neťemet beneret ent ṭāṭāt pet qemat ta ȧn en Ḥāpi*
5 *em tepḥet-f sesenet nifu neťem en meḥ ȧmt* 5. *ta sam renpit seśep āutu*
em bu nefer em

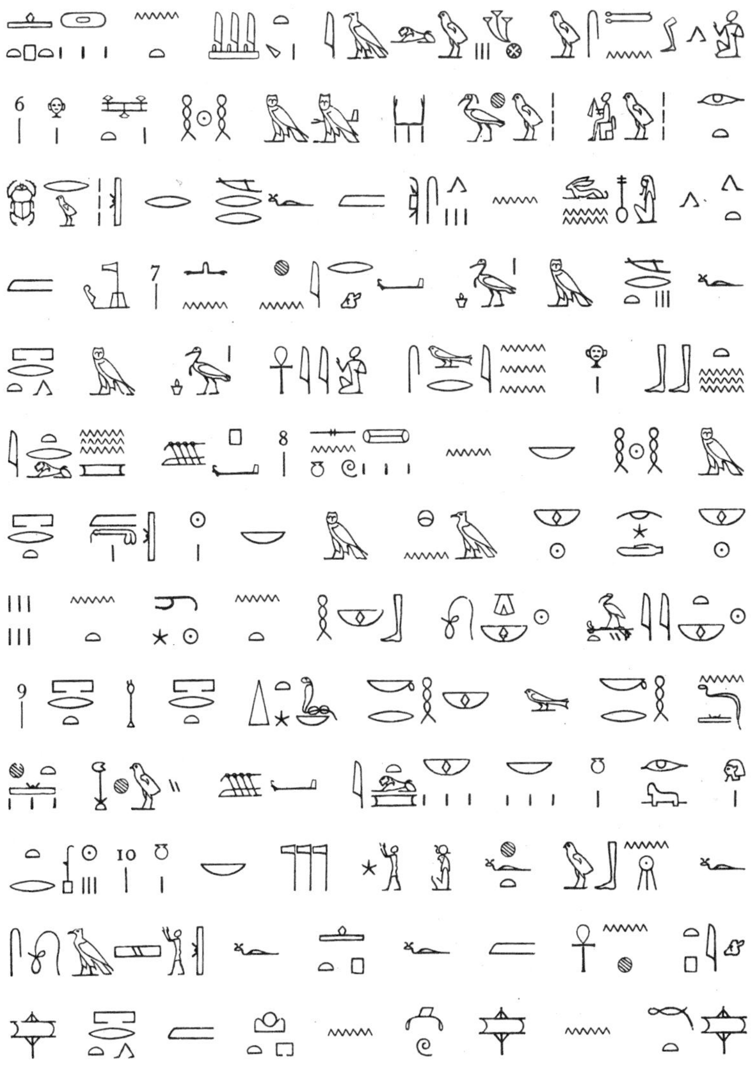

ḥetepet ent Seχet-Åaru usθen-å 6. *ḥer uat ḥeḥ emmā kau χu śepsu årit* 6
χeperu er merer-f em śesu en Un-nefer āq pert em Neter-χert 7. *ån χenår* 7
ba-å em mert-f pert em ba ānχi surå ḥer bebet åtr seśep 8. *sennu en neb* 8
ḥeḥ em pert embaḥ hru neb em pautna ḥeb åbeṭ ḥeb sås ent smat ent ḥeb Uaḳ
Teḥutit 9. *pert Åmsu* (or *Uṫut*) *pert Sepet rekḥ ur rekḥ neṫ[es] χet χaui* 9
seśep åtru nebu nu Åusår ṭep tråiu 10. *nu neb neteru ṭua Rā χeft uben-f* 10
suaś-f ḥetep-f em ānχ tepå nef pert em χut en āu nef en meḥt

11 *īt* 11. *ḥer āāui ṭem-tu ren-f ā qāḥu ḥer ḥetepet t̔efau perχeru χeft nȧs-f*
12 *seŝep mu ḥer āāui ḥen ka* 12. *seχem-f em ta seχem-f ḥeqet ḥer āb merer ka-f*
13 *ȧm-f ta ḥer χaut Neb-er-t̔er ḥer uthu en nebu ḥeḥ* 13. *erṭāt-f āri* (?) *ŝebu*
14 *āb em āutu ent Un-nefer t̔a-f māχent ent Neter-χert er ȧaiu nu* 14. *Seχet-*
15 *Ȧaru ȧp-f uat seŝen-f mātennu ŝes-f Sekeri em Re-stau ȧn ŝenāt-f* 15. *ḥer*
seba en ṭuat bāḥ ȧm em ȧrp ȧrtet seŝep met̔et urḥu mest̔em net̔em ȧb ḥebs
16 16. *menχ en ka en mer ŝenti sen en*

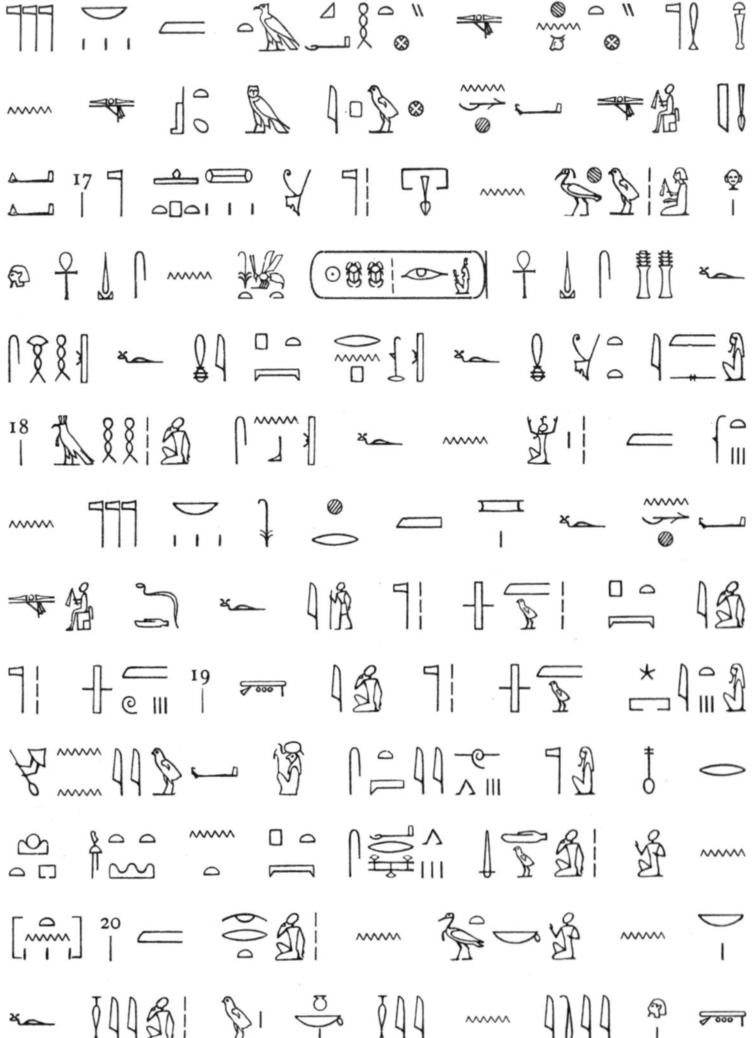

neteru nebu em Taqāḥti Àmsu Χenti neter ḥen ṭep en Àmsu Àuset em Àpu Neχt-Àmsu maāχeru ṭāṭā 17. *neter ḥetepet en neteru perχeru en χu ḥer ṭep* 17
ānχ uťa senb en suten net (*Rā-χeperu-àri-maāt*) *ānχ uťa senb ṭeṭṭeṭ-f seuaḥ-f mà pet renp-f mà entet Àmsu* 18. *neḥeḥ senb-f en ḥeḥ em renput en neteru* 18
nebu suten reχ maā meri-f Neχt-Àmsu ťeṭ-f à neteru àmu pet à neteru àmu 19. *ta à neteru àmu ṭuàt χenniu Rā staiu neter nefer er χut àmentet ent pet* 19
sār meṭu-à en ten em spertu en baket en neb-f ḥesiu-à nuk ḥesi en àθi ṭep ta

ṭā-f ḥetep-à em àuset-à ent ḥeḥ χnem-à [Seχet-ḥetepet]

THE BATTLE OF KADESH.

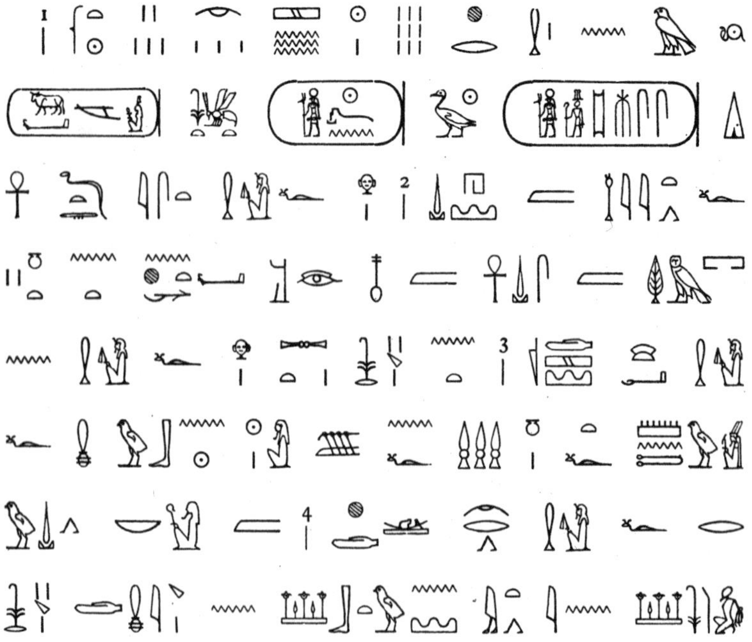

1. *Renpet ṭua àbeṭ χemt šemu hru paut χer ḥen en Ḥeru Rā (Ka-neχt-meri-maāt) suten net (Rā-user-maāt-setep-en-Rā) sa Rā (Rā-meses-meri-Àmen) ṭā ānχ t'etta àst ḥen-f ḥer* 2. *Ṭah em utit-f sent ent neχt res nefer em ānχ ut'a senb em àm en ḥen-f ḥer θest res ent* 3. *Qeṭeš χāā ḥen-f mà uben Rā sešep-nef χakeru nu tef menθu ut'a neb em* 4. *χeṭ sper ḥen-f er res ṭemà en Šabtun īt àn Šasu*

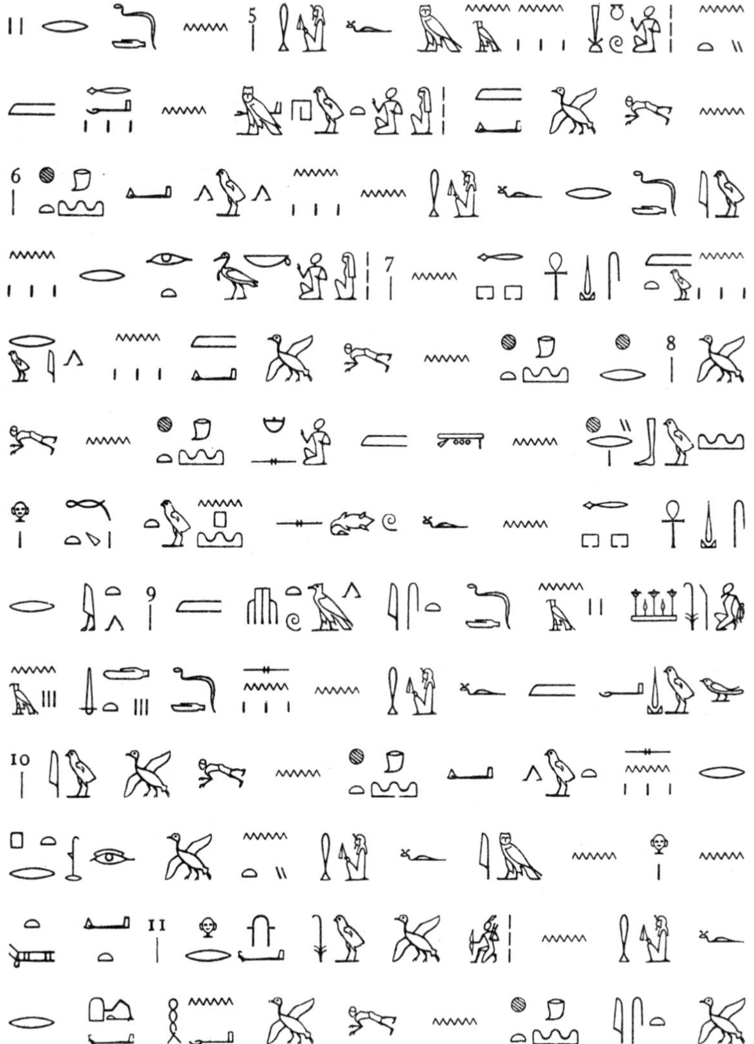

sen er t'eṭ en 5. *ḥen-f emnai-n sennu enti em āā en māhetu emmā pa χer*
en 6. *Χeta ṭā īu-n en ḥen-f er t'eṭ àu-n er àrit baku* 7. *en Āa-perti ānχ*
ut'a senb emtun ruà-n emmā pa χer en Χeta χer 8. *pa χer en Χeta ḥems em*
ta en Χirebu ḥer meḥt Tunep senṭu-f en Āa perti ānχ ut'a senb er īt 9. *em*
χentua àst t'eṭ na sen Śasu· nai meṭet t'eṭ-sen en ḥen-f em āt'au 10. *àu pa*
χer en Χeta ṭā īut-sen er petrà pa enti ḥen-f àm en ḥer en tem ṭāt 11. *ḥer*
su pa māša en ḥen-f er āba ḥnā pa χer en Χeta àst pa

χer en Χeta 12. *iu ḥnā ser neb en set neb māša-u neθeḥ-u ȧn-nef emmā-f em neχt āḥāu ḳeru* 13. *ḥer en ḥa en Qeṭeš ta ȧqesi ȧn reχ ḥen-f er ťeṭ-set ȧu uťa ḥen-f em χet sper er meḥt ȧmenti Qeṭeš . . . . māša en ḥen-f ȧm seneťem ḥen-f ḥer* 14. *ȧsteb en smu īt ȧn ḥapu enti em šesu ḥen-f ȧn-sen ḥapu sen en pa χer en* 15. *Χeta stu-u embaḥ ťeṭ-en-sen ȧn ḥen-f entuten ȧχ ťeṭ-en-sen tun er* 16. *pa χer en Χeta entef ṭā īut-n er petrȧ pa enti ḥen-f ȧm ťeṭ-en-sen ȧn* 17. *ḥen-f*

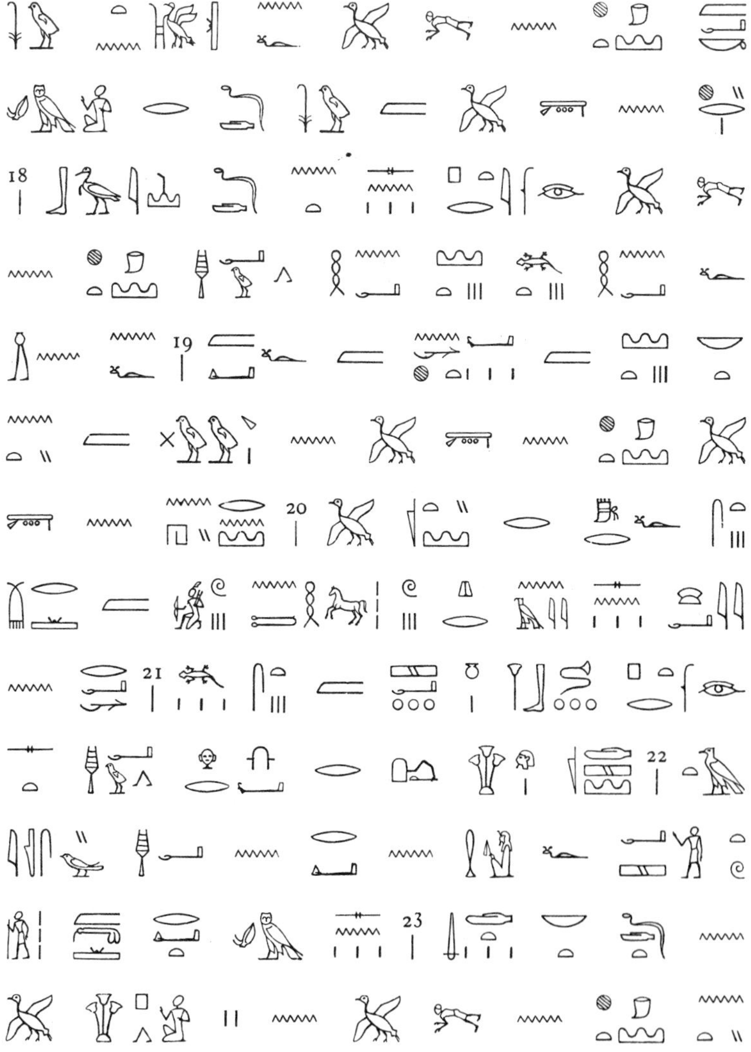

su ten-nef pa χer en Χeta māk setem-ȧ er ťeṭ su em pa ta en 18. *Χirebaȧ ťeṭ ent sen petrȧ pa χer en Χeta āḥāu ḥnā set āšt ḥnā-f ȧn-nef* 19. *emmā-f em neχ̣t em set nebt enti em uu en pa ta en Χeta pa ta en Nehiren* 20. *pa Qeti er ťer-f set āper em māša neθeḥ-u χer nai-sen χ̣āāi en rā* 21. *āšt set em šā nu uteb petrȧ set āḥāu ḥer er āba ḥa Qeṭeš* 22. *ta ȧqesi āḥā en erṭā en ḥen-f āš-tu seru embaḥ er ṭāt setem-sen* 23. *meṭet nebt ťeṭet en pa ḥap sen en pa χer en Χeta enti*

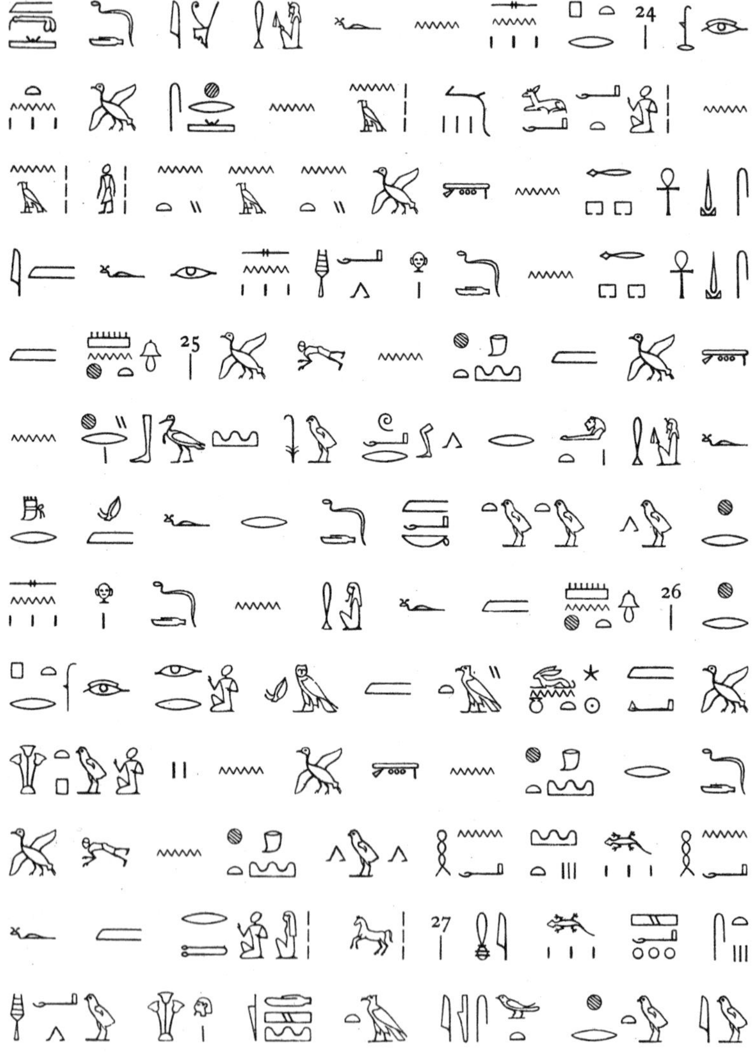

embaḥ t̆eṭ ȧn ḥen-f en sen 24. *petrȧ-ten pa seχer en nai meru āuāāt en nai seru enti na enti pa ta en Āa-perti ānχ ut̆a senb ȧm-f ȧri-sen āḥā ḥer t̆eṭ en Āa-perti ānχ ut̆a senb em menχet* 25. *pa χer en Χeta em pa ta en Χireba su uār er ḥāt ḥen-f t̆er setem-f er t̆eṭ māk tutu īu χer sen ḥer t̆eṭ en ḥen-f em menχet* 26. *χer petrȧ ȧri-ȧ setem em tai unnut emmā pa ḥaput sen en pa ta en Χeta er t̆eṭ pa χer en Χeta īu ḥnā set āšt ḥnā-f em reθ neθeḥ* 27. *mȧ āšt šā set āḥāu ḥa Qeṭeš ta ȧqesit χertu ȧu*

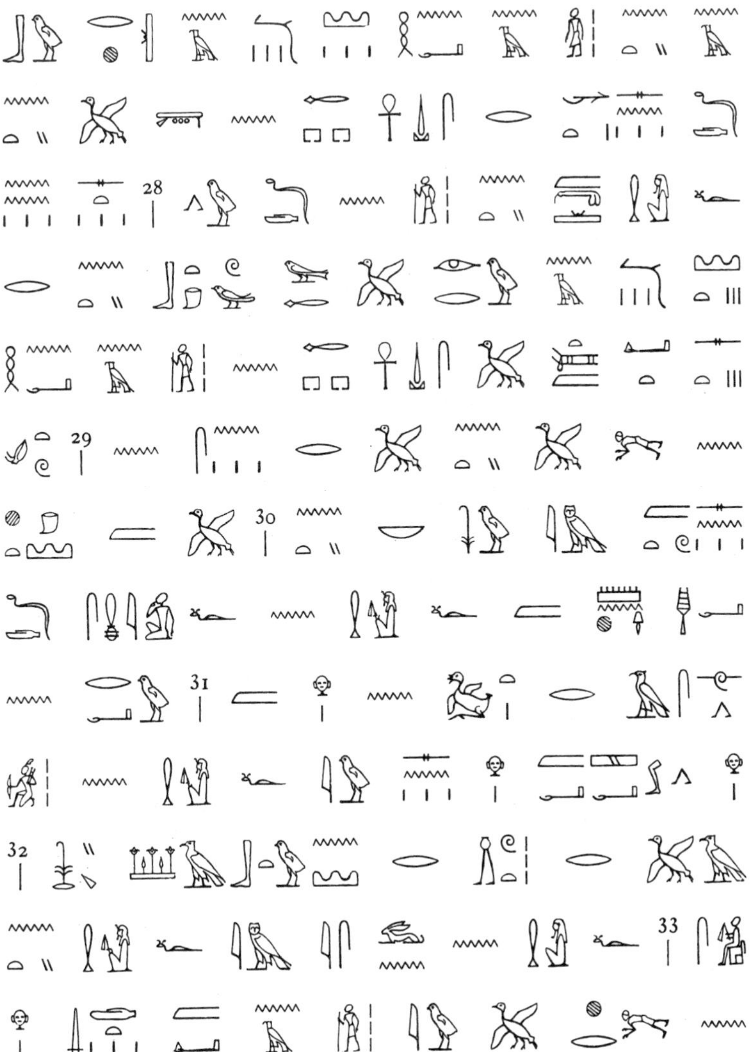

bu reχ na meru set ḥnā na seru enti na enti pa ta en Āa-perti ānχ uťa senb er χet-sen ťeṭ-en-n set 28. *īu ťeṭ en seru enti embaḥ ḥen-f er enti betau ur āa pa āru na meru set ḥnā na seru en Āa-perti ānχ uťa senb pa tem ṭāt-set setem-tu* 29. *en-sen er pa enti pa χer en Χeta em pa* 30. *enti neb su ȧm emtusen ťeṭ smȧ-f en ḥen-f em menχ āḥā en erṭāu* 31. *em ḥrȧ en ťat er asta māša en ḥen-f ȧu-sen ḥer māšā ḥer* 32. *res Śabtun er ȧn-tu er pa enti ḥen-f ȧm ȧs un en ḥen-f* 33. *sneťem ḥer meṭtet emmā na seru ȧu pa χer en*

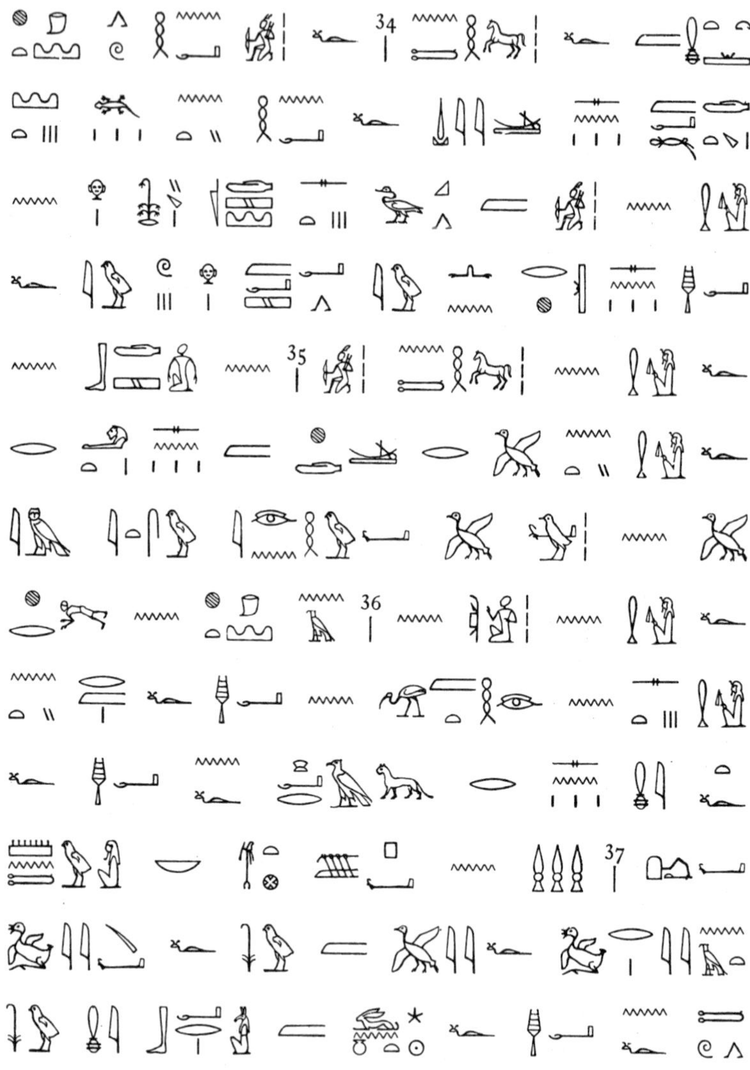

Xeta īu ḥnā māśa-f 34. *neθeḥu-f emmātet set āšt enti ḥnā-f ṭai-sen māseśeṭet en ḥer resi Qeṭeś set āq em māśa en ḥen-f àu-u ḥer māśā àu àn reχ-sen āḥā en beṭeś en* 35. *māśa neθeḥu en ḥen-f er ḥāt-sen em χeṭ er pa enti ḥen-f àm àstu ànḥu pa neχtu en pa χer en Xeta na* 36. *en śesu en ḥen-f enti er-ḳes-f āḥā en qemḥet-en-set ḥen-f āḥā-nef Xāāra er-sen mà tef Menθu neb Uast seśep en χakeru* 37. *āba ṭai-f su em paif ṭareinat su mà Bāru em unnut-f āḥā-nef θeu*

er sesumut-f ȧu-f ḥer 38. *χerp asta ȧu-f uā ḥer ṭep-f ȧu-f ḥer āq em pa χeruu na pa χer en Χeta ḥnā set āšt enti ḥnā-f ȧu ḥen-f mȧ Suteχ āa peḥt-peḥt* 39. *ȧu-f ḥer uānui ḥer sma ȧm-sen ȧu ḥen-f ḥer ṭāt ha-sen na uru em ḳebḳebet em uā ḥer uā er pa mu nut Ȧrenθ heṭ* 40. *-ȧ set nebt ȧu-ȧ uā-kuȧ ȧu χaāu-ȧ pai-ȧ māša tai-ȧ neθeḥ bu āḥā uā ȧm-sen er* 41. *ānnu en ānχ-ȧ meru-ȧ Rā ḥesiu-ă ȧtef-ȧ Tmu ȧr seχer neb ťeṭ en ḥen-ȧ ȧri-ȧ* 42. *set em maāti embaḥ* 43. *māša-ȧ neθeḥu-ȧ*

THE ANNALS OF RAMESES III.

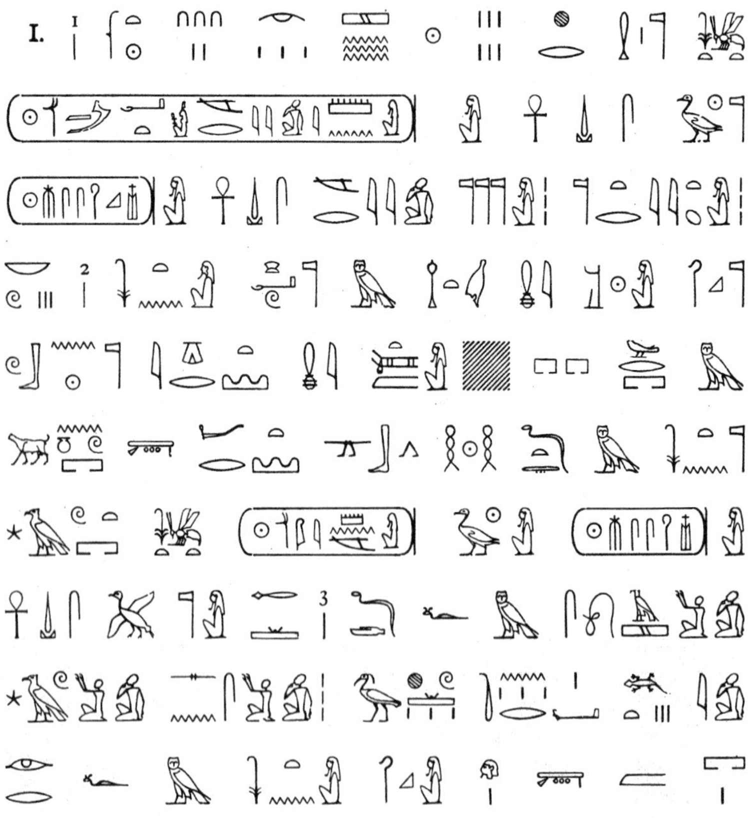

1 **I.** — 1. *Renpet māb sen ȧbeṭ χemt šemu hru sȧs χer ḥen suten net (Rā-user-*
Maāt-meri-Ȧmen) ānχ uťa senb sa Rā (Rā-meses-ḥeq-Ȧnnu) ānχ uťa senb
2 *meri neteru neterit nebu* 2. *suten χāāu em ḥeťet mȧ Res ḥeq uben Ȧḳert mȧ*
Tmu . . . . perti ur em χennu Tasert seb ḥeḥ ťetta em suten Ṭuaut suten net
(Rā-user-Maāt-meri-Ȧmen) sa Rā (Rā-meses-ḥeq Ȧnnu) ānχ uťa senb pa
3 *neter āa* 3. *ťeṭ-f em seuaš ṭuau senes χu θenre āšt ȧ ȧri-f em suten ḥeq ṭep*
ta em per

ȧtf-f śepsi Ȧmen-Rā suten neteru 4. *Mutet Χensu neteru nebu Uast per ȧtf-f* 4
śepsi Tmu neb taiu Ȧnnu Rā Ḥeru-χuti Iusāaset Nebt-ḥetep neteru nebu
Ȧnnu per ȧtf-f śepsi 5. *Ptaḥ Āa-qemā-ȧneb-f neb ānχ taiu Seχet āat meri* 5
Ptaḥ Nefer-Tmu χu taiu neteru nebu Ḥet-Ptaḥ-Ka ȧtfiu śepsiu neteru
neterit nebu qemāt 6. *meḥi em na χu neferu ȧ ȧri-nef er reθ en pa ta* 6
Qemt ta neb er seḥui-un er ťeru em sep uā er ṭāt āmamu 7. *ȧtfiu* 7
neteru neterit

nebu qemāt meḥi reθ neb pāt reχit neb ḥememu neb em na χu qennu θenre
8, 1 *āšt* 8. *ȧ ȧri-f ḥer ṭep ta em ḥeq āa en Qemt* **III.** — 1. *seχu senes*
θenre χu ȧ ȧri-f er per ȧtf-f šepsi Ȧmen-Rā suten neteru Mutet Χensu
2 *neteru nebu Uast* 2. *ṭeṭ ȧn suten* (*Rā-user-Maāt-meri-Ȧmen*) *ānχ uṭa senb*
sa Rā (*Rā-meses-ḥeq-Ȧnnu*) *ānχ uṭa senb pa neter āa em seuaš ȧtf-f neṭer*
3 *pen šepsi Ȧmen-Rā suten neteru paut χeperu χer ḥāt* 3. *neter neteri utet su*
ṭesef fa-ā seqau atf ȧri ent qemau

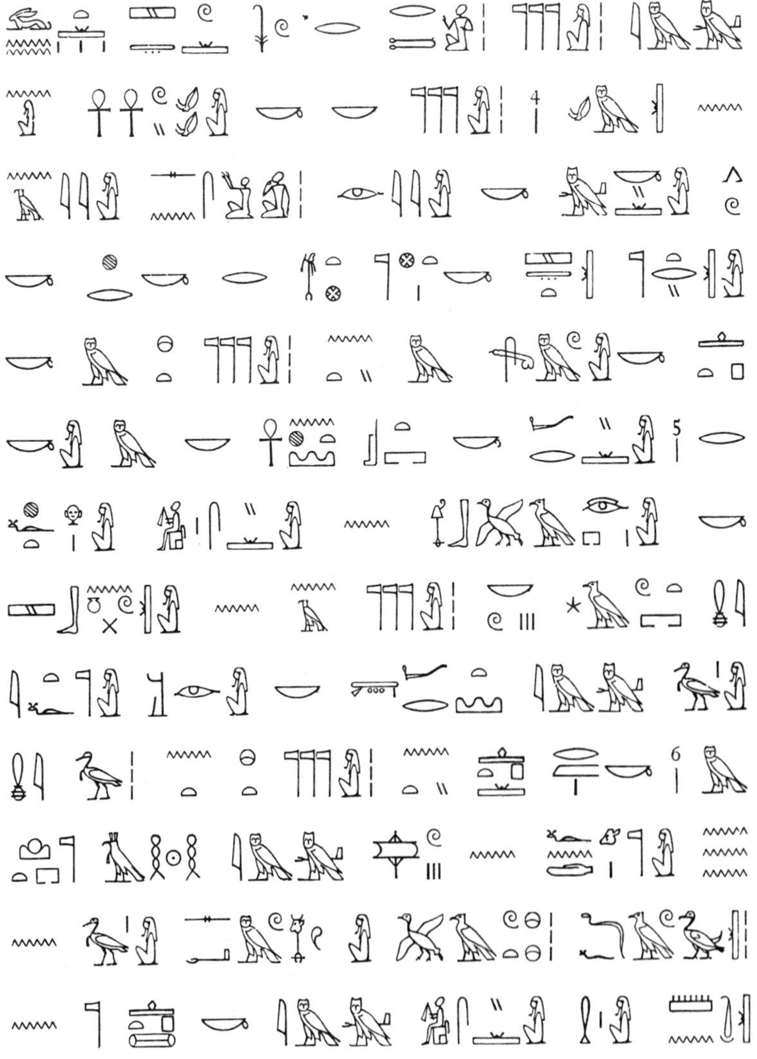

unenet šetau su er reθ neteru ȧmmā-nȧ ānχui-k neb neteru 4. *setem en nai-ȧ* 4
ṣenes ȧri-ȧ-k māki iu-k χer-k er Uast neter nut-k šetat neteri-k em paut neteru
enti em semu-k ḥetep-k em neb Ānχet ȧuset-k ťeseri 5. *er χeft šepsi en ābbaa-k* 5
šebennu-ȧ en na neteru nebu ṭuat mȧ ȧtf-ȧ Ȧusȧr neb Taťesert ȧmmā ba-ȧ
mȧ baiu ent paut neteru enti ḥetep er-ḳes-k 6. *em χut neḥeḥ ȧmmā nefu en* 6
fenṭ-ȧ mu en ba-ȧ seāmu-ȧ paut ťefau en neter ḥetep-k ȧmmā šepsi-ȧ
ḥen-ȧ men

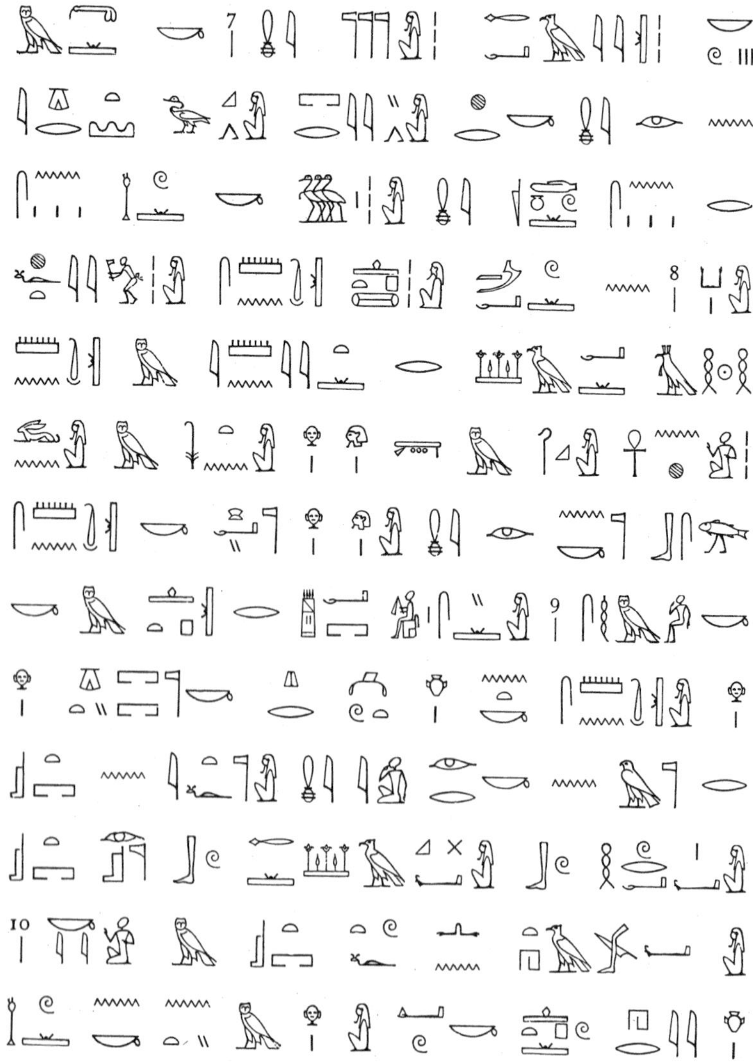

7 *embaḥ-k* 7. *mȧ neteru āāai nebu Ȧḳert āq-ȧ peri-ȧ χer-k mȧ ȧri en sen*
8 *utu-k baiu-ȧ mȧqeṭ-sen er χefti-ȧ s-men ḥetepu-ȧ maāu en* 8. *ka-ȧ men*
em ȧmenit er śaā neḥeḥ un-ȧ em suten ḥer ṭep ta em ḥeq ānχiu semen-k
9 *χāāi ḥer ṭep-ȧ mȧ ȧri-nek bes-k em ḥetep er ḥet-ā śepsi* 9. *s-neťem-k ḥer*
nesti-k χer āut ȧb entek semen-ȧ ḥer ȧuset en ȧtf-ȧ mȧ ȧ ȧri-k en Ḥeru er
10 *ȧuset Ȧusȧr bu āaśaq-ȧ bu ḥurā-ȧ* 10. *ki em ȧuset-tuf ȧn teha-ȧ utu-nek*
enti em ḥer-ȧ ṭāu-k ḥetepu heri ȧb

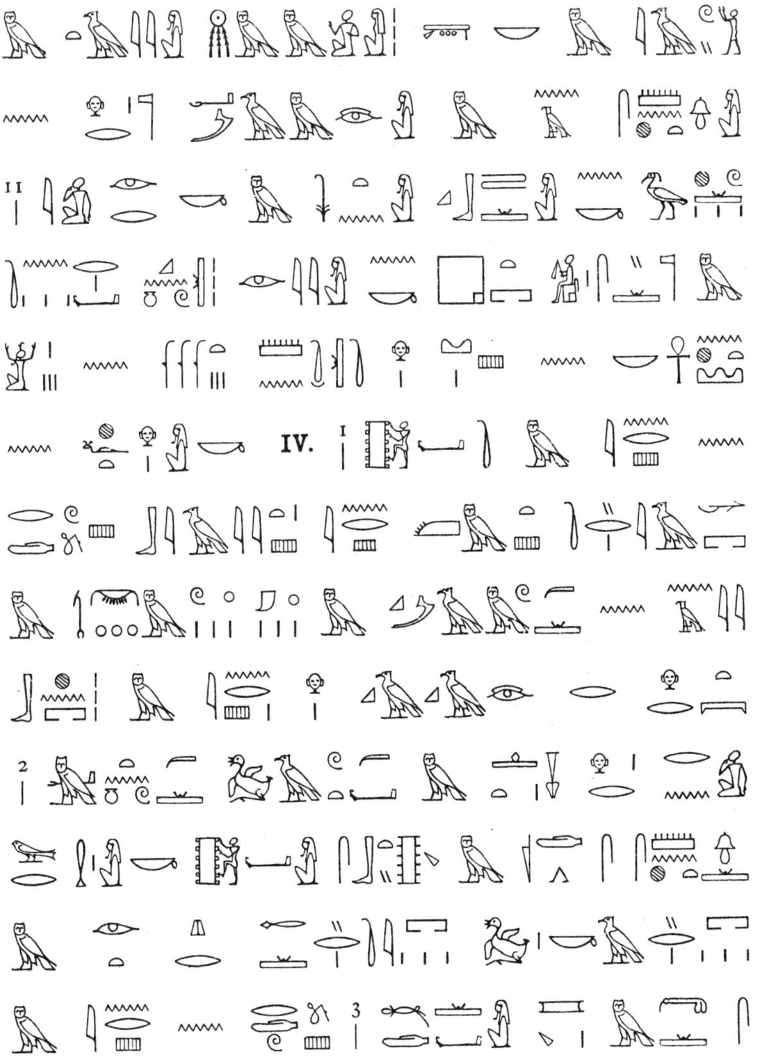

em tai-ȧ ḥememet ta neb em ȧaui en ḥrȧ-[k] āmam-ȧ em na smenχet-ȧ II. *ȧ* II
ȧri-k em suten qeb-ȧ nek χu θenre qennu ȧri-ȧ nek ḥet šepsi em ḥeḥ en
renput menθ ḥer ṭu en Neb-ānχet en χeft-k **IV.** — I. *qeṭθ em ȧner en* I
ruṭ bȧait ȧner Qemt θireȧa em smu χemt em qemamu en nai beχenu em ȧner
ḥer qaqa er ḥert 2. *mātennu ťaut em basanet* (?) *ḥer ren ur ḥen-k qeṭ-ȧ sebti* 2
em qeṭ-s s-menχet em ȧrit χer āaireθȧ ťakaire em ȧner en ruṭ 3. *sešeṭ-ȧ* 3
mer (?) *em-baḥ-s*

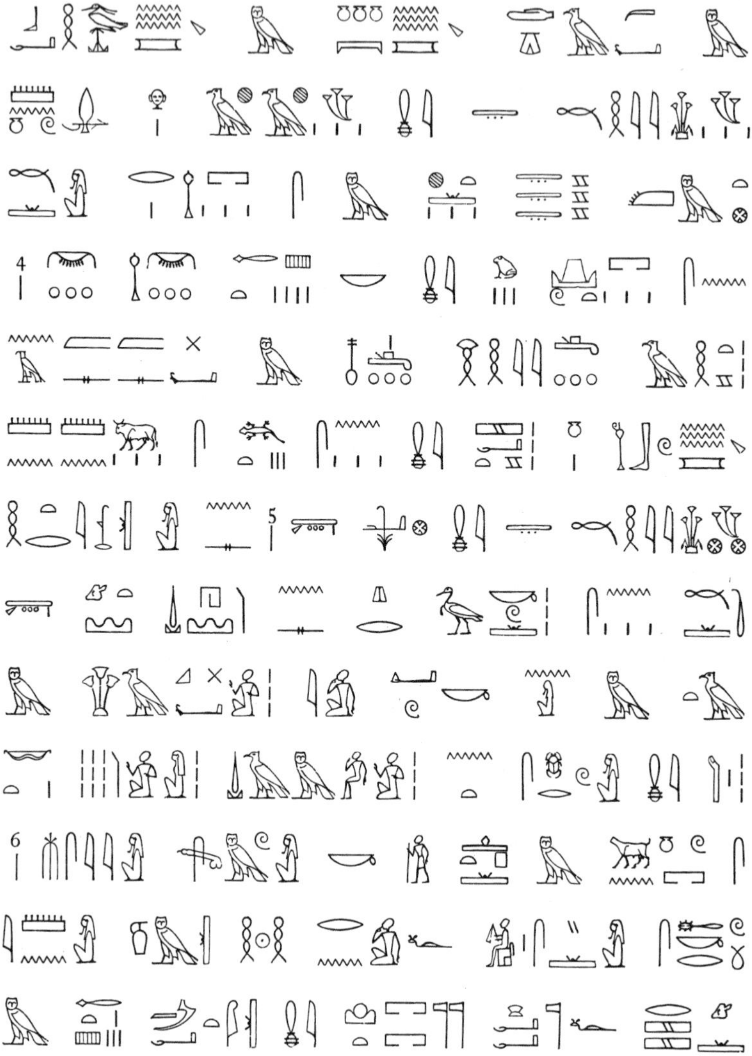

bāḥ em Nu ṭeka em mennu ḥer aχaχ mȧ ta Meḥi meḥ-ȧ re-ḥet'-s em χet
4 *taiu Qemt* 4. *nub ḥet' āat neb mȧ ḥefnu šentu-sen namesmes em neferu*
5 *uaḥi aḥet menmen seāšt-sen mȧ šāt nu utebu ḥetrȧ-ȧ nes* 5. *ta Qemā*
mȧ ta Meḥi ta Χent Tah nes χer baku-sen meḥθ em ḥaqu ȧ ṭāu-k-nȧ
6 *em ta pet paut t'am ent seχeperu mȧ t'ebā* 6. *mesi-ȧ semu-k ur ḥetep em*
χennu-s Āmen-χnem-ḥeh ren-f šepsi s-χakeru em āat maāt mȧ χuti
χāā-f rešeš-

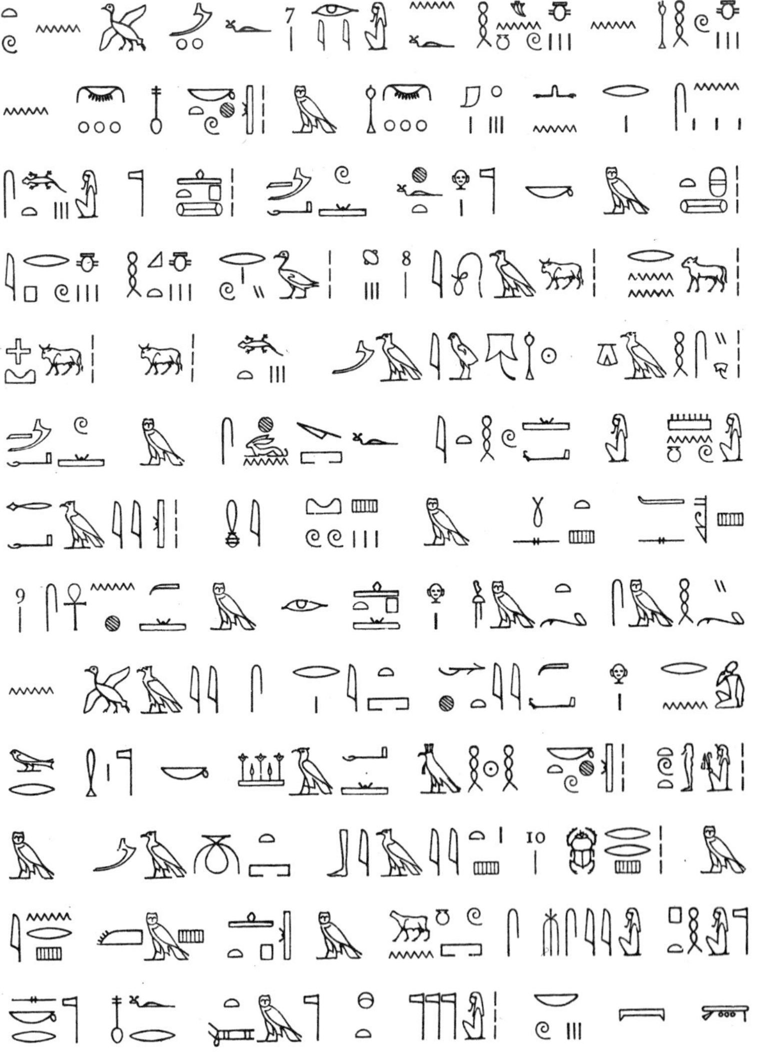

tu en pa maa-f 7. *ȧri-ȧ-nef ḥennu en utḥu en nub nefer keteχu em ḥet'* 7
χemt ȧn re-sen seāšt-ȧ neter ḥetepu maāu χeft-k em ta ȧrpu ḥeqt reui χepen
8. *ȧuaa renen ȧmṭu ȧḥ āšt maȧu ḳaḥsi maāu em seχunen-f ȧtḥu-ȧ* 8
menu āāai mȧ ṭuu em šeset beḥes (?) 9. *seānχ em ȧri ḥetep ḥer unemet* 9
semeḥi en pai-s reȧt χeti ḥer ren ur ḥen-k šaaā neḥeḥ keteχu tut em mat
bȧait 10. *χepereru em ȧner qem ḥetep em χennu-s mesi-ȧ Ptaḥ-Seker* 10
Nefer-Tem paut neteru nebu pet ta

11 *ḥetep em kerȧ-s baku em nub nefer* 11. *ḥet' em qemamu em meḥ em āat*
maāt menχet em ȧri ȧri-ȧ-nek ḥet-ā šepsi en suten em χennu-s mȧ ḥet-āat
12 *Tem enti em ḥert uχai* 12. *ḥetrȧ sebaut en smu sešeṭ āa en χāāii en*
1 *nub nefer ȧri-ȧ-nes quir atep em nefer uaḥi er χen er* **V.** — 1. *šent-s*
ȧn-nu urṭu ȧri-ȧ-nes re-ḥet' uȧa āāai ḥer ṭep ȧtur atep χer χet āšt er
2 *reḥet-s šepsi* 2. *reri-s em kamu ȧusetu āt-ent-χet atep χer ṭeka ḥurere en*
ḥātut-k qeṭ-ȧ en

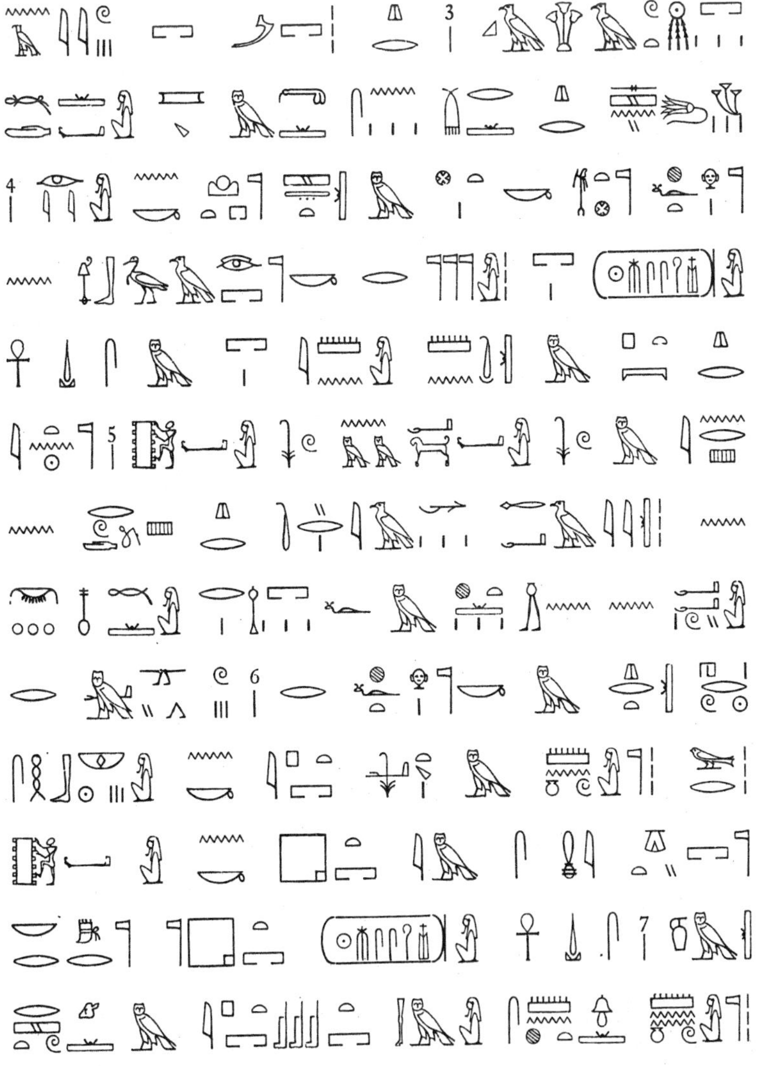

naiu peru-ma (?) *χer* 3. *qaḥaaut sešeṭ-ȧ mer embaḥ-sen āper χer sešeni* 3
4. *ȧri-ȧ-nek χut šetat em nut-k Uast χeft en ābbaa-k er neteru per* (*Rā-meses-* 4
ḥeq-Ȧnnu)| *ānχ uťa senb em per Ȧmen men em pet χer ȧten* 5. *qeṭ-ȧ su* 5
nemmā su em ȧner en ruṭ χer θireȧa āāaiu en nub nefer meḥ-ȧ reḥeť-f em
χet ȧn en āāui-ȧ er māsi-u 6. *er χeft-k em χert hru seḥeb-ȧ-nek ȧpet qemāt* 6
em menu uru qeṭ-ȧ-nek ḥet ȧm-s mȧ nesti Neb-er-ťer neter ḥet (*Rā-meses-*
ḥeq-Ȧnnu)| *ānχ uťa senb* 7. *χnem reštu em Ȧptet nem-ȧ semenχet mennu-* 7

k em Uast neχtuθ àuset ḥetep en àb-k er ḳes-tu ḥrà-k per (Rā-user-maāt-meri-
8 *Àmen) ānχ uťa senb em per Àmen* 8. *màtet kerà Neb-er-ťer qeṭ em àner mà*
9 *bàaiu semenχet em kat er neḥeḥ θireàa ḥer ḥràu em àner en ma sebaut* 9. *ḥetrà*
10 *em nub āper su em ťamu s-χeper-nà χer χet em ḥefnu* 10. *àri-à-nek kerà*
śeta em āt uāt em àner nefer en mat āāuit ḥer ḥrà-f em χemt em qemamu
11 *χeti ḥer ren-k neteri* 11. *semu-k ur ḥetep em χennu-f mà Rā em χuti-tuf*
smen ḥer àuset-f er śaā er

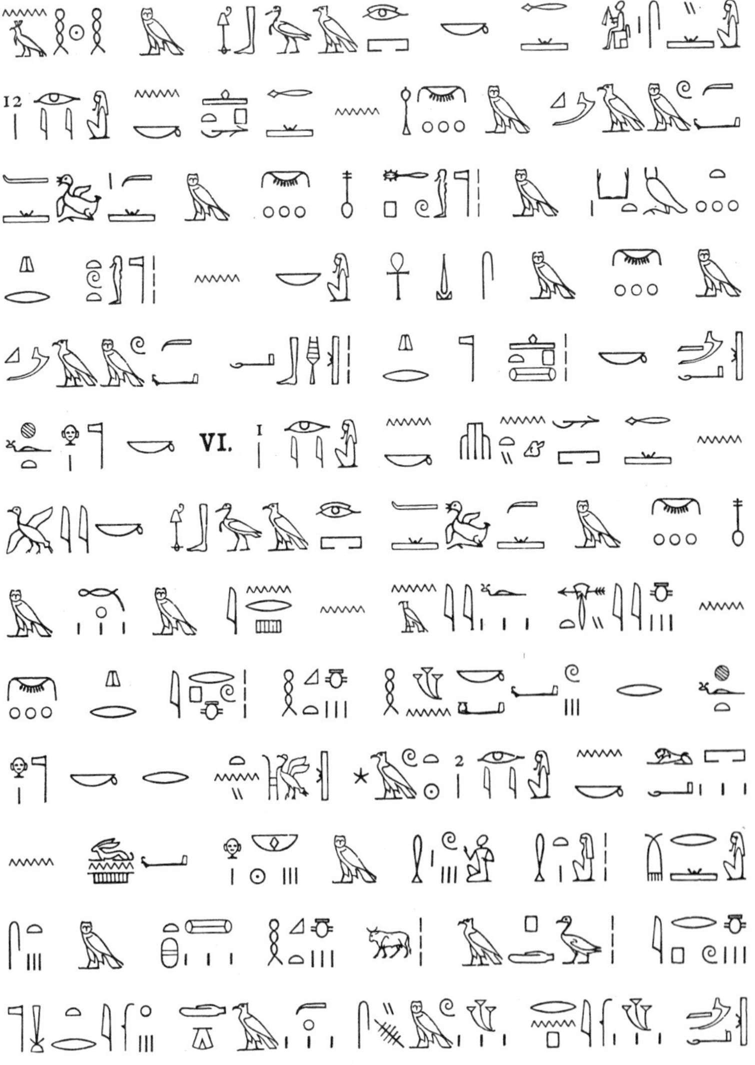

neḥeḥ em ābbaa-k āa šepsi 12. *ȧri-ȧ-nek ḥetep āa en ḥet' em qemamu ḥut'a em* 12
nub nefer χapu em katemet χer tut en neb ānχ ut'a senb em nub em qemamu
āb χer neter ḥetepu-k maā χeft-k **VI.** — 1. *ȧri-ȧ-nek χenti āa en paik* 1
ābbaa ḥut'a em nub nefer em meḥ em ȧner en naif satiï en nub χer ȧrpu
ḥeqt ḥenk-u er χeft-k er teni ṭuaut 2. *ȧri-ȧ-nek rā en un-ḥrȧ em* 2
ḥenu ḥenet āper-set em ta ḥeqt ȧḥ apṭ ȧrpu neter sentrȧ ṭeka simu
renpȧ maā

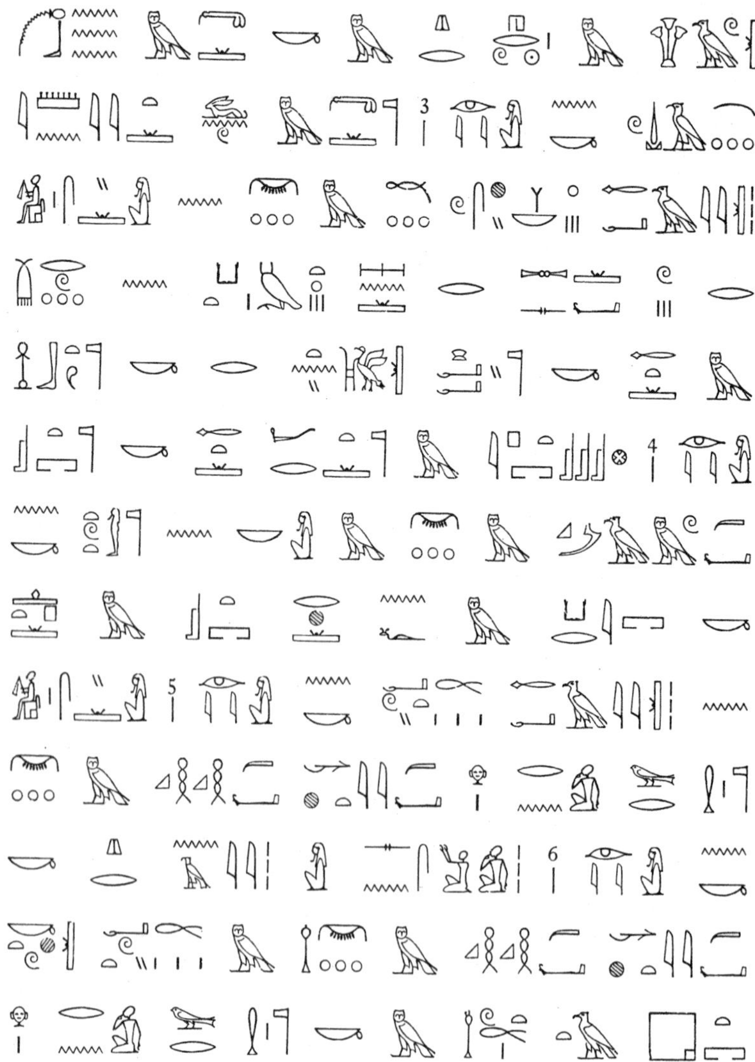

3 *āb embaḥ-k em χer hru em ḥau ȧmenit unu embaḥ* 3. *ȧri-ȧ-nek uťa*
šepsi en nub em meḥ useχi āāaiu āperu en katemet qen er θes-u er šenbet-k
4 *er teni χāāi-k āat em ȧuset-k āat ťesert em Ȧpt* 4. *ȧri-ȧ-nek tut en neb*
5 *em nub em qemamu ḥetep em ȧuset reχ-nef em kerȧ-k šepsi* 5. *ȧri-ȧ-*
nek āuti āāaiu en nub em qeḥqeḥ χeti ḥer ren ur ḥen-k χer nai-ȧ senes
6 6. *ȧri-ȧ-nek keteχu āuti em ḥeť em qeḥqeḥ χeti ḥer ren ur ḥen-k em utut*
ta ḥet

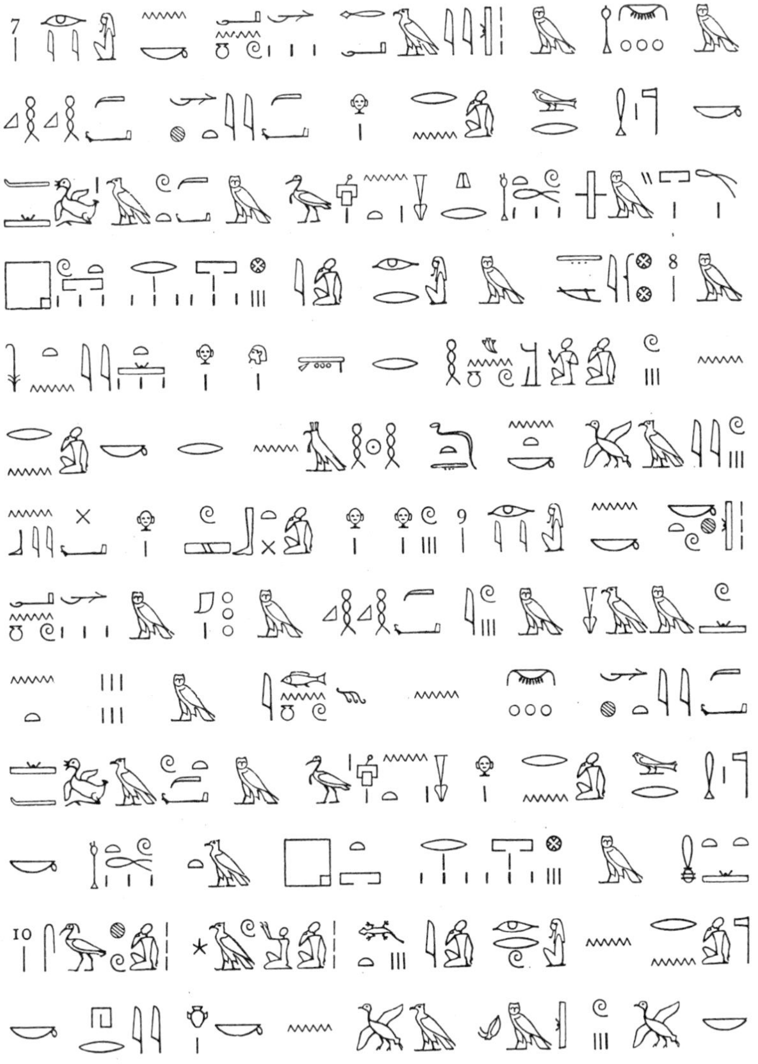

7\. *ȧri-ȧ-nek ānnu āāai em ḥet em qeḥqeḥ χeti ḥer ren ur ḥen-k ḥuťaut em* 7
basanet χer utut ȧmi ḥetu er-pau ȧ ȧri-ȧ em Ta-merȧ 8. *em sutenit ḥer* 8
ṭep ta er ḥennu-u en ren-k er neḥeḥ ťetta entek paiu nebi ḥer ušebt ḥer
ḥrȧu 9. *ȧri-ȧ-nek keteχu ānnu em χemt em qeḥqeḥ ȧu em samu ent sȧs* 9
em ȧnnu en nub χeti ḥuťaut em basanet ḥer ren ur ḥen-k utut ta ḥet er
pau em mȧtet 10. *seχu ṭuau āšt ȧ ȧru-ȧ en ren-k heri ȧb-k en pa setem-u* 10
pa neb

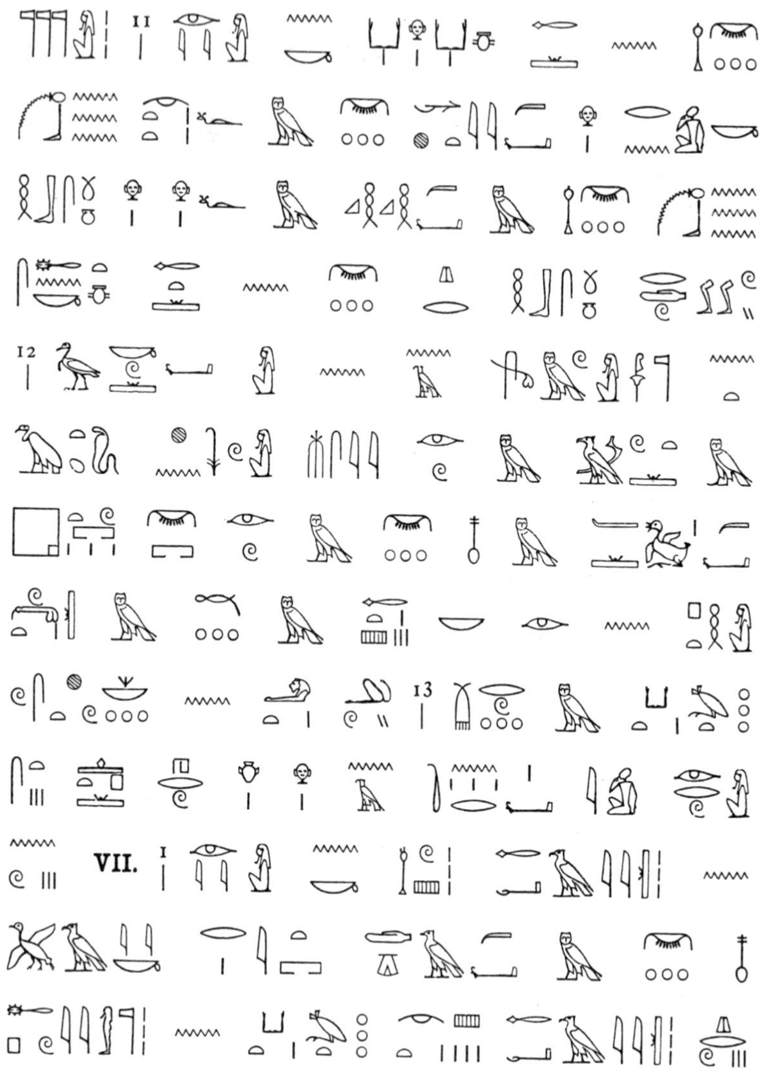

11 *neteru* 11. *ȧri-ȧ-nek ka-ḥrȧ-ka āa en ḥet' āb septet-f em nub χeti ḥer ren-k ḥebs ḥer ḥrȧ-f em qeḥqeḥ em ḥet āb seχaneket āat en nub χer ḥebs reṭuui*

12 12. *baku-ȧ en na semu ent Mut Χensu mesi ȧru em maut em ḥetu-nub ȧru em ṇub nefer em hut'a umet em meḥ em āat neb ȧri en Ptaḥ useχetu en*

13 *ḥāt peḥui* 13. *āperu em katemet-set ḥetep heru ȧb ḥer na θenre ȧ ȧru-ȧ-nu*

1 **VII.** — 1. *ȧri-ȧ-nek utu āāai en paik reȧt ṭeḳa em nub nefer χapui en katemet sept āāai χeru*

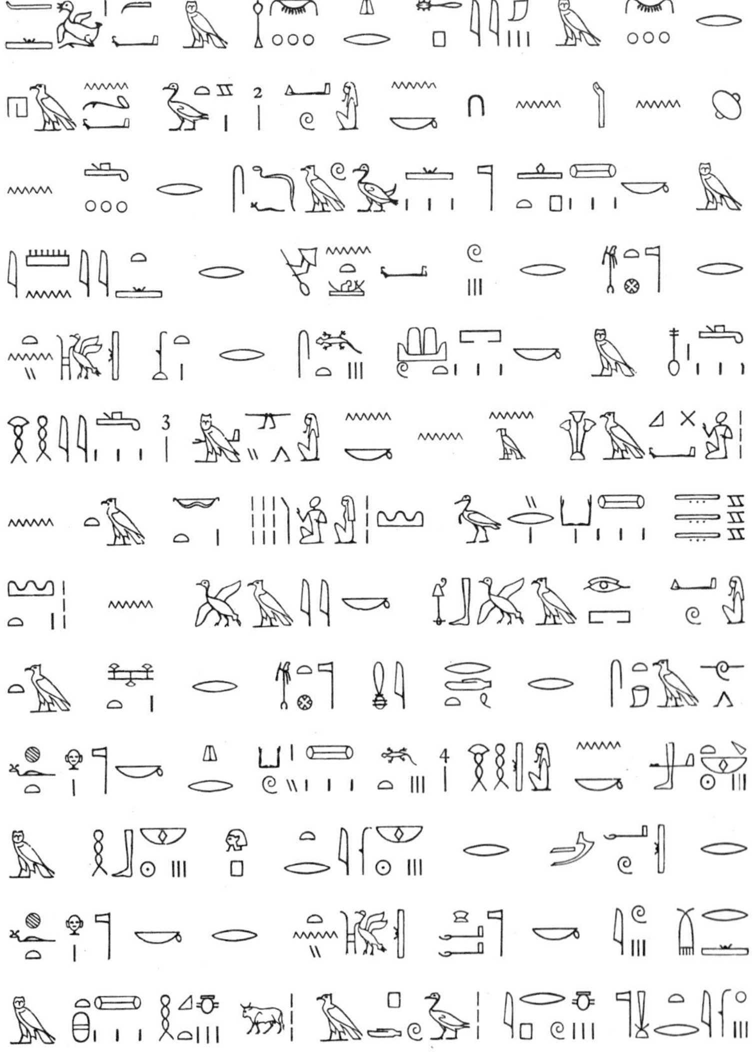

ḥuťa em ḥeť χer χapi em nub er han sat 2. *ṭāu-ȧ-nek met en ťebā en ṭep* 2
en neferu er seťefau neter ḥetepu-k em ȧmenit er χent-u er Uast er
teni renpit er seāšt šentu-k em neferu uaḥi 3. *māsi-ȧ-nek en na* 3
ḥaqu en ta pet paut baireka taiu set en paik ābbaa ṭāu-ȧ ta uat er
Uast mȧ reṭet er seta χeft-k χer kaui āšt 4. *uaḥ-ȧ-nek ābt em ḥebu* 4
ṭep trȧiu er maāu er χeft-k er teni χāā-k ȧu āper em ta ḥeqt ȧḥ apṭu
ȧrpu neter sentrȧ

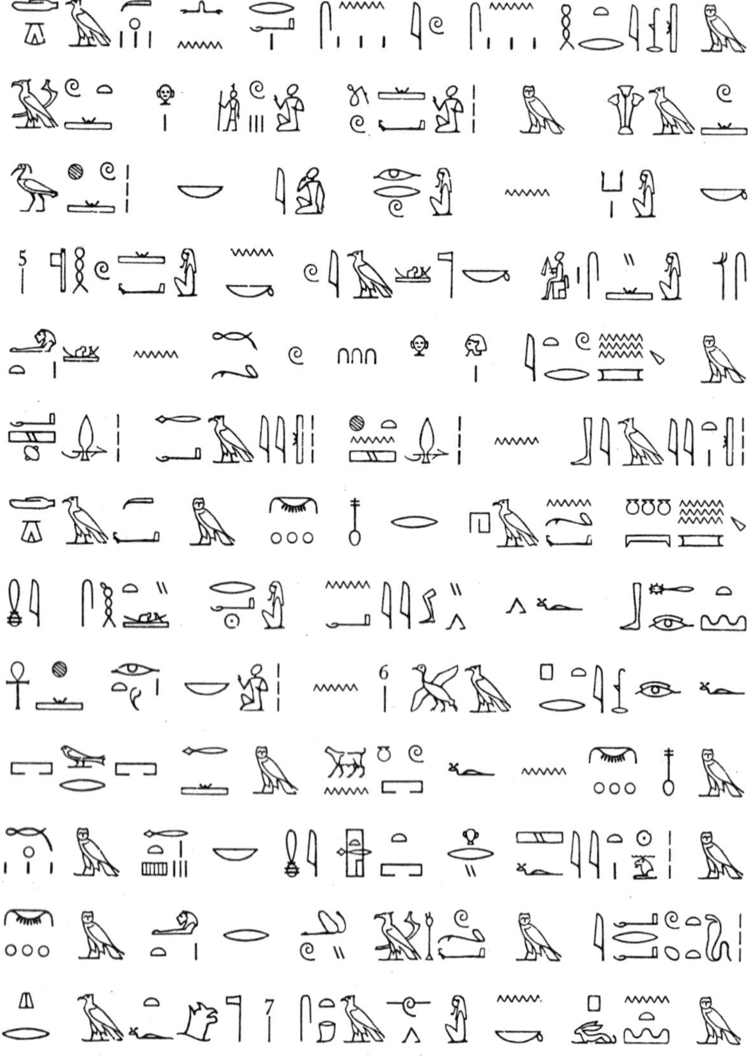

ṭeḳa ȧn rā sen ȧu-sen ḥetrȧ em maut ḥer seru ruṭu em ḥau χu neb ȧ
5 *ȧru-ȧ en ka-k* 5. *sāqḥu-ȧ-nek uȧa-k śepsi User-ḥāt en meḥ śaā māb*
ḥer ṭep ȧtur em āś āāai χenteś en bȧait ṭeḳa em nub nefer er han nu
6 *mȧ sekti Rā nāi i-f Beχat ānχ maat-nebu en* 6. *pa petrȧ-f peru-ur āa*
em χennu-f en nub nefer em meḥ em āat neb mȧ ḥet-āat ḥeri śefit
7 *em nub em ḥāt er peḥui mautu em ȧārāutet χer atf* 7. *seta-ȧ-nek*
Punt em

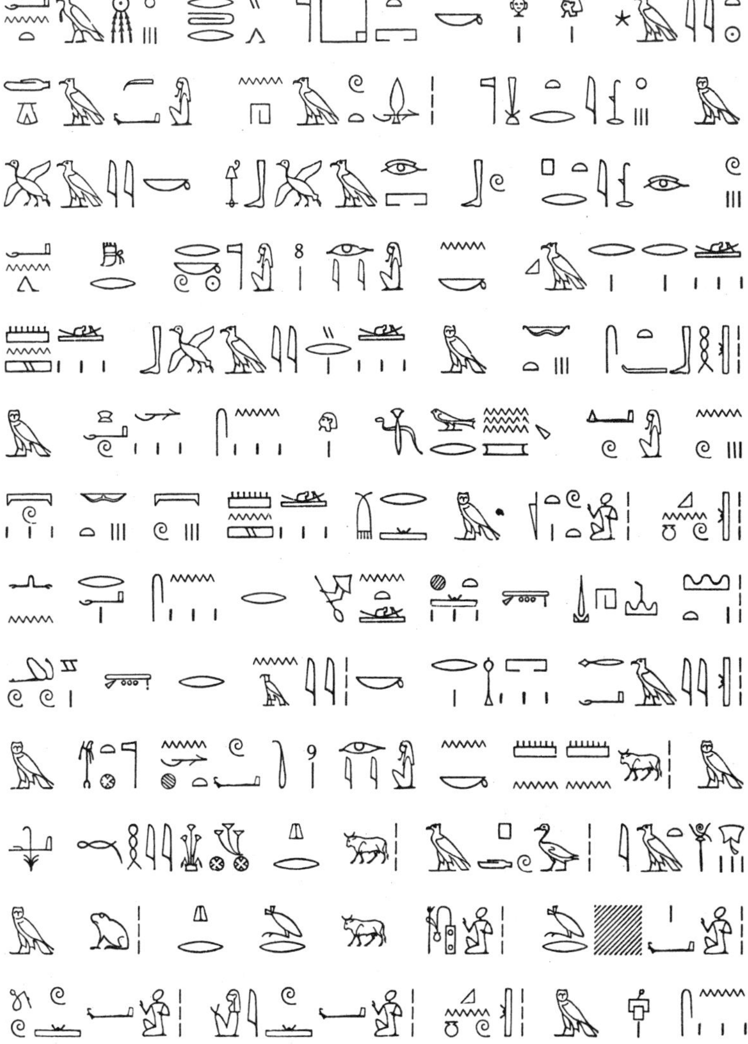

ānti reri neter ḥet-k ḥer ṭep ṭuait ṭeḳa-ȧ nehaut neter sentrȧ em paik
ābbaa bu petrȧ-u ān t́er reku-ȧ 8. *ȧri-ȧ-nek qarere meneš baaire em pet* 8
setebeḥ em χāu-sen ṭep uat́-ur ṭāu-ȧ-nu ḥeru pet ḥeru meneš āper
em qeṭut qennu ȧn rā-sen er χent χet ta T̆ah set peḥuu ta er naik re-ḥet́
āāai em Uast neχt́u-θ 9. *ȧri-ȧ-nek menmen em qemā meḥi χer ȧḥ apṭu* 9
ȧat em ḥefnu χer mer ȧḥ ānu mer . . . . ruṭuu sau qennu em-
sa-sen

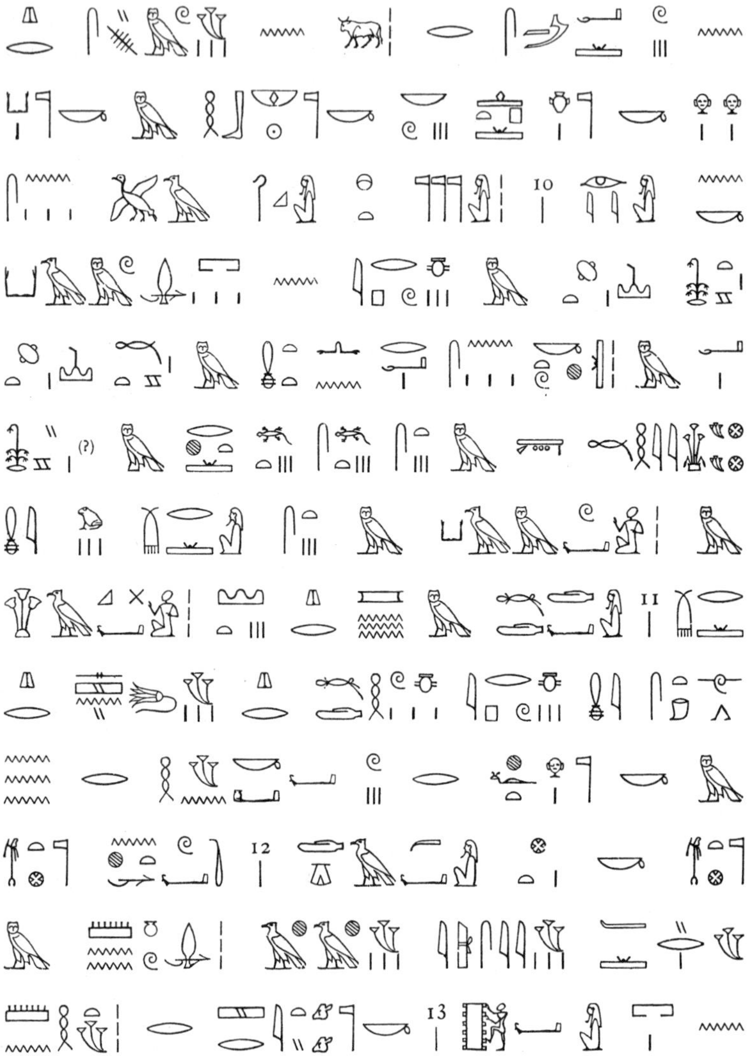

χer simu en āḥ er semaā-u en ka-k em ḥeb-k nebu ḥetep ȧb-k ḥer ḥrȧ-sen
10 *pa ḥeq paut neteru* 10. *ȧri-ȧ-nek kamu en ȧrpu em Ut-reset Ut-meḥet*
emmȧtet ȧn rā-sen keteχu em qemā em reχt āšt seāšt-set em ta meḥi
11 *mȧ ḥefnu āper-set em kamu em ḥaqu set χer mer* (?) *em sešeṭeṭ-ȧ* 11. *āper*
χer sešeni χer sešeṭḥu ȧrpu mȧ sta mu er ḥenk-u er χeft-k em Uast
12 *neχtuθ* 12. *ṭeka-ȧ nut-k Uast em mennu aχaχ ȧsi ḥu*(?)*-re menḥet er*
13 *šerȧti-k* 13. *qeṭ-ȧ pa en*

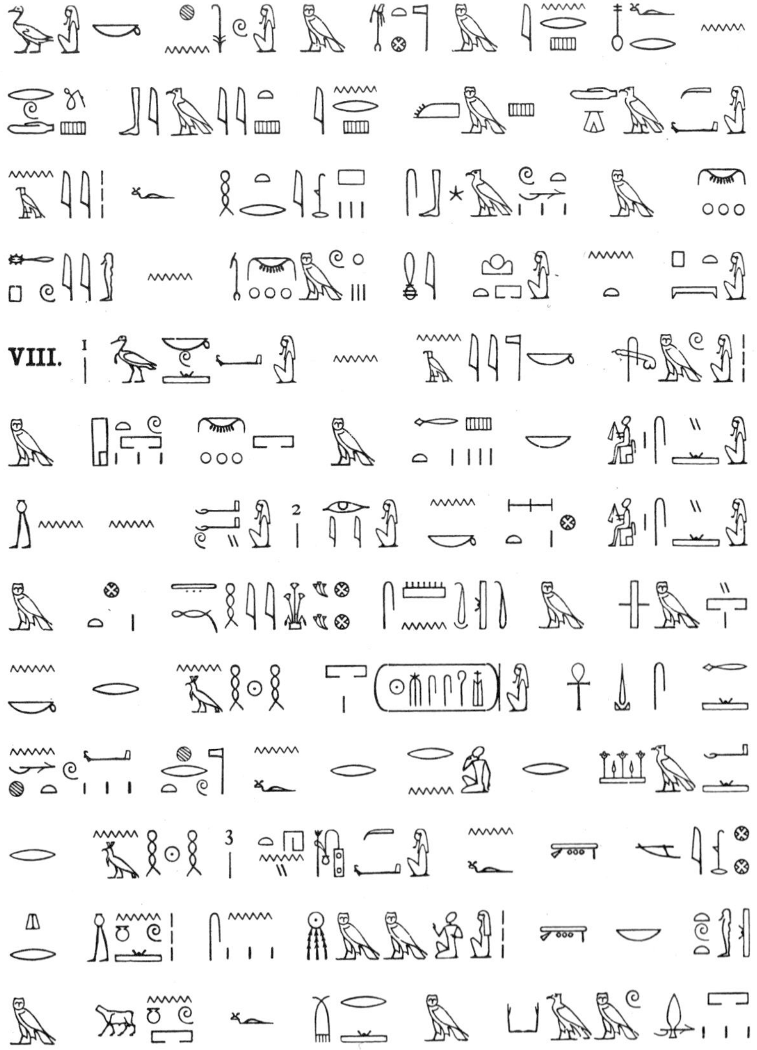

sa-k Χensu em Uast em ȧner nefer en ruṭ bȧait ȧner qem ṭeḳa-ȧ naif ḥetrȧ
sebaut em nub χapui en smu mȧ χut ent pet **VIII.** — 1. *baku-ȧ en naik* 1
semu em ḥetu nub em āat neb šepsi ȧn en āāui-ȧ 2. *ȧri-ȧ-nek ťaťat šepsi* 2
em nut ta meḥi semen-θ em ȧmi-nek er neḥeḥ per (Rā-meses ḥeq Ȧnnu)
ānχ uťa senb āa neχtu χertu nef er ren er šaā er neḥeḥ 3. *teheni-ȧ* 3
nef Ta-merȧ χer ȧnnu-sen ḥememu ta neb tut em χennu-f āper em kamu

4 *āāai ȧusetu sututi em śenti neb benerȧ atep* 4. *χer ṭeḳa-sen uat seθeḥen*
5 *em ḥurere ta neb ȧsi θufi ṭeṭemet mȧtet śā* 5. *ȧri-ȧ nef ka en Qemt*
bāḥ em taiu em ta-u āāai en ťeṭtu χer ȧrert ȧnḥu em sebti em qeṭ-u
6 *mȧ ȧtur ṭeḳa em mennu* 6. *āāai ḥer uat-u neb āśt neḥeḥ ȧm-sen er*
śāt nu utebu er māsi-u en ka-k er Uast neχtu-θ ȧrpu mȧ seta
7 *mu ȧn rā-sen er* 7. *ḥenk-u er χeft ḥrȧ-k em ȧmenit*
8 8. *qeṭ-ȧ-nek*
neter ḥet-k em

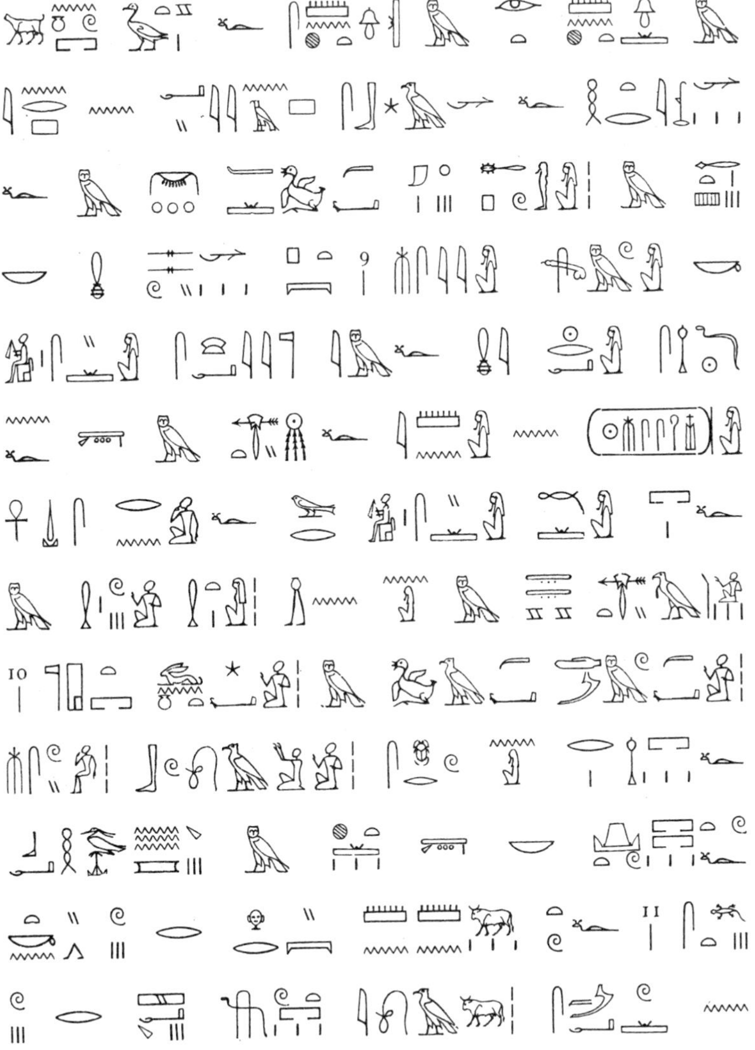

χennu sat-f semenχet em àrit menχet em àner en āiina seba-f ḥetrà-f em
nub ḥuťa χemt χapu em āat neb mà sesui pet 9. *mesi-à semu-k šepsi* 9
seχāāi àm-f mà Rā s-ḥeť-nef ta em sati-f Àmen en (*Rā-meses ḥeq Ànnu*)
ānχ uťa senb ren-f ur šepsi meḥ-à per-f em ḥenu ḥent àn-nà em taiu Sati
10. *neter ḥet unnut em ťa ṭemamu mesui buua s-χeperu-nà re-ḥeť-f bāḥ em* 10
χet ta neb šentutu-f tekeni-u er ḥeri menmen-tuf 11. *seāšt-u er šā meťetu* 11
àuaa semaāu en

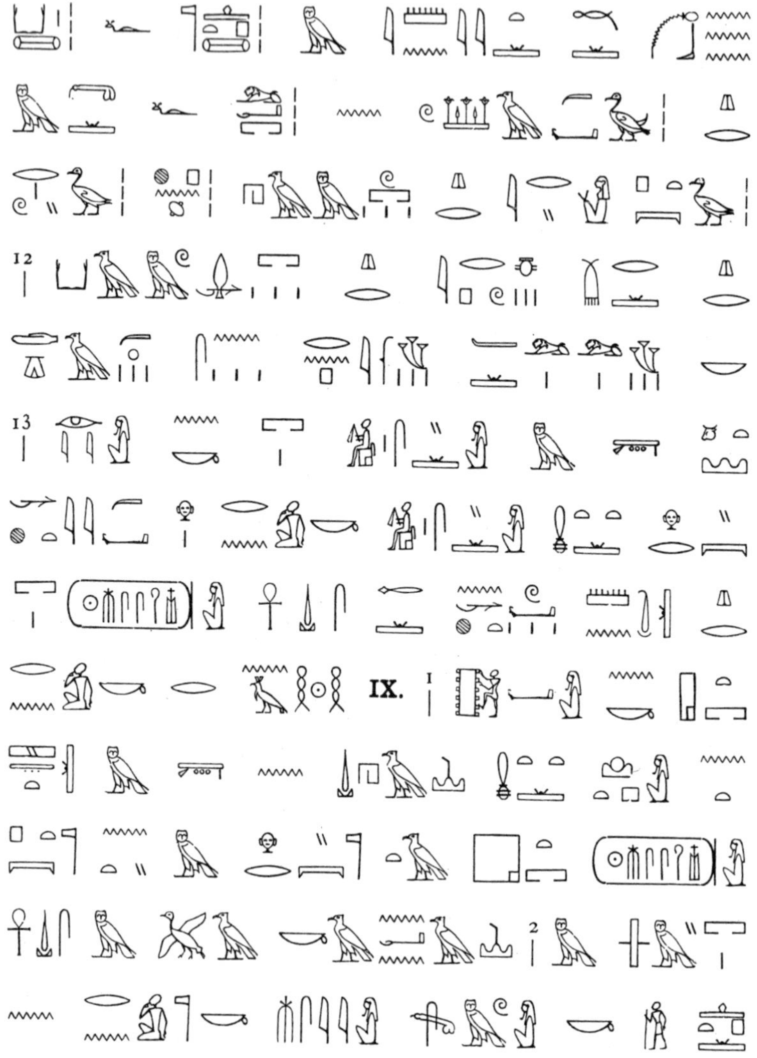

ka-f neter ḥetepu em ȧmenit meḥ āb embaḥ-f rā en uśa χer reui χepen
12 *hamu χer ȧri pet* 12. *kamu χer ȧrpu āper χer ṭeḳa-sen renpȧ ḥurere neb*
13 13. *ȧri-ȧ-nek per śepsi em ta Χent χeti ḥer ren-k śepsi mȧtet ḥeri per*
Rā-meses ḥeq Ȧnnu ānχ uťa senb āa neχtu men χer ren-k er neḥeḥ
1 **IX.** — 1. *qeṭ-ȧ-nek ḥet śeta em ta en Ṭaha mȧtet χut ent pet enti em ḥeri ta ḥet*
2 *Rā-meses-ḥeq Ȧnnu ānχ uťa senb em pa Kanāna* 2. *em ȧmi en ren-k mesi-*
ȧ semu-k ur ḥetep

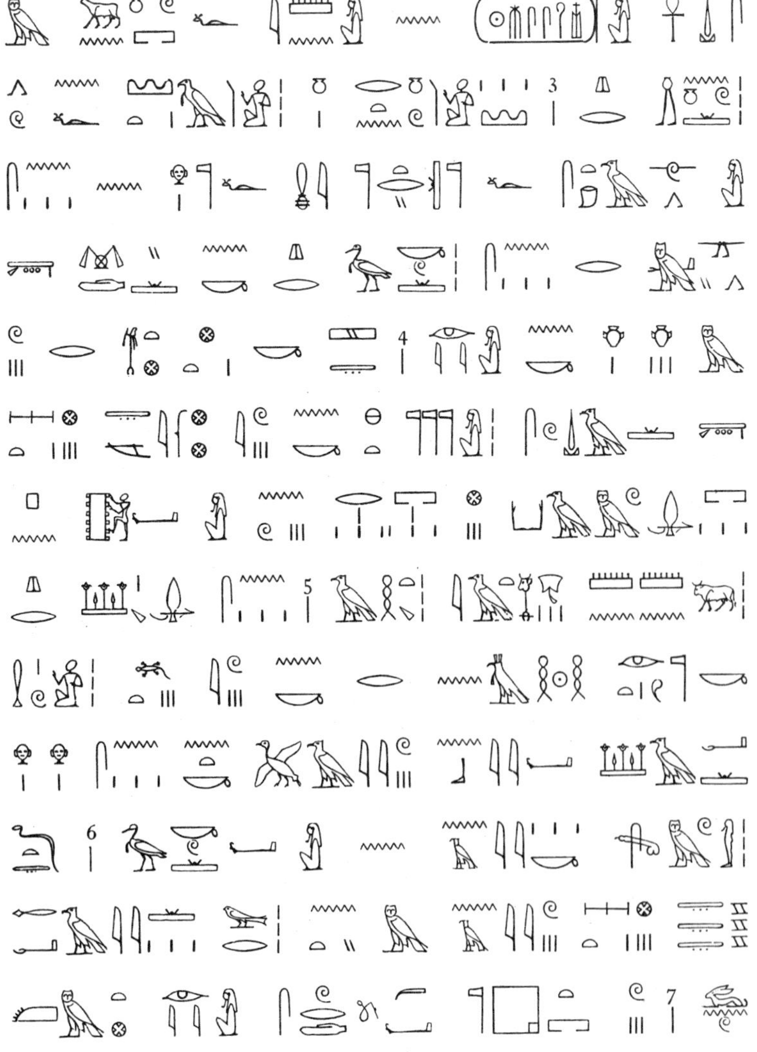

em χennu-f Ȧmen en (*Rā-meses ḥeq Ȧnnu*) *ānχ uťa senb iu-nef setu nu*
Retennu 3. *χer ȧnnu-sen en ḥrȧ-f mȧ neteri-f seta-ȧ ta ṭemṭi-nek χer* 3
baku-sen er māsi-u er Uast nut-k śeta 4. *ȧri-ȧ-nek ȧbiu em ťaťat Ta-merȧ* 4
ȧu-nek paut neteru seuťa ta pen qeṭ-ȧ-nu er-pau kamu χer śenti-sen 5. *aḥet* 5
ȧat menmen ḥenu āśt ȧu-nek er neḥeḥ mat-k ḥer ḥrȧ-sen entek paiu nebi śaā
ťetta 6. *baku-ȧ en naik semu āāai uru enti em naiu ťaťat taiu Qemt ȧri-ȧ* 6
surṭ neter ḥet-u 7. *unu* 7

XX *a.* 1.

2.

3.

4.

5.

6.

7.

smui qeb neter ḥetepu maāu en ka-sen em ḥau ȧmenit unu embaḥ-sen 8. *petrȧ seḥui-nȧ ȧri-nȧ neb embaḥ-k ȧtf-ȧ śepsi neteri neb neteru āmamu reθ neteru em nai-ȧ χu* 9. *ȧ ȧru-ȧ-nek em θenre ȧu-ȧ ḥer ṭep ta* **XX** *a.* — 1. *ťamaāu ťeruu ȧpt 3782.* 2. *nebṭu ȧpt 930.* 3. *ȧuaa 419.* 4. *renen en ȧuaa 290.* 5. *neḳa 18.* 6. *śent 281.* 7. *ḥer sa 3.*

8.

9.

10.

11.

12.

13.

14.

15.

16.

17.

XX *b.* 1.

2.

3.

4.

8. *ȧmtu 740.* 9. *tup 19.* 10. *ȧḥ 1122.* 11. *ḥetep ȧḥ šent 2892.* 12. *ȧuaa maȧu ḥet' 1.* 13. *maȧu ḥet' 54.* 14. *nerāu 1.* 15. *ḳaḥesi 81.* 16. *ḥetep 139.* 17. *ḥetep ȧat šent 3029.* **XX** *b.* — 1. *re ānχ 6820.* 2. *χet āa ānχ 1410.* 3. *turpu ānχ 1534.* 4. *t'aȧu ānχ 150.*

5. *mest ānχ* 4060. 6. *aptu en mu ānχ* 25,020. 7. *menȧt* 57,810. 8. *pāṭet ānχet* 21,700. 9. *paāšt ānχ* 1240. 10. *ḳaire pet* 6510. 11. *ḥetep apt šent* 126,254. 12. *qerḥ mer meḥ em remu χer χet χnemu* 440. 13. *remu ḥet'* 2200. 14. *reā māša* 15,500. 15. *remu uḳas* 15,500. **LXXV.** — 1. *Ṭeṭ ȧn suten* (*Rā-usr-maāt meri-Ȧmen*) *ānχ ut'a senb pa neter āa χer seru ḥāuti*

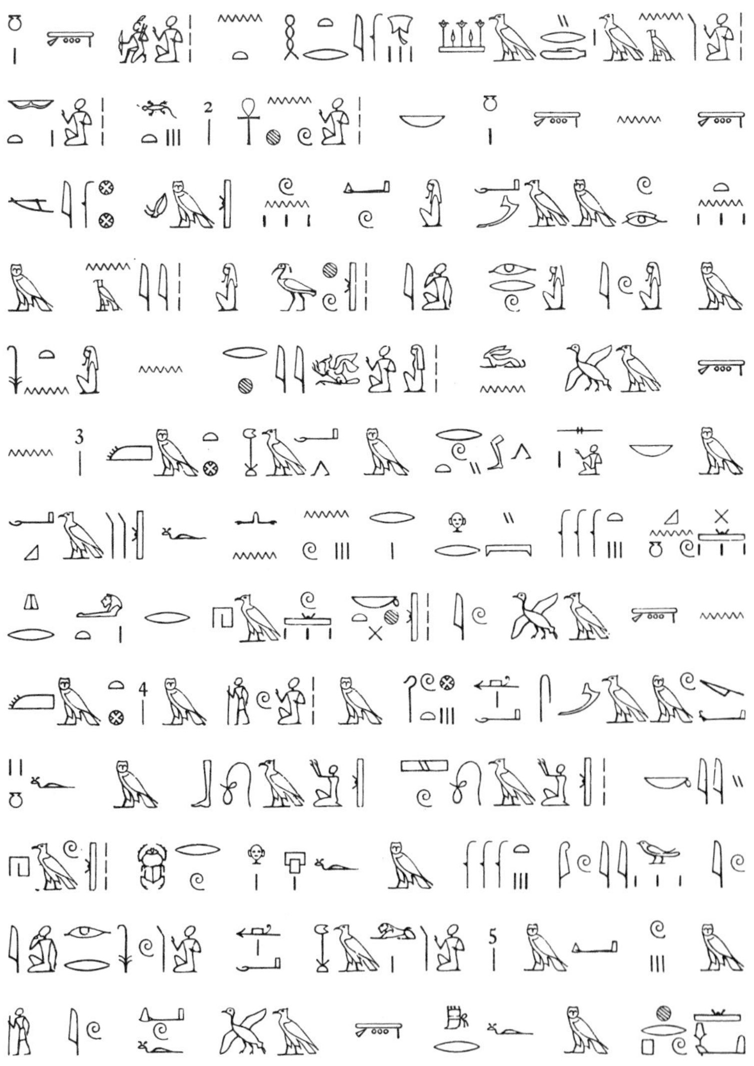

nu ta menfitu ent ḥetrȧ Śaireṭana pet āšt 2. *ānχu neb nu ta en Ta-* 2
merȧ setem-un ṭau-ȧ āmamu-ten em nai-ȧ χu ȧ ȧru-ȧ ȧu-ȧ em suten
en reχi un pa ta en 3. *Qemt χaā em ruti sa neb em āqa-f ȧn-nu re* 3
ḥeri renput qennu χer ḥāt er hau keteχ ȧu pa ta en Qemt 4. *em seru* 4
em ḥequt uā smamu sennu-f em buaa šuua ki hau χeperu ḥer-sa-f em
renput šui ȧu Ȧrsu uā Χaru 5. *emmā-u em ser ȧu māu-f pa ta t̔er-f* 5
em χerpu

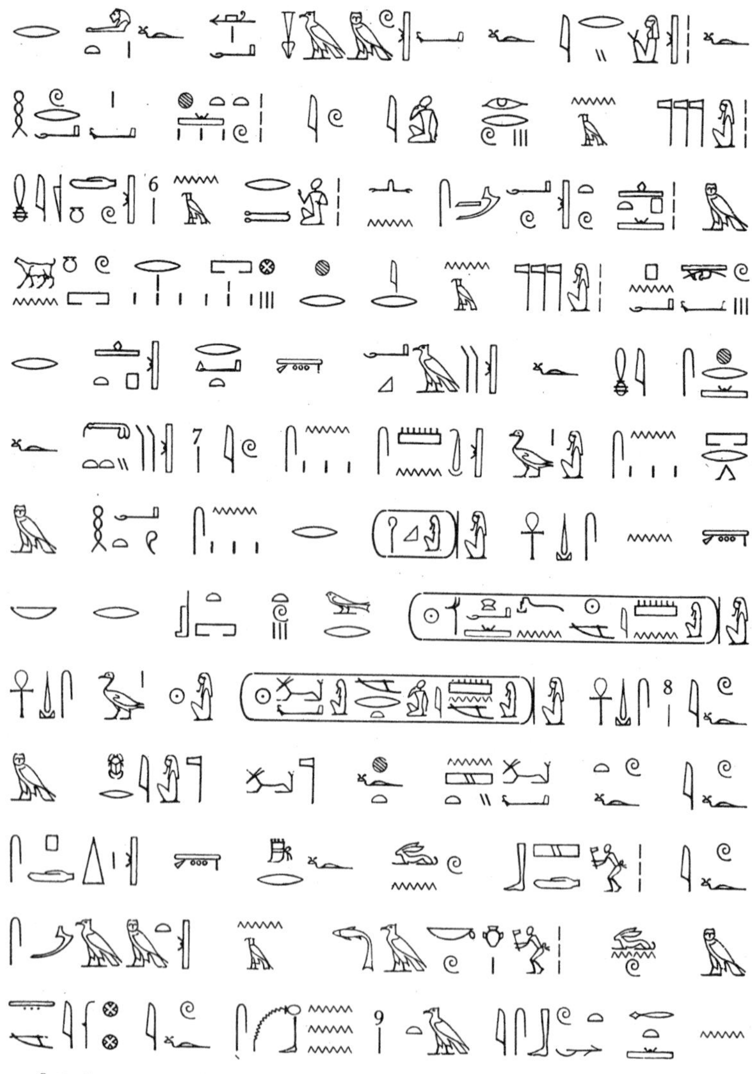

6 *er ḥāt-f uā samu-f ȧri-f ḥurā χettu ȧu ȧ ȧru na neteru mȧqeṭ* 6. *na reθ*
ȧn semaāu-tu ḥetepu em χennu er-pau χer ȧr na neteru penā-u er ḥetep er ṭāt
7 *ta āqa-f mȧ seχer-f metti* 7. *ȧu-sen smen sa-sen per em ḥāt-sen er* (*Ḥeq*)
ānχ uṫa senb en ta neb er ȧuset-tu ur (*Rā-user-χāā-setep-en-Rā-meri-Ȧmen*)
8 *ānχ uṫa senb sa Rā* (*Rā-Set-neχt-mert-Ȧmen-meri*) *ānχ uṫa senb* 8. *ȧu-f*
em Χeperȧ Set χeft nešti-tu-f ȧu-f sepṭ ta ṫer-f unu beṣṭ ȧu-f smamt na
9 *χaku-ȧbu unu em Ta-merȧ ȧu-f seāb* 9. *ta ȧsbut āat en*

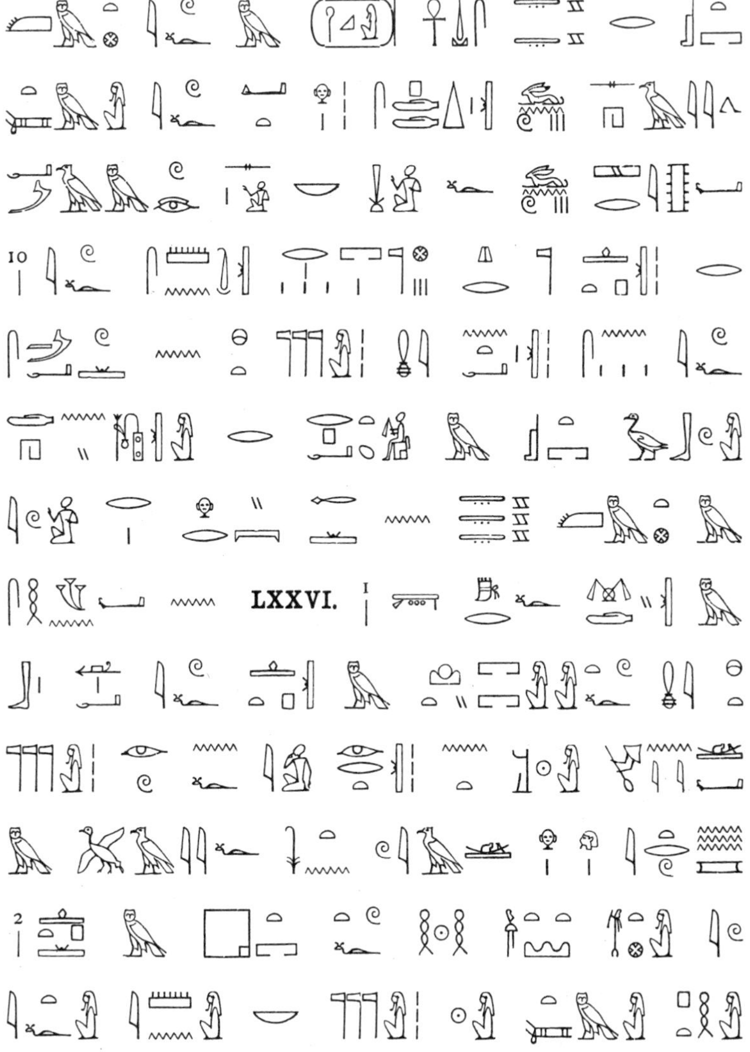

Qemt àuf em (*Ḥeq*) *ānχ uťa senb taiu er àuset Tmu àu-f ṭāt ḥràu sepṭeṭ unu*
sehai āmamu sa neb sen-f unu šerà 10. *àuf smen er-pau χer neter ḥetepu er* 10
semaāu en paut neteru mà entāu-sen àu-f ṭeheni-à er erpāt em àuset Sebu
àu-à re-ḥeri āa en taiu Qemt em seḥen en **LXXVI.** — 1. *ta ťer-f ṭemṭi em* 1
bu uā àu-f ḥetep em χuti-tuf mà paut neteru àru-nef à àrit ent Àusàr (?)
χeni em paif suten uàa ḥer ṭep àtru 2. *ḥetep em ḥet-tuf ḥeḥ Àmentet Uast* 2
àu àtf Àmen neb neteru Rā Tmu Ptaḥ

3 *nefer-ḥrȧ s-χāāu-ȧ em neb taui er ȧuset utet-ȧ seśep-ȧ ȧaut en ȧtf-ȧ* 3. *em*
ȧhahai ȧu ta ḥetep unf χer ḥetepu ȧu-u reśui en maa-ȧ em (*Ḥeq*) *ānχ*
4 *uťa senb taui mȧ Ḥeru seḥeq-f taui er ȧuset Ȧusȧr χāāu-k* 4. *em atf χer*
ȧārāret χnemu-ȧ χāā śuti ma Tatenen s-neťem-k em tenťat Ḥeru χuti ṭebu-k
5 *em χakeru mȧ Tmu* 5. *ȧri-ȧ seχeperu Ta-merȧ em ťamu āśt em ābuu* (?)
6 *en ḥet-ā seru āāai menfitu ent ḥetrȧ qennu mȧ ḥefnu Śaireṭana* 6. *Qeheq*
ȧn rā-sen

šesu em t'ebā semṭet Ta-merȧt ȧri-ȧ seuseχ na taš en Qemt er t'eru
seχer-ȧ na teha-set em nai-sen 7. *taui smamu-ȧ na Ṭaȧnȧuna em nai-* 7
sen ȧauu na T'akire Puir saθȧ ȧru em sesefi Šaireṭana Uašeš en pa
iumā 8. *set ȧru em tem unu ḥaq em sep uā ȧnnu em ḥaq er Qemt* 8
mȧ šā nu utebu senti-ȧ set em neχtu uāfi ḥer ren-ȧ āšt 9. *nai-sen* 9
t'amu mȧ ḥefennu ḥetrȧ-ȧ-set er t'eru em ḥebs sepṭ em re-ḥet' šenut
er teni

LXXVII.

10 *renpit åri-å seksek Saåaire em måhåut* 10. *Śasu χef-å nai-sen merhaire*
em reθ-tu χet-tu nai-sen åaut emmåtet ån rā-sen ṭenḥ ånnu em ḥaq
11 *em ånnut Qemt* 11. *ṭāu-å set en paut neteru em ḥenu er-pau petrå-å*
ṭāt āmamu-ten em keteχ seχeru åu-u åru em Tamerå t'er suteniut un
1 *Rebu Mā-* **LXXVII.** — 1. *śauaaśa senet'em ḥer Qemt åu θetetu na*
ṭemåut pa reṭ åmentet śaā em Ḥet-Ptaḥ-ka er Qarebana peḥu åtru āa
er reåai-

tuf neb 2. *entu ȧ feχ na ṭemȧut en Ḳutut* (?) *em renput qennu āśt* 2
ȧu-sen ḥer Qemt petrȧ ȧri-ȧ seksek-sen semamu em sep uā χer-ȧ pa
3. *Māśauaśa Rebu Mersabata Qaiqaśa Śai Hasa Baqana ḥeṭeb ḥer* 3
snef-sen ȧru em ȧnu ṭāu-ȧ χeti-sen 4. *er χenṭi taś Qemt ȧnu-ȧ* 4
sepi-ȧ ṭemu-ȧ em ḥaq āśt ṭenḥ mȧ apṭu er ḥāt sesemut-ȧ ḥemt-sen
χarṭu-sen mȧ t'ebā 5. *nai-sen ȧat em ṭennu mȧ ḥefennu ḳer-ȧ naiu* 5
ḥāuti

em neχt ḥer ren-ȧ ṭāu-ȧ-nu ḥeru pet āāai en māhaȧut ȧbu ȧru em
6 6. *ḥenu menši ḥer ren-ȧ ḥemt-sen χarṭu-sen ȧru emmȧtet māsi-ȧ*
nai-sen ȧaut er per Ȧmen ȧru-nef menmenut šaā ḥeḥ ȧri-ȧ χnemet
7 7. *āat urt em set Āina ȧu-set ȧnḥu-tu em sebti mȧ ṭu en bȧat em*
ťaut en ťaťaui em senti ta χi meḥ māb χer θesemet nai-f ḥetrȧ sebaut
8 8. *seqḥu em āš nai-u qerȧu em χemt χer maāui seqḥu-ȧ menš āāai baire*
er ḥāt-

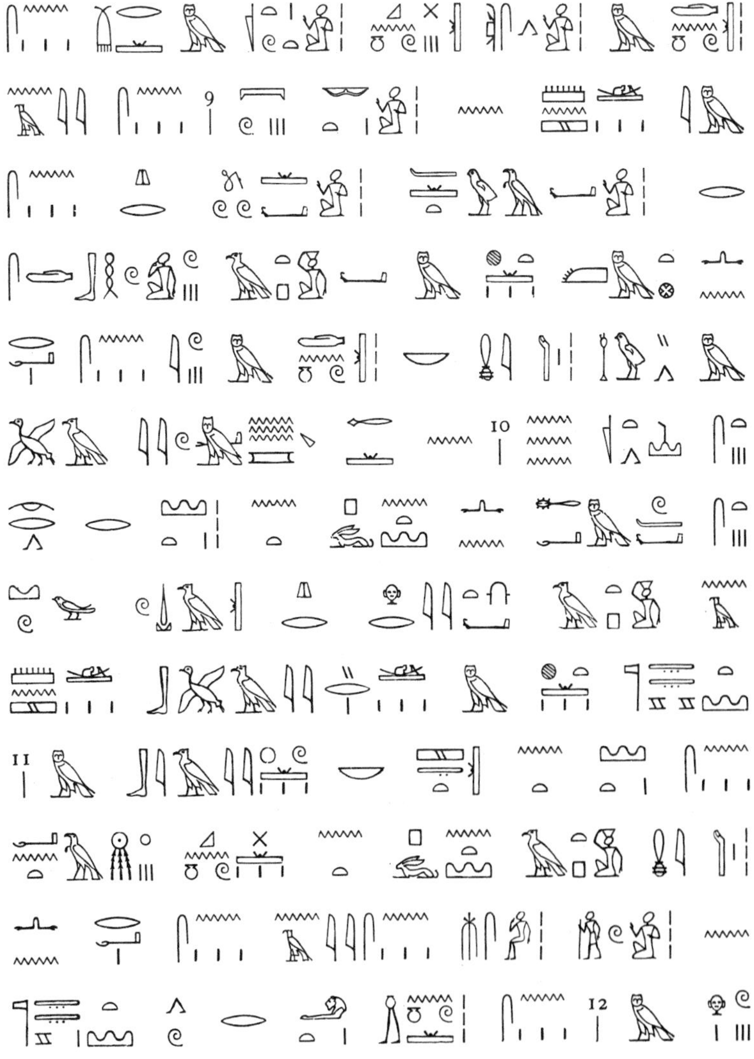

sen āper em qetut qennu šesu em ṭennu nai-sen 9. *ḥeru pet en menš* 9
ȧm-sen χer ruṭu ḥututi er seṭebḥu-u atep em χet Qemt ȧn rā-sen ȧu
em ṭennu neb mȧ ťebā utui em pa iumā āa en 10. *mu Qet set sper* 10
er set ent Punt ȧn χaāmu-set ṭu uťa χer ḥerit atep na menš baire em χet
Neter-tauit 11. *em bȧaiu neb šetat ent set-sen ānti qennu ent Punt atep* 11
mȧ ťebā ȧn rā-sen nai-sen mesu seru en Neter-tauit iu er ḥāt ȧnnu-sen
12. *em ḥrȧ-u* 12

er Qemt set sper àu seuťau er set Qebti set menàu em ḥetep χeri χet ànnu-
13 *set atep em ḥerti ḥer āaāaiu ḥer reθ atep er* 13. *āḥāu ḥer àtru merit Qebti*
utui em χet en ḥràu sper em Ḥeb māsi em ànnu embaḥ mà bàaiu nai-sen
1 *mesu seru em àaui en ḥrà-à* **LXXVIII.** — 1. *sensen-ta ḥeberber en χeft*
ḥrà-à ṭā-à set en paut neteru nebu ta pen er seḥetep ḥāuti-u ṭep ṭuat
2 *utui-à nai-à àputi* 2. *er set Āaθàka er na χau χemt āāaiu enti em àuset ten*
àu nai-sen menš

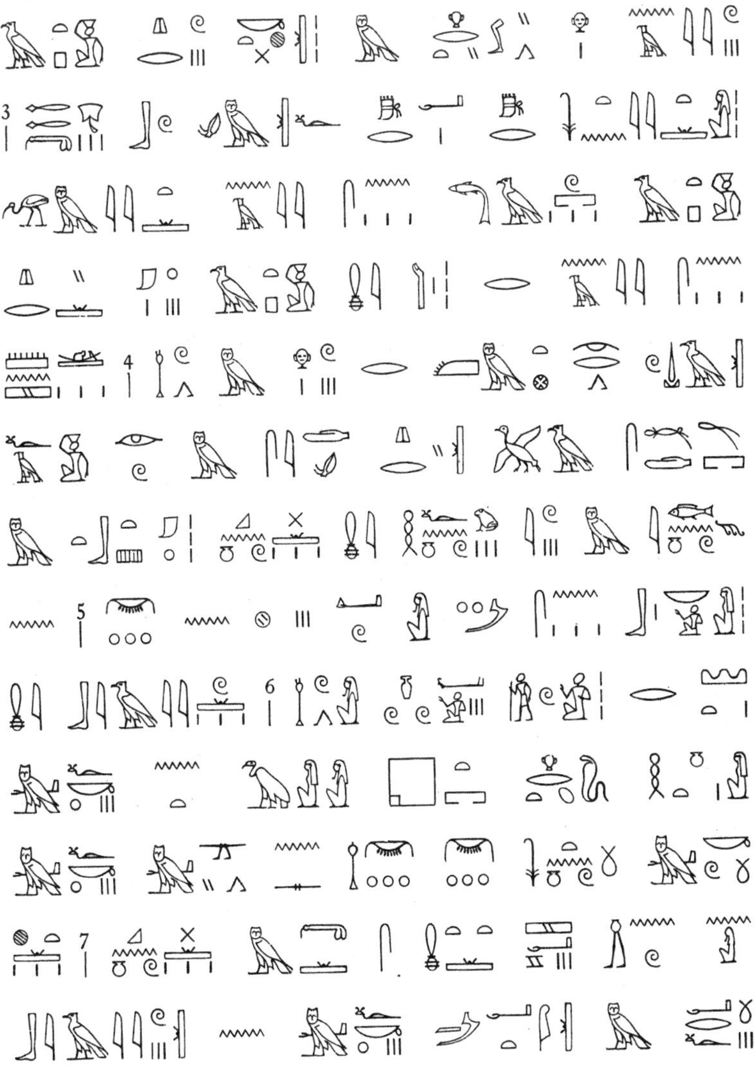

atep χeru keteχ em ḥerti ḥer nai-u 3. *āaāaiu bu setem-f t'er-ā t'er sutenit qemit* 3
nai-sen χau atep χeri χemt atep mȧ t'ebā er nai-sen menš 4. *utu em ḥrȧu* 4
er Qemt sper ut'a fa ȧru em Sȧṭen χeri pa sešeṭ em tebt χemt qennu mȧ
ḥefennu ȧu em ȧnnu en 5. *nub en sep χemt ṭāu-ȧ maa-sen bu-nebu mȧ bȧaiu* 5
6. *utu-ȧ ābuu seru er set māfek ent mut-ȧ Ḥet-ḥert ḥent māfek māsi-nes* 6
ḥet' nub sutennu māku χet 7. *qennu embaḥ-s mȧtet šā ȧnu-nȧ bȧaiu en* 7
māfek maāt em āref

8 *āśt māsi embaḥ-ȧ bu petrȧ-u ān* 8. *t'er sutenit ȧri-ȧ seruṭ ta t'er-f*
9 *em mennu ḥer aχaχ ṭāu-ȧ ḥems reχit em nai-u qubu ṭāu-ȧ śemi* 9. *ta*
set nu Ta-merȧ iut-s seuseχ-θ er ȧuset mer-nes ȧn teha-set kaiu bu-
10 *nebu ḥer uat ṭāu-ȧ ḥems māśa ent ḥetrȧ* 10. *em rek-ȧ Śaireṭana*
11 *Qeheq em nai-sen ṭemȧut st'er qa en atiu ȧn nu ḥeri ȧn seki* 11. *en*
Keś χerui en Χare pet-u χāāu-u śaremā em χennu rā-u ȧu-sen sau
teχu

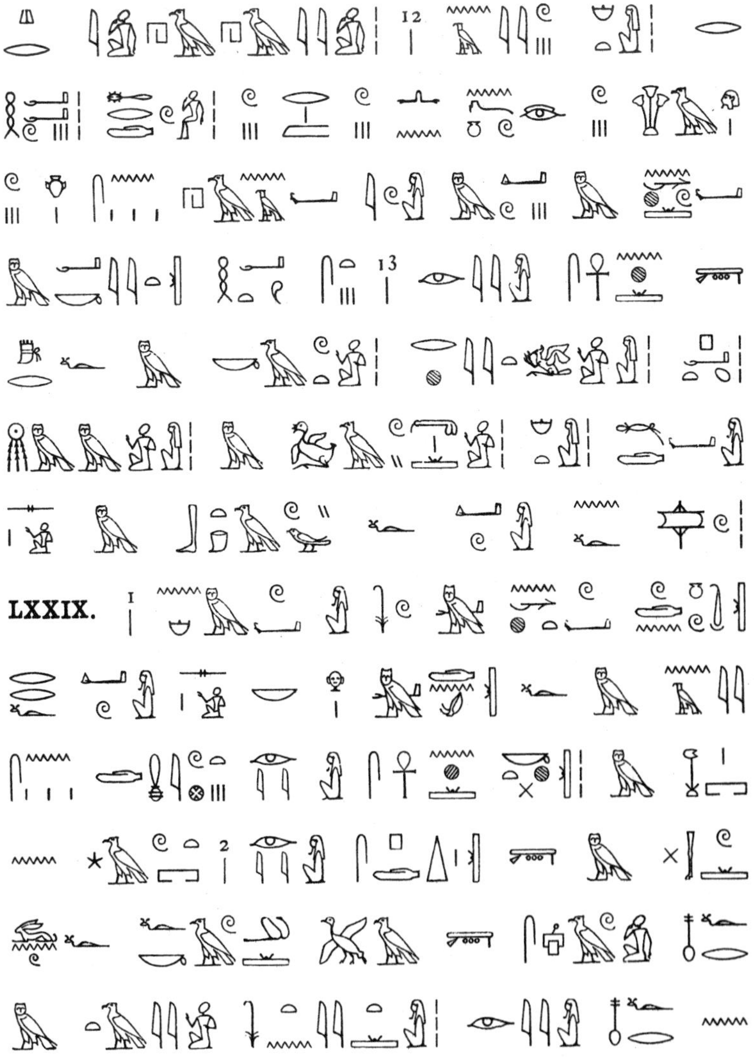

χer ȧhahai 12. *nai-u ḥemt er ḥāāu χarṭu-u er-ḳes-u ȧn ennu-u ḥa-u* 12
ȧb-sen hana ȧu-ȧ emmā-u em neχtu mākit ḥāt-set 13. *ȧri-ȧ seānχ ta* 13
t'er-f em kaut reχit pāt ḥamemu em t'aui ḥemt sešeṭ-ȧ sa em betaui-f ṭāu-ȧ-
nef nefu **LXXIX.** — 1. *neḥemu-ȧ su mā neχtu uṭennu err-ef ṭāu-ȧ* 1
sa neb ḥer māṭen-f em nai-sen ṭemȧut ȧri-ȧ seānχ keteχ em χa en sebaut
2. *ȧri-ȧ sepṭ ta em nemu unu-f fekau pa ta sau nefer em tai-ȧ sutenit ȧri-ȧ* 2
nefer en

3 *na neteru mȧ na reθ* 3. *ȧn-nȧ ent neb mā bu-nebu ȧri-ȧ sutenit ḥer ṭep ta em*
4 *(Ḥeq) taui ȧu-ten em ḥenu χer reṭiu-ȧ ȧn θek šašat ȧu-ten* 4. *nefertu ḥer ȧb-ȧ mȧ*
χut-ten meḥi-ten em nai-ȧ utut nai-ȧ ťeṭeṭet petrȧ ḥetep-ȧ em Ȧḳert mȧ ȧtef-ȧ Rā
5 5. *ṣ̌ebennu-ȧ paut neteru āat em pet ta ṭuat smen Ȧmen-Rā sa-ȧ er ȧuset-ȧ sešep-f*
6 *ȧaut-ȧ em ḥetep em (Ḥeq) taui seneťem ḥer ȧuset* 6. *Ḥeru em neb taiu χnem-*
nef em atf mȧ Tatenen (Rā-user-maāt-setep-en-Ȧmen) ānχ uťa senb sa-ȧ
7 *sems en Rā utet-su ťesef (Rā-meses-ḥeq-maāt-Ȧmen-meri) ānχ uťa senb* 7. *sifi*

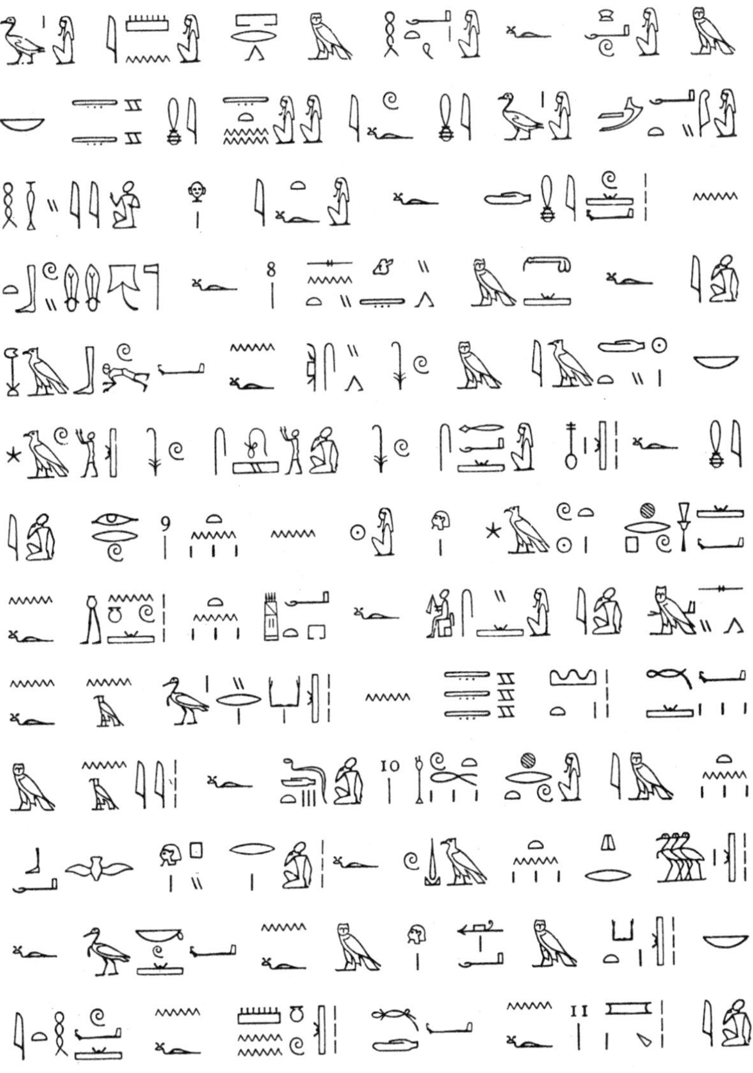

sa Ȧmen per em ḥāt-f χāāu em neb taui mȧ Tatenen ȧuf mȧ sa Maāti
ḥesi ḥer ȧtf-f ṭemȧu en tebui-f 8. *senti ta embaḥ-f ȧ χabu-nef śesi su* 8
em ȧaṭti neb ṭuau-su seuaś-su seāa-ȧ neferu-f mȧ ȧ ȧru- 9. *ten en Rā* 9
ṭep ṭuaut χerpu-nef ȧnnu-ten āt-f śepsi ȧ māsi-nef na baireka en
taiu set meḥ em nai-f ťeṭet 10. *utut χertu-ȧ ȧm-ten bā ṭepi-re-f uťa-* 10
ten χer baiu-f baku-nef em ṭep uā em kat neb ȧtḥu-nef mennu seśeṭ-nef
11. *meru ȧ* 11

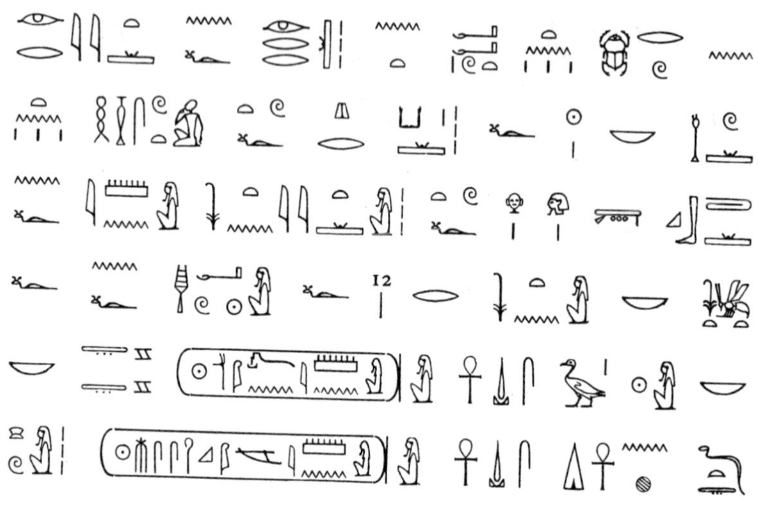

ȧrit-nef ȧrru ent āāut-ten χeperu en ten ḥestu-tuf χer kau-f hru neb utu-nef
12 *Ȧmen sutenit-tuf ḥer ṭep ta qeb-f nef āḥāu-f* 12. *er suten neb suten net neb taui* (*Rā-user-maāt-setep-en-Ȧmen*) *ānχ uṫa senb sa Rā neb χāu* (*Rā-meses-ḥeq-maāt-meri-Ȧmen*) *ānχ uṫa senb ṭā ānχ ṫetta*

THE STELE OF PI-ĀNKHI-MERI-ȦMEN.

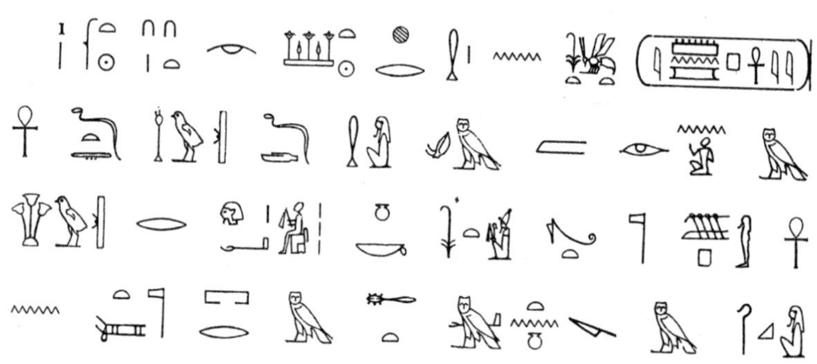

1 1. *Renpit ṫaut uā ȧbeṭ uā ṡat χer ḥen en suten net* (or *bȧt*) (*Ȧmen-meri P-ānχi*) *ānχ ṫetta utu ṫeṭ ḥen setem em ȧri-nȧ em ḥau er ṭepāu nuk suten tȧt neter seṡep ānχ en Tem per em χat mātennu em ḥeq*

senṭ-nef seru er-f . . . . . . 2. sa en mut-f ȧu-f er ḥeq em suḥt neter nefer neteru 2
meri sa Rā ȧrit em āāui-f (Ȧmen-meri P-ānχi) iu-entu er ťeṭ en ḥen-f ȧu un
ser en ȧmentet ḥā ur em Neter Tafneχθ em sept . . . . em Ḥeseb-ka em Ḥāp
em . . . . . . 3. em Ān em Per-nub em Ḥeť-ȧneb θet-nef ȧmentet em mȧqeṭ-f em 3
peḥiuu er θet-taui χent em māśa āśt taui ṭemṭ em χet-f ḥāu ḥequ ḥet (?) em θesem
em sau reṭui-f ȧn χetem en sebtet-[sen] 4. sept nu resu Mertem Per-(Rā-χerp(?)- 4
χeper) Neter-ḥet-sebak Per-māťa θekanś ṭemȧt nebt en ȧmentet seśes-sen āa

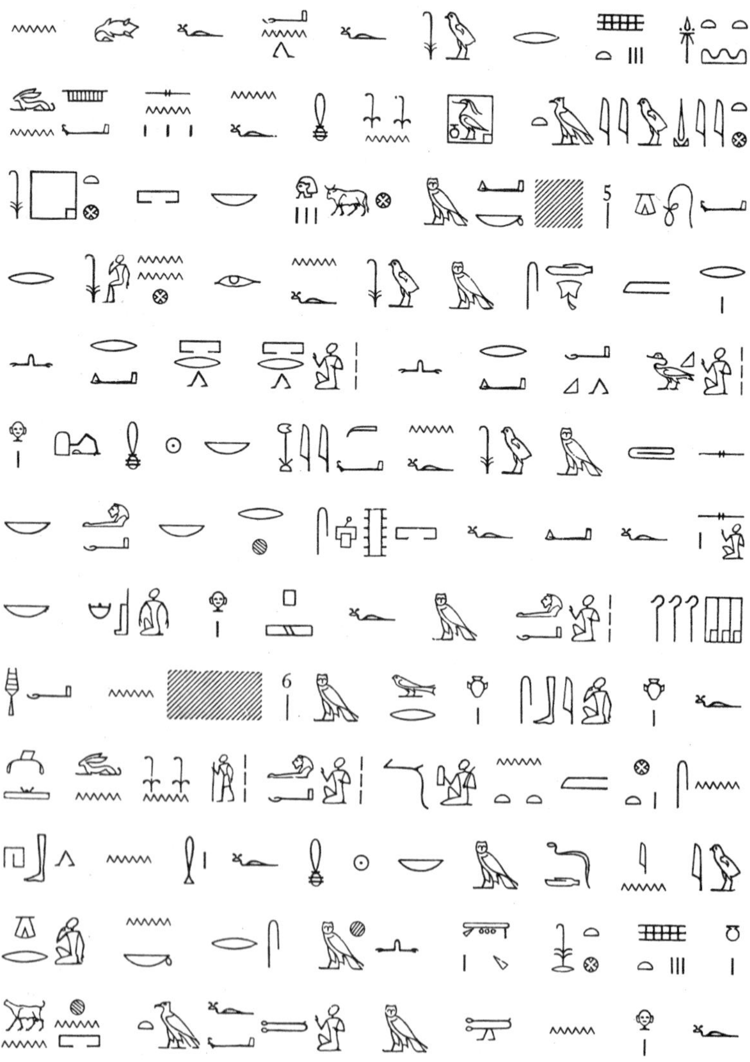

en senṭ-f ān-f su er sept ȧbtet un-sen nef mȧ enen Ḥet-bennu Taiuťait Suten-
5 *ḥet Per-neb-ṭep-ȧḥet māk* 5. *ḳua er Suten-ḥenen* (or *Ḥenen-su*) *ȧri-nef su*
em seṭ em re ȧn erṭā per peru ȧn erṭā āq āqu ḥer āba mȧ hru neb χai-nef
6 *su em rer-s neb ḥā neb reχ sa-f ṭā-f sa neb ḥems ḥer peś-f em ḥāu ḥequ ḥeṭu* (?)
āḥā en . . . . . . 6. *em ur ȧb sebȧ ȧb-f āu un enen seru ḥāu mer māśa entet*
em nut-sen hab en ḥen-f mȧ hru neb em ťeṭ ȧn ȧu ḳer-nek er es χem ta rest
sept nu Ťenχen Tafneχθ em θet en ḥrȧ-f

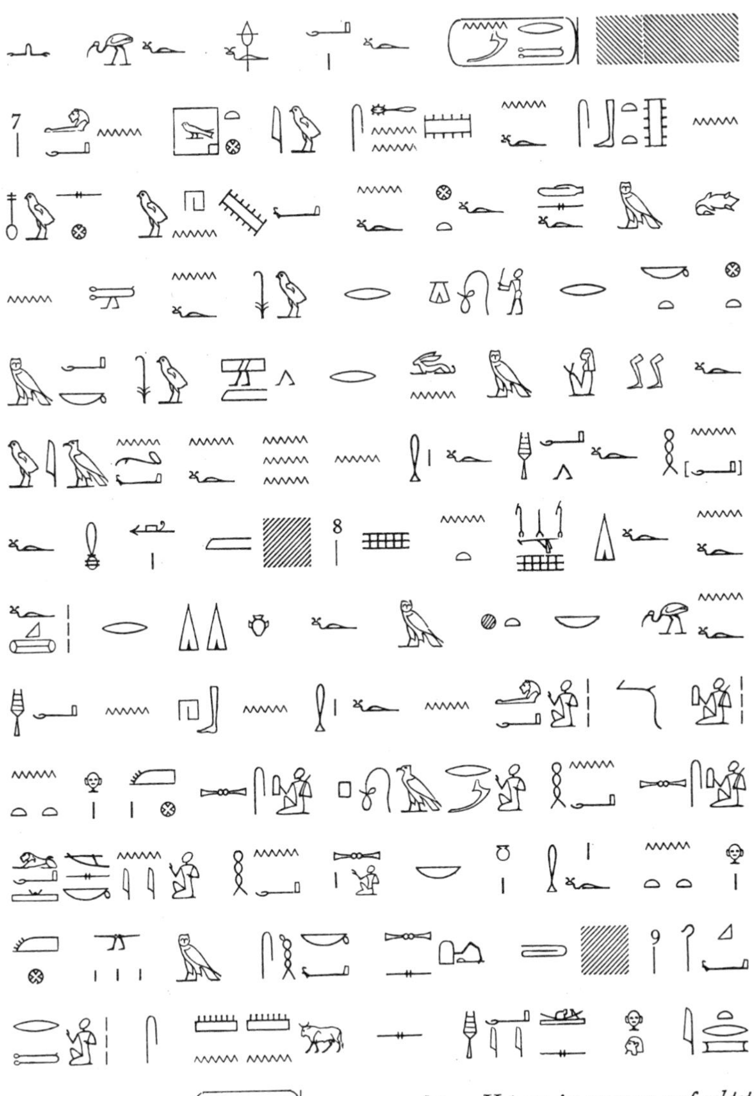

ȧn qem-f χesef ā-f (*Nemareθ*) . . . . 7. *ḥā en Ḥet-ur ȧu seχanen-nef sebtet* 7
en Neferus uhen-nef nut-f ṭesef em senṭ en θet-nef su er ḳua er ket nut māk su
šem er un em sau reṭui-f uȧan-nef mu en ḥen-f āḥā-f ḥen[ā]-f mȧ uā em . . . .
8. *sept ent Uab ṭā-f-nef fequ er ṭāṭā ȧb-f em χet neb qem-nef āḥā en hab en* 8
ḥen-f en ḥāu meru māša entet ḥer Qemt θes Puarma ḥenā θes Rā-mersekni
ḥenā θes neb nu ḥen-f entet ḥer Qemt seb em sek θes āba rer . . . . . . 9. *ḥeq* 9
reθ-s menmen-s āḥāi-s ḥer ṭep ȧter

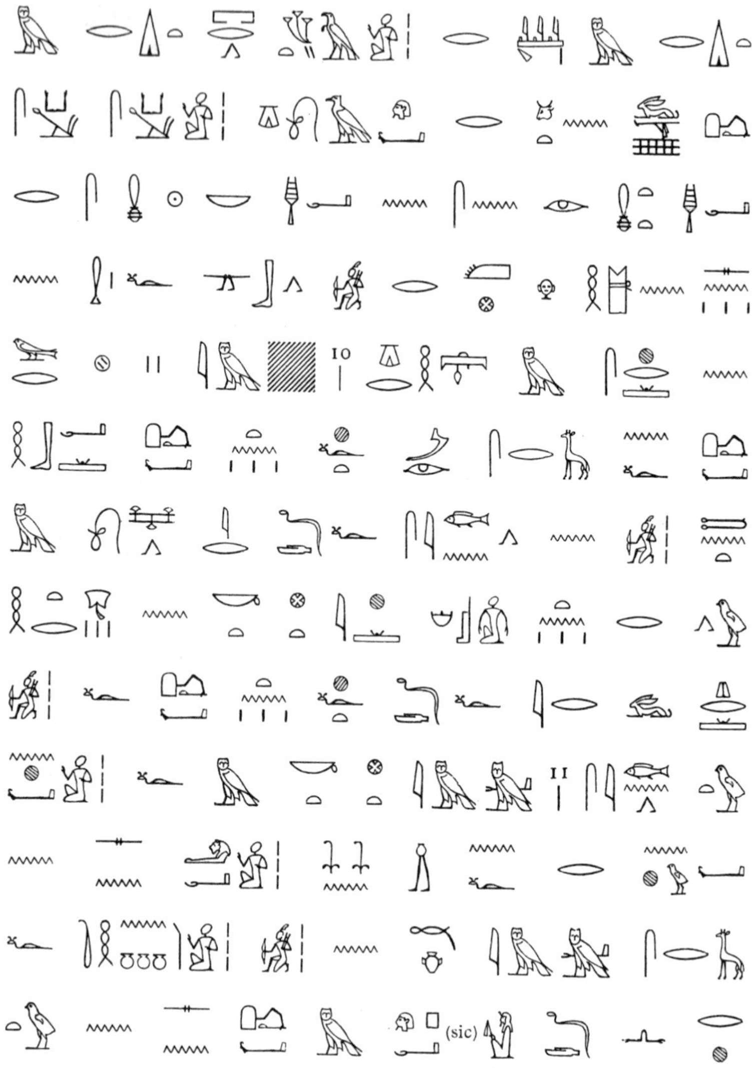

em erṭāt per ḥentiu er seχet em erṭāt seka sekau ḳua er χent en Un āba er-es
mȧ hru neb āḥā-en-sen ȧri mȧtet āḥā en ḥen-f seb māśa er Qemt ḥer ḥen-sen
10 *ur sep sen ȧm . . . . . .* 10. *ḳerḥ em seχer en ḥebā āba-ten χeft maa ser-nef āba*
em ua ȧr ťeṭ-f sȧn en māśa θent ḥetrȧ en ket nut ȧχ ḥems-ten er iu māśa-f
11 *āba-ten χeft ťeṭ-f ȧr un χer neχu-f em ket nut ȧmmā* 11. *sȧn-tu-en-sen ḥāu*
enen ȧn-nef er neχu-f θeḥennu māśa en meḥ ȧb ȧmmā ser-tu-en-sen āba
em ṭepāu ťeṭ ȧn reχ-

n āś-nef em seneh māśa neḥeb qennu ṭep en ȧḥ-k 12. *ȧ ȧrit sek em āba* 12
reχ-nek Ȧmen pa neter utu-n ȧr sper-θen er χennu en Uast χeft en Ȧpt
āq-θen em mu āb-θen em ȧter unχ-θen em ṭep śarem pet sefeχ āba em
ābā 13. *ser em neb peḥtpeḥt ȧn un peḥtpeḥt en θer em χem-f ȧri-f sau* 13
ā em neχt ā ȧu āśt ṭā sa en ānṭiu ȧu uā θet-f sa χa net-ten em mu nu
χau-f sen-ten ta χeft-f ťeṭ- 14. *ten nef ȧmmā en-n uat āba-n em χaibit* 14
χepeś-k ťamu

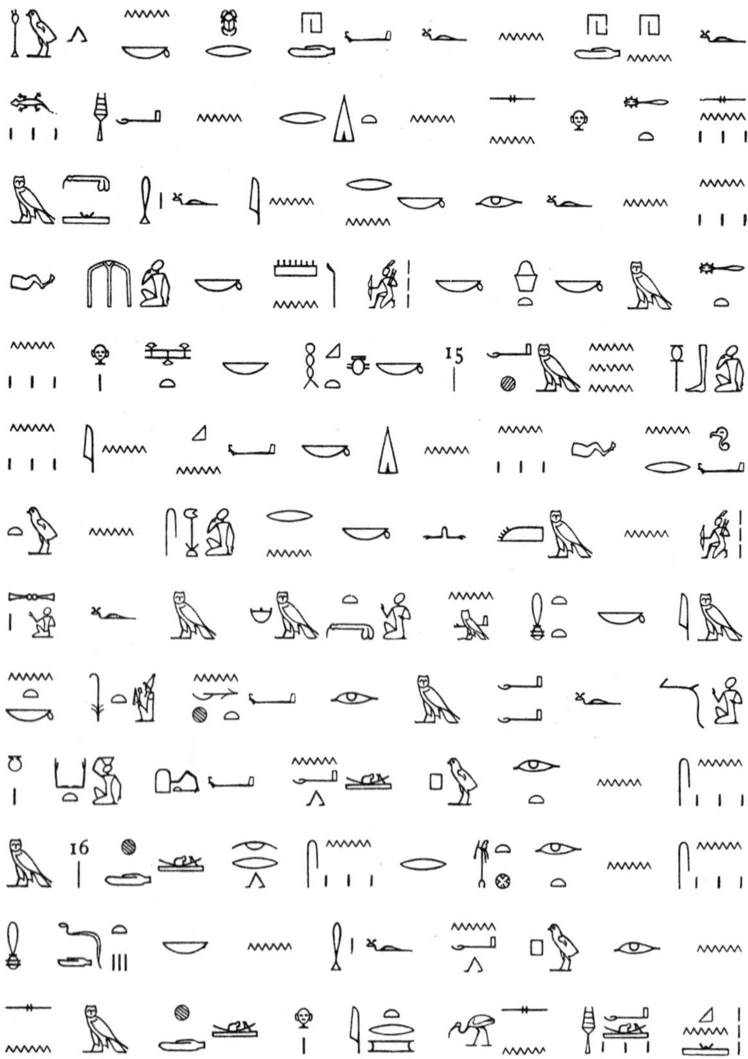

*utu-nek χeper heṭ-f en heṭhen-f āšt āḥā en erṭāt-en-sen ḥer χat-sen embaḥ
ḥen-f ȧn ren-k ȧri-f-en-n χepeš seḥi-k men māša-k ṭat-k em χat-n ḥer uat*
15 *neb ḥeqt-k* 15. *āχem ȧb-n ȧn qen-k ṭā-en-n χepeš nerȧ-tu en seχa ren-k
ȧn qem en māša θes-f em ḥemt nimā mȧtet-k ȧm entek suten neχt ȧri*
16 *em āāui-f mer nu kat āba nā pu ȧrit-en-sen em* 16. *χeṭ sper-sen er Uast
ȧrit-en-sen mȧ t̆eṭet neb en ḥen-f nā pu ȧri-en-sen em χeṭ ḥer ȧter qem-sen
āḥāu qenu*

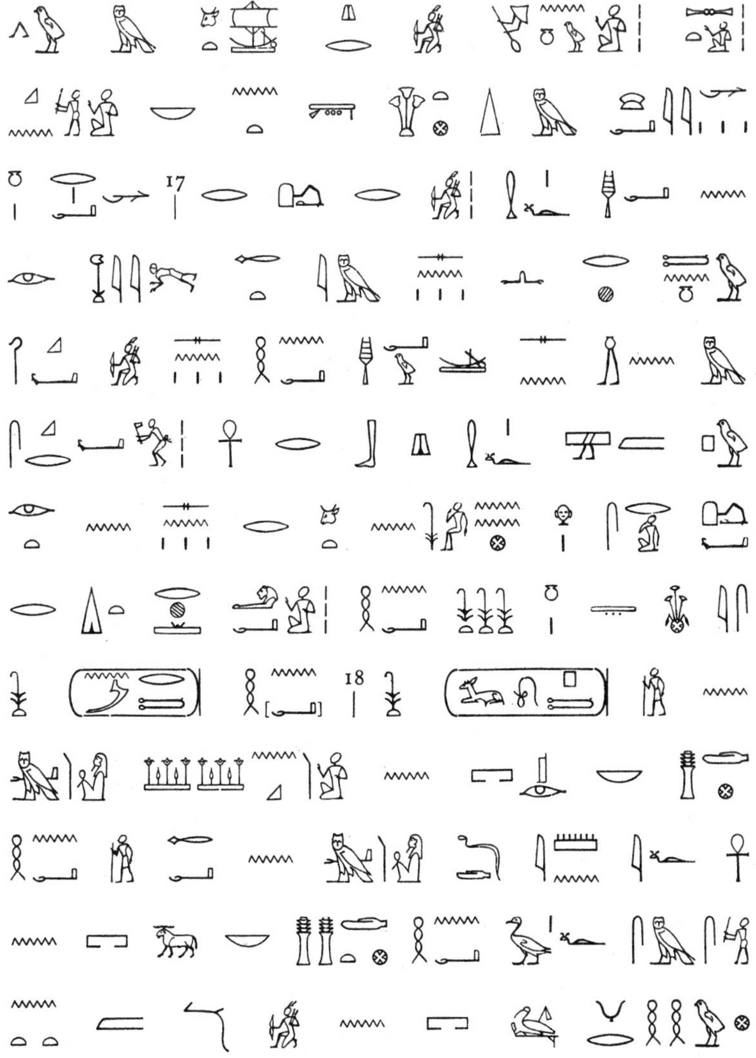

iu em χent χer māśa χennu θest qen neb ent ta meḥt sepṭ em χāāi nu
rā 17. *er āba er māśa ḥen-f āḥā en ȧri χai āat ȧm-sen ȧn reχ θennu* 17
ḥeq māśa-sen ḥenā āḥāu-sen ȧn em seqeru ānχ er bu χer ḥen-f śem pu
ȧrit-en-sen er χent en Suten-ḥenen ḥer ser āba er ṭāt reχ ḥāu ḥenā suteniu
nu ta resu ȧs suten (*Nemareθ*) *ḥen[ā]* 18. *suten* (*Āuuapeθ*) *ser en Māśuāś* 18
Śaśānq en Per-Ȧusȧr-neb-Ṭeṭṭeṭ ḥenā ser āa en Māśuāś T̓eṭ-Ȧmen-ȧf-ānχ en
Per-ba-neb-Ṭeṭṭeṭ ḥenā sa-f sems entet em mer māśa en Per-Tehuti-ȧp-reḥḥu

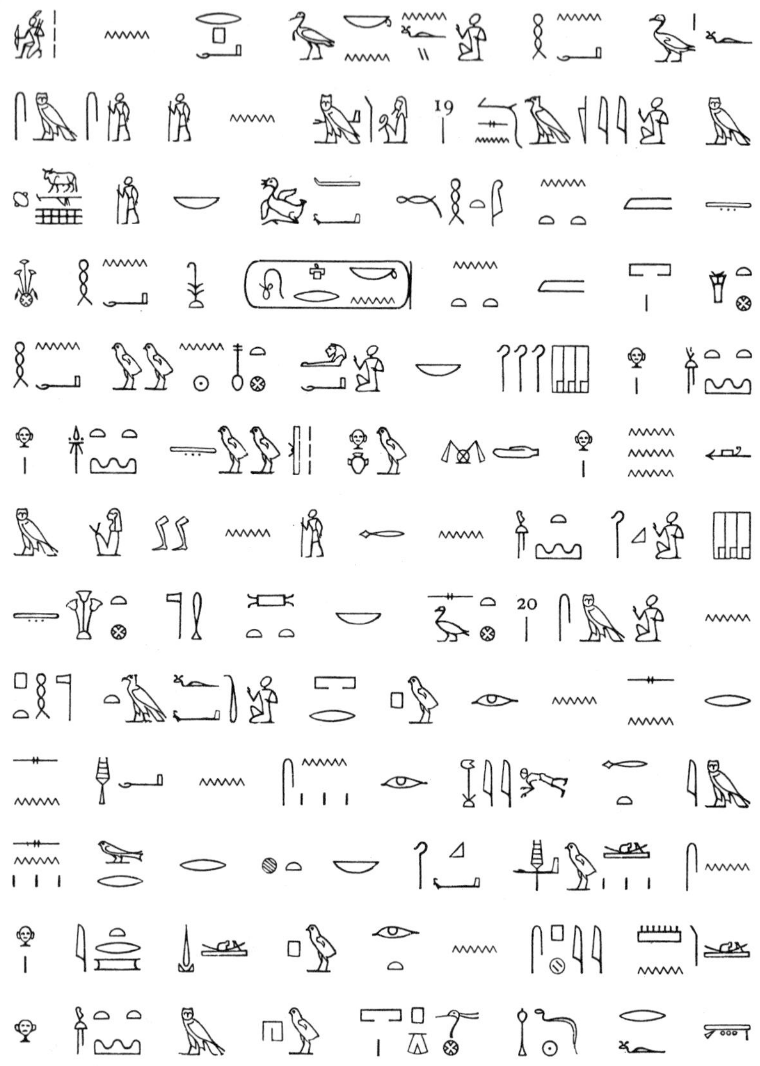

19 *māša en erpā Baken-nefi ḥenā sa-f sems ser en Māšuāš* 19. *Nesnaqṭi em Ḥeseb-ka ser neb ťa meḥet entet em ta resu ḥenā suten* (*Uasarken*) *entet em Per-Bast ḥenā Uu-en-Rā-nefert ḥā neb ḥequ ḥetu* (?) *ḥer àmentet ḥer àbtet tauu ḥer-àbu ṭemṭ ḥer mu uā em sau reṭui en ser āa en Àment ḥeq ḥetu ta*
20 *meḥt neter ḥen Netet neb Sat* 20. *sem en Ptaḥ Tafneχtθ per pu àri-en-sen er sen āḥā en sen àri χai āat àm-sen ur er χet neb ḥeq āḥāu-sen ḥer àter ťa pu àrit en sepi men ḥer àmentet em hu Per-peḳa ḥeť eref ta*

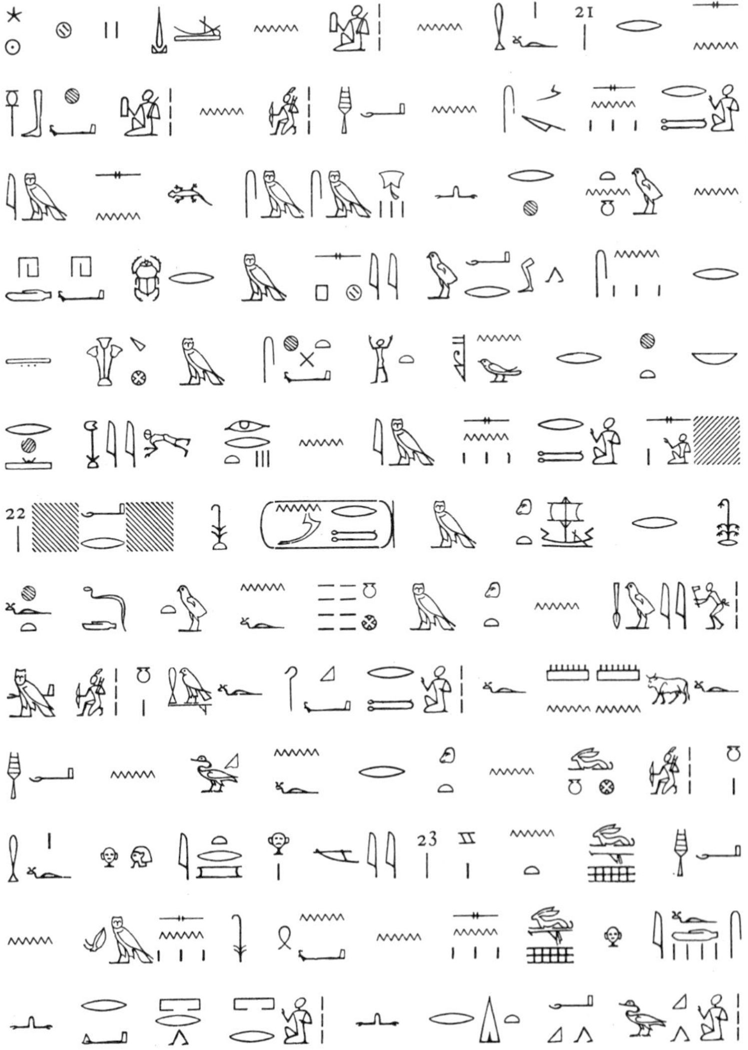

ṭuat sep sen ťa en menfitu en ḥen-f 21. *er-sen àbeχ menfitu en menfitu āḥā* 21
en sma-sen reθ àm-sen āś semsem àn reχ tennu en heṭeh χeper em sepi
uār-sen er ta meḥ em seχet qat qesen er χet neb reχ χai àrit en àm-sen reθ
sa . . . . . 22. . . . . *ār* . . . . *suten Nemareθ em χent er resu χeft ťeṭ-tu nef* 22
Χemennu em χent en χerui mā menfitu nu ḥen-f ḥeq reθ-f menmen-f āḥā en
āq-nef er χent en Unnu menfitu nu ḥen-f ḥer ṭep àter ḥer meri 23. *ent Un āḥā* 23
en setem-sen su śen-en-sen Un ḥer àfṭ-s àn ertā per peru àn erṭāt āq āqu

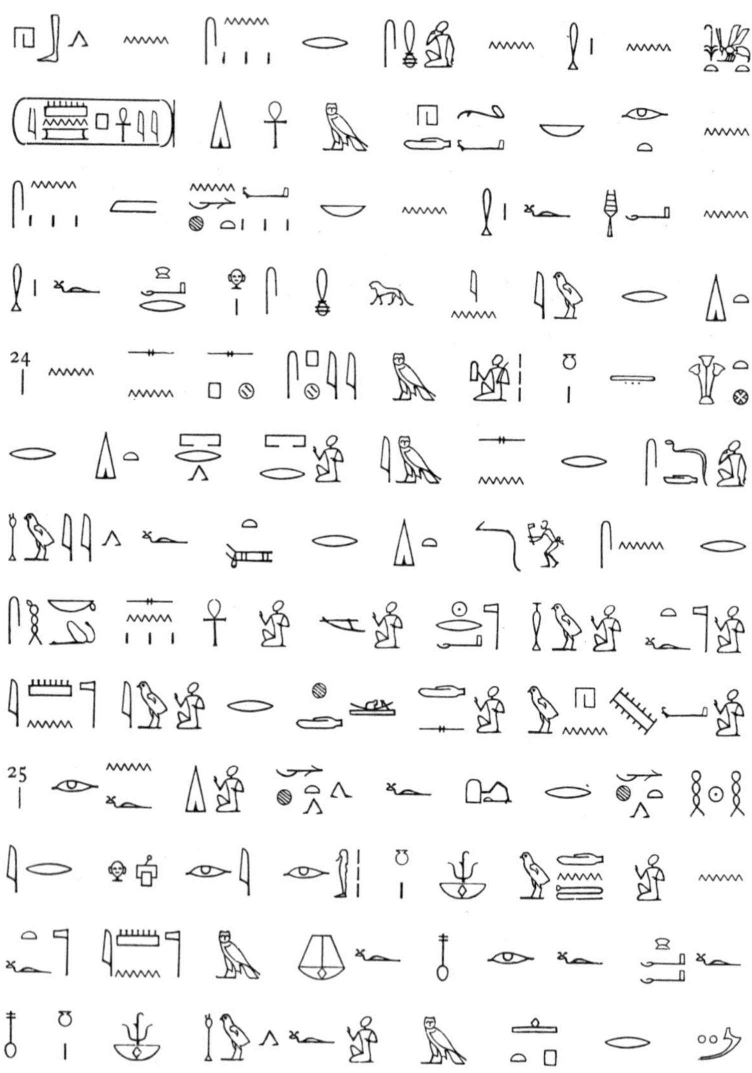

heb-en-sen er smȧ en ḥen en suten net (or *bȧt*) *Ȧmen-meri P-ānχi ṭā ānχ em*
heṭ neb ȧrit-en-sen em neχt neb en ḥen-f āḥā en ḥen-f χār ḥer-s mȧ ābu ȧn
24 *ȧu erṭāt-* 24. *en-sen sep sepi em menfitu nu ta meḥt er ṭāt per per ȧm-sen*
er seṭeṭ utui-f tem er ṭāt mer-sen er sek-sen ānχ-ȧ mer-ȧ Rā ḥesu-ȧ tef-ȧ
25 *Ȧmen ȧu-ȧ er χeṭ ṭes-ȧ uhen-ȧ* 25. *ȧri-nef ṭā-ȧ χet-f āba er χet ḥeḥ ȧr*
ḥer-sa ȧri-ȧ ȧru nu ȧp-renpit uṭen-ȧ en tef Ȧmen em ḥeb-f nefer ȧri-f
χāā-f nefer nu ȧp-renpit utu-f-ȧ em ḥetep er maa

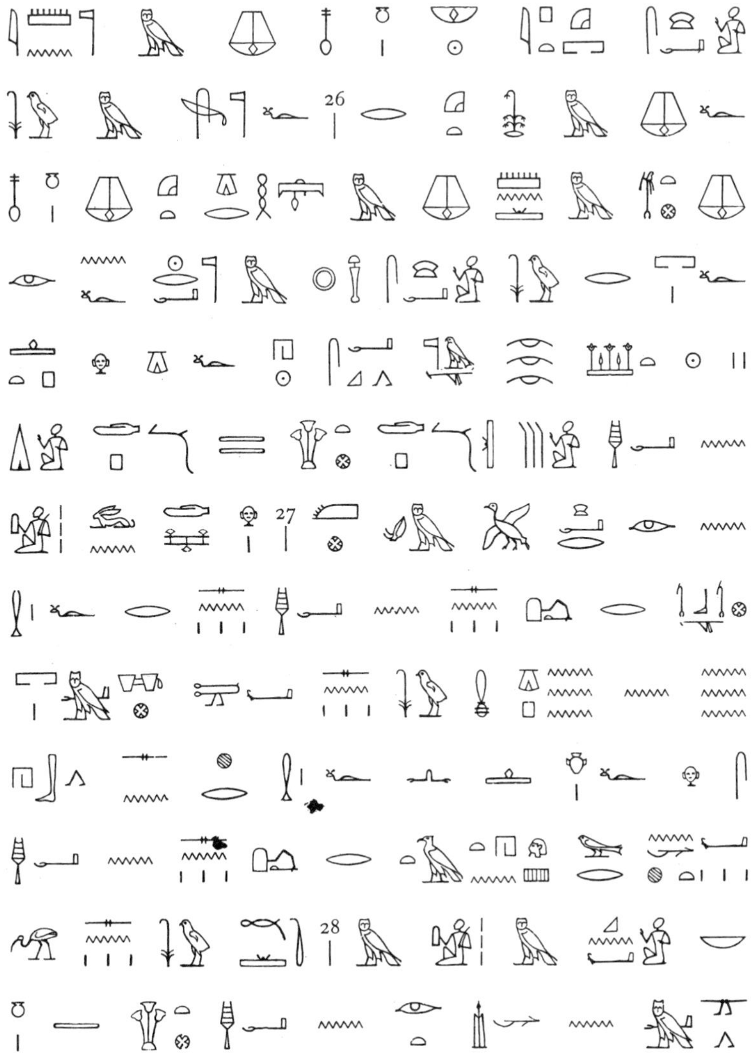

Àmen em ḥeb nefer nu ḥeb Àpt seχā-à su em sem-f 26. *er Àpt resu em ḥeb-f* 26
nefer nu ḥeb Àpt ḳerḥ em ḥeb men em Uast ḥeb àri-nef Rā em sep ṭep seχā-à
su er per-f ḥetep ḥer nest-f hru seāq neter àbeṭ χemet šat hru sen ṭā-à ṭep taui
meḥt ṭep ṭebā-à āḥā en menfitu un ṭi ḥer 27. *Qemt setem pa χār àri-en-ḥen-f* 27
er-sen āḥā-en-sen āba er Uaseb Per-māṭet θet-sen su mà ḳep en mu heb-sen
χer ḥen-f àn ḥetep àb-s ḥer-s āḥā-en-sen āba er Tatehen ur neχt qem-sen su
meḥ-θ 28. *em menfitu em qen neb nu ta meḥt āḥā en àrit àn* (?) *en māseb* 28

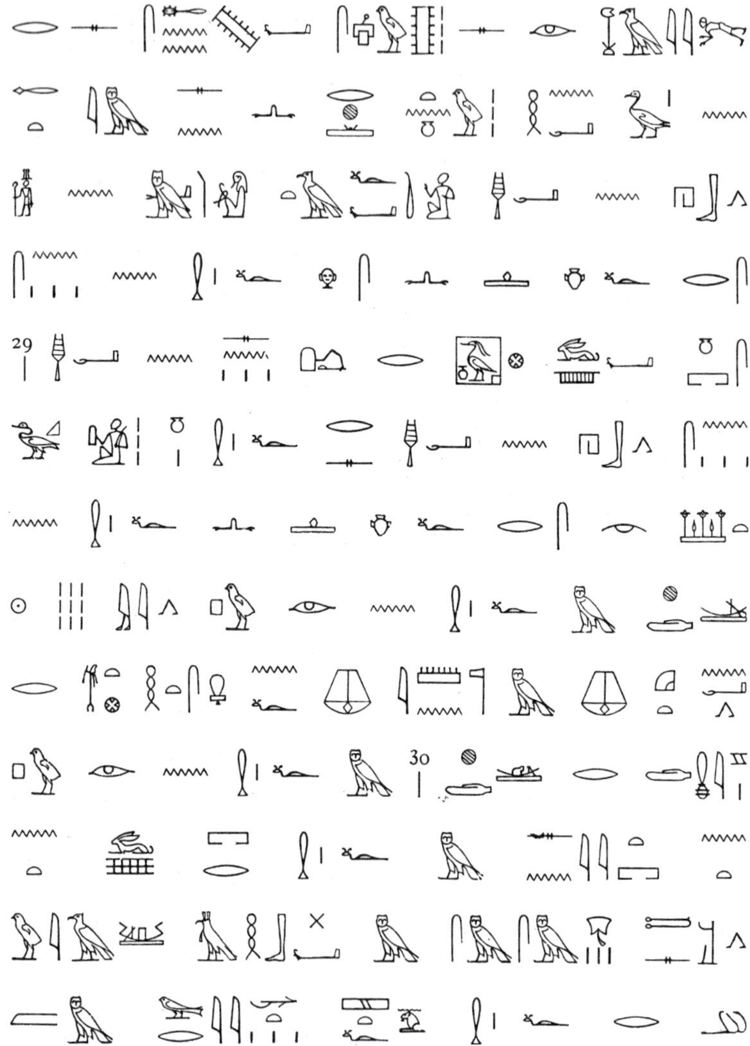

er-es seχanen sau-s àri χai āat àm-sen àn reχ tennu ḥnā sa en ser en Mā
29 *[šuaš] Tafneχtθ āḥā en heb-sen en ḥen-f ḥer-s àn ḥetep àb-f er-es* 29. *āḥā-en-sen āba er Ḥet-bennu un χen-s āq menfitu nu ḥen-f er-es āḥā en heb-sen en ḥen-f àn ḥetep àb-f er-es àbeṭ [uā] šat hru paut i pu àri en ḥen-f em χeṭ*
30 *er Uast ḥetes-nef ḥeb Àmen em ḥeb Àpet nā pu àri en ḥen-f em* 30. *χeṭ er ṭemà ent Un per ḥen-f em senit ent uàa neḥeb em semsem θes emem urit šeft ḥen-f er peḥ*

Satet ȧb neb χer seṭ-f āḥā en ḥen-f per em χaā er 31. *mesṭeṭu-f χāār* 31
eres mȧ ābi ȧn ȧu men en āba-ten enen uťefa uȧp-ȧ ȧn trȧt ḥetes peḥiu
ṭāṭā senṭet-ȧ em ta meḥ ȧri-en-sen seχet qat qesen em ḥu ȧrit-f-nef ȧm er
ȧmentet res Χemennu ḳua er-es 32. *mȧ hru neb ȧrit θereri er ḥebs sebti* 32
θes bak er seχi satetiu ḥer satet χaāā ḥer χaā ānnu ḥer sma reθ ȧm-sen mȧ
hru neb χeper en hru χemet ȧu Unnu seḥuua-s en fent ḳa em 33. *χenem-s* 33
āḥā en Unnu erṭāt su ḥer χat-s senemeḥ χeft en

[lacuna of 16 lines]

net (bȧt) ȧpu per h[a] χer χet neb nefer maa nub āat neb śeps ḥebsu em śens (?)
χāā un ḥer ṭep-f ȧārāt ṭāṭā śeft-f ȧn ȧb en hru āś ḥer se[n]emmeḥ en urer-f
34 *āḥā en erṭāt iu* 34. *ḥemt-f suten ḥemt suten sat Nes-θent-meḥ er senemmeḥ*
en suten ḥemt suten ȧpt suten sat suten sent erṭāt-en-s ḥer χat-s em per ḥemt
χeft en suten ḥemt māȧ-[t]en nȧ suten ḥemt suten sat suten sent seḥetep-ten
51 *Ḥeru nebt āḥāt ur baiu-f āau maāχeru-f ȧmmā* . . . . 51. *em-k nemā*
52 *semtu sep sen nemā ȧr sem-tu nemā semtu* . . . . 52. *nek uat en ānχ ȧn ȧu-*
53 *ȧ seḥi em śeser un-nȧ* . . . . . 53. *reset em*

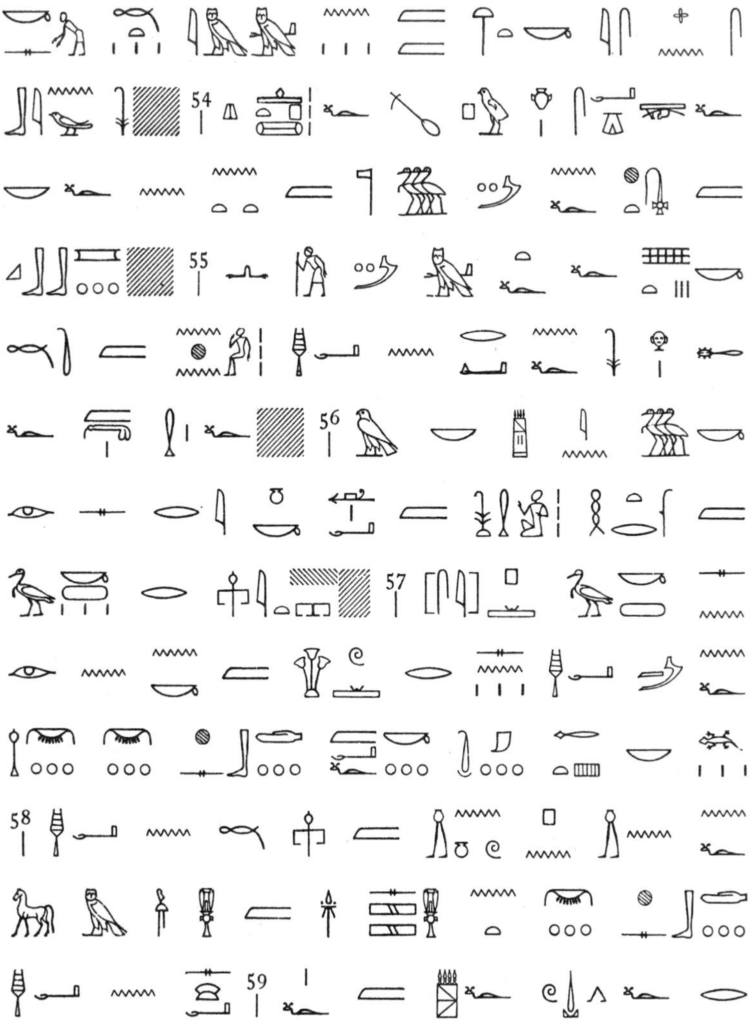

kes meḥt åmmā-n emem χaibet-k ås un-s bån su . . . . . . 54. *χer ḥetep-f* 54
ḥem pu åb sāḳ-f neb-f en entet em neter baiu maa-nef χet em qebeb . . . . .
55. *ån åau maa tef-f sept-k meḥθ em neχenu āḥā en erṭā-nef su ḥer χat-f* 55
embaḥ ḥen-f . . . . . . 56. *Ḥeru neb āḥāt ån baiu-k åri-s er-å nuk uā em* 56
suten ḥenu ḥetrå em bak er per-ḥet̄ . . . . . 57. . . *[så]p bak-sen åri-nå-nek* 57
em ḥau er sen āḥā maā-nef ḥet̄ nub χesbeṭ māfek χemt āat neb āś 58. *āḥā* 58
en meḥ per-ḥet̄ em ånnu pen ån-nef semsem em unemi seśeś em åbt seśeś ent
nub χesbeṭ āḥā en sχāā 59. *-f em āḥāt-f ut̄a-f er* 59

per Teḥuti neb Χemennu sma-nef ȧua unṭu apṭ en tef Teḥuti neb Χemennu
60 *χemennu em Per χemennu* 60. *un ȧn menfitu nu Un ḥer nehem χennu ťeṭ-sen*
61 *neferu Ḥeru ḥetep em* 61. *nut-f sa Rā P-ānχi ȧri-k en-n ḥebs mȧ χu-k Un uťa*
62 *pu ȧri en ḥen-f er* 62. *per en suten Nemareθ śem-nef āt neb ent suten per peru-*
63 *ḥeť-f uťa-f er ṭāt-nef sta-entu* 63. *nef suten ḥemt suten sat un ȧn-sen suaś*
64 *ḥen-f em χet ḥemt ȧn ťa en ḥen-f ḥrȧ-f er* 64. *sen uťa pu ȧri en ḥen-f er*
65 *ȧḥ nu semsem uťa en neferu maa-nef* 65. *seḥeqer-sen ťeṭ-f ānχ-ȧ meri-ȧ Rā*

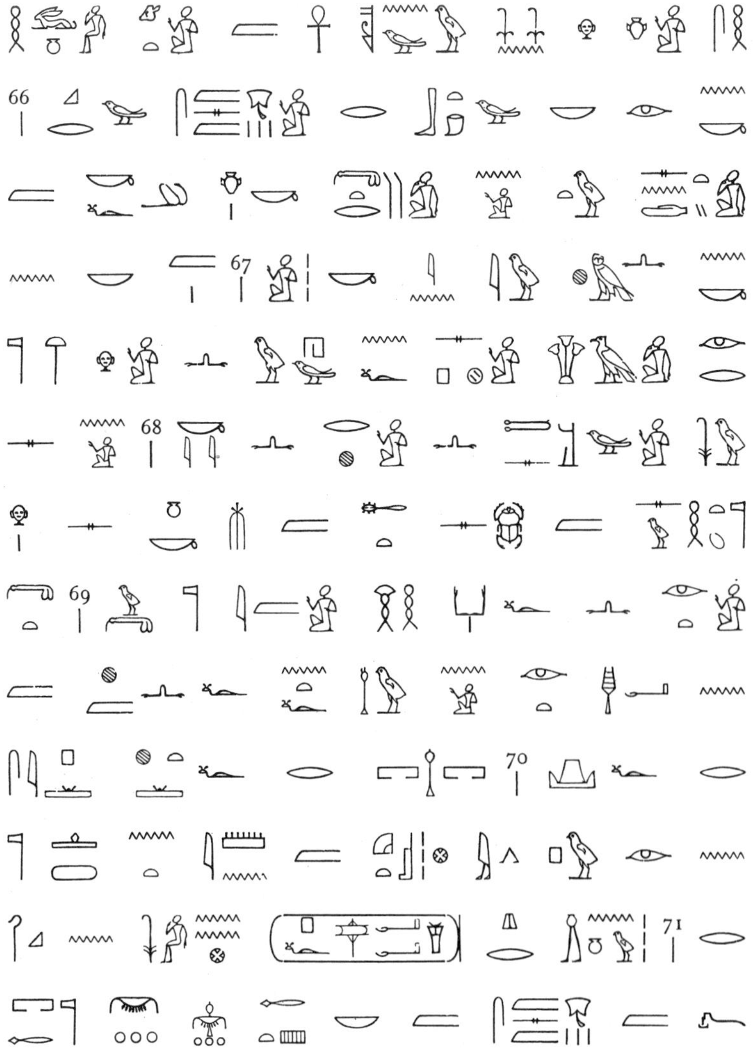

ḥunnu fent-å em ānχ qesenu enen ḥer åb-å seḥe- 66. *-qer semsemu-å er* 66
beta neb åri-nek em kef åb-k meter-nå-tu senṭit en neb ḳes 67. *ret-k ån* 67
åu χem-nek neter χaibit ḥer-å ån uh-nef sep-å ḥa åri-s-nå 68. *ki ån reχ-å* 68
ån θes-å su ḥer-s nuk mes em χat s-χeper em suḥt met- 69. *u neter åm-å uaḥ* 69
ka-f ån årit-å em χem-f entef utu-nå årit āḥā en såp χet-f er peru-ḥeṭ
70. *šent-f er neter ḥetep ent Åmen-em-Åpt i pu åri en ḥeq en Suten-ḥenen* 70
Pef-āā-Bast χer ånnu 71. *er per-āa nub ḥeṭ āat neb em semsem em setep* 71

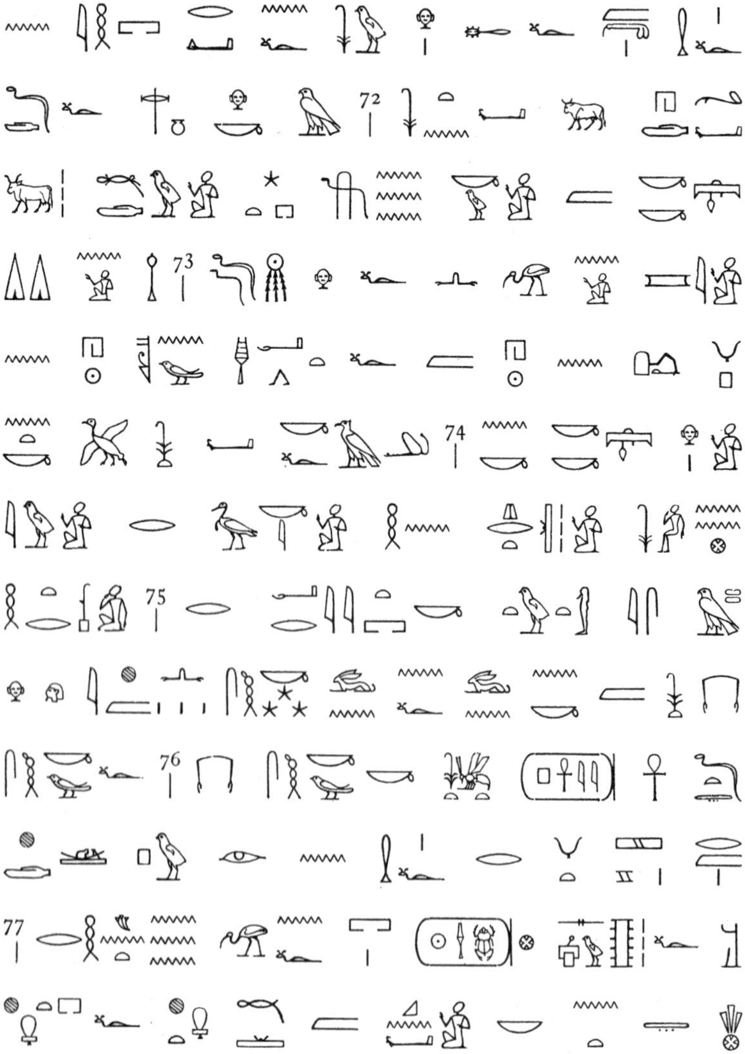

72 *en ȧḥ erṭā-nef su ḥer χat-f embaḥ ḥen-f t̕eṭ-f net̕ ḥrȧ-k Ḥeru* 72. *suten neχt*
73 *ka heṭ kauit seśeṭu-ȧ ṭuat met̕-kuȧ em kek ṭāṭā-nȧ* 73. *ḥet̕et̕ ḥer-f ȧn qem-nȧ*
74 *mer-ȧ en hru qesen āḥāt-f em hru en āba ȧp entek pa suten neχt kefa-* 74. *nek*
75 *kek ḥer-ȧ ȧu-ȧ er bakȧ ḥen χert-ȧ Suten-ḥenen ḥetrȧ* 75. *er ārit-k tut ȧs*
76 *Ḥeru-χuti ḥer ṭep ȧχemu seku un-nef un-nek em suten ȧn sek-f* 76. *ȧn sek-k*
77 *suten net* (or *bȧt*) *P-ānχi ānχ t̕etta χeṭ pu ȧri en ḥen-f er ȧp śe er ḳes* 77. *Reḥent*
qem-nef Per Χerp-χeper-Rā sau-f θes χetem-f χetem meḥ em qen neb ent ta meḥ

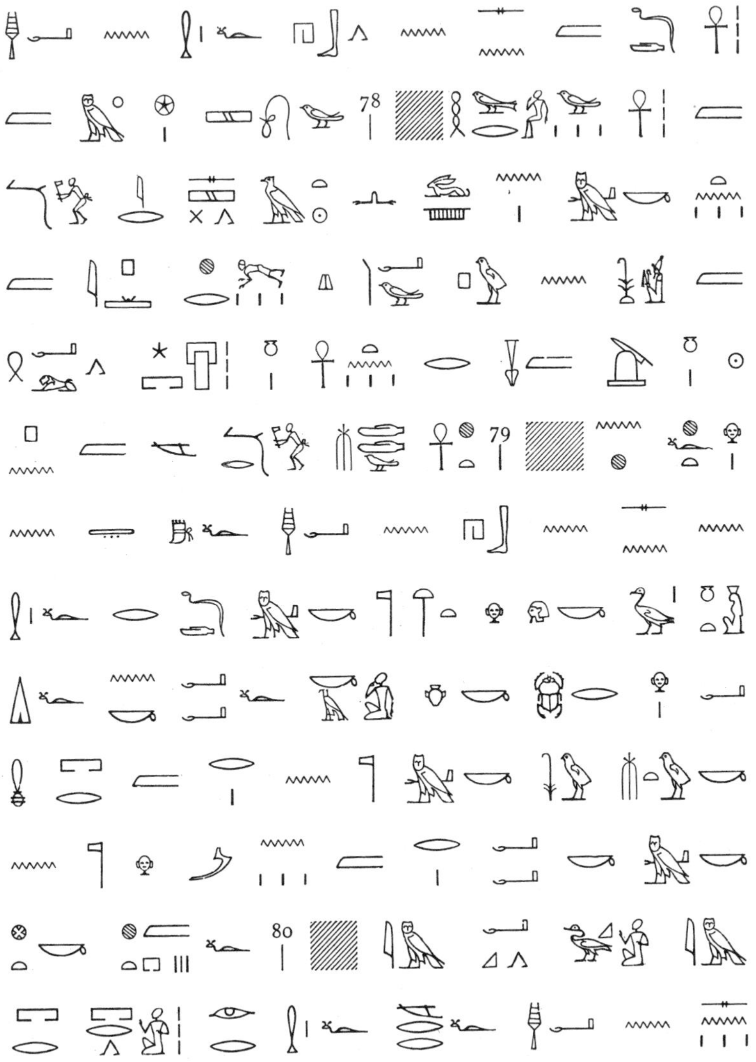

āḥā en ḥen-f heb-en-sen em ťeṭ ānχu em mit (?) . . . . . *śua* 78. . . . . . *ḥuru* 78
ānχu em mer ȧr seś at ȧn un-nȧ māk-ten em ȧp χer χerāā (?) *pu en suten*
em Śenār sebau nu ānχ-ten er sam nemmat nu hru pen em mer mer mesṭeṭ
ānχet 79. . . . . . *nχ χeft en ta ťer-f āḥā en heb-en-sen en ḥen-f er ťeṭ māk* 79
neter χaibit ḥer ṭep-k sa Nut ṭā-f-nek āāui-f ka ȧb-k χeper ḥer ā mȧ per
em re en neter māk su mestu-k en neter ḥer maa-n em re āāui-k māk nut-k
χetem-f 80. . . . . . *ȧm āq āq ȧm per peru ȧri ḥen-f merer-f āḥā-en-sen* 80

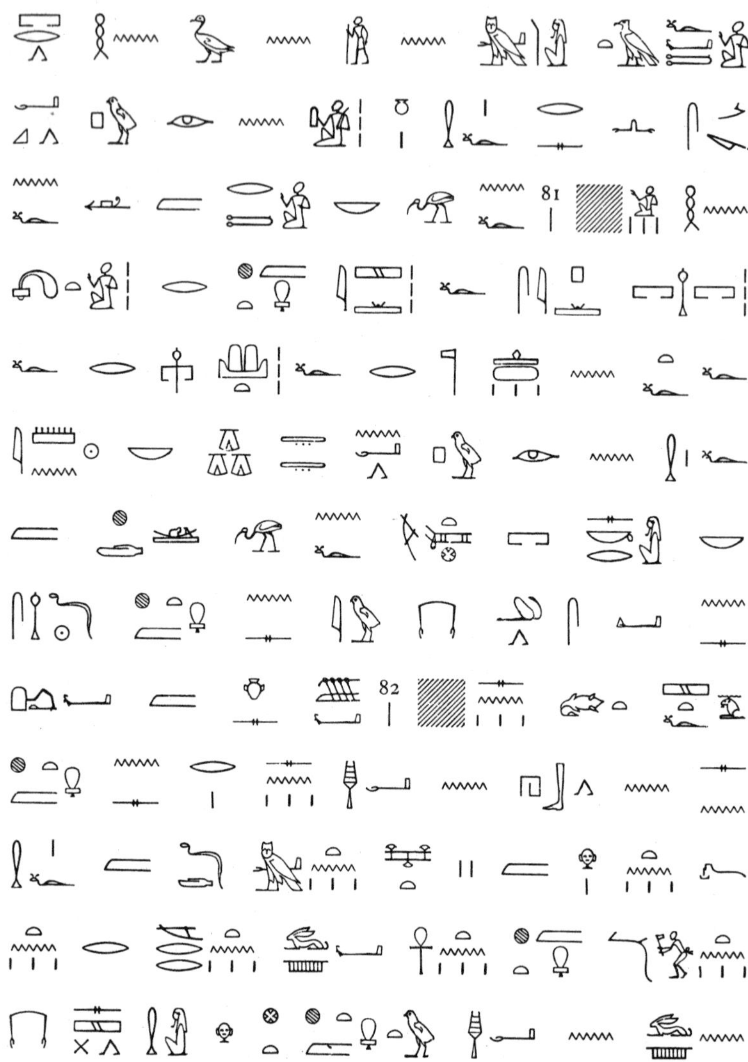

per ḥen sa en ser en Mā[šuaš] Tafneχtθ āq pu ȧri en menfitu nu ḥen-f er-es
81 *ȧn sma-nef uā em reθ neb qem-nef* 81. . . . . . *ḥen netu er χetem ȧš-f sȧp*
peru-ḥet-f er per-ḥeṭ šent-f er neter ḥetepu en tef-f Ȧmen-Rā neb nest taiu nā
pu ȧri en ḥen-f em χeṭ qem-nef Mertem Per-Seker neb seḥeṭ χetem-nes ȧu
82 *ȧn peḥ-s ṭā-nes āba em ȧb-s sešep* 82. . . . . . *sen senṭet šeft χetem-nes re-*
sen āḥā en heb-en-sen ḥen-f em ṭeṭ mā-ten uat sen em ḥrȧ-ten setep-ten er
merer-ten un ānχ-ten χetem mer-ten ȧn seš ḥen-ȧ ḥer nut χetemtu āḥā-en-un-

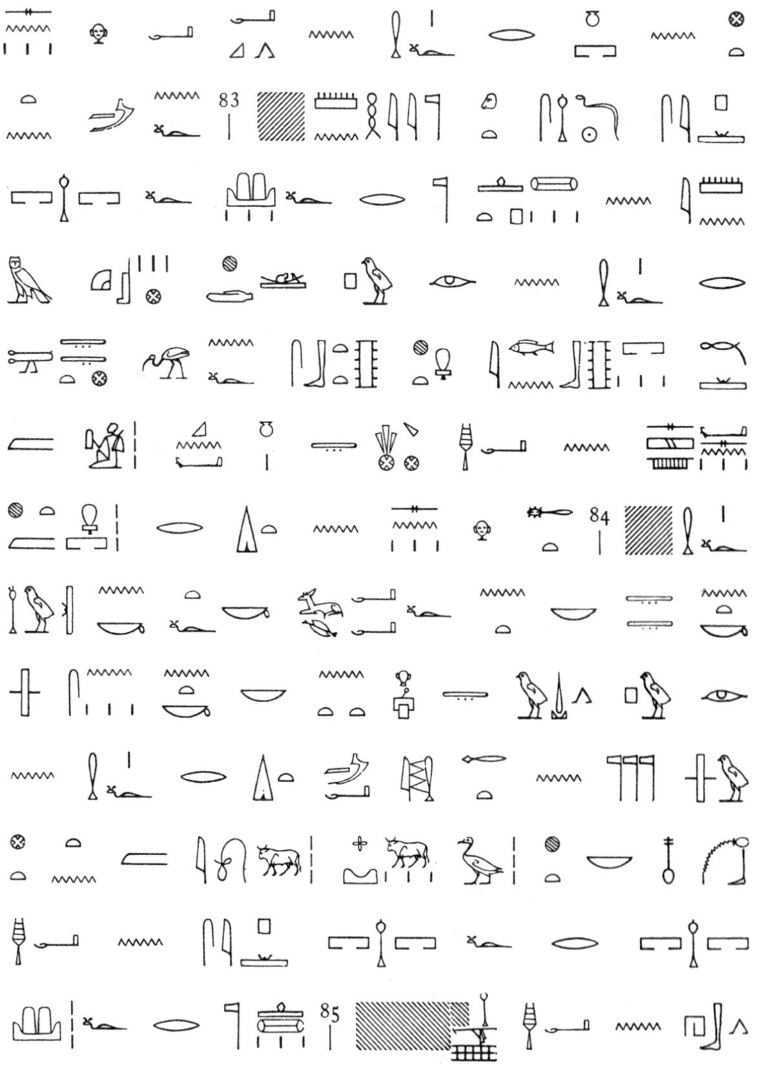

sen ḥer ā āq en ḥen-f er χennu en nut-ten maā-nef 83. . . . . . *Menḥi χent* 83
seḥet' sȧp peru-ḥet'-f šent-f er neter ḥetepu en Ȧmen-em-ȧpt χeṭ pu ȧri en ḥen-f
er Θettauit qem-nef sebtet χetem ȧnebu meḥ em menfitu qen nu Ta meḥ āḥā en
seš-sen χetem er-ṭāt-en-sen ḥer χat 84. *[sen]* . . . . . . *ḥen-f utu-nek tef-k āuāā-f* 84
ent neb taui entek ȧm-sen entek neb entet ḥer-sa ta ut'a pu ȧri en ḥen-f erṭāt
maā āb āat en neteru ȧmu nut ten em ȧua unṭu apt χet neb nefer āb āḥā en
sȧp peru-ḥet'-f er peru-ḥet' šent-f er neter ḥetepu 85. . . . . . *Ȧneb-ḥet' āḥā en heb-* 85

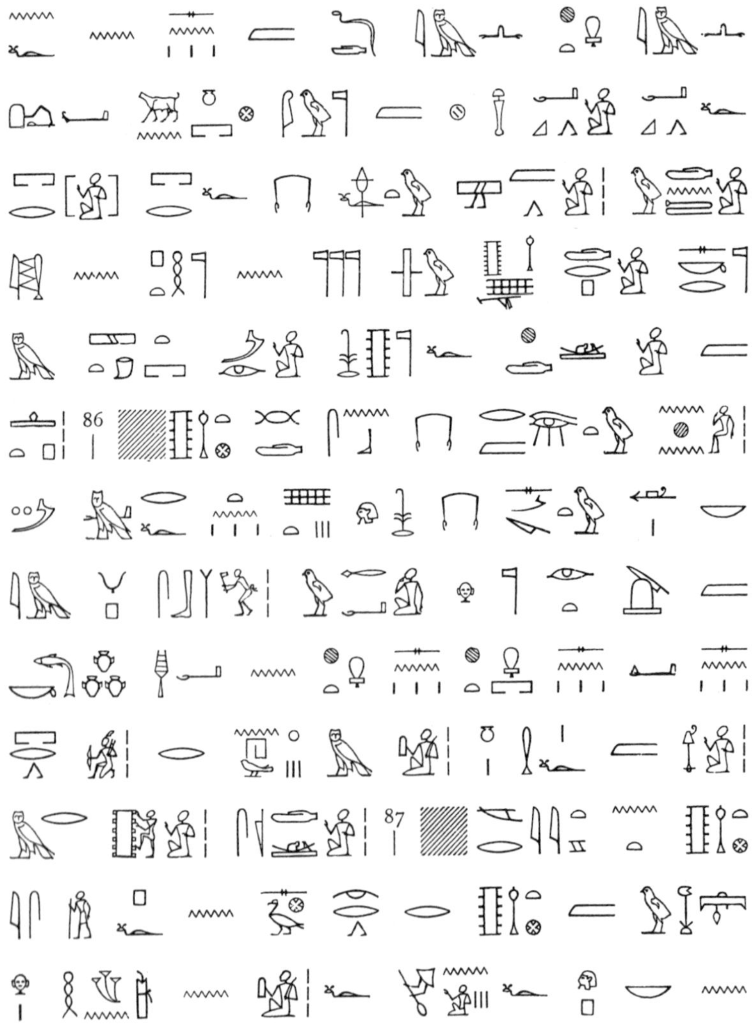

nef en sen em t̓eṭ ȧm χetem ȧm āba χennu Ś u em sep ṭep āq-ȧ āq-f per-[ȧ]
per-f ȧn χeseftu śemu uṭen-ȧ āb en Ptaḥ en neteru ȧmu Ȧneb-ḥet̓ ṭerp-ȧ
86 *Seker em śetat maa-ȧ ȧneb-resu-f χeṭ-ȧ em ḥetep* 86. . . . . . *Ȧneb-ḥet̓ āṭ*
senb ȧn rem-tu neχenu maa mā ref-ten sept ṭep res ȧn smatu uā neb ȧm
ȧp sebȧu uāā ḥer neter ȧrit nemmat em χak ȧbu āḥā en χetem-sen χetem-
sen ṭā-sen per menfitu er neh em menfitu nu ḥen-f em ḥemu mer qeṭ seqeṭu
87 87. . . . . *merit ent Ȧneb-ḥet̓et ȧs ser pef en Sa sper er Ȧneb-ḥet̓et em uχa*
ḥer ḥen en menfitu-f χennu-f ṭep neb en

menfitu-f [ṭem]t reθ 8000 ḥer ḥen en sen ur sep sen māk Men-nefer meḥ em menfitu em ṭep neb nu ta meḥt pert [?] beṭet per neb šent ḥer nemesmes χāi neb nu 88. . . . . . sebtet qeṭ θesem ur em ȧrit en ḥemt er χet ȧter em rer ȧbtet 88
ȧn qemtu āba ȧm meťet ṭi meḥ em ȧua peru-ḥeť āper em χet neb ḥeť nub χemt ḥebs neter senθrȧ āšen seft šem-ȧ ṭā-ȧ χet en seru meḥ un-ȧ en-sen sept-sen χeper-ȧ em 89. . . . . hru er i-ȧ ḥems pu ȧri-nef ḥer semsem ȧn neḥti- 89
nef uri-f χeṭ pu ȧri-nef em senṭ en ḥen-f ḥeť ta er-f ṭua sep sen sper ḥen-f er Ȧneb-ḥeťet menȧ-

90 *nef ḥer meḥt-s qem-nef mu ār er sau āḥāu menȧ er* 90. *[merit ent] Men-nefer*
āḥā en ḥen-f maa-s em neχt sebtet χi em qeṭ nemau θesemu āper em neχt ȧn
qemtu uat ent āba er-es un ȧn sa neb ḥer t̀eṭ re-f em menfitu nu ḥen-f em
91 *ṭep-reθ neb en āba sa neb ḥer t̀eṭ ȧmmā ḳuaa-n* 91. . . . . . . *māk menfitu-s*
āš neb χet ḥer t̀eṭ ȧri sta er-es seχi-n sa er-es sau-s seneḥ-n bak seāḥā-n
χetu ȧri-n ḥetau em t̀eru er-es pešt-n su em enen er ḳes-s neb em θerθer
92 *ḥenā* 92. . . . . . . *ḥer meḥt-s er*

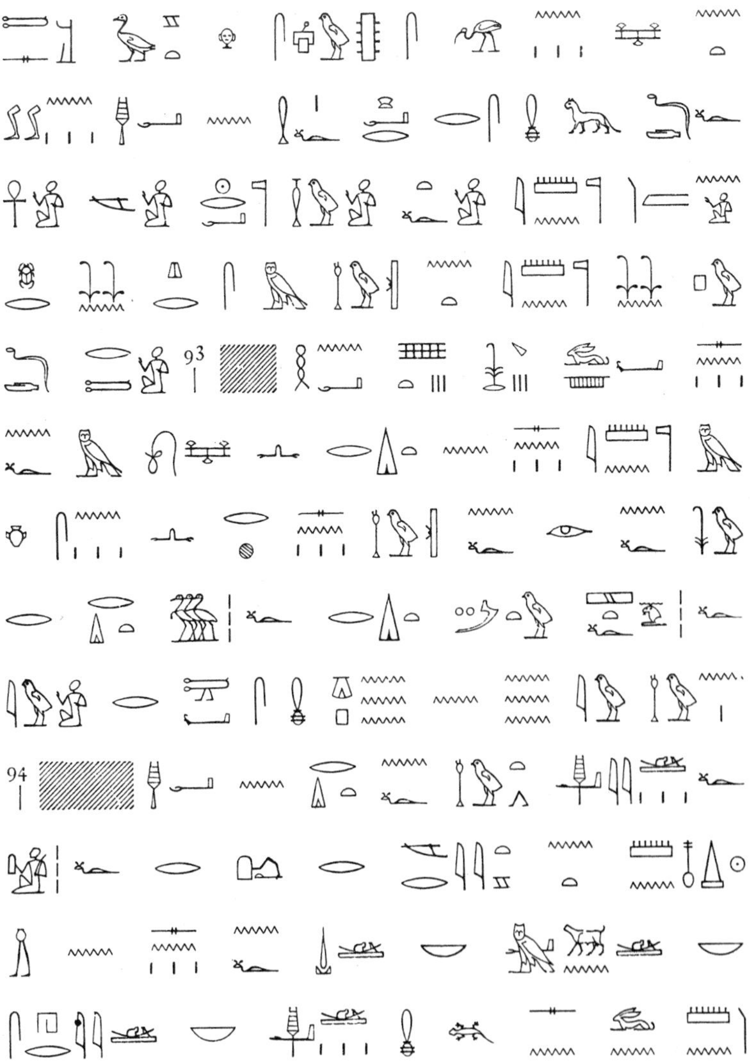

θes sat ḥer sau-s qem-n ua ent reθ-n āḥā en ḥen-f χār er-es mȧ ȧbu ťeṭ-f
ānχ-ȧ mer-ȧ Rā ḥesu-ȧ tef-ȧ Ȧmen qem-nȧ χeper enen χer-s em utu ent
Ȧmen enen pu ťeṭ reθ 93. . . . . *ḥnā sept reset un-sen nef em ua ȧn erṭāt* 93
en sen Ȧmen em ȧb-sen ȧn reχ-sen utu-nef ȧri-nef su er erṭāt baiu-f erṭāt
maatu śefit-f ȧu-ȧ er θet-s mȧ ḳep en mu ȧu utu-nȧ 94. . . . . *āḥā en* 94
erṭāt-nef utut āḥāi-f menfitu-f er āba er merit ent Mennefer ȧn en-sen nef
ťa neb māχen neb seheri neb āḥāu mȧ āś-sen un menȧ

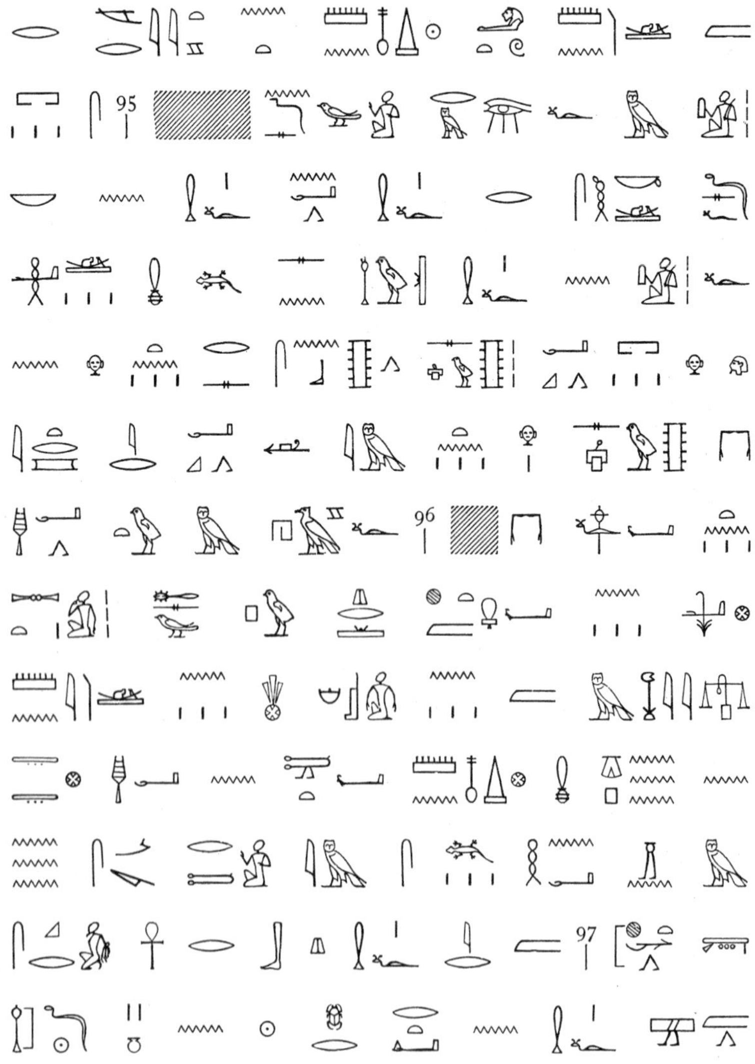

95 *er merit ent Mennefer ḥātu menȧ em peru-s* 95. . . . . *neťes rem-f em men-*
fitu neb en ḥen-f nā ḥen-f er sek ťesef āḥāu mȧ āś-sen utu ḥen-f en menfitu-f
en ḥrȧ-ten er-es senb sau āq peru ḥer ṭep ȧter ȧr āq uā ȧm-ten ḥer sau ȧn
96 *āḥā-tu em ha-f* 96. . . . . . . *ȧn χesef-ten θest χas pu χer χetem-n qemā*
menȧ-n meḥt ḥems-n em māχai taui āḥā en θet Mennefer mȧ ḳep en mu
97 *sma reθ ȧm-s āś ḥnā ȧn em seqer ānχ er bu χer ḥen-f ȧr em* 97. *[χet ta*
ḥeť] sen en hru χeper erṭāt en ḥen-f śem

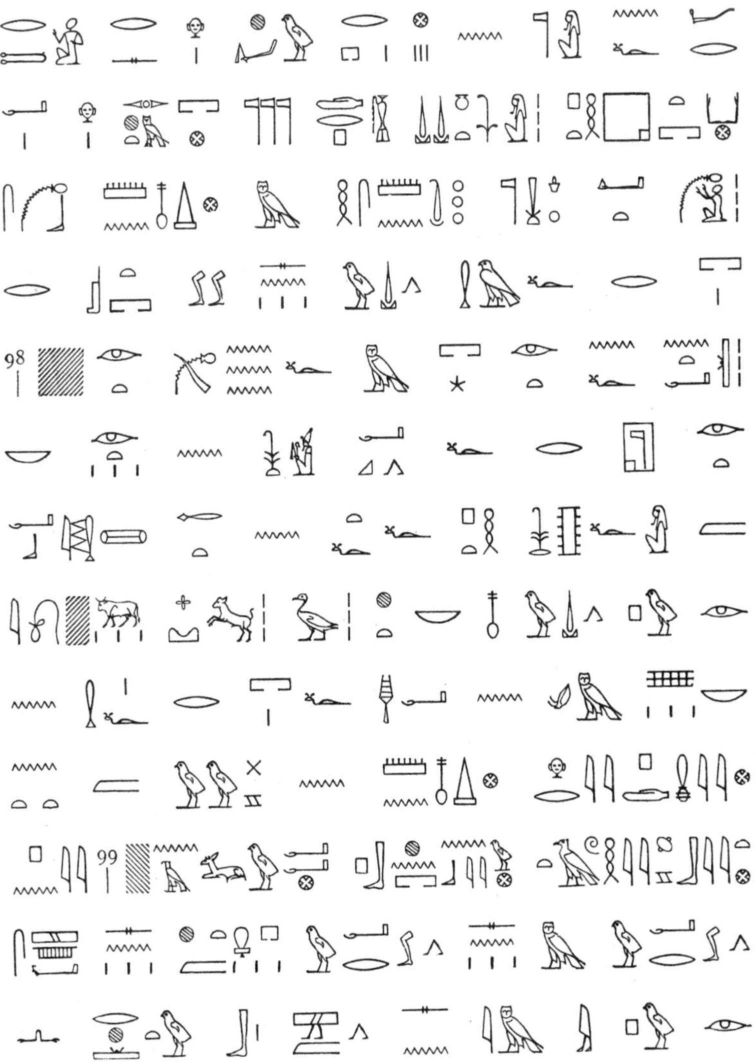

reθ er-es ḥer χu er peru en neter nef ser (or *ťeser*)*-ā ḥer Seχem neteru ṭerp*
ťaťatsu Ptaḥ-ḥet-ka seāb Mennefer em ḥesmen neter sentrȧ ṭāt ābu er ȧuset
reθ-sen uťa ḥen-f er per 98. *[Ptaḥ] ȧrit āb-f em seba* (?) *ȧrit-nef entāu neb* 98
ȧrit en suten āq-f er neter ḥet ȧrit āb āat en tef-f Ptaḥ ȧneb res-f em ȧua
unṭu reu χet neb nefer uťa pu ȧri en ḥen-f er per-f āḥā en setem sept neb
entet em uu en Mennefer Ḥeripṭemȧi Peni 99. . . . . *naāuāā Pebeχennebiu* 99
Tauḥibit seś-sen χetem uār-sen em uār ȧn reχtu bu śem-sen ȧm i pu ȧri

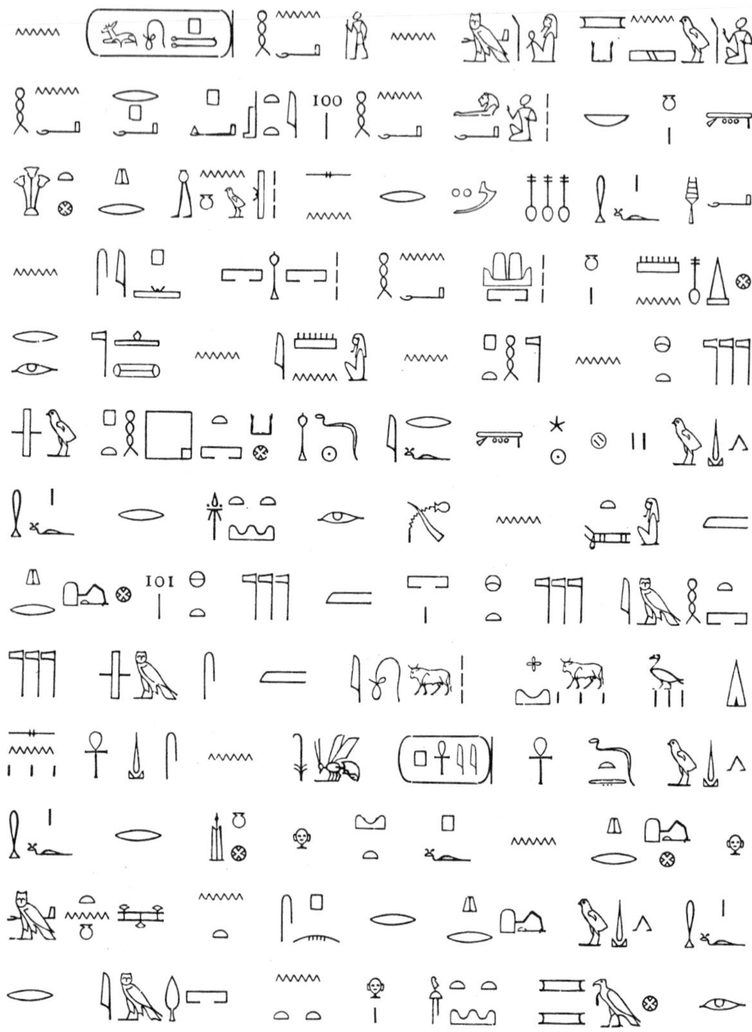

en Āuuapeθ ḥnā ser en Mā [šuaš] Merkanešu ḥnā erpā Peṭā-Ȧuseteṭȧ
100 *100. ḥnā ḥāu neb nu ta meḥt χer ȧnnu-sen er maa neferu ḥen-f āḥā en sȧp*
peru-ḥetʼ ḥnā šent nu Mennefer er ȧri neter ḥetep en Ȧmen en Ptaḥ en paut
neteru ȧmu Ptaḥ-Ḥet-Ka ḥetʼ ȧref ta ṭua sep sen uṫa ḥen-f er ȧbtet ȧri āb en
101 *Ȧtmu em Χerāba* 101. *paut neteru em per paut neteru ȧmaḥet neteru ȧm-s em*
ȧua unṭu reu ṭā-sen ānχ uṫa senb en suten net (or *bȧt*) *P-ānχi ānχ ṫetta*
uṫa ḥen-f er Ȧnnu ḥer ṭut pef en Χer-āba ḥer mātennu ent Sep er Χer-āba
uṫa ḥen-f er ȧm entet ḥer Ȧmentet Merti ȧri

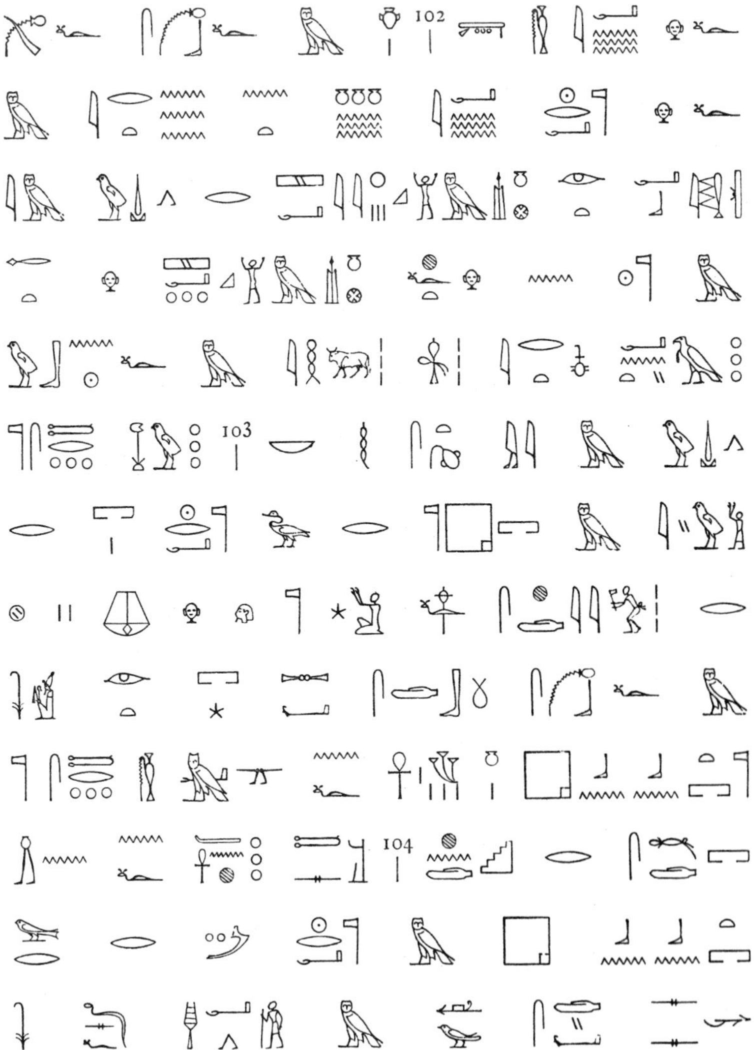

āb-f scāb-f em ȧb 102. *Ta-qebḥ ȧā ḥrȧ-f em ȧrt ent Nu ȧā Rā ḥrȧ-f ȧm* 102
uťa er Śāiqa-em-Ȧnnu ȧrit āb āat ḥer Śāiqa-em-Ȧnnu χeft en Rā em uben-f
em ȧḥu ḥeť ȧrt ānti neter senθer χau 103. *neb neťem set i em uťa er per Rā* 103
āq er neter-ḥet em ȧiu sep sen χer-ḥeb ḥer neter ṭua χesef seχeṭi er suten ȧrit
per ṭua θes seṭeb seāb-f em neter senθer qebḥ mās-nef ānχu nu Ḥet-benbenet
ȧn-nef ānχu θes 104. *χenṭ er seśeṭ ur er maa Rā em Ḥet-benbenet su ťesef* 104
āḥā em uā seṭi ses

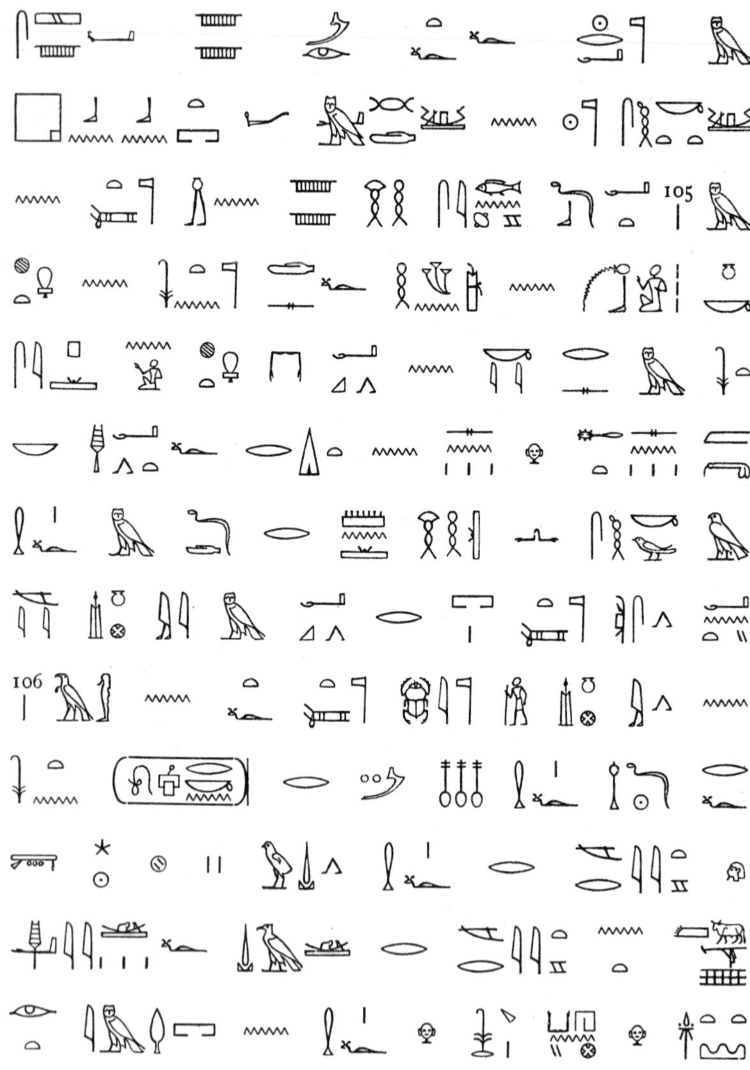

seš āaui maa tef-f Rā em Ḥet-benbenet ťeser māāṭ en Rā sektet en Tmu ȧn
105 *āaui uaḥ sȧn ťebāt* 105. *em χetem en suten ṭes-f ḥen en ābu nuk sȧp-nȧ*
χetem ȧn āq en ki eres em suten neb āḥāt-f er ṭāt en-sen ḥer χat-sen em-baḥ
ḥen-f em ťeṭ er men uaḥ ȧn sek Ḥeru meri Ȧnnu i em āq er per Tmu šes
106 *ānti* 106. *en tef Tmu-Χeperȧ ser Ȧnnu i en suten Ua-sar-ken er maa neferu*
ḥen-f ḥet' eref ta ṭua sep sen uťa ḥen-f er merit ṭep āḥāiu-f ťa er merit ent
Ka-qem ȧrit ȧm en ḥen-f ḥer res Kaheni ḥer ȧbtet

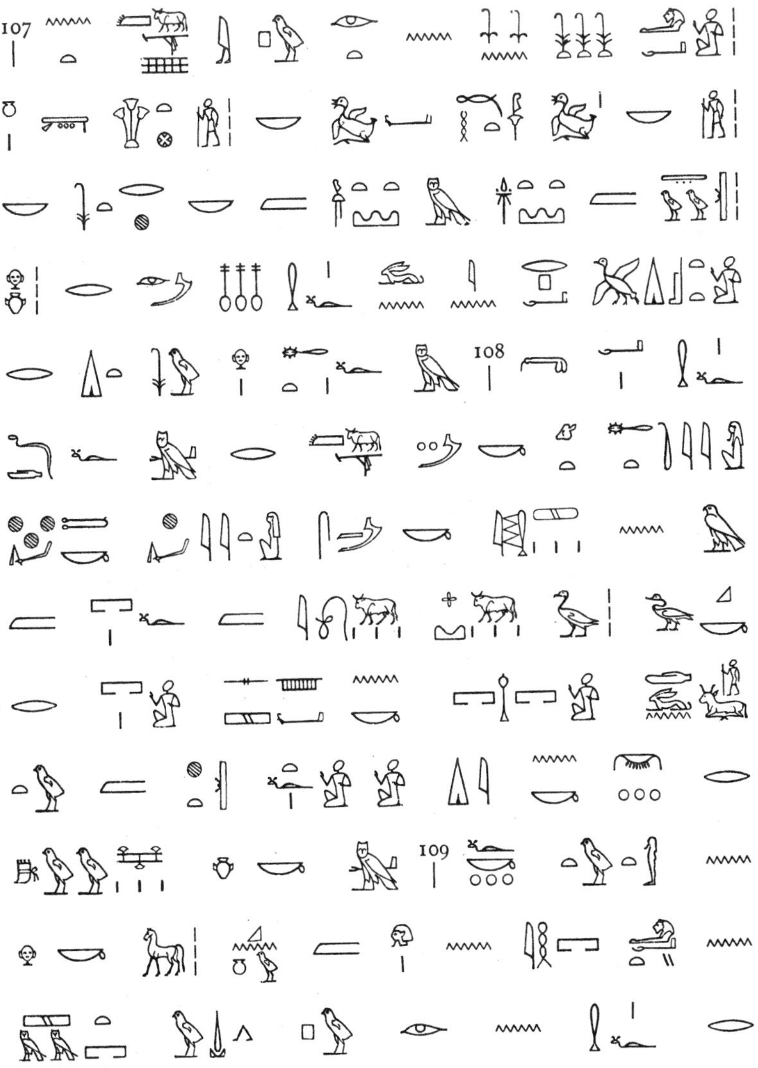

107. *ent Ka-qem i pu ȧrit enen suteniu ḥāu nu Ta-meḥt seru neb ťa-meḥt* 107
ťa neb seru neb sutenet reχ neb em ȧmentet em ȧbtet em taiu ḥerȧbu er maa
neferu ḥen-f un ȧn erpā Pa-ṭā-Ȧusetet er ṭāt su ḥer χat-f em- 108. *baḥ ā* 108
ḥen-f ťeṭ-f mā er Ka-qem maa-k Χent-χatθi χuθ-k Χuit semaā-k ābu en
Ḥeru em per-f em ȧua unṭu reu āq-k er per-ȧ seš-nek perui-heť-ȧ ṭun-tu em
χet tef-ȧ ṭā-ȧ nek nub er ťeruu ȧb-k mā- 109. *fek tut en ḥrȧ-k semsemu* 109
qennu em ṭep en ȧḥ ḥāti en šememet uťa pu ȧri en ḥen-f er

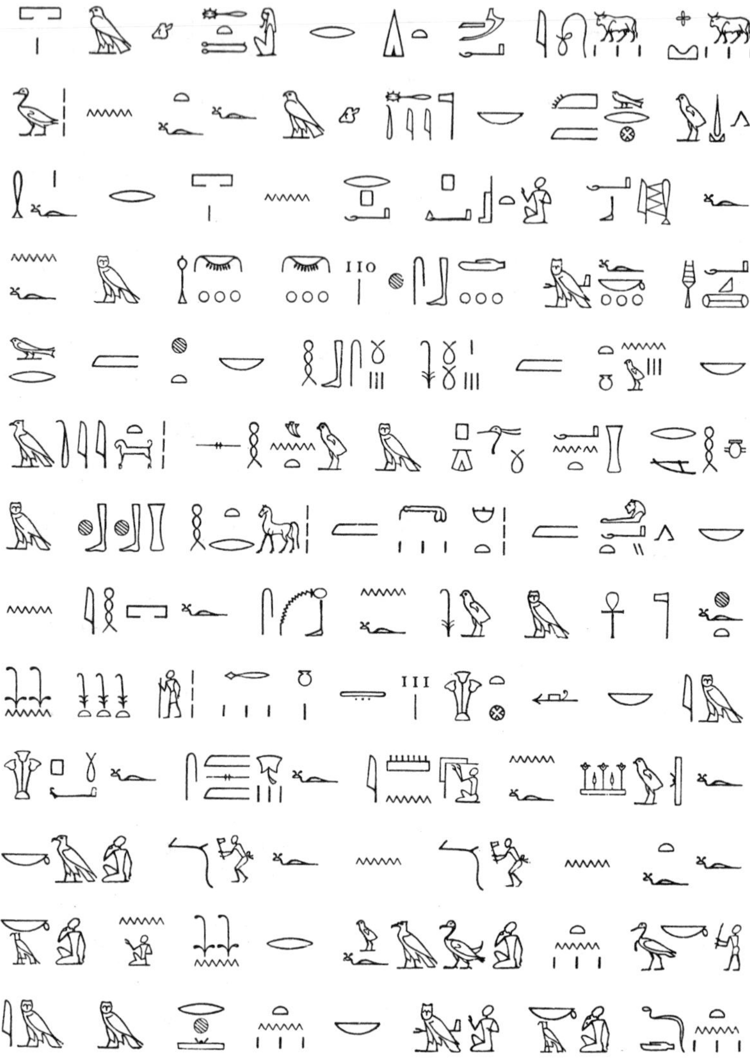

per Ḥeru-χent-Χatθ er ṭāt maā ȧua unṭu reu en tef-f Ḥeru-χent-Χaθi neb
110 *Qem-ur uťa ḥen-f er per en erpā Pe-ṭā-Ȧusetet āb-f nef em ḥeť nub* 110. *χesbeṭ*
māfek āḥāq ur em χet neb ḥebs suteniu śesu em tennu neb aθit seḥentu em
peḳ ānt merḥ em χebχeb ḥeter em ťaiu ḥemt em ḥāti neb en ȧḥ-f seāb-nef su
111 *em ānχ neter χeft enen suteniu seru āaiu nu ta* 111. *meḥt uā neb ȧm ḥap-f*
semsemu-f ȧmen-nef śau-f ka mer-f en mer en tef-f ka-nȧ enen er ufa-
ten bak ȧm em reχ-ten neb mā-ȧ ka ťeṭ-ten

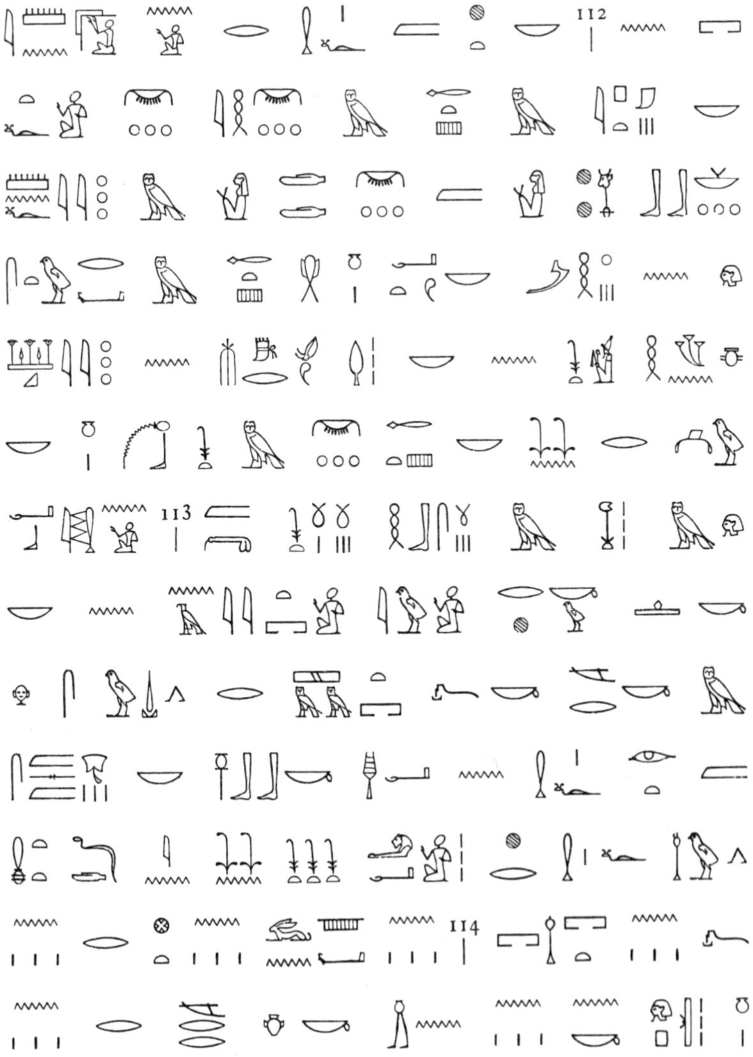

ȧmen-nȧ er ḥen-f em χet neb 112. *en per tef-ȧ nub ȧḥ em āat em ȧpt neb* 112
menfiu em ȧri ṭeṭ nub em ȧri χeχ bebu setur em āat sa nu āt neb maḥu en
ṭep śaqi en mesťer ȧmu neb en suten ḥen neb nu āb suten em nub āat neb
enen er āu āb-nȧ 113. *em-baḥ suteniu śesu ḥebs em χa em ṭep neb en nait* 113
ȧu-ȧ reχ-ku[ȧ] ḥetep-k ḥer-s uťa er śememet setep-k mer-k em semsemu neb
ābeb-k āḥā en ḥen-f ȧriť emmȧtet ťeṭ ȧn enen suteniu ḥāu χer ḥen-f utu-n er
nut-n un-n 114. *per-ḥeťet-n setep-n er merer ȧb-k ȧn-n nek ṭepu nu* 114

šemem-n ḥāutti nu semsemu-n āḥā-n ḥen-f årit måtet reχ ren åri suten Ua-
sar-ken em Per-Bast Uu-en-Rā-nefer suten Āuuapeθ em θent-remu Ta-ån
115 *ḥā Ṭeṭ-Åmen-åf-ānχ-å* 115. *em Per-Ba-neb-Ṭeṭṭeṭ Ta-ā-Rā sa-f semsem*
mer menfitu em Per-Teḥuti-åp-reḥeḥ Ānχ-Ḥeru ḥā Merkaneš em Neter-θeb
em Per-χerḥebi em Sam-beḥuṭet ḥā ur en Māšuaš Paθenef em Per-Sept em
116 *Ā-pen-åneb-ḥet'et* 116. *ḥā ur en Māšuaš Pema em Per-Åusår-neb-Ṭeṭṭeṭ*
ḥā ur en Māšuaš Nesnaqeṭi em Ka-ḥeseb ḥā ur en Māšuaš Neχt-Ḥeru-na-
šennut em Per-ḳerer ur en Māšuaš

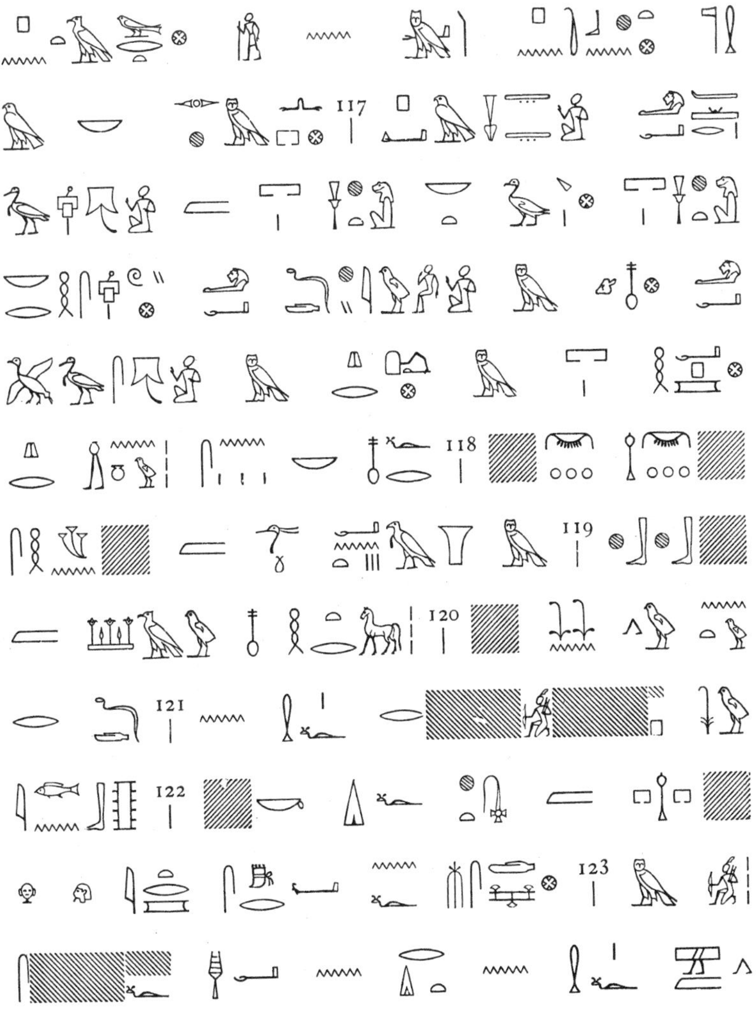

Penta-urt ser en Māšuaš Penθ-beχent neter ḥen Ḥeru neb Seχem 117. *Pe-ṭā-* 117
Ḥeru-sam-taiu Ḥāre-basa em Per-seχet nebt Sa Per-Seχet-neb-reḥessaui
ḥā Teṭχiȧuχerṭ em Χent-nefer ḥā Pabas em Χer-āba em Per-Ḥāp χer
ȧnnu-sen neb nefer 118.... *nub ḥet'* .... *[aθit] seḥen[tu] em peḳ ānti em* 118
119. *χebχeb* ...... *em šau nefer ḥeter* 120...... *enen* .... *iu-en-tu er t'eṭ* 119 120
121. *en ḥen-f* .... *menfitu* ..... *p su ȧneb-* 122. *[f en senṭ-]k ṭā-f χet* 121
em peru-ḥet' .... *ḥer ṭep ȧter st'er-nef Mesṭ* 123. *em menfitu* ..... *-f* 122 123
āḥā en erṭāt en ḥen-f šem

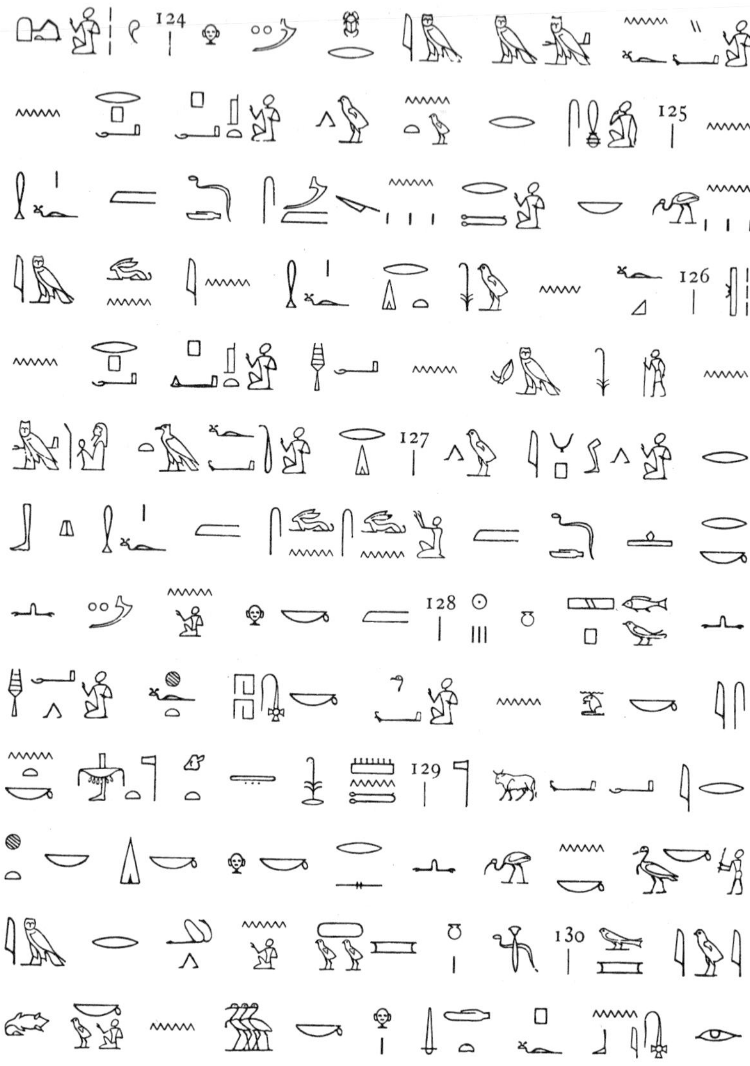

124 *àbaiu-f* 124. *ḥer maa χeper àm emmā nefi en erpā Pe-ṭā-Àuset iu-en-tu er smà*
125 125. *en ḥen-f em t'eṭ semam-n reθ neb qem-n àm un àn ḥen-f erṭāt su en*
126 *fequ* 126. *en erpā Pe-ṭā-Àuset āḥā en setem su ser en Māšuaš Taf-neχθ er ṭā*
127 127. *iu àp er bu χer ḥen-f em sunsun em t'eṭ ḥetep er-ek àn maa-nà ḥrà-k em*
128 128. *hru nu šep àn āḥā-à χeft heh-k neràu-à en šefit-k às entek Nubt χent Ta-*
129 *resu Menθ* 129. *ka neχt ā àr χet neb ṭā-k ḥrà-k er-es àn qem-nek bak àm er*
130 *peḥ-nà àuu nu Uat'-ur* 130. *àu-à senṭ-kuà en baiu-k ḥer meṭet pef nebà àri*

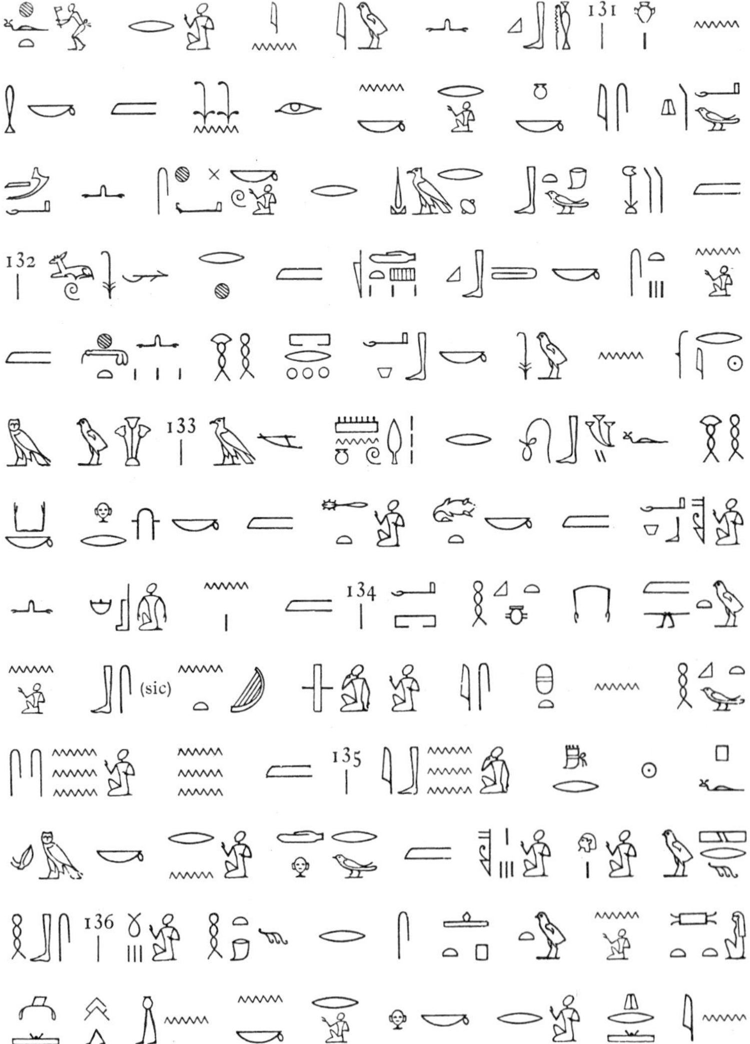

χeft er-ȧ ȧn ȧu ȧn qebḥ 131. *ȧb en ḥen-k em enen ȧri-nek er-ȧ nuk ȧs χer* 131
ā maā ȧn seχ-kuȧ er t'ar beta χa em 132. *āusu reχ em qeṭet qeb-k set nȧ* 132
em χemet uaḥ peru āb-k su en trȧ em uḥa 133. *mennu er uabi-f uaḥ ka-k* 133
ḥer-k em χat-ȧ senṭet-k em āb-ȧ ȧn ḥems-nȧ em 134. *ā ḥeqt ȧn mas-tu-nȧ* 134
bȧnt ȧm-ȧ ȧs ta en ḥeqet ses-ȧ mu em 135. *ȧb t'er hru pef setem-k ren-ȧ* 135
ṭeḥer em ḳesu-ȧ ṭep-ȧ ušer ḥebs 136. *-ȧ ḥeta er-s ḥetep-tu-nȧ Nitet āu ḥāp* 136
ȧn-nek er-ȧ ḥrȧ-k er-ȧ χer ȧn

137 *trȧt se-* 137. *peχa ka-ȧ seāb bak em θes-f ȧmmā seśep-θ χet-ȧ er per-ḥeť em*
138 138. *nub ḥenā āat neb ḥātu ȧs nu semsemu ṭebu em χet neb ȧmmā iu-nȧ ȧpt*
139 139. *em sȧn ṭer-f senṭet em ȧb-ȧ ka pert-ȧ er neter-ḥet em ḥrȧ-f seāb-ȧ em*
140 *ānχ* 140. *neter erṭāt en ḥen-f śem χer-ḥeb ḥer Pe-ṭā-Ȧmen-[neb] nest-taiu*
141 *mer menfitu Puarma feq* 141. *-nef su em ḥeť nub ḥebs āat neb śeps per-*
142 *nef er neter ḥet ṭua-nef neter se-* 142. *āb-nef su em neter ānχ em ťeṭ ȧn teh-ȧ*
143 *suten utu ȧn uȧn-ȧ* 143. *ťeṭet ḥen-f ȧn ȧri-ȧ āu er ḥā em χem-k ȧrit-ȧ em*
144 *ťeṭ-* 144. *et en suten ȧn teh-ȧ*

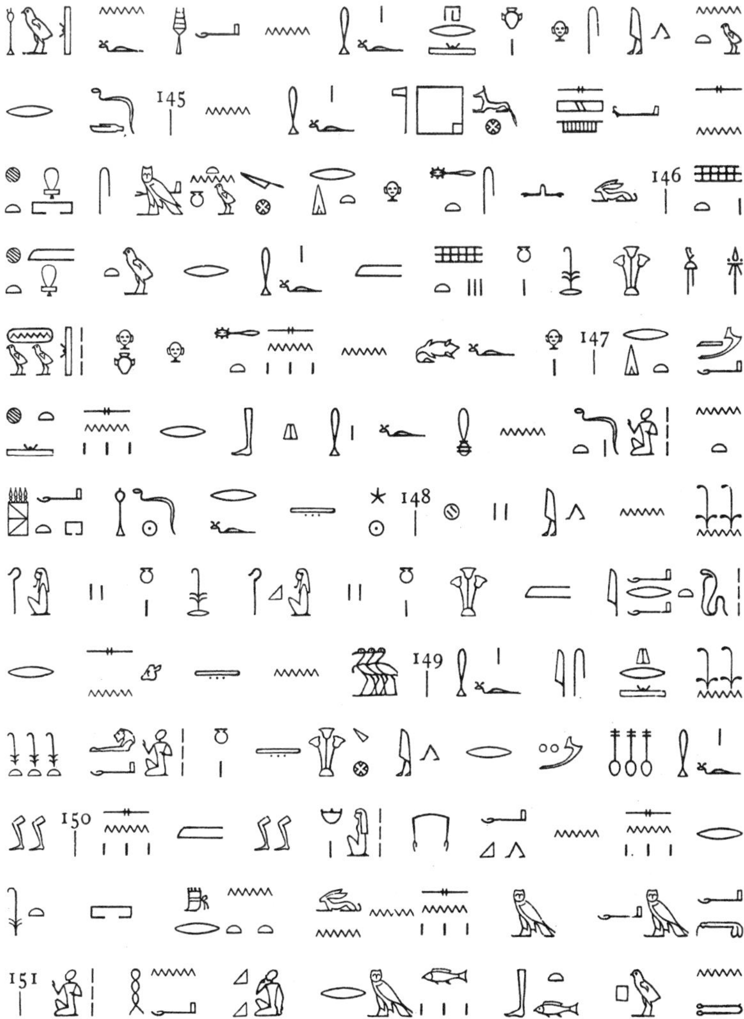

utu-nef āḥā en ḥen-f her ȧb ḥer-s i-en-tu er ťeṭ 145. *en ḥen-f Neter-ḥet-Ȧnpu* 145
seś-sen χetem-s Mātennu erṭāt ḥer χat-s ȧn un 146. *sept χetem-tu er ḥen-f* 146
em sept nu resu meḥt ȧment ȧbt ȧuu ḥer-ȧbu ḥer χat-sen en senṭ-f ḥer 147. *er-* 147
ṭāt maā χet-sen er bu χer ḥen-f mȧ en ťet ent ḥet-āt ḥeť eref ta ṭua 148. *sep* 148
sen i en enen ḥequi sen nu resu ḥequi sen nu meḥt em ȧārāt er sen-ta en baiu
149. *ḥen-f ȧs χer enen suteniu ḥāu nu ta meḥt i er maa neferu ḥen-f reṭ-* 149
150. *sen em reṭ ḥemt ȧn āq-en-sen er suten per ťerenťet unen-sen em āmāu* 150
151. *ḥenā qeq remu bet pu enθ* 151

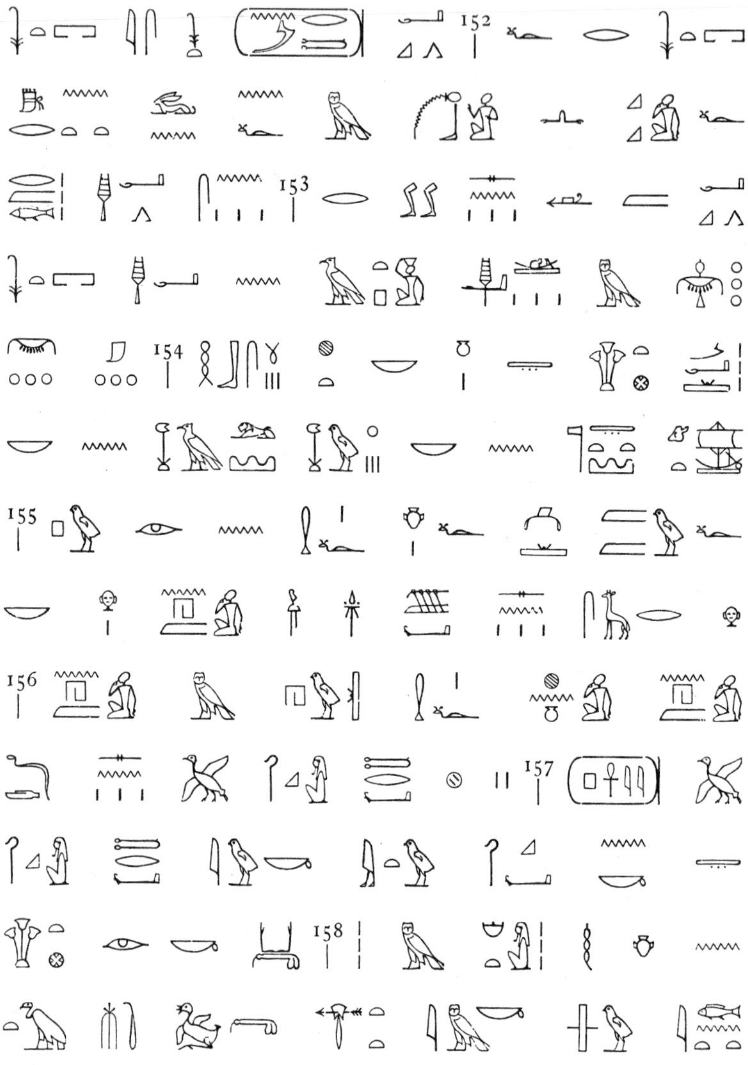

152 *suten per ȧs suten Nemareθ āq-* 152. *f er suten per t̉erentet un-nef em āb*
153 *ȧn qeq-f remu āḥā-sen* 153. *er reṭ-sen uā em āq suten per āḥā en atep āḥāu*
154 *em ḥet̉ nub χemt* 154. *ḥebs χet neb nu ta meḥt maā neb en Χar χau neb en*
155 *Neter-ta χent* 155. *pu ȧri en ḥen-f ȧb-f āu memu-f neb ḥer nehem ȧment*
156 *ȧbt seśep-sen ser ḥer* 156. *nehem em hu ḥen-f χennu nehem t̉eṭ-sen pa ḥeq*
157 *θer sep sen* 157. *P-ānχi pa ḥeq θer ȧu-k i-tu ḥeq-nek ta meḥt ȧri-k kau*
158 158. *em ḥemt net̉em ȧb en mut mes-θ t̉a satet ȧm-k ȧmu ȧntet*

ȧrit-nes ȧu kaut 159. *mes ka ȧu-k er neḥeḥ neχt-k men pa ḥeq mer Uast.*

THE DECREE OF CANOPUS.

1. *Renpit pest Apaliusa sesu seχef ṭep per sesu met-seχef en ȧmu Ta-mert* 1
χer ḥen suten net (or *bȧt*) *Ptualmis ānχ ṫetta Ptaḥ meri sa en Ptualmis*
Ȧrsenat neterui senui āb en Ȧleḳsanṭeres maātχeru ḥā neterui senui ḥā
neterui menχui Apualaniṭes 2. *sa en Māauaskian ȧu Māanaqeraṭa sat* 2
Pailamna fa ṭenȧ en embaḥ Ȧrsenat sen meri hru pen seχau ȧu

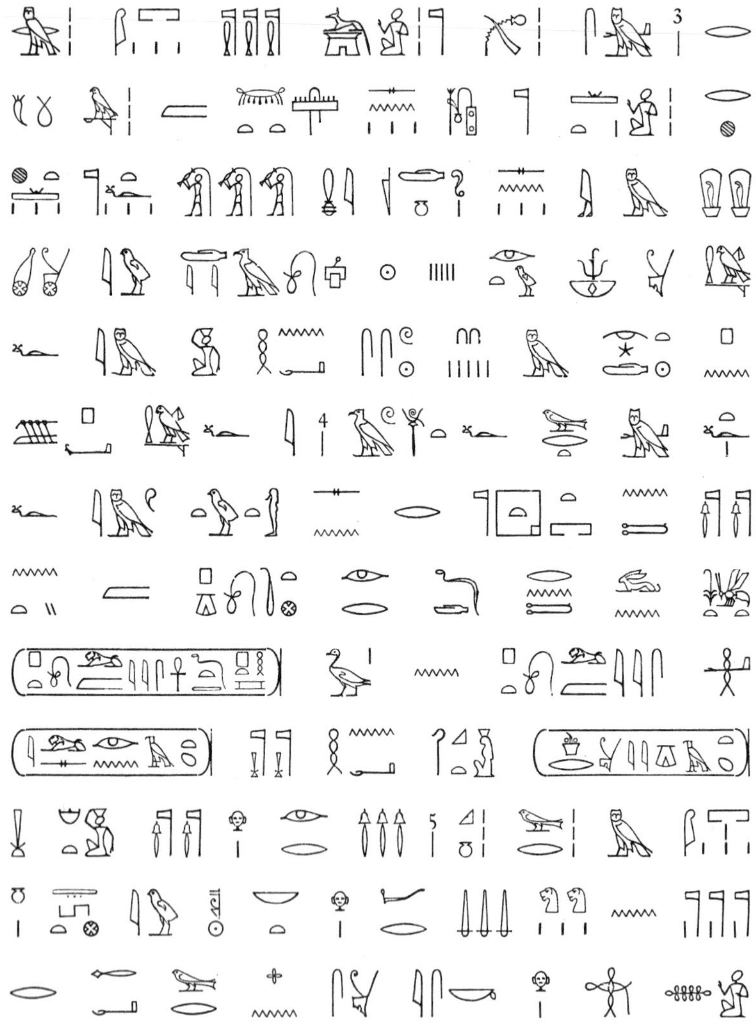

3 *meru maāu neteru ḥenu ḥer seśeta neteru ābu semā* 3. *er mār neteru em satet-*
sen ānu neter śāt reχ χet neter tefu ābu mà qeṭ-sen i em àterti taui àu Ṭiauasa
sesu ṭua àritu ṭep renpit en neter ḥen-f àm-f ḥnā sesu ťaut ṭua em àbeṭ
4 *pen seśep neter ḥen-f à-* 4. *aut-f urt mā tef-f àm-f tut-sen er neter ḥet enθ*
neterui menχui enti em Peḳuaθet àri ťeṭ erenθ un suten net Ptualmis ānχ ťetta
Ptaḥ meri sa en Ptualmis ḥā Àrsenat neterui senui ḥnā ḥeqt Bareniḳat sent
5 *ḥemt neterui menχui ḥer àri* 5. *menχu qenu uru em maāu nu Tamert àu*
ḳant nebt ḥer ser meṭu peḥpeḥ en neteru er āā ur un-sen àsk ḥer meḥ sa

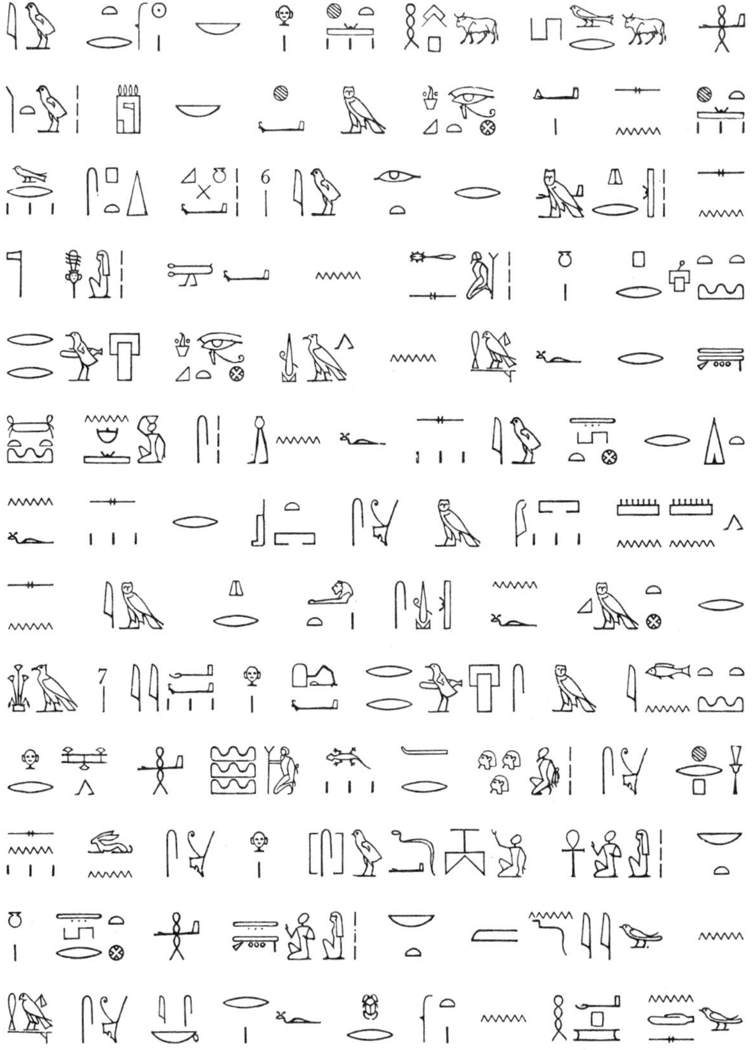

ȧu trȧ neb ḥer χet Ḥāp Mer-ur ḥā āutu neter ḥet neb χu em Baqet ṭā-sen χet
uru sept qenu 6. *ȧu ȧrit er māχer-sen neteru seχemu θet en χas nu Per-* 6
satet ererṭu Baqet uťa en neter ḥen-f er taiu Satet neḥem-f-s ȧn-f-s ȧu Tamert
er ṭāt-nef-s er ȧuset-sen em maāu menmen-sen ȧm χer ḥāt seuťa-nef Qemt er
7. *ḥaiā ḥer āba ererṭu-s em Ȧntet ḥer ḥā setu āš ḥer ṭepu-sen χerp-sen un-* 7
sen ḥer seuťā ānχu nebt nu Tamert ḥā taiu nebt em neťi en neter ḥen-sen
ȧsk er-f χeper renpit en Ḥāp neṭes

8 *em* 8. *hau-sen un ānχu nebt nu Baq àb-sen ķesen ḥer χeper àsk em seχen*
χefti seχau-sen χerit χep χentet em rek suteniu ṭepāu er χeper seχen Ḥāp
9 *neṭes en àmu Tamert em ha-sen àu neter ḥen-f ťesef ḥā sent-f* 9. *ḥer meḥ-*
sau er àb-sen emχa ḥer àmu neteru peru ḥnā àmu Baqet àu āu-sen un-sen
ḥer mau āš sep sen ḥer er ṭāt sa-sen àu ḥetràt qenu en àb en seānχ reχit
àu-sen ḥer erṭāt àntu peru àu Qemet em Retenetet àbt em ta en Keftet em
10 *aà Nebinaitet enti em ḥer àb Uať* 10. *ur ḥnā setu uru ḥer er ṭāt ḥeť āš àu*

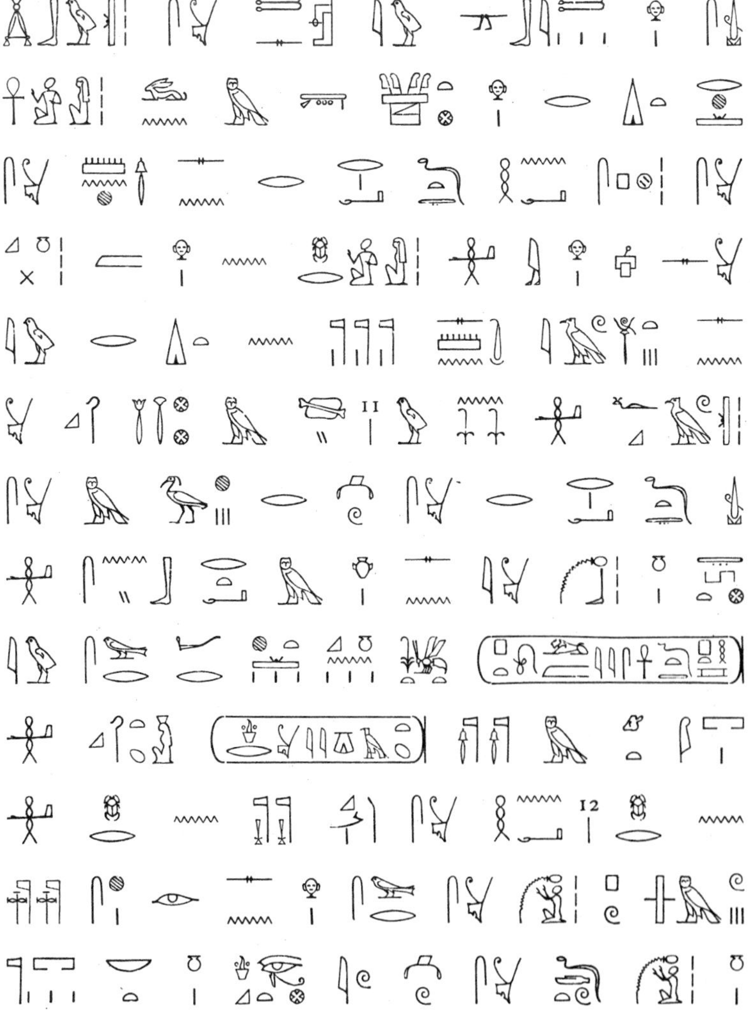

ṭebu-sen θes ȧu sebȧθ ḥer seuťa ānχu un em Ta-netert ḥer er ṭāt reχ-sen menχ-sen er rā ťetta ḥnā sepu-sen qenu em ḥrȧ en χeperu ḥā i ḥer sa-sen ȧu erṭāt en neteru smen ȧaut-sen en ḥeq taiu em 11. *ȧsiu enen ḥā feqau-sen em* 11
χu er āu-sen er rā ťetta uťa ḥā senib erṭā em ȧb-sen ȧn ābu nu Tamert ȧu seur ser χet qenu suten net Ptualmis ānχ ťetta Ptaḥ meri ḥā ḥeqt Bareniḳat neterui menχui em χent maā ḥā χeper en neterui senui qema-sen ḥnā χeper
12. *en neterui neťui seχ ȧri-sen ḥer seur-sen ābu pu ȧmu neter peru nebt nu* 12
Baqet ȧu āu-sen ťeṭtu ābu nu

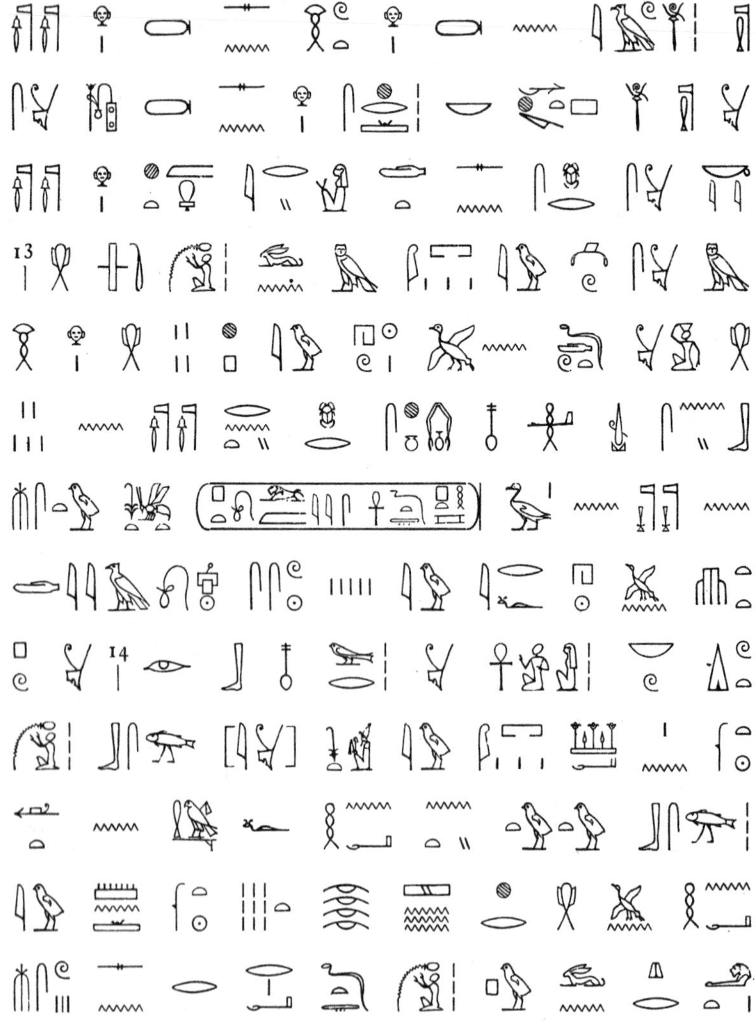

neterui menχui ḥer ren-sen uaḥ-tu ḥer ren en ȧau neter ḥen-sen āp ren-sen ḥer seχeru neb χet ȧau neter ḥen en neterui menχui ḥer χetem ȧri ṭet-sen seχeper-sen
13 *ki* 13. *sa ȧmθ ābu un em maāu ȧu āu-sen em uaḥ ḥer sa fṭu χep ȧu hru pen t̓eṭtu-nef sa ṭua en neterui menχui er-enti χeper seχen nefer ḥā ut̓a senib mestu suten net Ptualmis ānχ t̓etta Ptaḥ meri sa en neterui senui en Ṭiauasa sesu ṭua*
14 *ȧu ȧref hru pen χentet pu en* 14. *ȧri bu-nefer uru en ānχu nebu ṭātu ābu bes ȧn suten ȧu maāu šā en renpit uāt en neter ḥen-f ḥnā enti utut besu ȧu men renpit pest ȧbeṭ fṭu šemu χer sa pen ḥnā mesu-sen er rā t̓etta ābu pu un χer ḥāt*

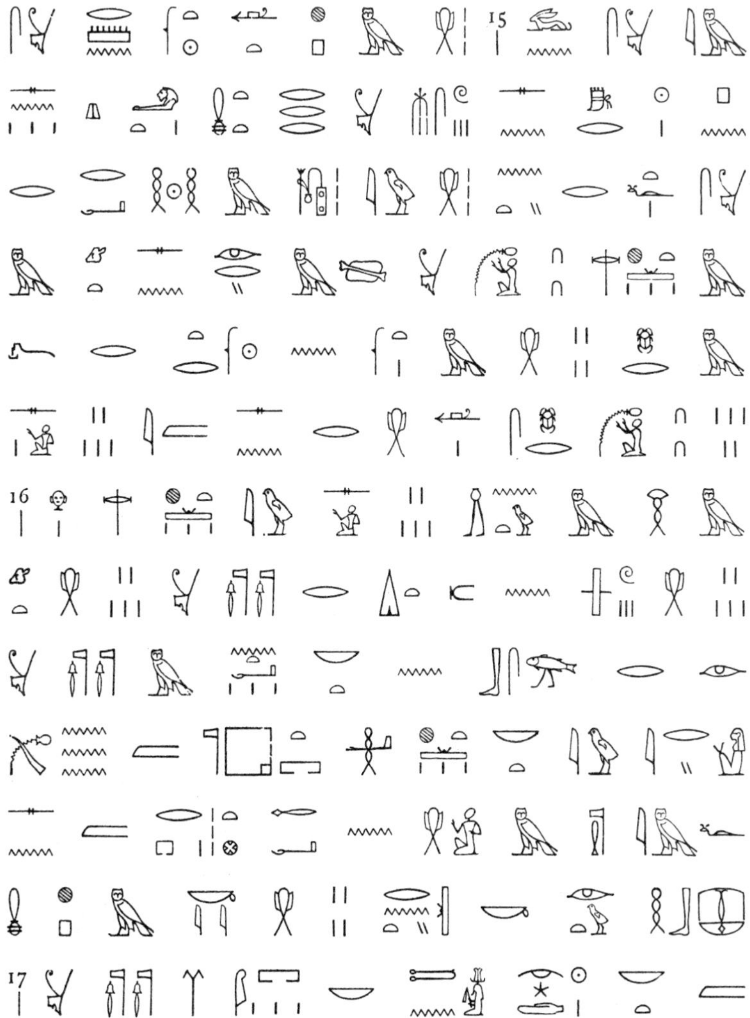

sen ermen renpit uāt χep em sau 15. *un-sen ȧm-sen χer ḥāt mȧtet ererer en mesu-* 15
sen ťer hru pen er rā ḥeḥ em ānu ȧu sau enti er tef-sen em χent-sen ȧri em ȧsiu
en ābu ťaut neť χet em setep er trȧ en renpit em sau fṭu χeper em sa ṭua ȧm-
sen er sa uā seχeper ābu ťaut ṭua 16. *ḥer neť χet ȧu sa ṭua ȧntu em uaḥ em* 16
χent sa ṭua en neterui menχui er ṭāt ṭenȧ en ȧmu sa ṭua en neterui menχui
em entā nebt en bes er ȧri āb em neter ḥet ḥā χet nebt ȧu ȧri-sen em erperut
āā-en-sa em neter ḥen ȧm-f mȧ χep em ki sa fṭu erenti k ȧritu ḥeb 17. *en* 17
neterui menχui em maāu neb θen ȧbeṭ nebt em

sesu ṭua sesu pest sesu ťaut ṭua em ȧri seχau serer χer ḥāt ȧu ḳer ȧritu ḥeb en
neteru uru χā āa rer em Tamert ȧu ḳant-f en renpit em-tutu ȧri χā āa ȧu ḳant-
18 *f en renpit en suten net Ptualmis ānχ ťetta Ptaḥ meri* 18. *ḥā heqt Bareniḳat*
neterui menχui em χent ȧterti taui ḥer Baqet er āu-s em hru per neter Sepṭet
ťettu ṭep renpit em ren-f ḥer ānu nu per-ānχ em-tutu ȧri-f em renpit pest
ȧbeṭ sen šemu sesu uā er ȧritu ḥeb en ṭep renpit ḥeb en Bast ḥer χā āa en Bast
19 *em ȧbeṭ pen ťerenti ḳant en* 19. *setut reṭu neb ḥai Ḥāp ȧm-f ȧs ȧu ȧref·un*
seχen ȧs-k uṭeb χā en neter Sepṭet ȧu ki hru tennu renpit fṭut er ȧn sentu hru

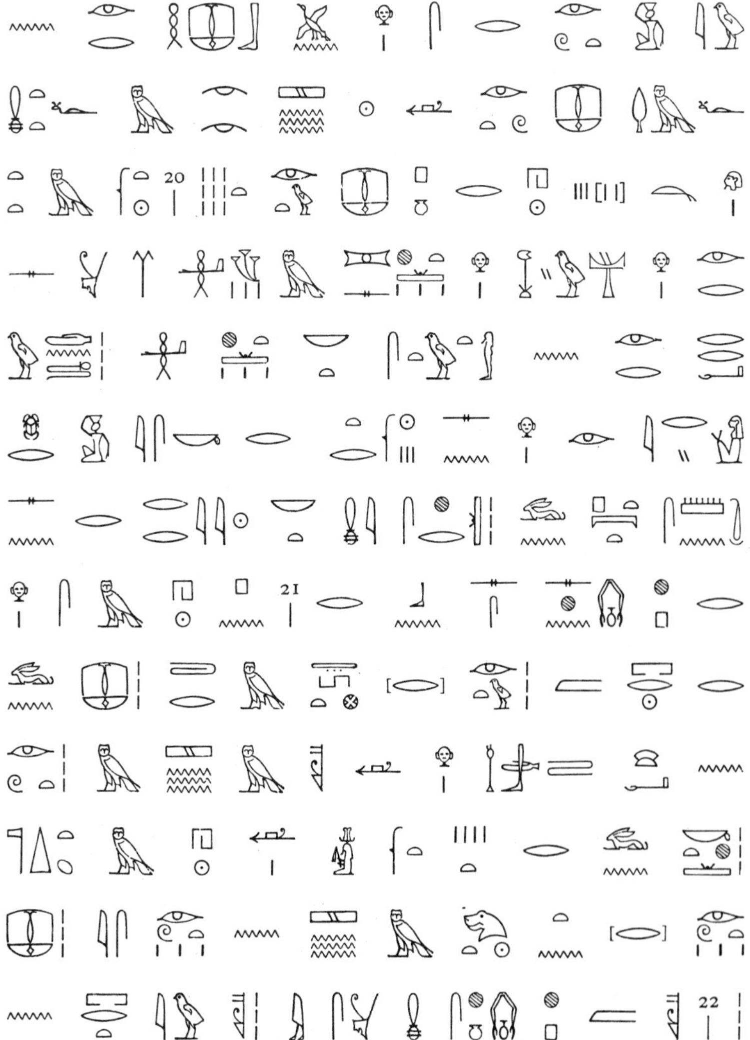

en àri ḥeb pen ḥer-s er àritu-f àu màtet-f em àbeṭ sen šemu sesu uā àritu ḥeb àm-f
tet em renpit 20. *pest àritu ḥeb pen er hru ṭua sent ṭep-s en em ḥāu em mesχet* 20
ḥer χaui ḥer àri uṭen ḥā χet nebt setut en àri errā χeper-f àsk er trà-sen ḥer
àri àri-sen er reri nebt mà seχeru un petet smen ḥer-s em hru pen 21. *er ben* 21
ses seχen χep er un ḥebu rer em Tamert er àritu em per er àritu em šemu em
ḳant uā ḥer uṭeb χā en neter Sepṭet em hru uā ten renpit fṭut er un keteχ ḥebu às
àritu en šemu em at ten er àritu en pert àu ḳant i-sen mà seχen χep em ḳant 22. 22

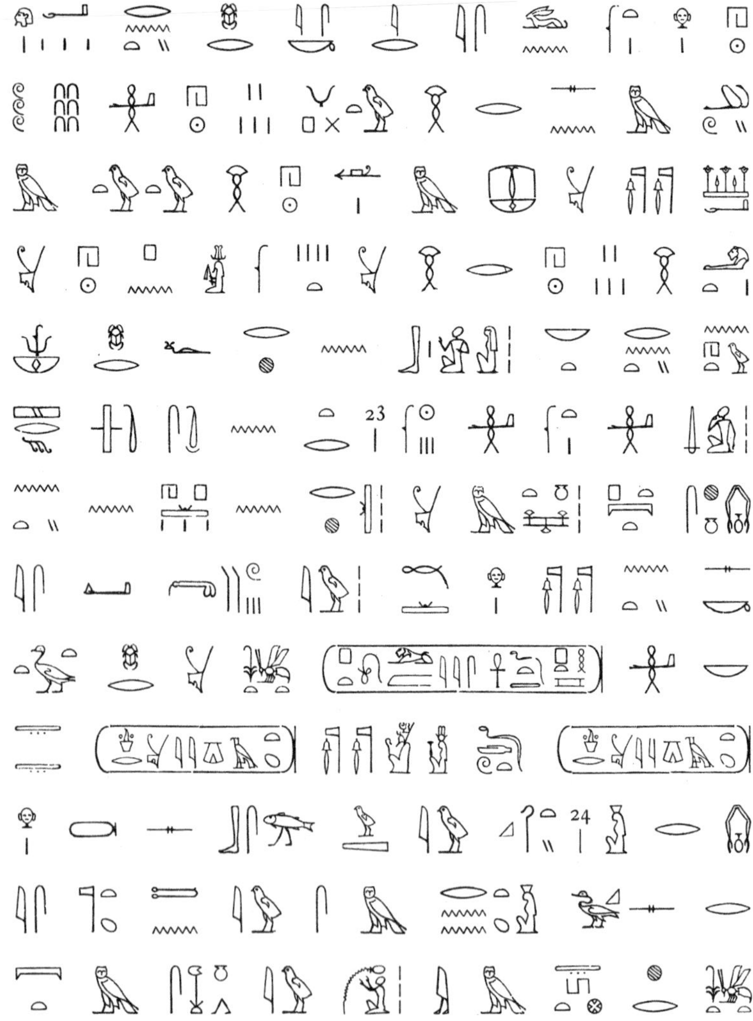

ṭepāu erenti χeper àsk àr às un renpit ḥer hru šaā χemet . . . . . ḥā hru ṭua
àput uaḥ er sen em peḥui em-tutu uaḥ hru uā em ḥeb en neterui menχui šā en
hru pen ten renpit fṭut en uaḥ er hru ṭua uaḥ ḥāt ṭep renpit χeper-f reχ en
23 *bu-nebt erenti nehtu šer àmθ smen en* 23. *trà ḥā renpit ḥā meṭu enti en hep*
en reχ en mātenu petet seχen às ṭā metu àu meḥ ḥer neterui menχui enti sek satet
χeper en suten net Ptualmis ānχ ṫetta Ptaḥ meri ḥā neb taui Bareniḳat neterui
24 *menχui ṫeṭtu Bareniḳat ḥer ren-s bes ut àu* 24. *ḥeqti er seχen às neteret θen*
àu-s em renenet āq-s er pet em seχan àu ābu i em Tamert χer suten net

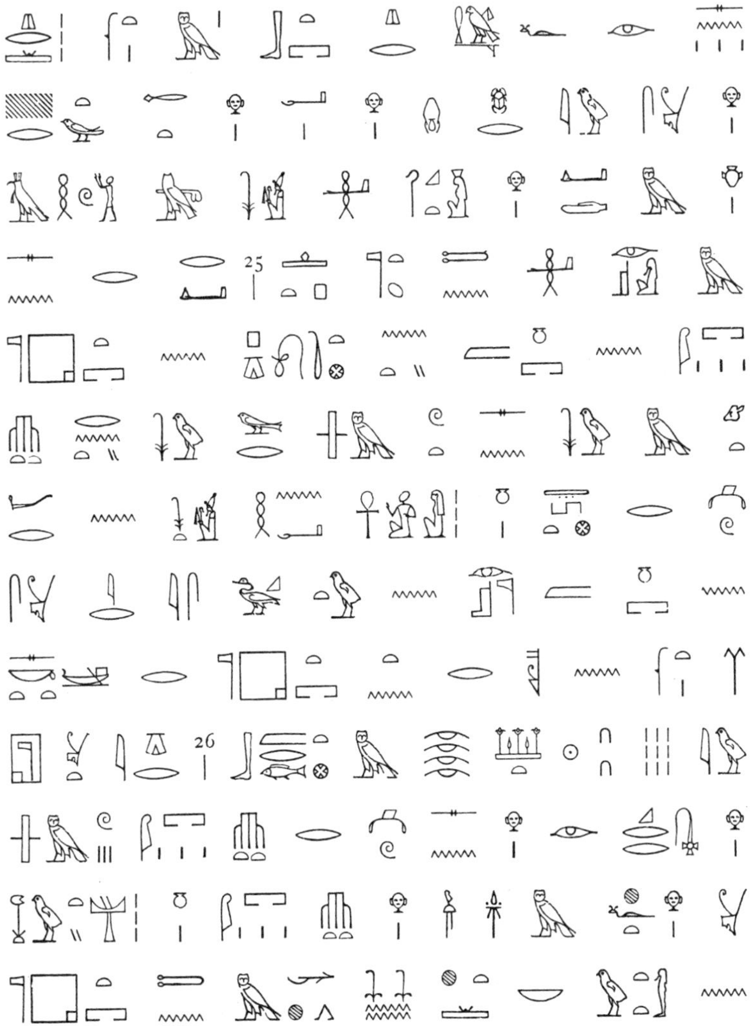

χer renpit em bet χer neter ḥen-f ȧri-sen .... rt āat ḥer-ā ḥer seχen χeper ȧu
sen ḥer neḥu embaḥ suten ḥā ḥeqet ḥer ṭāṭ em ȧb-sen er erṭā 25. *ḥetep neteret* 25
θen ḥā Ȧusȧr em neter ḥet en Peḳuaθet enti emχen en maāu χentet erenti su
ur ȧm ut-sen-su em χent serer en suten ḥnā ānχu nu Tamert er āu-sen ȧr ȧs
āq-tu en Ȧusȧr em χen en sektet er neter ḥet ten er ḳant en renpit em neter ḥet
ent Ȧḳer 26. *-bemremet em ȧbeṭ fṭu śat sesu t́aut pest ȧu ȧmu maāu χentet er* 26
āu-sen ḥer ȧri qerer ḥer χauti nu maāu χentet ḥer unami semeḥi em χeft
en neter ḥet θen emχet enen χet neb tut en

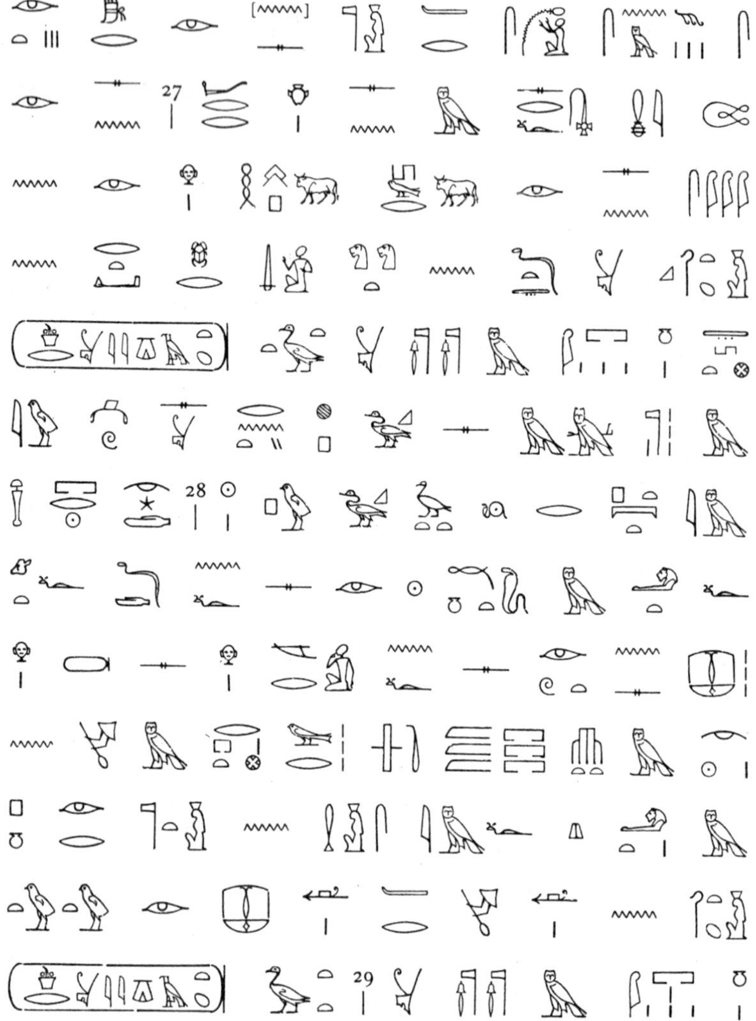

27 *ȧrit ṭer ȧri-nes netert ḥer seāb senem-s ȧri-sen* 27. *serer ȧb-sen em seref mȧ sent en ȧri ḥer Ḥāp Mer-ur ȧri-sen semaāu en erṭāt χeper meṭ peḥpeḥt en ṭetta en ḥeqt Bareniḳat satet en neterui menχui em maāu nu Tamert ȧu āu-sen*

28 *erenti χep āq-s emmā neteru em ṭep per* 28. *ȧbeṭ pu āq satet Rā er petet ȧm χent-f ṭeṭ-nef-s ȧri Rā meḥenet em ḥāt-f ḥer ren-s ḥer mer-nef-s ȧritu-nes ḥebu en χen em erperut uru ȧmθ maāu χentet em ȧbeṭ pen ȧri netert en ḥen-s ȧm-f*

29 *χer ḥāt em-tutu ȧri ḥeb uā ḥer χen uā en ḥeqt Bareniḳat satet* 29. *en neterui menχui em maāu nu*

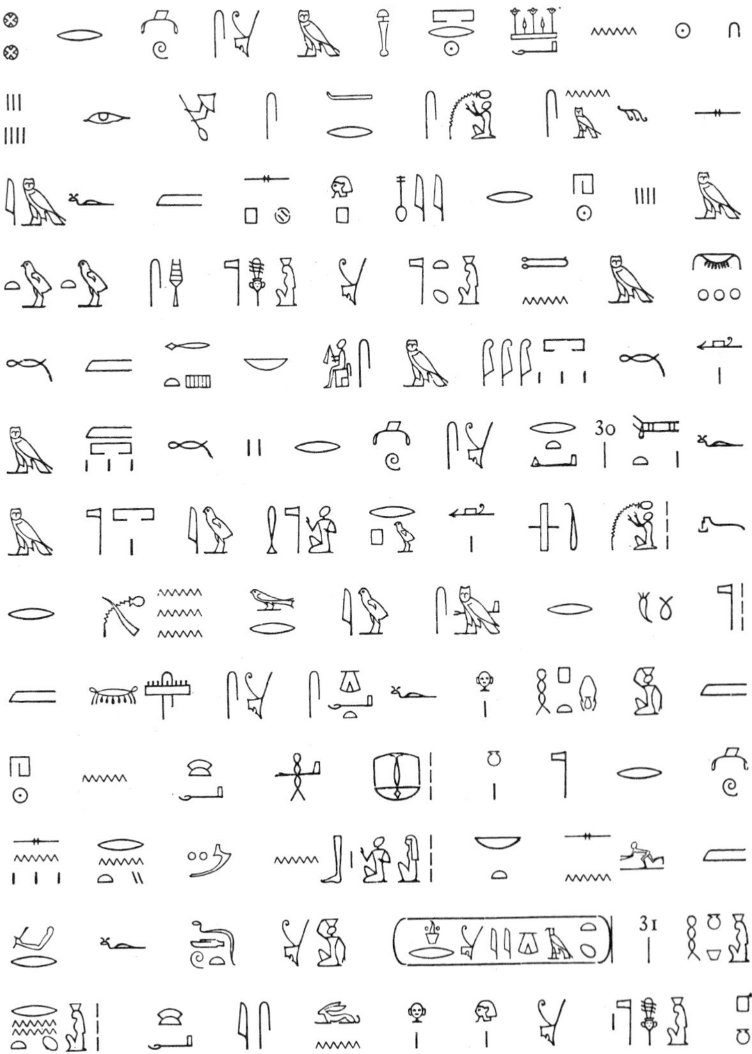

taui er āu-sen em ṭep per šā en sesu met seχef ȧri χen-s ḥer seāb senem-s ȧm-f em sep ṭep neferi er hru fṭu em-tutu seāḥā neter seχem en netert θen em nub meḥ em āat neb šeps em maāu meḥ uā em maāu meḥ sen er āu-sen erṭāt 30. *temt-f em neter per ȧu neter ḥen erpu uā ȧmθ ābu setep er āb ur* 30
ȧu smā er mār neteru em sati-sen seḳāt-f ḥer ḥept-f em hru en χā ḥā ḥebu nu neter er āu-sen erenti maa [en] nebu nebt sen em serer-f ťeṭtu-nef Bareniḳat
31. *ḥent renenet χā ȧs un ḥer ṭep en neter seχem pen* 31

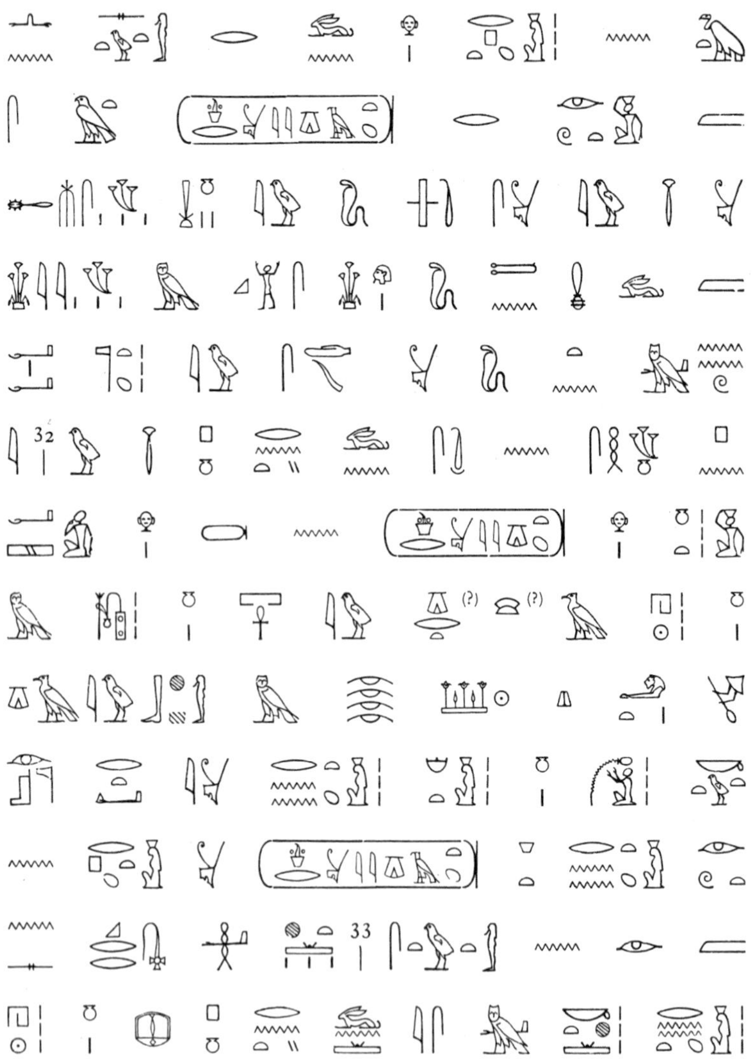

ȧn setut er un ḥrȧ erpet en mut-s neteret Bareniḳat er ȧritu-f em χames
sen ȧu ārāt ȧmθ-sen ȧu uat′ en ḥai em qa-s ḥa ārā θen mȧ un em āāui
32 *neteret ȧu seṭ en ārā-ten mānenu* 32. *ȧu uat′ pen erenti un smen en seḥen*
pen āś ḥer ren en Bareniḳat ḥer net-f em ānu nu per ānχ ȧu . . . . . . hru
nu Ḳaȧubeχ . . . . em ȧbeṭ fṭu śa χer ḥāt χen Ȧusȧr er ṭāt ȧn renenet ḥemt
nu ābu ketut en erpet en Bareniḳat ḥent renenet ȧri-tu-nes qerer-ḥā χet
33 33. *setut en ȧri em hru nu ḥeb pen erenti un ȧs mā keteχu renenet*

ȧri em setut enen en neteret ten er mer-sen ṭuau-tu neteret-θen ȧs ȧn qemāt setep er ŝes neteru tām χāu nu neteru un-sen em ābu-sen ȧr ȧs qurt em ḥāt ererer fa χames ȧn qemāt ȧu χentet 34. *ṭā en neter seχem en neteret θen* 34 *ḥes-ut en seχem-s ȧn ṭemau ḥesu t̄au ḥemt em χā ḥā ḥebu nu neteru em ṭuau serer en θet per ānχ ṭā en ṭemseb nu ḥesu ān mȧtet ḥer ŝefta nu per ānχ erenti ȧs ṭātu ḥetepu en ābu em χent maāu χeft bes-sen* 35. *ȧn suten ȧu neter* 35 *ḥet ȧu māi ṭātu χeru en mesu ḥemt nu ābu t̄er hru mes-sen ȧm-f em χent neter ḥetepu nu neteru*

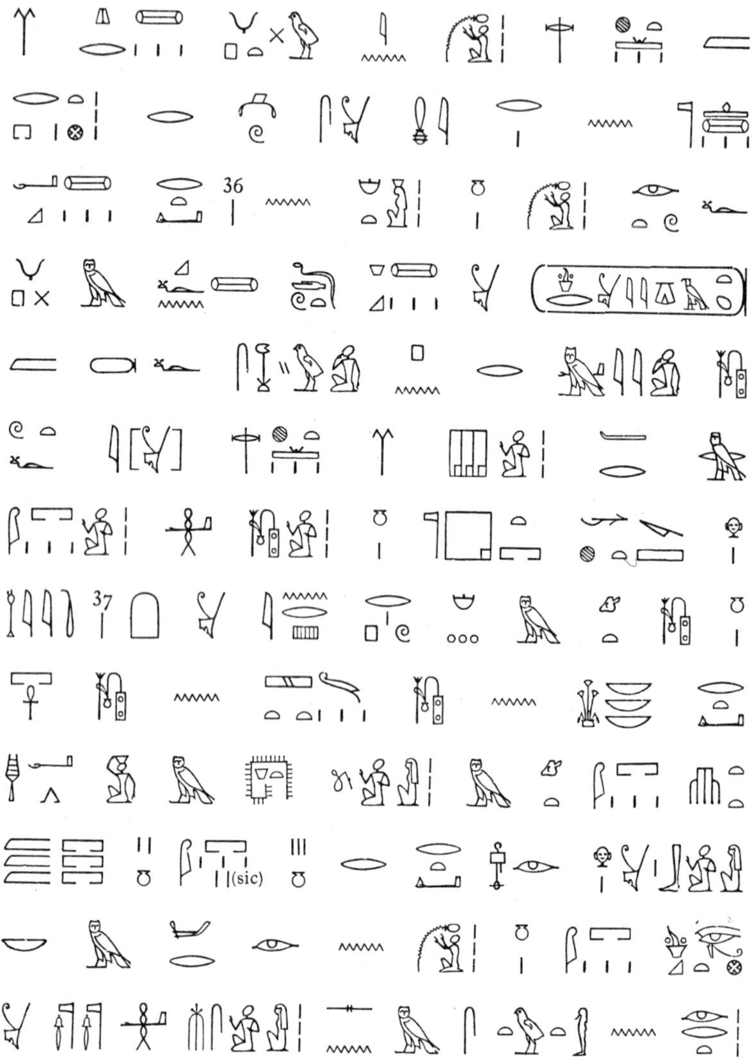

em χeru àptu àn ābu net'χet em erperut er āu-sen mà re en neter ḥetepu āqu
36 *erṭāt* 36. *en ḥemt nu ābu àritu-f àp em qefen t'eṭtu āqu en Barenikat em ren-f seχaiu pen er māi ān-tu-f àn net' χet em ḥetu ḥer mer maāu ḥā ānu nu*
37 *neter ḥet χet ḥer utiθ* 37. *en àner repu χemt em-χent ān nu per ānχ ān en šetet ān en Ḥa-nebu erṭāt āḥā-f em useχt reṭu em χent maāu χentet maāu sen maāu χemet er erṭāt āb ḥrà-nebu neb em serer àri en ābu nu maāu Baqet en neterui menχui ḥā mesu-sen em setut en àritu.*

THE PRECEPTS OF KAQEMNȦ.

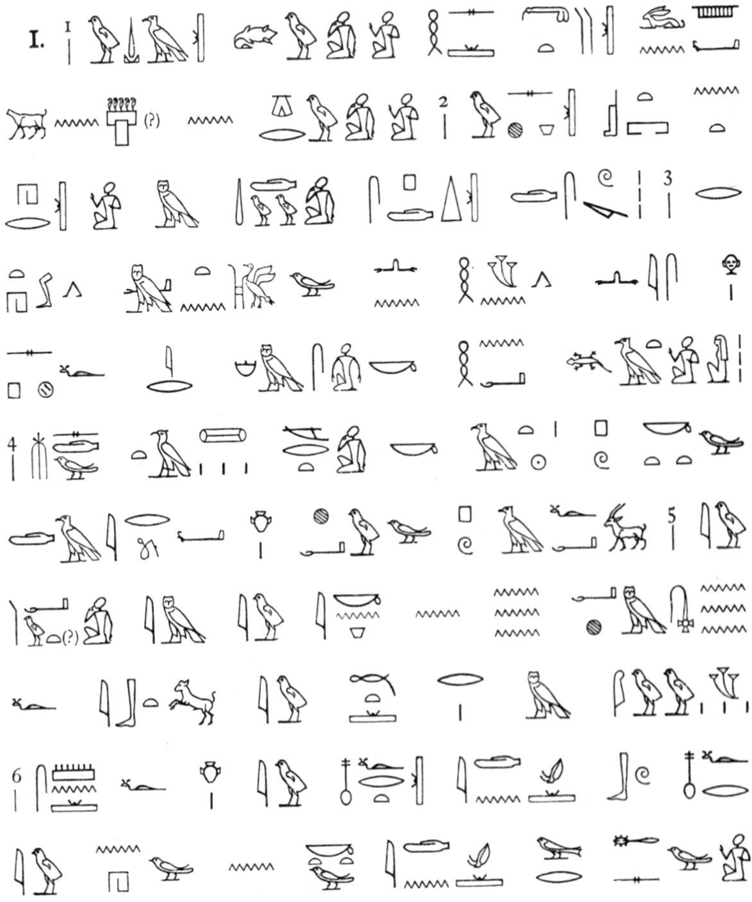

I. — 1. *uťa senṭu-ȧ ḥes met un χen en ḳeru-ȧ* 2. *useχ ȧuset ent her-ȧ* 1, 2
em meṭuu sepṭ ṭesu 3. *er teh māten ȧn ḥen ȧn-ȧs ḥer sep-f ȧr ḥems-k ḥnā* 3
āšta 4. *mesṭ tau mert-k at pu ketet ṭaȧr ȧb χāu pu afā* 5. *ȧu āut ȧm ȧu* 4, 5
ȧken en mu āχem-f ȧbt ȧu meḥt re em šuu 6. *semen-f ȧb ȧu nefert ȧṭen* 6
bu nefer ȧu neh en ketet ȧṭen ur χas

7, 8 7. *pu ḥent en χat-f seua trȧ-s χem-nef usten χat em per-sen ȧr* 8. *ḥems-*
9 *k ḥnā afā ȧm-ka χeft-f seua ȧr surȧ-k ḥnā* 9. *teχu sešep-k ȧu*
10 *ȧb-f ḥetepu em atu er ȧuf er-ḳes seken* 10. *sešep ṭā-f nek em uȧn-set*
11 *ka sesefet pu ȧr šuu em sereχ en sa* 11. *ȧn seχem en meṭet nebt ȧm-f*
12 *χeṭer en ḥrȧ er ṭefa-ȧb ȧmam-nef* 12. *kahes er mut-f meru-f pu bu*
1 *nebu ȧmmā per ren-k* **II.** — 1. *ȧu ḳer-k em re-k nȧst-k em āāa*
ȧb-k ḥer

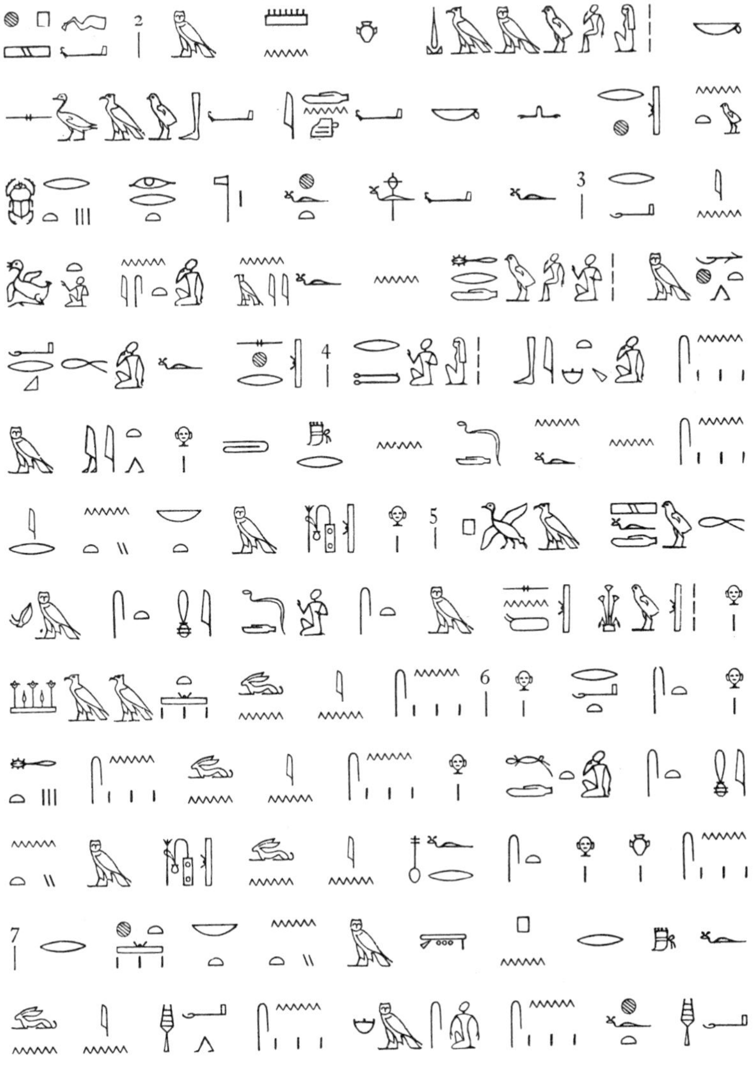

χepeś 2. *em men ȧb ťamu-k saub ȧṭen-k ȧn reχ entu χepert ȧrit neter* 2
χeft χesef-f 3. *erṭā ȧn ťat nȧst naif en χarṭu emχet ārq-f seχer* 3
4. *reθ bȧt-sen em it ḥer . . . . . . ťer en ťeṭ-nef en sen ȧr enti nebt em ān* 4
ḥer 5. *pa śefṭu setem set mȧ ťeṭ-ȧ-set em sen ḥau her śaat un ȧn sen* 5
6. *ḥer erṭāt-set ḥer χat-sen un ȧn sen ḥer seśeṭ-set mȧ enti em ān un ȧn* 6
nefer-set ḥer ȧb-sen 7. *er χet nebt enti em ta pen er ťer-f un ȧn āḥā-sen* 7
ḥems-sen χeft āḥā

8 *en ḥen en suten net* (or *bȧt*) *Ḥunȧ* 8. *menȧ-nef āḥā en seāḥā ḥen en suten*
9 *net Se-nefer-u em suten menχ em ta pen er t̔er-f āḥā en erṭā* 9. *Kaqemnȧ*
er mer nut t̔an (sic). *Iu-f pu.*

THE PRECEPTS OF PTAḤ-ḤETEP.

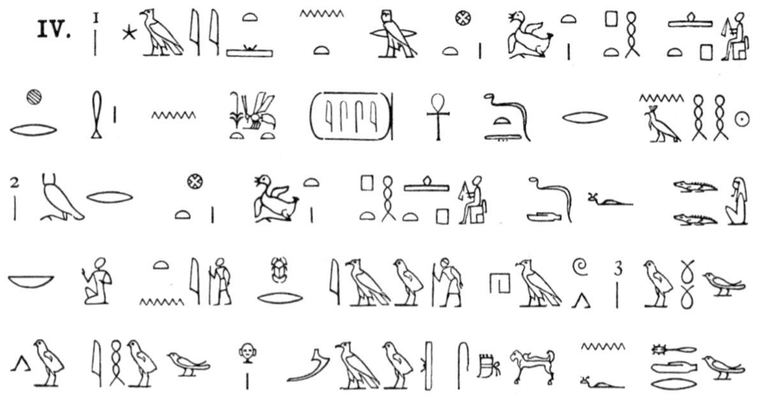

1 **IV.**[1] — 1. *Ṭuait ent mer nut t̔at Ptaḥ-ḥetep χer ḥen en suten net Ȧssȧ*
2 *ānχ t̔etta er neḥeḥ* 2. *mer nut t̔at Ptaḥ-ḥetep t̔eṭ-f Ḥenti neb-ȧ tenȧ*
3 *χeper ȧau hau* 3. *uqesqes iu ȧḥu ḥer mau set̔er-nef χaṭer*

1. Page three is left blank in the papyrus.

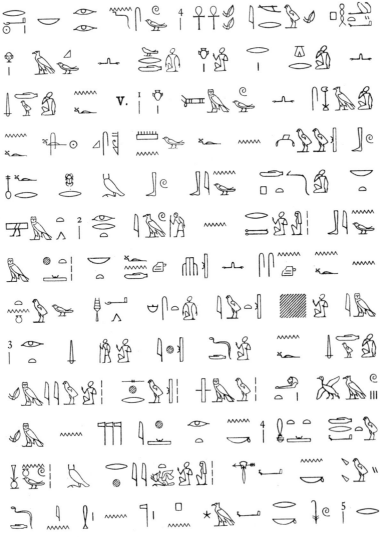

rā neb maati neťesu 4. *ānχui àmeru peḥti ḥer aq àn urṭ àb re ḳer àn meṭu-nef* 4
V. — 1. *àb temu àn seχa-nef sef qes men-f en āuu bu nefer χeper em* 1
bu bàn ṭept nebt šemet 2. *àrit àau en reθ bàn em χet nebt fenṭ χent àn* 2
sesen-nef en tennu āḥā ḥemst àut . . . . àm 3. *àrit meṭ ser àχ* 3
ťeṭ-à nef meṭu setemiu seχeru àmu ḥāt pau setem en neteru àχ àrit nek
4. *màtet ṭertu šennu em reχit sati-nek . . . ui ťeṭ àn ḥen en neter pen sba* 4
erek su 5. *er* 5

6 *meṭet χer ḥāt ȧχ ȧri-f bȧ en mesu seru āq setem ȧm-f metet ȧb neb* 6. *t'eṭ-*
nef ȧn mesi saau ḥā em ʽθesu en meṭet nefer t'eteṭet en erpāt ḥā neter ȧtef
7 *neter meri suten sa* 7. *ur en χat-f mer nut t'at Ptaḥ-ḥetep em sba*
8 *χemu er reχ ṭep ḥesb en meṭet nefert em χut en en[ti]* 8. *setemet-fi em*
qesqeset en enti er tehet set t'eṭ ȧnef χer sa-f em āāa ȧb-k ḥer reχ-k net'net'
9, 10 *erek* 9. *ḥenā χem mȧ reχ ȧn ȧntu t'eru ābet ȧn ābuu āper χu-f* 10. *ṭeḳu*
meṭet nefert er

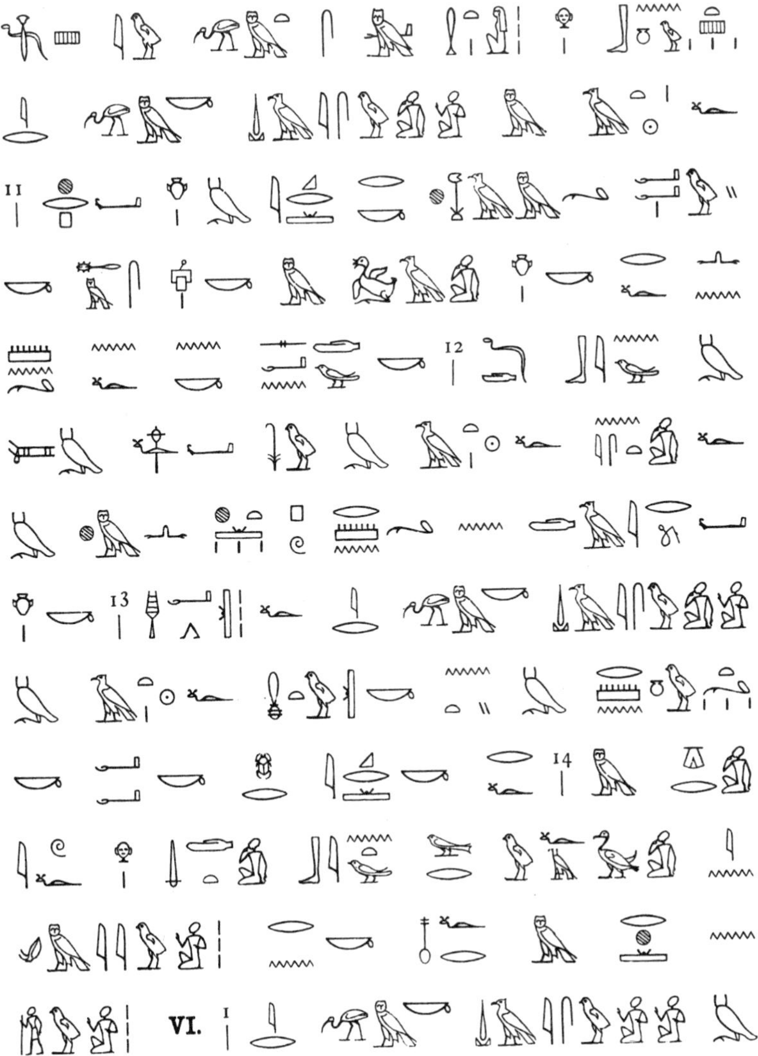

uat' àu qemt-s mā ḥent ḥer bennut àr qem-k t'aàsu em at-f 11. *χerp àb* 11
em àqer erek χam āāui-k χames sa-k em t'a àb-k er-ef àn men-nef-nek
sānṭ-k 12. *t'eṭ bàn em tem χesef-su em at-f nàst-f em χem χet pu* 12
ermen en ṭaàr àb-k 13. *āḥā-f àr qem-k t'aàsu em at-f màtu-k enti em* 13
ermennut-k āāui-k χeper àqer-k eref 14. *em ḳer àuf ḥer meṭet bànt* 14
ur ufa àn setemiu ren-k nefer em reχ en seru **VI.** — 1. *àr qem-k* 1
t'aàsu em

2 *at-f em ḥuru ȧn ȧs mȧtu-k em aṭ ȧb-k er-f χeft χases-f* 2. *ȧmmā su*
er ta χesef-f er-f ṫesef em useśeṭ-su er ḥesi ȧb-k em ȧā ȧb en enti χeft-k
3 *qesen pu* 3. *ḥeṫṫu ḥuru ȧb tu er ȧrit enti em ȧb-k ḥu-k su em χesef*
4 *en seru ȧr un-nek em* 4. *semi ḥer utu en seχer en āśta ḥeḥ-nek sep neb*
5 *menχ er unt seχer-k ȧn āu* 5. *ȧm-f ur maāt uaḥ ṫat ȧn χenenet-s*
6 *ṫer rek Ȧusȧr ȧu χesef-tu en seś ḥer hepu seśet* 6. *pu em ḥrȧ en āun ȧb*
ȧn neṫit

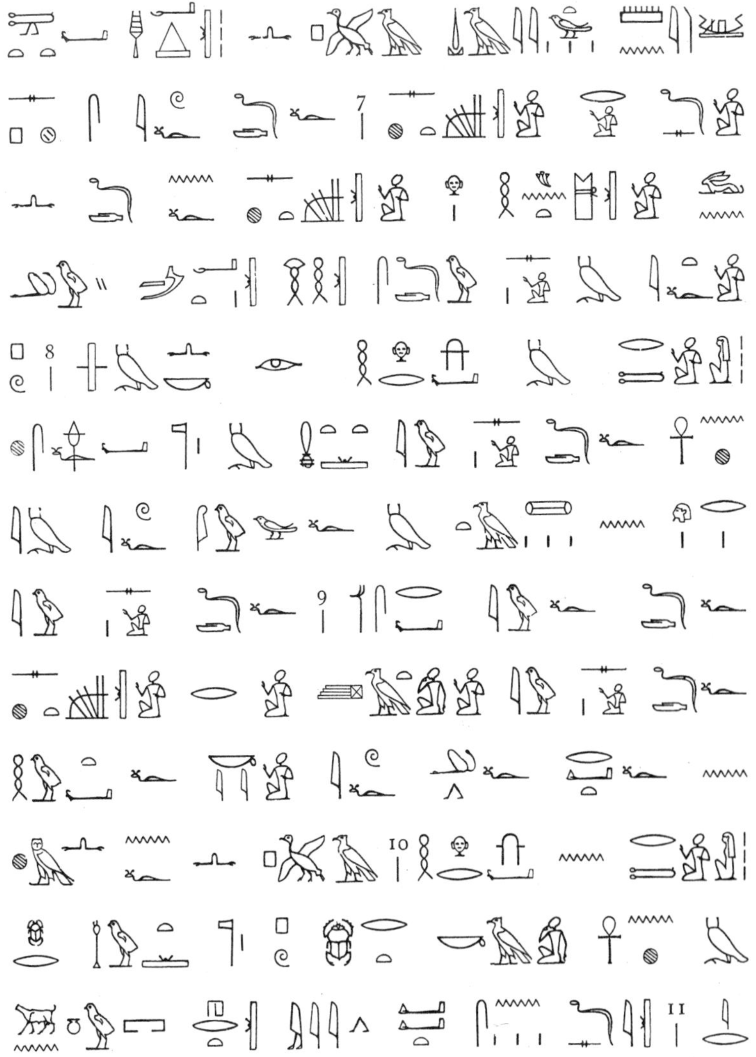

θetet āḥā ȧn pa ťait menȧ sep-s ȧu-f ťeṭ-f 7. *seχet-ȧ er-ȧ ťes-ȧ ȧn ťeṭ-nef* 7
seχet-ȧ ḥer ḥent-ȧ un peḥui maāt uaḥ seťeṭu sa em ȧtef pu 8. *ȧm-k* 8
ȧri ḥer em reθ χesef neter em mȧtet ȧu sa ťeṭ-f ānχ ȧm ȧu-f šu-f
em ta en ṭep-re ȧu sa ťeṭ-f 9. *user ȧu-f ťeṭ-f seχet-ȧ er-ȧ sat-ȧ ȧu* 9
sa ťeṭ-f ḥut-f ki ȧu-f peḥ-f erṭāt-f en χem-nef ȧn pa 10. *ḥer en* 10
reθ χeper utut neter pu χepert ka ānχ em χennu hert i ṭāṭāt-sen ťesȧ
11. *ȧr* 11

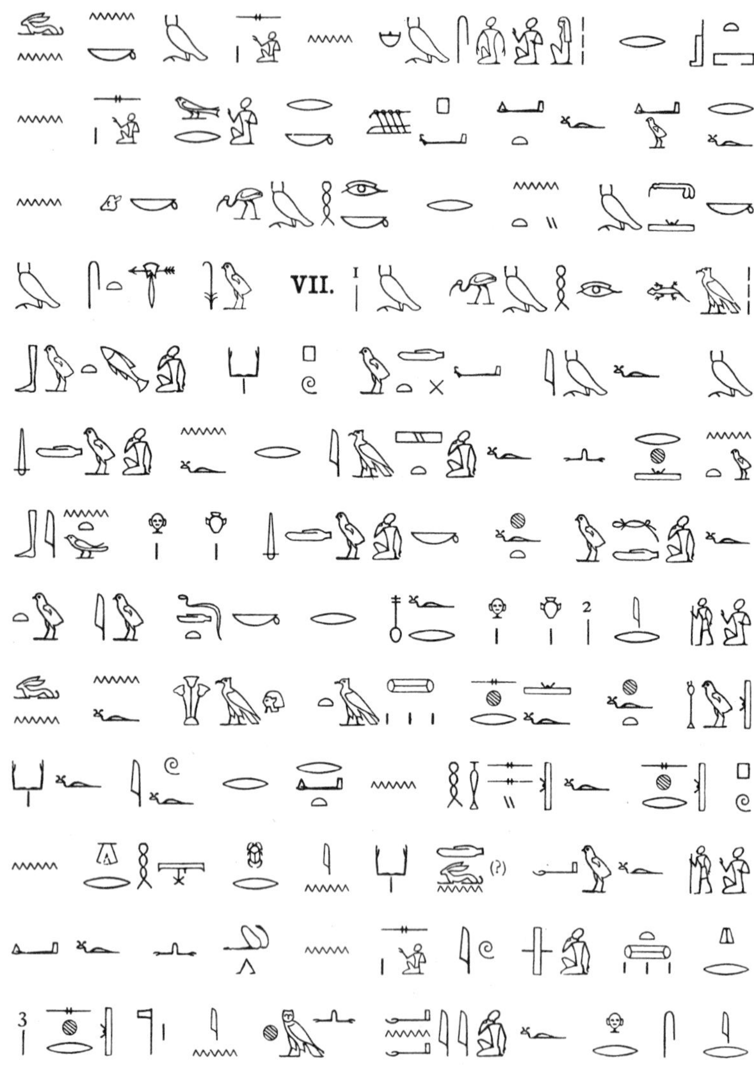

un-nek em sa en ḥems er àuset en sa ur erek sešep ṭāt-f ṭāu er-ef en fenṭ-k
1 *qemeḥ-k er enti embaḥ-k em set su* **VII.** — 1. *em qemeḥ āša betu*
ka pu uṭet àm-f em meṭu-nef er àašet-f àn reχ entu bànt ḥer àb meṭu-k
2 *χeft useśeṭ-f-tu àu ṫeṭet-k er nefer ḥer àb* 2. *àr ur un-nef ḥa ta seχer-f*
χeft utu ka-f àu-f er erṭāt en ḥesesi-f seχer pu en ḳerḥ χeper àn ka ṭun
3 *āu-f ur ṭā-f àn peḥ en sa àu àm ta χer* 3. *seχer neter àn χem ānāi-f*
ḥer-s àr

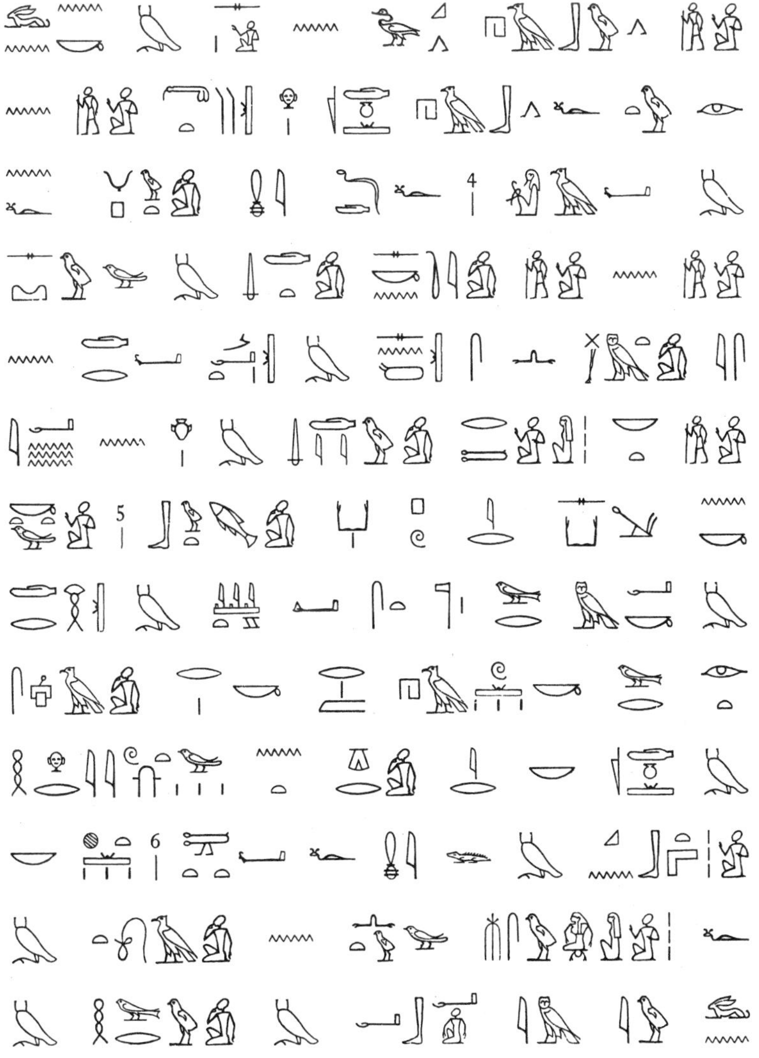

un nek em sa en āq habu uru en uru met ḥer qeṭ hab-f-tu ȧri-nef
ȧput mȧ ṭeṭ-f 4. *sa em seṭu em meṭet sekenθȧ uru en uru en ṭer maāt* 4
em sen-s ȧn uḥemt ȧs ȧā en ȧb em meṭiu reθ nebt uru ketet 5. *betu* 5
ka pu ȧr seka-nek ṭer em seχet ṭā-set neter ur māk em sesa re-k
er ḳes hau-k ur ȧrit ḥeriut ent ḳer ȧr neb qeṭ em neb χet 6. *θetet-f* 6
mȧ emsuḥ em qenbet em tua en ȧtu mesu-f em ḥuru em ābā ȧm
ȧu un

7 *ur àtf em ahu mut mest ḥetep ket er-es àn uā* 7. *seχeperu neter àu*
neb àḥit neḥ sešes-f àr χas-k šes sa àqer nefer sem-k neb χer neter em
8 *reχ-nek neťesu χentu àm-k āāa* 8. *àb-k er-f ḥer reχt-nek àm-f χentu senṭ-*
nef χeft χepert-nef àn i às χet ťes hep-sen pu en merru-sen àr uāt-f
9 *àu sāq-nef ťes àn neter àri àqer-f* 9. *χesef-f ḥer-f àu-f šeter šes àb-k*
trà en un-nek em àri ḥau ḥer meṭṭetu em χeb trà en šes àb betu ka pu
ḥeťet at-f em neḳeb

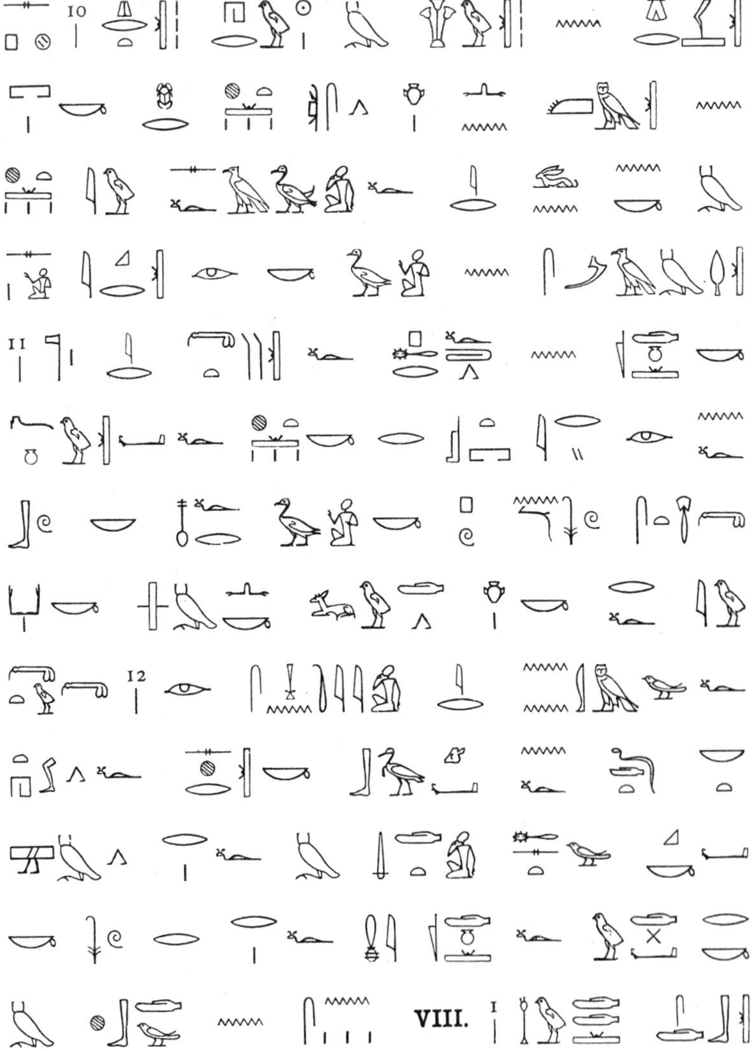

sep 10. *χert hru em ḥau en ḳer per-k χeper χet ṡes àb àn qem en* 10
χet àu sefa-f àr un-nek em sa àqer àri-k sa en smam 11. *neter* 11
àr met-f peχarer-f en qeṭ-k ennu-f χet-k er àuset àri àri-nef bu neb
nefer sa-k pu nes-su sat ka-k àm-k āuṭ àb-k er-f àu metut 12. *àri* 12
senθi àr enenem-f teh-f seχer-k ba-nef ṫeṭet nebt ṡem re-f em meṭet
χast qek-k su er re-f mà qeṭ-f uṭ erek em χebṭ-en-sen **VIII.** — 1. *uṭeṭ* 1
seṭeb-

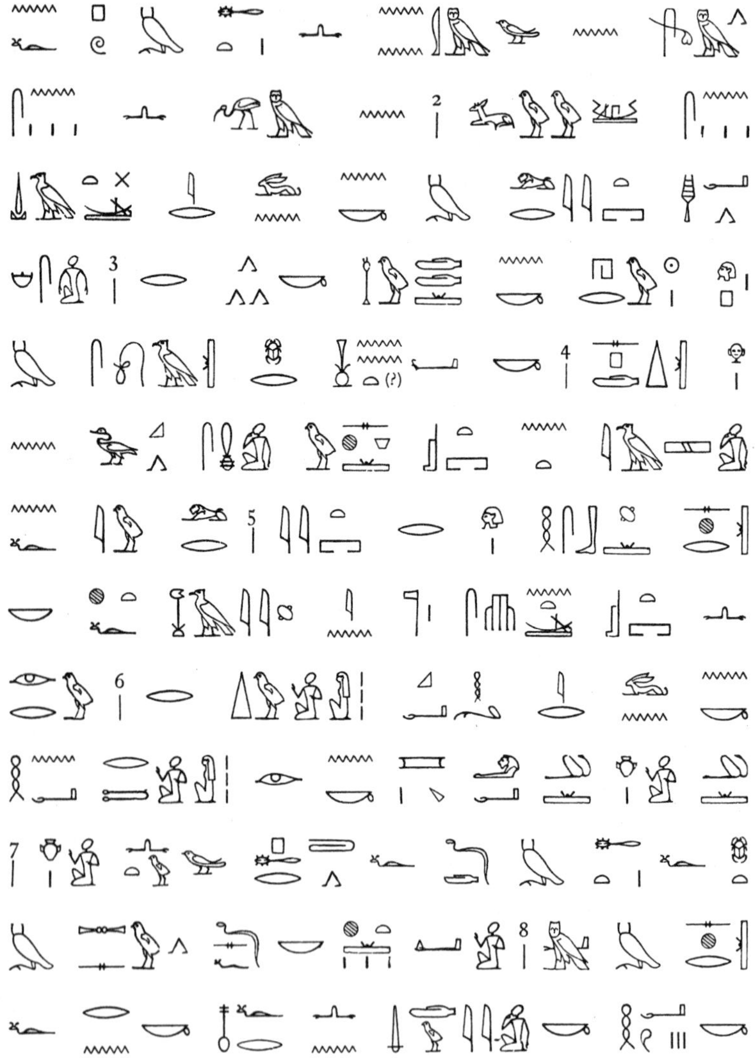

2 *nef pu em χat ȧn enenem en sem-sen ȧn qem en* 2. *āuu-sen ťat ȧr un-*
3 *nek em rerit āḥā ḥems* 3. *er nemmat-k uṭeṭ-nek hru ṭep em seua χeper*
4, 5 *śennet-k* 4. *sepṭ ḥrȧ en āq smȧ useχ ȧuset ent ȧaś-nef ȧu* 5. *rerit er ṭep*
6 *ḥesb seχer neb χeft χai ȧn neter seχent ȧuset ȧn ȧru* 6. *er sepṭu qāḥ ȧr*
7 *un-nek ḥnā reθ ȧri-nek mer ḥā peḥ ȧb-ȧ peḥ* 7. *ȧb-ȧ ȧtu peχarer-f ťeṭ*
8 *em χat-f χepert em θesu ťes-f neb χet ṭā-ȧ* 8. *mā em seχer-f ren-k nefer*
ȧn meṭui-k ḥāu-k

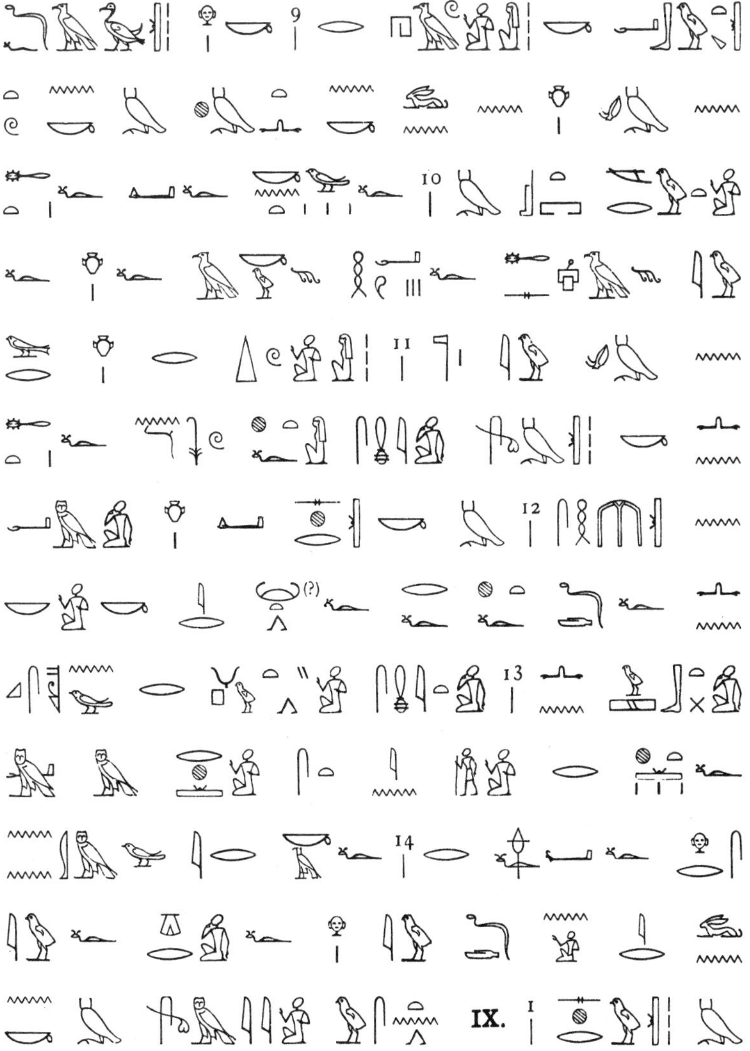

ťefa ḥrȧ-k 9. *er hau-k ābut-tu nek em χemt nek un en ȧb setem en* 9
χat-f ṭā-f kent-f 10. *em ȧuset mertu-f ȧb-f aku ḥāu-f χasa ȧu ur ȧb* 10
er sepṭu 11. *neter ȧu setem en χat-f nessu χeft* (?) *smȧ sem-k ȧn ām-ȧb* 11
ṭā seχer-k em 12. *seḥ en neb-k ȧr uāt-f er-f χeft ťeṭ-f ȧn qesen er* 12
ȧputi semȧt 13. *ȧn uśebt mā em reχ set ȧn ur er χet-f enenem ȧr ka-f* 13
14. *er χesef-f ḥer-s ȧu-f ḳer-f ḥer ȧu ťeṭ-nȧ ȧr un-nek em semi usten* 14
IX. — 1. *seχeru em* 1

2 *utut-nek ȧri erek χet tennu seχa-nef* 2. *hru i ḥer sa ȧn i meṭet em*
3 *qab ḥeset* 3. *beses kapu χeper sefat ȧr un-nek em semi her setem-k*
4, 5 4. *meṭu speru em ḳen-f su er seket χat-f em kat* 5. *nef ṫeṭ-nek set mer*
6 *χer āu ȧāt ȧb-f er ȧrit it-nef ḥer-s ȧr* 6. *ȧri ḳennu spert ȧu ṫeṭtu*
7 *ȧu trȧ er mā teh-f set ȧn* 7. *spert-nef nebt ḥer-s em χepert-sen senān*
8 *ȧb pu setem nefer ȧr mer-k* 8. *seuāḥ χenemes em χennu āq-k er-f*
em neb em

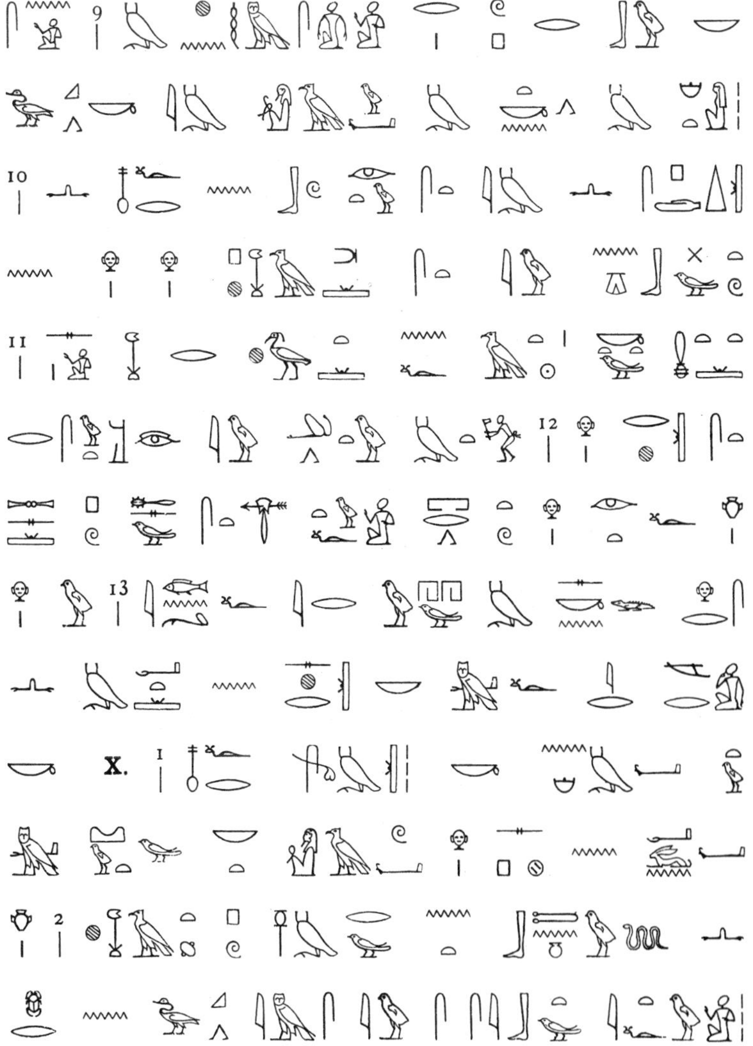

sen 9. *em χenemes re pu er bu neb āq-k ȧm sau em teken em ḥemt* 9
10. *ȧn nefer en bu ȧritu set ȧm ȧn sepṭ en ḥrȧ ḥer peχa-set ȧu neḳeb-tu* 10
11. *sa χa er χut-nef at ketet mȧtet resut ȧu peḥ-tu mit* 12. *ḥer reχ-set θes* 11,12
pu χas set-tuf pertu ḥer ȧrit-f ȧb ḥer u- 13. *ȧn-f ȧr uheh em seken ḥer-s* 13
ȧn māt en seχer neb mā-f ȧr mer-k **X.** — 1. *nefer semu-k neḥem-tu mā* 1
ṭut nebt sau ḥrȧ sep en āun ȧb 2. *χat pu mer ent beθennu ȧn χeper en āq* 2
ȧm-s ȧu sesȧbt ȧtfu

3, 4 *ťait* (?) 3. *ḥenā sennu nu ťait* (?) *ȧu neś-s ḥemt ťai ťaut pu bȧnt* 4. *nebt*
5 *ārf pu neχebṭet nebt uaḥ sa āqa-f maāt śem er nemtet-f* 5. *ȧu-f ȧri-f*
6 *ȧmt ȧm ȧn uni per āun ȧb em āun ȧb-k ḥer peseśet* 6. *em ḥent ȧnȧs er*
7 *χert-k em āun ȧb-k er hau-k ur ṭua en* 7. *sefu er neχt ānṭ pu perer*
8 *er χer hau-f śu em ȧnt en meṭet ȧn* 8. *nehut en āunt ḥer-s seχeper śenθi*
9 *em qebḥ χat ȧr ȧqer-k ḳer-k per-k* 9. *mer-k ḥemt-k em χen meḥ χat-s*
ḥebs sa-s

peχaret pu ent ḥāu-s merḥet-s 10. *āu ȧb-s trȧ en unent-k aḥet pu χut en* 10
neb-s ȧm-k n perā (?) *serit* 11. *seḥer-s er seχem aθeṭȧ* (?)*-s ťā-s pu maat-s* 11
maa-s seuaḥ-s 12. *pu em per-k šenāi-s mu* (?) *pu kat er-s en āāui-s šenenet-* 12
s ȧri-nes mer **XI.** — 1. *seḥetep āqu-k em χepert-nek χepert en ḥesesu* 1
neter ȧr uheh em seḥetep 2. *āqu-f ȧu ťeṭtu ka pu āāab ȧn reχ-en-tu χepert* 2
sa-f ṭua 3. *ka pu ka en met ḥetepu ȧm-f ȧr χeper sepu nu ḥesesu ȧn āqu* 3
ťeṭ 4. *i-ui ȧn* 4

5 *ȧn-tu ḥetepet er ṭemȧ ȧu ȧn-tu āqu un aq* 5. *ȧm-k uḥem meskȧ en meṭet ȧn*
6 *setem-k su peru pu ent ta χat* 6. *uḥem meṭet maa ȧn setem en set er ta em*
7 *t'eṭ er-s s t n māk χeft-k reχ* 7. *ȧqer ȧu utu-tu t'aut ȧrit-s seχeperu er θetet-s*
8 *em mesṭet* 8. *mȧ hepu māk-s seun resut pu ḥebs er ḥer-s ȧr un-nek em sa*
9, 10 9. *ȧqer ḥems em seḥ en neb-f saq ȧb-k er bu ȧqer ḳer-k* 10. *χu-set er*
11 *teftef meṭi-k reχ-nek āb-k ȧn ābuu* 11. *meṭuu em seḥi*

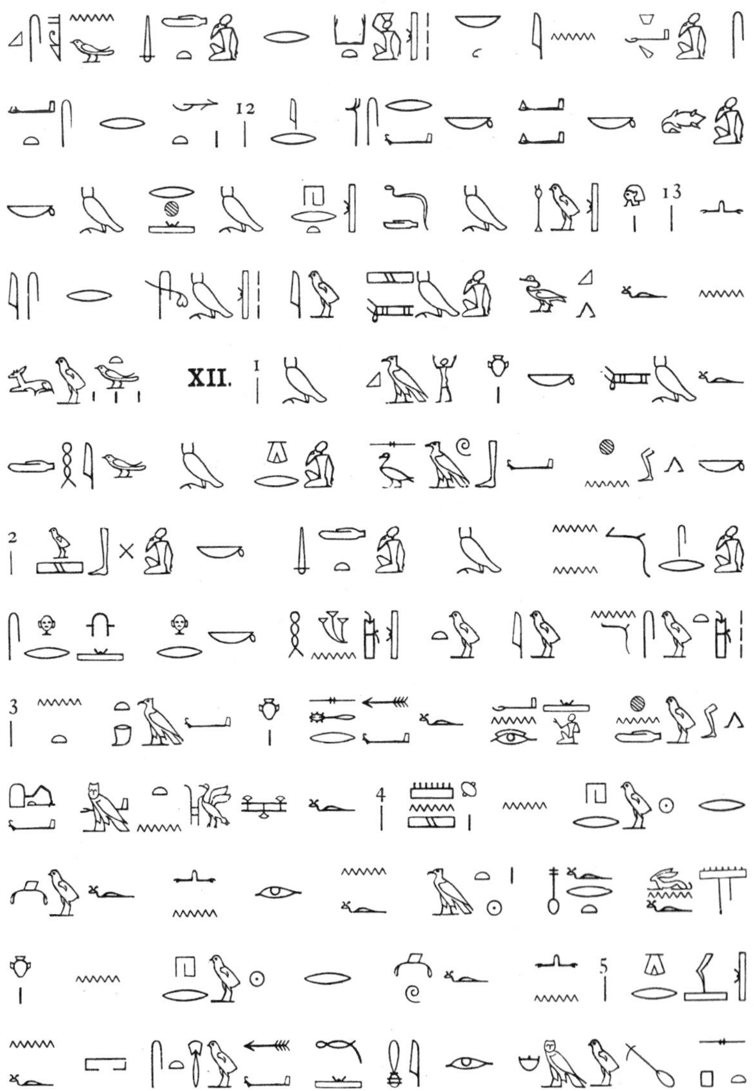

qesen meṭet er kat nebt ȧn āb-s ṭāt-s er χet (?) 12. *ȧr usr-k ṭāṭā-k senṭ-k* 12
em reχ em hert t̔eṭ em utu ṭep 13. *ȧn ȧs er semu ȧu śetem āq-f en āut* 13
XII. — 1. *em qa ȧb-k tem-f ṭeḥȧ em ḳer saub χen-k* 2. *uśeb-k meṭet em* 1, 2
nenser seḥer ḥrȧ-k ḥen-tu ȧu nesut 3. *ent ta ȧb seχar-f ān χenṭu āba* 3
māten-f 4. *menś en hru er āu-f ȧn ȧri-nef at nefert unf ȧb en hru er* 4
āu-f ȧn 5. *ḳer-nef per setu meḥ mȧ ȧri ḥemu sept* 5

6 *er ta ki neťeru* 6. *ȧu setem en ȧb-f er ḥen am χesef tu em at ur em se-*
7 *ḥeťennu ȧb en enti* 7. *atepu χeper seṭebȧ-f er šent su sefeχ ka em merer su*
8 *ṭāṭā kau pu* 8. *ḥenā neter merert-f ȧrit-nef seqeṭ erek ḥrȧ em-χet nešen ȧu*
9 *ḥetep χer ka-f* 9. *ȧu seṭebȧ χer χeft kau pu seruṭ merut seba ur er χut-*
10 *nef* 10. *seχeper sešep-f em ḥer-ȧb reθ ṭā-k χer saa-f ḥer neb-f unen ťefa-*
11 *nek* 11. *χer ka-f ȧu ṭāt ent merut er ḥetepu ȧu sa-k er ḥebs χer-s un*
12 *sešep-f ḥrȧ-k* 12. *er*

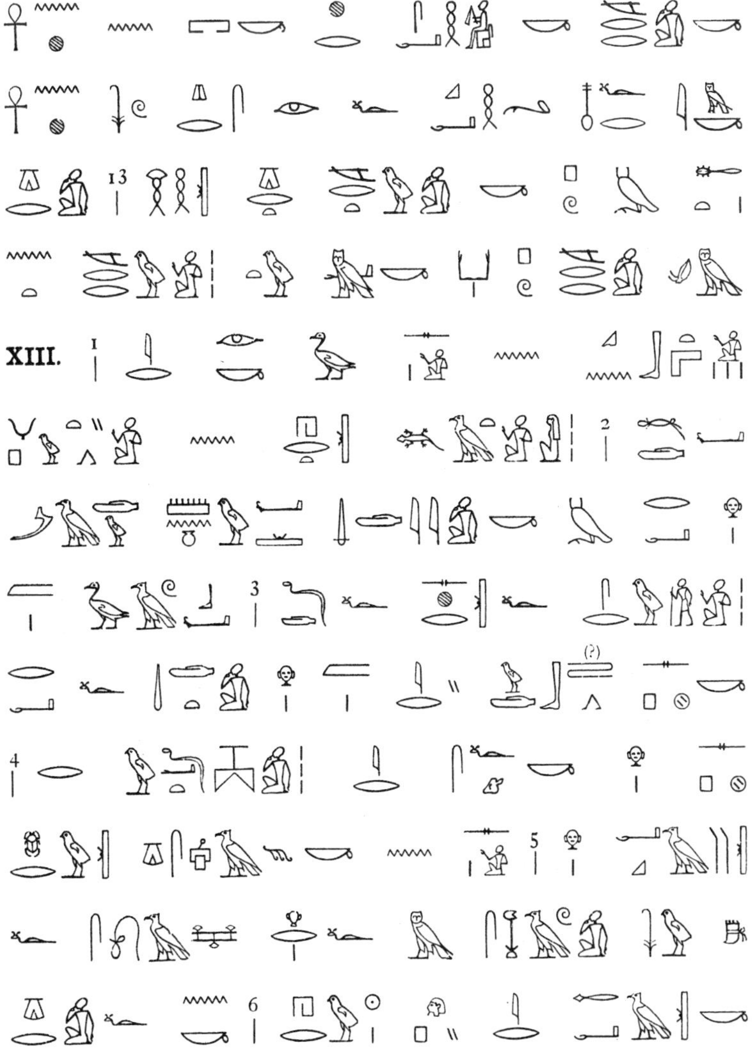

ānχ en per-k χer sāḥ-k merer-k ānχ su χer-s ȧri-f qāḥ nefer ȧm-k ḳer
13. *uaḥ ḳert merut-k pu em χat ent merru tu māk ka pu merer setem* 13
XIII. — 1. *ȧr ȧri-k sa sa en qenbet ȧputi en hert āšat* 2. *sešeṭ* 1, 2
maṭu mennu meṭi-k em rā ḥer ḳes saub 3. *t'eṭ-f seχer-f seru erṭā-f* 3
meṭet ḥer ḳes ȧri uṭeb sep-k 4. *er ut'āt ȧr sef-k ḥrȧ sep χeperu ḳessa-k* 4
en sa 5. *ḥer āqa-f seua ḥer-f em seχau su t'er ḳer-f-nek* 6. *hru ṭepi* 5, 6
ȧr āāa-k

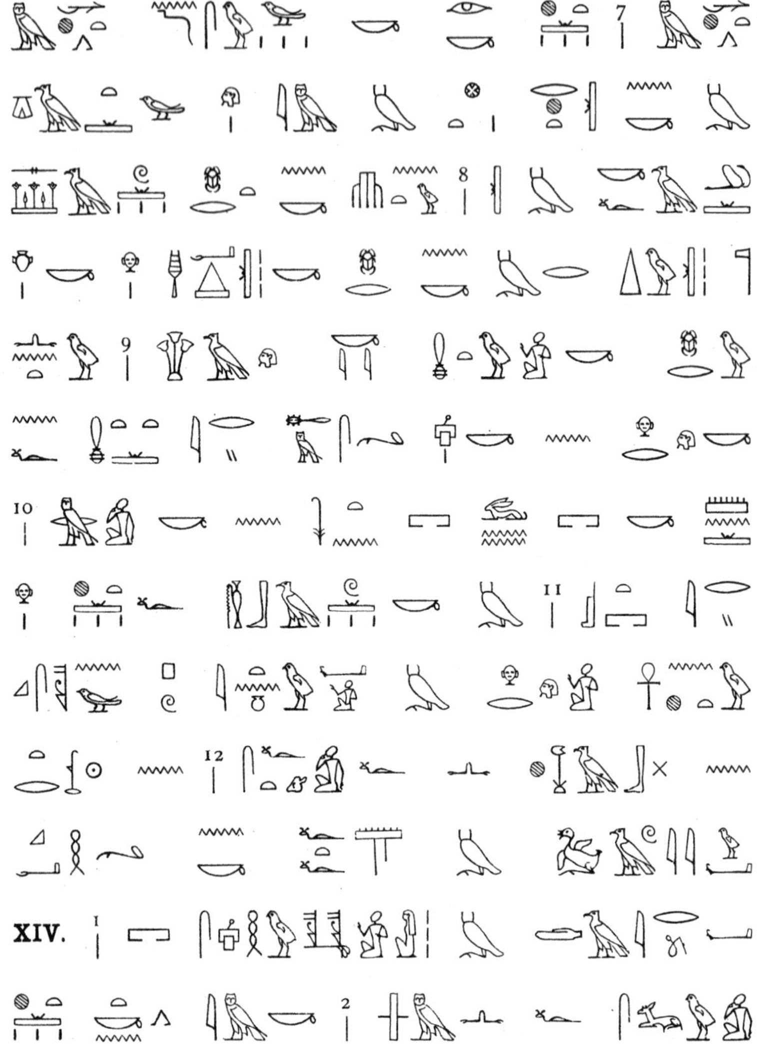

7 *emχet neťesu-k ȧri-k χet* 7. *emχet ḳat ṭep ȧm em nut reχt-nek em sešau*
8 *χepert-nek χentu* 8. *em kefa ȧb-k ḥer āḥā-k χeper-nek mer sepṭu neter*
9, 10 *ȧn-tu* 9. *ḥa ki mȧtu-k χeperu-nef mȧtet ȧri χames sa-k en ḥer-k* 10. *mer-k*
11 *en suten per unen per-k men ḥer χet-f qebḥau-k em* 11. *ȧuset ȧri*
12 *qesen pu ȧtennu em ḥer ānχ-tu trȧ en* 12. *seft-f ȧn χab en*
1 *qāḥ-nek fetf em ťauiu* **XIV.** — 1. *per saḥu em ṭaȧr χet teken ȧm-k*
2 2. *ȧm-f seāu*

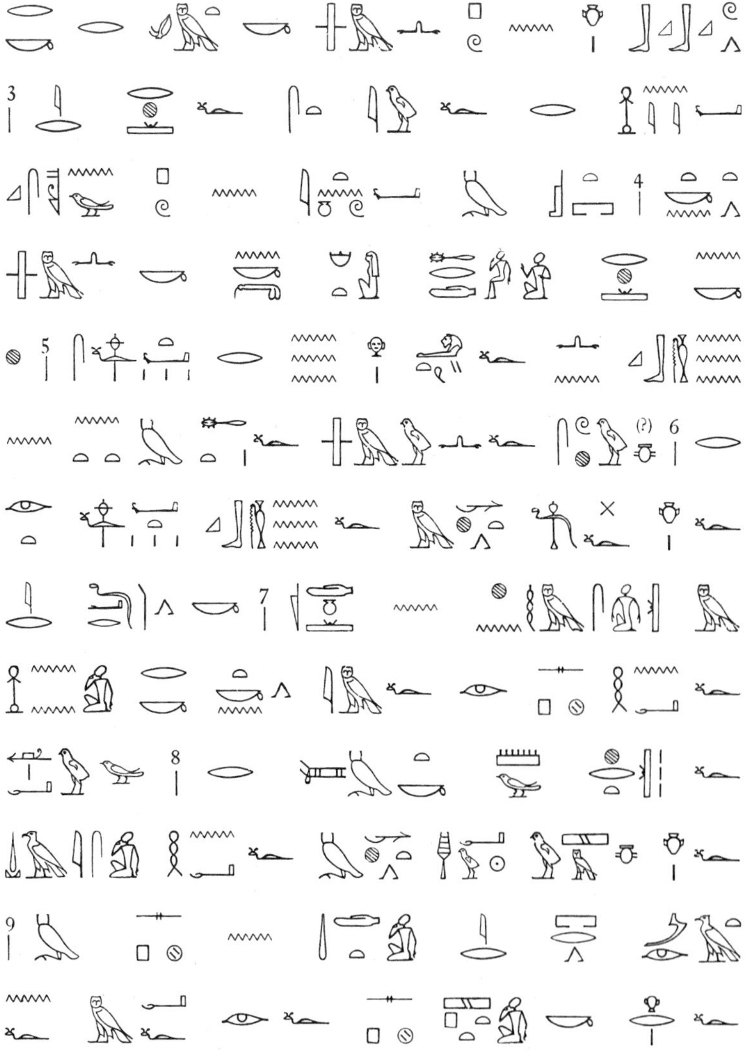

erek er setemet-k ȧm pu en ȧb beqbequ 3. *ȧr reχ-f set ȧu-f er ṡeni qesen* 3
pu en ȧtennu em ȧuset 4. *tekent ȧm-k nek ḥemt χarṭ reχ-nek* 5. *χesefet* 4, 5
er mu ḥer ḥāti-f ȧn qebḥ en entet em χat-f ȧmu-f seuχu 6. *er ȧriṭ χesefet* 6
qebḥ-f em-χet ḥet́-f ȧb-f ȧr ṭ́ār-k 7. *qeṭ en χenemes em ṡenen erek* 7
teken ȧm-f ȧri sep ḥenā-f uāu 8. *er temt-k men χert-f ṭ́aȧs ḥenā-f emχet* 8
āḥāu uṡem ȧb-f 9. *em sep en meṭet ȧr per maat-nef mā-f ȧri-f sep ṡeptet-k* 9
ḥer-f

10,11 10. *χenemes su re-pu en θetetu ḥer saqu em āba-nef meṭet em* 11. *uśeb em*
12 *sep en seha em uȧtu eref em hebu su ȧn pa* 12. *sep-f tem iu ȧn uh entu*
13 *em śa-su ḥeť ḥrȧ-k trȧ en un-nek* 13. *ȧr per em māχer en āq en ȧn ta en*
1 *peseśet* **XV.** — 1. *ḥenti ḥrȧ-f sereχi pu śu em χat-f χeper ȧtennu em*
2 *seahhu* 2. *em ȧri su er teken ȧm-k seχau pu en sa amt en qeṭ ȧm . . . .*
3 *χet ťam reχ śut-k* 3. *unen χet-k em χas bȧt-k er χenemes-k ḥeb . . . . f*
4 *pu meḥ-f ur su* 4. *er*

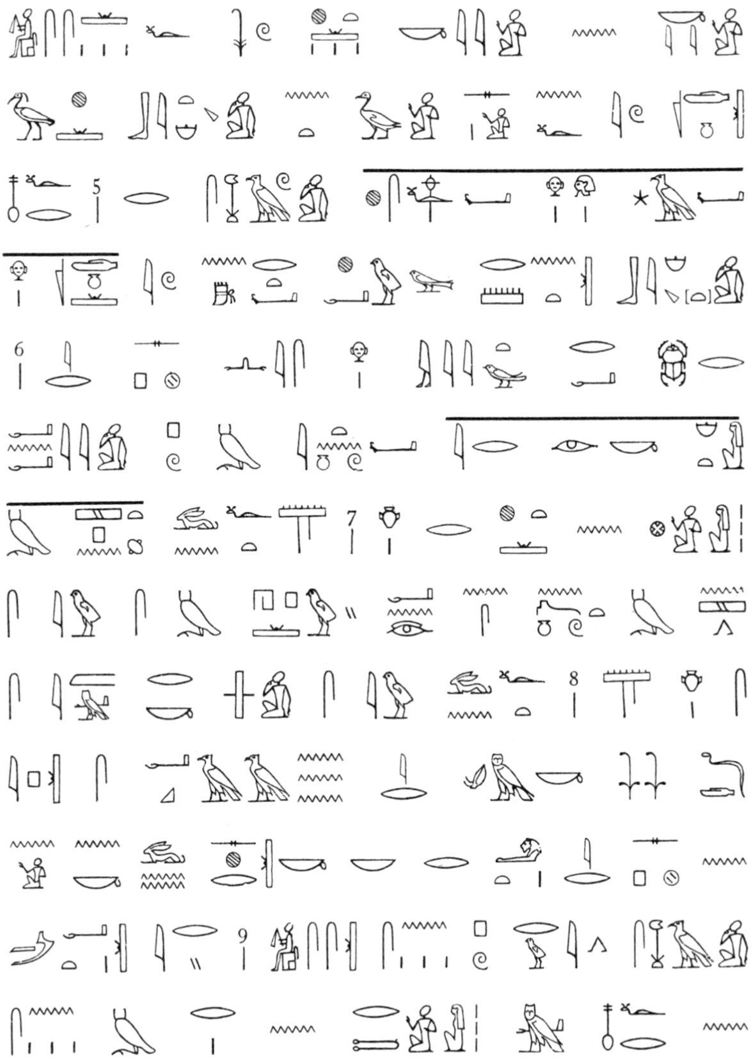

šepses-f su χet ki en ki χu bȧt ent sa sa nef ȧu qeṭ nefer 5. *er seχau* 5
χesef ḥer s-a ḥer qeṭ ȧu neťert χāu erment bȧt 6. *ȧr sep ȧnȧs ḥer it erṭā* 6
χeper ānāi pu em ȧtennu ȧr ȧri-k ḥemt em šepent unfet 7. *ȧb er χet* 7
en nu-s ȧu-s em hepui ān nes ennut em neš-s ȧmmā erek ȧm-s ȧu
unfet 8. *ȧb-s ȧp-s āqaa ȧr setem-k enen ťeṭ-nȧ-nek unen seχer-k neb* 8
er ḥāt ȧr sep en maāt ȧri 9. *šepses-sen pu ruȧ seχa-sen em re en reθ mā* 9
nefer en

θesu-sen ȧn-entu meṭet nebt ȧn 10. *sek en em ta pen ťetta ȧrit-s qesert er nefer*
11 *meṭu seru er-s seba sa pu er ťeṭ en* 11. *emχet setem-f set χeper em ābuu*
setemu nefer ťeṭ en emχet ent setem-f set ȧr χeper sep nefer mā unen em
12 12. *ḥer un-nef menχ en neḥeḥ ȧu saa-f neb er ťetta ȧn reχt semit-f em*
13 *sment nefer-f ȧm-f* 13. *ṭep ta sa-tu reχ ḥer reχt-nef ȧn ser ḥer sep-f nefer*
1 *mā en ȧb-f nes-f āqa* **XVI.** — 1. *sept-fi ȧu-f ḥer ťeṭ maati-fi ḥer maa*
2 *mesťerui-f tet* 2. *ḥer setem χut en sa-f*

ȧri maāt śu em ḳer 3. *χu setem en sa setemu āq setem em setemu χeper* 3
setemu 4. *em setemȧ nefer setem nefer meṭet setemu neb χut χut* 5. *setem* 4, 5
en setemu nefer setem er entet nebt χeper merut nefert neferui 6. *seśep* 6
sa ťeṭ ȧtf-f χeper-nef ȧaut χer-s mertu 7. *neter pu setem ȧn setem en* 7
mesṭeṭu neter ȧn ȧb seχeper 8. *neb-f em setem em tem setem ānχ uťa senb* 8
en sa ȧb-f ȧn setemu 9. *setem ťeṭ merer setem pu ȧri ťeṭet neferui setem sa* 9
en 10. *ȧtf-f reś-ui ťeṭti-nef enen sa ān-f em neb* 11. *setem* 10,11

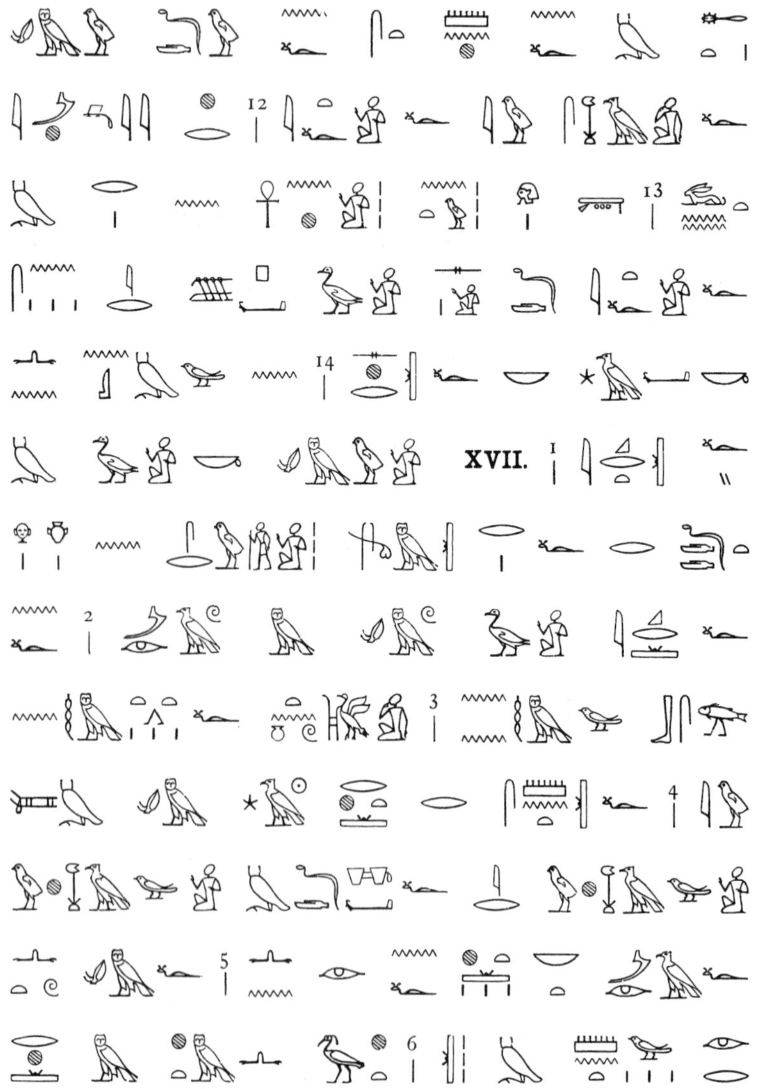

12 *setemu ťeṭu-nef set menχ-nef em χat àmaχi χer* 12. *àtf-f àu seχa-f em re*
13 *en ānχu entu ṭep ta* 13. *ūnent-sen àr seśep sa sa ťeṭ àtf-f àn nem en*
14, 1 14. *seχer-f neb seba-k em sa-k setemu* **XVII.** — 1. *àqert-fi ḥer-àb en seru*
2, 3 *sem re-f er ťeṭet-nef* 2. *maau em setemu sa àqer-f nemtet-f tennu* 3. *ennem*
4 *bes tem setem ṭua reχt er sment-f* 4. *àu uχa meťeṭ-f àr uχa àtu setem-f*
5, 6 5. *àn àri-nef χet nebt maa-f reχ em χetem χut* 6. *em ment àri-*

f χebṭet nebt er uā seset (?) 7. *àm rā neb ānχ-f em metet χer-s āqu-f pu* 7
χeben ťeṭ 8. *bàt-f àm em reχ en seru ḥer mit ānχ rā neb* 9. *seuat ḥer* 8, 9
sepu-f mā āša en it ḥer-f rā neb 10. *sa setemu em šes Ḥeru nefer nef* 10
emχet setem-f àau- 11. *u-f peḥ-f àmaχ seťeṭ-f em màtet en χarṭu-f* 11
em semau 12. *sebau àtf-f sa neb seba mà àri-f seťeṭ-f χer* 13. *mesu* 12, 13
àχ ťeṭ en sen χarṭu-sen àri bà **XVIII.** — 1. *em rāā ťeṭet-k seruṭ maāt* 1
2. *ānχ mesu-* 2

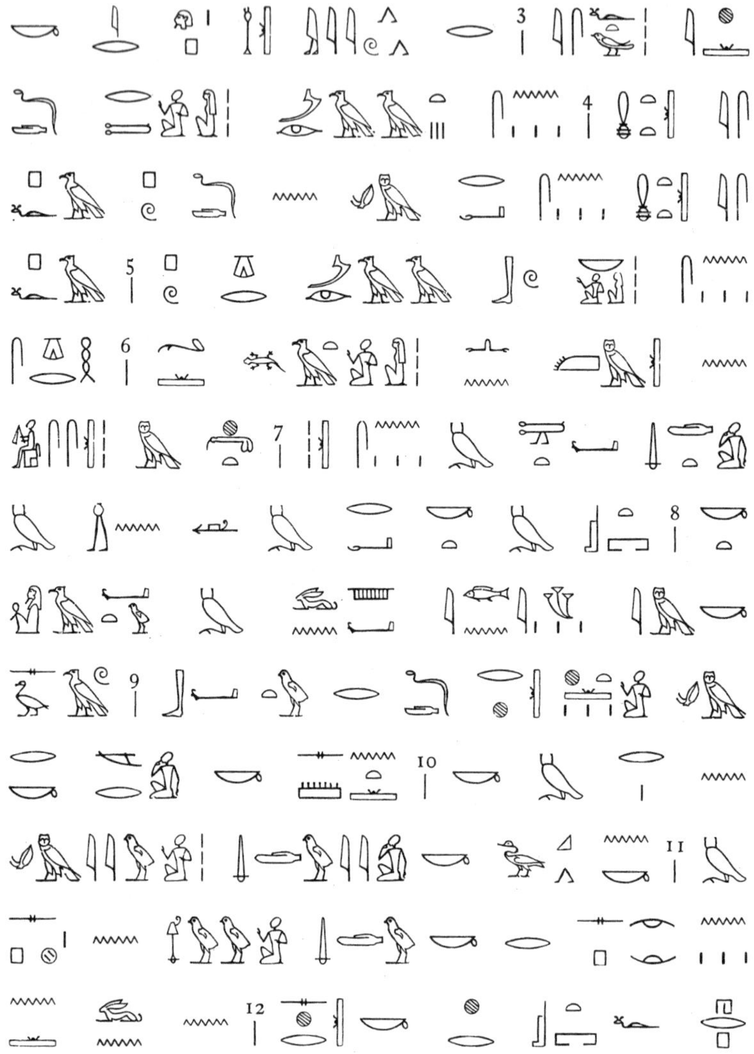

3, 4 *k ȧr ṭep utu iu er* 3. *ȧsfet ȧχ t'eṭ reθ maat-sen* 4. *mȧtet ȧs pefa pu*
5 *t'eṭ en setem erṭā-sen mȧtet ȧs pefa* 5. *pu ḳer maa bu-nebu-sen s-ḳerḥ*
6, 7 6. *āšat ȧn qem en šepses em χemt* 7. *sen em θet meṭet em ȧn uā em*
8, 9 *erṭā ket em ȧuset* 8. *ket sautu em un ȧnȧ ȧm-k sau-* 9. *b-tu er t'eṭ*
10 *reχ χet setem erek mer-k smen-* 10. *t-k em re en setemiu meṭui-k āq-nek*
11, 12 11. *em sep en ābuu meṭu-k er septi-n en un en* 12. *seχer-k χer ȧuset-f*
herp

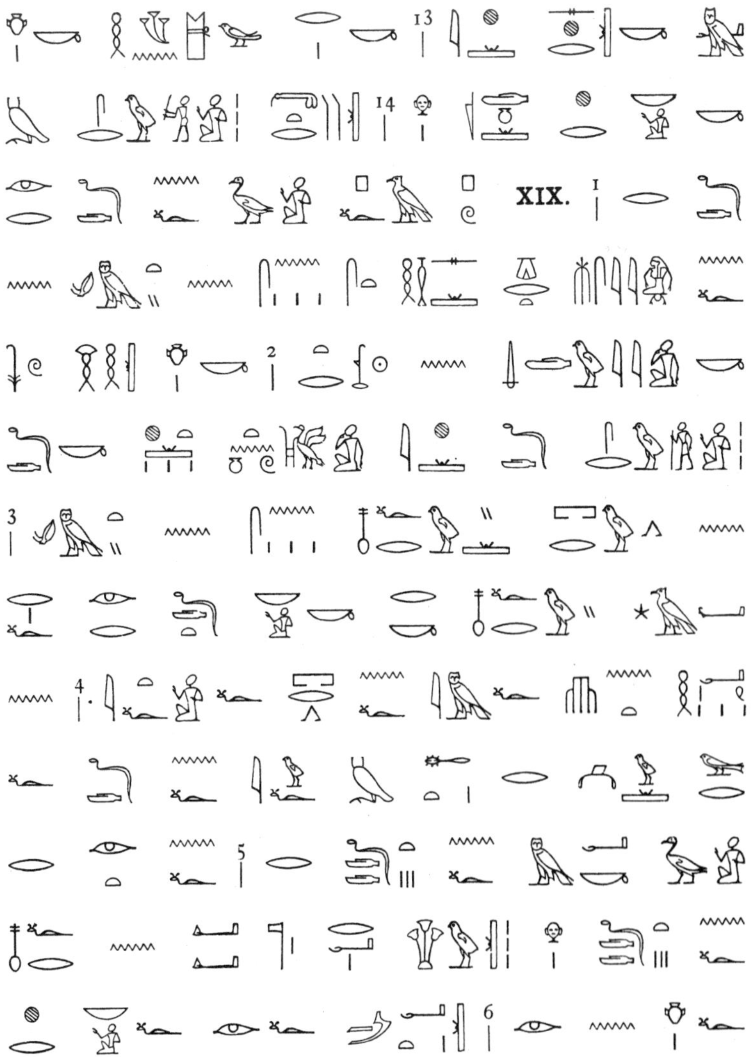

àb-k ḥen re-k 13. *àχ seχer-k mā em seru meter* 14. *ḥer qeṭ χer neb-k* 13,14
àri ṭeṭ-nef sa pefa pu **XIX.** — 1. *er ṭeṭ en setemti-en-sen set ḥes ḳert* 1
mesi-nef su uaḥ àb-k 2. *trà en meṭui-k ṭeṭ-k χet tennu àχ ṭeṭ seru* 3. *setemti-* 2, 3
en-sen neferui peru en re-f àri ṭeṭet neb-k erek neferui seba en 4. *àtf-f* 4
per-nef àm-f χent ḥā-f ṭeṭ-nef àu-f em χat er āu ur er àrit-nef 5. *er* 5
ṭeṭṭet-nef māk sa nefer en ṭāṭā neter erṭā ḥau ḥer ṭeṭṭet-nef χer neb-f àri-f
maāt 6. *àri en àb-f* 6

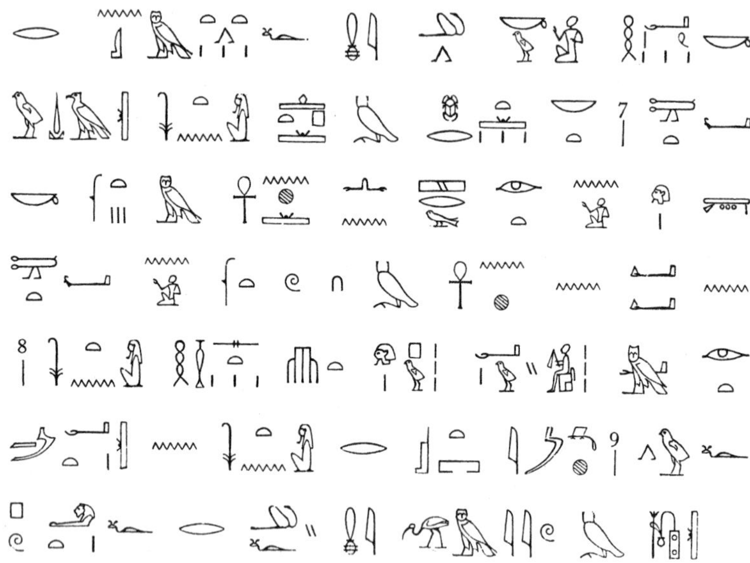

7 *er nemtet-f mà peḥ-kuà ḥā-k uťa suten ḥetep em χepert nebt* 7. *θet-k renpit em ānχ àn šer àrit-nà ṭep ta θet-nà renpit šaā met em ānχ en ṭāṭā en*
8 8. *suten ḥeset χent ṭepu ā-ui mā àrit maāt en suten er àuset àmaχ*
9 9. *iu-f pu ḥāt-f er peḥ-f mà qemiu em ān*

THE TRAVELS OF AN EGYPTIAN.

(British Museum Papyrus No. 10, 247.)

3 **XVIII.** — 3. *Taïk šāi āšθà em nasaqu atep-tu em meṭet āāiu petrà*
4 *feqau-tu em na uχaχu atep* 4. *atep-*

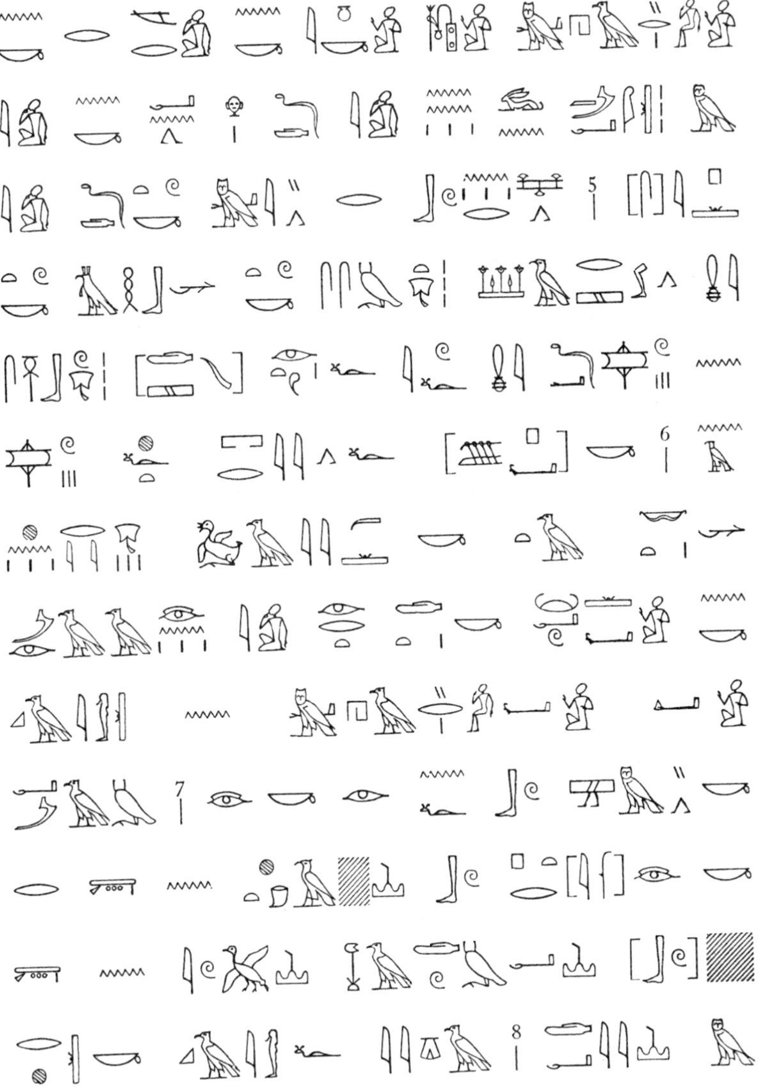

nek er mer-nek ȧnuk ān māhaire ȧ nek ān ḥer t̆eṭ ȧ en-n un maā em ȧ
t̆eṭ-tuk māȧi er bu-n-re 5. *sȧp-tuk neḥeb-tuk sesemet šareš mȧ sābu ṭeš* 5
maat-f ȧu-f mȧ t̆āu en nifu χeft peri-f sešep-k 6. *na χenri t̆ai-k ta* 6
pet maa-n ȧ ȧrit ṭet-k uāu-nek qaȧ en māhaire ṭā-ȧ āmam 7. *-k ȧri-* 7
nef bu šemi-k er ta en Χeta bu petrȧ-k ta en Ȧupa Ꭓaṭumā bu reχ-k qaȧ-f
Iḳaṭāi 8. *em* 8

mȧtet su mȧ ȧχ pa ṫar en Sesetsu ānχ uṫa senb pa ṭemȧt en Χirebu ḥer taif
1 *merṫareȧat* **XIX.** — 1. *paif χet mȧ ȧχ bu ȧru-k utui er Qeṭeś ḥenā*
2 *Tubaχet bu śemi-k er enen Śasu* 2. *χeri ta pet māśa bu ṭeḳas-k uat er*
3 *Pamaḳar.pet . . . . . θȧ em hru su* 3. *ruṭ em āunt ḥer ȧnrena āś peḥutu*
4 *ḥeri āśt maȧu ṭȧbi ḥetemet* 4. *ȧnḥu em Śasu ḥer uat-f bu θes-k er ṭu Śaua*
5 *bu ṭeḳas-k āāui-* 5. *k uaḥ ḥer . . . . .*

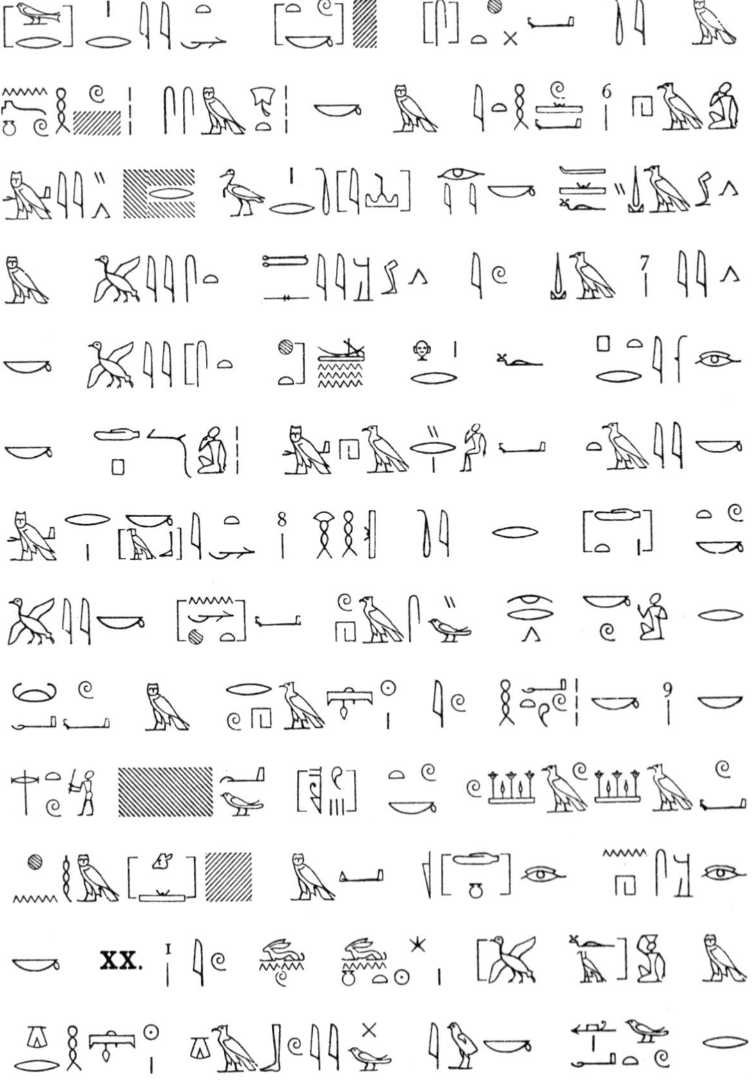

urerit-tuk . . . seχet-θȧ em ennuḥu sesemet-k em ȧtḥu 6. *ha māi . . . er* 6
Bareθȧ ȧri-k ḥufiťa em paiset θesi ȧu ťa 7. *i-k paiset χet ḥer-f petrȧ-k ṭep* 7
māhaire taik mārekabȧt 8. *uaḥ-θȧ er ṭet-tuk paik neχt uhasi sper-ku er* 8
uāu em ruha ȧu ḥātu-k 9. *neb netťu . . . . . . ḳesen-tuk uśauśau χenem-[tu]* 9
emmā qeṭ nehes-k **XX.** — 1. *ȧu unu unnut pa fa em ḳerḥ ḳabui ȧu-k* 1
uā-tu er

2 *neḥeb-k bu i sen en sen ta neha* 2. *-reȧua āq-f paif ȧhait pa sesemet θef-tu*
3 *pa sen em χetχet-tu em ḳerḥ* 3. *ȧťa naik ḥebs paik māreȧa nehes em ḳerḥ*
4 *āmamu-f em ȧri-nef θetet-nef sepit su* 4. *āq na enti bȧn su śebennu em*
5 *na māhaȧut Śasu ȧri-f su em qȧa en Āamu* 5. *pa χerui iu er ȧrit śamā*
6 *em ťaut qem-tu enen-tu nehes-k bu qem-k* 6. *ā* (?) *uārt-*(?) *sen ȧriu ermen χet-tuk*

χeperu-tu em māhaire seṭebḥu meḥ-k em mesťert-k 7. *seťeṭ-nek ki ṭemȧt* 7
šetaau er ťeṭ Kepuna ren-f su mȧ ȧχ tai-sen netert ki sep bu 8. *ṭekas-k* 8
su metett māi er Bareθȧ er Ṭiṭuna er Ṭairepuθȧ pa χeṭ **XXI.** — 1. *en* 1
Naťana tennu Ȧuθu mȧ ȧχ set ḥer ťen ki ṭemȧt em pa iumā Ṭaire en
2. *meru ren-f ȧťa-tuf mu em na barei user su em remu er šāt ťeṭ-nek ki ṭep* 2
3\. . . . . . *neťeset pa seš Ṭaireāu ȧu-k er ťeṭ uṭeṭ su* 3

4 *er ṫeṭbu mer usi māhaire* 4. *māi ṭāu-k ḥer ta uat em χentiθi er Pakākna*
5 *χeperu pa mātennu en Āksapu tennu* 5. *er re merṫa ṭemȧt metett māi er ṭu*
6 *en User paif reśaȧu mȧ* 6. *ȧχ χeperu pa ṭu en Ikama tennu nimāu er*
7 *meḥ-tuf pa māhaire ȧ ȧri-f māśā* 7. *er Ḥuṫare tennu paif χet mȧ ȧχ*
8 *ȧmmāu-ȧ pa ā en śemi er Ḥamaθȧ* 8. *Ṭeḳare Ṭeḳare-ȧaire ta ȧuset sutsut*
en pa māhaire

XXII.

neb metett **XXII.** — 1. *māi er taif mȧt ṭā-k petrȧ-ȧ Iāah ȧr ȧutu ḥer* 1
māšai er Merṭamem un 2. *ḥer tennu em ȧri seḥen er ḥen er sebaitu-tuk* 2
semu en en-n reχ-sen māȧi teṭ-ȧ nek keteχet 3. *ṭemȧt enti ḥeri-sen bu šemi* 3
erek ta en θaχisa Kafire-Māirerena θȧmenti 4. *Qeṭeš Ṭepur Ȧťai Haire-* 4
nemmȧta bu petrȧ-k Qaireθȧ-ānbu emmā 5. *Baθȧ-θupair bu reχ-k Ȧṭurmā* 5
Ṭiṭipuθȧ em mȧtet bu reχ-k ren

6 *en* 6. *Χanrieťa enti em ta en Ȧupa ka ḥer taauśet-f ta ȧuset maa seki*
7, 8 7. *en per-ā neb metett-ȧ māi er pa [se]ťȧ en Sina ṭāu-k reχ-ȧ* 8. *Re-*
1 *ḥubu uāu-kuȧ Baiθȧ-Śaȧare ḥenā θȧire-Qaire pa χet* **XXIII.** — 1. *en*
Ireṭuna ťaȧu-tuf mȧ ȧχ ṭā-ȧ reχ-ȧ pa ā-en-senen er seś Mākθȧ enti ḥer-f
2 *ementek māhaire* 2. *seśsaui em kat per-ā-ȧb qem-tu māhaire mȧ-qetu er*
saḳa er ḥāt māśa pa

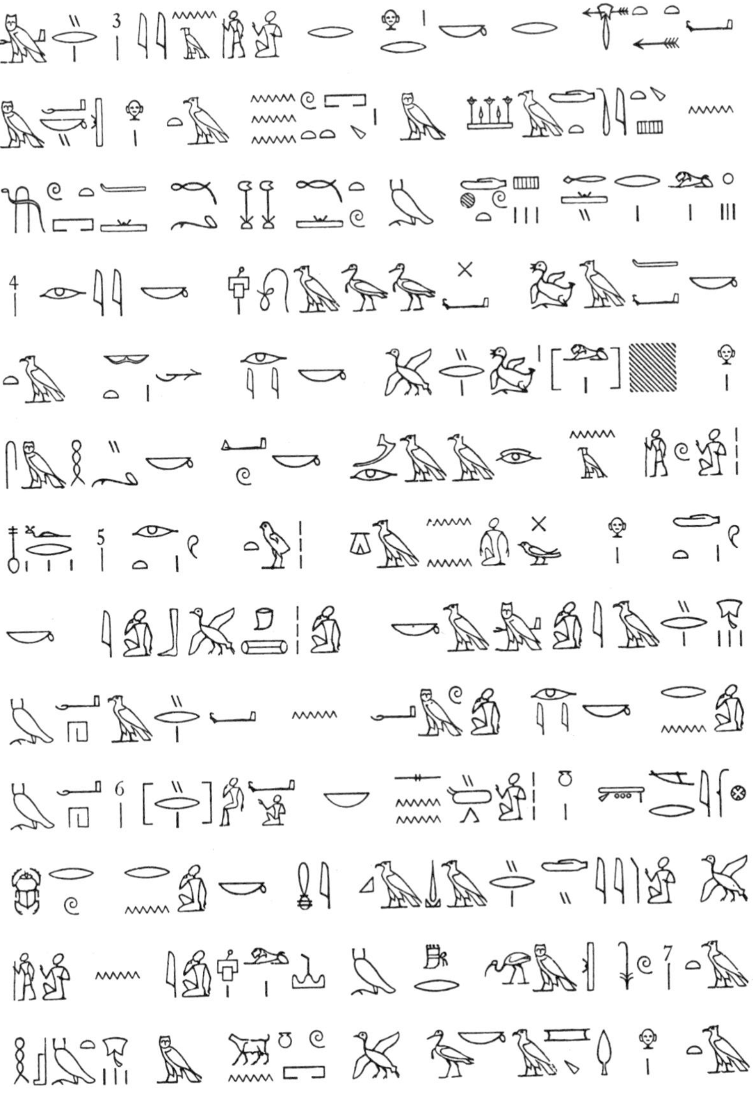

3. *māireina er ḥer-k er satet māki ḥer ta mutet em šaṭetθȧt en meťut meḥ* 3
MM meḥtu em ṭeχut āairere 4. *ȧri-k sauababa ťa-k ta pet ȧri-k paireťar* 4
ḥer semeḥi-k ṭāu-k maa na seru neferu 5. *maat-tu ḳanen ḥer ṭet-k ȧbata* 5
kamāȧire māhaire en āmu ȧri-k ren māhaire 6. *neb seneni nu Ta-merȧ* 6
χeperu ren-k mȧ Qaťaireṭi pa ser Ȧsare em ťer qem su 7. *ta ḥetemet em* 7
χennu pa baka ḥer ta

8 *ḳautet naḥaθȧ em Śasu kepu χeri na baȧa* 8. *unu ȧm-sen en meḥ fṭu en*
9 *ā fent-sen en trȧt ḥesai ḥer bu ān ȧb-sen bu setem-u en sununnu* 9. *ȧu-k*
uātu ben ťaire er ḥenā-k ben ťaba . . . . ḥa-k bu qem-k pa marmar ȧri-f
1 *nek ā-en-* **XXIV.** — 1. *seś uťā re-tu em śemi en ḥer-k ȧu bu reχ-k pa*
2 *mātennu ȧťai ḥer-k pa ťanna ťaťa-k śanre* 2. *en paik bau uaḥ ḥer ṭetu-k*
uat-tuk meḥθȧ em ṭeχtu āanre ben

sasaḥ senen ruṭ-tu em àsburere 3. *ḥer qaťa naḥa θut unšàu na šatireθàt* 3
ḥer taïk uā reàai pa ṭu āḥā ḥer taïk 4. *ketθà à à šemi-k em ha-set kaθà* 4
urireit-tuk ḥer ḳes set senṭu-tu er māťeṭ 5. *sesemet-tuk àr χaā-tuf er sebat* 5
taïk ṭet χaā-θà kefau-θà taïk kauišana hai-entu seš-k pa 6. *ḥetrà er* 6
smamu ta ṭet em ḥeru ta ḳautet ben tu àpt-θà em qaà en meru set bu reχ-k
ḳauatennu-tu 7. *set ta*

XXV.

ȧnqefqefet χaā-θȧ em ȧuset-set pa ḥetrȧ ṭensmen er atep set ḥāti-k fet fai
8 8. *tuk er θenθen ta pet un ȧb χer-k pa χerui en ḥa-k ťa-k pa isaṭiṭi*
1 **XXV.** — 1. *ḥanre-nek uā ā unbu śennu ṭā-k su ḥer ta ketθȧ reȧai χaāqu-tu*
2 *pa ḥetrȧ* 2. *er ennuit qem-k sťeri petrȧ-k ṭep mert-tuk āq-θȧ er Ip*
3 3. *qem-k pa śent* (?) *aχaχ er trȧ-f ȧri utennu en ȧmu qem-k ta śerȧu*
4 4. *nefer ta enti*

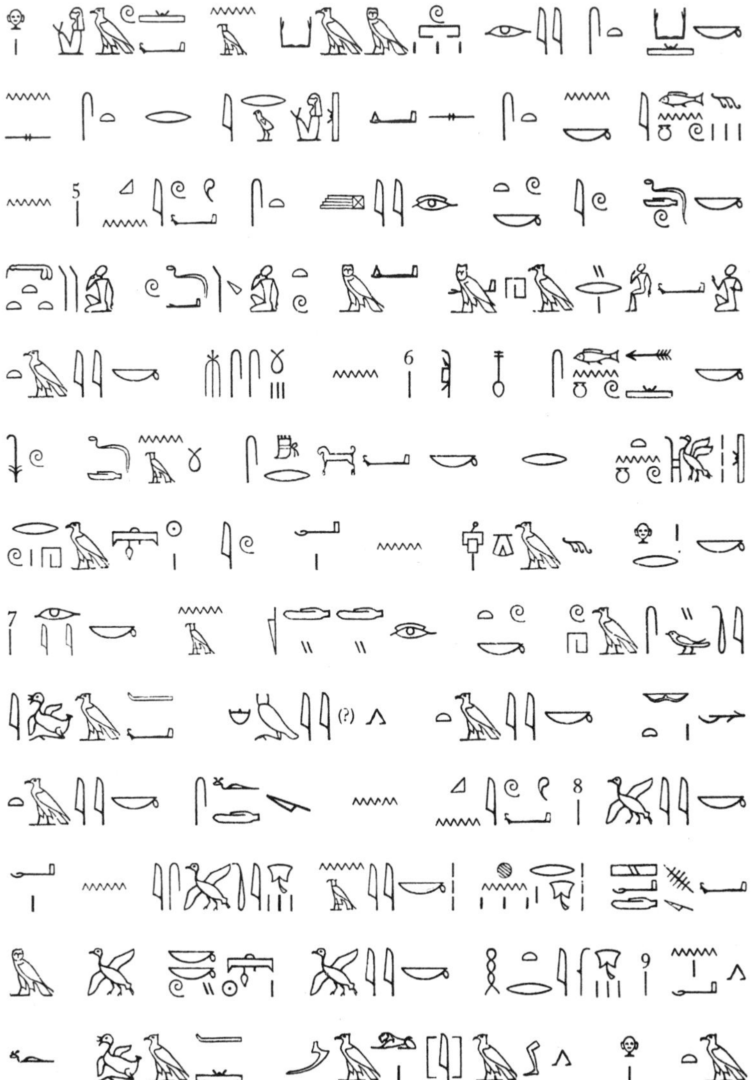

ḥer sau na kamu ȧri-set ka-k nes set er ȧru ṭā-s set nek ȧnnu en 5. *qenȧu-* 5
set sai-tuk ȧu t̓eṭu-k metett ut̓ā-tu emmā māhaire taik meses en 6. *ŝes* 6
nefer sȧnnu-k su t̓eṭna st̓er-k er tennu ruha ȧu ā en saḳa ḥer-k 7. *ȧri-k* 7
na qeṭiṭi-tuk uhasi-θȧ ȧt̓a ḥemi taik pet taik sefeṭ en qenȧu 8. *paik* 8
ā en ȧspaθȧ naik χenre ŝāṭ em pa kekui paik hetrȧ 9. *nā-f t̓a mareȧa* 9
ḥer ta

XXVI.

1 *χireqaθȧθȧt ta mȧt ṭuni-θȧ er ḥāt-f ȧri-f* **XXVI.** — 1. *uśauśa taik*
2 *mārekabuθȧt ȧri-f paik em . . . . . . naik χāāu hai er āuṭent* 2. *set ḥepu*
em pa śā . . . . χeperu em śuit ṭebḥ āťau-k pa neťet re-k ȧ ṭāu-ten śebeb ḥer
3 *mu . . . . ȧu* 3. *peḥ-ȧ ȧu-ȧ uťa-k ȧriu seχa-ḥrȧ bu ȧru setem bu han-u*
4 *naik seťeṭ besi ṭāt* 4. *beset em χennu pa χepeś ȧu qeṭi-tu ābut ȧu ābuu*
5 *θebu em re uat-tuk ȧriu* 5. *mertu-nek neb ennuit-u taik*

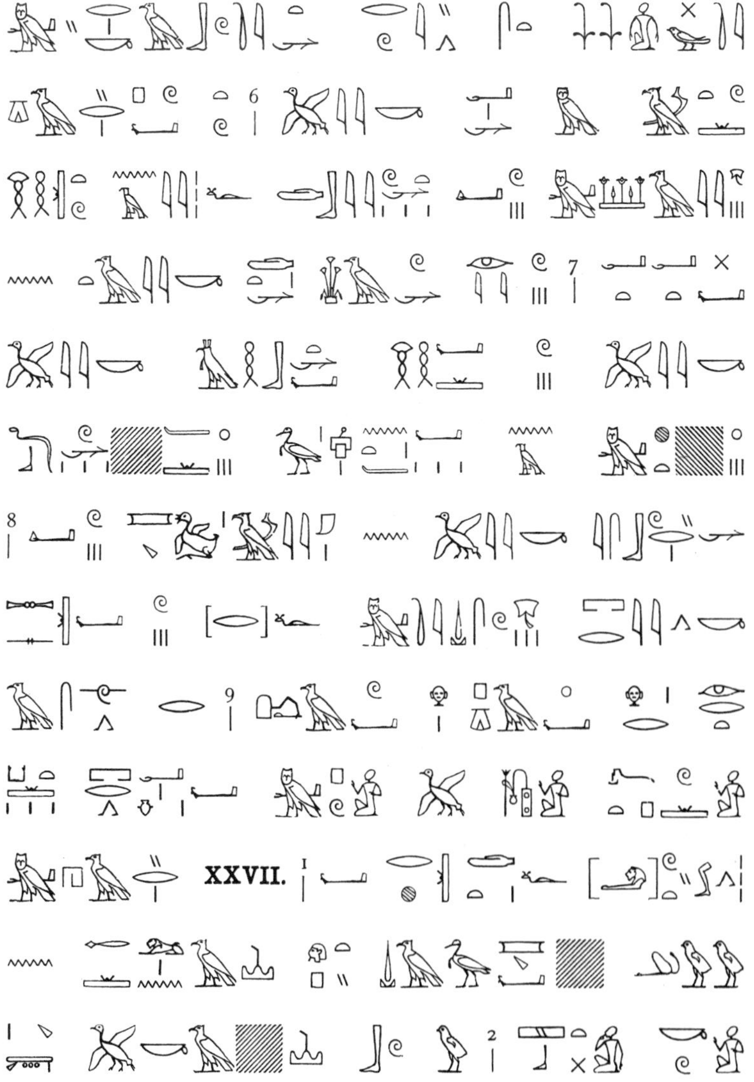

mārekabuθȧt ruȧi set enen-θȧ ḳairepu-tu 6. *paik ā* (or *ṭet*) *em matu uaḥ-tu* 6
naif ṭebitu ṭā-u māśaai en taik ṭet ḥau ȧri-u 7. *ātāt paik neḥebet uaḥ-u* 7
paik ťebu . . . basanet na māχet . . . . 8. *ṭā-u merťamai en paik ȧsbuire* 8
θes-u eref māθȧťasu peri-k asta er 9. *ābau ḥer peḳa ḥer ȧrit kat per-ā-ȧb* 9
Māpu pa ān setepu māhaire **XXVII.** — 1. *reχ ṭet-f ḥāuti en Āarena ṭepti* 1
ťaba . . . . peḥuu ta Paka . . . . . bu uśebt 2. *kuȧ* 2

nefer bȧn bu ān-ku na semȧi māȧi t̓eṭ-ȧ nek [χet neb n]ek pa χetemu
3 *. . . . . uat-tuk ṡaā-* 3. *ȧ nek em ta āt en Sesetsu ānχ ut̓a senb bu ṭeḳas-k*
4 *su em kefau bu ȧmu-ku remu [en] . . . . . .* 4. *bu āb-ku em χennu set*
5 *hana māi seχa-ȧ nek Ḥut̓aina paiset χetem er tennu* 5. *māȧi erek er*
ā en Uat̓it Sesetsu ānχ ut̓a senb em paif neχet User-Maāt-Rā ānχ ut̓a
6 *senb Sa . . . aire* 6. *ḥenā Ȧbsaqbu set̓eṭ-ȧ-nek qaȧ en Ātinini bu reχ-k paif*
7 *ṭep-reṭ Naχai* 7.

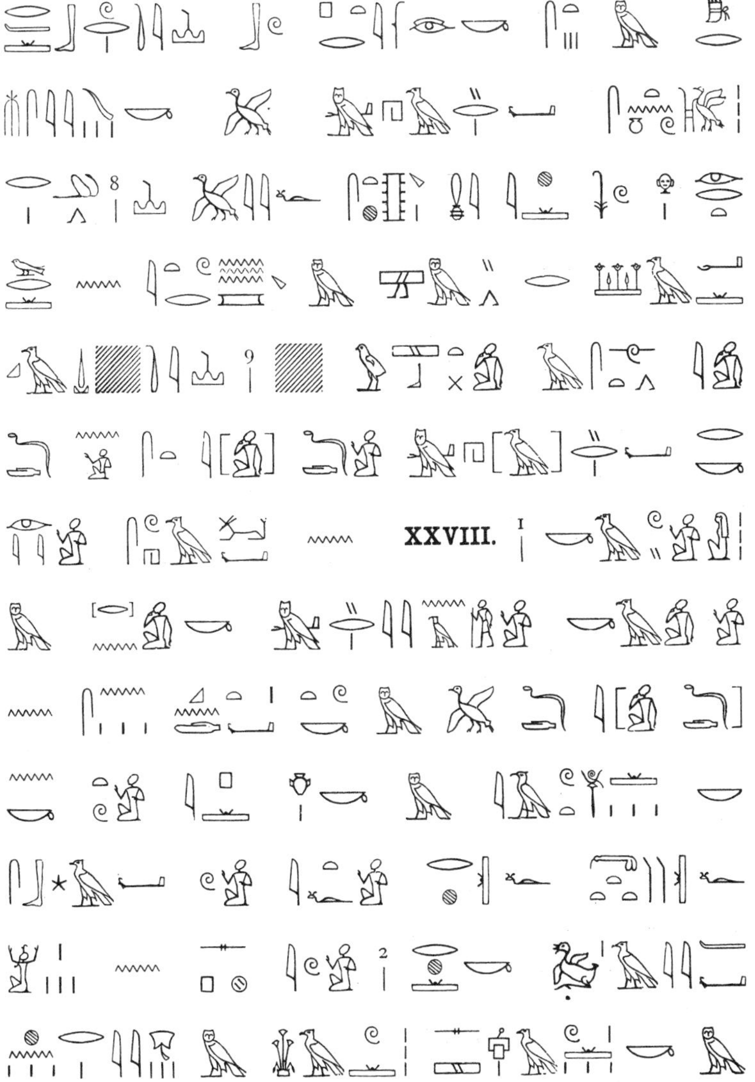

Reḥubureθȧ bu petrȧ-k set em t́er mesi-k pa māhaire setennu Repeḥ
8. *paif seteχ mȧ ȧχ su ḥer ȧrit ur en ȧtur em śemi er śaā Qat́a . . .* 8
θȧ 9. . . . *uśebt asta ȧ t́eṭ-nȧ set ȧ t́eṭ-ȧ māhaire erek ȧri-ȧ suha en* 9
XXVIII. — 1. *kaui em ren-k māireina ka-ȧ en sen qenṭet-tuk em pa t́eṭ* 1
ȧ t́eṭ-nek tuȧ ȧp ȧb-k em ȧaut neb seba-uȧ ȧtf-ȧ reχ-f metett-f ḥeḥ en sep
ȧu-ȧ 2. *reχ-k t́ai χenrei em ḥau seśesau-k em* 2

rā . . . . ȧn per-ā-ȧb seθenȧ-f er ḥāt-ȧ un-kuȧ em utu en Menθu ḥet' usi
3 *per neb ḥer nest-k* 3. *uȧauȧa usi θes-k i-k nȧ baṭenu em teχteχ atep-tu em*
4 *āt'au-u peχa-k meṭet em āq en ḥer-k ȧn fet-k er qemqem* 4. *θenre-tu em ḥer-k*
ȧmmā χesasa-tu ben hai-k su mȧ ȧχ χem peḥ-nef χer peḥ enen em ȧχ bu hai-
5 *ȧ māk-kuȧ sper-kuȧ han-tu ṭensmen* 5. *ḥāti-k ȧb-k smen em ȧri ḥet'ennuna*
seti en ȧmu χaāqu-ȧ nek peḥ en śāt-tuk

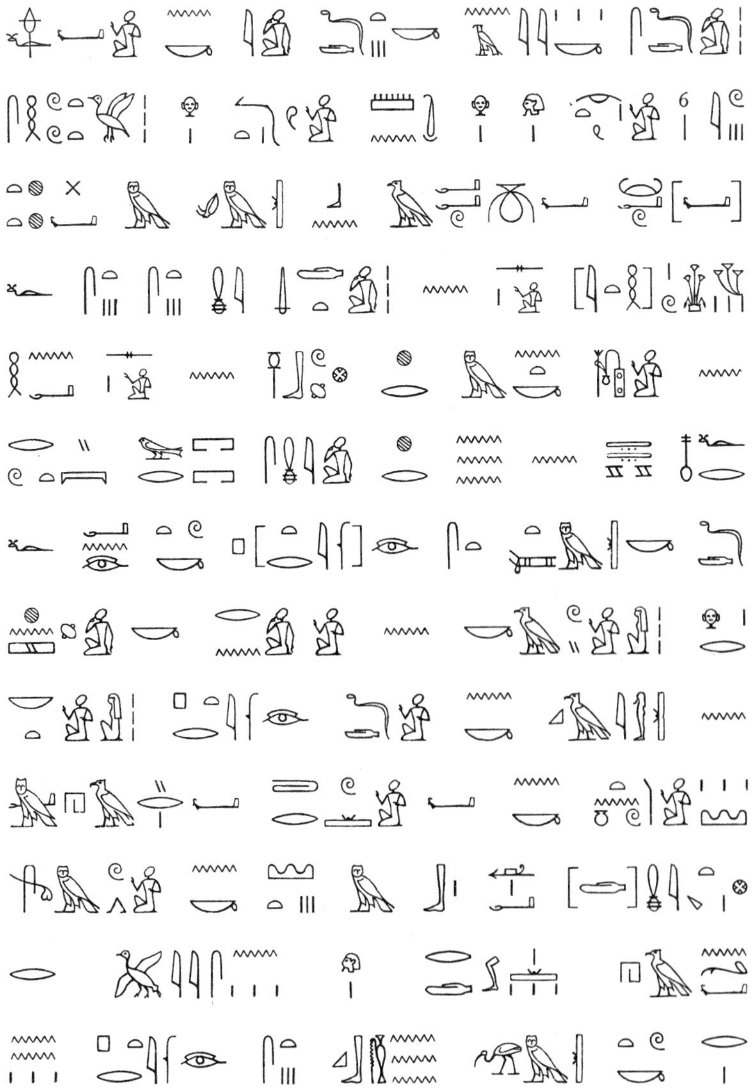

χesef-ȧ nek ȧ ťeṭet-k naik seťeṭ seḥtutu ḥer nest-ȧ men ḥer ṭep sept-ȧ 6. ȧu 6
teχteχ em setem ben aāāu uāu-f set set mā meṭet en sa ȧtḥu ḥenā sa en Ābu
χer ementek ān en ruti peru ur semȧ χer mu en taui nefer-f ān-tuk petrȧ-
set tem-k ťeṭ χenš-k ren-ȧ en kaui ḥrȧ nebt petrȧ ťeṭ-ȧ nek qaȧ en māhaire
reru-ȧ nek tennu semu-ȧ nek set em bu uā ṭemȧt er paisen ṭep reṭ han-en-n
petrȧ-set qeb[ḥ] qem-tuk re

seťeṭ-u χeperu neb emmā pa Sire-uah.

HYMN TO ȦMEN-RĀ.

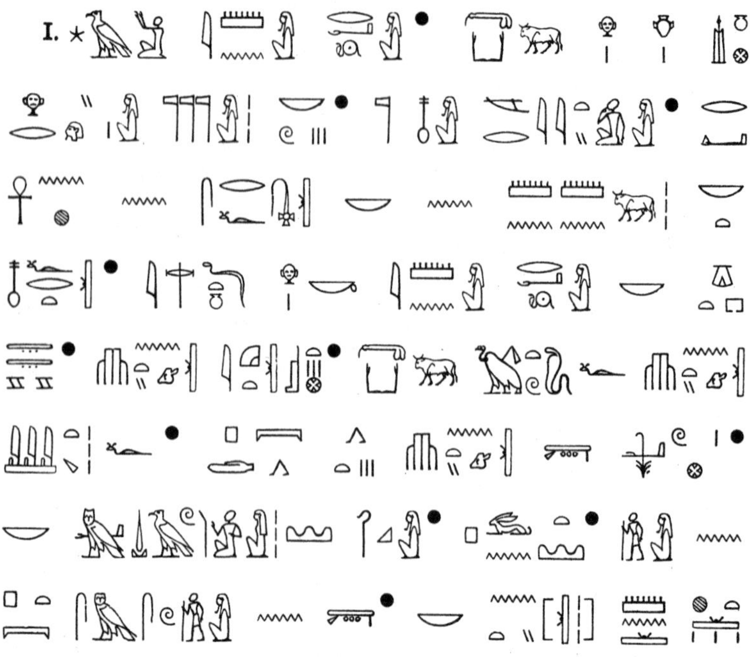

I. *ṭua Ȧmen-Rā • ka ḥer ȧb Ȧnnu ḥeri neteru nebu • neter nefer meriti • erṭā ānχ en seref neb en menmenu nebt nefert • ȧneťet ḥrȧ-k Ȧmen-Rā neb nest taiu • χenti Ȧptet • ka mut-f χenti seχet-f • peṭ nemmat χenti ta qemāu • neb māťau ḥeq • Punt • ser en pet semsu en ta • neb enti men χet*

men χet nebt • *uā ḥer sepu-f mȧ emmā neteru* • *ka nefer en paut neteru* • *ḥeri neteru nebu* • *neb maāt ȧtf neteru* • *ȧri reθ qemam āut* • *neb enti qemam χet en ānχu* • *ȧri simu seānχ menmenet* • *seχem nefer ȧri en Ptaḥ* • *ḥun nefer en* **II.** *mertu* • *ṭāṭāu-nef neteru ȧau* • *ȧri χeru ḥeru seḥet́-f taiu* • *t́a ḥert em ḥetepu* • *suten net Rā maātχeru ḥeri taiu* • *āāa peḥti neb šefit* • *ḥeri ȧri ta maqeṭ-f* • *ten seχeru er neter neb* • *ḥāāu neteru em neferu-f* • *ṭāṭāu-nef hennu em peru ur* • *seχāu em peru seref* (?) •

merru neteru sti-f • χeft i-f em Punt • ser ȧaṭt ha-f Māťau • nefer ḥer i neter ta • χenχen neteru reṭ-fi • χeft sa-sen ḥen-f em neb-sen • neb senṭet āāa nerȧu • ur baiu seχem χā • uať ḥetepu ȧri ťefau • hennu-nek ȧri neteru • āχ pet ṭer satu **III.** *res uťa Ȧmsu Ȧmen • neb neḥeḥ ȧri ťetta • neb ȧau χenti Ȧptet • men kerti nefer ḥrȧ • neb urerit qa šuti • nefer sešeṭ qa ḥeťet • meḥennu uaťti na ḥrȧ-f • qemȧti-f ȧmi ḥet-ā • seχti*

* Restored from Plate V, line 5.

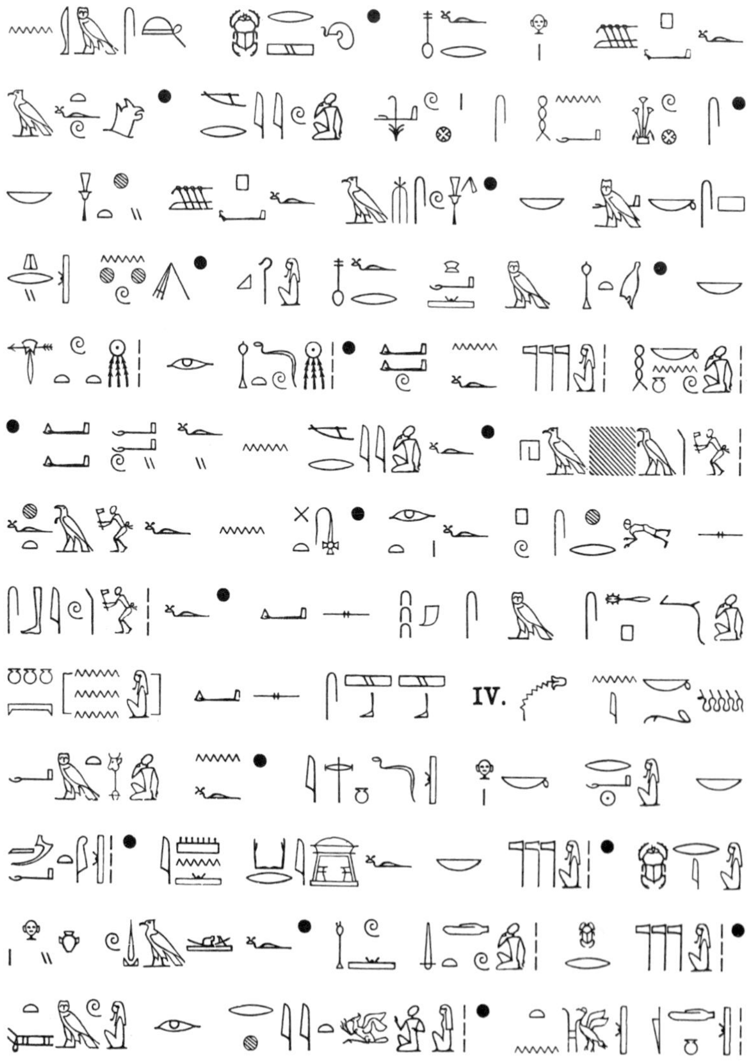

nemmes χeperś • nefer ḥrà seśep-f atfu • meriu qemāu-s ḥenā meḥu-s • neb seχti seśep-f amesu • neb mākes χeri neχeχu • ḥeq nefer χāā em ḥeťet • neb satut àri ḥeťtu • ṭāṭāu-nef neteru ḥekennu • ṭāṭā āāui-fi en meri-f • ha . . . . ti χefti-f en seśet • maat-f pu seχer-s sebàu-f • ṭā-s māb-s em seχap Nu ṭā-s seśebśeb **IV.** *Nàk āmt-nef • àneť ḥrà-k Rā neb maāt • Àmen karà-f neb neteru • Χeperà ḥeri àb uťa-f • utu meṭtu χeper neteru • Tmu àri reχit • ten qeṭ-*

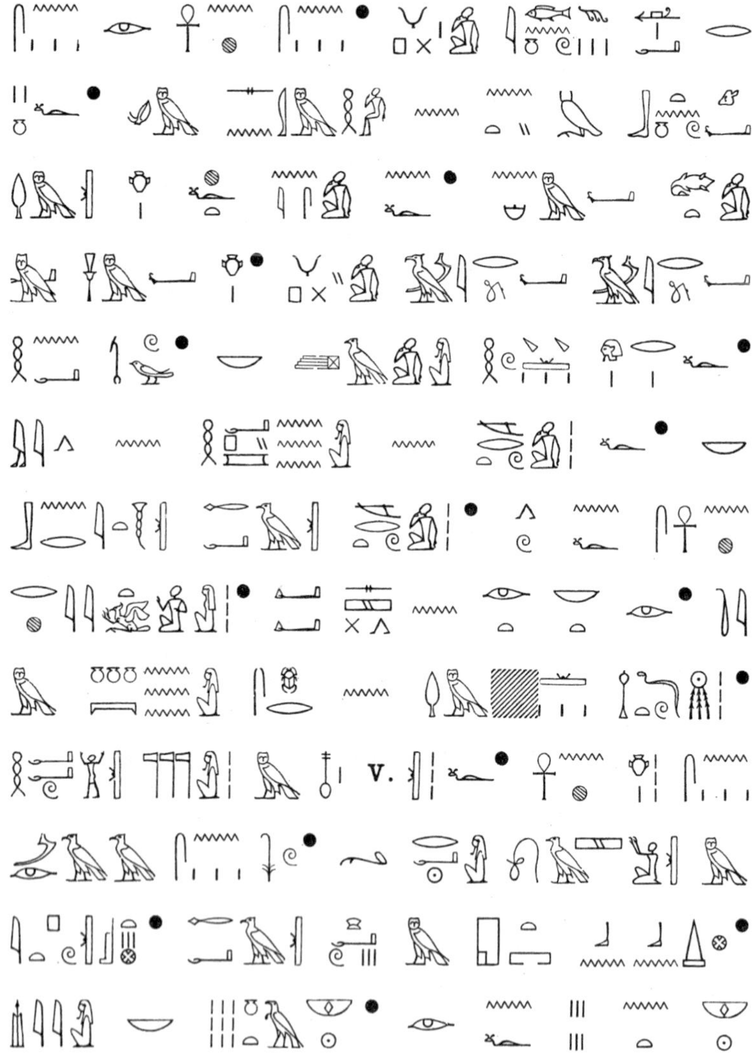

sen àri ānχ-sen • àp ànnu uā er sen-f • setem senemeḥ en enti em betennu • àm àb χeft nàs-nef • neḥem senṭet mā seχem àb • àpi maàr maàr ḥenā usu (?) • *neb sa ḥu ṭep-re-f • i en Ḥāpi en mertu-f • neb beneràt āāa mertu • iu-nef seānχ reχit • ṭāṭā seś en àrit nebt àri- • θà em Nu seχeper en àm . . . . . ḥettu • ḥāāu neteru em neferu* **V.** *-f • ānχ àb-sen maa-sen su •. Rā uaś em Àptut • āāa χāāu em ḥet Benben • Àni neb pautti • àri-nef sas ent ḥeb* *ṭenȧt* • *Ȧθi ānχ uťa senb neb neteru nebu* • *qemḥu-f-su ḥeri-ȧb χut* • *ḥeri pāt Ȧuḳer* • *ȧmen ren-f er mesu-f* • *em ren-f pu en Ȧmen* • *ȧneť ḥrȧ-k ȧmi em ḥetepu neb āut ȧb seχem χāāu* • *neb ureret qa šuti* • *nefer sešeṭ qa ḥeťet* • *mertu neteru maa-nek* • *seχti men em ȧpt-k* • *mertu-k seš-θȧ χet taui* • *satut-k χāā-θȧ em maati neferu pāt uben-k* • *beṭeš āut pesṭ-k* • *ȧu mertu-k em pet rest* • **VI.** *benerȧt-k em pet meḥtet* • *ȧu neferu-k ḥer θetet ȧbu* • *mertu-k ḥer* • *sešebeṭ āāuit* •

qemam-k nefer ḥer s-ḳenen ṭet • ḥāti māhuu en maa-nek • tut uā ȧri enti nebt uā uāu ȧri unent • perer en reθ em maati-f • χeper neteru ṭep-re-f • ȧri simu seānχ mennmen • χet en ānχu en hamemet • ȧri ānχ-θȧ remu en ȧtru • ȧpuṭ ḳenχapet (?) • erṭā nifu en enti em suḥt • seānχ ....• ȧri ānχ-θȧ χennus ȧm • ťeṭfet pui mȧtet ȧri • ȧri χerti • pennu em baba-sen • seānχ pui em χet nebt • ȧneť ḥrȧ-k ȧri enen er āu-u • uā uāu āšt āāui • seťer **VII.** *resu*

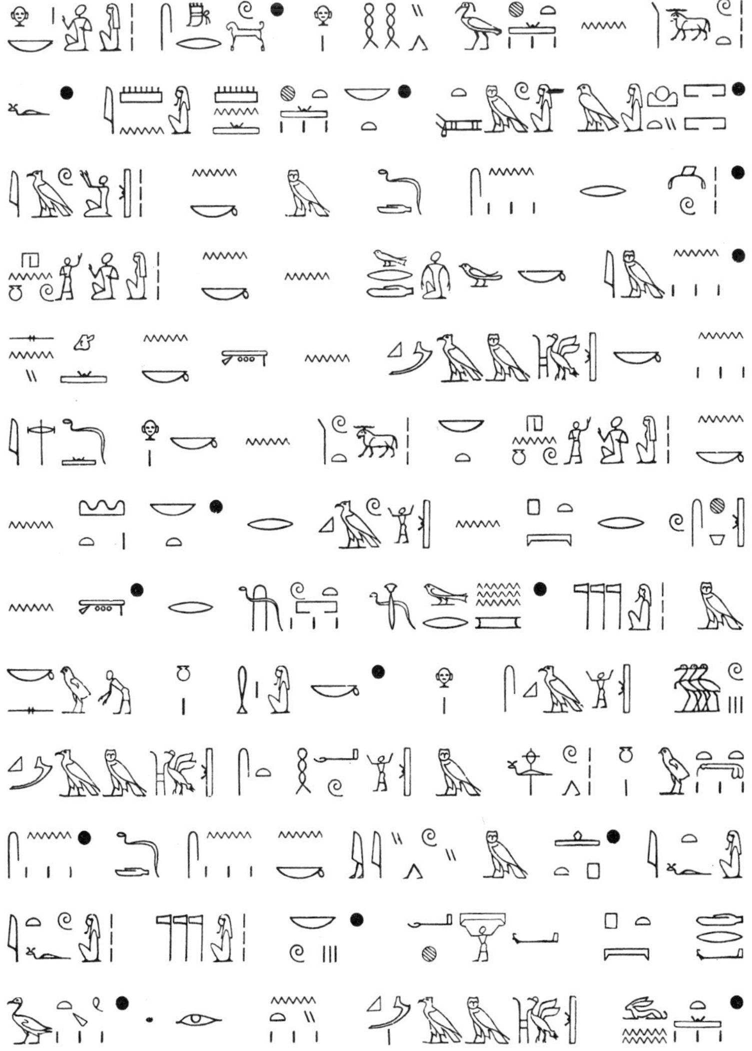

ḥrȧ-nebu • seťeru ḥer ḥeḥi χut en āut-f • Åmen men χet nebt • Temu Ḥeru-χuti • ȧau-nek em ťeṭ-sen er āu-u • hennu-nek en urṭ-k ȧm-n • seni-nek ta en qemam-k-n ȧneť ḥrȧ-k en āut nebt hennu-nek en set nebt • er qau en pet er useχ en ta • er meťut uať-ur • neteru em kesu nu ḥen-k • ḥer seqa baiu qemam-set ḥāu em χesefu nu utet-sen • ťeṭ-sen-nek iui em ḥetep • ȧtf ȧtfu neteru nebu • āχ pet ṭer satu • ȧri enti qemam unenet •

ȧθi· ānχ uťa senb ḥeri neteru • ṭua-n baiu **VIII.** *-k mȧ ȧri-k-n • ȧri-nek ḥer mestu-k-n • ṭā-n-nek ḥekennu ḥer urṭ-k ȧm-n • ȧneť ḥrȧ-k ȧri enti nebt • neb maāt ȧtf neteru • ȧri reθ qemam āut • neb neperȧ • ȧri ānχ āut enti set • Ȧmen ka nefer ḥrȧ • meriti em Ȧptet • āāa χāāu em ḥet Benben • nem* (or *uḥem*) *seśeṭu em Ȧnnu • ȧpi Reḥui em useχt āāat • ḥeri paut neteru āāat • uā uāu ȧti sen-f • χenti Ȧptet • Ȧni χenti paut neteru-f • ānχ em maāt rā*

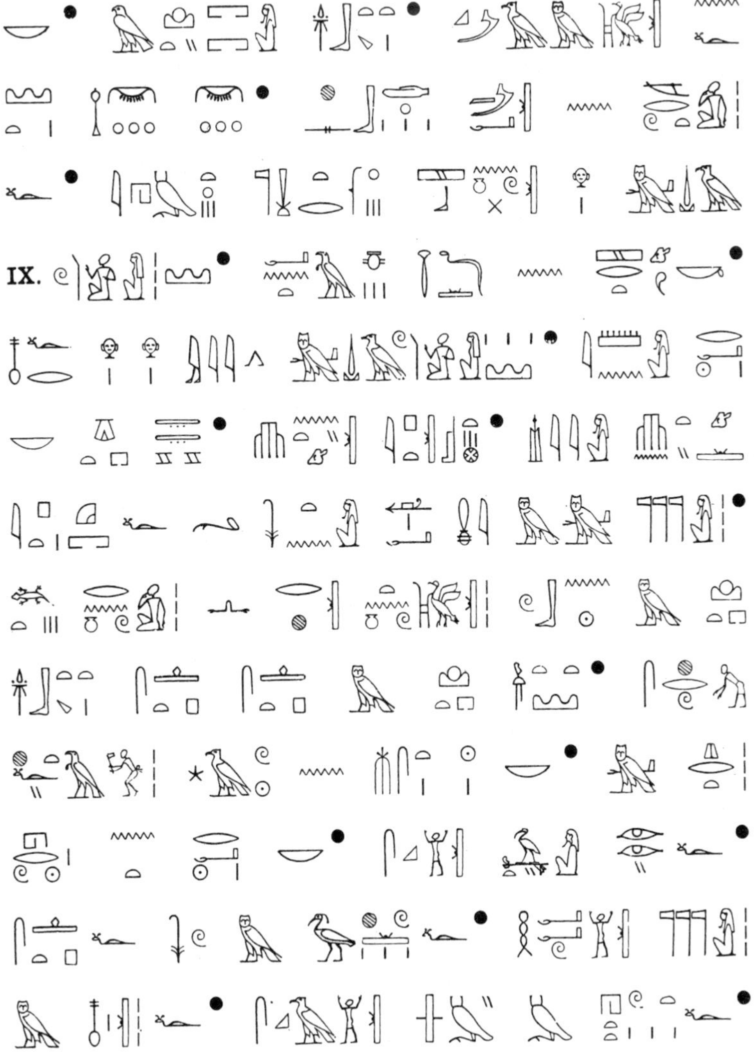

neb • Ḥeru χuti Ȧbtet • qemam-nef set ḥet' nub • χesbeṭ maā en mertu-f • ȧhemt neter sentrȧ šebennu ḥer māt'au • **IX.** *ānti uat' en šert-k • nefer ḥrȧ ḥer i Māt'au • Ȧmen-Rā neb nest taiu • χenti Ȧptet • Ȧni χenti Ȧpt-f. Suten uā mȧ emmā neteru • āšt rennu ȧn reχ tennu uben em χut ȧbtet seḥetep seḥetep em χut ȧmentet • seχeru χefti ṭuau en mest hru neb • mā χert hru ent rā neb • seqa Teḥuti maati-f • seḥetep-f su em χu-f • ḥāāu neteru em neferu-f • seqa ȧmi em hetetut-f •*

neb sektet āṭet • nemȧta-sen-nek Nu em ḥetep • seqeṭet-k ḥāāut • maa-sen seχeru Sebȧu • seχap ḥāu-f em ṭes • ȧm **X.** *en su χet • sesunnu ba-f er χaut-f • Nȧk pef neḥem nemmat-f neteru em ḥāāut • seqeṭet Rā em ḥetepu • Ȧnnu em ḥāāut • seχeru χefti nu Temu Ȧptet em ḥetepu Ȧnnu em ḥāāut • Nebt-ānχ ȧb-s neṭem • seχeru χefti nu neb-s • neteru χer-āba em hennu ȧmu χemu em sen-ta • maa-sen su usr em seχem-f • seχem neteru • maāti neb*

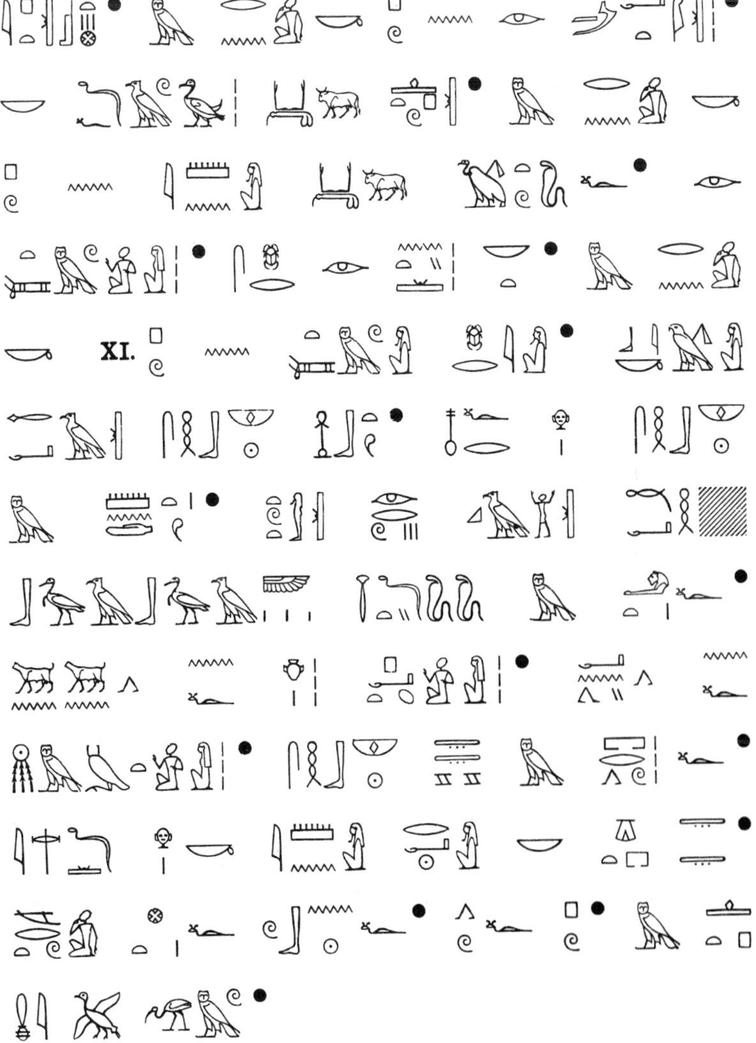

Åptet • *em ren-k pu en åri maāt* • *neb t̓efau ka ḥetepu* • *em ren-k pu en Åmen ka mut-f* • *åri temu* • *seχeper åri enti nebt* • *em ren-k* **XI.** *pu en Temu-χeperå* • *båk āāa seḥeb šenbt* • *nefer ḥrå seḥeb em menṭet* • *tut åru qa māh . . . . baba uatti em ḥāt-f* • *χenχen-nef åbu pāt* • *āni-nef hememet* • *seḥeb taiu em peru-f* • *ånet̓ ḥrå-k Åmen-Rā neb nest taiu* • *mertu nut-f uben-f* • *iu-f pu* • *em ḥetep må pa qemu* •

THE SPOLIATION OF THE TOMBS.

1 **I.** — 1. *Renpit met sȧs ȧbeṭ χemet śat hru met χemennu χer ḥen suten*
2 *net neb taui Nefer-ka-Rā-setep-en-Rā ānχ uťa senb sa Rā neb χ̣āu* 2. *Rā-*
messu-merer-Ȧmen ānχ uťa senb meri Ȧmen-Rā suten neteru Ḥeru-χuti ṭā
3 *ānχ ťetta ḥeḥ* 3. *hru en ṭāt śemi na ruṭuu en pa χer āa śeps pa ān en ťat*
4 *pa ān en pa mer perti ḥeť en Āa-perti ānχ uťa senb* 4. *er sȧp na meru ȧsit*
5 *na suteniu ṭepāu ḥnā na merāḥāit ȧusetu en ḥetep en na ḥesiu* 5. *ťerti ānχ nu*

nut ent em ta ȧmentet nut ȧn mer nut ťat Χā-em-Uast suten ābuu Nes-Ȧmen pa
ān 6. *en Āa-perti ānχ uťa senb āa en per en per neter ṭuaut ānχ uťa senb-θ en* 6
Ȧmen-Rā suten neteru suten ābu Nefer-ka-Rā-em-per-Ȧmen pa uḥemu en
Āa-perti ānχ uťa senb 7. *na seru āāaiu ḥer pa enti ȧriu na ȧťa em ta ȧmentet* 7
nut ȧ ťeṭu ḥā ḥer māťai Pa-ser-āa en pa χer āa šeps 8. *ḥnā pa ān en Āa-* 8
perti ānχ uťa senb enti em ta ȧmentet Uast smäi ȧm-u en ťat na seru ābuu en
Āa-perti ānχ uťa senb 9. *na reθ enti utui em* 9

10 *hru pen ḥnā ḥā ḥer māṫai Pa-ser-āā en pa χer* 10. *ḥer māṫai*
11, 12 *Bakenurenre en per āa* 11. . . . . *en pa χer* 12. . . . . *en* . . . . .
13, 14 *per āa* 13. . . . . *en* . . . . *per āa* 14. . . . . *Ȧmen*
15, 16 15. *ḥer māṫai Menθu-χepeš-f en per āa* 16. *ān Paaïbȧuk en ṫat*
17, 18 17. *ān āa en uṫa Pai-neferu en pa mer perti heṫ* 18. *neter ḥen Pa-ān-χāu*
19 *en per Ȧmen-ḥetep ānχ uṫa senb* 19. *neter ḥen Ur-Ȧmen en per Ȧmen ent*
20, 1 *per ȧrp* 20. *na māṫai en pa χer enti ȧre māu* **II.** — 1. *na meru ȧsi*

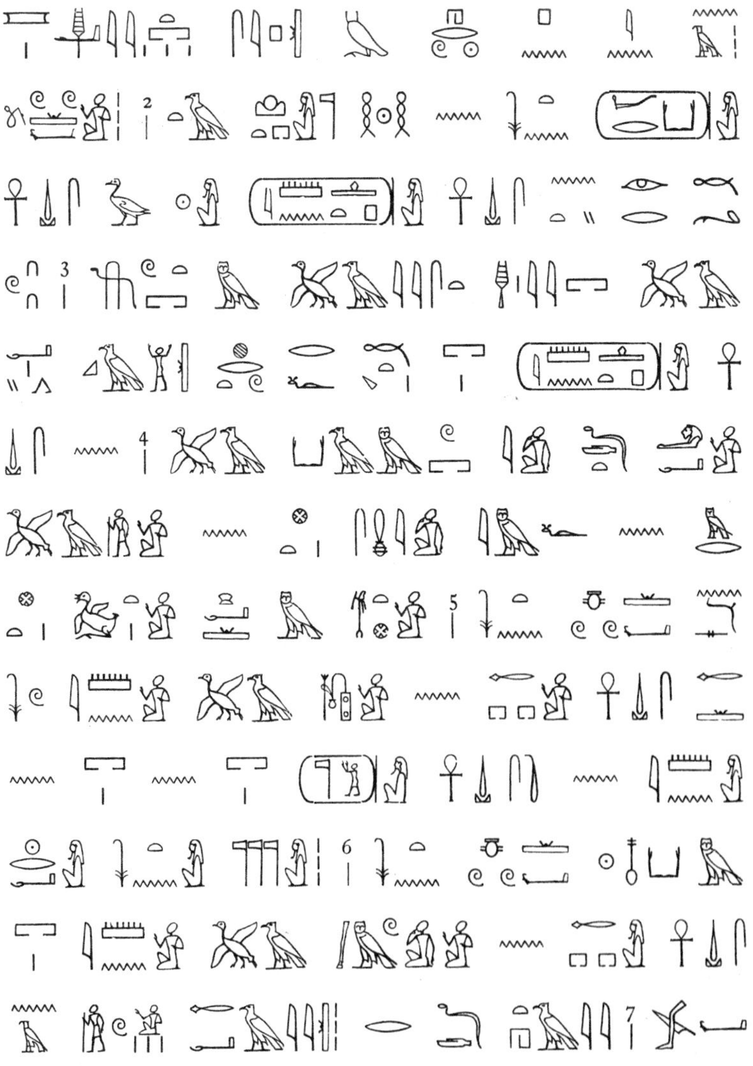

merāḥāit sȧp em hru pen ȧn na ruṭuu 2. ta χut ḥeḥ en suten Ser-ka-[Rā] 2
ānχ uťa senb sa Rā Ȧmen-ḥetep ānχ uťa senb enti ȧri meḥ śaā ťaut 3. meťut 3
em paiset āḥāi pa āi qa χertu eref meḥt per Ȧmenḥetep ānχ uťa senb en
4. *pa kamu ȧ ťeṭet ḥā Pa-ser en nut smȧ ȧm-f en mer nut ťat Χā-em-Uast* 4
5. *suten ābu Nes-su-Ȧmen pa ān en Āa-perti ānχ uťa senb āa en per en per* 5
Neter ṭuau ānχ uťa senb-θ en Ȧmen-Rā suten neteru 6. suten ābu Rā-nefer- 6
ka-em-per-Ȧmen pa uḥemu en Āa-perti ānχ uťa senb na uru āāaiu er ťeṭ tehai 7. 7

8 *su na àťau sàp em hru pen su qemi uťai àn na ruṭuu* 8. *pa mer en suten*
Sa-Rā-Àn-āa ānχ uťa senb enti meḥt per-Àmen-ḥetep ānχ uťa senb en
9 *pa ābu* 9. *enti paif mer ṭer ḥer-f enti paif utu smen embaḥ-f àu pa*
10 10. *tu en pa suten āḥā ḥer pai utu àu paif θesemu er āuṭ reṭu-f*
11, 12 11. *ťeṭ-nef Beḥu-ka sàp em hru pen su qemi uťai* 12. *pa mer en suten Rā-*
nub-χeper ānχ uťa senb sa Rā Àntuf ānχ uťa senb qemi-f em

rā 13. *uṭennu em ṭet na àťau àu àruiu meḥ sen ḳes* (?) *em utennu em paif* 13
ťeruu meḥ uā 14. *em ta useχt en bun-re en ta merāḥāt en ḥer māsi* 14
utennu Àurei en per Àmen 15. *enti em āu su uťai bu pui na àťau reχ peḥ-f* 15
16. *pa mer en suten Rā-āḥā-em-àpu-maāt ānχ uťa senb sa Rā Àntuf-āa ānχ* 16
uťa senb su qemi 17. *em rā utennu em ṭet na àťau em ta àuset smen paif utu* 17
en paif mer 18. *sàp em hru pen su qemi uťa bu pui na àťau* 18

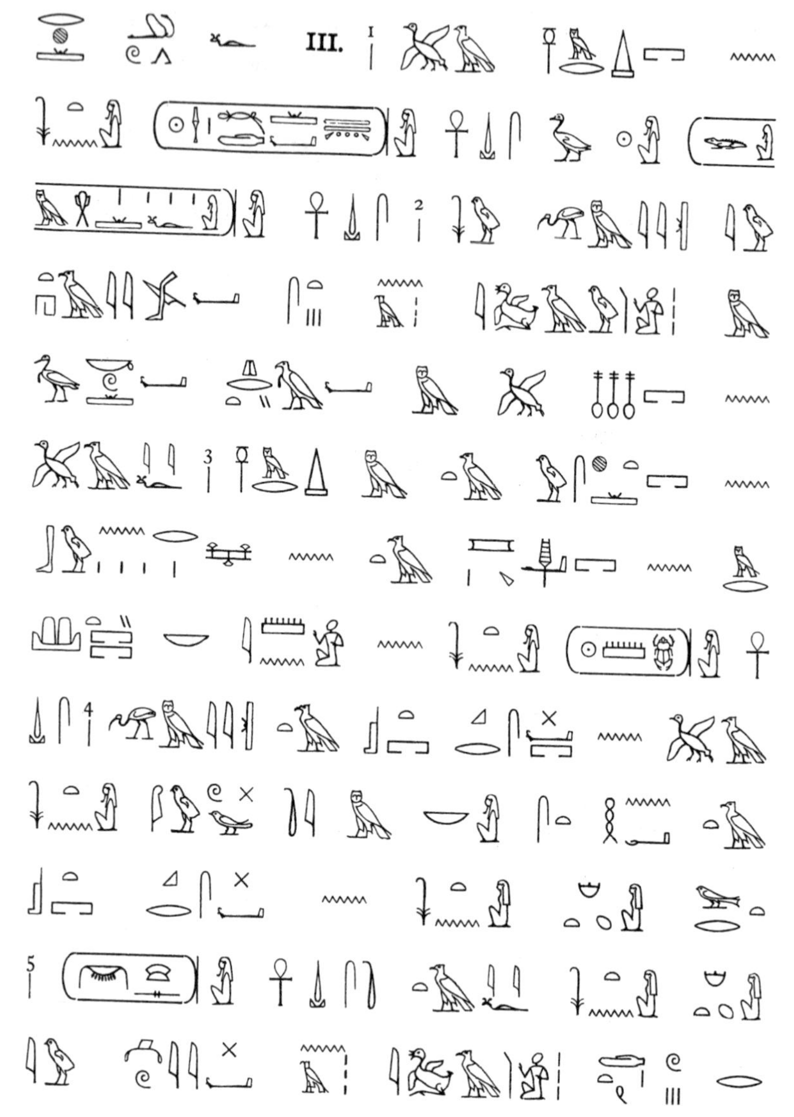

1 *reχ peḥu-f* **III.** — 1. *pa mer en suten Rā-seχem-šešeṭ-taui ānχ uťa senb sa*
2 *Rā Sebek-em-sa-f ānχ uťa senb* 2. *su qemi ȧu tehai-set na ȧťau em baku χerti*
3 *em pa neferu en paif* 3. *mer em ta useχt en bun-re en ta merāḥāt en mer*
4 *šenti Neb-Ȧmen en suten Rā-men-χeper ānχ uťa senb* 4. *qemi ta ȧuset*
qeres en pa suten šuu-θȧ em neb-set ḥnā ta ȧuset qeres en suten ḥemt urt
5 5. *Nub-χā-s ānχ uťa senb-θ taif suten ḥemt ȧu āui na ȧťau ṭet-u er*

re-u åriuiu ṭat 6. *na uru ābu semti er-ef qemi pa seχeru en āu ṭet er re-u* 6
å åru 7. *na åṭau er pai suten ḥnā taif suten ḥemt* 8. *pa mer en suten Rā-* 7, 8
seqenen ānχ uṭa senb sa Rā Tau-āa ānχ uṭa senb såp em hru pen 9. *ån na* 9
ruṭuu su qemi uṭa 10. *pa mer en suten Rā-seqenen ānχ uṭa senb sa Rā* 10
Tau-āa-āa ānχ uṭa senb er meḥ suten Tau-āa ānχ uṭa senb sen 11. *såp em* 11
hru pen ån na ruṭuu su qemi uṭai 12. *pa mer en suten Rā-uaṭ-χeper ānχ* 12
uṭa senb sa Rā Ka-mes ānχ uṭa senb

13 *sȧp em hru pen su [qemi] uťai* 13. *pa mer en suten Ȧāḥ-mes-sa-pa-ȧri ānχ*
14 *uťa senb sȧp [em hru pen su] qemi uťai* 14. *pa mer en suten Rā-neb-χerut*
15 *ānχ uťa senb sa Rā Menθu-ḥetep ānχ uťa senb enti em Ṭesert su uťai* 15. *ḥetep*
16 *meru en na suteniu ṭepāu sȧp em hru pen ȧn na ruṭuu* 16. *qemi ȧu-u uťai*
17 *mer paut qemi tehai uā ḥetep met* 17. *na merāḥāuit en na qemāi en per*
18 *Neter-ṭuau ānχ uťa senb-θ en Ȧmen-Rā suten neteru qemi uťai sen* 18. *qemi*
ȧu tehai set na ȧťau sen ḥetep

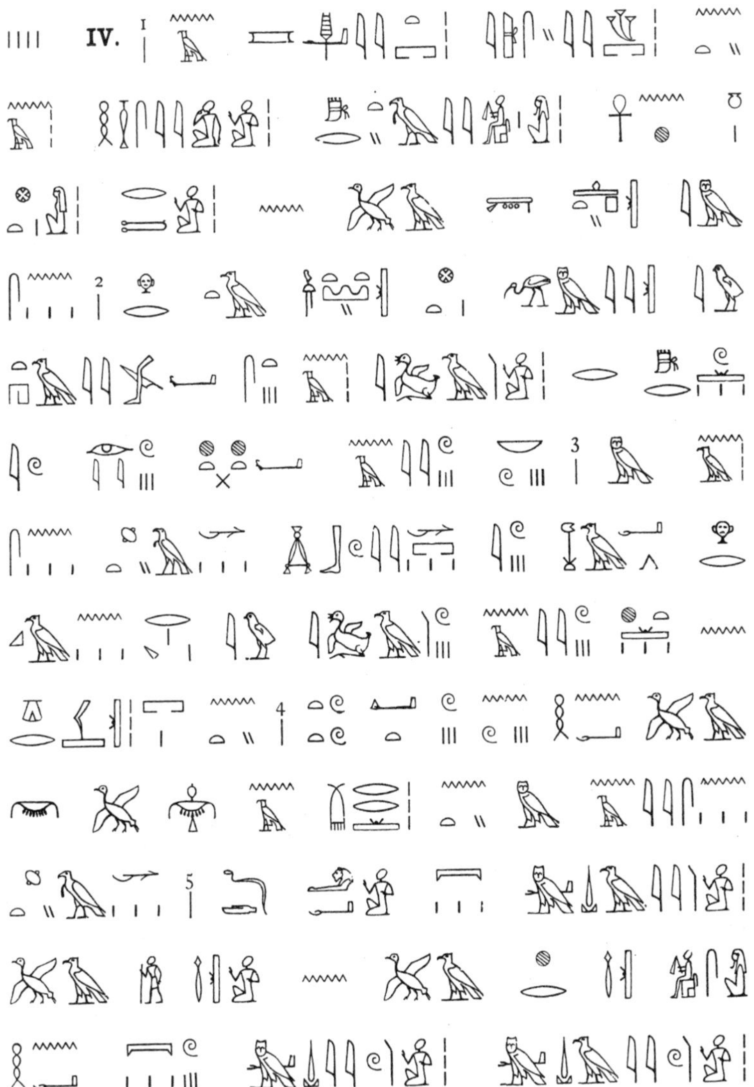

fṭu **IV.** — 1. *na merāḥāit ȧsi enti na ḥesi t̛erti ānχ nu nut reθ en pa* 1
ta ḥetepi ȧm-sen 2. *ḥer ta ȧmenteti nut qemi ȧu tehai set na ȧt̛au er t̛eru* 2
ȧu ȧriu χetχet naiu nebu 3. *em naisen uti ṭebui ȧu χaā ḥer qan-re ȧu* 3
ȧt̛au naiu χet en ḳer enti 4. *tutu ṭāt-u-nu ḥnā pa nub pa ḥet̛ na āpereru enti* 4
em naisen uti 5. *t̛eṭ ḥā ḥer māt̛ai Pa-ser-āa en pa χer āa ṡeps ḥnā ḥeru* 5
māt̛aiu māt̛aiu

6 6. *ruṭuu en pa χer pa ān en pa ťat pa ān en pa mer perti-heť unu àrimā-u*
7 *smāi àm-u en* 7. *mer nut ťat Χā-em-Uast suten ābu Nes-su-Àmen pa ān en*
Āa-perti ānχ uťa senb āa en per en Per-Neter-ṭuau ānχ uťa senb-θ en
8 8. *Àmen-Rā suten neteru suten ābuu Rā-nefer-ka-em-per-Àmen pa uḥemu en*
9 *Āa-perti ānχ uťa senb na uru āāaiu* 9. *ṭāu ḥā en àmentet ḥer māťaiu Pa-*
10 *ser āa en pa χer pa ren en na àťau em ānu* 10. *embaḥ ťat na uru ābuu meḥ*
àm-u set ťeṭḥu àru semetti-u ťeṭu

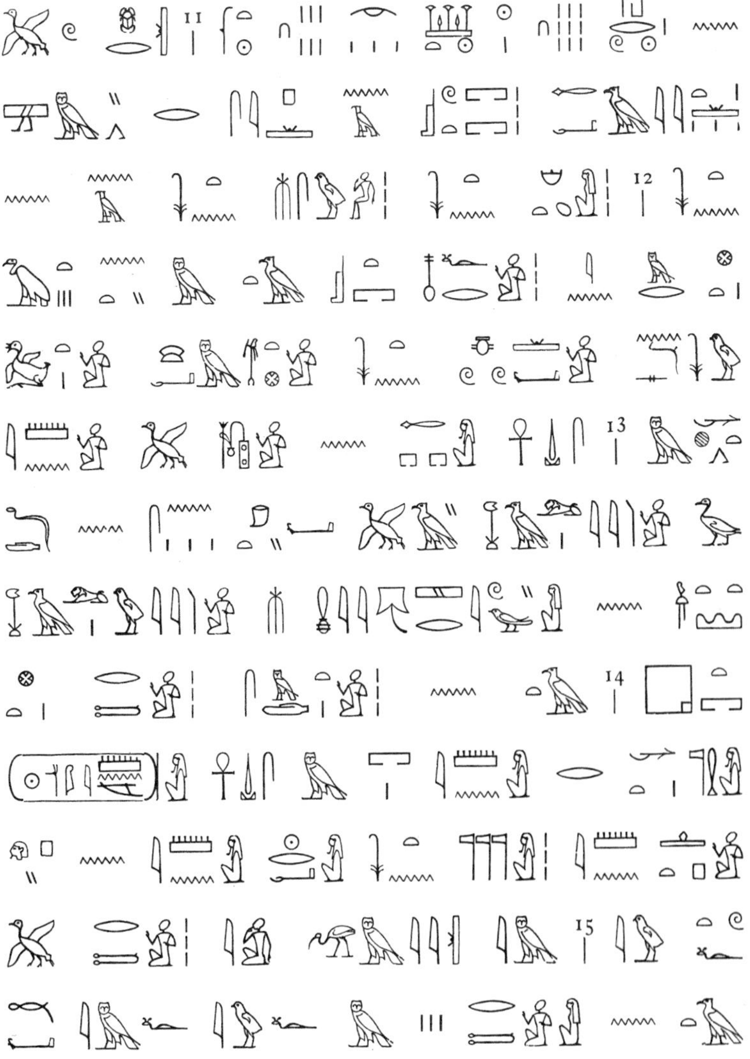

pa-u χeper 11. *Renpit met sȧs ȧbeṭ χemet śat hru met paut hru en śemi er sȧp* 11
na ȧusetut āāait en na suten mesu suten ḥemt 12. *suten mut enti em ta ȧuset* 12
neferu ȧn mer nut ṭat Χā-em-Uast suten ābuu Nes-su-Ȧmen pa ān en Āa-perti
ānχ uṭa senb 13. *emχet ṭet-en-sen χemti* (?) *Pai-χarei sa Χareui mes Mȧi-* 13
śerȧui en ȧmentet nut reθ semṭet en ta 14. *Ḥet Rā-user-maāt-meri-Ȧmen ānχ* 14
uṭa senb em per Ȧmen er χet neter ḥen ṭepi en Ȧmen-Rā suten neteru Ȧmen-
ḥetep pa reθ ȧ qemi ȧm 15. *ȧu-tuf meḥ ȧm-f ȧu-f em χemet reθ en ta* 15

16 *ḥet er ḳes na ȧusetut ȧ ȧrui mer nut t'at Rā-neb-maāt-neχt paif* 16. *semetti em*
renpit met fṭu er t'eṭ unu-ȧ em pa χer en suten ḥemt Ȧuset ānχ ut'a senb-θ
17 *en suten Rā-user-maāt-meri-Ȧmen ānχ ut'a senb ȧn-ȧ nehai* 17. *en uχet ȧm*
1 *ȧriu-ȧ hai-u χer ȧr t'at pa ābuu ṭāt ȧt'a-tu pa χemti er ḥāt-u er* **V.** — 1. *na*
ȧusetut ȧu-f āfnu em reθ sauu t'erȧuu ȧu-tuf ṭāt-nef maat-f em t'er peḥu-f
2 *set ȧu na uru* 2. *t'eṭ-nef ȧ šemi er ḥāt-n er pa χer ȧ t'eṭ erek ȧn-ȧ na uχet*
3 *ȧm-f ȧu pa χemti šemi er ḥāt na uru* 3. *er uā χer*

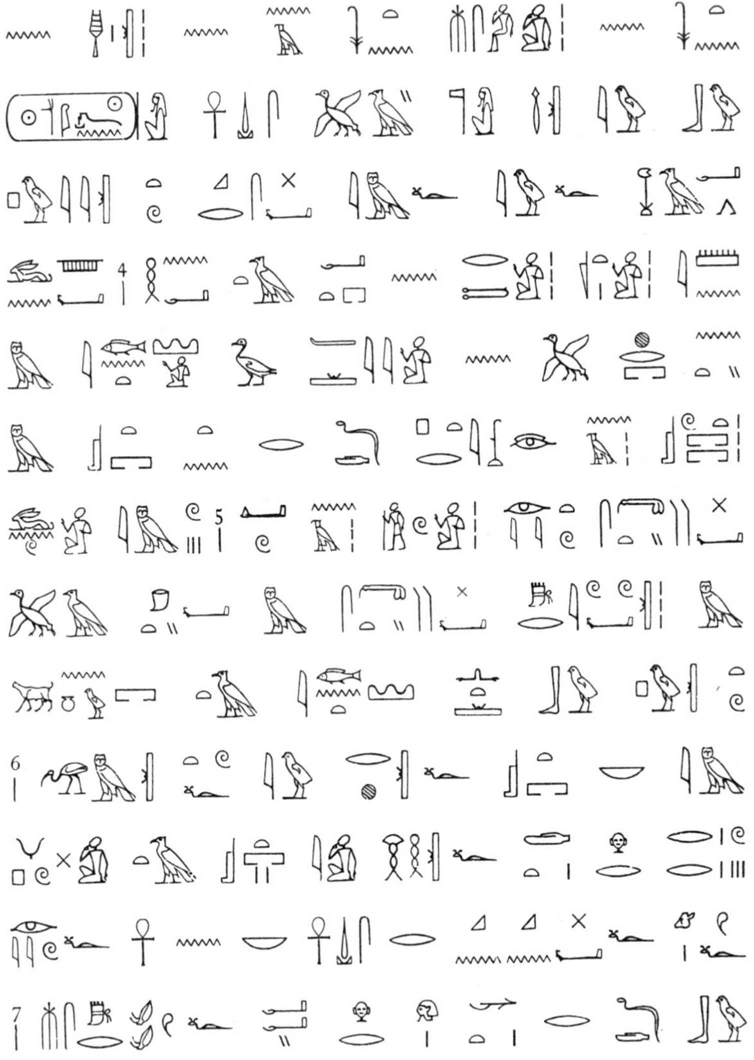

en āḥā en na suten mesu en suten Rā-user-maāt-setep-en-Rā ānχ uťa senb
pai neter āa àu bu pui-tu qeres àm-f àu-f χaā un 4. *ḥnā ta āt en reθ qeṭet* 4
Àmen-em-ànt sa Ḥui en pa χer enti em àuset ten er ťeṭ petrà na àusetut unu-à
àm-u 5. *ṭāu na uru àri-tu semetti pa χemti em semetti ťeràuu em χennuu ta* 5
ànt àt bu pu-tu 6. *qem-tu-f àu reχ-f àuset neb àm àpu ta àuset sen à uaḥ-f* 6
ṭet ḥer er re-u àriu-f ānχ en neb ānχ uťa senb er qenqen-f fenṭ-f 7. *mesťerui-f* 7
āāui ḥer ṭep χet er ťeṭ bu

8 *reχ-à àuset nebt ḥer em χennuu nai àusetut àpu pai χer enti un χer* 8. *mā tai*
āt à uaḥ ṭet-ten ḥer er re-u sàp na uru na χeru na àusetut āāait enti em na
9 *àuset-* 9. *neferu enti na suten mesut suten ḥemt suten mut itef met nefer*
10 *en Āa-perti ānχ uťa senb ḥetep em χen-sen set* 10. *qemi uťa ṭāu na uru*
11 *āāait reri na ruṭuu ḥututi reθ qeṭ en pa χer ḥeru* 11. *māťai māťai semṭet neb*
12 *en pa χer ta àmentet nut em àpiu āāait er śaā nut* 12. *Renpit met sàs àbeṭ*
χemet śat hru met paut

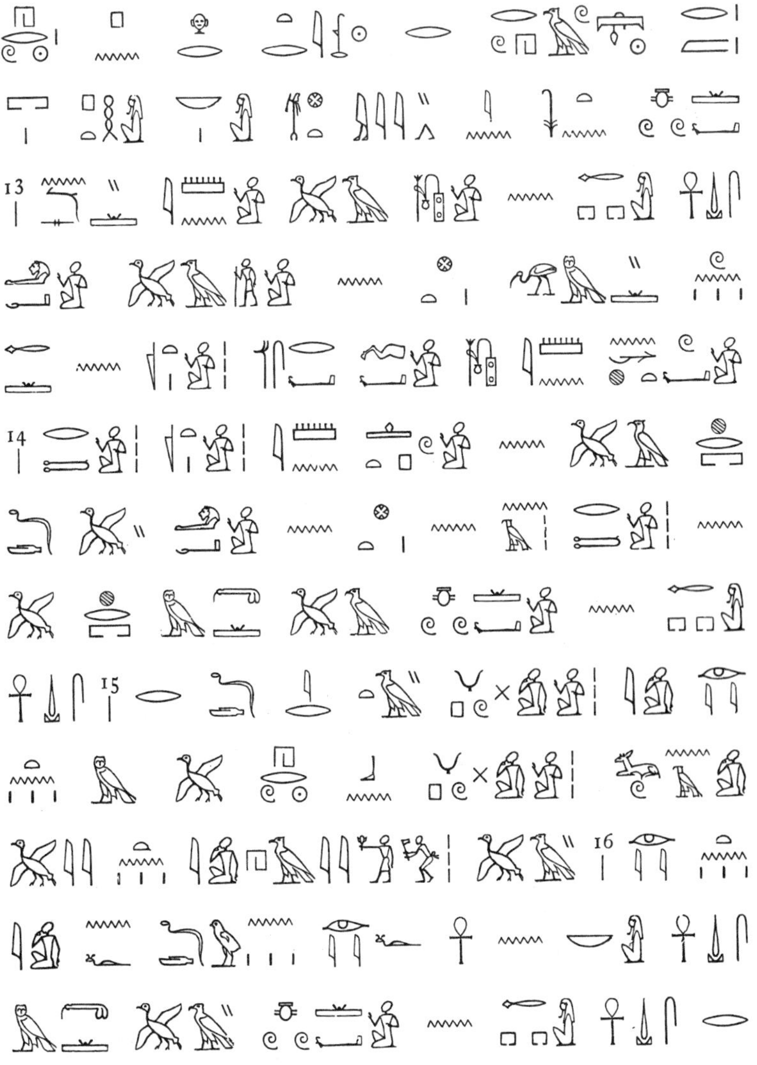

hru pen ḥer trȧ er ruhau er ḳes Per-Ptaḥ neb Uast i ȧn suten ābuu 13. *Nesi-* 13
Ȧmen pa ān en Āa-perti ānχ uťa senb ḥā Pa-ser en nut qemi-un āa en qeṭet
User-χepeš ān Ȧmen-neχtu 14. *reθ qeṭet Ȧmen-ḥetepu en pa χer ťeṭ pai ḥā en* 14
nut en na reθ en pa χer embaḥ pa ābuu en Āa-perti ānχ uťa senb 15. *er ťeṭ* 15
ȧr tai ȧpu ȧ ȧri-ten em pa hru ben ȧpu āuna paiten ȧhai pai 16. *ȧri-ten* 16
ȧ nef ťeṭ-un ȧri-f ānχ en neb ānχ uťa senb embaḥ pai ābuu en Āa-perti ānχ
uťa senb er

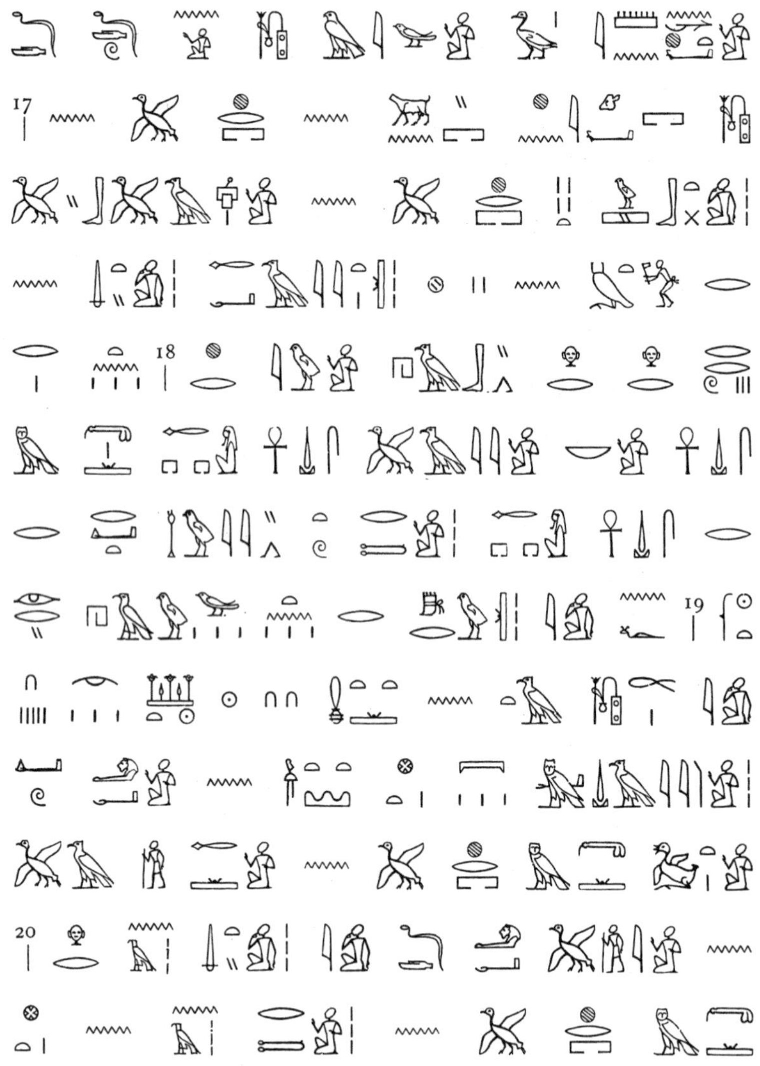

17 *ťeṭ ťeṭu-nȧ ān Ḥerȧ-śerȧu sạ Ȧmen-neχt* 17. *en pa χer en χeni χenȧ ān Pai-*
18 *baasa en pa χer fṭut uśebet en meṭti āāait sep sen en mit er re-ten* 18. *χer ȧu-ȧ*
habi ḥer ḥer er re-u embaḥ Āa-perti ānχ uťa senb pai-ȧ neb-ȧ ānχ uťa senb er
19 *erṭāt utui-tu reθ Āa-perti ānχ uťa senb er ȧri hau-ten er ťeru ạ-nef* 19. *Renpit*
met sȧs ȧbeṭ χemet śat hru ťaut mȧtet en ta ān ȧ ṭā-u ḥā en ȧmentet nut
20 *ḥer māťai Pa-ser-āa en pa χer embaḥ ťat* 20. *ḥer na meṭti ȧ ťeṭ ḥā Pa-serȧ*
en nut en na reθ en pa χer embaḥ

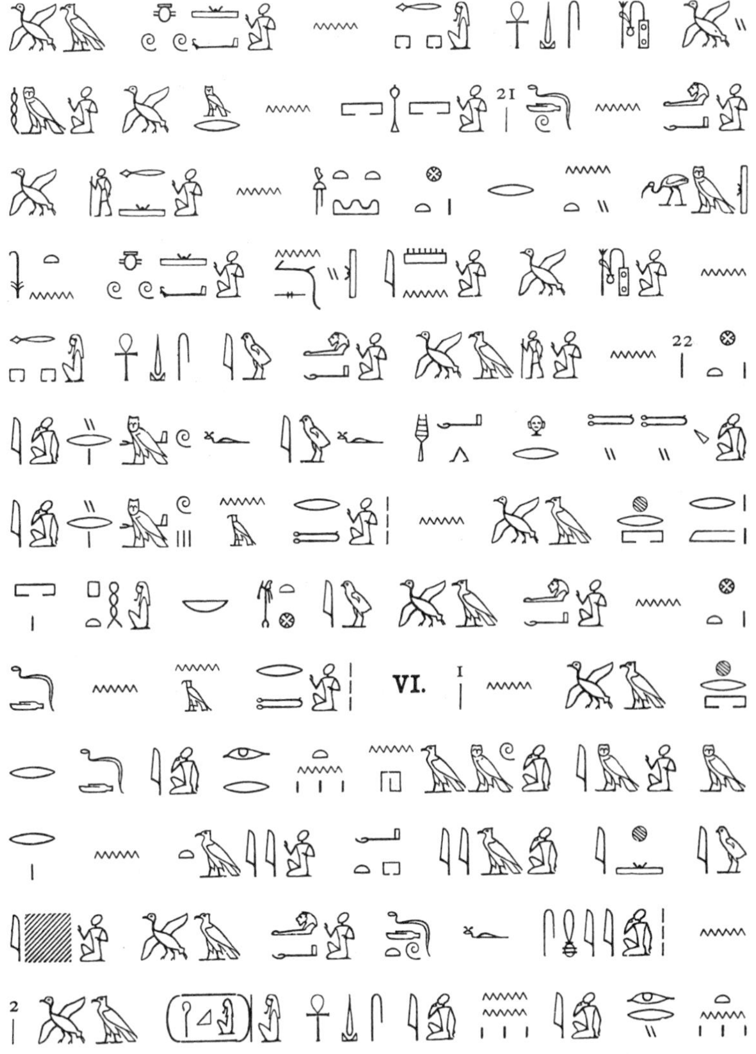

pa ābuu en Āa-perti ānχ uťa senb ān Pai-neťem pa mer en peru ḥeť 21. *ťeṭu* 21
en ḥā Pa-ser-āa en ȧmentet nut er enti qem suten ābuu Nesi-Ȧmen pa ān
en Āa-perti ānχ uťa senb ȧu ḥā Pa-ser en 22. *nut ȧire-māu-f ȧu-f āḥā* 22
ḥer θiθi ȧire-māu na reθ en pa χer er ḳes Per-Ptaḥ neb Uast ȧu pa ḥā en
nut ťeṭ en na reθ **VI.** — 1. *en pa χer er ťeṭ ȧ ȧri-ten nehamu ȧm-ȧ em re* 1
en tai-ȧ āt ia ȧχ ȧu ȧ . . . . pa ḥā ťeṭtu-f smȧi en 2. *pa Ḥeq ānχ* 2
uťa senb ȧ en-n ȧ ȧri-ten

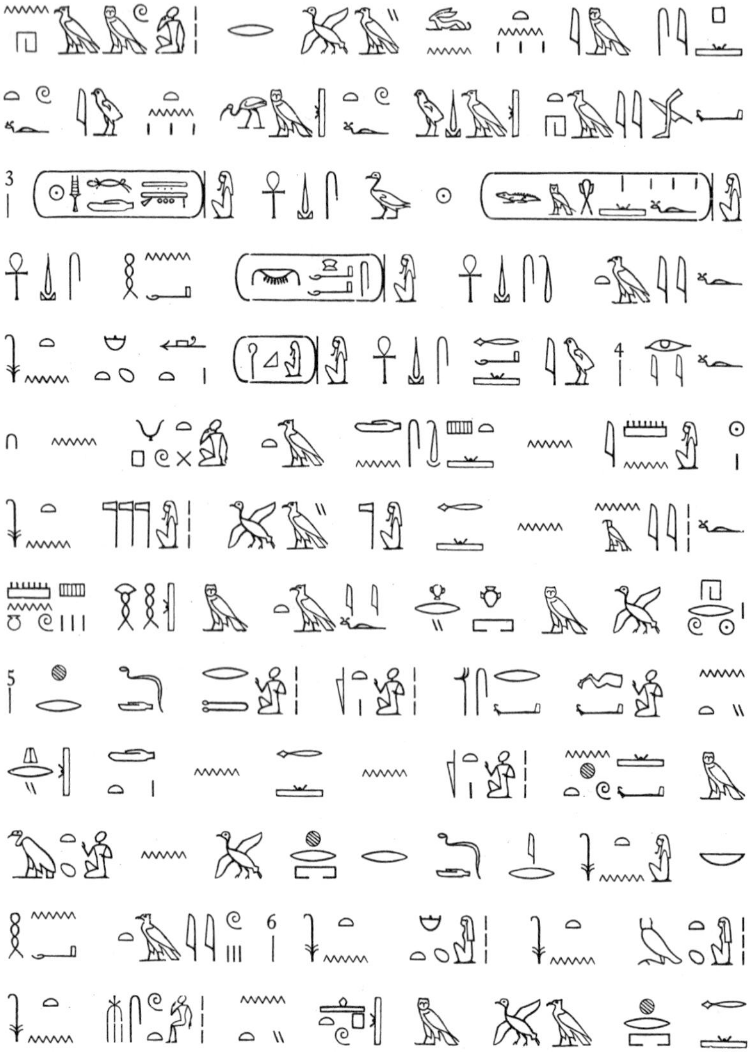

3 *nehamu er pai un-ten ȧm sȧp-tuf ȧu-ten qem-tuf uťa tehai* 3. *Rā-āḥā-seśeṭ-*
taui ānχ uťa senb sa Rā Sebek-em-sa-f ānχ uťa senb ḥnā Nub-χāā-s ānχ
4 *uťa senb-θ taif suten ḥemt uāt Ḥeq ānχ uťa senb āā ȧu* 4. *ȧri-f met en*
ȧput ta ṭenset en Ȧmen-Rā suten neteru pai neter āa en naif mennu uaḥ
5 *em taif ḥeri-ȧb pa hru* 5. *χer ťeṭ reθ qeṭet User-χepeś enti χeri ṭet en āa en*
6 *qeṭet Neχtu-em-mut en pa χer er ťeṭ ȧr suten neb ḥnā taiu* 6. *suten ḥemt*
suten mut suten mesut enti ḥetepu em pa χer āa

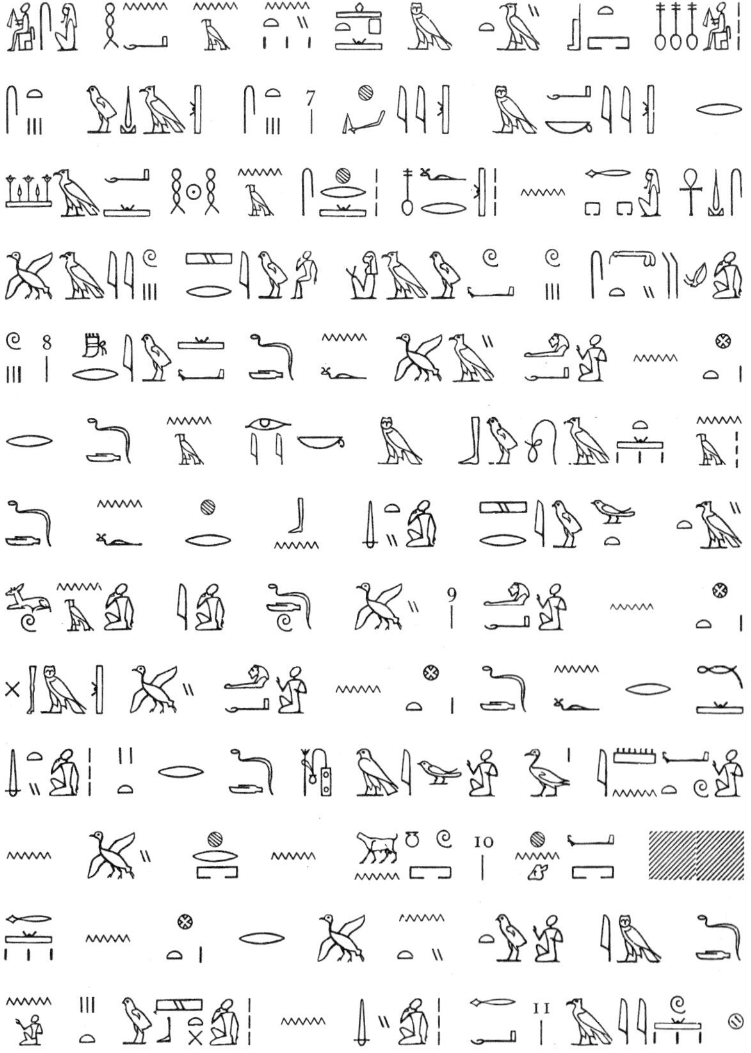

šeps ḥnā na enti ḥetep em tai ȧuset neferu set uťa set 7. *χui māki er* 7
šaā ḥeḥ na seχeru neferu en Āa-perti ānχ uťa senb paiu šerȧu sauu-u
semetti-u 8. *ťerȧu ťeṭ-nef pai ḥā en nut er ťeṭ na ȧri-k em buuat na ťeṭ-* 8
nef χer ben meṭti šerȧu tai āuna ȧ ťeṭu pai 9. *ḥā en nut nem* (or *uḥem*) 9
pai ḥā en nut ťeṭ-nef er meḥ meṭti sent er ťeṭ ān Ḥeruȧšerȧu sa Ȧmen-neχtu
en pai χer en χennu 10. *χen . . . . . āa en nut er pa enti tuȧ ȧm ťeṭ-nȧ* 10
χemet ušebet en meṭi āāaiu 11. *sep* 11

sen ān un paiȧ ānu-ȧ ḥnā pa ān ťaťat sen en nut χer ťeṭu-nȧ ān Paibasa
12 *en pa χer ketθȧ* 12. *meṭti sent ḥetep ṭuat ānu-un emmȧtet ȧu ben nesi-set*
13 *āu-entu χeru āuna ȧu em betauu āāait neχebu* 13. *en ṭāt ḥer menȧu neb*
en ȧri sebait nebt ḥer ḥer er re-u χer ȧu-ȧ habi ḥer er re-u embaḥ Āa-perti ānχ
14 *uťa senb pai neb-ȧ ānχ uťa senb* 14. *er erṭāt utui-tu reθ Āa-perti ānχ uťa*
senb er ȧri hau-ten ȧ-nef un em pai ḥā en nut ȧri-f met en ānχ en neb ānχ
15 *uťa senb er ťeṭ* 15. *ȧu-ȧ ȧri em mȧtet*

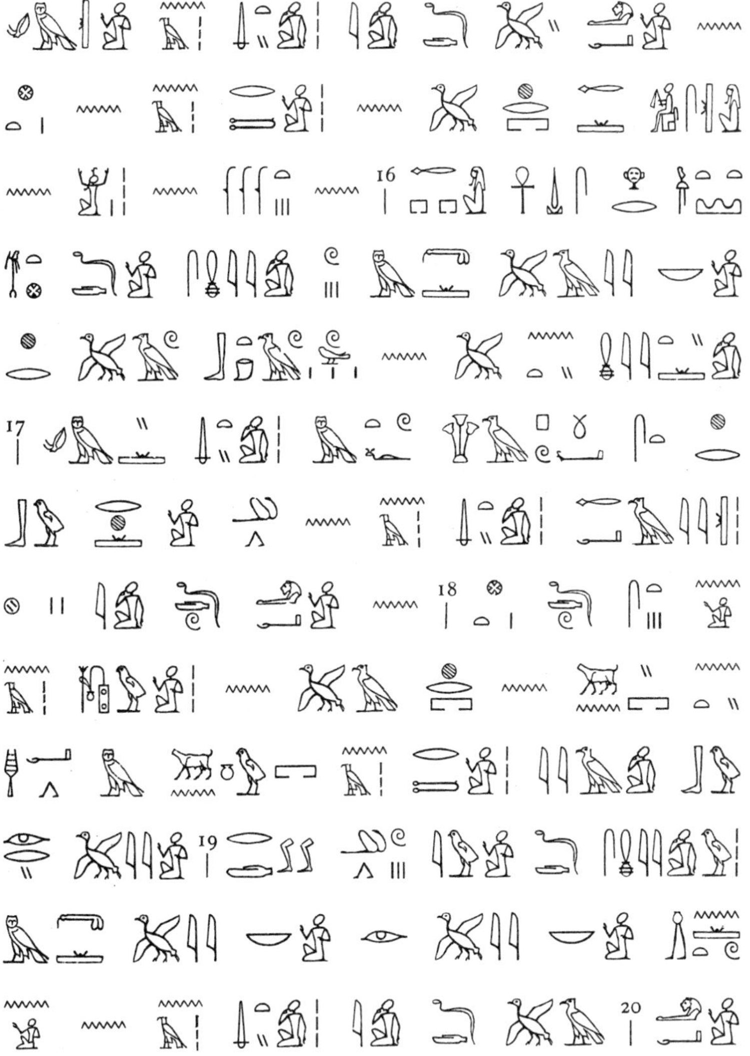

setem-ȧ na meṭti ȧ ťeṭ pai ḥā en nut en na reθ en pa χer āa šeps en ḥeḥ
en renput en 16. *Āa-perti ānχ uťa senb ḥer ȧmentet Uast ťeṭ-ȧ smȧi-u* 16
embaḥ pai neb-ȧ χer pau betauu en pa enti mȧiti 17. *setemi meṭti emtuf ḥapu* 17
set χer bu reχ-ȧ peḥ en na meṭti āāai sep sen ȧ ťeṭu ḥā en 18. *nut ťeṭu-set* 18
nȧ na ānu en pa χer en χeni enti āḥā em χennu na reθ ia bu ȧri pai-ȧ
19. *reṭ peḥ-u ȧu-ȧ ťeṭ smȧi-u embaḥ pai neb-ȧ ȧri pai neb-ȧ ȧntu-nȧ en na* 19
meṭti ȧ ťeṭ pa 20. *ḥā* 20

en nut ťeṭu set nȧ na ānu en pa χer χer ȧu-ȧ habi ḥer er re-u embaḥ Āa-
21 *perti ānχ uťa senb ȧ nef pau betauu* 21. *en pai ān sen en pa χer paiu peḥ*
22 *pai ḥā en nut er ťeṭ-nef smȧi ȧu bu pui naiu itef ťeṭ-nef* 22. *smȧi ȧu ȧ*
ťeṭu smȧi en ťaṭ ȧu-f em ā resu χer un-nef χeper em ā meḥt ȧu na māťai
23 *šesi en* 23. *ḥen-f ānχ uťa senb en pa χer χeṭ er pa enti ťat ȧm χer naiu*
24 *seχai ȧrui nȧ meter Renpit met-sȧs ȧbeṭ χemet šat ḥru ťaut* 24. *em na*
meṭti ȧ setem em ṭeti pa

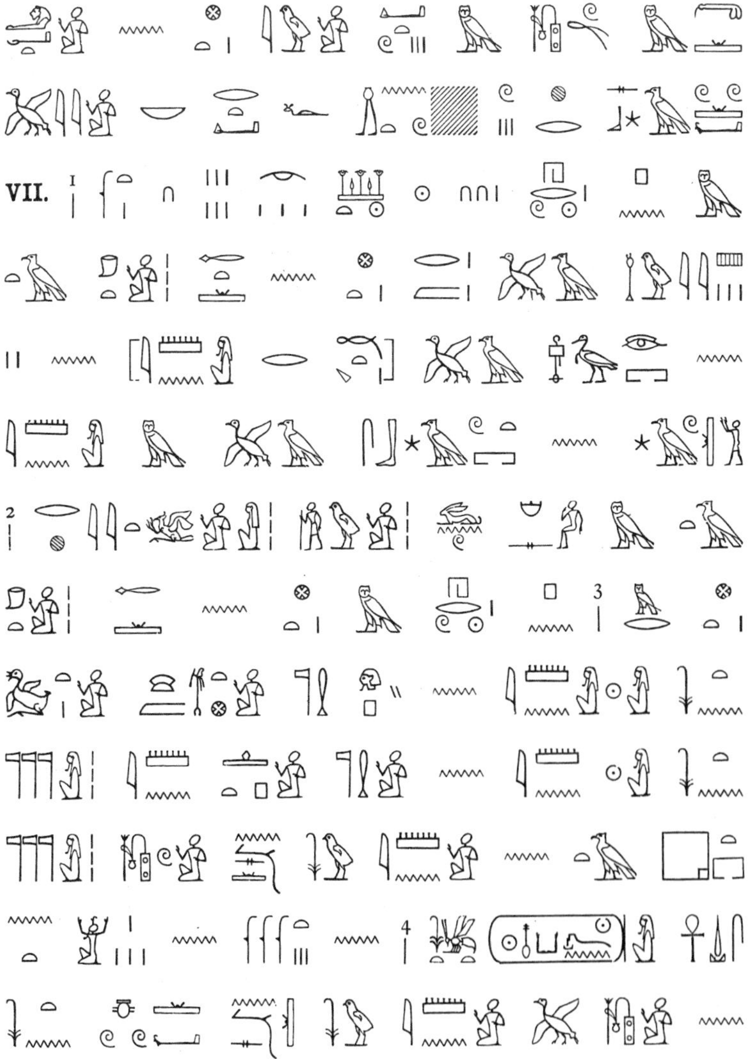

ḥāt en nut àu-à ṭāt-u em ānu embaḥ pai-à neb erṭāt-f àntu . . . . . . u χer sebauu
VII. — 1. *Renpit met-sàs àbeṭ χemet śat hru ťaut-uā hru pen em ta tat āat en* 1
nut er ḳes pa utui sen en Àmen er meḥt pa āba en Àmen em pa sebaut en ṭuau
2. *reχit seru unu ḥems em ta tat āa en nut em hru pen* 3. *mer nut ťat Χā-* 2, 3
em-Uast neter ḥen ṭepi en Àmen-Rā suten neteru Àmen-ḥetep neter ḥen en
Àmen-Rā suten neteru ānu Nes-su-Àmen en ta ḥet en ḥeḥ en renput en 4. *suten* 4
net Rā-nefer-ka-setep-en-Rā ānχ uťa senb suten ābuu Nes-su-Àmen pa ān en

Āa-perti ānχ uťa senb āa en per en per neter ṭuau ānχ uťa senb-θ en Ȧmen-
5 *Rā suten neteru* 5. *suten ābuu Rā-nefer-ka-em-per-Ȧmen pa nemu en Āa-*
perti ānχ uťa senb ȧṭennu Ḥeruȧ en [na] . . . . . . ent per . . . .
6 *sirei Ḥeruȧ en* 6. *na χenu ḥā Paserȧ en nut āḥā en ṭāu mer nut ťat Ϗā-em-*
7 *Uast ȧntu χemti Paχaru sa Ϗareui* 7. *χemti Ťarei sa Ϗā-em-ȧpt χemti*
8 *Pakamen sa Ťarei en ta ḥet Rā-usr-maāt-Ȧmen-meri* 8. *ānχ uťa senb er χet*
pa neter ḥen ṭep en Ȧmen ťeṭ ȧn ťat en na seru āāaiu en ta tat āat en

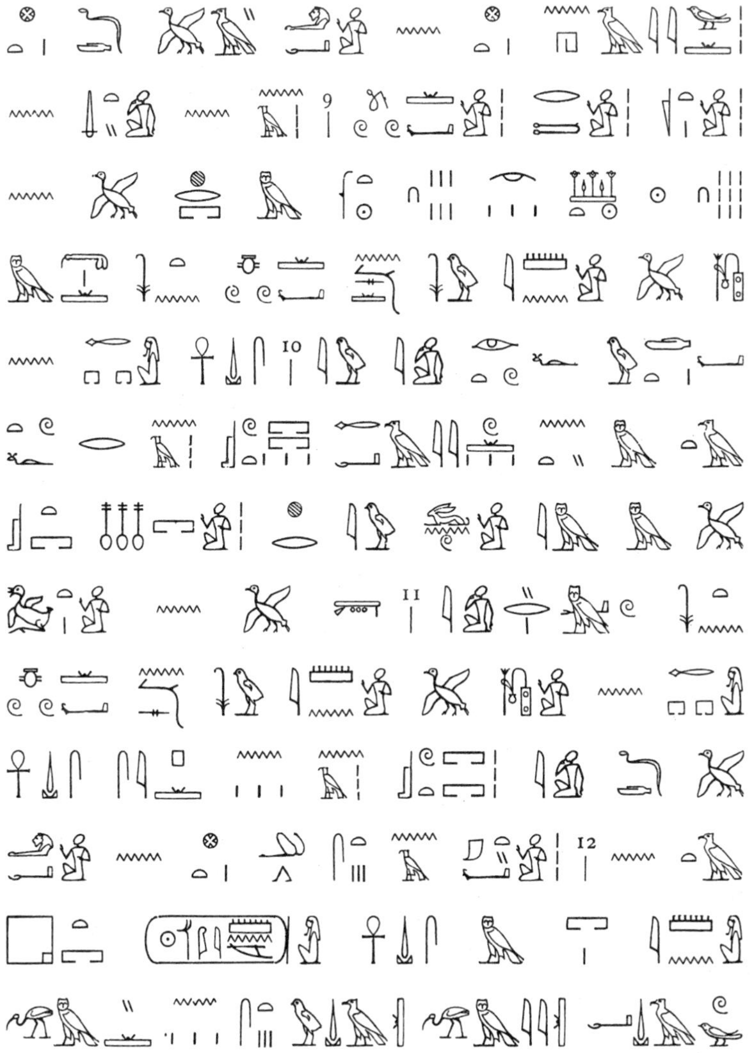

nut t'eṭ pai ḥā en nut nehai en meṭti en na 9. *ruṭuu reθ qeṭet en pa χer em renpit* 9
met-sȧs ȧbeṭ χemet šat hru met-paut embaḥ suten ābuu Nes-su-Ȧmen pa
ān en Āa-perti ānχ ut'a senb 10. *ȧu ȧ ȧritu-f uṭet-tuf er na ȧusetut āāaiu* 10
enti em ta ȧuset neferu χer ȧu unu-ȧ ȧm em pa t'at en pa ta 11. *ȧiremāu* 11
suten ābuu en Nes-su-Ȧmen pa ān en Āa-perti ānχ ut'a senb sȧp-n na ȧusetut
ȧ t'eṭ pa ḥā en nut peḥ set na χemti 12. *en ta ḥet Rā-usr-maāt-Ȧmen-meri* 12
ānχ ut'a senb em per Ȧmen qemi-n set ut'a qemi āt'au

13 *em pa ťeṭtu-f neb χer petrȧ* 13. *na χemti āḥā embaḥ-ten ȧu ťeṭu pa χeper*
14 *neb ȧru neťneť re-u qemi na reθ* 14. *ȧu bu pui-u reχ ȧuset neb em ta ȧuset*
15 *neferu ȧ ťeṭu pai ḥā na meṭtet eres set su ȧru āťau ȧm set* 15. *ṭāu na seru*
āāaiu ṇifu en na χemti en ta ḥet Rā-user-maāt-Ȧmen-meri ānχ uťa senb em
16 *per Ȧmen er χet en neter ḥen ṭep en Ȧmen-Rā suten neteru* 16. *Ȧmen-*
ḥetep hru pen ānu-un āuti-set . . . . . em χa en ān en ťat.

VOCABULARY

A.

aa		field **117**. 12
aȧ (read ***ȧa***)		island **228**. 12
aāāu		uncouth, boorish, fool **293**. 3
auu		marshy places (?) **102**. 12
apṭ		duck, feathered fowl **56**. 13
apuṭ (or ***ȧpṭu***)		ducks, wild-fowl **157**. 13; **175**. 11
Do.		ducks, wild-fowl **85**. 13
Do.		Do. Do. **130**. 8
aput en mu		water fowl **168**. 2
apṭ		to flutter **71**. 7
Apaliusa		Apellaeus (Ἀπελλαῖος) **225**. 3
Apualaniṭes		Apollonides (Ἀπολλωνίδης) **225**. 7
afa		greedy man, glutton **242**. 3

afa greediness **241.** 7

ȧm (?) = not **262.** 2

amesu sceptre **297.** 3

ȧrt hair (?) **61.** 1

aha grief, sorrow, grievous **54.** 2

aha " " " **80.** 13

ahu " " " **54.** 2

aha cow **72.** 2

aḥet field, fields **4.** 2; **115.** 1; **127.** 11; **259.** 2

aḥet to pray **124.** 10

aχaχ flowers, flowering plants **148.** 2; **160.** 12; **180.** 3; **286.** 11

aχaχ to put forth bloom, to flourish **89.** 12

asta to bring, to lead, to hasten,

astat to haste, haste **139.** 7; **141.** 2; **289.** 9

aku to become weak (?) **255.** 4

aq to diminish, be wanting **245.** 2; **260.** 2

at, aṭ moment, [evil] moment **62.** 7; **203.** 3; **233.** 12; **241.** 6

atu to be angry, to reject (?) **242.** 6

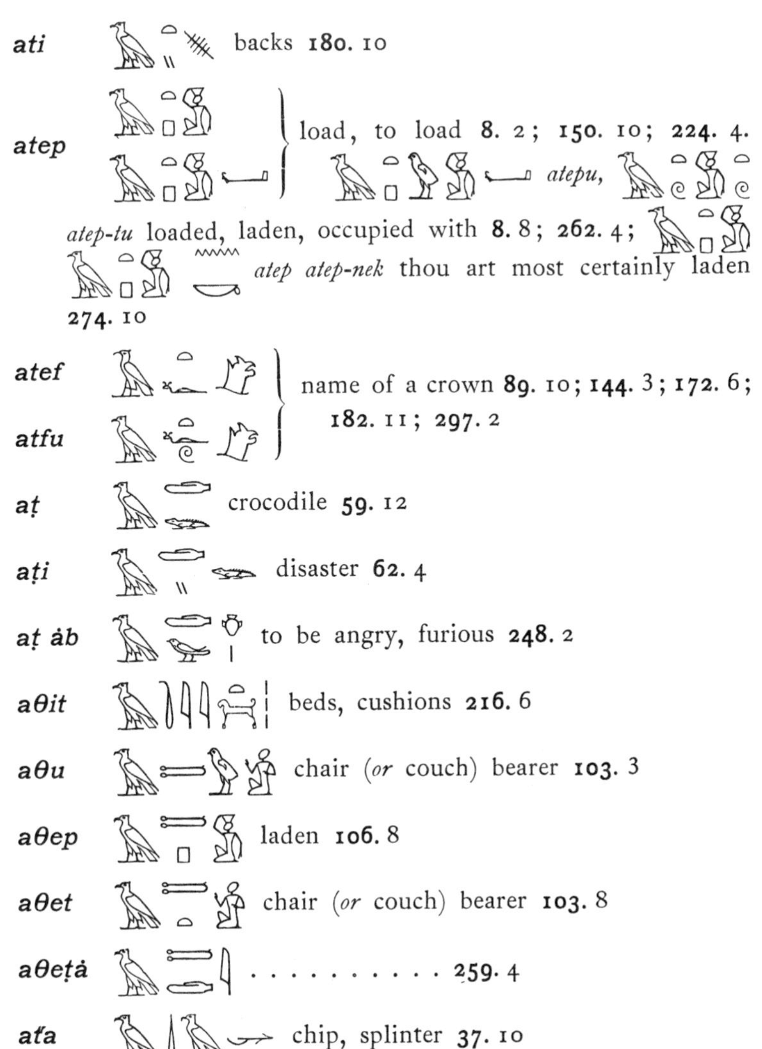

ati backs **180.** 10

atep load, to load **8.** 2; **150.** 10; **224.** 4. *atepu,* *atep-tu* loaded, laden, occupied with **8.** 8; **262.** 4; *atep atep-nek* thou art most certainly laden **274.** 10

atef, **atfu** name of a crown **89.** 10; **144.** 3; **172.** 6; **182.** 11; **297.** 2

aṭ crocodile **59.** 12

aṭi disaster **62.** 4

aṭ àb to be angry, furious **248.** 2

aθit beds, cushions **216.** 6

aθu chair (*or* couch) bearer **103.** 3

aθep laden **106.** 8

aθet chair (*or* couch) bearer **103.** 8

aθeṭà **259.** 4

at'a chip, splinter **37.** 10

Ȧ.

à I, me, my **5.** 9, 13; **7.** 2; **10.** 1; **121.** 7, 10; **128.** 11; **129.** 7; **131.** 4; **134.** 1; **241.** 1

à O, hail! **50.** 3; **53.** 7; **58.** 7; **62.** 13;

93. 3; 133. 8; "O go, O open" 5. 11

ȧ to say, to call out to one 323. 13

ȧ he who, that which, that what 1. 5; 4. 6, 7; 24. 12; 142. 9; 146. 10; 309. 6

ȧa meḥt island of the north 101. 5

ȧauu islands 132. 8; 173. 5; 220. 12; 223. 5

ȧau, ȧauu , old age, to grow old 244. 9; 245. 6; 271. 7

ȧau , old age, old man 129. 10; 199. 4

ȧaut old 269. 7

ȧau
ȧaui to praise, praises 147. 1; 178. 8; 295. 7; 296. 10; 301. 3

ȧaut , , , rank, dignity, honour 96. 9; 97. 1; 99. 4; 103. 12; 129. 9; 172. 2; 226. 6; 291. 10

ȧaut , beasts, cattle 1. 7; 3. 4

ȧat cattle 159. 11; 165. 8

Ȧam name of a city 106. 6

ȧamet acceptable 113. 10

àar lock of hair **63.** 6

àaru a fruit **28.** 8

àareret vines **101.** 13

àaχeχ sinews **65.** 8

àaś, *àaśet* to ask for, an asking **250.** 6; **254.** 7

àaṭ climes, regions **59.** 4: **60.** 13; **70.** 9

àatet, *àat* backbone, the middle **108.** 12; **109.** 6; **110.** 5; **115.** 21

àaṭet dew **296.** 2

àaṭeti moment **183.** 5

àā to wash **26.** 11; **213.** 1, 2

àā àb, *àāt àb* to gratify oneself **248.** 5; **251.** 6; **256.** 7

àābet offering **113.** 1

àārāt uraeus **90.** 2; **198.** 3

àārāret, *àārāutet* uraei, the serpents on the crown of Rā **158.** 12; **172.** 7; **223.** 8

àāḥ the moon, Moon-god **81.** 12; **90.** 6

Àāḥmes-sa-pa-àri a king of the XVIIth dynasty **314.** 2

àiu [hieroglyphs] to praise, praise **213**. 7

àu [hieroglyphs]
àuu [hieroglyphs] } praise **42**. 12; **225**. 1

àu [hieroglyphs] to be (auxiliary verb). With personal pronouns:— [hieroglyphs] I am **198**. 13; **220**. 12; [hieroglyphs] thou art **16**. 13; [hieroglyphs] thou art (fem.) **33**. 7; [hieroglyphs] he is **1**. 6; [hieroglyphs] she is **6**. 12; **9**. 10; [hieroglyphs] we are **30**. 3; [hieroglyphs] ye are; [hieroglyphs], [hieroglyphs] **3**. 6, 10; **4**. 2; [hieroglyphs] they are **3**. 2; **178**. 1. [hieroglyphs] was one **5**. 6; **22**. 9; **25**. 11; [hieroglyphs] being **185**. 4

àu = er [hieroglyphs], [hieroglyphs] = [hieroglyphs] to **49**. 7; **51**. 9; **228**. 10; **229**. 1; for **96**. 4; from **228**. 9; against **55**. 6; more **63**. 9

àu āu = er āu [hieroglyphs] to the whole extent **228**. 7; **229**. 13

àu ḥer = er ḥer [hieroglyphs] above **73**. 6

àu men = er men [hieroglyphs] until **230**. 12

àuaa [hieroglyphs] oxen **149**. 4; **163**. 13; **166**. 10

àuf [hieroglyphs] flesh, meat **59**. 11; **72**. 6; **128**. 1; **242**. 6

Àupa [hieroglyphs] a city in Syria **275**. 12; **282**. 2

Àurei [hieroglyphs] a proper name **311**. 5

Àusàr [hieroglyphs], [hieroglyphs] Osiris **49**. 5; **126**. 6; **130**. 5

Àusàr χent Àmentiu [hieroglyphs] "Osiris at the head of those in Amenti" **78**. 3; **95**. 10

Àuset — Isis 50. 2; 53. 3; 56. 8; 63. 4; 75. 8; 123. 9

Àuset — a queen of Rameses III. 318. 4

àuset — seat, throne, place, position, abode, house 3. 7; 14. 3; 40. 1; 42. 8; 90. 3; 103. 9; 117. 2; 128. 9; 180. 6; 227. 7; 250. 1; 272. 13. Plur. *àusetu* seats 150. 12; tombs 317. 2; 318. 8; 319. 6; 320. 4; 331. 6

àuset àmaχ — a place where honour is shewn to one 274. 6

àuset-ā — pain, sickness 51. 6; 71. 10

àuset neferu — "the abode of the blessed", *i. e.*, the tomb 317. 4; 320. 5; 325. 1; 331. 7; 332. 5

àuset re — "place of the mouth", *i. e.*, occasion for speech 15. 12; 32. 10; 36. 7

àuset reṭ — "place of the feet", *i. e.*, accustomed position 211. 4

àuset ḥeḥ, *àuset ent ḥeḥ* — "eternal abode", *i. e.*, the tomb 129. 12; 134. 1

àusetu en ḥetep — "abodes of peace", *i. e.*, the tomb 306. 10

àusetu sutut — promenades 162. 1

Àuḳertet — the underworld 299. 3

Àuθu — a country near Tyre 279. 8

ȧb , the heart **245**. 2; interior (of a city) **204**. 9

ȧb mind **5**. 12; **122**. 6; sense, wisdom, understanding, intelligence **43**. 9; **257**. 7; **268**. 11; attention **128**. 10; intention **6**. 3; disposition, manner **284**. 4; will, courage **122**. 10; **245**. 3; **262**. 2; wish, longing, desire, lust **6**. 11; **58**. 11; **228**. 9; **241**. 7; **242**. 5; self, *e. g.*, thyself **203**. 91. *Ȧb* with verbs:— to enrage **248**. 2; **256**. 7; to desire greatly **68**. 3; to be gracious **298**. 3; to gratify oneself **248**. 4; **251**. 6; **252**. 6; to be proud **242**. 13; **246**. 10; to rejoice **259**. 1; to be violent **257**. 11; **258**. 6; to hide **255**. 7; to be joyful **261**. 11; **267**. 7; right hearted **246**. 3; to be content **273**. 1; to please **248**. 4; to be master **247**. 3; to confine the attention **260**. 11; to be hard-hearted **298**. 4; to be distracted **262**. 3; to follow one's desires **252**. 11; to vex, to grieve **264**. 3; to be haughty **261**. 5; to be hot-tempered **261**. 9; to rage **247**. 4

ȧbu hearts **70**. 2

ȧbu or **ȧbiu** heart amulets **165**. 5

ȧb to desire **68**. 3

ȧb , thirst **190**. 5; **221**. 10

ȧb, ȧbt , thirst **241**. 9; **286**. 4

ȧb left hand **64.** 3 (see *semeḥi*)

ȧb , to depart **68.** 9; **198.** 3

ȧba to dance **117.** 6

ȧbata servant **283.** 8

ȧbi to come **61.** 5

ȧbu to wish for, to love **3.** 9; **9.** 2; **21.** 1

ȧbu to burn with desire **176.** 2

ȧbu panther **7.** 3; **11.** 2

Ȧbhat a country in or to the south of Nubia **104.** 7; **105.** 3

ȧbeχ (or **abeχ**) to join in battle **193.** 2

Ȧbsaqbu a city in Syria **290.** 11

ȧb, ȧbt , east, left **65.** 1; **199.** 12; **224.** 8

ȧbtet , , , east, left **107.** 5; **108.** 8; **109.** 7; **303.** 1

ȧbeṭ , , month **42.** 6; **45.** 8; **82.** 12; **226.** 5

ȧbṭet

ȧbeṭ monthly festival **112.** 10; **124.** 7. The Egyptian year contained twelve months of 30 days each, or three seasons , and , each containing four months. Compare the following examples of dating:— **184.** 7; **196.** 8; **306.** 1;

195. 5; 49. 6; 76. 8; 78. 4; 126. 3; 130. 1; 235. 10; 49. 2; 124. 6; 42. 6; 232. 8; 233. 2; 105. 13; 134. 3; 142. 1; 124. 7; 230. 12

ȧbṭ name of a fish 90. 10

ȧbṭ left 52. 10

Ȧbṭu Abydos 49. 5; 77. 4; 126. 7

ȧp, ȧpu , except 202. 5; 206. 8; 86. 9; 319. 11; 320. 2

ȧp er except 99. 1

ȧpu ḥer but, except 121. 13; 125. 5

ȧp to open 58. 2; 132. 9

ȧp renpit new year 232. 9

ȧp renpit festival of the new year 112. 7

ȧpt śe "the beginning of the lake", *i. e.*, the Fayyūm 202. 11

ȧp to count, to estimate, to prize 104. 1; 203. 4; 267. 10; thought highly of 265. 12

ȧpt measure, reckoned 104. 2; 166. 8

ȧp , envoy, messenger 42. 9; 43. 11; 74. 4; 220. 6; embassy 117. 5

ȧpu messengers 198. 1

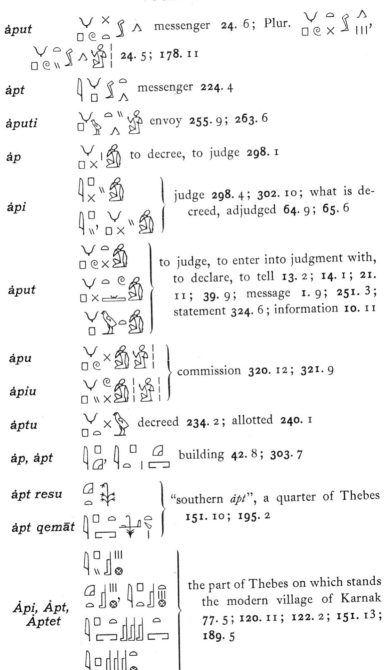

ȧput messenger **24**. 6; Plur. , **24**. 5; **178**. 11

ȧpt messenger **224**. 4

ȧputi envoy **255**. 9; **263**. 6

ȧp to decree, to judge **298**. 1

ȧpi judge **298**. 4; **302**. 10; what is decreed, adjudged **64**. 9; **65**. 6

ȧput to judge, to enter into judgment with, to declare, to tell **13**. 2; **14**. 1; **21**. 11; **39**. 9; message **1**. 9; **251**. 3; statement **324**. 6; information **10**. 11

ȧpu, **ȧpiu** commission **320**. 12; **321**. 9

ȧptu decreed **234**. 2; allotted **240**. 1

ȧp, ȧpt , building **42**. 8; **303**. 7

ȧpt resu, **ȧpt qemāt** "southern *ȧpt*", a quarter of Thebes **151**. 10; **195**. 2

Ȧpi, Ȧpt, Ȧptet the part of Thebes on which stands the modern village of Karnak **77**. 5; **120**. 11; **122**. 2; **151**. 13; **189**. 5

ȧpt to open (?), be opened (?) **49**. 8; **52**. 9

ȧpu those **95**. 1

Ȧpu Panopolis **129**. 3; **133**. 2

Ȧp-uat (?) "opener of ways", a name of Osiris **60**. 1; **65**. 8

ȧpuṭ ducks, geese **300**. 7

ȧpś to illumine **70**. 3

ȧpt exudation (?) **90**. 11

ȧpet metal vases **217**. 2

ȧpt brow **299**. 8

ȧpṭu planks **37**. 4

ȧfṭ the four cardinal points **56**. 3; four (sides of a city) **193**. 12

ȧm, **ȧmu** to eat **2**. 12; **3**. 5; **33**. 8; **127**. 5

ȧmt eating **130**. 11

ȧm camp **134**. 6; **197**. 6; **212**. 13; **214**. 13

ȧm favour **115**. 8; acceptable unto **107**. 2; *ȧm ā* kind (?) **110**. 2; *ȧm ȧb* gracious **298**. 3

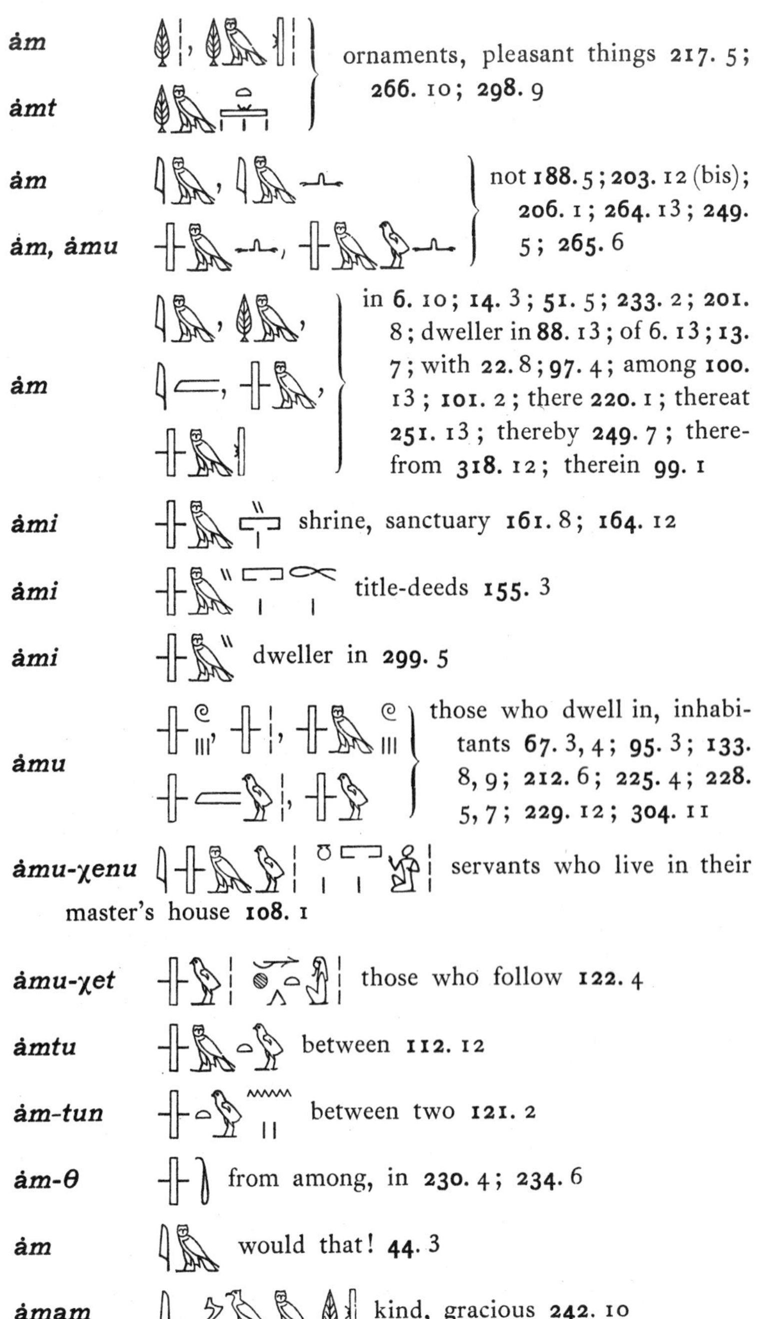

ȧm, **ȧmt** ornaments, pleasant things **217.** 5; **266.** 10; **298.** 9

ȧm, **ȧm, ȧmu** not **188.** 5; **203.** 12 (bis); **206.** 1; **264.** 13; **249.** 5; **265.** 6

ȧm in **6.** 10; **14.** 3; **51.** 5; **233.** 2; **201.** 8; dweller in **88.** 13; of 6. 13; **13.** 7; with **22.** 8; **97.** 4; among **100.** 13; **101.** 2; there **220.** 1; thereat **251.** 13; thereby **249.** 7; therefrom **318.** 12; therein **99.** 1

ȧmi shrine, sanctuary **161.** 8; **164.** 12

ȧmi title-deeds **155.** 3

ȧmi dweller in **299.** 5

ȧmu those who dwell in, inhabitants **67.** 3, 4; **95.** 3; **133.** 8, 9; **212.** 6; **225.** 4; **228.** 5, 7; **229.** 12; **304.** 11

ȧmu-χenu servants who live in their master's house **108.** 1

ȧmu-χet those who follow **122.** 4

ȧmtu between **112.** 12

ȧm-tun between two **121.** 2

ȧm-θ from among, in **230.** 4; **234.** 6

ȧm would that! **44.** 3

ȧmam kind, gracious **242.** 10

Ȧmam name of a country **100.** 1

ȧmaχ to be held in veneration, honoured **110.** 8

ȧmaχi
ȧmaχi
ȧmaχu one honoured, esteemed **107.** 3; **113.** 9; **270.** 2

ȧmaχiu venerable beings **127.** 10

Ȧmmu a sanctuary of Hathor **92.** 5

Ȧmem a name of the city of Buto **92.** 13

ȧmmā (or ***ȧmem***) ,
ȧmāt give, grant, let I pray, place **3.** 13; **24.** 5; **43.** 4; **145.** 1; **188.** 10; **242.** 12; **267.** 9; **280.** 10; put us **199.** 1

ȧmmu boat **119.** 3

ȧmen , to hide, hidden, hidden one **59.** 8; **89.** 8; **297.** 11; **299.** 3

Ȧmen , the "hidden" god, Ammon **41.** 1; **76.** 6; **189.** 3; **294.** 3 etc.

Ȧmen-Rā , Ȧmen-Rā **40.** 10; **42.** 7; **76.** 6; **294.** 3

Ȧmen-sepṭ-ābui "Ȧmen the Two-horned" **77.** 1

Ȧmen-em-ȧnt a proper name **319.** 4

Ȧmen-meri-Rā-meses Rameses XII. (?) **40.** 10

Ȧmen-em-ḥāt a proper name **108**. 6; **109**. 2

Ȧmen-neχtu a proper name **321**. 5; **322**. 1; **325**. 10

Ȧmen-ḥetep Amenophis I. **308**. 10; **309**. 3

Ȧmen-ḥetep a high-priest **317**. 11

Ȧmen-ḥetepu a cemetery official **321**. 6

Ȧmen-χnem-ḥeḥ "Amen the uniter of eternity" **148**. 12

Ȧmen-χnem-Ḥāt-śepset Queen Ḥātshepset **119**. 8

Ȧmen-qa-ȧuset a proper name **77**. **4**

ȧmenit perpetuity **146**. 5; **154**. 2; **166**. 2

ȧment the west **224**. 8

Ȧmentet the west, the underworld **58**. 2; **110**. 7; **307**. 1

Ȧmenteti the west, the underworld **315**. 4

ȧmentiu those in the underworld **49**. 5; **53**. 10; **61**. 6; **62**. 3

ȧmentet resu west-south **197**. 7

ȧmeru to be deaf **245**. 1

ȧmḥet hall of a tomb **212**. 8

ȧm-χent at the head of, in **236**. 7

Àmsu , , , (?) the god of generation **77.** 11; **120.** 7; **128.** 2; **129.** 3; **131.** 9; **133.** 1; **133.** 5

Àmes

Àmsu-Àmen name of a double deity **296.** 9

Àmsu-χenti (?) name of a city (?) **133.** 1

Àm-seḥti name of a god **64.** 11

àmt darling **119.** 9

àmt abode, habitation **258.** 5

àmt **111.** 4

Àmtes name of a queen **98.** 12

àmtu (for *unṭu*) cattle **149.** 5; **167.** 1

àn , to bring, to carry **5.** 4; **41.** 10; to close doors **214.** 3; to add a word to a book **272.** 7

àn , offerings, tribute **41.** 10, 12; **42.** 10; **48.** 7

àn , marks a subject in a sentence, and is a mark of emphasis **4.** 6; **5.** 2; **129.** 1; **134.** 10; **136.** 13; **199.** 6

àn interrogative particle. Is it? shall it? is it that? **190.** 6; **201.** 4; **248.** 13; shall it be? **186.** 11; **197.** 3; shall then? **197.** 4; is it that not? **221.** 1

Àn Moon-god **79.** 3, 11; **81.** 9; **84.** 6

àn battering ram **195.** 13

ȧn not 2. 1; 7. 12; 50. 6; 51. 8; 202. 9; unless, without 249. 1; is not? 59. 10

ȧn ȧs except, only, not as yet 50. 9; 51. 9; 68. 9; 241. 4; 248. 1; 258. 7; 267. 5; . . . . only 251. 5; 252. 7

ȧn āu faultless 248. 10

ȧn ābu ceaselessly 127. 3

ȧn uā no one 19. 1

ȧn un, **ȧn unt** there is not 83. 7; 105. 13

ȧn urṭ unceasingly 245. 2

ȧn maati (?) eyeless, blind 62. 12

ȧn ennu blindly 58. 3

ȧn re, **ȧn rā** (?) numberless 149. 2; 158. 1; 159. 8; 172. 13

Ȧn-reχ a proper name 60. 7

ȧn reχ unknown (of a god) 89. 8

ȧn useχt without join 124. 4

ȧn sep never 59. 3; 60. 8; (or) never before 98. 2; 99. 5

ȧn sek — indestructible 94. 10; never failing 123. 13; 214. 7

ȧn setem — deaf 62. 12

ȧn kat — no work 82. 9

ȧn ṭennu — divisionless 124. 5

ȧnȧ — flowers, branches of trees 272. 8

Ȧni — Moon-god 298. 13; 302. 13; 303. 6

ȧnu — graves, cemeteries 175. 8

Ȧneb — a city near Pelusium 92. 11

ȧneb, **ȧnebet** — walls 91. 9; 205. 5; 219. 10

Ȧneb resu — "Southern Wall", a part of Memphis 206. 5

Ȧneb-ḥeťet — "White Wall", a name of Memphis 87. 2; 185. 7; 206. 4, 6

Ȧnpu — the god Anubis 126. 7

Ȧnpu — the Nome of the Jackal 110. 3; 114. 1, 7; 115. 3

Ȧnpu — a proper name 1. 2

ȧnemem — skin 73. 7

ȧnlana — oak-tree 276. 9

ȧner — stone 116. 10; 147. 6; 149. 12; 240. 8

ȧner uā monolith 124. 4

ȧner en ruṭ sandstone 147. 6

ȧner ḥet' limestone (?) 97. 10

ȧner qem black basalt (?) 147. 7

Ȧnna name of an author 40. 5

ȧnnu hairy skin, hair 30. 1; 155. 9; 287. 2; 298. 1; outside of a metal 179. 7

ȧnnu ,
ȧnnut } offerings, income, produce, burdens 115. 9; 161. 12; 165. 2; 174. 6; 178. 3; 201. 12; 212. 3; 219. 6

Ȧnnu On, Heliopolis 90. 7; 119. 1; 212. 11; 294. 3

Ȧnnu resu Hermonthis 120. 5

ȧnḥ
ȧnḥu } to surround, to enclose 140. 7; 162. 7; 176. 8; 276. 11

ȧnuk , I 10. 7; 14. 12

ȧnq to collect, to embrace 52. 7; 65. 5

ȧnqefqefet part of a horse's harness (?) 286. 1

ȧnt , conduct, the bringing of, lead 97. 10; 258. 10; carried off, removed 246. 12; 260. 1

ȧnt valley 14. 5; 17. 1; 18. 5; 19. 7; 24. 7; 25. 1; 319. 9

Ȧntuf a king of the XIth dynasty 310. 13

Ȧntuf-āa a king of the XIth dynasty **311.** 9

ȧntet valley **224.** 13; **227.** 9

ȧr marks emphasis **1.** 1; **10.** 11; **46.** 12; **188.** 7; **242.** 7

ȧref an emphatic word **125.** 1; **230.** 8

ȧr ȧs behold if **234.** 1

ȧr en ṭertu when **10.** 2

ȧr-ḳert but **112.** 11

ȧri , at, belonging to **57.** 1, 12; **125.** 9; **217.** 3 (bis); **218.** 2; **230.** 3; **231.** 10; **264.** 6; **300.** 10

ȧri, **ȧru** guardian, companion, lover, helpmeet **20.** 9; **29.** 10; **57.** 12; **170.** 1; **287.** 2

ȧru those which are at **42.** 1; **96.** 7; **112.** 1

ȧru attribute **51.** 1, 10; **53.** 2; **56.** 10; **60.** 10

ȧr, **ȧri** , , , to make, to do, doer, to be done, begotten of **6.** 13; **11.** 1; **44.** 9; **96.** 6; **105.** 3, 4; **107.** 5; **200.** 11; to write a book **40.** 4; to recite a book **49.** 4; **78.** 3; **79.** 2; one having done **123.** 4; working **298.** 8; matter **305.** 4; execution of work **150.** 3

ȧru to make **85.** 12

åri ān to act as scribe 99. 3

åri netert to deify 236. 11

åri ḥebsu to weave clothes 1. 6

åri ḥemt to marry a wife 267. 6

åri ḥer to terrify 249. 5

åri χet to acquire wealth 264. 1

åri seχeru to perform duties 4. 7

åri seka to plough 1. 8

åri ṭeṭ to say 226. 8

årit setep sa to protect 98. 9

årit , matter, thing, something done, made of, child of 76. 6; 108. 12; 184. 1; 298. 8; handicraft 207. 5; fine work 163. 1

åritu to celebrate a festival 226. 4

åru celebration 194. 11

åru ceremonies 305. 7

årru works, acts, deeds 116. 8; 184. 1

årret works, acts, deeds 116. 8; 184. 1

åri pet birds which fly in the air 164. 3

åremā with 308. 13

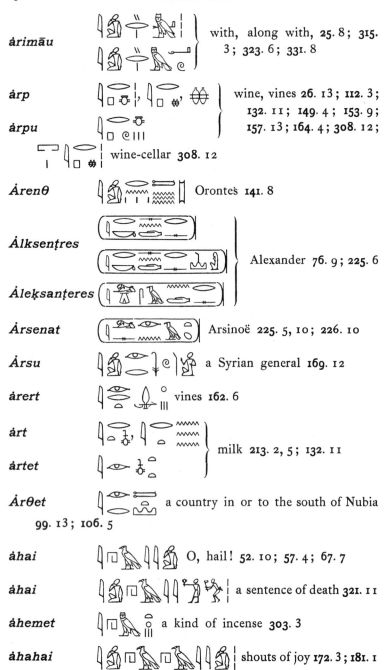

årimāu with, along with, 25. 8; 315. 3; 323. 6; 331. 8

årp, **årpu** wine, vines 26. 13; 112. 3; 132. 11; 149. 4; 153. 9; 157. 13; 164. 4; 308. 12;

wine-cellar 308. 12

Årenθ Orontes 141. 8

Ålksenṭres, **Åleḳsanṭeres** Alexander 76. 9; 225. 6

Årsenat Arsinoë 225. 5, 10; 226. 10

Årsu a Syrian general 169. 12

årert vines 162. 6

årt, **årtet** milk 213. 2, 5; 132. 11

Årθet a country in or to the south of Nubia 99. 13; 106. 5

åhai O, hail! 52. 10; 57. 4; 67. 7

åhai a sentence of death 321. 11

åhemet a kind of incense 303. 3

åhahai shouts of joy 172. 3; 181. 1

ȧhait cow-byre, stable, any farm outhouse 2. 13; 6. 2; 278. 3.

ȧḥ silver 217. 2

ȧḥ field, pastureland 110. 6

ȧḥ ox, oxen 11. 12; 12. 4; 85. 13; 130. 8

ȧḥ stable 189. 2; 216. 8

ȧḥ nu semsem stable for horses 200. 12

ȧḥi to embrace 70. 13

ȧḥi sistrum-bearer 50. 7; 52. 12; 58. 7; 61. 4; 62. 13; 76. 6

ȧḥit people, tribe 252. 3

ȧḥu decay, senility 244. 10

ȧḥeti
ȧḥetit throat 78. 8; 88. 2

ȧχ why? what? what manner of? 6. 5; 7. 10; 14. 10; 136. 11; 245. 9; 246. 1; 323. 11; sign of the optative 16. 11; 20. 6; 188. 8; 271. 11; 272. 1; 273. 1; 276. 1, 4

ȧχemu seku the stars that never set 202. 9

ȧχer because 98. 3, 4, 5

ȧs behold, but 2. 2; 10. 7; 41. 7; 124. 9; 221. 2; 232. 11; 233. 12; but with 223. 9

ȧs, ȧsi , tomb 107. 9; 116. 13; 118. 4; 126. 9

ȧsit tombs, sepulchres 306. 9; 308. 13; 315. 1

ȧsu reward 125. 8; 229. 6; 231. 4

ȧsi flowers, shrubs 160. 12; 162. 3

Ȧsare Assyria 283. 12

ȧsut ancient custom (?) 109. 13; 114. 10

ȧsbuire whip 289. 7

ȧsburere thorny growth 285. 1

ȧsbut throne 170. 13

ȧspaθȧ quiver 287. 11

ȧsfet injustice, wrong 109. 8; 272. 1

ȧser cornland (?) 110. 6

Ȧssȧ a king of the Vth dynasty 244. 7

ȧsk behold 42. 6; 43. 8; 226. 13; 232. 12; behold moreover 227. 13

ȧst, ȧstu , behold 1. 9; 16. 8, 9; 121. 7; 134. 5; 135. 8; 140. 7

ȧsteb throne 136. 7

Ȧstennu a form of Thoth 74. 2

àś 204. 4

Àśer a district of Thebes 77. 4

àśta persea tree 77. 3

àkebu to weep 63. 6

àken vessel 241. 8

àqer , **àqert** , mental or physical strength, superiority, able, perfect 3. 11; 95. 4, 8; 98. 3; 129. 2; 247. 3, 10; 270. 6

Àqertet a name of the underworld 60. 9

àqesi, àqeset , vile 136. 4; 138. 13

àḳeru dwellers in *Àḳert* (?) 89. 6

Àḳerbemremet the Heracleum * 235. 10

Àḳert a name of the underworld 142. 5; 146. 2; 182. 6

àt fruitless, in vain 319. 8

àti , the destitute 128. 4; 302. 12

àtu , not, destitution 251. 12; 254. 11; 270. 12

àturti the eastern and western horizons 74. 3; 85. 11

àtur river, basin of water 90. 10; 158. 5; 291. 4

* = ἐν τῷ Ἡρακλείῳ ἱερου (Greek text, l. 51).

ȧtur a measure of length **162.** 8

ȧtep to be laden **2.** 7

ȧtef father **1.** 2; **50.** 10; **116.** 9; **121.** 4; "divine father", *i. e.*, a kind of priest **246.** 5

ȧtfu, ȧtfiu fathers, parents **50.** 12; **84.** 3; **143.** 8; **257.** 13; **301.** 12

Ȧtem, Ȧtmu the god Atmu or Tmu **50.** 11; **77.** 12

ȧten disk of the sun **13.** 13; **74.** 4; **125.** 11

ȧtennu herald **65.** 2

ȧtennu vicar, deputy **77.** 7; **78.** 1; **264.** 9; **265.** 3; **266.** 9; **267.** 6; **330.** 4

ȧter

ȧtru Nile, river flood, stream, canal **108.** 11; **131.** 6; **178.** 4; **210.** 6; **300.** 7

ȧtru Nile festivals **131.** 10

ȧterti north and south Egypt **226.** 3; **232.** 6

ȧtḥu to drag, to haul, to pull **149.** 6; **183.** 13; **277.** 2

ȧtḥu papyrus plants **293.** 4

Ȧṭulmā a city of Syria **281.** 12

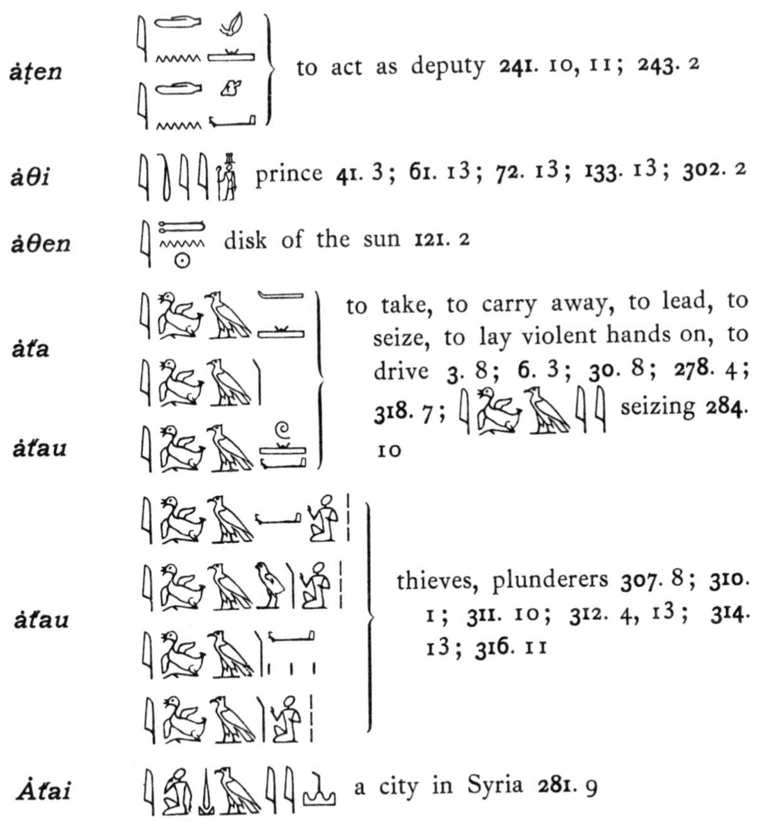

áṭen to act as deputy **241.** 10, 11; **243.** 2

áθi prince **41.** 3; **61.** 13; **72.** 13; **133.** 13; **302.** 2

áθen disk of the sun **121.** 2

áťa, **áťau** to take, to carry away, to lead, to seize, to lay violent hands on, to drive **3.** 8; **6.** 3; **30.** 8; **278.** 4; **318.** 7; seizing **284.** 10

áťau thieves, plunderers **307.** 8; **310.** 1; **311.** 10; **312.** 4, 13; **314.** 13; **316.** 11

Áťai a city in Syria **281.** 9

Ā.

ā hand **132.** 1; *ḥer ā* forthwith **43.** 6; at once (see under)

āāui the two hands, sides **49.** 9; **56.** 8; **60.** 12; **132.** 1; **247.** 3; **259.** 7; **299.** 13

ā uārt (?) a going, a travelling **278.** 13

ā unbu a kind of flower **286.** 6

ā fent tip of the nose (?) 284. 3

ā meḥt the side of the north 328. 8

ā-en-ȧspaθȧ a quiver 287. 11

ā-en-senen a journeying, a going 282. 9

ā-en-seś a journeying, a going 284. 9

ā-en-saḳa piece of sackcloth 287. 7

ā-en-śemi a going, a journeying 280. 11

ā resu the side of the south 328. 8

ā = āt *q. v.* 290. 9

ā ḥeqt beer shop 221. 8

āā , door 115. 12; 118. 3

āāui, āaut , doors 86. 11; 104. 11; 118. 4; 152. 10; 214. 1

āā wretched, miserable 203. 4; 221. 2

āa cover of a sarcophagus 98. 1; 104. 8

āat stone 217. 2

āat stones 148. 4, 13; 156. 8; 158. 11; 217. 2

āāa to become or be great 263. 13

āa , great (of age) 1. 2; 46. 4; 108. 12; 105. 7; 109. 6; 121. 5;

āāa , very great 77. 1

āāi, āau great 49. 5; 198. 10

āāai great 146. 1

āāaiu great 35. 1; 39. 6; 331. 6

āāait great 317. 2; 320. 4

āāiu nobles, princes, magnates 135. 2

āāat great 46. 11; 59. 5; 110. 1, 10; 111. 8; 191. 4; 302. 11; great lady 25. 12

āāa-ȧb to magnify the heart, *i. e.*, be proud 242. 13; 246. 10

Āa-perti Pharaoh 22. 11; 23. 1; 24. 1; 30. 8; 32. 8; 135. 4; 139. 5; 306. 8

āa-en-uťa chief of the storehouse 308. 8

āa-en-per major-domo 307. 3; 309. 9; 316. 5; 330. 1

āa-en-χen "large of interior" (of a barge), *i. e.*, broad-beamed (?) 98. 1

āa-en-sa chief of a priestly order 231. 11

āa-en-qeṭet chief of the sailors 321. 5; 324. 10

āāa ner[*ȧu*] very terrible 296. 5

āa neχtu very mighty 161. 10

āā-re to speak insolently 128. 5

āāa ḥāti exceedingly courageous 295. 10

āāa χāu great or mighty of crowns **298**. 12; **302**. 9

āa śeps most venerable **306**. 6; **307**. 10; **315**. 12

āā en śefit }
āāi śefi } very terrible **85**. 8; **89**. 11

āaāaiu asses **178**. 3; **179**. 2

āāuit colonnade **122**. 12

āāab offerings, sacrifices **259**. 10

āaireθȧ **147**. 12

āanre }
āairre } rocks, stones **283**. 3; **284**. 13

Āarena a city in Syria **289**. 12

āaśaq to injure **146**. 11

Āaθȧka a city in Syria **178**. 12

ā-i (?) a going (?) **309**. 5

Āiina a kind of stone **163**. 2

Āiina a city in Syria **176**. 7

āu hand (?) **250**. 11

āu jackals, dogs **18**. 10

āu fault, defect, injury, calamity, evil **35**. 8 **65**. 13; **66**. 12; **222**. 12; **248**. 10; **256**. 7

āut calamity 261. 5

āu ruin, smashed 311. 6

āu heir 68. 3; 74. 3

āuāā heir 53. 12; 63. 3; 205. 8

āuāt heritage, inheritance 108. 1; 110. 8; 111. 7; 114. 1

āuāāt tribesmen 138. 2

āu to make long, to dilate, length 95. 2; 105. 12; 111. 9; 186. 10

āuu throughout 245. 4

āu ȧb to make the heart glad 259. 1

āut ȧb joy, gladness 146. 9; 299. 5

āu nif a full wind (?) 131. 13

āu ḥāp to go quickly (?) 221. 13

āui to be strong 312. 13

āu violence 313. 3

āuait to do work 1. 8

āuu to divert (?), to turn aside (?) 254. 2

Āuapeθ a royal name 191. 9; 212. 1; 218. 3

āun ȧb to be violent 257. 11; 258. 5, 6, 7

āun ȧb the violent man **248**. 13

āunt violence, to be violent **258**. 11

āuna to decree **321**. 10; **325**. 8; **326**. 5; decreed, condemned **326**. 5

āunt a kind of tree **276**. 9

āuur to conceive **37**. 12

āuḥānu to flood (?) **55**. 10

āusu scales, balance **221**. 4

āut beasts, animals, quadrupeds **83**. 3; **227**. 2; **295**. 4; **299**. 10; **301**. 1; **302**. 6

āut the attribute of an animal (?) **241**. 8

āuti plaques **154**. 9

āuti register **332**. 11

āutu joy **130**. 12

āutu food **132**. 7

āuṭ to separate **13**. 5, 6; **310**. 9; see also between

āuṭ to put away, to remove **253**. 8

āuṭent ground **12**. 10; earth, dust **17**. 8; **18**. 8; **288**. 5

āb court (?) **240**. 11

āb to approach, to meet **59**. 9; **61**. 9; **95**. 13; **221**. 5

āb opposite 116. 4; the opposite 260. 12; 261. 1

āb body, person 221. 7

āb , , offering, sacrifice 46. 11; 47. 2; 205. 10; 211. 7

āb altar 95. 6; 132. 4

āb tables of offerings 153. 5

ābtu offerings 88. 13

āb , to be ceremonially pure, to wash, to purify 49. 7; 189. 5; 290. 6; pure 120. 3; 130. 8

āb , purification, washing, pure 132. 6; 217. 6

āb libation 211. 5; 231. 10; 237. 8

āb , libationer, a man ceremonially pure 77. 5; 224. 2; 225. 6

ābu , , libation priests 129. 5; 211. 3; 299. 12; 226. 1, 3; 229. 8; 230. 4; 239. 4

ābt a meat-offering ceremonially pure 112. 3

ābet place of purification 32. 3; 33. 2

āba to invade, to harass (?) 266. 2

āba to offer 65. 8

āba to advance to or into **93.** 6

āba courtyard, hall **145.** 7; **151.** 4; **153.** 1, 7; **157.** 8; **159.** 3; **329.** 5

āba to fight, battle, battle gear (?), opposition **21.** 10; **44.** 1; **135.** 13; **137.** 10; **189.** 7; **261.** 10

ābaiu fighting men **220.** 1

ābauti strife **22.** 13; **23.** 3

ābā to speak against, to be in opposition **125.** 5; **189.** 7; **251.** 13

ābi (or **abi**)
ābu (or **abu**) panther **194.** 4; **197.** 3

ābu festivals **157.** 10

ābtu festivals **31.** 7; **34.** 3

ābuu (or **ḥemu**)
ābu (or **ḥemu**) workman, artisan, artist, skilled worker **34.** 4; **246.** 12; **272.** 12

ābuu (or **ḥemuu**) workmen **37.** 7; **288.** 12

ābut (or **ḥemut**) workshops **288.** 11

ābuu (or **ḥemuu**) skilled, learned **268.** 4

ābuu (or **ḥemuu**) art, handicraft **260.** 13

ābet (or **ḥemt**) work, art **246.** 12

ābut (or **ḥemut**) skilful, able, handicraft 43. 8; 118. 13

ābu courtyard 310. 5

ābuu workmen 307. 2, 5, 12; 318. 6; 321. 13; 323. 1; 172. 11; 179. 9

ābu (or **abu**) cessation 127. 3; 129. 8; ceaselessly 127. 3

Ābu (or ***Abu***) Elephantine 99. 11; 103. 5; 104. 10; 293. 5

ābui two-horned 77. 1

ābut obstacle, opposition 255. 1

ābeb (or **abeb**) to desire 217. 10

ābeχ, ābeχu (or **abeχ**) , × to enter, to penetrate 43. 3; 122. 11

āpi to fly 64. 5; 75. 3

Āpenȧnebḥeṫet a city near Per-sepṭ 218. 9

āper, **āperi** , to be provided with, accompanied by 64. 3; 82. 8; 83. 9; 137. 8; 151. 2; 246. 12 manned by a crew 159. 7

Āper a city in the Delta 84. 7

āperu, **āpereru** ornaments, fittings 154. 4; 315. 10

āfennu to be fettered 318. 8

ām ȧb to hide, to act deceitfully 255. 6

āmāu impure men 223. 12

Āmu nomad Nubian tribes 99. 9

Āmu an Asiatic 278. 10

āmamu
āmamu
āmu } to eat, to consume, to swallow 16. 1; 29. 1; 37. 12; 275. 10; 283. 9

āmamu to see, to understand, to perceive 15. 6; 17. 4, 13; 32. 8; 143. 13; 278. 6; to shew, to instruct 39. 7; 169. 3

āmt something eaten 297. 10

ān a district in Lower Egypt 185. 6

ān pleasant, gracious 267. 8; 269. 13; 284. 4; 293. 7

ān a man of peace 261. 9

ān , to return 7. 12; 17. 12; 20. 3; 30. 4; 51. 7; 186. 1; to send back 290. 1; turning back 305. 9; to be seen again 159. 4; 180. 1; to seek again 28. 8; to repeat 275. 2

ān , to write, writing 230. 2; 243. 7 to put in writing 99. 3; document 322. 9

ānu titledeeds 109. 13

ānu	book, pages of a book, written papers **40.** 6; **76.** 8; **316.** 11
ānu en per ānχ	hieroglyphic writing **232.** 7; **238.** 8; **240.** 8
ān en ḥa-nebu (?)	Greek writing **240.** 9
ān en śātet	"writing of books" (demotic) **240.** 9
ān, *ānuu*	scribe **40.** 2; **76.** 4; **306.** 7 (bis); **307.** 3; educated, learned **43.** 9
ānu	scribes **23.** 13; **159.** 12; **240.** 7; **327.** 9; **328.** 1
ān suten	royal scribes **43.** 10
ān t̓at̓at	scribe of the municipality **326.** 2
ān śāt neter	sacred scribes **226.** 2
ānāi	to gainsay, to contradict **250.** 13; **267.** 6
Ānep	a name of the city Mendes **83.** 13
ānen	to take back, to retract **124.** 13
ānnu	to turn back **141.** 11
ānnu	tablets **155.** 1
ānnu	stones **197.** 10
ānnu	beautiful **52.** 13; **56.** 12; **116.** 10

ānχ — life, to live, alive **10.** 11; **49.** 3; **53.** 6; **168.** 4, 5; *ānχi* living one **131.** 5

ānχu — living men and women **65.** 2; **126.** 2; **129.** 4; **146.** 6; **169.** 2; **203.** 1; **228.** 1; **227.** 10; **230.** 9; **270.** 3; "living ones", *i. e.*, the dead **104.** 8

ānχet — living one **116.** 13; **119.** 7; **168.** 4, 5

ānχ — to swear an oath by the life of any one **123.** 5; **141.** 11; **194.** 8; **319.** 12

ānχ neter — to swear an oath by God **216.** 8; **222.** 6, 10; — to swear a ten-fold oath **326.** 12

ānχ mesut — living one of births **110.** 11

ānχ t'etta — ever-living **244.** 7

ānχ ut'a senb — "life, health, strength" **22.** 11; **23.** 1; **24.** 1; **25.** 3; **26.** 1; **32.** 9; **33.** 2; **34.** 5; **135.** 4; **269.** 10; **307.** 4

ānχ ṭeṭ user — "life, stability and strength" **78.** 10

ānχu — incense, flowers **213.** 11

ānχu — flowers **213.** 10

ānχui — the two ears **145.** 2; **245.** 1

ānχ nu nut — the dwellers in a town **307.** 1; **315.** 2

Ānχ-Ḥeru — a proper name **218.** 6

Ānχet the place of sunset 145. 6

ānt
ānti ,
ānti
ānti
} unguent 61. 2; 72. 12; 92. 4; 159. 1; 177. 11; 213. 5; 214. 9; 216. 6; 219. 7; 303. 4

ānṭ to be without, lacking, lack 258. 9

ānṭiu destitute men 189. 10

ār to rise up 208. 1

āri a kind of offering (?) 132. 6

ārāt uraeus, uraei 74. 9; 88. 4

ārit palace, hall 202. 8

ārf purses, bags 179. 13; 258. 3

ārfet to embrace 122. 4

ārq to conclude 243. 5

ārq renpit festival of the last day of the year 112. 7

ārqu to swear an oath 15. 7; 33. 6; to swear by God 36. 12

ārqi the end of a period 124. 7

āret (?) shrine 98. 1

ārtu shrine 104. 11

āḥā, *āḥāu* — to stand up, to stand still, to withstand 5. 7; 18. 3; 103. 9; 136. 3; 137. 4; 213. 13; 220. 9; 244. 3; opposition 247. 8. For as an auxiliary verb compare:— 5. 7; 41. 12; 110. 1; 9. 13; 45. 9; 140. 9; 187. 9; 195. 7

āḥā — provisions, wealth, wealthy condition, stores 111. 12; 249. 1; 264. 4; 319. 1

āḥā — the stony sides of a mountain 285. 4

āḥā, *āḥāu* — time, period, duration of life 87. 10; 184. 4; 265. 11

āḥā — palace 106. 10

āḥāi — hall 309. 4

āḥāu — boats, barges 178. 10; 190. 13; 208. 2; 222. 4

āḥāi — boats 187. 13; 209. 10; 214. 12

āhāq — a kind of food 216. 4

āχ — to spread out 296. 8; 301. 12

āχ — to fly 60. 6

āχai — to fly 48. 1

Āa-χeper-ka-Rā — prenomen of Thothmes I. 122. 13

āχamu branches 127. 4

āχem to quench thirst 190. 5; 241. 8

āś to cry out 13. 11; 16. 8; 22. 7; 238. 7

āś, āśt , to call 137. 10; 189. 1; to summon 43. 7

āś acacia tree 17. 2, 6; 18. 5; 19. 3; 21. 9; 25. 1; 32. 9; 276. 9; plur. 14. 6; 158. 6; 176. 11

āśa to be abundant 115. 9; abundant 274. 8

āśa overmuch 250. 4; a large company 271. 5

āśu many 99. 10

āśt many 42. 10; 137. 4; very many 48. 7, 8; myriads of hundreds of thousands; a vast multitude 102. 4

āśta a company, a public assembly 241. 5; 248. 9; 263. 6; 272. 5

āśen (or ***bȧt***) honey 207. 8

Āksapu a city in Syria 280. 4

āq , to enter 6. 1; 65. 6; 126. 9; 129. 6; 131. 3; 206. 2; to rush on (of soldiers) 140. 3

āqu ingoers 186. 5; 193. 13

āqu — bread, cakes, food, provisions 3. 3; 240. 3, 4; 271. 2

āqu — dependants 259. 8, 10, 13; 260. 1

āqa — to act rightly, just, justice, right 23. 9; 169. 7; 170. 5; 258. 3; 263. 11; 268. 11

āqaa — guidance (?) 267. 10

āt — chamber 118. 5; 200. 7; 319. 4

āt ent χet — summer-houses 150. 12

āt — limb, member 127. 1; 217. 4

āt uāt em ȧner — monolith 152. 9

ātāt — to strengthen 289. 4

Ātinini — a city in Syria 290. 12

āṭ, āṭi — firm, safe (?) 59. 3; 206. 6

āṭi — dirt, filth 52. 5

āṭu — dirty grease (?) 9. 1

āṭet — the boat of the setting sun 123. 10; 304. 1

āť — child 84. 3

āťau, **āťau** — wrong, falsehood, deceit, violence 9. 8; 13. 3; 135. 9; 331. 13; 332. 6

āťau — to speak violently 288. 6; strong words 292. 5

āṭau robber **9.** 2

āṭeṭu young man **6.** 1; **7.** 3; **14.** 8; young woman **22.** 2

I.

i, ***i, iu*** to go, to come **10.** 2; **65.** 3; **81.** 13; **101.** 8; **272.** 1; coming **10.** 12; one who comes **4.** 3. come! **259.** 13; having gone out **19.** 2; coming **135.** 10; **136.** 12; a coming, a going **109.** 8; **134.** 10; **243.** 6; comer **301.** 11; to come to the end of a book **40.** 2; **305.** 12; as an auxiliary **139.** 3

i-ḥer-sa what comes after, *i. e.*, posterity **229.** 4

ia O **323.** 11; **327.** 10

iȧ **64.** 11

Iāah a city in Syria **281.** 2

iui **70.** 1

imā, ***iumā*** sea, river **21.** 5; **22.** 4; **173.** 7; **177.** 6; **279.** 9

Iusāaset name of a goddess **143.** 4

Ip Joppa (?) **286.** 11

Ireṭuna [hieroglyphs] a city in Syria **282.** 8

I-ḥetep [hieroglyphs] a proper name **101.** 5

isaṭiṭi [hieroglyphs] trembling **286.** 5

Ikama [hieroglyphs] a city in Syria **280.** 7

Iḳaṭāi [hieroglyphs] a city in Syria **275.** 13

it [hieroglyphs] evil deeds (?), evil way (?) **267.** 5; **271.** 6

itf [hieroglyphs] fathers **320.** 6; **328.** 6

[hieroglyphs], [hieroglyphs] U.

u [hieroglyphs] they, them, their **2.** 10; **3.** 8; **8.** 10; **96.** 4; **136.** 2, 10; **137.** 8; **307.** 12; **318.** 6

un [hieroglyphs] ye, you, they, them, their **96.** 2, 3; **143.** 12; **169.** 3; **321.** 4, 12; **326.** 1, 4, 11; **332.** 11

Uaua [hieroglyphs]
Uauat [hieroglyphs] } a country in Nubia **92.** 12; **100.** 2; **106.** 5

uauai [hieroglyphs] to say (to oneself) **47.** 8

ua [hieroglyphs] to march **188.** 7

ua [hieroglyphs] way, road **209.** 6

uat [hieroglyphs], [hieroglyphs], [hieroglyphs] } way, road, path **5.** 13; **58.** 12; **98.** 9; plur. [hieroglyphs] **132.** 9

uat [hieroglyphs] a garden walk **162.** 2

uab to be pleasant 98. 4; 99. 2

uabi flower, bud 221. 6

Uab the Oxyrhynchite nome 187. 7

Uabet (or ***Uaseb***) Oxyrhynchus 115. 1; 195. 8

uaḥ to put in position, to place, to set down, to leave, to let remain, permanent 2. 10; 25. 2; 129. 10; 258. 3; to sow seeds 221. 5; to plant trees or shrubs 221. 6; besides, in addition to 230. 1; set in position; placed 277. 7 to increase, to grow steadily 83. 6; 86. 4; 94. 10

uaḥ àb to apply the mind 273. 5

uaḥi wheat 148. 5; 150. 8; 157. 6

Uasarken Osorkon 192. 4; 214. 10; 218. 2

Uast Thebes 41. 1; 44. 5; 45. 6; 47. 6; 49. 1; 89. 12; 140. 11; 225. 2

uaś to praise 106. 11

Uaśeś name of a class of people or of a nation 173. 7

Uaḳ name of a festival 131. 8

uat' sceptre 238. 3

uat' emerald 247. 1

uat' to make green, fertile, new, fresh 92. 1; 296. 6; 303. 4

uaṭuaṭ green herbs **63.** 12

Uaṭ-ur "Great Green", *i. e.*, the Mediterranean Sea **159.** 6; **220.** 12; **228.** 12; **301.** 8

uaṭet green, youthful **119.** 7

Uaṭit a goddess **92.** 2

Uaṭit name of a city or country **290.** 9

Uaṭti the two serpents over the brow of Rā **296.** 12; **305.** 8

uȧ I **129.** 2; **133.** 13

uȧ to make an end of **266.** 3

uȧa boat **45.** 6; **95.** 5; **158.** 4; plur. **150.** 9

uȧa ḥeḥ "boat of millions of years", a name of the boat of the sun **88.** 7

uȧauȧa to be loose or disjointed **292.** 3

uȧan to leave, to forsake **187.** 6

uȧpt (or **up**) order **197.** 4

uȧn to depart from, to put aside **222.** 11; **242.** 7; **257.** 8

uā , a, one **1.** 1; **45.** 8; **169.** 12; **187.** 7; One, *i. e.*, God **52.** 13; each **14.** 7; to speak with one voice **19.** 12

uā one, a man, a person 13. 7; 14. 7; 252. 2

uā uāu "the only One" 300. 3, 13; 302. 11; one from another 298. 1; one on top of another 141. 7; one by virtue of his seasons 295. 1

uā neb any one, every one 41. 11; 216. 9

uā as the indefinite article:— one of the prophets 237. 7; an evil thing 16. 9; a house 19. 6; a stream 13. 5; any thing 16. 10; a good thing 16. 10; a side 13. 7; a knife 15. 12; a woman 20. 7; a young woman 24. 3; a vessel 18. 2; a bull 29. 12; a pot 17. 11

uā, *uāu*, *uāu* to be alone, alone 10. 4; 59. 7; 97. 5; 265. 10; solitary 57. 12; only 99. 4; 300. 3; alone by himself 141. 12

uā-tu, *uā-θȧ* alone 20. 1; 277. 13

uāi solitude 54. 7

uātet only one (fem.) 119. 9

uāā to curse 206. 8

uāu to return, to bring back, to recall (?), to understand 2. 6; 8. 6; 275. 8; 293. 3

uā the opposite (?) 271. 1

uāt (?) (?) 252. 9; 255. 8

uāfi to bind round 173. 10

uānui to kill 141. 5

uār to flee, to escape 138. 6; 193. 4; 212. 12

uārt tablet (?) 101. 5

uāt goat 101. 3

ui mark of the dual; compare:— 259. 13; 267. 8; 269. 12; 273. 8

uu district, region 211. 10

uu borders, frontiers 137. 6

Uu-en-Rā-nefer a city near Bubastis 192. 5; 218. 3

uben , to shine 13. 13; 14. 7; 64. 2; 121. 2; rising and setting 83. 1

ufa applause, approval 216. 12; 247. 11

ufiḥ to blaze 52. 10

umet (?) 118. 9

umet studded 156. 8

Un the nome of Hermopolis 188. 2; 193. 11; 196. 11; 200. 3

Unnu Hermopolis 193. 10

un, ***unu*** to be, to exist, to become 2. 2; 75. 3; 199. 1; 226. 13; being 11. 1; 238. 13; becoming 41. 6; to be 292. 2; *unen* being 46. 12; there is 102. 9; being 107. 1. For as an auxiliary compare *passim.*

unu, ***unu*** those who were 113. 2; things that were 171. 2

uneniu beings who are 129. 4

unenet things which are or shall be 145. 1; 300. 3; 301. 13

un to rise 53. 6; 64. 7

un to open 5. 11; 74. 5; 186. 2; 203. 3

un re opener of the mouth 90. 4

un maā very truth 125. 13

un-ḥrȧ festivals of the "shewing the face" (of the god) 153. 11

Unȧ name of an officer of Pepi I. 107. 3

uni place 258. 5

unbu a plant or shrub 286. 6

unf to have pleasure 172. 3

unf ȧb / ***unfet ȧb*** to be glad 261. 11; joy, gladness 267. 7, 9

unemi, unemet , right hand 87. 1; 149. 8; 199. 13; 235. 12

Un-nefer a name of Osiris 63. 7; 74. 12; 79. 12

Unen-nefer a name of Osiris 130. 7

unnut , hour 7. 1; 104. 3; 140. 13; 277. 12; at once 38. 9

unnut priests who took it in turn to serve in the temple for a certain period 163. 9

unχ to dress, to arrange the dress 189. 6

unχu to arrange (the hair) 10. 5

unt fortresses 101. 11

Unt the XVth nome of Upper Egypt 110. 4, *i. e.*, Hermopolis

unṭu calves 200. 1

ur to be great 112. 13; greatness, size 291. 4

ur ȧb pride, insolence 186. 9

ur great **41**. 7; **165**. 11; superior **247**. 11; much **241**. 11; plur. great ones **48**. 7; mighty men **141**. 6; a man greater than **250**. 2; worth more than **258**. 8; **266**. 13; greatest of all **192**. 11; doubly great **188**. 5; exceedingly great **139**. 4; dual *urui* **120**. 12; **124**. 1; *urti* **122**. 12

ur eldest **98**. 11; **110**. 7

urt eldest (fem.) **41**. 1; **120**. 7

ur mighty one (a god) **51**. 13

ur mansion **142**. 5

ur a large piece (of meat) **128**. 1

ur baiu mighty willed **296**. 6

Urti-ḥekau "great one of words of power", a name of Isis **120**. 4

Ur-Ȧmen a proper name **308**. 11

uri, ***urit*** chariot **207**. 11; **196**. 13

urer, ***urerer*** name of a crown **88**. 5; **198**. 4

ureret name of a crown **296**. 6, 11

uriret, ***urireit*** chariot **35**. 11; **45**. 7; **48**. 5; **277**. 1; **285**. 5

urer } chariot 35. 11; 45. 7; 48. 5; 277. 1; 285. 5
ureret

urḥu unguent 132. 12

urḥu smeared with 18. 7

urś } to pass the time, to occupy oneself 19. 1; 21. 2; 64. 13
urśu

urṭ, urṭu , to stop (of the heart), to rest 62. 10; 150. 9; 301. 4; 302. 4

Urṭu-àb "Still-heart", a name of Osiris 80. 1; 88. 9

uh , to fail 201. 5; 266. 5

uheh to lack, to fail in 257. 8; 259. 9

uhen to lay waste, to overthrow 187. 3; 194. 9

uhasi to diminish, to be careless of 277. 8; 287. 8

uḥa , to quarry stone 105. 9; 221. 6

uhem , , × to repeat, see *nem.*

uχ pillars (?) 117. 13

uχa portico 117. 11

uχa night 206. 12

uχa an unlearned man, a fool, a boor 270. 11

uχaā to let fall **5**. 13

uχai pillars **150**. 5

uχaχ to seek, to search into **17**. 8, 9; **24**. 6; **27**. 10; **28**. 6; **79**. 8; **274**. 10

uχet things **318**. 5

usi much **280**. 1; **292**. 3, 4

usu feeble **298**. 5

usr , = , to be strong, strong, strength, power **40**. 9; **62**. 1; **108**. 7; **126**. 8; to become rich **249**. 8; to be abundant in **279**. 11; strong one **119**. 7; **78**. 10

Usr-Maāt-Rā-setep-nu-Rā prenomen of Rameses II. **40**. 9; **45**. 12

User name of a mountain in Syria **280**. 6

User-ḥāt name of a boat **158**. 5

User-χepeś a proper name **321**. 5; **324**. 9

Usertsen a king of the XIIth dynasty **110**. 12; **114**. 6

useχ , ; *useχt, useχtu* , open space **241**. 2; hall **254**. 6; hall of the universe **302**. 10; breadth **105**. 12; **301**. 7

useχt en bunre outside hall **311**. 3; **312**. 6

useχt reṭu people in the outer court of the temple **240**. 10

useχt a broad, flat barge **105**. 1

useχi / **useχtu** collars **154**. 3; **156**. 9

useśeṭ to ask, to seek **248**. 4; **250**. 7

ust destroyed **109**. 10

usten to lead, to advance **242**. 2; **255**. 13

usθen to walk **131**. 1

uś decayed **114**. 8; effaced **116**. 2

uśa to fatten **164**. 2

uśauśau to be smashed **277**. 10; **288**. 2

uśeb / **uśebt** to answer **17**. 12; **20**. 4; **30**. 5; **59**. 9; **155**. 7; **261**. 7; **266**. 2; statement, deposition, defence **322**. 3; **325**. 13

uśem to be softened, persuaded (?) **265**. 11

uśer , lack of **60**. 4; **221**. 11

uqesqes (?) senile weakness **244**. 9

uḳas to cut, to split **168**. 12

ut (?) **234**. 11

Ut-meḥt the oasis of El-Baḥriyyeh **160**. 5

Ut-reset the oasis of El-Khârgeh 160. 4

uti coffins 315. 7

utet , to beget, begotten, begetter 41. 2; 63. 9; 120. 7; 144. 12; 172. 2; 301. 10; engendered 41. 1

utet su t̆esef self-begotten 182. 12

utu, utui , to send forth, to set out 43. 4; 177. 5; 179. 5; 189. 4

utui } expedition 134. 5; 276. 4; to go 307. 13; to escape 194. 7
utit

utiθ tablet, stele 240. 8

utu } stele, tablet 129. 7; 310. 8; 311. 11

utui, utu , } stelae, tablets 110. 3; 156. 11; 329. 4

utu , } to command, to decree 44. 3; 184. 8; 222. 11; 248. 8; decreed 41. 5; decree 249. 12; command 105. 6
utu ,

utu, utut , , decrees 45. 12; commands 121. 11; decrees for the foundation of a temple 155. 3

utu ṭep chief command 261. 3

utu crown, garland 35. 10

uteb, utebu } furrow, furrows 137. 9; 148. 6; 173. 10; 292. 2

uṭennu to breach a wall, breach, breached **286.** 12; **311.** 2, 10

uṭḥu table **132.** 5

uṭḥu altars **149.** 1; to drink wine **33.** 3

uṭ to inscribe **42.** 4

uṭ to shoot out **52.** 6; **54.** 3; to cast forth **253.** 12

uṭeb to change, movement **232.** 12; **233.** 10; **263.** 9

uṭen to make an offering **194.** 11; **206.** 3

uṭen, *uṭennu* offerings **34.** 3; **35.** 7; **181.** 8; **233.** 5

uṭennu damaged **311.** 1

uṭet to shoot out, to depart from (?) **250.** 5; **331.** 5

uṭeṭ what is decreed **253.** 13; **254.** 4

uṭeṭ to burn **279.** 13

uθes to support, to bear **75.** 2; **120.** 2

uθeset support **122.** 3

uṯ to decree **112.** 5

uṯ boundary stone, landmark **108.** 10; **109.** 5; **114.** 11, 13; plur. **109.** 12

uṯa amulets **154.** 2

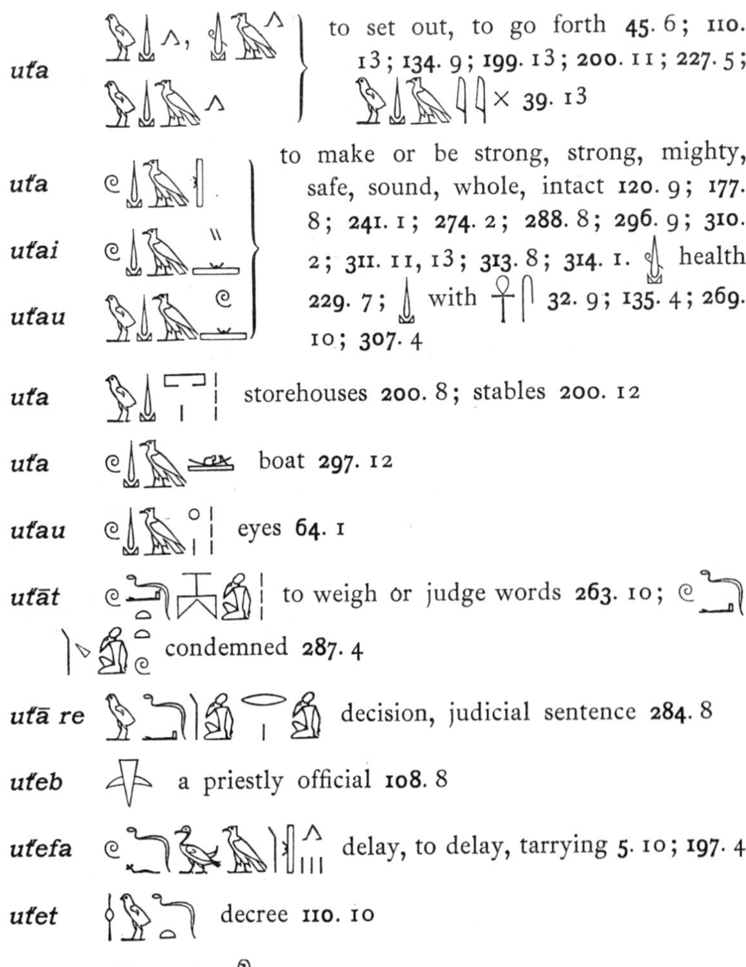

uťa — to set out, to go forth **45**. 6; **110**. 13; **134**. 9; **199**. 13; **200**. 11; **227**. 5; × **39**. 13

uťa, **uťai**, **uťau** — to make or be strong, strong, mighty, safe, sound, whole, intact **120**. 9; **177**. 8; **241**. 1; **274**. 2; **288**. 8; **296**. 9; **310**. 2; **311**. 11, 13; **313**. 8; **314**. 1. health **229**. 7; with **32**. 9; **135**. 4; **269**. 10; **307**. 4

uťa storehouses **200**. 8; stables **200**. 12

uťa boat **297**. 12

uťau eyes **64**. 1

uťāt to weigh or judge words **263**. 10; condemned **287**. 4

uťā re decision, judicial sentence **284**. 8

uťeb a priestly official **108**. 8

uťefa delay, to delay, tarrying **5**. 10; **197**. 4

uťet decree **110**. 10

uťat eye, eye of Rā **81**. 13; **122**. 2

B.

ba to hoe up, to lay waste **101**. 8

ba to mock, to sneer at **253**. 10

ba soul **127**. 4

bau soul 284. 12

ba divine soul 55. 2; 64. 5

ba damned soul 304. 5

baiu souls, will 84. 2; 145. 10
Do. Do. 41. 9; 119. 1; 121. 5; 128. 9
Do. Do. 296. 6; 302. 2

baȧa underwood, bushes 284. 2

Baiθȧ-Śaȧạre a city in Syria 282. 7

baireka tribute 157. 7; 183. 9

baba to fly 305. 8

baba holes of animals, dens 300. 11

baire boats, barges 159. 5; 176. 13; 177. 9

barei boats, barges 279. 11

Bareniḳat Berenice 226. 10; 229. 10; 232. 5; 234. 10; 236. 5; 237. 12; 238. 2; 240. 4

Bareθȧ Beyrût, a city in Syria 277. 3; 279. 6

basanet chisel, graver 147. 10; 155. 3, 10

basanet graven objects **289**. 6

Bast the goddess of Bubastis **91**. 12; **232**. 9

bak ladder **197**. 8; **208**. 10

bak to work, to do **216**. 12; to subjugate **125**. 11; wrought **124**. 1; resistance **220**. 11

baku to toil **4**. 12; **8**. 4; to work metal **156**. 5; work **312**. 5; wrought **150**. 1

baku works **148**. 8; products **165**. 4

bak , tribute, service **199**. 8

bak servant **97**. 4; **222**. 1

baku , servants **113**. 6; **135**. 4

bakȧ servant **202**. 7

Bakȧu "Worker", a name of the Sun-god **94**. 4

baket servant **133**. 12

baka cleft in the rock, gorge **283**. 13

Bakenurenre an official of Rameses X. **308**. 3

Bakennefi a proper name **192**. 1

Baqana name of a nation **175**. 7

Baqet Egypt **227**. 2; **228**. 7; **229**. 13; **232**. 6; **240**. 12

Baqet a woman's name **107**. 6; **119**. 5

Baqet name of an official **119**. 6

Batau a proper name **1**. 2

baṭenu to be involved in **292**. 4

Baθȧ-θupaire a city in Syria **281**. 12

bȧa steel **73**. 7

bȧa bushes, plants **59**. 8

bȧt to wonder at **271**. 3

bȧat a wonderful thing **30**. 9

bȧaiu, ***bȧait*** wonders, marvels, wonderful **35**. 4; **152**. 4; **158**. 6; **177**. 10; **178**. 7; **179**. 9; most wonderful turquoises **179**. 13

bȧ, bȧt honour, credit, worth **243**. 5; **246**. 1; **266**. 12; **267**. 4

bȧat a kind of stone **176**. 8

bȧait ,, **147**. 7; **149**. 11; **161**. 2

bȧf to look, to see **52**. 9

bȧn evil, wrong, evil thing **7**. 4; **247**. 5; **278**. 8

bȧnt displeasing **250**. 7; evil thing **247**. 11

bȧnt evils, vices **258**. 2; worst of all, in most evil case **245**. 6

bȧnt harp 221. 9

bȧt (?) honey 198. 2

bȧk hawk 47. 13; 305. 5

bā to be complied with (?), to be obeyed (?) 183. 11

Bāre or **Bāru** name of a god 143. 13

bāḥ , to flood 121. 1; 132. 11; filled to overflowing 148. 1

bāḥu to inundate 61. 12; overflowing, abundance 84. 9

bu not 9. 10; 10. 1; 16. 9; 24. 13; 139. 1; 141. 10; 146. 11; 179. 2; 319. 13; not? 275. 11, 12; 276. 4, 5, 7, 12, 13; 278. 1, 12; 279. 5. there is not 311. 6; there was not 319. 3; there was not 319. 9; there is no one 10. 1

bu , , place, wherever 191. 6; 210. 12; 257. 3; 171. 9; 293. 11

bu neb everywhere 257. 1

bu ȧqer strength, wisdom 260. 11

bu ān ungracious 284. 4

bu bȧn misery, wretchedness 245. 5

bu nefer happiness, comfort 130. 12; 241. 10; 245. 4; prosperity 230. 9

bu-en-re "place of the mouth" (or opening), *i. e.*, outside **21.** 5; **275.** 3; **311.** 4; **312.** 7. See *er bu-en-re*.

bu neb anybody, everybody **180.** 7

bu nebt | ***bu nebu*** all people, everybody **179.** 8; **182.** 2; **234.** 5; **242.** 11; **272.** 4

buaa | ***buaa*** great men **163.** 10; **169.** 10

buaat strength **325.** 6

buaitu wonder, marvel **31.** 7

beb collars, necklaces **217.** 3

Bebi the son of Osiris **70.** 13

bebet depth of a stream **131.** 5

bef to see **60.** 4

ben not **7.** 13; **10.** 7; **129.** 8; **233.** 8; **321.** 10; Behold, was it not when I . . . . ? **15.** 2

benbenet pyramidion **104.** 9; **122.** 11

benen virile **53.** 11

Benenet a district of Thebes **77.** 2

bennut emerald ore (?) **247.** 1

benerȧ pleasant **162.** 2

benerȧt [hieroglyphs] palm 298. 7; grateful, pleasant 130. 9; 299. 11

Benθ-reś [hieroglyphs]
Bent-reśti [hieroglyphs]
Bent-enθ-reśt [hieroglyphs] } daughter of the Prince of Bekhten 43. 2; 43. 13; 46. 1

Beχat [hieroglyphs] the place of sunrise 158. 8

beχenu [hieroglyphs] pylon towers 147. 9

beχenti [hieroglyphs] two pylons 122. 12

beχennu [hieroglyphs] house 19. 6; 27. 5

Beχten [hieroglyphs] a country in Western Asia 41. 12; 42. 10; 43. 11; 46. 2

Beχten [hieroglyphs] the city of Bekhten 44. 8. 13; 46. 11

beḥu [hieroglyphs] to hunt, to slay 19. 1

beḥes [hieroglyphs] to hunt, to slay 21. 3, 13

beḥes [hieroglyphs] a kind of stone 149. 7

Beḥ-ka [hieroglyphs] the name of a dog 310. 11

bes [hieroglyphs] to come forth, to pass 93. 8; 146. 7; 230. 10; 231. 9; 234. 11; 270. 9; train, following 121. 4; [hieroglyphs] 230. 11

besi [hieroglyphs] passing 288. 10

best [hieroglyphs] passage 288. 10

beses [hieroglyphs] to lead to 256. 3

beś drenched, to be steeped in some liquid mess **9.** 11

beśṭ revolt **170.** 11

beśeθ to revolt **102.** 7

bet unguent **72.** 11

bet place, house **45.** 13 ; **46.** 7 ; **47.** 5 ; **235.** 1

bet abominable thing **223.** 13

beta evil, wickedness **201.** 2 ; **221.** 3

betau, betaui evil thing **7.** 11 ; breach of duty **139.** 4

betaui evil case, crime **181.** 7

betauu crimes **326.** 6 ; **327.** 5 ; **328.** 3

betu accursed **64.** 8 ; hateful **250.** 5

betu ka a hateful person **250.** 5 ; **251.** 7 ; **252.** 13

betu to come forth **75.** 13

beti barley **6.** 4

betennu sore trouble **298.** 2

betek rebel **103.** 2

betek rebellion, rebels **102.** 9

beṭ — barley 207. 3

beṭeś — to collapse, to sink down exhausted 140. 5; 299. 10

beθennu (?) — (?) enmity (?) 257. 12

beθet — to escape 60. 2

Beq — Egypt 228. 1

beqbequ — to walk, to travel 265. 1

P.

p — the 44. 12

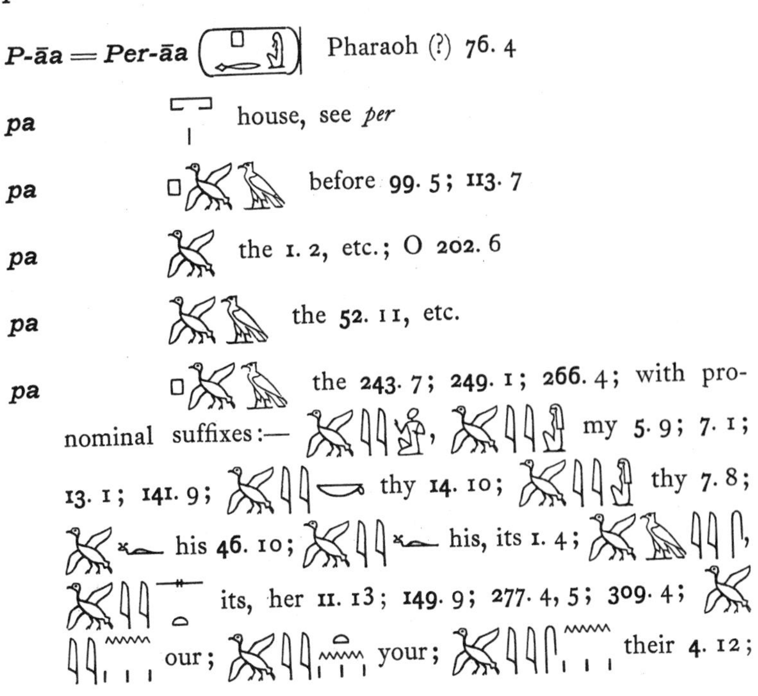

P-āa = Per-āa — Pharaoh (?) 76. 4

pa — house, see *per*

pa — before 99. 5; 113. 7

pa — the 1. 2, etc.; O 202. 6

pa — the 52. 11, etc.

pa — the 243. 7; 249. 1; 266. 4; with pronominal suffixes:— , my 5. 9; 7. 1; 13. 1; 141. 9; thy 14. 10; thy 7. 8; his 46. 10; his, its 1. 4; , its, her 11. 13; 149. 9; 277. 4, 5; 309. 4; our; your; their 4. 12;

8. 4; their 155. 6; 165. 10; 325. 4; 328. 4; 317. 1

pa = *pai* this

pau those 245. 10

pau cakes (of Memphis) 87. 1

paut cakes 145. 12

paut primeval matter 144. 11

pautet matter 87. 8

paut , matter. matter or company of the gods 19. 9; 41. 1; 54. 1; 55. 5, 6; 145. 5; 302. 11

pautna new moon festival 131. 7

pautti Do. Do. 298. 13

paut nine 40. 9; 41. 4; 42. 13

pai this 7. 10; 33. 9

Paānχāu a prophet of Amen 308. 10

paāśt a kind of pigeon 168. 5

Pabas a governor of Kher-āba 219. 5

Pamaḳare a city in Syria 276. 7

Paχet name of a deity 108. 8

Pa-ser a proper name 309. 7; 321. 4; 323. 5

Pa-serȧ Do. 322. 12; 330. 6

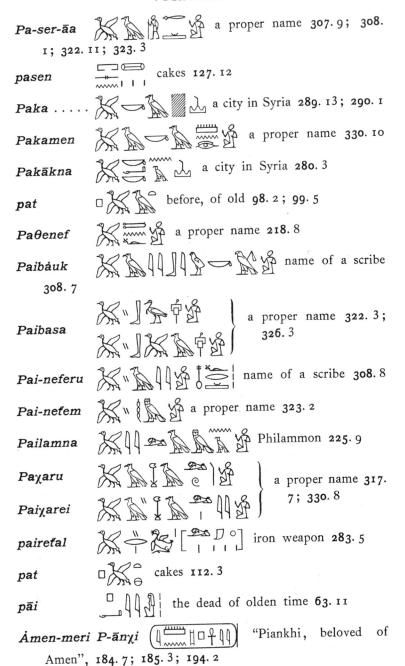

Pa-ser-āa a proper name 307. 9; 308. 1; 322. 11; 323. 3

pasen cakes 127. 12

Paka . . . . . a city in Syria 289. 13; 290. 1

Pakamen a proper name 330. 10

Pakākna a city in Syria 280. 3

pat before, of old 98. 2; 99. 5

Paθenef a proper name 218. 8

Paibȧuk name of a scribe 308. 7

Paibasa a proper name 322. 3; 326. 3

Pai-neferu name of a scribe 308. 8

Pai-neťem a proper name 323. 2

Pailamna Philammon 225. 9

Paχaru
Paiχarei a proper name 317. 7; 330. 8

paireťal iron weapon 283. 5

pat cakes 112. 3

pāi the dead of olden time 63. 11

Ȧmen-meri P-ānχi "Piankhi, beloved of Amen", 184. 7; 185. 3; 194. 2

pāt — a class of human beings, dead or living 116. 12; 120. 6; 144. 1; 181. 5; 299. 2, 9; 305. 9

pāṭet — pigeon 168. 4

pu — this, it is 18. 8; 19. 8; 46. 5; 230. 9; 241. 6

pui — this 9. 10; 311. 6; 81. 12; 82. 1; 91. 1

Puarma — a proper name 187. 10; 222. 8

pui — to fly 37. 10; 39. 4

pui — birds, fowl 300. 10

Puirsaθȧ — a proper name 173. 5

Punt, *Puntet* — Arabia or Somali land 71. 4; 158. 13; 177. 7; 294. 9; 296. 1

Pepi — a king of the VIth dynasty 97. 1

Pebeχennebiu — a city near Memphis 211. 11

pef — that 206. 12; 221. 10; 304. 6

pefa — that 272. 3, 4

pefi — that 91. 5

Pef-āā-Bast — a rebel king 201. 12

Pema governor of Busiris **218.** 10

pen , this **43.** 11; **97.** 13; **233.** 3; **237.** 13

pan this **47.** 11; **230.** 5; **232.** 10

penā overturned, prostrated **80.** 11; **170.** 4; a story wrongly told **15.** 5

Peni . . . naāuāā a city near Memphis **211.** 11

pennu mouse **300.** 10

Pentaurt a proper name **219.** 1

Penθbeχenet a proper name **219.** 1

per grain, wheat, corn **207.** 3

peru , corn, seed **221.** 5; **228.** 10

pert Do. Do. **207.** 3

pertu , Do. Do. **4.** 4; **5.** 4; **6.** 4

pertet Do. Do. **120.** 8

per issue **184.** 10

per to come forth **6.** 5; **19.** 8; to flow **72.** 12; outcome **260.** 3; coming out **275.** 6; **146.** 2; coming out, come **4.** 2

perer to come or go out **300.** 3

peru , those who come out **186.** 5; **193.** 13; appearances **305.** 10

pert [hieroglyphs], [hieroglyphs] appearance **131**. 7; rising of a star **131**. 9; offspring **120**. 3; that which comes forth **108**. 13; a coming forth **126**. 9; **131**. 3

per [hieroglyphs]
pert [hieroglyphs] } the season of the year in which things grow, *i. e.*, the spring; it contained four months **49**. 2; **124**. 6; **233**. 9

per [hieroglyphs] house, house of a god, *i. e.*, temple **1**. 3; **48**. 10

peru [hieroglyphs] houses **210**. 5

Per-Ȧusȧr-neb-Ṭeṭṭeṭ [hieroglyphs] Busiris **191**. 10; **218**. 10

Per-Ȧmen [hieroglyphs] the Ȧmen shrine at Thebes **77**. 6; **151**. 5; **308**. 11

Per Ȧmen-ḥetep [hieroglyphs] Temple of Amenophis **308**. 10; **309**. 5; **310**. 4

per ȧrp [hieroglyphs] wine-cellar **308**. 12

per-āa [hieroglyphs], [hieroglyphs] "great house", *i. e.*, Pharaoh **96**. 10; **201**. 13

per-āa [hieroglyphs] a name of the cemetery **308**. 3

per mer χent [hieroglyphs]
per mer χent [hieroglyphs] } "governor (or governors) of the shore of Pharaoh" **98**. 7; **99**. 4; **100**. 11

per seḥeṫ χent [hieroglyphs] inspector of the shore of Pharaoh **96**. 10

peru ānχ [hieroglyphs] the double house of life **43**. 5

peru ur [hieroglyphs] the eastern and western horizons **91**. 13; **293**. 6; **295**. 13; part of a boat **158**. 10

Per-ba-neb-Ṭeṭṭeṭ Mendes 131. 12; 218. 5

Per-Bast Bubastis 192. 4; 218. 3

Per-Ptaḥ the Ptah temple 321. 2; 323. 8

peru-ma bowers, summer-houses 151. 1

Per-māṭa Oxyrhynchus 185. 12; 195. 9

Per-nub name of a city 185. 7

Per-neb-ṭep-åḥet Aphroditopolis 186. 3

Per-neter-ṭuat temple of the "Morning Star" 307. 4; 309. 10; 316. 6; 330. 1

Per-Rā-user-maāt-meri-Åmen temple of Rameses III. 152. 2

Per-Rāmessu-ḥeq-Ånnu temple of Rameses III. 151. 4

Per-Ḥāp Nilopolis 219. 5

per ḥemt womens' apartments 198. 7

peru ḥeṭ treasury 40. 2; 200. 8; 201. 10

per ḥeṭ treasury 199. 11; 204. 5

Per-χemennu the temple of the eight gods of Hermopolis 200. 2

Per-Rā-χerp-χeper a city of Upper Egypt 185. 12; 202. 12

Per-χerḥebi a city near Sebennytus 218. 7

Per-sepṭ a city in the Delta **218.** 9

peru-seref ? the places of sunrise and sunset **295.** 13

Per-Seχet-neb[t]-reḥesȧui a city near Sais **219.** 4

Per-Seχet-nebt-sa a city near Sais **219.** 4

per-śāt library **56.** 9

per-Teḥuti temple of Thoth **200.** 1

Per-Teḥuti-ȧp-reḥḥu Hermopolis **191.** 13; **218.** 6

per ṭua (?) the chapel of a tomb **211.** 5

Per-ḳerer a city in the Delta **218.** 12

Per-peḳ a city near Abydos **192.** 13

per-ā , , strength, power, violence **41.** 5; **259.** 3

per-ā fighting men **282.** 3

per-ā-ȧb brave **289.** 10, 12; **292.** 1

per-χeru , , funeral offerings of meat and drink **63.** 13; **85.** 13; **95.** 6; **112.** 5; **133.** 3

Perses a proper name **79.** 1; **84.** 12

Persatet Persia **227.** 4

pert vigour **71.** 13

perti mighty one **51**. 7, 8

pertet Do. **54**. 10

peḥ, *peḥu* to arrive at a place or condition, to penetrate **65**. 4; **128**. 12; **204**. 8; **249**. 10; **311**. 7; **312**. 1

peḥ, peḥui the end **249**. 4; **292**. 13; the back of the neck **156**. 9; the stern of a boat **158**. 12

peḥ ȧb the heart's desire **254**. 10, 11

peḥu remote districts, borders, limits **102**. 12; **174**. 13

peḥuu borders, boundaries **289**. 12; "ends of the earth" **159**. 8

peḥu swamps, marshes **41**. 10

peḥiuu Do. Do. **185**. 8

peḥiu revolt (?) **197**. 5

peḥpeḥ valour, mighty deeds **126**. 4; **130**. 2; **226**. 12

peḥpeḥt fame, renown **236**. 4

peḥtpeḥt strength, strong, valour **41**. 7; **141**. 5; **189**. 7, 8

peḥti strong, valour, vigour, strength **6**. 9; **62**. 1; **245**. 1; **295**. 10

peχa to divide, to cut off, to separate, to take part in **90**. 10; **257**. 4; **292**. 5

peχarer going, conduct **253**. 5; **254**. 11

peχaret method of procedure **259**. 1

pesset to bake, to cook **3**. 2

peseśet divisions, borders, parts of the world **123**. 8; **258**. 6; **266**. 7

pest nine **225**. 3; **230**. 12

pest, ***pesṭ*** back, backbone **30**. 3; **31**. 2; **41**. 11

pesṭ to shine, shining one **64**. 6; **82**. 5; **88**. 2; **299**. 10

peś part, place **186**. 8; to spread out **57**. 9

peśes to divide **108**. 11; **109**. 6; **115**. 2

peśet to divide, division **208**. 12

pet sky, heaven **39**. 5; **50**. 5; **51**. 9; **58**. 13; **149**. 13; **233**. 7

pet bow **40**. 9; **41**. 4; **42**. 13; **180**. 12; **275**. 7

pet foreign sailors **159**. 5; **169**. 2; **176**. 1

pet paut foreign mercenary troops **85**. 9; **126**. 5; **130**. 3; **148**. 10; **157**. 7

pet māśa foreign bowmen **276.** 6

Ptualmis Ptolemy **225.** 5; **226.** 9

Ptualmis-ānχ-t'etta-Ptaḥ-meri "immortal Ptolemy, beloved of Ptah" **225.** 4; **226.** 9; **229.** 9; **230.** 7; **232.** 4; **234.** 9

peten these **100.** 10; **101.** 7

petrȧ to see, to look, behold! **6.** 10; **10.** 12; **12.** 7; **135.** 11; **136.** 12; **137.** 3; **166.** 3; **274.** 9

Ptaḥ the god Ptah **130.** 7; **143.** 7; **192.** 9

Ptaḥ-nefer-ḥrȧ "Ptah of the Beautiful face" **171.** 13

Ptaḥ-res-ȧneb-f "Ptah of his Southern Wall", a title of Ptaḥ of Memphis **211.** 7

Ptaḥ-āa-qemā-ȧneb-f a title of Ptah of Memphis **143.** 6

Ptaḥ-ḥetep a famous writer **244.** 6, 8; **246.** 6

Ptaḥ-ḥet-ka "house of the *ka* of Ptah", *i. e.*, Memphis **211.** 2; **212.** 6

Ptaḥ-Sekri-Ȧusȧr the triune god of the Resurrection **130.** 7

Ptaḥ-Seker Ptah-Socharis **149.** 13

peṭ to stretch, to be wide or spacious **128.** 6; **294.** 8

Peṭā-Åuset / ***Peṭā-Åusetetå*** / ***Peṭā-Åusetet*** a proper name 212. 2; 216. 3; 215. 4; 220. 2, 5

Peṭā-Åmen-neb-nest-taiu a proper name 222. 7

Peṭā-Åmen-suten-taiu a proper name 76. 6

Peṭā-Ḥeru-sam-taiu a proper name 219. 2

peṭes to lay waste 101. 10

peḳ , byssus 216. 6; 219. 7

peḳa some object of metal 289. 9

Peḳuaθet Canopus 226. 8; 235. 5

F.

f , he, his, its 2. 2; 34. 5; *et passim*

f he, his, its 218. 5; 220. 1; 226. 7

f he, his, its 226. 5; 227. 6; 228. 6; 232. 4; 233. 1, 6; 237. 3, 9, 12; 238. 2; 240. 10

fa , / ***fa*** to lift up, to take up, to bear 8. 1; 12. 11; 77. 12; 239. 4; to lift down 179. 6; to betake oneself to flight 22. 5; 286. 3

Fa-ā the god who "lifts the hand" 144. 12

fa ṭenȧ = χανηφόρος basket-bearer 225. 9

fi = *f* + sign of the dual, his 13. 5; 123. 11; 125. 4; 246. 8; 268. 12 (bis); 270. 6; 296. 4; 297. 6

fi to be disgusted 17. 10

fent , } nose 197. 12; 284. 3; 145. 11; 245. 7

fenṭ

feχ to clothe, to dress 175. 1

feχt garments, raiment 117. 4

fekau see 181. 12

feq to reward 222. 8

fequ , gifts, rewards 187. 8; 220. 4

feqau reward, profit 274. 10

feqau to endow 229. 6

fet disuse, decay 118. 13

fet to sink (of the courage) 286. 3

fetef garment (?) to dress (?) 264. 11

fṭu , , } four, fourth 28. 1; 75. 2; 77. 8; 232. 13

fṭut

M.

em in, into 1. 9; out of 53. 6; from 2. 9; 5. 4; 126. 10; at 45. 7, 4; as 111. 1; over 92. 4; with 64; 8. 8; 252. 5; against 128. 5; 131. 4; about, concerning 194. 2; before 204. 11; among 53. 1; according to 4. 5; 108. 13; in the form of 299. 9; in the position of one 251. 1; in the condition of 191. 13; in the capacity of 103. 5; introduces a sentence 9. 3; 9. 12, etc.

em in, from 228. 5; 231. 13; 233. 4; 235. 9; 240. 1

em not, without 5. 9; 7. 11; 62. 10; 188. 1; 189. 7; 201. 3; 261. 7; not by any means 247. 6; let it not be! 256. 11

em åmenit in perpetuity 157. 4; 162. 13; 164. 1

em åsu
em åsiu as a reward for, in return for 125. 8; 229. 6; 231. 4

em āb upon, against 116. 4

em uaḥ besides 231. 7

em uaḥ ḥer in addition to 230. 5

em uā alone 213. 13

em unnut immediately 26. 7

em nem (or **uḥem**) a second time 55. 3

em baḥ before, in the presence of 2. 10; 14. 1; 39. 9; 43. 10

em baḥ ā from of old time 215. 5

em peḥui endwise 234. 2

em maut anew 158. 1

em mȧtet likewise, thus 4. 3; 12. 5; 140. 1; 217. 10

em mȧqet in the manner of 185. 8

em ment daily 6. 11; 23. 4, 8

em rāā 271. 12

em re pu or, on the contrary 16. 10

em rer round about 207. 6

em ḥa behind 54. 2

em ḥau in addition to 154. 1; 158. 2; 166. 2; 184. 8; 199. 9

em ḥāt before, in front of 90. 11; 91. 2

em ḥrȧ on behalf of 229. 4

em ḥeri above 164. 11

em ḥeru above 91. 12

em ḥeru over 285. 11

em ḥer upon, about 139. 7; 146. 13

em ḥer ȧb within 228. 12

em ḥetep successfully, satisfactorily 106. 1; 305. 12

em χem without 189. 8; 201. 9

em χen , in, within, inside 44. 5; 81. 11; 320. 7

em χennu within 142. 6; 170. 4; 319. 9; 320. 1

em χent in 229. 10

em χent en in 193. 8

emχet after, according to, in the train of 2. 3; 50. 8; 96. 6; 123. 2; 129. 10; 200. 10; 243. 4

em χer among 95. 9

em sa at the back or side of, after, following 1. 6; 2. 4; 36. 1, etc.

em sep uā at one time, all together 80. 4; 143. 12

em seḥeť evident, plain 11. 1

em seχan suddenly 234. 13

em seśeta secretly 98. 12

em setut rightly (?) 240. 13

em qeb double 127. 10

em qeṭ round about 147. 11; 162. 7

em ṭebu in return for 96. 7

em ṭep upon, on top of 54. 11; 92. 5

em ṭeti from, at the hand of 328. 13

em t'er when, since, as soon as, because 16. 6; 283. 12; 291. 1; 318. 10

em t'erti when 27. 8; 32. 8

ma , ,

ma

maa — to see 43. 4; 50. 7; 125. 3; 203. 11; 275. 8. sight 123. 1; vision 259. 5; visible 121. 1

maat , eye 165. 8; 259. 5; 318. 9

maati , , the two eyes 52. 9, 13; 93. 9; 245. 1; 300. 4

maat nebu every eye, *i. e.*, all people 158. 9

maat nebt any person 86. 9

maat stupidity (?) 265. 12

maa setem (?) the god of seeing and hearing 63. 4; 74. 2

maaut

maut — radiance 52. 10; splendour 60. 3; , splendours 64. 3, 5

maut joyfully 52. 8; 61. 1

mat a kind of stone 152. 6, 9

maȧu lions 276. 10

maȧu ḥet' a kind of antelope 149. 5; 167. 5, 6

maȧr strong 298. 4

maȧuset the two legs **54**. 11

maā a piece of land **127**. 3

maā to send, to bring **101**. 4 ; **102**. 5

maā products **224**. 5

maā , indeed, truly **107**. 3 ; **221**. 3 ; very truth **125**. 13 ; veritable **69**. 9

maāu right **125**. 6

maā
maāt , ,
maāt
maāt , — right, truth, justice, law **13**. 3 ; **14**. 2 ; **101**. 6 ; **108**. 5 ; **110**. 1 ; **111**. 8 ; **114**. 5 ; **126**. 4 ; **128**. 7 ; **130**. 3 ; **195**. 3 ; **248**. 11 ; **251**. 5 ; **267**. 12 ; the king's law **274**. 6

maā ,
maāu — to offer, to pay what is due, to make obligatory offerings, due **125**. 12 ; **146**. 4 ; **153**. 13 ; **157**. 11

maāti veritable, true **183**. 2

maāti truth **141**. 13

***ma*[*ā*]
maāt — real, actual **133**. 7 ; real, genuine (of precious stones or turquoises) **148**. 13 ; **179**. 13

maāχeru ,
maātχeru , — "true of word", triumphant (?) **79**. 1 ; **107**. 5, 6 ; **122**. 13 ; **198**. 10 ; **225**. 6

Maāt-ka-Rā prenomen of Queen Ḥātshepset **119**. 8 ; **120**. 10

maā to slaughter 34. 5

maāui bronze fastenings, staples (?) 176. 12

maāu temples 226. 11; 227. 7; 229. 10; 236. 10; 237. 5, 6. temples of the first rank 240. 10; temples of the second rank 240. 11; temples of the third rank 240. 11

maāset liver 33. 9

mau to ponder on 228. 8

mau new, youthful freshness 156. 6; 244. 10

mautu to load, to be laden with 158. 12

mareȧa attendant 287. 13

marmar (or *meremere*) name of an official 284. 7

maḥu crowns 217. 4

Maḥeṭ the XVIth nome of Upper Egypt 110. 3; 111. 6

mas to bring 42. 11; *mastu* brought 221. 8

mat, matu , new 111. 3; 117. 13; 289. 2

mat plinth, pedestal 149. 11

mat granite, the granite region 111. 3; 120. 12

mat ruṭ "granite growing", *i. e.*, living granite 124. 4

see under *Merṭamem*

maṭu ignorance (?) **263**. 7

maθ granite **104**. 11

maθ granite slabs **106**. 8

mȧ , like, as, according to, inasmuch as, since, as well as, together with **1**. 5; **7**. 3; **40**. 8; **53**. 2; **54**. 11; **75**. 8; **125**. 4; **243**. 8; gods as well as men **182**. 1; in marvellous (quantities) **179**. 9; by hundreds of thousands **179**. 9; by tens of thousands **179**. 4; in the form of, in the guise of **1**. 5

mȧn daily **59**. 1; **67**. 8

mȧ enti like one who, like that which **9**. 1; **51**. 6; **243**. 11

mȧ re in proportion to (Gr. κατὰ λόγον) **240**. 2

mȧ hru neb daily **186**. 6, 11; **188**. 3; **197**. 7, 10

mȧ qeṭ

mȧ qeṭu like, in such wise **21**. 7; **98**. 10; **106**. 2; **146**. 3; **170**. 3; **226**. 3

mȧit way **288**. 1

mȧiti likewise (?) **327**. 6

Mȧi-śerȧui a proper name **317**. 8

mȧtet , the like, likewise, thus, in this wise **12**. 5; **83**. 8; **96**. 6; **113**. 6; **245**. 11; copy, likeness **152**. 3; **322**. 9; like the sand (for number) **179**. 12

måteti like, as **56.** 2 ; **78.** 5

måtu fellow, companion **248.** 1 ; **264.** 5

måtu likeness, pattern **247.** 9

mā grant, prithee, with, from, by, by reason of **42.** 13 ; **43.** 7 ; **45.** 1 ; **97.** 13 ; **181.** 8 ; **199.** 4 ; **226.** 6 ; **247.** 1 ; **267.** 13 ; let be given **239.** 12

mā ref grant then **206.** 7

Māanaqeraṭa Menekrateia **225.** 8

māāṭ name of the boat of the setting sun **214.** 2

māāṭet name of the boat of the setting sun **81.** 12

māå, ***māåi***, ***māi*** come **6.** 13 ; **15.** 4 ; **50.** 6 ; **53.** 7 ; **54.** 4 ; **93.** 1 ; **275.** 3 ; come thou **10.** 4

māåi O give **81.** 2 ; **240.** 5

māåu hair **5.** 13

māireina (or ***mārina***) chief **283.** 1 ; **291.** 8

māirekabuθåt chariot **289.** 1

Māuaskian Moschion **225.** 8

māutet (?) lake (?), abyss (?) **283.** 2

māb thirty **105.** 12 ; **142.** 1 ; **49.** 2

māb spear, dart **297.** 8

Māpu a title of honour (?) 289. 10

māfek turquoise 41. 10; 73. 5; 91. 3; 179. 10; "turquoise land" (*i. e.*, Sinai) 92. 11; real turquoise 179. 13

mānen to entwine 238. 5

mār to dress, to clothe 226. 2; 237. 8

māreȧa groom, servant (?) 278. 5

mārekabȧt, **mārekabuθȧt** chariot 277. 7; 288. 3

māh to hesitate, to delay 121. 5

māhȧut, **māhaȧut** tribes 174. 2; 176. 2; 278. 9

māhaire an official title 275. 1, 9; 277. 6; 279. 1; 280. 13; 282. 12

māhi to hesitate 128. 11

māhuu to tremble 300. 2

māhut tribes 135. 2

māḥ 305. 7

māk verily, behold, grant 138. 7; 186. 3; 203. 3; 260. 6, 8; 263. 4; *māki* 145. 3; 283. 2

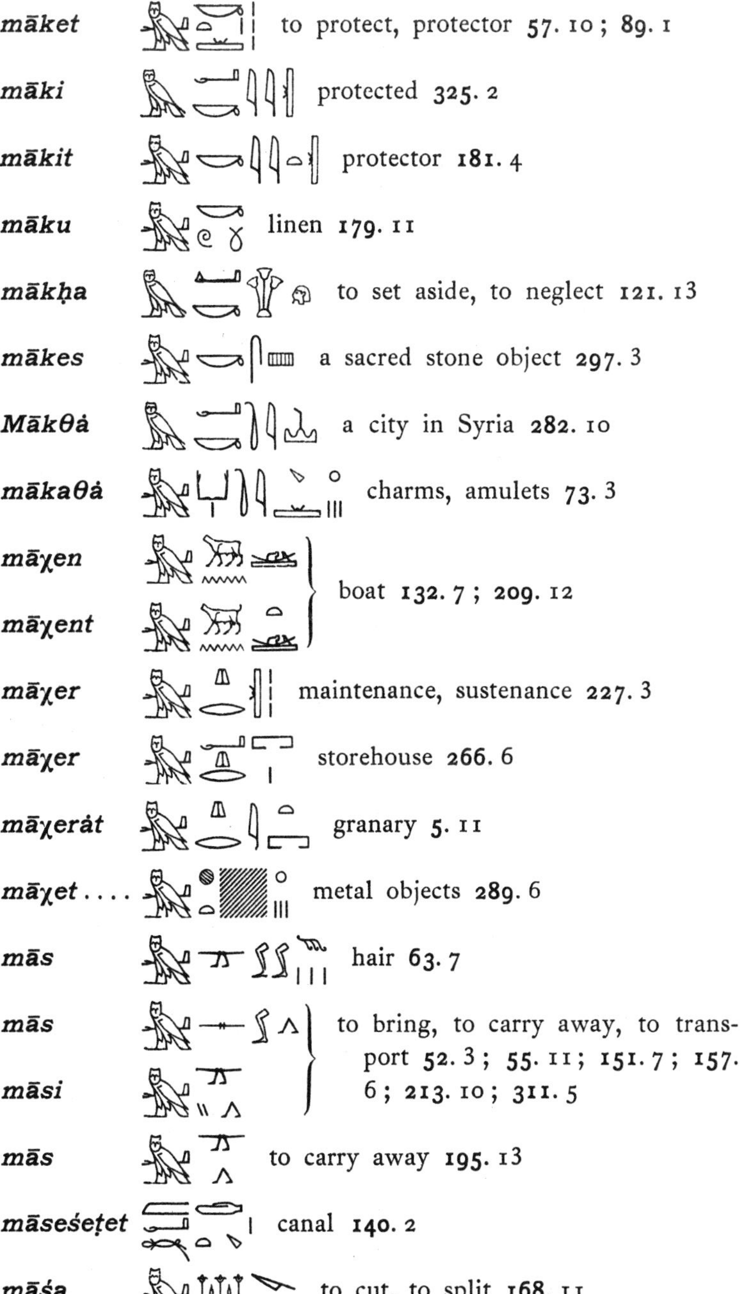

māket to protect, protector 57. 10; 89. 1

māki protected 325. 2

mākit protector 181. 4

māku linen 179. 11

mākḥa to set aside, to neglect 121. 13

mākes a sacred stone object 297. 3

Mākθȧ a city in Syria 282. 10

mākaθȧ charms, amulets 73. 3

māχen
māχent } boat 132. 7; 209. 12

māχer maintenance, sustenance 227. 3

māχer storehouse 266. 6

māχerȧt granary 5. 11

māχet .... metal objects 289. 6

mās hair 63. 7

mās
māsi } to bring, to carry away, to transport 52. 3; 55. 11; 151. 7; 157. 6; 213. 10; 311. 5

mās to carry away 195. 13

māseśeṭet canal 140. 2

māśa to cut, to split 168. 11

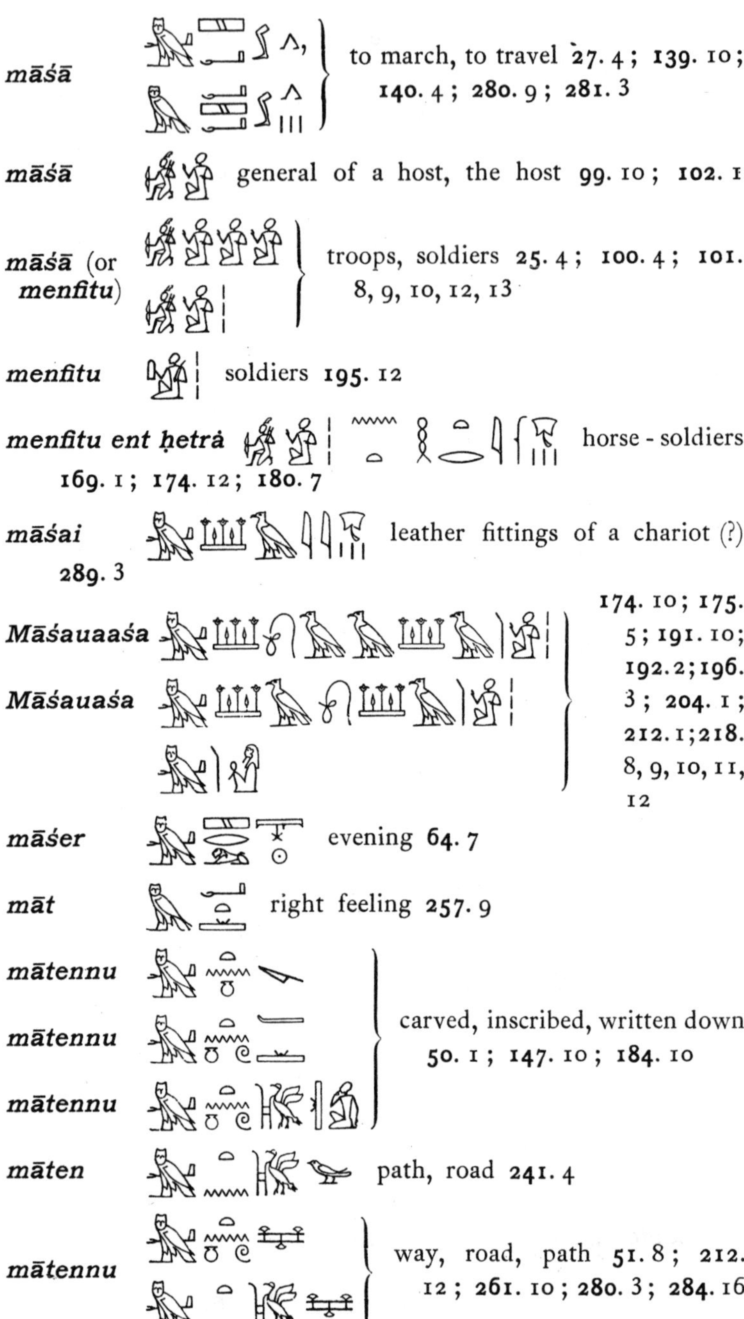

māśā — to march, to travel 27. 4; 139. 10; 140. 4; 280. 9; 281. 3

māśā — general of a host, the host 99. 10; 102. 1

māśā (or *menfitu*) — troops, soldiers 25. 4; 100. 4; 101. 8, 9, 10, 12, 13

menfitu — soldiers 195. 12

menfitu ent ḥetrȧ — horse - soldiers 169. 1; 174. 12; 180. 7

māśai — leather fittings of a chariot (?) 289. 3

Māśauaaśa, *Māśauaśa* — 174. 10; 175. 5; 191. 10; 192. 2; 196. 3; 204. 1; 212. 1; 218. 8, 9, 10, 11, 12

māśer — evening 64. 7

māt — right feeling 257. 9

mātennu, *mātennu*, *mātennu* — carved, inscribed, written down 50. 1; 147. 10; 184. 10

māten — path, road 241. 4

mātennu — way, road, path 51. 8; 212. 12; 261. 10; 280. 3; 284. 16

mātennu ways, roads 132. 9

Mātennu Aphroditopolis 223. 3

māṭen to obey, obedience 181. 9

māθȧťasu leather thongs 289. 8

māťai
māťaiu the town-guard 307. 9; 308. 11, 12; 315. 11, 13; 316. 10; 320. 10; 322. 10

māťau name of a nation 294. 9; 296. 2; 303. 4, 5

māťeṭ force, blow 285. 6

mu water, lake, stream, water supply 9. 9; 87. 1; 109. 12; 187. 6; 241. 8; 279. 1, 6; essence 24. 3; "knowing my water", *i. e.*, "knowing from what I have sprung" 115. 6; "of one water", *i. e.*, of one kidney 192. 6; water-flood 195. 9

Mu-Qet a proper name (?) 177. 6

mui essence, seed 50. 11

mut mother 7. 8; 41. 3; 50. 13; 242. 11

muθ, muθet mother 1. 1; 10. 7

Mut
Mutet the divine mother, the goddess Mut 143. 2; 144. 7; 294. 7; 305. 3

mut[ti] the two mothers of Egypt, one of the North and one of the South 123. 11.

emem in, upon, among **124**. 5; **196**. 13; **199**. 1

emmā with, among **1**. 4; **23**. 1; **51**. 7; **127**. 10; **131**. 2; **135**. 2; **137**. 5; with him **1**. 4; with her **7**. 6

memu read *ḳesui* "the two sides" (of the Nile) **224**. 7

men to abide, to be permanent or established **53**. 11; **129**. 12; to persist in, to continue (fighting) **197**. 3; established **145**. 13; **146**. 5; established **147**. 5

men ȧb to be resolute, harsh **41**. 5; **243**. 1

men to allow (?) **247**. 5

men monuments, buildings, funeral edifice **107**. 6; **114**. 7; **117**. 10; **118**. 9; **127**. 4

men to pain, to be diseased, sickness, disease **43**. 3; **245**. 4; **265**. 10

men, ***menȧ*** to arrive by boat, to land, to bring into port, to die, to moor a boat **106**. 1; **190**. 4; **192**. 12; **207**. 13; **208**. 2; **209**. 13; **244**. 1; **249**. 1

menȧu to arrive in port **178**. 2

menȧu punishment by death **326**. 7

menȧnȧu death **94**. 6; **96**. 6

menȧtu arrival in port (*i. e.*, death) **40**. 1

menȧt a kind of bird **168.** 3

menāt nurse **38.** 5

Menāt-χufu a city in Upper Egypt (the modern Beni-hasan) **108.** 9; **109.** 4

menfi bracelets **217.** 3

menmen, ***menmenut***[1] cattle **148.** 6; **159.** 10; **163.** 12; **176.** 6; **294.** 5; **295.** 6

menmen to stand **227.** 7

menmen to carry off **95.** 12

mennu colossal statue of a deity **149.** 6; plur. **151.** 10

mennu , monuments **183.** 13; **324.** 8

mennu , trees, plantations **148.** 2; **160.** 12; **162.** 8; **180.** 3; **221.** 6

mennu offerings **90.** 2

mennu vigorously **263.** 7

Men-nefer Memphis **207.** 2; **209.** 11; **210.** 1

Menḥi name of a deity **205.** 2

menḥet flowers **160.** 13

menχ (?) linen bandages **130.** 8; **132.** 13

1. The variant occurs on p. 300. 5.

menχ to stablish **270.** 1

menχ good **116.** 5; well-doing **128.** 13; beneficent **244.** 3; benevolence **229.** 3; firm **117.** 1; a lasting good **268.** 7

menχet perfect, to perfect, correct **63.** 3; **66.** 4; **138.** 5; **150.** 3

menχu benefits **226.** 11

menχ permanent servants (?) **108.** 1

menś sad, diseased in mind (?) **261.** 10

menś ship **159.** 5; **177.** 9

menśi ships **176.** 3

see

ment such and such **3.** 7

ment , to fail **119.** 2; disasters **270.** 13

ementuf he, it **1.** 1

ementek thou **32.** 6; **282.** 11; **293.** 5

menṭet bosom, breast **305.** 7

menṭ breasts **84.** 9

Menθ , the god Mentu **41.** 6; **134.** 8; **140.** 11; **220.** 10; **292.** 2

Menθu ,

Menθu-ḥetep a king of the XIth dynasty **314.** 5

Menθu-χepeś-f an officer of Rameses X. 308. 6

mer pool, any collection of water 160. 8

meru (?) cisterns, reservoirs 183. 13

meru port, harbour 279. 9

meri river bank 193. 11

merit quay, river bank or side 23. 6; 178. 5; 206. 11; 209. 11; 210. 1; 214. 11

mer to grieve, be sick, sad, dire, deadly 20. 5; 33. 12; 257. 12; 280. 1; sick 9. 8

mer to die, death, dead 10. 12; 20. 13; 26. 7; 194. 7; 203. 3, 6; 204. 12; 216. 11

mert death 286. 10

mer tomb 310. 3, 5; 311. 7, 12; 312. 1; 313. 5, 8; 314. 4

meru tombs 306. 9; 308. 13; 314. 6

mer love, will, pleasure 6. 11; 93. 10; 254. 10

merȧ friend 202. 4

meru friends 242. 11

mer (or *meri*) to love, to be loved 41. 1; 130. 5; 185. 2

meri beloved, loving 142. 3; 143. 7; 306. 3

meriu darling 123. 6

merit
meriti } beloved one 107 1; 294. 4

mert will, desire 131. 4

merer , to love, desire, will 110. 1; 111. 8; 131. 3; 204. 12; 217. 13

merru , to love 107. 4; 296. 1

merru friends 252. 8; 263. 4

merert love 262. 6

mertu to love, love, loved one 25. 10; 53. 3; 255. 3; 262. 12; greatly beloved 51. 2

mer , } chief, foreman, superintendent 96. 9; 107. 4; 119. 6; 159. 12; 264. 7

meru , governors 138. 2; 226. 1

mer per ār superintendent of the chamber 96. 9

mer ma
mer maā } chief of temple servants 100. 8; 240. 6

mer māśa inspector of soldiers 186. 10

mer nut governor of the town 111. 5; 244. 4; 307. 1

mer ḥenu neter } inspector of priests 100. 7; 129. 3

mer resu governor of the South **103.** 5

mer set ȧbtet governor of the eastern lands **108.** 8

mer śenti governor of granaries **132.** 13

mer kat clerk of the works **129.** 11; **190.** 10

meru āuāāt chiefs of tribes **138.** 2

meru maā[*u*] temple governors **226.** 1

meru set governors of districts **139.** 1

merāḥāṭ tomb **311.** 4; **312.** 7

merāḥāit tombs **306.** 10; **309.** 1; **314.** 10; **315.** 1

Meriti a name of Rā **88.** 11

meru to tie up **265.** 12

Mer ur Mnevis Bull **227.** 1; **236.** 3

Mer-em-ȧptu name of a scribe **40.** 4

Mer-en-Rā prenomen of Pepi I. **103.** 4; **104.** 9, 13

Mer-nefert a city in Upper Egypt **116.** 9

merhaire huts (?), tents **174.** 3

merḥ wax **216.** 6

merḥet to anoint **259.** 1

Mersabata name of a nation **175.** 6

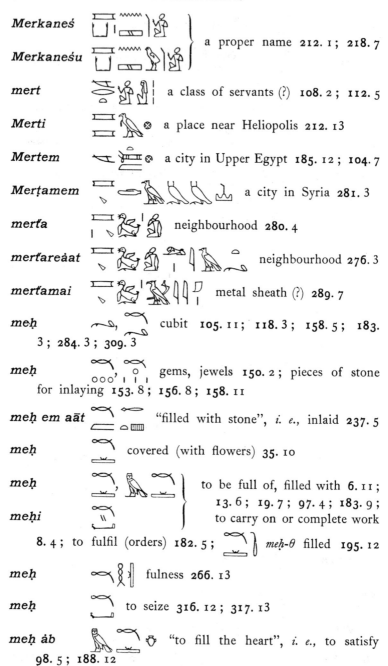

Merkaneś } a proper name 212. 1; 218. 7
Merkaneśu

mert a class of servants (?) 108. 2; 112. 5

Merti a place near Heliopolis 212. 13

Mertem a city in Upper Egypt 185. 12; 104. 7

Merṭamem a city in Syria 281. 3

merťa neighbourhood 280. 4

merťareȧat neighbourhood 276. 3

merťamai metal sheath (?) 289. 7

meḥ , cubit 105. 11; 118. 3; 158. 5; 183. 3; 284. 3; 309. 3

meḥ , gems, jewels 150. 2; pieces of stone for inlaying 153. 8; 156. 8; 158. 11

meḥ em aāt "filled with stone", *i. e.*, inlaid 237. 5

meḥ covered (with flowers) 35. 10

meḥ , } to be full of, filled with 6. 11; 13. 6; 19. 7; 97. 4; 183. 9; to carry on or complete work
meḥi
8. 4; to fulfil (orders) 182. 5; *meḥ-θ* filled 195. 12

meḥ fulness 266. 13

meḥ to seize 316. 12; 317. 13

meḥ ȧb "to fill the heart", *i. e.*, to satisfy 98. 5; 188. 12

meḥ mesṭert "to fill the ear", *i. e.*, to listen with great attention 279. 2

meḥt re mouthful 241. 9

meḥ-sa
meḥu-sa } to have a care for 226. 13; 228. 6

meḥ sekau to carry out ploughing 4. 5

meḥ to pour out water, to inundate 53. 4; 57. 4; 63. 9

meḥ to float 106. 8

meḥi inundation 71. 12

meḥ a word placed before ordinal numbers 237. 5; 237. 6; 325. 10

meḥ
meḥt } north wind 130. 11; 131. 13

meḥ
meḥi } north 99. 12; 148. 2. South and North 143. 9; 160. 6

meḥu north 297. 2

meḥt
meḥtet } north 99. 11; 135. 7; 191. 2; 199. 1; 299. 12; 309. 5

meḥt Àmenti north-west 136. 6

meḥti northern 108. 11; 109. 5; 114. 11; 115. 1

meḥtet the beings of the north 61. 1

meḥi sorrow **54.** 5

meḥt to grieve **59.** 6

Meḥennut, *Meḥenut* } name of a serpent goddess **236.** 8; **296.** 12

Meḥit name of a goddess **77.** 12

meḥu crowned **49.** 9

meḥt plume **192.** 3

meχa greatly **228.** 6

m[ā]χai balance, scales **210.** 9

mes , to give birth to, to be born, born of **41.** 1; **201.** 7

mesi } to give birth to, to produce, bearer **38.** 2; **246.** 3; **273.** 4; birth **291.** 2

mesut (or *mestu*), *mesut, mest*, *mestu* } birth, born **53.** 12; **109.** 1; **110.** 13; **230.** 7; **303.** 10

mest genetrix **252.** 1

mesu , ; *mesu* , ; *mesut* } young boys and girls **96.** 4; **240.** 13 children **246.** 2; **251.** 12; **271.** 11, 13; **317.** 3; **319.** 1
Do. **320.** 6

mesui Do. **163.** 10

mesu divine children 299. 3

mesu ḥemt female children 239. 12

mesu Ḥeru children of Horus 86. 2

mesu seru children of nobles 177. 12; 178. 7

mesi to carve 148. 11; 156. 6; 163. 4

emsuḥ crocodile 251. 11

emseḥu crocodiles 13. 6; 16. 7

mesχet ribbons, veils 233. 4

mest to plate (with gold) 123. 4

meses belt, girdle 287. 5

meska superabundance (of speech) 260. 2

mest a kind of goose (?) 168. 1

Mesṭ a city in Lower Egypt 219. 11

mesṭ , to haste 94. 6; 241. 6

mesṭet hateful, abominable 260. 8

mesṭeṭ
mesṭeṭu } to hate 203. 6; 269. 8

mesṭeṭu enemies, foes 197. 2

mesťem stibium 132. 12

mesťer ear 217. 5

mesṭerui the two ears **268.** 13; **319.** 13

met ten **157.** 2; = XII **76.** 8; **112.** 10; = XV **42.** 6; **82.** 4; = XVII **105.** 8; = XIX **49.** 2; **111.** 11

met sȧs "Lady of [the city of] Sixteen", *i. e.*, Hathor, lady of Lycopolis **93.** 1

met , seed **41.** 6; **126.** 1

metu seed, affinity **201.** 8; **253.** 9

met en ȧuset a title (?) **100.** 11

met, ***metti***, ***metet*** to regulate, to put right, to be exact, right, truth **124.** 9; **170.** 6; **234.** 8; **241.** 1; **251.** 2; **253.** 5

metet uprightness **128.** 12

mettet examination **282.** 4; **287.** 4; **291.** 11

metet ȧb a right disposition **246.** 3

emtuȧ I **17.** 5

emtuk thou **4.** 3; **17.** 8

emtuf he **2.** 10

emtutu one **18.** 1; **26.** 2; **30.** 9; **232.** 3; **234.** 3; **236.** 11; **237.** 3

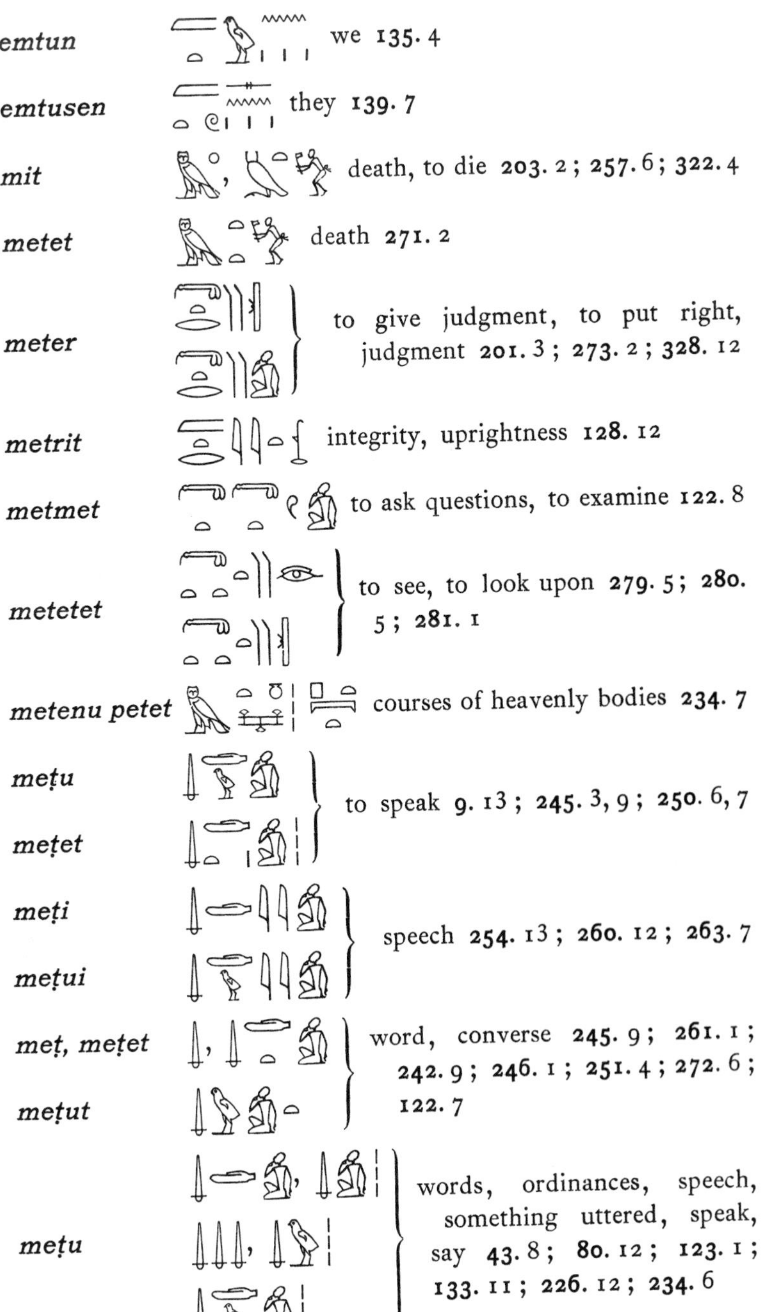

emtun — we 135. 4

emtusen — they 139. 7

mit — death, to die 203. 2; 257. 6; 322. 4

metet — death 271. 2

meter — to give judgment, to put right, judgment 201. 3; 273. 2; 328. 12

metrit — integrity, uprightness 128. 12

metmet — to ask questions, to examine 122. 8

metetet — to see, to look upon 279. 5; 280. 5; 281. 1

metenu petet — courses of heavenly bodies 234. 7

meṭu, *meṭet* — to speak 9. 13; 245. 3, 9; 250. 6, 7

meṭi, *meṭui* — speech 254. 13; 260. 12; 263. 7

meṭ, meṭet, *meṭut* — word, converse 245. 9; 261. 1; 242. 9; 246. 1; 251. 4; 272. 6; 122. 7

meṭu — words, ordinances, speech, something uttered, speak, say 43. 8; 80. 12; 123. 1; 133. 11; 226. 12; 234. 6

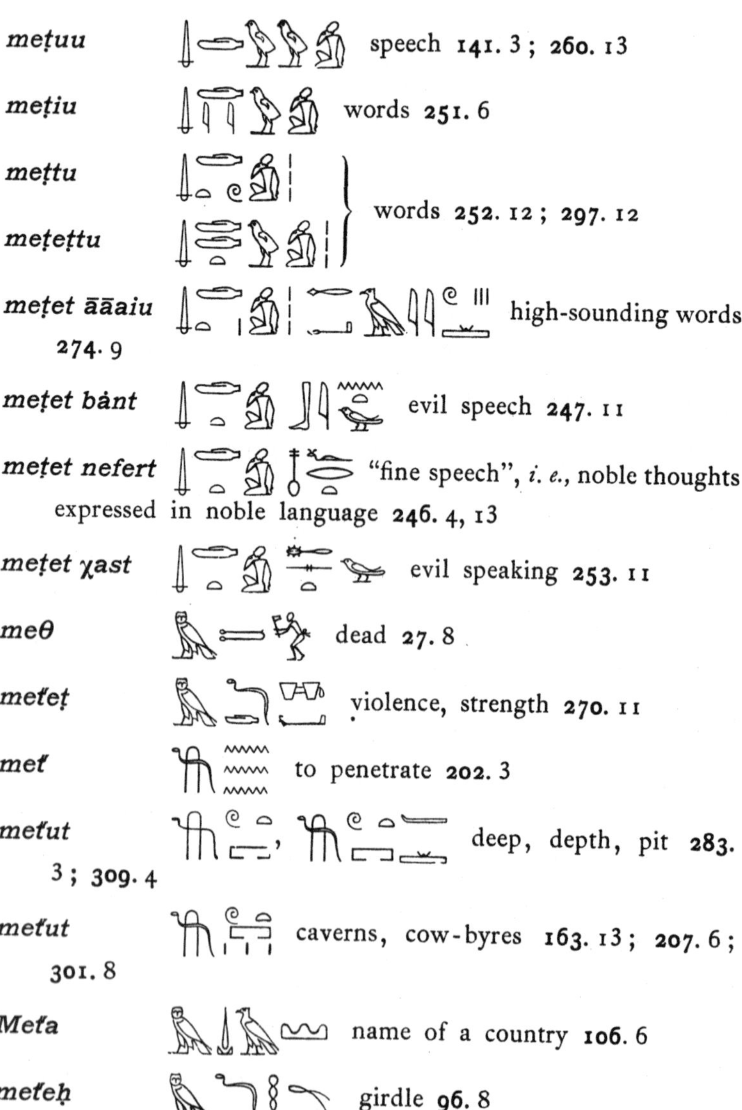

meṭuu speech **141.** 3; **260.** 13

meṭiu words **251.** 6

meṭṭu
meṭeṭṭu } words **252.** 12; **297.** 12

meṭet āāaiu high-sounding words **274.** 9

meṭet bȧnt evil speech **247.** 11

meṭet nefert "fine speech", *i. e.*, noble thoughts expressed in noble language **246.** 4, 13

meṭet χast evil speaking **253.** 11

meθ dead **27.** 8

met̄eṭ violence, strength **270.** 11

met̄ to penetrate **202.** 3

met̄ut deep, depth, pit **283.** 3; **309.** 4

met̄ut caverns, cow-byres **163.** 13; **207.** 6; **301.** 8

Met̄a name of a country **106.** 6

met̄eḥ girdle **96.** 8

met̄et ointment **132.** 12

N.

en mark of the genitive, for, to, in, by 1. 1; 4. 1; 8. 1; 9. 2; 41. 2; 76. 8; 133. 3; 225. 6; among 193. 6; in addition to 234. 4; before 225. 9; 119. 1, so that 124. 2; for ever 107. 8; behind 11. 5; 12. 8; 136. 3; 286. 5. at 140. 3; with, by 113. 9; for ever 107. 9

n = *nȧ* me 105. 5

n to turn, to come 6. 1

n to come 14. 9; 32. 6

en 272. 13

n we, us 4. 1; 10. 5; 50. 7; 51. 1; 133. 3

na the (plur.) 16. 6; 18. 10; 22. 12; 23. 1, 7; 29. 1; 34. 7; 35. 12; 135. 8, 9; 138. 2; 147. 2; 173. 3, 4, 5

na en these, these crocodiles 16. 7; these dogs 18. 10; these garments 22. 12; 23. 2; these washermen 23. 1; these people 34. 7; these followers 140. 8; those belonging to 138. 3

nai-ȧ [hieroglyphs] my 39. 6; 145. 3; 166. 5

nai-k [hieroglyphs] thy 6. 10; 159. 9; 165. 11

nai-f [hieroglyphs] his 1. 6; [hieroglyphs] his children 243. 4

nai-n [hieroglyphs] our 135. 1

nai-sen [hieroglyphs] their 4. 10; 26. 3; 137. 8

nai-u [hieroglyphs] their 151. 1; 175. 13; 176. 11; 179. 1; 180. 4; 315. 6; 328. 6, 11

nait [hieroglyphs] house 217. 8

namesmes [hieroglyphs] to heap up, to make run over 148. 5

naḥa [hieroglyphs] crowded or blocked up behind 284. 1

naḥa [hieroglyphs] a species of plant or shrub 285. 2

Naχai [hieroglyphs] a city in Syria 290. 13

nasaqu [hieroglyphs] breaks, divisions 274. 8

Naťana [hieroglyphs] a place near Tyre

nȧ [hieroglyphs] I, me 5. 7; 112. 5; 127. 1, 6

nȧs [hieroglyphs] to cry aloud, to invoke, to be invoked 78. 3; 80. 4; 132. 2; 298. 3

nȧst [hieroglyphs] to address, cry 242. 13; 243. 4

nȧsbeť (?) [hieroglyphs] to proclaim 34. 2

Nȧk name of a fiend **297.** 9; **304.** 6

nā to travel **204.** 6; **210.** 3; **287.** 12

nā to sail **105.** 9; **190.** 10

nāi travelling, coming, to sail **75.** 6; **83.** 4; **89.** 4; **158.** 8

nāru a kind of fish **16.** 1

nārt sycamore **89.** 12

nimā
nimāu who? **9.** 13; **32.** 6; **190.** 8; **198.** 11 (bis)

Nini a proper name **84.** 11

nu of **27.** 3; **39.** 12; **100.** 6; **104.** 13

nu they, them **150.** 8; **165.** 7; **169.** 7; **176.** 1; **180.** 10; **315.** 9; us (?) **81.** 2

nu babe, child **51.** 13; **70.** 8

nu sky **213.** 2

nu water **148.** 1; **158.** 7

Nu the Sky-god **297.** 9

nui dagger, weapon **11.** 3; **12.** 7; **15.** 10

nui (?) tools **26.** 3

nub gold **30.** 7; **153.** 7; **179.** 8, etc.

nub nefer fine gold **149.** 2; **151.** 8; **153.** 7; **158.** 7

nub en sep χemt "gold of three times", *i. e.*, much refined gold **179.** 8

nub "Golden one", a name of a god **91.** 8

nub , places where gold is smelted (?) **156.** 7

nubȧu to fashion, to form **58.** 5

nubi to smelt, to work metals by fire **124.** 10

nubu moulded **73.** 8

Nub-χās / ***Nub-χāā-s*** name of a queen **312.** 12; **324.** 4

Nubt name of a god **220.** 10

nu neḥeḥ ever, everlasting **107.** 8

nuk , , I **46.** 6; **53.** 3; **99.** 3; **133.** 13

nut of **141.** 8

nut (?) towns-folk **267.** 7

nut town **20.** 1

nut , , towns, cities **42.** 7; **85.** 8; **100.** 9; **111.** 3

nut pyramid district **97.** 2

nuti (?) double city **237.** 1

Nut — the goddess of the sky **41**. 7; **52**. 7; **55**. 11; **57**. 9, 13; **72**. 8; **123**. 9

neb — all, any, each, every, of every sort or kind **1**. 9; **2**. 8; **156**. 8; **177**. 10; **207**. 3; every one **195**. 12; any, each, every **8**. 1; **15**. 6; **35**. 6; **95**. 11; **242**. 9

nebu, **nebut** — all **41**. 1; **52**. 4; **121**. 5; **126**. 2

neb — lord **13**. 2; **50**. 3; **97**. 10; **103**. 4; **104**. 8; **115**. 12; a man of property, owner **256**. 13; **259**. 3; lord **49**. 5; **51**. 3; **62**. 4; **67**. 6; plur. *nebu* lords, owners **315**. 6

neb åmaχ — possessor of reverence, *i. e.*, revered one **110**. 8; **111**. 5

neb ānu — "master of books", *i. e.*, an author, scribe **40**. 5

neb χet — "lord of things", *i. e.*, a wealthy man **251**. 11

neb śeta neb åārā (?) or **smauti** — lord of the North and South, or uniter of the North and South **108**. 5; **109**. 1; **110**. 11; **114**. 5; **124**. 4; **130**. 2

neb qeṭ — "master of manner", *i. e.*, one who knows how to act properly (?) **251**. 10

nebt — lady, mistress **91**. 1, 3, 4, etc.

Nebt-Åmmu — a name of the goddess Uatchet **92**. 5

Nebt-ānχ a name of Isis 304. 9

nebt per "mistress of the house", *i. e.*, wife, married woman 80. 1; 107. 6

Nebt-ḥet , Nephthys 50. 2; 77. 10

Nebt-ḥetep } a name of Hathor 91. 6; 143. 4

Neb-Àmen a proper name 312. 8

Neb-er-t'er
Neb-er-t'ert } a name of Osiris 41. 2; 75. 12; 91. 10; 119. 10; 122. 3

nebà
nebàt } flame 68. 12; 220. 13

nebi protector 155. 7; 165. 10

Nebinaitet Cyprus 228. 12

nebṭ to tie, to plait the hair 5. 6

nebṭ lock of hair 22. 8

Nebṭ , } name of a cloud 54. 9; 55. 6; 64. 9

nebṭu plaited mats 166. 9

neperà grain, Corn-god 302. 6

nef , he, it, him 219. 3, 6; 230. 5; 237. 12

nefi, *nefiȧ* — foe, enemy, evil one 59. 2; 60. 2; 220. 1

nefer — to be good or beautiful, good 44. 7; excellent 2. 1; beautiful 41. 1; gracious 33. 4; happy (of days) 33. 3; sweet (of pasture) 3. 6; pretty 286. 13; good (look-out) 134. 6; happily 40. 2; prosperity 181. 12; to recover from a sickness 46. 2; good or bad 290. 1; very fine indeed 3. 11; 24. 9; the best of all 243. 12; *nefer-ui* doubly good 269. 6; 273. 7, 8

neferu — fair, good, excellent, lovely, beautiful, beauties 7. 2; 37. 4; 53. 2; 57. 8; 70. 3; 71. 9; 122. 3; 143. 10; 183. 6; 200. 4; 295. 12; 299. 9

neferu — "the happy beings", *i. e.*, the dead 317. 4

neferi — beautiful one 62. 13

nefert — what is good 3. 9; 130. 8; 241. 10; 269. 6; 294. 6

nefert — fair women 80. 12

nefertu — pleasant 182. 4

nefer-θȧ — favourable 4. 2

neferi — fire 92. 4

Neferus — name of a city 187. 3

Nefer-Tem — a god of Heliopolis 143. 7; 149. 13

Nefer-ḥrȧ "beautiful face", a name of Rā 51. 2; 52. 11

Nefer-ḥetep a name of Khonsu 44. 5

Nefer-ḥetep-pa-āā Nefer-ḥetep Major 77. 8

Nefer-ḥetep-pa-śere Nefer-ḥetep Minor 77. 9

neferi er / **neferit er** up to, until 49. 6; 124. 6; 237. 3

neferu grain 148. 5; 150. 7; 157. 3, 5

neferu young horses 200. 12

neferu door (?) 312. 5

nifu air, wind, breath 68. 1; 96. 2; 118. 8; 130. 11; 181. 7; 300. 8

nem mistake, error 270. 5

nem (or **uḥem**) to repeat 43. 1; 44. 2, 7; 109. 1; 151. 13; 302. 9

nemt (or **uḥemt**) to repeat 251. 5

nemu (or **uḥemu**) herald 307. 6; 309. 12; 316. 8; 330. 3

nemau new 208. 4

Nemareθ Nimrod (?) 187. 1; 191. 9; 200. 7; 224. 1

nemmat block of slaughter **51**. 13 ; **74**. 11

nemt stride, walk, gait **128**. 6

nemmat (or **nemtet**) steps **294**. 8 ; **304**. 6

nemmȧt couch **64**. 1 ; **80**. 10

nemȧta to stride over **304**. 1

nemmā to build, to construct **151**. 6

nemāu boats **102**. 11

nememtau to stride **56**. 2

nemtet steps **254**. 4 ; **258**. 4 ; **270**. 9 ; **274**. 1

nemmes to enlighten **89**. 9

nemesmes to heap up to overflowing **207**. 4

nemmes a headdress **297**. 1

nemmeset libation vases **86**. 5, 13

enen (?) these (?) **276**. 6

enen this, these **65**. 12 ; **121**. 3 ; **186**. 2 ; **208**. 12

enennai to delay (?) **79**. 9, 10

enen-tu broken remains **278**. 12

enen-θȧ broken, useless **289**. 1

ennu to occupy oneself **253**. 6

ennu to bind together **65**. 12

ennut bond **267**. 8

ennu to look, to see **28**. 7 ; **29**. 2 ; **58**. 3

ennu to look, to see **12**. 6 ; **181**. 2

ennu time, period **50**. 9 ; **64**. 2

ennuit moment **286**. 8

ennuit to put in good order **288**. 13

ennuit to tend, to care for **16**. 12 ; **17**. 3

ennuḥ to tie up, to fasten **51**. 4

ennuḥ cordage **89**. 4

ennuḥu traces, harness **277**. 2

enenem error, to act wickedly **253**. 9 ; **254**. 1 ; **255**. 11 ; **270**. 9

nenser excitement (?) **261**. 7

ner to have terror of **190**. 6

nerȧu to be in terror of, to hold in awe, to vanquish, to defeat, awe, terror **56**. 12 ; **70**. 3 ; **85**. 9 ; **220**. 9 ; **296**. 5

nerit to strike awe into 120. 6

nerāu 167. 7

Neh a district of Athribis 92. 9

neh , few, little, small quantity 206. 10; 241. 11

nehai few 318. 5; 331. 1

nehaut neter sentrȧ trees which produce incense 159. 2

nehamu rejoicing 323. 10; 324. 1

nehamu people who rejoice 25. 9; 30. 10

nehareȧu chattels (?), things (?) 278. 2

nehat walls 59. 5

Nehiren Mesopotamia 137. 7

nehut little 258. 10

nehem to rejoice 47. 7; 200. 3; 224. 8

Neher Mesopotamia 41. 7

nehes } to wake 48. 2; 277. 11; 278. 6, 12

nehet sycamore trees 127. 5

neh-tu diminished 234. 5

neḥ to trust in 252. 3

neḥu (?) (?) to worship, to pray 235. 3

neḥeb neck 34. 8; thyself 278. 1

neḥeb harness 275. 4

neḥeb to yoke 189. 1; 196. 12

neḥebet yoke 289. 5

neḥem , , to pillage 100. 13; to deliver 45. 2; 63. 5; 227. 6; 298. 3

neḥemu to deliver 21. 6; 181. 8

Neḥra father of Khnemu-ḥetep 107. 5; 111. 5; 113. 11

neḥeḥ , , , eternity, everlastingness 14. 3; 88. 1; 116. 11; 117. 1; 152. 5; 225. 2; 244. 7; for ever and ever 124. 3

neḥeḥ ḥenti an eternity of *ḥenti*, *i. e.*, periods of 120 years 129. 5

neḥeḥ to pray 133. 6

Neḥes Negro-land 95. 12

Neḥes negroes 99. 13; 100. 1, 2, 3

neḥti to trust 207. 1

neχu to support 188. 11

neχeb title 42. 4

neχebu to be described 51. 8

neχebu slaughter, punishment **326.** 2

neχebṭet wickedness **258.** 3

Neχen a city in Upper Egypt **97.** 3

neχen humility **113.** 8; **117.** 7

neχen babe **68.** 7; **94.** 3; plur. **199.** 5; **206.** 6

neχeχu flail **297.** 4

neχt , strong, mighty, violent, strength, power, force **40.** 8; **42.** 6; **122.** 13; **258.** 9; victory **134.** 6; strong **152.** 1; **160.** 11; strongly fortified **195.** 11

neχt , strength, mighty deeds **41.** 4, 6

neχt troops **136.** 3

neχtu power, force **181.** 8; mighty one **181.** 3

neχtu troops **188.** 10

neχtu strongly fortified places **173.** 10

neχtu (?) forces **140.** 7

neχt-ā strong of arm, *i. e.*, mighty **189.** 9; **220.** 10

Neχt a proper name **110.** 7; **113.** 13

Neχt-Ȧmsu a proper name **128.** 2; **129.** 3, 13; **133.** 2

Neχtu-em-Mut a proper name **324**. 10

Neχt-Ḥeru-na-śennut a proper name **218**. 12

neχtu proclaimed **55**. 4

nes, ***nest*** tongue **113**. 8; **268**. 11; **292**. 3

nes, nesi, ***nes***, ***nest*** belonging to **24**. 2; **73**. 5; **124**. 4; **253**. 7; **255**. 6; **326**. 4

nesut hastiness **261**. 8

Nes-Åmen, ***Neṣi-Åmen***, ***Nes-su-Åmen*** a proper name **307**. 2; **309**. 8; **316**. 4; **317**. 5; **323**. 4; **329**. 13; **331**. 9

Nes-Åmsu a proper name **76**. 5

Nesnaqeṭi a proper name **192**. 2; **218**. 11

Nes-θent-meḥ a proper name **198**. 5

nesert flame **65**. 4

nest throne, seat **78**. 9; **112**. 13; **120**. 5; plur. **40**. 11; **42**. 7; double throne **146**. 9

neś to tremble **29**. 1

neś to enter in, to rush upon 258. 1; 267. 8

neśu leaf of a door (?) 34. 9

neśen grief, trouble 262. 7

neśeni disasters 62. 7

neśti to rage 170. 10

nek *coire* 265. 4

Nekȧu name of a fiend 52. 2

neken to attack 64. 11

neket things 16. 10; 17. 4; 18. 1; 30. 6; 33. 10

neḳa to hew 65. 9

neḳa to open out 75. 5

neḳa a kind of wood 118. 4

neḳa pain 78. 8

neḳa bull 166. 12

neḳeb to be destroyed, to come to an end 252. 13; 257. 4

ent , of 42. 8; 235. 10

net thou 7. 11

ent which 110. 10

net to sprinkle 189. 11

Net , the goddess Neith 84. 7; 192. 8; 221. 12

net (?) ***netu*** (?) treasurer, chancellor **77**. 6; **97**. 11; **104**. 9; **119**. 6; plur. **204**. 4

net treasurers **100**. 5

net (or ***bȧt***) king of Lower Egypt **60**. 6; **62**. 10; **66**. 10; **111**. 4

net rules, regulations **238**. 7

entā rule, custom **41**. 8

entāu litany, prescribed rites **87**. 6; **171**. 5; **211**. 5; **231**. 9

ent creatures, things which exist **144**. 13; **182**. 1

enti things which are **294**. 10; **295**. 4; **300**. 3; **301**. 13

enti who, which **1**. 9; **6**. 6; **9**. 1; **136**. 8; everything which **243**. 7

entu those who **175**. 1; **270**. 3

entuten ye, you **136**. 10

entef he **121**. 8; **136**. 12

neter god **20**. 11; **49**. 5; **189**. 3; **195**. 5; God **243**. 3; **249**. 6; **250**. 13; **251**. 8; **252**. 2, 4; **233**. 5; **255**. 5; **259**. 9; **262**. 6; **264**. 4; **269**. 8; **273**. 12; god among gods **53**. 13

neteru gods 19. 10; 41. 1; 51. 7; 90. 4; 114. 5; 133. 3; 142. 3; 226. 2, 12; 294. 4

neteret goddess 238. 2

neterit goddesses 88. 11; 95. 1; 142. 3; 143. 9; 238. 5

neter strong, divine 41. 6; 55. 1; 123. 11

netrȧ divine one 90. 7

netri divine 144. 12; 145. 4; 165. 3

neterer power 121. 7

neterui menχui the two divine benefactors, Θεῶν Ἐυεργετῶν 225. 7; 226. 7; 229. 10; 230. 1; 231. 8

neterui neťui the two divine saviours 229. 12; = Gr. τοῖς προγόνοις Θεοῖς Σωτῆρσιν αὔξειν

neterui senui the two divine brethren, Θεῶν Ἀδελφων 225. 5; 226. 10; 229. 11; 230. 7

neterui ḥet-āt the two divine temples 56. 4

Neter a city near Sais 185. 5

neteru peru divine temples 228. 7

neter meṭu divine speech or tradition **129**. 6

neter net (?) divine treasurer **77**. 6; **97**. 11

neter ḥen priest **76**. 3; **97**. 2; **308**. 9

neter ḥen ṭep high-priest **128**. 2; priesthood **230**. 1

neteru ḥenu priests **100**. 7; **226**. 1

neter ḥet temple, shrine **61**. 13; **112**. 2; **227**. 2

neter ḥet unnut priests who serve for certain periods in the temple **163**. 9

neter ḥetep, ***neter ḥetepet*** property or offerings dedicated to a god **133**. 3; **201**. 11

neter sentrȧ, ***neter senθer*** incense **153**. 13; **211**. 3; **213**. 6

neter tefu "divine fathers", an order of priests **226**. 3

neter ṭua the divine morning star **213**. 8

neter ȧtef Ȧi neter ḥeq Uast "Ȧi, divine father, divine prince of Thebes", a king of the XVIIIth dynasty **126**. 6; **130**. 5

Neter ḥet Ȧnpu Cynopolis 223. 2

Neter-ḥet-Sebek Crocodilopolis 185. 12

Neter-χert
Neter χertet } the underworld 89. 6; 107. 9; 126. 9

Neter Sepṭet Sothis 83. 1; 232. 7

Neter-ta Arabia 41. 11; 296. 3

Neter-tauit } the lands on each side of the Red Sea 72. 12; 177. 9, 13; 224. 6

Neter-θeb Sebennytus 218. 7

entek thou 13. 2; 146. 9; 165. 10; 202. 6

entet , who, which 118. 6; 133. 5; 186. 10; 191. 13; 211. 10; everything which is 269. 5

neṭes little, low (of the Nile) 227. 13; 228. 4

enθ of 43. 6; 226. 7

neθeḥ horses 136. 2; 137. 8; 138. 12; 140. 1; 141. 10

net̄
net̄ti } to avenge 55. 13; 68. 2

net̄ intercession 115. 7

net̄tet avenger 120. 6

neťetre to speak for, to be eloquent **288.** 7

neťti ren to proclaim the name of **86.** 4

neť ḥrȧ to honour, to pay homage to **24.** 4

neť ḥrȧ to honour, to pay homage to **52.** 2

neť χet counsellor = βουλευτής **231.** 4 ; **240.** 1, 6

temple counsellors **240.** 1, 6

neťi subjection **227.** 12

neťit to be degraded, degradation **248.** 13

neťem to be glad, glad, sweet, pleasant **4.** 11 ; **23.** 11 ; **304.** 10

neťemi happy, rejoicer **81.** 4 ; **93.** 4 ; sweet-smelling **94.** 1

neťemťem love **51.** 3 ; **56.** 13 ; **60.** 5 ; **67.** 7

neťemet love **130.** 9

neťneť to converse **246.** 11

neťneť re to justify **332.** 3

neťer to smite **103.** 1

neťeru
neťert work, labour, exertion **262.** 1 ; **267.** 4

neťeș little **131.** 9

neťes child 210. 2

neťesu to become weak, to fail 245. 1

neťesu humble men 252. 5

neťesu lowly condition 264. 1

neťtu broken 277. 10

R.

er at 2. 7; from 13. 3; to, into 1. 7; 2. 6; 145. 1; toward 48. 1; so as 10. 10; against 20. 4; 241. 3; belonging to 136. 11; dedicated to 50. 2; rather than 263. 10; so that 98. 8; until 13. 13; more than:— more beautiful than any woman 20. 10; thou art greater than the gods 70. 10; they were more numerous than the sand 163. 13; more than any thing 98. 11; 193. 5; 207. 5

er ȧmtu between 122. 12

er ȧqer exceedingly 3. 11

er āu all, entirely 95. 2

er āa ur exceedingly 42. 3; 47. 1

er āuṭ between 13. 5, 6; 310. 9

er āq exactly opposite 23. 9

er bun-re outside 275. 3

er peḥ to the uttermost **196.** 13

er men as far as **109.** 7; **110.** 6; **115.** 3; until **231.** 1

er neḥeḥ for ever **14.** 3; **94.** 11

er ennuit straightway, instantly **286.** 8

er nefer successfully (?) **100.** 12, 13; **101.** 1, 3; **103.** 13

er enti , so that, because **139.** 4; **230.** 6; **231.** 12; **234.** 1; inasmuch as **323.** 3

er entet according to that which **109.** 13

erenθ inasmuch = ἐπειδὴ **226.** 8

er ruati outside **47.** 13

er hau towards **67.** 11

er ḥāā read *er ḥenā* with **181.** 2

er ḥāt
er ḥāti } before **8.** 10; **20.** 1; **22.** 5; **138.** 6; **170.** 1

er ḥenā with **33.** 3; **284.** 6

er ḥer in addition to **87.** 6

er ḥer over and above **57.** 7

er ḥeri
er ḥert } upwards **48.** 1; **163.** 12

er χeft opposite, in the face of **84.** 4; **145.** 7

er χent before 188. 2; 193. 10

er χer with 258. 9

er χet in the following of 139. 2; 194. 10; 317. 10; 330. 11

er ḳes near 22. 3; 35. 5; 80. 10; 91. 10, 11; 140. 9; 145. 10; 242. 6; 251. 9; 318. 1; 329. 4; 152. 2

er śaā until, unto 146. 5; 320. 13; 325. 3; for ever 153. 1; 161. 11

er ťer to the utmost limit 4. 8; 137. 7; 143. 12; 315. 5

re a kind of goose 167. 11

re door, gate, mouth 7. 13; 69. 3; 115. 12; plur. *reu* mouths 115. 11

re āāui "mouth of the two hands", *i. e.*, actions of the two hands 203. 11

re uat "mouth of the way", *i. e.*, neighbourhood 288. 12

re-tu uā (with) "one mouth" 20. 13

re ḥeri "upper mouth", *i. e.*, commander 169. 7; 171. 7

re without number 149. 2

reȧai
reȧat side 13. 8, 12; 34. 11; 175. 1; 285. 3; 286. 7

reȧt doorway 149. 9; 156. 12

rā barracks 180. 13

rā chambers 164. 2; storehouses 153. 10

reā a kind of fish 168. 11

rā day 271. 2; daily 245. 1

rā tool 137. 9; 191. 3

rā tools 27. 3

rā , in very deed, actually, to do, work, action to work indeed 4. 12; 8. 4; in very deed he 18. 3; really dead, or in the condition of one dead 27. 9; I am really alive 32. 5; , for ever 229. 3, 7; 230. 13; 231. 3; see also 14. 12; 263. 7; 311. 1

Reāu the quarries of Ṭura 97. 11

Rā , , , , , the Sun-god 13. 3; 40. 10; 42. 12; 64. 6; 131. 11; 171. 13; 213. 2; 295. 9; Rā the living one 126. 3

Rā-āḥā-em-ȧpu-maāt prenomen of Ȧntuf-āa 311. 8

Rā-uaṭ-χeper prenomen of Kames 313. 13

Rā-user-Maāt prenomen of Rameses II. 290. 10

Rā-user-Maāt-meri-Ȧmen 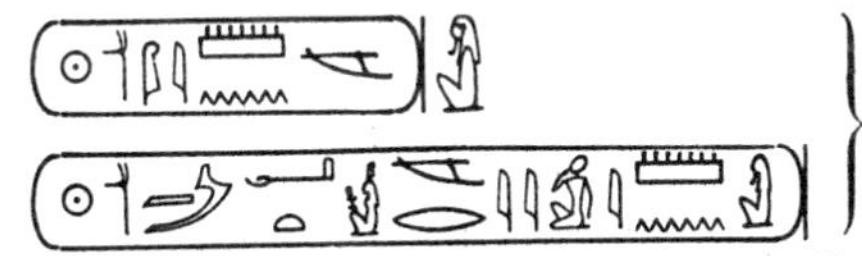 prenomen of Rameses III. **142.** 2, 7; **144.** 8; **317.** 10; **318.** 4; **319.** 2; **330.** 11; **332.** 8

Rā-user-Maāt-setep-en-Rā  prenomen of Rameses II. **134.** 4

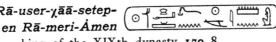

Rā-user-χāā-setep-en Rā-meri-Ȧmen 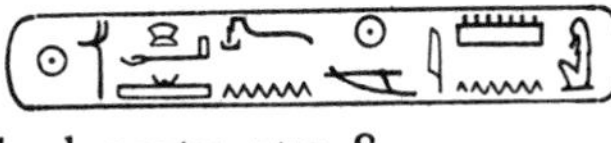 prenomen of Set nekht, a king of the XIXth dynasty **170.** 8

Rā-men-χeper 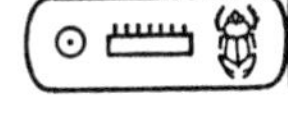 prenomen of Thothmes III. **312.** 8

Rā-mersekni 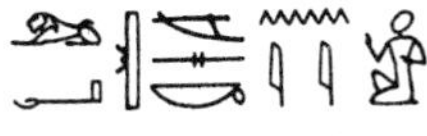 a proper name **187.** 11

Rā-messu-merer-Ȧmen  Rameses X. **306.** 3

Rā-meses-meri-Ȧmen  Rameses II. **134.** 4

Rā-meses-ḥeq-Ȧnnu  Rameses III. **142.** 3; **144.** 9

Rā-nub-χeper  prenomen of Antuf **310.** 12

Rā-nub-kau 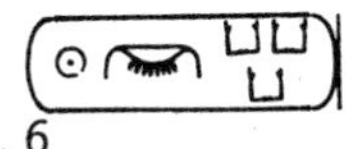 prenomen of Ȧmenemḥāt II. **108.** 6; **111.** 6

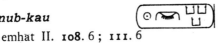

Rā-neb-maāt-neχt  a proper name **318.** 2

Rā-neb-χerut 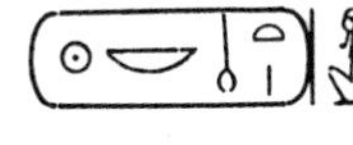 prenomen of Menθu-ḥetep **314.** 5

Rā-neferu 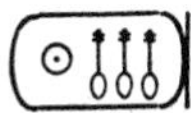 a princess of Bekhten **42.** 4

Rā-nefer-ka-em-per-Ȧmen a proper name **307.** 6; **309.** 11; **316.** 7; **330.** 3

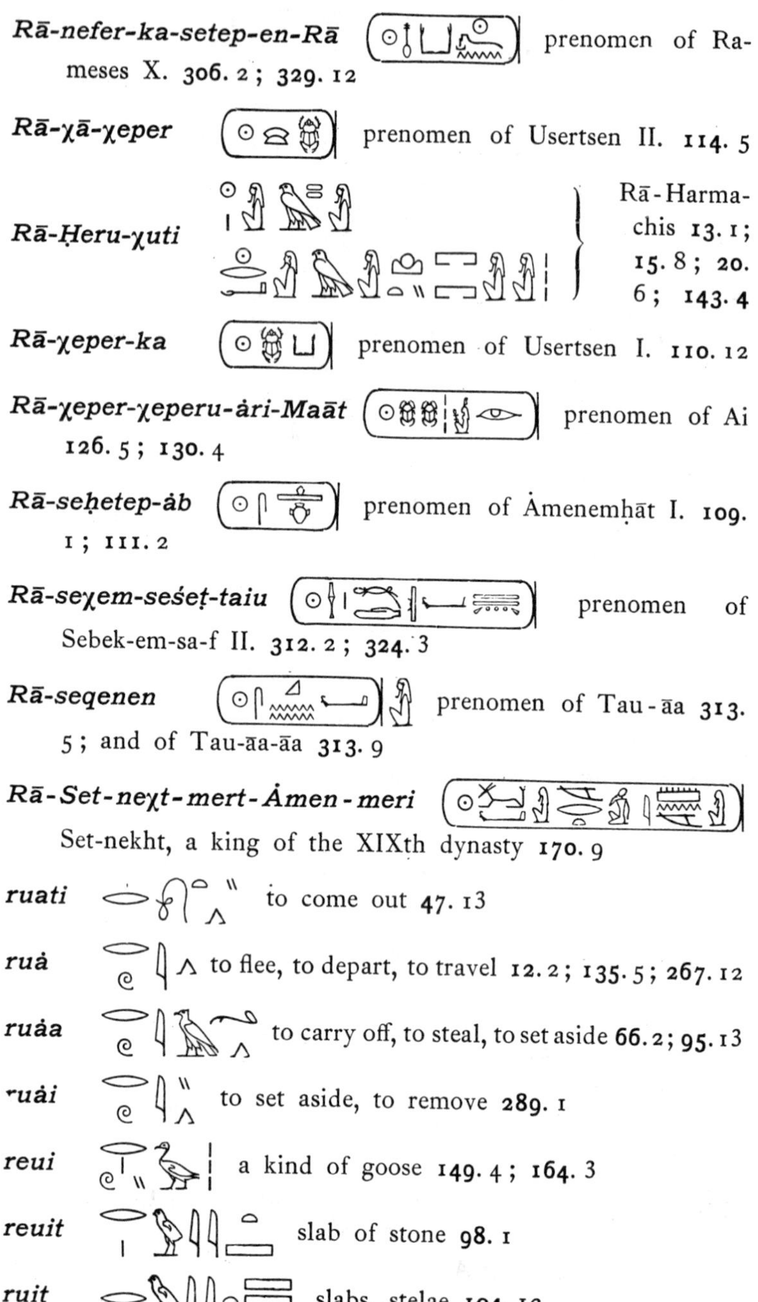

Rā-nefer-ka-setep-en-Rā prenomen of Rameses X. **306**. 2; **329**. 12

Rā-χā-χeper prenomen of Usertsen II. **114**. 5

Rā-Ḥeru-χuti Rā-Harmachis **13**. 1; **15**. 8; **20**. 6; **143**. 4

Rā-χeper-ka prenomen of Usertsen I. **110**. 12

Rā-χeper-χeperu-ȧri-Maāt prenomen of Ai **126**. 5; **130**. 4

Rā-seḥetep-ȧb prenomen of Ȧmenemḥāt I. **109**. 1; **111**. 2

Rā-seχem-seśeṭ-taiu prenomen of Sebek-em-sa-f II. **312**. 2; **324**. 3

Rā-seqenen prenomen of Tau-āa **313**. 5; and of Tau-āa-āa **313**. 9

Rā-Set-neχt-mert-Ȧmen-meri Set-nekht, a king of the XIXth dynasty **170**. 9

ruati to come out **47**. 13

ruȧ to flee, to depart, to travel **12**. 2; **135**. 5; **267**. 12

ruȧa to carry off, to steal, to set aside **66**. 2; **95**. 13

ruȧi to set aside, to remove **289**. 1

reui a kind of goose **149**. 4; **164**. 3

reuit slab of stone **98**. 1

ruit slabs, stelae **104**. 12

ruha evening 2. 7

ruhau evening 321. 1

ruti decay, ruin 169. 6

ruti portico, porch 293. 6

reṭ limit, border 174. 11

ruṭ to grow 34. 13; 35. 3; 89. 2; 127. 1; 276. 8; vigour 129. 1; overgrown with bushes 285. 1

ruṭu things which grow 232. 11

ruṭu granite 147. 4; 151. 7

ruṭet hard (of granite) 120. 12

ruṭu inspectors (?), workmen 158. 2; 159. 13; 177. 3; 306. 6; 309. 2; 310. 2; 313. 7; 314. 8; 316. 1; 320. 9; 331. 2

Rebu name of a nation 174. 9; 175. 5

er pā, *er pāt*, *er pāṭet* the hereditary head of a tribe 107. 4; 108. 7; 110. 2; 192. 1; fem. 39. 1; 111. 1; 171. 6; 246. 5

erpu or 237. 7; 240. 8; 257. 1; 266. 1

er per temple 121. 10

er peru, *er perut* temples 87. 10; 155. 4; 165. 7; 231. 11

Re-peḥ a city in Syria **291.** 3

erpet statue **238.** 11

erpet statues **238.** 1

erpetet the two female counterparts of Osiris, *i. e.*, Isis and Nephthys **55.** 8 ; **66.** 6

ermen the two arms **50.** 1 ; arms **86.** 12

ermeni shoulders **34.** 7

erment shoulder **6.** 6

ermen to carry on the shoulder **278.** 13

ermen passiveness **247.** 7

erment idleness **267.** 4

ermennut inactivity **247.** 9

rem, *remi*, *remit* to weep **68.** 13 ; **80.** 3 ; **210.** 2 ; **27.** 8 ; **16.** 4

remu fish **168.** 8, 12 ; **223.** 13 ; **224.** 3 ; **279.** 11 ; **290.** 5 ; **300.** 7 ; white fish **168.** 10

ren name **1.** 2 ; **52.** 4 ; **97.** 6 ; **129.** 8 ; **173.** 11 ; **230.** 1 ; accursed name **54.** 2 ; renown **254.** 13

rennu names 303. 8; 316. 11

renp to grow 50. 9; 51. 11; 52. 13; 89. 5; 133. 5; to rejuvenate 61. 11

renpet year 17. 9; 27. 13; 124. 6

renput years 28. 1; 119. 7; 147. 5; 169. 7

renpet āa festival of the great year 112. 7

renpet śerȧt festival of the little year 112. 7

renpȧ flowers 153. 13; 164. 5

renpit flowers 127. 2; 130. 12

renen heifer 166. 11; plur. 149. 4

renenet child, babe 120. 4

renenet virgin 234. 12; plur. 237. 13; 238. 10, 11

rer to revolve 51. 9; 53. 13; 55. 6; 56. 4; 59. 12

rer circuit 186. 6

rer circuit, disk 87. 9

rer general, common, throughout 232. 3; 233. 9

err upon 181. 9

reri to go round, to be surrounded, to pervade 150. 11; 159. 1; 320. 9

reru to go round **293.** 10

errā (?) besides **233.** 5

rerem to weep **70.** 8; **80.** 5

ererer (?) again **231.** 2; **239.** 4

reri time **233.** 7

rerit (or ***ārit***) chamber of council or state **254.** 3, 7

rertu dandled **57.** 7

rerṭu out of, outside **227.** 5, 9

reha evening **8.** 5

Reḥui the two opponents, *i. e.*, Horus and Set **302.** 10

Reḥubu a city in Syria **282.** 7

Reḥubureθȧ a city in Syria **291.** 1

Reḥent "mouth of the canal", *i. e.*, Illahun **202.** 12

Reḥesau a town near Letopolis **92.** 10

Reḥti Isis and Nephthys **56.** 4

re-ḥet treasury **150.** 9; plur. treasuries **148.** 3; **151.** 8; **159.** 9

reχ to know **6.** 11; **16.** 5; **154.** 8; to understand **246.** 7; to be sensitive to **221.** 4; being trained **116.** 2; knowing **121.** 7

reχ knowledge 6. 11; 246. 10; 261. 3; list 218. 2; science 234. 7; opinion 247. 12; , royal kinsman 107. 4; 117. 7

reχt knowledge 268. 8; enumeration 160. 6

reχ a wise or learned man 125. 4; 246. 11; 268. 10

reχ-χet sage, sages 43. 4; 226. 3; 272. 9

reχ ṭet cunning of hand 289. 11

reχi skilful (workmen) 37. 7

reχi χet sages 23. 13

reχit a class of beings, men and women 89. 8; 144. 2; 169. 5; 181. 5; 245. 12; 297. 13; 329. 7

reχit , men and women 120. 6; 123. 1; 63. 11; 228. 10

reχti washers 22. 11; 23. 1

res, resu , , south, southern 42. 8; 99. 10; 106. 4; 108. 10

reset southern 198. 13; south, north, west, east 223. 4

res (?) to exalt (?) 103. 3

res, resu , to watch, to guard 128. 8; 134. 6; 300. 13

Res Watcher, a name of Rā **296.** 8

Res (or ***Åusår***) a name of Osiris **142.** 4; **145.** 9; **171.** 10

resut unveiling **260.** 8; vision **257.** 6

re-stau
re-statet the opening into the tomb **90.** 2; **130.** 7; **132.** 10

reśaȧu top, summit **280.** 6

reśui to rejoice **172.** 4

reś-ui twofold joy **269.** 12

reśeś to be glad, to rejoice **148.** 13

reśtu joy **31.** 7; **151.** 13

rek time **180.** 8; **228.** 3; **248.** 11

reku time **159.** 4

rekeḥ heat **112.** 8

rekeḥ āa festival of the great heat **112.** 8

rekeḥ ur festival of the great heat **131.** 9

rekeḥ neťes
rekeḥ śerȧ festival of the little heat **112.** 8; **131.** 9

req to revolt from **125.** 9

ret men **80.** 3; **128.** 3

Retennu Syrians **165.** 2

Retennutet Syria **228.** 11

reṭ men and women **240.** 11

reṭet foot **157.** 9

reṭ , feet **12.** 7; **182.** 3; **296.** 4

reṭuui, reṭui , legs, legs of a vessel **156.** 4; **310.** 9

erṭā, erṭāt , , , , to give, to place, to appoint, to allow, to hand over, to cause, to make **43.** 7; **97.** 1; **125.** 1; **188.** 1; **244.** 4; causing, making **105.** 9; to lay to heart **243.** 9; to turn the back, to yield **228.** 8. As an auxiliary:— **44.** 3; **98.** 10; **240.** 10; **186.** 5; **186.** 5

erṭuu emanations, humours **61.** 9

reθ , , people, inhabitants **8.** 1; **24.** 8; **46.** 6; **101.** 4; **143.** 11

reθ (?) peoples, tribes **102.** 1

reθ qeṭet sailors **319.** 4; **320.** 10; **321.** 6; **324.** 9

H.

ha O! **36.** 3; **277.** 2

ha to come forth **95.** 3; to advance **198.** 1

ha to walk over **296.** 2

ha . . . . to throw down **297.** 6

ha to descend **127.** 7; **285.** 5

ha to fall **141.** 6

ha place **210.** 7

ha time **228.** 5

hai O, hail **68.** 2, 13; **81.** 9; **83.** 7; acclamation **88.** 10

Hai a fiend **69.** 12

hai husband **7.** 8; **9.** 3; **25.** 13; **61.** 2

hai to come in **98.** 12

hai destruction **318.** 6

hai falling **17.** 7; **285.** 9; one to go down **23.** 10

hait fall **26.** 7

Haire-Nemmȧta a city of Syria **281.** 10

hau hail **19.** 12

hau , time, period **105.** 4; **228.** 1

hau to advance **244.** 9

see *er hau* **67.** 11

hau time **169.** 8, 11

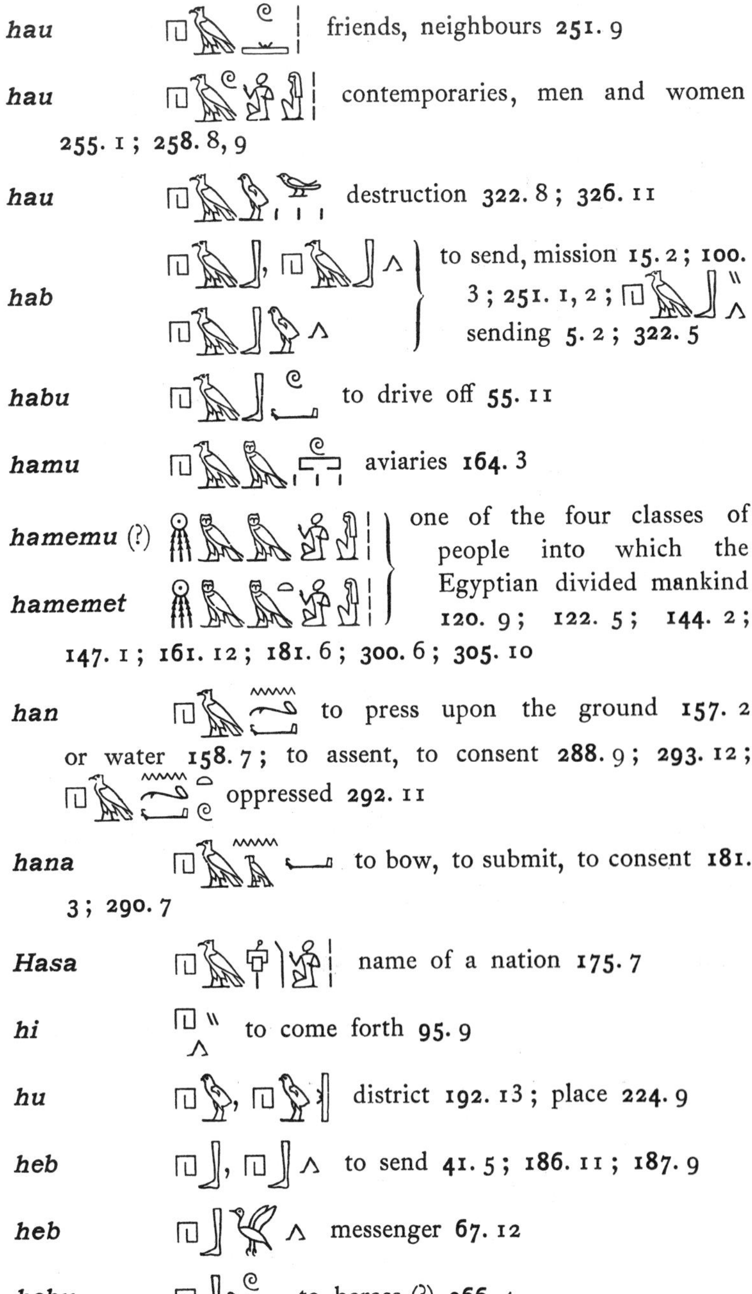

hau friends, neighbours 251. 9

hau contemporaries, men and women 255. 1; 258. 8, 9

hau destruction 322. 8; 326. 11

hab to send, mission 15. 2; 100. 3; 251. 1, 2; sending 5. 2; 322. 5

habu to drive off 55. 11

hamu aviaries 164. 3

hamemu (?) / *hamemet* one of the four classes of people into which the Egyptian divided mankind 120. 9; 122. 5; 144. 2; 147. 1; 161. 12; 181. 6; 300. 6; 305. 10

han to press upon the ground 157. 2 or water 158. 7; to assent, to consent 288. 9; 293. 12; oppressed 292. 11

hana to bow, to submit, to consent 181. 3; 290. 7

Hasa name of a nation 175. 7

hi to come forth 95. 9

hu district 192. 13; place 224. 9

heb to send 41. 5; 186. 11; 187. 9

heb messenger 67. 12

hebu to harass (?) 266. 4

hebt granary, storehouse **55.** 12; **56.** 5

hep, hepu , law **252.** 8; **260.** 8

hepu laws **248.** 12; scientific laws **234.** 7

hep-ui twice tied **267.** 8

hen to invoke **65.** 4; invocation **69.** 3

hen to incline (the head) in assent **44.** 13; **45.** 3; **46.** 9

hen sarcophagus **104.** 8

Heni Gracious one (?) **69.** 10

hennu praises **296.** 7; those who praise **295.** 13

her , peace, rest **241.** 3; **256.** 4

her ȧb to be content **223.** 1

heri ȧb rest, quietness **146.** 13; **155.** 13

heru gracious **63.** 9

h[r]u day **195.** 5; **225.** 10; **230.** 5; **232.** 6; **233.** 3; **234.** 2, 4

hru , day **3.** 1; **306.** 5; *hru neb* **2.** 6; **127.** 1; a happy day **46.** 9; unlucky day **202.** 5; daily **303.** 11; the first moment of day **254.** 4; **263.** 13

hru , days **3.** 3; **198.** 3; the five epagomenal days **234.** 2, 4

herp åb to be contented with 273. 1

hereret things which satisfy 128. 3

hert rest, peace 249. 13; welfare 263. 6

hert satisfaction (?) 103. 13

hert ťeṭ soft speech 261. 3

heh flame, fire 220. 9

hetetut those who sing praises 303. 13

heṭ to subdue, to overcome 141. 8; 202. 2; to vanquish 190. 1

heṭ defeat, overthrow 194. 2

heṭeh panic, terror 193. 4

Ḥ.

ḥa O, verily 201. 5

ḥa behind 137. 10; 238. 4

ḥa behind 11. 5; 50. 13; 53. 2; 54. 2; 60. 11; 69. 6; 136. 3; 181. 2; 250. 9; to put behind 264. 5

ḥai to weep 66. 12

ḥai papyrus 238. 4

ḥai rise (of the Nile) 232. 11

ḥai advantage, benefit 227. 9

ḥau part of a chariot 289. 4

ḥau more, increment, addition, besides 158. 2; 243. 8; 252. 11; 253. 11; 273. 12; 291. 13

ḥap
ḥapu to hide 216. 10; 327. 6

ḥap spy 137. 13

ḥapu spy 136. 8, 9

ḥaput spy 138. 10

ḥapt to embrace 51. 1

Ḥamaθȧ Hamath 280. 11

ḥanre obstacle, opposition 286. 6

ḥaq to capture, be captured 173. 8

ḥaqu captives 148. 9; 157. 6; 175. 10

ḥaθȧtu rain storms 74. 6

ḥā and 225. 6; 227. 1, 10; 228. 6; 229. 4; 233. 5; 234. 2, 6; 235. 3; 237. 10; 238. 12; 239. 7; 240. 7

ḥāu flowers 233. 4

ḥā
ḥāt limb, member, body 43. 3; 49. 7, 8; plur. 51. 3; 55. 3 (see *ḥāt*)

ḥā before, the front of, first, the beginning 42. 1; 49. 4; 76. 10; 254. 10 (see *ḥāt*) *ḥā* a title of very high rank 103. 5; 107. 4; 108. 7; 110. 2; fem. 111. 1

ḥāu , men holding the rank of *ḥā* 100. 4; 185. 10; 186. 8; 215. 1

ḥāā , , to rejoice, exultation 64. 13; 71. 5; 75. 5; 181. 2

ḥāāu , to rejoice 295. 12; 298. 10; 301. 10

ḥāāut joy 304. 7, 8, 9

ḥāu staff (?) 27. 1

ḥāuti , first, foremost 11. 1; 12. 4

ḥāutii divine preeminence 178. 10

ḥāuti leader 289. 11

ḥāuti leaders, governors 168. 14; 175. 13

ḥāutti best, finest 218. 1

ḥāp to hide (?) 221. 13

Ḥāp Apis bull 227. 1; 236. 3

Ḥāp a district near Sais 185. 6

Ḥāp ; *Ḥāpi* the Nile, the Nile-god 127. 1; 227. 13; 298. 6

ḥān with 42. 11; 43. 11; 44. 1; 45. 1; 46. 3; 46. 9; 47. 3

ḥāt the front (of an army) **100.** 4; brow **305.** 8; front of the neck **156.** 9; the bows of a boat **158.** 12; **210.** 1; those who lived in olden time **245.** 10; of olden time **246.** 1

ḥāti what is in front, the best, finest **215.** 12; **216.** 7; **222.** 3

ḥāt limb, member, body, person **29.** 2; **181.** 4; **277.** 9; **20.** 9

ḥāti heart **4.** 11; **17.** 5; **121.** 11; heart **28.** 9; courage **286.** 2; self:— himself **16.** 3; **28.** 4; plur. **300.** 2

ḥātut the two faces of the Sun-god **150.** 13

ḥāθȧ mattress **27.** 7

ḥu to strike, to fight against, to drive away **13.** 9; **94.** 6; **197.** 6; **248.** 6

ḥu to dash water after **22.** 4

ḥuaut to be sick, to stink **23.** 7

ḥuaut musty (of wine) **26.** 13

ḥu provisions (?) **298.** 5

ḥu entirely **106.** 2

Ḥu name of a god **75.** 1

Ḥui a proper name **319.** 5

ḥuire flowering trees **160.** 12

ḥufiťa to hasten **277.** 3

ḥun
ḥunnu } to refresh **123.** 7 ; **201.** 1

ḥun
ḥunnu } boy, a name of the Sun-god **50.** 6 ; **51.** 9 ; **295.** 6

Ḥunȧ a king of the IIIrd dynasty **244.** 1

ḥurā to do harm, to destroy, to expel **146.** 11 ; **170.** 2

ḥuru to curse **203.** 2 ; **248.** 1 ; **251.** 13

ḥuru ȧb odious (?), detestable (?) **248.** 6

Ḥurebasa a proper name **219.** 2

ḥurere flowers **17.** 6 ; **19.** 4 ; **21.** 9 ; **26.** 5 ; **150.** 13 ; **162.** 3 ; **164.** 5

ḥut to smite, to strike **249.** 10

ḥut to fashion **54.** 9

ḥututi a class of soldier servants **177.** 3 ; **320.** 9

ḥuťa
ḥuťaut } inlaid, encrusted **153.** 3,7 ; **155.** 3, 10 ; **156.** 7 ; **157.** 1 ; **163.** 3

Ḥuťaina a city in Syria **290.** 7

Ḥuťare Hazor (?) 280. 9

ḥeb 266. 13

ḥeb festival 42. 8; 49. 4; 82. 1; 93. 3; 112. 6; 131. 8; 194. 12; 195. 1

ḥebu festivals 157. 11; 233. 12

ḥeb to keep the festival 93. 5

ḥeb the book of the festival service 86. 1; 93. 13

ḥeb ȧpt the festival of Apt 195. 1, 3; 196. 9

ḥeb ur the "great" festival 112. 8

ḥebu en χen festivals wherein processions of the god formed a prominent part 236. 10

ḥebā to play as in a game, to jest 188. 6; , a game, a jest

ḥeberber to bow in homage 178. 9

ḥebs festivals 200. 5

ḥebs / *ḥebsu* clothing, apparel, garments 173. 13; 216. 5; 217. 7; 221. 12; 278. 5; 1. 6; 7. 2

ḥebs clothing, to be clothed 132. 13; 207. 8; 260. 9; 262. 13

ḥebs to cover the walls of a city by throwing up mounds 197. 8

ḥebs the cover of a vessel (?) **156.** 3, 4

ḥepu to disappear **288.** 5

ḥepḥep to turn **65.** 7

ḥept , to embrace, embrace, arms **57.** 2; **71.** 7; **237.** 9

ḥefnu , } hundreds of thousands **60.** 3; **148.** 4; **152.** 8; **168.** 7; **172.** 12; **173.** 12

ḥefennu

ḥemu (or *āβu*) } workmen **108.** 3; **206.** 10

ḥemut (or *ābut*) (?)

ḥemt (or *ābt*) the builder's craft **207.** 5

ḥemu , rudder **199.** 2; **261.** 13

ḥemi (?) to go away with **287.** 9

ḥems , } to sit down **2.** 11; **221.** 8; **241.** 5; to be encamped **135.** 6; to dwell **20.** 9; **186.** 8; sitting **245.** 8; sitting down to do the hair **5.** 6

ḥems , sitter **93.** 12; fem. **21.** 2

ḥemsu dwellers **250.** 1

ḥemt , wife, woman **1.** 4; **2.** 11; **37.** 9; plur. , **53.** 1; **223.** 11; mares **216.** 7

ḥemt coward, knave **190.** 8

ḥen and, along with 202. 7; 204. 1, 3

ḥenā with, and 2. 11; 45. 9; 102. 11

ḥen vase 217. 5

Ḥen a proper name 90. 13

ḥen to go in 241. 4

ḥen to go out 281. 4

ḥen to constrain 273. 1

ḥen to exhort, to admonish 188. 4; 200. 13; 214. 4

ḥen admonition 261. 8

ḥen order, command 262. 2

ḥen majesty 24. 9; 96. 8; 135. 1; 142. 1; 211. 4; 227. 5; 228. 4; fem. *ḥent* 236. 11

ḥen slave, servant 46. 6; 126. 10

ḥenu menservants 153. 11; 163. 8; 176. 3; servants male and female 46. 5

ḥent maidservants 153. 11; 163. 8; 247. 1

ḥen neter servant of the god, *i. e.*, priest 46. 10 (see also under *neter ḥen*).

ḥen ka priest of the *ka* or double 112. 4; 132. 3

ḥent / *ḥenut* mistress, lady 93. 1; 104. 10; 179. 10

ḥenuti labourer 2. 1

ḥenuḥ terror 48. 2

ḥennu measure 6. 2, 3; plur. 149. 1

ḥennu to run, to journey 5. 3; 24. 10

ḥennu phallus 15. 13

Ḥennu a name of the Sun-god 61. 6; 89. 5

ḥennu to proclaim 155. 5

ḥenk to make an offering, offering 153. 9; 160. 10

ḥenksti / *ḥenksti* women with dishevelled hair, *i. e.*, a name given to the two priestesses who personated Isis and Nephthys 50. 5; 53. 10; 58. 7

ḥent wife, mistress 42. 6; 58. 10

ḥent what is ordered by law 249. 3

ḥent to act with violence (?) 258. 6

ḥenti severity (?) 266. 7

ḥent animal emotion (?) 242. 1

Ḥenti a proper name 244. 8

ḥenti labourers, husbandmen 188. 1

ḥenti — two periods of 60 years 121. 1; 122. 6; 129. 5

ḥer — and 232. 6, 9; 236. 1; 237. 2; 240. 6

ḥer — to set in array 135. 12; 136. 3; 137. 10

ḥer — fear, terror 221. 7; 249. 5

ḥer — plain 227. 10

ḥer — a sign of the infinitive or participle, *passim*

ḥer — , , at 3. 12; 4. 12; by 5. 13; by way of 212. 11; on 13. 12; upon 26. 6; 87. 6; for, because of 4. 12; 98. 11; 242. 13; through 129. 7; in respect of 124. 12; on account of 43. 2; besides 320. 1; those on 99. 9; to the north 102. 13

ḥer ȧb — among 262. 10; within 215. 4; in the opinion of 42. 3; 98. 3, 4; 250. 7, 8; in my opinion 201. 1

ḥer ȧbu — , interior (plur.) 192. 6; 215. 4

ḥeri-ȧb — within, in 297. 12; 299. 2

ḥer ā — at once, straightway, instantly 43. 6; 46. 2; 203. 9; 205. 1; 238. 2

ḥer uat — he on the road, *i. e.*, traveller 101. 1

ḥer baḥ — before 64. 9

ḥer ḥer (or ḥrȧ) — because of, on behalf of 152. 5; 155. 7; 160. 2

ḥer er re-u } concerning them, for them 322. 5, 326. 8

ḥer ḥer er re-u

ḥer mā by 123. 4

ḥer ḳes at the side of 263. 7, 9

ḥer χeru beneath 127. 5

ḥer sa after, moreover 34. 6; 169. 11; 194. 11; according to 128. 7; by reason of, because of 53. 4; 69. 2; on the back of, *i. e.*, upon 3. 3

ḥer sa animals with young 166. 14

ḥer ṭep "on the head", *i. e.*, upon 80. 7; 144. 4; before (?) 233. 3; by himself 141. 2

ḥer above 65. 3

ḥer (or *ḥer ṭep*) chief, governor 66. 2; 110. 2; 267. 3

ḥer , chief 86. 9; 264. 6, 9; 268. 6

ḥeri chief 294. 4; 295. 2; 299. 2; 302. 1; plur. chiefs 100. 6

ḥer , } chief, president, master, captain 23. 5; 53. 2; 57. 8; 63. 8; 103. 4

ḥeru captains 159. 7; 176. 1; chiefs of foreign mercenaries 177. 2; chief of the transport 311. 5; captain of the guard 307. 9; 308. 1, 6; 315. 11; captains of the guard 315. 13; 320. 10

ḥeri besides, in addition to **281**. 7

ḥeri áb sanctuary **324**. 8

ḥeru except **10**. 1

ḥeru to go away **51**. 1; **53**. 4; **56**. 11; **63**. 5

ḥrá , face **44**. 11; **263**. 12; yellow face **52**. 12; plur. **59**. 13; **87**. 8; **88**. 4

ḥrá nebt
ḥrá nebu
ḥrá nebu neb } people, every body **240**. 11; **293**. 9; **301**. 1

ḥeri terror **70**. 5; **180**. 10

ḥerit terror **177**. 8

ḥeriut terror **251**. 10

ḥeri śefit the terrible one, a name of Rā **158**. 11

Ḥeri peṭemái a city near Memphis **211**. 10

Ḥeru , , } Horus **40**. 8; **52**. 2; **56**. 1, 7; **58**. 5; **61**. 8; **66**. 11; **69**. 12; **75**. 12; **108**. 5; **110**. 11; fem. **120**. 6

Ḥeru-á a proper name **40**. 4; **330**. 4, 5

Ḥerui the two Horus gods **123**. 8

Ḥeru-p-Rā Horus-Rā **76**. 11

Ḥeru nub "Horus the golden" **40.** 8; **108.** 5; **109.** 2; **114.** 5

Ḥeru-χuti "Horus of the double horizon", *i. e.*, Harmachis **41.** 2; **172.** 8

Ḥeru-χent-χateθ a proper name **216.** 1

Ḥeru-χent-χaθi a proper name **216.** 2

Ḥeru-ȧ-śerȧu a proper name **322.** 1; **325.** 10

ḥert sky, heaven **48.** 1; **104.** 13; **122.** 11; **295.** 8

ḥeru upper parts **73.** 11; things celestial **295.** 8

ḥert way **103.** 1

ḥer[u] seśeta "those over the mysteries", *i. e.*, a class of priests **226.** 1

ḥeru śā "those who are on the sand", *i. e.*, the dwellers in the desert **101.** 9; **102.** 7, 13

ḥert hall of a tomb **116.** 7

ḥert watercourse **119.** 2

ḥerti to transport **178.** 3; **179.** 1

ḥeḥ to seek **56.** 7; **59.** 4; **248.** 9

ḥeḥi to seek **301.** 1

ḥeḥ a long, indefinite period of time **60.** 6

ḥeḥ t'etta for ever and ever 64. 8; 81. 8

ḥeḥ en renput millions of years 88. 1; 147. 5; 133. 6; 327. 3 millions of times 291. 12

ḥes
ḥeset to sing, to praise, to recite 50. 2; 113. 7; hymned 53. 5

ḥes praise, song 241. 1; 273. 4

ḥeset praise 256. 3

ḥesti
ḥestu praise, praises 113. 4, 5

ḥesiu singers 239. 7, 9; 306. 11; 315. 2

ḥeset to please, pleasing, to be pleased with 98. 8

ḥesi ȧb to please 248. 4

ḥestu favour 184. 2

ḥesu favourable 259. 13

ḥeset favours, graciousness 117. 2; 274. 5

ḥesut act of grace 113. 12

ḥesi favoured one 107. 1; 133. 13; 183. 3; plur. 127. 10; 95. 9

ḥes will, pleasure 42. 7; 93. 11

ḥesesi will 250. 10

ḥessu favoured one 259. 9

ḥeseset pleasing things 128. 3

ḥesai ḥrȧ fierce-looking, savage, uncouth 284. 4

ḥesb a measure 6. 7

ḥesb something reckoned or computed "the very best *or* finest language that can be imagined" 246. 8

Ḥeseb-ka the XIth nome of Lower Egypt 185. 6; 192. 3

ḥesmen natron 211. 3

ḥesq to cut off 90. 13

ḥeken to adore, adored 108. 4

ḥekennu praise 88. 6; 297. 5; 302. 3

ḥeq to rule, to reign, to take possession of, to seize, to take 117. 3; 125. 8; 187. 12; 193. 9; 224. 11; rule 229. 6

ḥeq divine ruler, prince 170. 7; 171. 1; 172. 4; 182. 3; 323. 13; 324. 5

ḥeq prince 41. 3; 60. 6; 126. 4; 130. 3; plur. 106. 5; 100. 9

ḥeqt [hieroglyphs], [hieroglyphs] } princess 226. 10; 229. 10; 234. 11
ḥeqti [hieroglyphs] }

ḥeqa [hieroglyphs] governor 111. 1

ḥeqa [hieroglyphs] governorship 110. 8; [hieroglyphs] 111. 7

ḥequt [hieroglyphs] governors of cities 169. 9

ḥeq ḥet [hieroglyphs] governor of a temple 192. 7

ḥequ ḥet [hieroglyphs] [hieroglyphs] } governors of temples 100. 6; 185. 10; 186. 8; 192. 5

ḥeqer [hieroglyphs] hungry man 128. 4

ḥeqet [hieroglyphs], [hieroglyphs] beer 18. 2; 26. 12; 112. 3; 132. 4; 149. 4; 153. 9; 157. 13

ḥeqet [hieroglyphs] misery 221. 9

ḥet [hieroglyphs] lands 112. 4

ḥet [hieroglyphs] temple, palace 53. 8; 111. 2; plur. [hieroglyphs] 89. 1; [hieroglyphs] 100. 9; [hieroglyphs] chapters, or sections of a book 49. 4; 50. 2

ḥetut [hieroglyphs] temple buildings 155. 4

Ḥet [hieroglyphs] Diospolis parva 76. 4

ḥet āat [hieroglyphs], [hieroglyphs] "great house", palace 56. 4; 89. 3; 100. 5

ḥet āt [hieroglyphs], [hieroglyphs] "great house", palace 68. 1; 223. 7

Ḥet urt name of a city 187. 2

Ḥet-benben the temple of the two pylons 213. 10; 214. 2; 298. 12; 302. 9

Ḥet-bennu the capital of the XVIIIth nome of Upper Egypt 186. 2; 196. 5

Ḥet-Ptaḥ-ka "House of the Double of Ptaḥ", *i. e.*, a name of Memphis 143. 8; 174. 12

Ḥet-nub Alabastronpolis 105. 7

ḥetu nub smelting houses for gold 161. 6

ḥet ent ḥeḥ en renput "house of millions of years" 329. 12

Ḥet-Rā-usr-Maāt-meri-Ȧmen palace or temple of Rameses III. 317. 9; 330. 11; 331. 12; 332. 8

Ḥet-Rā-χeper-χeperu-ȧri-Maāt palace of Ȧi, a king of the XVIIIth dynasty 129. 12

Ḥet-ḥert Hathor 77. 11; 91. 2

Ḥet-ḥert the Hathor goddesses 20. 11

ḥet sȧs the "six houses" 97. 7

Ḥet-suten-ḥenen Heracleopolis 89. 11

Ḥet-seχem the capital of the VIIth nome of Upper Egypt 77. 11

ḥet-ka a *ka* temple 116. 9

ḥeta rags 221. 12

ḥetau masts, poles 208. 11

ḥeteb to lament 70. 9

ḥetep measure 6. 7

ḥetep sum total 6. 7; 167. 4, 10, 168. 7; 314. 9

ḥetep , peace 40. 2; 41. 9; contented, happy 252. 1

ḥetep to repose (of a statue) 148. 11; to rest (of the heart) 46. 7; to lie at peace (of a dead body) 134. 1; to set (of the sun) 11. 9; 64. 6

ḥetepu , to be satisfied 242. 5; contentment 259. 12; peace 146. 13; 295. 9; 299. 5

ḥetepet peace 46. 4; to be welcome 45. 12

ḥetep an altar or table for offerings 105. 8; 153. 2

ḥetepu offerings 63. 12; 72. 8; 73. 12; 118. 7; 127. 2; 262. 12; offerings legally due 166. 1

ḥetem
ḥetemet to stop, to be restrained 56. 10; 115. 11

ḥetemet hyaenas 276. 10; 283. 13

ḥeter
ḥetrȧ horses 25. 5; 36. 1; 169. 1; 216. 7; 285. 10; 286. 2; 287. 12

ḥetrȧi teams for ploughing 4. 1

ḥetrȧ to levy tribute, to become liable to pay tribute 148. 7; 158. 1; 173. 12; 199. 7; 202. 8

ḥetrȧt tax, tribute 228. 9

ḥetrȧ leaves of a door (?) 152. 5; 152. 6; folding doors (?) 161. 3; 176. 10

ḥetes to celebrate 196. 9; 197. 4

ḥetet shameful deed 15. 11

ḥeṭeb to slay 175. 7

ḥeť
ḥeťet to waste, to destroy 252. 13; 265. 7; 292. 3

ḥeť shrine 47. 13

ḥeť to become light, to shine 3. 1; 26. 8; to make bright 266. 5

ḥeť ta dawn, daybreak 13. 13

ḥeťet to illumine 71. 3; dawn 84. 4; 87. 3

ḥeťtu light, splendour 297. 5; 298. 9

ḥeť white 97. 10; 213. 5

ḥeť white metal, silver 30. 7; 73. 8; 149. 2

ḥeť
ḥeťet white crown, indicating Upper Egypt 88. 4; 93. 3; 123. 7; 142. 4; 297. 4

ḥeťeť [hieroglyphs] } radiance, light **74.** 6; **202.** 4

ḥeťeťa [hieroglyphs]

ḥeťennuna [hieroglyphs] to be sad, heavy (of the heart) **292.** 12

ḥeťeťu [hieroglyphs] abominable (?) **248.** 5

KH or CH (χ).

χa [hieroglyphs] thousand **130.** 8; plur. [hieroglyphs] **217.** 1

χa [hieroglyphs] to weigh, to measure **221.** 3

χa [hieroglyphs] to measure **125.** 2

χa [hieroglyphs] dead body **65.** 12; **78.** 7; **95.** 11

χa en ān [hieroglyphs] library, record chamber **332.** 11

χa en sbaut [hieroglyphs] chamber of the door **181.** 10

χaā [hieroglyphs] to leave, to forsake, to let go, to fall, to place, to fall upon **20.** 1; **28.** 11; **141.** 9; **169.** 6; **197.** 2; to throw **15.** 13; **18.** 10; **197.** 10; thrown aside, left **285.** 7; **315.** 7; **319.** 3; [hieroglyphs] thrown aside **285.** 8; **286.** 1

χaāā [hieroglyphs] slings **197.** 9

χaāmu [hieroglyphs] to afflict, to harm **177.** 7

χaāqu [hieroglyphs] } to cut, to shave, to wound **286.** 8; **292.** 13

χai [hieroglyphs] defeat **191.** 4; **192.** 10; **196.** 1

χai to enclose, to shut in **186.** 6

χai what is hateful **254.** 8

χaibit shadow **59.** 1; **67.** 8; **189.** 13; **199.** 1

χau to protect **57.** 4; **60.** 13; **67.** 1

χau various kinds of woods **41.** 10

χau spices made from woods **213.** 6; **224.** 6

χau mines (of copper) **178.** 12; **179.** 3

χau altars **189.** 11

χaui, *χaiui*, *χauti* altar, altars **131.** 10; **233.** 4; **235.** 12

χaut altar **128.** 1; **132.** 5

χaut carcase, dead body **304.** 5

χab to bend (?), to bow (?) **264.** 10

χabu to do homage **183.** 5

χapi, χapu, *χapui* figured designs or patterns in metal work **153.** 3; **156.** 13; **157.** 1; **161.** 4

χam to let fall **247.** 3

χames to bend, to turn aside **247.** 4; **264.** 6

χames ears of corn **238.** 3; **239.** 5

χames ears of corn **238.** 3; **239.** 5

Χanrieṭa a city in Syria **282.** 1

χar (?) name of a city **84.** 1

χare Syria **95.** 12; **180.** 12; **224.** 6

χare a Syrian **169.** 12

χareui a proper name **317.** 8

χarṭ, **χarṭet** boy, child **118.** 10; **129.** 10; **265.** 4

χarṭu children **175.** 12; **176.** 4; **243.** 4; **271.** 9, 12

χarti the two widows, *i. e.*, Isis and Nephthys **53.** 13

χas to be lowly, humble, feeble, sick, helpless **16.** 3; **252.** 3; **266.** 12; an evil thing **210.** 8; a brute of a man **241.** 11

χases to be in evil case (?) **248.** 2

χast evil **253.** 11

χas abominable folk **227.** 4

χasa to rest, to be at peace **255.** 4

χak åbu rebels **94.** 4; **170.** 12; **206.** 9; *χak-en-åbu* **90.** 13

χaker to decorate 57. 8

χakeru , decorations, ornaments 57. 8; 134. 8; 140. 1; 172. 9; a name of Rā 62. 3

χat sickness, failing 257. 12

χat , , womb, belly, body 40. 10; 41. 4; 45. 11; 50. 13; 51. 3; 130. 4; 184. 10; 242. 1. coolness, calm demeanour 258. 11; a man heated by anger 260. 4

Χati a proper name 113. 13; 115. 13

Χaṭumā a city in Syria 275. 12

χaṭbu to slay 11. 6; 12. 2; 13. 19; 14. 10; 15. 9

χaṭer decrepitude (?) 244. 10

χat' bread 101. 1

χāā, *χāāu* to be crowned 88. 4; 142. 4; crowned one (fem.) 120. 3

χāā , crown 172. 7; 237. 13; 296. 6; plur. , 40. 8; 119. 8; 120. 2

χāā , to rise like the sun 35. 9; 64. 8; 121. 2; 148. 13; 109. 9

χāāi , riser 90. 5; 150. 6

Χāā-em-Ȧpt a proper name 330. 9

χāā-em-Uast a proper name **307.** 2; **309.** 8; **316.** 4; **317.** 5; **330.** 7

χā-nefer the name of a pyramid **104.** 9

χāāi weapons, tools **207.** 4

χāāi-nu-rā, *χāāi-en-rā* tools for work **137.** 9; **191.** 2

χāāu wooden tools or weapons **27.** 3; **159.** 6; **180.** 12

χāāu some objects made of leather **288.** 4

Χāu disgraceful, shameful **241.** 7; **267.** 4

χāār, *χāāra* to rage furiously, rage **140.** 10; **194.** 4; **195.** 7; **197.** 3; **209.** 2

χā . . . . . (?) a kind of wood **118.** 3

χāātu inscribed **86.** 12

χi babe, child **51.** 8; **53.** 2, 11; **57.** 13; **58.** 1; **62.** 5

χi high, exalted **56.** 4; **176.** 9; **208.** 3

Χirebaȧ, *Χirebu* Aleppo **135.** 6; **137.** 2; **138.** 6; **276.** 2

χireqaθȧθȧt slippery places **288.** 1

χu to protect **85.** 1; **200.** 6; **211.** 1; **215.** 7

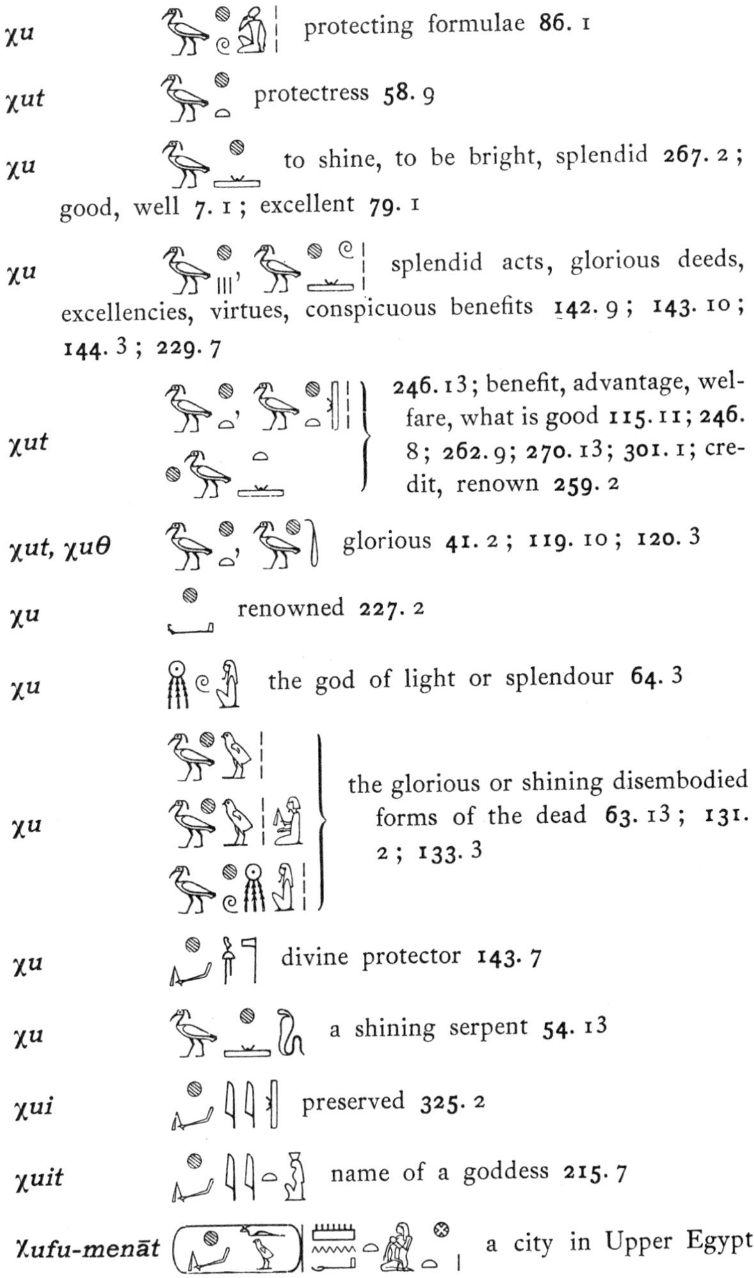

χu protecting formulae **86.** 1

χut protectress **58.** 9

χu to shine, to be bright, splendid **267.** 2; good, well **7.** 1; excellent **79.** 1

χu splendid acts, glorious deeds, excellencies, virtues, conspicuous benefits **142.** 9; **143.** 10; **144.** 3; **229.** 7

χut **246.** 13; benefit, advantage, welfare, what is good **115.** 11; **246.** 8; **262.** 9; **270.** 13; **301.** 1; credit, renown **259.** 2

χut, χuθ glorious **41.** 2; **119.** 10; **120.** 3

χu renowned **227.** 2

χu the god of light or splendour **64.** 3

χu the glorious or shining disembodied forms of the dead **63.** 13; **131.** 2; **133.** 3

χu divine protector **143.** 7

χu a shining serpent **54.** 13

χui preserved **325.** 2

χuit name of a goddess **215.** 7

Χufu-menāt a city in Upper Egypt **110.** 9; **111.** 11

χut horizon 64. 1; 82. 8; 121. 3

χuti the god of the two horizons 120. 3

χuti double horizon 148. 13; 152. 12

χut ḥeḥ "eternal horizon", a name of the tomb of Amenophis I. 309. 2

χut śetat "hidden horizon", *i. e.*, part of a temple 151. 3

χuti spirit, demon 43. 13; 46. 3; 47. 4

χeb to diminish (?), to hinder (?) 252. 12

χeba in spite of 36. 5

χebait cave, hole, den 52. 3

χeben defect 271. 3

χebχeb vase, vessel 216. 7; 219. 7

χebṭ evil, restraint 253. 13

χebṭet evil deeds 271. 1

χep to die 52. 5

χep to happen, being, existing 228. 3; 230. 5; 231. 1; 233. 8; 263. 6

χepen fat 149. 4; 164. 3

χeperȧ the god of creation 120. 3; 170. 10

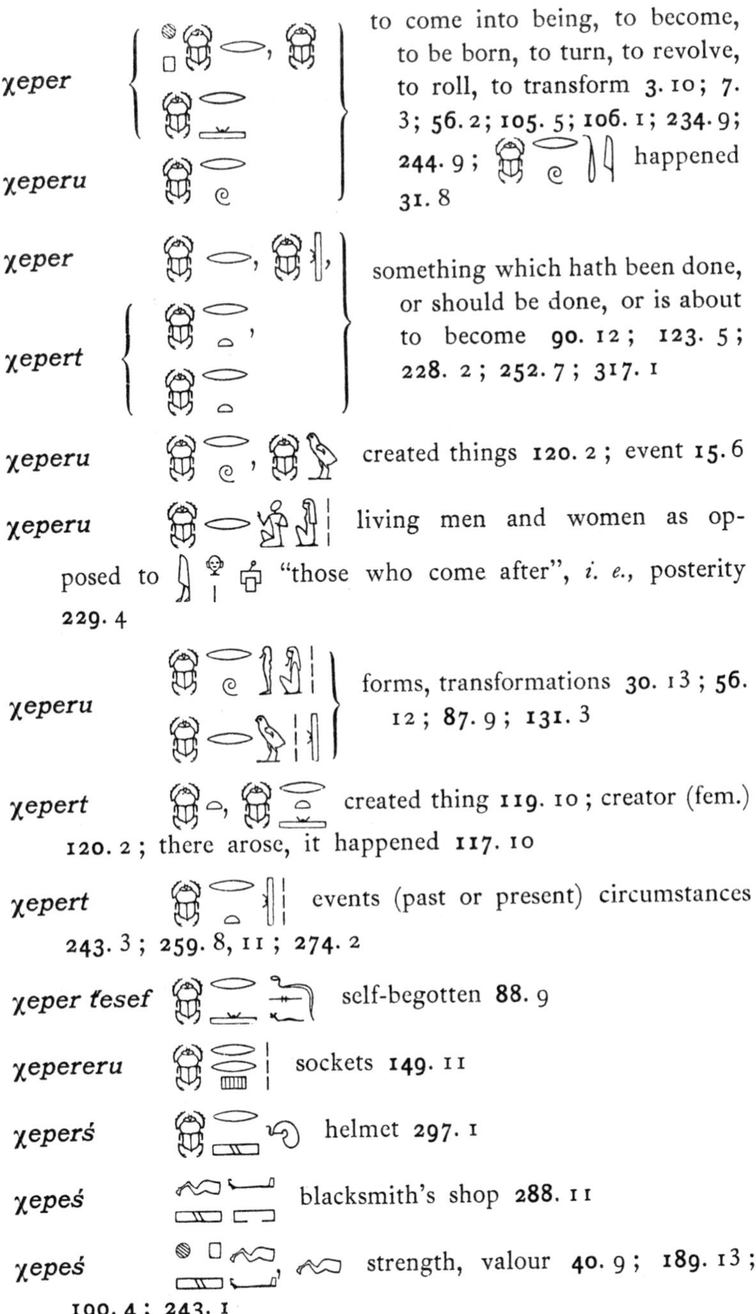

χeper — to come into being, to become, to be born, to turn, to revolve, to roll, to transform **3.** 10; **7.** 3; **56.** 2; **105.** 5; **106.** 1; **234.** 9; **244.** 9; happened **31.** 8

χeperu

χeper — something which hath been done, or should be done, or is about to become **90.** 12; **123.** 5; **228.** 2; **252.** 7; **317.** 1

χepert

χeperu — created things **120.** 2; event **15.** 6

χeperu — living men and women as opposed to "those who come after", *i. e.*, posterity **229.** 4

χeperu — forms, transformations **30.** 13; **56.** 12; **87.** 9; **131.** 3

χepert — created thing **119.** 10; creator (fem.) **120.** 2; there arose, it happened **117.** 10

χepert — events (past or present) circumstances **243.** 3; **259.** 8, 11; **274.** 2

χeper ťesef — self-begotten **88.** 9

χepereru — sockets **149.** 11

χeperś — helmet **297.** 1

χepeś — blacksmith's shop **288.** 11

χepeś — strength, valour **40.** 9; **189.** 13; **190.** 4; **243.** 1

χef — to seize 174. 2

χeft — 255. 6; 262. 8

χefti
χefti
χeftet
— enemy, enemies, foes 65. 5; 92. 3; 146. 4; 297. 7; 303. 10

χeft — when, at that time, according to, opposite, before 107. 10; 151. 3; 170. 10; 188. 6; 216. 8; 243. 13; 260. 6

χeft ḥu — conformably 106. 2, 13

χeftu — similar 113. 4 *(bis)*

χefti — when 228. 2

χefṭ — at, during 44. 4

χemu — breezes 61. 2

χem — to be ignorant, not to know, to come to an end, to finish 186. 12; 201. 4; 222. 12; 242. 2; without wanting 189. 8; ignorance, inability 249. 11

χem — an ignorant man 125. 3; 246. 11; plur. 246. 7

χem χet — an incapable man 247. 7

χemet — to disregard 124. 12; oblivion, ignorance 221. 5; 255. 2; 270. 13

χemu — secret places 304. 11

Xemennu the city of Hermopolis 193. 8; 197. 7; 200. 1

Xemennu the "eight" gods of Hermopolis 200. 2

Xemennu eight 87. 3

χemt three 6. 7; 87. 3; third 76. 4; *em χemt* as a third person 317. 13

χemt copper, bronze (?) 147. 8; 149. 2; 152. 10; 155. 8; 199. 10; 224. 5; 240. 8; copper mines 178. 12; copper ingots 179. 7

χemti worker in metals, coppersmith 317. 7; 318. 7; 319. 8; 330. 9; 331. 11; 332. 8

χen insincerity (?) 258. 13

χen, **χeni** interior, within, inner court 57. 11; 99. 13; 117. 11; 118. 6; 196. 5; 241. 2; 322. 2

χennu inner apartment of a house 256. 13; the interior of a barge 98. 1; the interior of a city 206. 2; an abode 249. 13; court, palace 104. 2

χen to transport 150. 7; transporting 171. 10

χen a periplus 236. 12; 237. 2

χen Ȧusȧr a periplus of Osiris 238. 9

χen to cause to advance **261**. 6

χen

χeni to hover, to alight, to flutter over **56**. 3; **68**. 11; **127**. 3

χennu

χenȧ to be fettered **127**. 9

χenȧ , prison, place of restraint **84**. 1; **322**. 2

χenȧr shut in **131**. 4

χnem , to unite, to be united to, to attain to **55**. 3; **123**. 11; **127**. 11; to build up, to join together **51**. 5

χnem one who is united to another, spouse **119**. 8

Χnemu the god who formed man **20**. 6

Χnemu-ḥetep a proper name **107**. 5; **113**. 12; **115**. 5, 13; **117**. 10

χnemu a wooden object in fish-pools **168**. 9

χenem smell, odour, stink **197**. 12

χenem to be drowsy, to sleep **277**. 11

χenemem waiting-women **38**. 6; **93**. 4

χenemes the manner and habits of a man of good birth (?), to treat with respect **256**. 12; **265**. 8; **266**. 1

χenemes[u] men of high birth and rank **257.** 1; **266.** 12

χnemet well, cistern **176.** 6

χeneniu carriers **133.** 10

χenenet , to sweep away **112.** 11; disturbed, broken **248.** 11

χennu to cry out **224.** 9

χennu priests, prophets, singers **200.** 4

χennu child **117.** 6

χennu , sailors **191.** 1; **206.** 13

χennu relatives **54.** 4; **55.** 5

χennus a kind of bird **300.** 9

χenrei reins (?) **275.** 7; **287.** 11; **291.** 13

χenχen to run away terrified **296.** 3

χenχen to leap towards **305.** 9

χenχen Middle Egypt (?) **186.** 13

χensu name of a god **77.** 2; **143.** 2; **144.** 7

Χensu pa àri seχer "Khensu the worker of plans" **44.** 12; **45.** 5, 6; **46.** 4; **47.** 2

Χensu nefer-ḥetep name of a god **44.** 6; **45.** 4; **48.** 10

χenś to stink **293**. 8

χent transportation **157**. 4

χent to sail up the river **185**. 9; **193**. 7; **224**. 6

χent image **120**. 9

Χent a country of Western Asia **148**. 8; **164**. 6

χent to be shut up, closed **245**. 7

χent court, inner chamber (?) **96**. 10

χent , , before, forward, at the head of **49**. 5; **53**. 8; **54**. 5; **99**. 11; **103**. 5; **108**. 2; **120**. 11; **273**. 9; **117**. 9; **113**. 1

χenti , acting as chief of **128**. 10; **228**. 3; **294**. 7, 8; **302**. 12
χentet

χentet first rank or grade **235**. 12; forerunner **230**. 8

χentu pre-eminence, exalted condition **252**. 5; **264**. 3

Χent-nefer a city in the Delta **219**. 4

Χent-χatθi a proper name **215**. 6

χenta , lake, reservoir **106**. 3, 10

χentȧ sepulchres **66**. 13

χenti shrine **153**. 6

χentua to advance **135**. 8

χenti } drawing nigh, advancing 50. 8; 280. 2

χentiθi

χenteś to be fettered 71. 8; 72. 3

χenteś a kind of tree 158. 6

χenṭ to tread, to walk 54. 12; 75. 2

χenṭ steps of an altar 213. 11

χenṭ dignified walk 128. 7

χenṭu } to advance 175. 9; 261. 9

χenti

χer cemetery, tomb 306. 6; 307. 10; 308. 2; 316. 1; 318. 3

χer en āḥā storehouse for funereal appliances 319. 1

χer , to subdue, to be subdued 81. 6; 175. 4

χer , to fall down 69. 12; 135. 2, 10; 262. 10; wretched one 135. 2, 10; 140. 8; 141. 3

χer slain 203. 4

χerit misery 228. 3

χer under, in the reign of 96. 8; 97. 1; 306. 1; under the majesty of, in the reign of 126. 3; 130. 1; 134. 3; 225. 4; 244. 7

χer by, with, from, now, with reference to 6. 10; 7. 7; 42. 2; 50. 3; 128. 11; 168. 14; 246. 10

χertu as for, now, with reference to 1. 1; 49. 6; 138. 13; 161. 10; 183. 10

χer år now, then 1. 3; 170. 4; 318. 6

χer, **χeri** under, with, having 6. 5; 12. 6; 19. 2; 42. 10; 121. 7; 179. 6; 324. 10; for 210. 8; by reason of 269. 7; lower (?) 127. 5; 157. 1

χer to have, to hold, to possess 83. 8; 85. 9; 93. 2; one possessed of (a devil) 43. 13; possessor 1. 3; with 179. 1; having grain 4. 4

χer renpit yearly 235. 1

χer hru, **χert hru** that which hath the day, *i. e.*, daily 95. 6; 151. 7; 154. 1; 303. 10

χeru things terrestrial 295. 8

χer-ā under the hand, *i. e.*, in charge of 97. 12

χer ḥāt before, in front of, formerly, originally 100. 4; 118. 12; 144. 12; 169. 9; 227. 8; 230. 13; 231. 2; 238. 9

χer ḥeb the man who hath the service book, reader, title of a priest 50. 4; 62. 13; 86. 9; *χer ḥeb ṭep* the chief reader 213. 8; plur. 129. 5

χeru provisions 239. 12; 240. 1

χer-āba a city near Memphis 212. 8; 219. 5

χerāba (?) to fight, to do battle with 304. 11

χeru voice, to cry 72. 2; 80. 6; 90. 9

χeru low-lying lands (?) 114. 13

χeruu forces 141. 3

χerui foes, enemy 54. 9; 180. 11; 193. 8; 286. 4; 278. 10

χerp to rule 227. 10; to lay under tribute 169. 13; to be master or foreman of 108. 2; 119. 5; to undertake 122. 10; 125. 12; to be in front 141. 1; to do more than some one else 41. 11; ruler 126. 4; 130. 2; to offer 183. 7; *χerp ȧb* to be superior 247. 3

χert affairs, dictates 121. 12; 265. 10

χert things which belong to, goods, possessions 202. 7; 258. 7; things 87. 3

χerti provisions 300. 10

χerti mason, worker with a chisel or graver 312. 5

χersek to remove 49. 8; 57. 1; 71. 9

χeχ to run 58. 11; 69. 1

χeχ throat 94. 7; 217. 3

χeχut neck 35. 10

χesasa to hasten 292. 8

χesbeṭ
χesbeṭet lapis-lazuli 35. 10; 216. 4; real lapis-lazuli 303. 2

χesef [hieroglyphs] to meet, to come upon some one **54**. 1; **262**. 2; to go with hostile intent, to fight against, to be in opposition to **98**. 8; **243**. 3; **249**. 6; to repulse **54**. 4; **55**. 7; to be repulsed **248**. 7; [hieroglyphs] repulsed **206**. 3

χesefet [hieroglyphs] obstacles **265**. 5, 7

χesef-ā [hieroglyphs] to resist the power of **187**. 1

χesteb [hieroglyphs] lapis-lazuli **41**. 10; **73**. 5

χet [hieroglyphs] thing **42**. 3; **187**. 8; property **201**. 10; a matter (*i. e.*, expedition) **99**. 9; a trial, a judicial enquiry **97**. 4; **98**. 11; plur. [hieroglyphs] wealth, property, things **8**. 8; **61**. 5; **123**. 5; **170**. 2; **252**. 8; **253**. 2

χet neter tauit [hieroglyphs] the produce of the lands on each side of the Red Sea **177**. 9

χet en ķer [hieroglyphs] things of the cemetery **315**. 9

χet Qemt [hieroglyphs] products of Egypt **177**. 4

χet [hieroglyphs] to engrave **230**. 2; inscribed **240**. 7

χeti [hieroglyphs] inscribed **149**. 9; **152**. 11; **154**. 10; **155**. 2; **156**. 2; **164**. 7

χet [hieroglyphs] wood, timber **106**. 7; **168**. 9; stick, canon **261**. 2; walking stick **319**. 13; staff (of life) **63**. 12

χet en ānχu [hieroglyphs] plants which yield life-stuffs **295**. 5; **300**. 6

χetu [hieroglyphs] masts **208**. 11

χet, *χeti*, *χetχet* } to retreat 175. 8; 194. 10; 278. 4; to turn back 55. 12

χet to follow; *ȧmu χet* those in the train of 122. 4 (see *em χet*)

χet across 299. 8

χet to investigate 122. 6

χet fire, heat 52. 3; 53. 8; 102. 1; 199. 3; 219. 10; 304. 4

χet ford 276. 4; 277. 5

χet āa a kind of goose 167. 12

χeta a country in Western Asia 135. 3; 136. 1; 137. 1; 140. 1; 141. 3; 275. 11

χetem } to close, to shut 185. 11; shut 202. 13; shut 204. 13; a shut in place, a fort, a citadel 202. 13; 223. 3; 290. 8; a closed in place (?) 290. 2

χetem , fortresses 203. 12; 205. 7

χetem , to seal 204. 4; ring, seal 214. 4; 230. 3

χetχet to break in pieces 315. 6

χeṭ to float or sail down the Nile 104. 13; 134. 9; 136. 5; 140. 6

χeṭ ford 279. 7

χeṭer (or *χeṭrȧ*) shame (?) 242. 9

S.

s she, her, it 5. 10 *et passim*; they 108. 3; their 127. 2

s they, them, their 108. 3; 127. 2; 227. 6

s *senb* health, in *q. v.*

sa person, one of a number 95. 11; 250. 1; one thousand men 257. 5; fem. a maiden 42. 2; 96. 2; plur. women 49. 7

sa en åqer a wise man, a man of high rank 252. 4; 253. 4

sa en Ābu a man of Elephantine (as opposed to a man of the Delta) 293. 5

sa en åtḥu [] a man of the papyrus swamps, *i. e.*, a man of the Delta 293. 5

sa neb every one 169. 6; any body 96. 5

sa son 41. 1

sa son 116. 4; 246. 10; 270. 6; fem. , daughter 42. 1; 45. 2; 68. 8; 225. 9

sa Rā , "son of the Sun", a royal title 142. 2; "daughter of the Sun" 119. 8

Sa-Rā-ån-āa a royal name 310. 3

sa (?) earth 208. 9

sa goose 38. 3

Sa the city of Sais 206. 12

sa a measure 125. 2

sa to protect 81. 7

sa , protection 45. 1; 80. 10; *sau* protectors 69. 5

sa a grade or order of priests 76. 4; 78. 1; 230. 4; plur. 231. 1

sa wall-tower 186. 7

sa , amulet, ornament, spell, charm 46. 1; 93. 9; 217. 4

sa back, side, body 58. 8; 247. 4; 258. 13; see *em sa*

sa to guard against 251. 3

sa , to see, to know 259. 11; to recognise 185. 1; recognised 185. 1; divine knowledge 121. 11

sa, *sat* knowledge 249. 9; renown 298. 5

sa to fill, to satisfy, to be satisfied 251. 9; 268. 9; satiety 262. 10; 268. 7

sau, *sau*, *sauu* to watch, to guard, to protect, protector 120. 5; 123. 3; 257. 2; 287. 1; 318. 9; 325. 4

sau-ā weak of arm, *i. e.*, feeble one **189**. 9

sau reṭui watcher of the two feet, *i. e.*, follower **185**. 10; **187**. 5; **192**. 7

saȧu keepers, guards **11**. 13; **159**. 13

sau walls **196**. 1; **202**. 12; **208**. 1; **210**. 5

sau to be filled with food **180**. 13

sau surfeit **246**. 3

Sau the city of Sais **73**. 1; **84**. 6

Sau name of a god **84**. 6

saub to teach, to instruct, to inform **243**. 2; **261**. 6; **263**. 8; **272**. 9

Saāaire name of a people **174**. 1

sauababa to go round about **283**. 4

sai to see **287**. 3

Sa . . . aire a city in Syria **290**. 11

sab judge **97**. 3; *sab ȧr Neχen* a judge belonging to the city of Nekhen **97**. 3; **98**. 6; **99**. 4

sap to dig **118**. 8

sam to gather (flowers) **130**. 12

sam couch **47**. 12; platform **203**. 5

sam hair **92**. 6

sam to make clear **58.** 12

sam phallus **51.** 12; **53.** 9; **60.** 5; **67.** 7

sam to unite **58.** 13; **123.** 8

sam ta union with the earth, *i. e.*, burial **65.** 9

samu composition **155.** 8

samu to join, to unite **170.** 1

Sam-beḥuṭet the XVIIth nome of Lower Egypt **218.** 7

saheh loathing (?) **266.** 9

saḥ passage **285.** 1

Saḥu Orion **82.** 13

saḥu neighbours **264.** 12

saq to collect **260.** 11; with to collect the senses, to confine the attention **260.** 11

saqu to act haughtily **266.** 2

saḳa to march **282.** 13

saḳa a piece of sackcloth **287.** 7

Sati, Satet name of a goddess **92.** 1

Sat Sais **192.** 8

sat ground **157.** 2; domain, estate **163.** 1

satu [hieroglyphs] earth, earth's surface 296. 8; 301. 13

sat [hieroglyphs], [hieroglyphs]
satet [hieroglyphs] } to shoot arrows, to send forth to emit rays of light 102. 1; 197. 9; 245. 12; 261. 13; 283. 1

satetiu [hieroglyphs] archers 197. 9

sat, satu [hieroglyphs], [hieroglyphs]
sati [hieroglyphs]
satuu [hieroglyphs] } beams of light, rays, radiance 74. 7; 81. 10; 95. 10; 121. 1; 163. 6; 297. 5

sati [hieroglyphs] to emit water 83. 5

sat [hieroglyphs]
sati [hieroglyphs] } to sow seed, to beget, to fecundate 52. 12; 83. 13

satet [hieroglyphs]
sat [hieroglyphs] } seed 96. 3; 224. 13; [hieroglyphs] emanations 57. 1

sat-tu-f [hieroglyphs] a man of a lascivious nature 257. 7

Sati [hieroglyphs] Asiatics 163. 8

satii [hieroglyphs] vases 153. 8

sata [hieroglyphs] adoration 93. 7

sata [hieroglyphs], [hieroglyphs] adorations 55. 11; 93. 3

sati [hieroglyphs]
satet [hieroglyphs] } ornamental or festal garments 226. 2; 237. 9

Satet [hieroglyphs] Asia 126. 4; 130. 2; 227. 6

Satetti [hieroglyphs] Asiatic lands 197. 1

saθ a barge **97.** 13 ; **105.** 2

saθ to bring (?), to carry (?) **106.** 6

sabu jackals **275.** 5

sȧbet the making of strife **257.** 13

sȧp to count, to reckon **109.** 13 . **199.** 8 ; **204.** 4 ; to decree **214.** 5 ; to provide for **112.** 3 ; to examine, to make an inventory of **201.** 10 ; **306.** 8 ; examination, scrutiny **309.** 1 ; **310.** 1 ; **311.** 12

sȧp visitor **89.** 7

sȧn material for sealing **214.** 3

sȧn, ***sȧnnu*** to hasten **5.** 9 ; **188.** 7, 10 ; **222.** 5

sȧnnu to pay for something **287.** 5

sȧs six **82.** 1

ses (?) sixty **105.** 11

sȧṭ heap **179.** 6

seāa to magnify **183.** 6

seāu to curse, to cry out excitedly **264.** 13

seāuur to make to conceive **58.** 2

seāb to purify **170.** 13 ; **211.** 3 ; **213.** 1 ; **–36.** 1

sāb ornaments, jewellery **25.** 6

seāmu to give to eat **145.** 12

seān to bring back **25.** 5

seānχ , to feed, to vivify **63.** 10; **116.** 1; **295.** 5; **298.** 7

seānχ to carve a life-like image **149.** 8

seānṭ to break in upon **247.** 5

seār to be brought **133.** 11

sāḥ to become ennobled **110.** 13; governorship **111.** 4

sāḥ nobleman **97.** 8; plur. **113.** 1

sāḥ dignity, honour **116.** 6; **263.** 1

seāḥā , to raise up, to exalt **81.** 11; **244.** 2; to set up (a statue) **237.** 4

sāḥu , the glorified form or spiritual body of the dead, mummy **58.** 3; **64.** 5

seāśt to multiply **53.** 9; **62.** 12; **149.** 3; **157.** 5

seāq to make to enter **195.** 5

sāqḥu (or **seqḥu**) to build **158.** 4; **176.** 11, 12

sāk to capsize, to overturn **199.** 2

su , , he, him, it **1.** 3; **15.** 5; **50.** 12; **109.** 3; **120.** 2; **186.** 1; they **63.** 9

su ṭesef he himself **144.** 12; **213.** 13

seua to make to depart, to go to a distance, to

seuat be remote 254. 5; 263. 12; 271. 5; to commit an excess 242. 1, 4

seuaḥ to be firm, to make to remain or endure 123. 10; 256. 12; 259. 5

seuaś to worship, to adore, to praise 42. 1; 64. 12; 131. 12; 142. 8; 144. 10

seuaṭ to transmit in a flourishing condition 129. 9

suut to travel, to walk about 127. 2

seun to atone for 260. 8

sununnu blandishment 284. 5

sunsun to make supplication 220. 7

seur to increase 229. 9, 12

surȧ to drink 2. 11; 29. 7; 126. 10; 131. 5; 242. 4

surṭ to build up 165. 13

suha to frighten 291. 7

suḥt egg 41. 5; 64. 1; 120. 3; 185. 2; 201. 7; 300. 8

suḥt egg 90. 12

suχu 265. 6

seuseχ to widen 173. 2

seuseχ-θ walking boldly with long steps **180**. 5

sutut
sutsut } to walk about, to frequent, to come **162**. 1 ; **280**. 13

suten , , } king, king of Upper Egypt **97**. 6 ; **111**. 4 ; **115**. 7 ; **200**. 7 ; **202**. 6 ; **211**. 6 ; **214**. 4

sutenet queen **122**. 4

suteniu , kings **105**. 4 ; **191**. 8 ; **215**. 1

suteniu ṭepāu , royal ancestors **228**. 4 ; **306**. 9 ; **314**. 6

suteni ,
suteniut , } reign, sovereignty **40**. 8 ; **120**. 10 ; **155**. 5 ; **174**. 9 ; **179**. 2

suten ȧpt royal harem **97**. 6 ; **98**. 11 ; **99**. 6

suten ȧpt women of the royal harem **198**. 6

suten ābu (or **ḥemu**) royal workman **34**. 4

suten ābuu royal inspector (?) **307**. 2 ; **309**. 8, 11 ; **316**. 4, 7 ; **317**. 5 ; **323**. 4 ; **329**. 13 ; **330**. 2 ; **331**. 4

suten uȧa royal barge **171**. 11

suten per , royal palace **35**. 12 ; **115**. 9 ; **200**. 8 ; **223**. 12 ; **224**. 1

suten mesu royal children **317**. 3 ; **319**. 1 ; **320**. 6 ; **324**. 13

suten mut royal mothers **317**. 4 ; **320**. 6 ; **324**. 12

suten net (or ***bȧt***) king of the North and South **40.** 9; **60.** 7; **126.** 5; **130.** 3; plur. **95.** 8

suten reχ , royal kinsman (?) **107.** 4; **133.** 7; **215.** 3

suten ḥemt , royal woman, queen **37.** 9; **42.** 4; **98.** 11; chief royal wife **312.** 11

suten ḥemt , queens, royal women **198.** 5, 6, 8; **200.** 9; **317.** 3; **320.** 6; **324.** 12

suten ḥenu royal servants **199.** 7

Suten ḥenen Heracleopolis **89.** 11; **91.** 8; **186.** 4; **191.** 7; **201.** 12

Suten ḥet capital of the XVIIth nome of Upper Egypt **186.** 3

suten sa royal son, prince **38.** 10; plur. fem. **198.** 6, 9; **200.** 9

suten sent , royal sisters **198.** 7, 9

suteniu śesu / ***sutennu*** (?) royal linen, fine linen **179.** 11; **216.** 5; **217.** 7

Suteχ name of a god **141.** 4

seuťa , to make strong, to keep safe and sound **72.** 5; **165.** 6; **178.** 1; **227.** 8

seuťā to make happy **227.** 11

sifi son, child 182. 13

simu field produce, green herbs 2. 8; 153. 13; 160. 1; 295. 5; 300. 5

Siȧna a city in Syria 282. 5

Sire-uah a proper name 294. 1

sirei bearers of fans or fly-flappers 330. 5

Seb, Sebu the god of the earth 53. 12; 62. 2; 171. 6

Seb (?) the god of the earth 68. 9

seb to send, to traverse, to march 142. 6; 187. 12; 188. 4

sba to teach, to instruct 118. 12; 245. 13; 246. 7; 262. 8; 268. 3; instruction 267. 3

sbait, sbaitu wisdom, instruction, teaching, correction 244. 6; 281. 5; 326. 7

sbauu punishment 329. 2

sba door 12. 6, 9; 101. 5; 118. 4; 132. 10

sbaut door 329. 6; 11. 5

sebau doors 104. 12; 116. 2; 203. 5

sebaut 150. 5; 152. 6; 161. 3; folding doors 163. 2

seba (?) gate (?) 211. 5; 213. 9

sebat (?) part of a chariot, socket (?) 285. 8

sebȧ hostile (?), rebellious (?) 186. 9

sebȧu the Fiend, foes, devils 54. 4; 55. 9; 56. 5; 66. 1; 206. 8; 297. 8; 304. 3

sebȧθ provisions (?) 229. 1

sebeχtut pylons 95. 2

Sebek-ānχ a proper name 117. 8

Sebek-em-sa-f a king of the XIIIth dynasty 312. 2; 324. 3

sebti
sebtet wall, walls, ramparts 147. 11; 162. 7; 176. 8; 185. 11; 197. 8; 205. 5; 208. 3

Sep name of a god 212. 12

sep a time; *sep sen* twice 3. 11; 13. 9; *sep ftu* four times 45. 5; 102. 6; , *sep tep* primeval time 42. 8; 121. 5; 195. 4; 206. 2; season 241. 5; period 257. 11; time, turn 261. 13; occasion, opportunity 265. 9, 12, 13; a case, matter 263. 10; duty 263. 9; work 107. 7; manner (?) 121. 6; fortune, luck, ill-luck, destiny 7. 13; 201. 5; *sep uā* altogether 173. 9; at a blow 175. 4; plur. occasions 259. 12; dispositions 229. 3 ; abilities 115. 10 ; in a crushing manner 266. 3 ; prosperity, success 268. 6 ; favourable opportunity 248. 9 ; the time of the things of the day 253. 1

sep to leave, to remain 194. 5

sepi, *sepit* remnant, remainder 175. 10 ; 192. 12 ; 193. 4 ; 194. 5 ; 278. 7

sper, *speru* to go or come out, a going forth 8. 3 ; 9. 6 ; 18. 8 ; 43. 12 ; 55. 3 ; 134. 9 ; 136. 5 ; 177. 7 ; 198. 4

speruu plaintiff 256. 5, 9

sper, speru, *spert* words, utterances 13. 4 ; 115. 4 ; 133. 12

sepeḥu to drive away 70. 13

sepeχa to divide, to separate 222. 1

sept , nome 57. 5 ; 60. 9 ; 185. 5 ; plur. , 85. 8 ; 93. 8 ; 185. 11 ; 186. 1 ; 206. 7

sept 105. 12

septi , the two lips 268. 12 ; 272. 12

sept plinths (?), bases (?) 156. 13

septet edge of a vessel, lip, rim 156. 2

sepṭ , to be provided with **77.** 1; **181.** 11; **227.** 3; **241.** 3

sepṭu those endowed with things, *i. e.*, the wealthy **254.** 9; **255.** 5

sepṭu things provided (by God) **264.** 4

sepṭ rations, provisions **173.** 13

Sepṭet Sothis **131.** 9

sepṭ ḥrà to watch diligently **254.** 5; **257.** 3

sepṭ, ***sepṭeṭ*** to set in order **170.** 11; **171.** 2

sef yesterday **245.** 4

sef to suffer vexation **263.** 10; to be longsuffering **54.** 8

sefa to be idle, slack **253.** 3

sefat disgust (?) **256.** 4

sefi babe **82.** 12; **88.** 5

sefu to annoy **258.** 8

sefenṭ knife, dagger **15.** 12

sefeχ to flee, to escape, to put off **59.** 1; **189.** 7; **262.** 5

seft oil **207.** 8

sefeṭ knife, dagger **287.** 10

sem a kind of priest 192. 8

sem, **semu**, **semi** to lead, to guide, leader, guide, director 75. 9; 88. 7; 92. 1; 114. 4; 121. 8; 195. 2; 198. 11; 248. 8; 281. 5

sem action 255. 6; conduct 252. 4

semi leader 255. 13; a leader of peace, *i. e.*, peacemaker 256. 4

sma to slay 102. 2; 103. 2; 141. 5; 193. 2; 200. 1

semaā, **semaāu** to make an offering or to offer a sacrifice legally due 112. 2; 170. 3; 215. 7

semaāu decrees, something ordered 236. 3

semaāt to cry out for justice 13. 1

semau to make new 271. 9

smam to please 253. 4

semam, **smamu** to kill, to slay, to break, to cut 169. 9; 173. 4; 220. 3; 285. 10; a killing 170. 12

smat (?) festival of the halfmonth 112. 10; 131. 8

smȧ to report, to declare, to announce, to give an order 139. 8; 194. 1; 220. 2; 254. 6; 255. 6; 309. 7

smȧ speech, word, words 7. 4; 8. 13

smȧu speech 56. 7

smȧt utterance 255. 9

smȧi report, story 10. 13; 307. 11; 316. 3

semā deputed to do something, charged with 226. 1; 237. 8

semu image 145. 5; 148. 11; 152. 11; 156. 5; plur. 165. 11

smu fine copper 35. 11; 120. 10; 122. 11; 124. 2; 147. 8; 150. 6; 161. 4

smui ruin, decay 166. 1

semi fiends 71. 2

semen to establish, to make permanent, to found 23. 8; 90. 3; 108. 10; 109. 5; 114. 12; 146. 4; 152. 13; 170. 6; 229. 5; 234. 6; 241. 10; 310. 7; 311. 11; *semen-θ* established 161. 8

sement stability 268. 9

semenχ to beautify, to set in order 107. 7, 10; 108. 10; 114. 7

semenχet ornamented 147. 11; 152. 4; fine actions 147. 2

smer a title of high rank 97. 2; plur. 115. 8; *smer* overseer of the prophets 97. 2

smer uāt [hieroglyphs] } "one (or only) *smer*", a title of high rank 98. 6; 113. 1; 114. 2; 115. 7;
smer uāti [hieroglyphs] } plur. [hieroglyphs] 100. 5

smeru nub [hieroglyphs] *smers* of high rank 100. 7

smeri [hieroglyphs] a class of priests 93. 1

semeḥ [hieroglyphs] he that dippeth himself 88. 12

semeḥi [hieroglyphs], [hieroglyph] left, the left hand 87. 2; 149. 8; 235. 12; 283. 6

semeḥtet [hieroglyphs] left hand (but read *àbtet*) 45. 8

sems [hieroglyphs], [hieroglyphs] } eldest 50. 12; 74. 1; 87. 8;
semsu [hieroglyphs] } 182. 12; 294. 10

semsem [hieroglyphs] eldest 218. 5

semsem [hieroglyphs], [hieroglyphs] [hieroglyphs] } horses 45. 7; 48. 8; 193. 3; 199. 12; 200. 12; 201. 2; 216. 10; 218. 1

semti [hieroglyphs] [hieroglyphs] } to inspect, to make a judicial examination 313. 2; 316. 13; 318. 2; 319. 7; 325. 4

semti [hieroglyphs] course of life (?) 268. 8

semṭet [hieroglyphs] workmen (?), servants 173. 1; 317. 9; 320. 11

sen [hieroglyphs], [hieroglyphs], [hieroglyphs] they, them, their 3. 7; 101. 4; 226. 13

sen [hieroglyphs] two 1. 1; [hieroglyphs] the next day 3. 1; [hieroglyphs] *sent* two 86. 10

sen [hieroglyphs] second 77. 6; 84. 3; [hieroglyphs] (fem.) 134. 6

senu [hieroglyphs] fellow, neighbour, companion 41. 11; 100. 12; 104. 1

sen, *senȧ* [hieroglyphs] brother 1. 1; 58. 10; 257. 1; [hieroglyphs] *sen-meri* = φιλάδελφος 225. 10

senu, sennu [hieroglyphs] brethren 107. 2; 135. 1; 258. 1

senȧ, senȧt, *sent* [hieroglyphs] sister 43. 2; 53. 3; 57. 1, 6; 58. 10; 109. 10; [hieroglyphs] sister-wife 226. 11

senti [hieroglyphs] the two sisters, *i. e.*, Isis and Nephthys 51. 5, 10; 65. 10; 81. 1

sen [hieroglyphs] thief 278. 1, 4

sen [hieroglyphs] to offer, to be offered 237. 11

sen [hieroglyphs] to follow in the track of 116. 7; to pass over 232. 13; 243. 8; passage 251. 5

sen-ta, *seni-ta* (or *sensen ta*), *senti-ta* [hieroglyphs] to smell the earth, *i. e.*, to bow to the ground in homage 43. 1; 178. 8; 183. 4; 223. 9; 301. 5

senȧ ta [hieroglyphs] adorer 93. 6

senān to depict, to describe 256. 11

senit cabin 196. 11

senb to surround 210. 5

senb, *senib* to be in good health, sound, healthy, 133. 6; 206. 6; 229. 8. This word is contracted to in 22. 11; 23. 1; 24. 1; 25. 3; 26. 1; 32. 9; 33. 2; 34. 5; 135. 4; 269. 10; 307. 4

snef blood 34. 9; 175. 8

seneferi to make happy 78. 8

Seneferu a king of the IVth dynasty 244. 2

senem grief, sorrow 236. 1; 237. 2

senemeḥ, *senemmeḥ* to entreat, to make supplication 197. 13; 198. 4, 6

senemeḥ prayer 298. 2

senen to pass 285. 1

senen image 50. 10; 51. 2; 75. 4

sennu cakes 127. 13; 131. 6

seneni chiefs, leaders 283. 10

seneh to group, to set soldiers in array 189. 1

seneḥ to bind, to fetter 208. 10

senes to glorify, glorifications 142. 9; 144. 4; 145. 3; 154. 11

sensen to smell, to breathe 67. 13

sent to be crowned 233. 3

sent habit, custom 236. 2

senti to found, to establish 173. 10

senti ta to establish, or found, the earth 176. 9

sentrȧ , incense 95. 7 ; 112. 3

senṭu to fear 7. 5 ; 135. 7 ; being afraid 8. 12

senṭu , fear, reverence, to fear, timid 47. 1 ; 52. 1 ; 58. 6 ; 197. 5 ; 252. 7 ; 261. 2 ; 298. 3

senṭet ,

senθi crying out 253. 9

seneťem , to sit, to dwell, to make to sit, to encamp 86. 11 ; 122. 9 ; 136. 7 ; 139. 12 ; 146. 8 ; 172. 8 ; 174. 10 ; 182. 10

seneťemi making to rejoice 80. 9 ; 88. 2

senťes 106. 9

ser wool 49. 9

ser tambourine, drum 49. 9

ser to be fettered 56. 1

ser to challenge 191. 7

ser to dispose, to arrange **41**. 4; **188**. 6, 12; **224**. 8

ser prince, chief **41**. 12; **42**. 10; **44**. 1; **45**. 3; **53**. 7; **82**. 4; **96**. 10; **97**. 8; **99**. 7; **136**. 1; **245**. 9; **294**. 9

seru chiefs, nobles, elders, princes **39**. 6; **41**. 8; **98**. 10; **158**. 2; **168**. 4; **246**. 2; **247**. 13; **248**. 7; **263**. 8; **268**. 3; **270**. 7; **273**. 2

seru āāaiu nobles in chief **307**. 7; **309**. 13; **316**. 9

seru ābuu chief inspectors **307**. 12; **313**. 1; **316**. 12; **320**. 8; **332**. 7

sert the office of governor (?) **104**. 4

ser (or *ṫeser*) to make holy **226**. 12; honour **229**. 9; **240**. 12

ser (or *ṫeser*)-*ā* to hold out the hand to **211**. 1

seri (or *ṫeseri*) exalted **50**. 10

Ser- (or *ṫeser*)-*ka*-[*Rā*] prenomen of Amenophis I. **309**. 2

seruṭ to make to grow **89**. 13; **107**. 7; **111**. 13; **180**. 2; **262**. 8

seri written **49**. 6

serer to write **232**. 1; **239**. 8

serit kindness, gentleness **259**. 3

seref warmth, heat 236. 2 ; 294. 5

sereχ to know how to behave (?) 242. 8

sereχi to make to know 266. 8

seha to crush 266. 3

seha to make to come 105. 8 ; 119. 3

sehai making to go 171. 2

seheb to send forth 52. 7

seheri boat 209. 13

seḥ to travel 52. 8 ; 53. 5

seḥ council chamber 129. 2 ; 255. 7 ; 260. 10

seḥ, seḥi counsel 190. 4 ; 260. 13

seḥapu to conceal 59. 9

seḥāā to make to rejoice 78. 7

seḥua to stink 197. 11

seḥui to collect 143. 12 ; 166. 3

seḥi to mount, to ascend 198. 13

seḥeb to make to keep holiday or to rejoice 151. 10 ; 305. 6 (bis)

seḥen a thief 95. 13

seḥen to rule 171. 8

seḥen crown **238.** 6

seḥentu provided with **216.** 6; **219.** 7

seḥen to make to turn back **281.** 4

seḥer to set on the way **259.** 4; **261.** 8

seḥer, seḥerȧu , to drive away **46.** 4; **53.** 8; **57.** 11; **62.** 7; **85**

seḥerȧut

seḥeqer to starve **200.** 13; **201.** 1

seḥetep to appease, to propitiate, to do good to **178.** 10; **198.** 9; **259.** 8; to set (of the Sun) **303.** 9

seḥtutu to tremble **293.** 2

seḥeṯ overseer **96.** 10; **97.** 2

seḥeṯ to illumine, radiance **163.** 5; **204.** 8

seḥeṯennu ȧb to distract the attention **262.** 3

seχ to be cut off, cast away **221.** 3

seχ to beget (?) **229.** 12

seχa ḥrȧ to be deaf **288.** 9

seχa , to remember **122.** 9; **129.** 7; **190.** 7; **228.** 3; **245.** 3; memory **66.** 1; recollection **263.** 12; decree, or deed of commemoration **225.** 10; **232.** 1

seχau

seχai to remember **16.** 9; instructions **328.** 11

seχap to stab, to pierce **297.** 8; **304.** 3

seχanen to throw down, to breach a wall **187.** 2; **196.** 1

seχan to hasten **234.** 13

seχaneket vessel **156.** 4

seχar to break through **261.** 9

seχakeru to ornament **148.** 12

seχā to make to rise like the sun, to crown oneself with splendour like the rising sun **114.** 5; **195.** 1; making to rise (of a statue) **163.** 5

seχāt crowned one (fem.) **120.** 4

seχāu celestial bodies which rise like the Sun **295.** 13

seχu to glorify **78.** 6; **125.** 13; to do good things for **86.** 2

seχu glorifications **78.** 3

seχun slaughter-house **149.** 6

seχi to scale the walls of a city **195.** 9; **208.** 9

seχef seven **17.** 9; **20.** 11; **225.** 3

seχeper , to form, to create, to make to become, to provide food for **3.** 1; **4.** 9; **7.** 10; **114.** 2; **126.** 5; **130.** 3; **163.** 10; **201.** 7; **230.** 3; **252.** 2; **258.** 11; **260.** 7; **305.** 4

seχeperu

seχem [hieroglyphs] to have or to gain the mastery over any one or any thing 92. 2; 132. 4; to strengthen 65. 10; master, mighty one 69. 10; 296. 6; possessor 299. 5; rule 304. 13

seχem ȧb [hieroglyphs] violent

seχem [hieroglyphs] divine or spiritual form 61. 13; 62. 2; 295. 6; 304. 13

seχem [hieroglyphs] image (?) 237. 4; plur. 227. 4

Seχem [hieroglyphs] the capital of the IInd nome of Lower Egypt 219. 2

seχemet [hieroglyphs] shrine 211. 2

seχen [hieroglyphs] to hover 54. 9

seχen [hieroglyphs] occurrence, event 228. 2, 4; 230. 6; 232. 12; 233. 8; 234. 11; 235. 2

seχent, *seχenti* [hieroglyphs] to make to approach, to bring nigh to 65. 13; 73. 12; 254. 8; to promote 129. 1

seχer, *seχeru* [hieroglyphs] to overthrow 71. 2; 91. 6; 173. 3; 303. 9

seχer [hieroglyphs] plan, design, intention 138. 2; 263. 8; plan (of a campaign) 100. 10; mode of life, behaviour 250. 9; advice, opinion 255. 7; character, education 267. 11; act 141. 12; affair, condition 248. 10; [hieroglyphs] dispensation of God 250. 13; [hieroglyphs] the scheme of human affairs 243. 5; [hieroglyphs] the affairs of the people 248. 9

seχeru [hieroglyphs] things, matters, plans 4. 7; 174. 8; 295. 11; devices 44. 9; schemes, plots 55. 10; counsels 245. 10; condition 1. 5; 25. 13; traces, marks 313. 2; documents 230. 2; kind, species 30. 2; wont, manner, habit 2. 5; 9. 9; [hieroglyphs] like 7. 8; 43. 13

seχseχ [hieroglyphs] to flee 12. 11

seχet [hieroglyphs] to capture 249. 2, 3, 9

seχet [hieroglyphs] join 124. 5

seχet [hieroglyphs] defeat 193. 5; 197. 6; to break 277. 1

seχet [hieroglyphs] field, fields, meadows 1. 7; 71. 13; 251. 8

seχet [hieroglyphs] fields 114. 12

Seχet-Åaru [hieroglyphs] a section of the Elysian Fields 127. 11; 131. 1

Seχet-ḥetepet [hieroglyphs] the Elysian Fields of the Egyptians 127. 12

Seχet [hieroglyphs] name of a goddess 92. 4; 143. 6

seχti [hieroglyphs] the crowns of the North and South 296. 13; 297. 3; 299. 7

seχetχet [hieroglyphs] to repulse 59. 7

seχeṭi [hieroglyphs] fiends 213. 8

ses [hieroglyphs] once 233. 8

ses [hieroglyphs] to drink 221. 10

ses [hieroglyphs] bolt 213. 13

sesui bolts 163. 4

sesa to fill with food, to satisfy 128. 4

sesu day 225. 3; 226. 5; 230. 8; 232. 1

sesemet horses 275. 4; 277. 2; 278. 3

sesumut horse 141. 1

sesemut horses 175. 11

sesunnu to be destroyed 304. 5

sesefi to cleanse by fire 173. 6

sesefet ill-mannered 242. 7

sesen, *seseni* } to smell, to breathe 96. 2; 245. 7

sesenet breaths 130. 10

seset noble words 271. 1

Sesetsu Sesostris 276. 2; 290. 4, 9

seś to unbolt, to open 205. 6; 214. 1; 215. 9; 223. 2

seśes to unbolt 185. 13

seś } to pass, to traverse, to follow 129. 7; 203. 3; 248. 12; 285. 10; motion 298. 8; an entrance 279. 12; moving 299. 8

seś courses 82. 8

seśet an open way 248. 12

seśau to take advantage **264.** 3

seśa a skilled or learned man **129.** 6

seśebśeb to vomit **297.** 9

seśebeṭ to make to sink down exhausted **299.** 13

seśep to shine **64.** 1

seśep image **184.** 9

seśep players on tambourines **94.** 8

seśep to receive, to accept, to take upon oneself, what is received **28.** 1; **56.** 9; **127.** 13; **132.** 12; **140.** 11; **242.** 5; **262.** 9, 13; acceptable **222.** 2

seśepet chamber (?) **104.** 13

seśen to undermine a wall, to overthrow **101.** 11

seśen to make a way through **132.** 9

seśeni lilies **151.** 2; **160.** 9

seśes to make to follow **252.** 3

seśsaui skilful **282.** 11

seśeś sistrum **199.** 12

seśet fire **297.** 7

seśeta confidential matter, secret **97.** 5; a secret of the harem **99.** 5

Seśeta (?) name of a deity **63.** 13; **70.** 9

seśeṭ, **seśeṭu** — to dig 147. 13; 151. 2; 181. 6; 183. 13; 202. 2

seśeṭet — a recitation 243. 10

seśeṭ, **seśeṭu**, **seśeṭet** — to recite a prayer, to be recited or proclaimed, to pronounce letters or words 66. 3; 86. 1; 87. 4; 93. 13; 116. 3; 129. 7; to enchant 17. 5

seśeṭ — to finish, to work out 263. 6

seśeṭ — opening in a wall, window, cavity 35. 9; 150. 6; 179. 6; 213. 11

seśeṭ, **seśeṭu** — diadem, turban 296. 12; 299. 6; 302. 10

seśeṭḥu — vases 160. 9

seśeṭeṭ — to dig, to excavate 160. 8

sek (or **åsk**) — behold 234. 8

sek — the end, death 194. 8

sek — to drag a boat 210. 3

sek — to perish, to fail, to dwindle away, injury, defect 94. 10; 123. 13; 202. 10; 268. 1

sek, **seki** — to fight, to do battle with 180. 11; 187. 12; 189. 3

seki — warriors, athletes (?) 282. 3

seka } to plough 1. 8; 3. 12; 127. 10; 251. 7
seka
sekau

sekau ploughmen 188. 2

seken , glutton (?), greedy person (?) 242. 6; 257. 8. *seken-θȧ* to act like a glutton 251. 4

Seker } the god Seker 87. 6; 130. 7; 132. 10; 204. 7
Sekeri

seksek to cut down, to crush, to destroy 26. 2; 32. 9; 174. 1; 175. 3

seket χat to make the courage to fail 256. 6

sekti } name of the boat of the rising sun 89. 4; 123. 10; 158. 8; 214. 2; 235. 9; 304. 1
sektet ,

seqa (or *saq*) , to collect 61. 9; 72. 7; 252. 9

seq } to exalt 128. 9; 144. 13; 301. 9; 303. 11
seqa
seqau

seqebeb to cool, to be cool 127. 5

seqem to continue 39. 2

seqer captive 210. 12

seqer captives 102. 4; 191. 6

seqernu conqueror 54. 8

seqeṭ to turn 262. 6

seqeṭet, *seqeṭu* sailors 206. 11; 304. 2

seḳāt to carry round 237. 9

seḳenen to make weak 300. 1

seḳenen perfume 23. 2

seḳerḥ to pacify, to bring to rest 272. 5

set she, it, her 5. 6; 18. 10

set they, them, their 3. 9; 4. 3; 112. 12; 124. 10; 136. 5; 178. 1, 3; also written 108. 3; 127. 2; 227. 6

set to clothe 57. 13

set smell 213. 6

set babe 63. 2

set desert, foreign land, mountainous country, mountain 19. 2; 23. 9; 24. 5; 109. 8; 118. 11; 178. 11; 301. 7; 302. 7

set plur. of above 95. 11; 100. 9; 106. 5; 107. 5; 110. 7; 115. 4, 12; 125. 9

seta foreign barbarian land 102. 9

setu foreign captives 227. 10

setiu mountaineers (?) 165. 2

Set the opponent of Horus 52. 6; 54. 1; 170. 10

sta to bring, to be brought 43. 6; 157. 9; 200. 9

staiu bringers 133. 10

sta a mound of earth cast up about a city by a besieging host 208. 9

sta mu (?) watercourse 160. 10; 162. 11

statet (?) 102. 13

stastau rebels 52. 9

stau to kindle a light or fire 9. 10

stu to bring 136. 10

setur worked, inlaid 217. 4

setut to collect, to gather together 232. 10; 233. 5; 238. 1; 239. 1

seti to convey (?) 292. 12

sti , smell, scent 22. 11; 23. 11; 71. 4; 94. 1; 296. 1

sti sweet-smelling unguent 73. 10

setebḥ provided with 159. 5

setep to choose, to be chosen 120. 5; 231. 5; 237. 7

setepu chosen one 289. 10

setep en àḥ the pick of the stable 202. 1

setep sa the court, palace 98. 9; 103. 9; 112. 13; 117. 3

setep sa protected by an amulet 93. 9

stef bubbles in a liquid 18. 3; 26. 12

setem a priestly title 86. 9, 10

setem, **setemet**, **setemu** to hear, to hearken, to obey 3. 7; 10. 7; 56. 7; 98. 13; 125. 4; 138. 7; 263. 4; to hear a case in court 97. 4; to obey the dictates of the body 255. 2

setemu one who listens, the hearing one 269. 2, 3, 4; 270. 6; hearers 273. 4, 7

setemu, **setemiu** listeners 115. 10; 245. 10; 247. 12; 272. 11

setennu noble, splendid 291. 2

set ḥemt woman 20. 7; 21. 7; 25. 5

seteχ wall, rampart 291. 3

setet to tremble 70. 4; trembling 88. 3

seṭ to break open, to pierce 62. 1

seṭ , tail, rump 186. 4; 238. 5

seṭ to be afraid of 197. 1

seṭu to make evil 251. 4

seṭi to draw back 213. 13

seṭeb a portion of the priestly apparel 213. 9

seṭeb activity 253. 13

seṭebȧ , endeavour, anxiety 262. 7

seṭebḥu to provide with food 177. 4

seṭebḥu to be alert 279. 1

seṭennu prince 87. 7

seθ (or *ȧsθ*) behold 98. 5; 99. 4; 100. 4; 102. 13; 105. 13

seθ a libation basin 98. 2; 104. 11; plur. 104. 12

seθenȧ to be upright 292. 1

seθeḥen to shine with a yellowish green colour 162. 3

[se]*ťȧ* form (?) 282. 5

seťebu opposition 68. 2

seťefau to provide for 157. 3

sṫer to fortify **219.** 11

sṫer fort, strong place **99.** 13; plur. **99.** 13

sṫer, **sṫeru** to lie down, to make to lie down **7.** 1; **19.** 2; **244.** 10; **300.** 13; **301.** 3; to put cattle in their stalls for the night **8.** 10; **9.** 7

sṫeri lying down **47.** 12; **286.** 9

seṫet babe **117.** 4

seṫeṭ, **seṫeṭet** to tell, to relate, to describe **123.** 2; **194.** 6; **271.** 8, 10; **279.** 2

seṫeṭ exhortations **288.** 10

seṫeṭu precept **249.** 4

SH.

śe lake, pool **118.** 8; **126.** 13

śe (**śemut**) the period of harvest and beginning of the inundation season **42.** 6; **124.** 7; **233.** 10

śa the period when crops grow **49.** 6

śa to begin **124.** 5

śa to propose **128.** 11

śa to rejoice **70.** 2

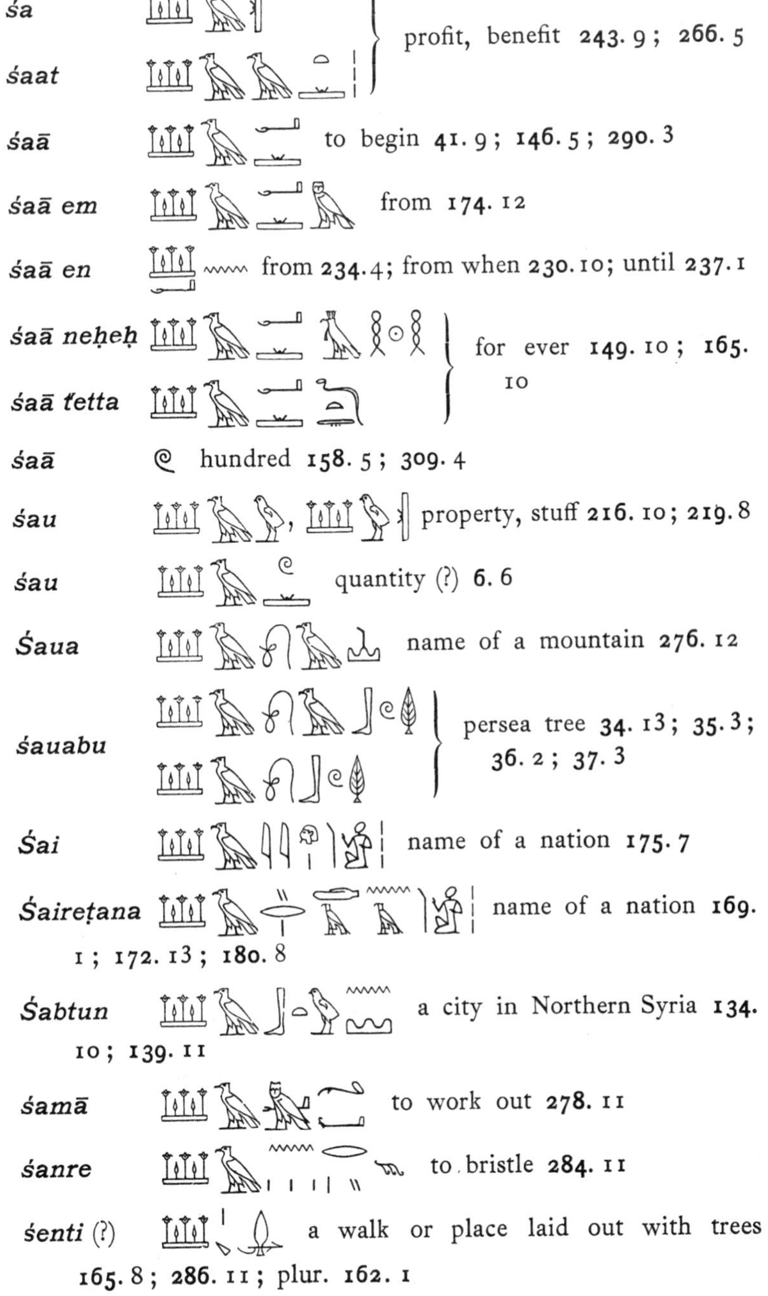

śa, *śaat* — profit, benefit **243.** 9; **266.** 5

śaā — to begin **41.** 9; **146.** 5; **290.** 3

śaā em — from **174.** 12

śaā en — from **234.** 4; from when **230.** 10; until **237.** 1

śaā neḥeḥ, *śaā t'etta* — for ever **149.** 10; **165.** 10

śaā — hundred **158.** 5; **309.** 4

śau — property, stuff **216.** 10; **219.** 8

śau — quantity (?) **6.** 6

Śaua — name of a mountain **276.** 12

śauabu — persea tree **34.** 13; **35.** 3; **36.** 2; **37.** 3

Śai — name of a nation **175.** 7

Śaireṭana — name of a nation **169.** 1; **172.** 13; **180.** 8

Śabtun — a city in Northern Syria **134.** 10; **139.** 11

śamā — to work out **278.** 11

śanre — to bristle **284.** 11

śenti (?) — a walk or place laid out with trees **165.** 8; **286.** 11; plur. **162.** 1

śarem to remove, to carry off 189. 6

śaremā to lie idle 180. 12

śareś swift 275. 4

Śasu nomad Arabs who lived on the N. E. of Egypt 134. 10; 135. 8; 276. 6, 11; 284. 1

Śasu the land of the Shasu 278. 9

Śaśanq a proper name 191. 10

śaśat to tread upon 182. 4

śaqi rings 217. 5

śat beginning 124. 8

śat proposition 121. 6

śat to make in primeval times 126. 1

śatireθȧt gulfs, precipices 285. 3

śaṭ to dig 106. 3

śaṭetθȧt cave, rocky cavern 283. 2

śā to cut down trees 101. 12

śā to hollow out a boat 105. 10

śā, śāt sand 99. 9; 137. 9; 279. 12

śā uncultivable land 110. 6

śāi letter 274. 8

Śāi-qa-em-Ånnu a place near Heliopolis 213. 3, 4

śāt , , book, letter, writing 40. 2; 50. 2; 56. 9; 87. 4; 95. 1; plur. 43. 6

śāt to cut, to cut down 15. 13; 17. 7; 52. 4; 287. 11

Śu , name of a god 11. 9; 206. 2

śu to want, lack of, cessation, emptiness, without 70. 11; 249. 7; 258. 10; 266. 8; 269. 1; empty 312. 10

śuu a man lacking a quality 242. 8

śua to be weak, helpless (?) 203. 2

śuua beggars (?), mean men 169. 10

śui , a few 44. 1; 169. 11

śuit want, lack of 288. 6

śuu green herbs, vegetables 241. 9

śuit shadow 126. 10

śut friends (?) 266. 11

śuti , the two plumes 117. 5; 172. 7; 296. 11; 299. 6

śeb 57. 4

śebu pieces of meat 127. 13

śebu food 132. 6

śebeb food 288. 7

śebennu to mingle with, to be united, to join oneself to 145. 8; 182. 7; 278. 8; 303. 3

śep palm of the hand 118. 5

śep what is abominable 220. 8

śepenṭ sickness, disease (?) 267. 7

śeps august, venerable, sacred, honourable, precious 38. 11; 83. 2; 237. 5

śepsi venerable or sacred being 143. 1, 8; fem. 25. 11; 32. 4; 37. 11

venerable, sacred 145. 13

śepsu the venerable ones, *i. e.*, the dead 131. 2; 306. 6

śepses to honour, honour, sacred majesty, sacred beings 106. 11; 267. 1, 12; 272. 6

śepset sacred, venerable 118. 6

śepset "venerable one", a name of Isis 75. 12

śepsti the two venerable women, *i. e.*, Isis and Nephthys 71. 5

śeptet words which cause shame 265. 13

śefi, *śeft*, *śefit* — awe, terror **63**. 8; **70**. 4; **82**. 3; **196**. 13; **204**. 9; **295**. 10

śefta, śefṭu — , book, writing **239**. 9; **243**. 7

śem — , to go, to march **45**. 13; **128**. 6; **187**. 5; **191**. 6; **200**. 7; goer **1**. 6

śemu — advancing hosts **206**. 3

śem re — to speak evil of any one **253**. 11

śem ta — to pilot, to guide **50**. 9

śema — demons, devils **44**. 10; **46**. 5

śememet — stable **215**. 13; **217**. 9; **218**. 1

śen — circuit **55**. 7; **70**. 13

śenui (?) — the two circuits or orbits **60**. 13

śen — to shut in, to beleaguer a city **193**. 12

śenāi — to treat harshly **259**. 6

śenā, *śenār* — to turn back, to be repulsed **127**. 8; **132**. 10; **203**. 5

śeni — to be fettered, hindered **265**. 2

śenit — men in high positions **85**. 10; **128**. 6; the four children of Horus **82**. 2

śenbet neck, body 154. 5; 305. 6

śenen, *śenenet* to cry out, to call 259. 7; 265. 9

śennu to tell, to relate 10. 13

śennu to grieve sorely 79. 8

śennu to abuse, to curse 16. 3

śennu hair 49. 8; 65. 13; 72. 12

śennu evil 245. 12

śennu a kind of plant 286. 7

śennet weariness 254. 5

śens (?) some woven material 198. 2

śent to surround 262. 4

śent a going out 98. 11

śent princes 113. 10

śent miscellaneous 166. 13; 167. 4

śent granary 150. 8; 201. 10

śenti double granaries (?) 132. 13; 312. 8

śentu granaries 148. 4; 157. 5; 163. 11; 204. 5

śenti tresses, hair 22. 9

śenti to grieve sorely 33. 11

śentu the circuit of the sun 125. 11

śentet things abominable 127. 9

śenθi sadness, sickness, trouble 258. 11

Śenθit name of a deity 73. 2

śenť acacia wood 105. 11; 106. 4

śer little 234. 1

śer offspring 41. 2

śere son 76. 11

śerȧ to wall up, to stop a gap 171. 3

śerȧu child, boy, young boy or girl 1. 3; 2. 4; 325. 4; 24. 3; 286. 13

śer evil 26. 7; diminution 274. 3

śerȧut of little value 325. 7

śert nose 303. 4

śerȧti nostrils 160. 13

śes to follow, to serve 67. 6; 94. 4; 132. 9; 252. 4; 287. 5

śesu, *śesi* followers, servants 140. 8; 173. 1; 328. 9

śes ȧb to follow one's inclination 252. 11, 12; 253. 2

śes ānti to perform the ceremony connected with the *ānti* perfume **214.** 8

śesu Ḥeru , "followers of Horus", a class of mythological beings **127.** 7; **271.** 7

śes (?) a kind of stone **125.** 2

śeser arrow **198.** 13

śeset , alabaster **105.** 7; **149.** 7

śeta , secret, hidden, hidden things **50.** 11; **61.** 5; **83.** 9; **165.** 5

śetau hidden one **145.** 1

śetai mystery **87.** 6

śetat mystery **145.** 4; rare, curious **177.** 10

śetat , shrine, hidden place **86.** 4; **88.** 8; **206.** 5

śetem **261.** 4

Śet-ṭeśert "Red pool", a district near Memphis **91.** 11; **92.** 10

śeťet to dig up **112.** 9; *śeťet śā* the festival of digging up sand **112.** 9

K.

k I **98.** 8; **99.** 1; **101.** 4; **145.** 4; **288.** 8; **291.** 10, 12, 13

k thou, thee, thy **5.** 3 *et passim*

k also 231. 12 ; another 238. 10

ka thou 242. 3

ka word, speech, to say, to cry out, to tell 7. 2 ; 37. 1 ; 69. 8 ; 121. 8 ; 203. 9 ; 216. 11 ; 255. 11 ; 291. 8

ka then 249. 12 ; verily 17. 12 ; 222. 5 ; 242. 7

kat saying 256. 6

ka , , the double 70. 11 ; 78. 7 ; 106. 13 ; 127. 9 ; plur. , 119. 7 ; 131. 2 ; person 259. 10 ; 287. 1 ; plur. 262. 5, 8 ; myself 222. 1 ; himself 250. 10 ; a benevolent person 263. 4 ; a just man 259. 12 ; a hateful person 250. 5 ; 251. 7 ; 252. 13. chapels of the *ka* 112. 1 ; by the person of 40. 2

ka, ***kaui*** food, provisions 157. 10 ; sustenance 166. 1 ; products 162. 4 ; 164. 1

ka , bull 19. 13 ; 32. 12 ; 34. 3 ; 41. 2 ; 51. 10 ; 56. 13 ; 120. 7 ; 294. 3 ; male 224. 12 ; 225. 1 ; plur.

Ka-neχt-meri-Maāt a title of Rameses II. 134. 4

Ka-ḥeseb the XIth nome of Lower Egypt 218. 11

Ka-qem the city Kochome 214. 12 ; 215. 1

kaut cow 58. 2 ; 225. 1 ; plur. 202. 3

kauti the two cows, *i. e.*, Isis and Nephthys 52. 12 ; 53. 1

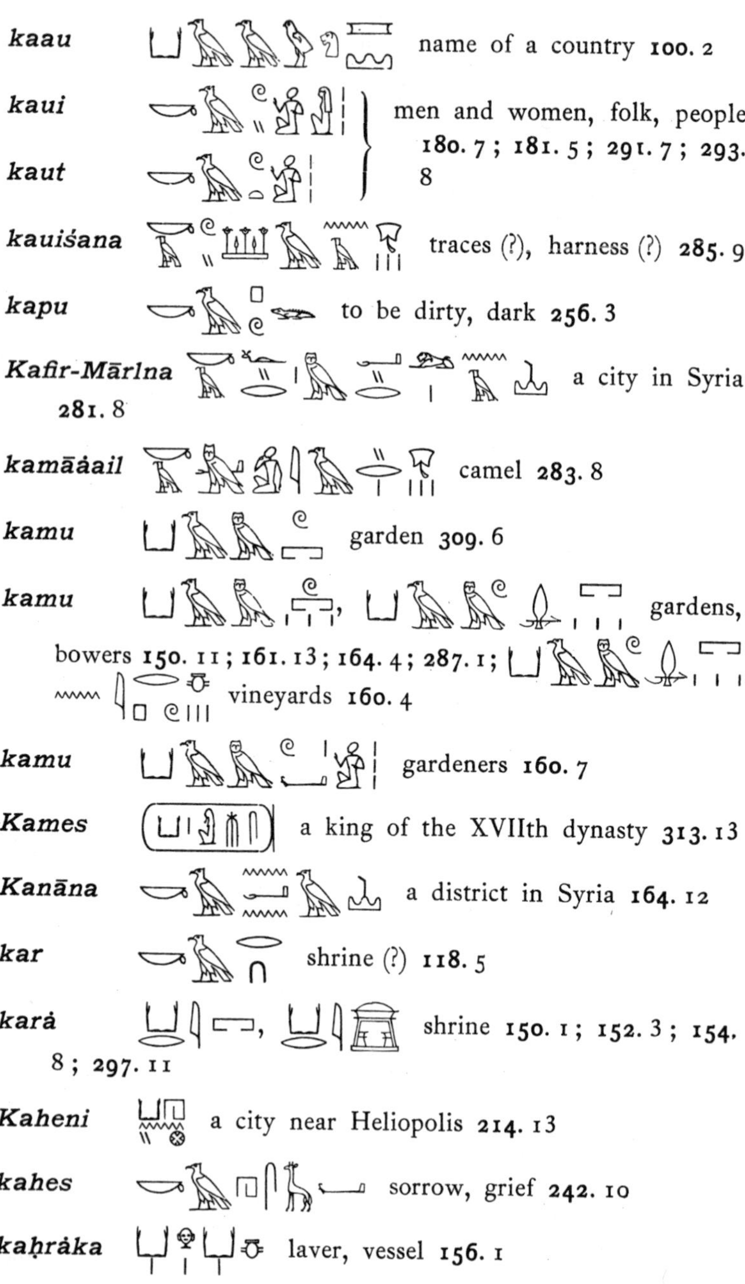

kaau name of a country 100. 2

kaui }
kaut } men and women, folk, people 180. 7; 181. 5; 291. 7; 293. 8

kauiśana traces (?), harness (?) 285. 9

kapu to be dirty, dark 256. 3

Kafir-Mārlna a city in Syria 281. 8

kamāȧail camel 283. 8

kamu garden 309. 6

kamu , gardens, bowers 150. 11; 161. 13; 164. 4; 287. 1; vineyards 160. 4

kamu gardeners 160. 7

Kames a king of the XVIIth dynasty 313. 13

Kanāna a district in Syria 164. 12

kar shrine (?) 118. 5

karȧ , shrine 150. 1; 152. 3; 154. 8; 297. 11

Kaheni a city near Heliopolis 214. 13

kahes sorrow, grief 242. 10

kaḥrȧka laver, vessel 156. 1

Kaqemna an Egyptian writer 244. 4

kat bosom, breast (?) 259. 6

kat to work 124. 6

kat workman 104. 1

kat work, labour, building works 82. 9; 121. 8; 129. 11; 152. 5; 183. 12; 261. 1; 282. 12

katu hidden 15. 11

katemet fine gold 153. 3; 154. 4; 156. 9, 13

kaθȧ to rush headlong 285. 5

ku, ḳua I 217. 8; thou 30. 2; 277. 8; 289. 13

kuȧ I 10. 4; 93. 10; 121. 4; 24. 4

ki another 13. 8; 21. 10; 146. 12; 214. 5; 249. 10; 169. 10; one to another 267. 1

ki ťeṭ otherwise said 72. 3; 73. 9

kepu to hide 284. 2

Kepuna a city in Syria 279. 3

kefa to spread out, to unfold 202. 6

kefau to reach the end of 290. 5

kefa ȧb to harden the heart to do evil 201. 3; 264. 3; 285. 8

Keftet Phoenicia 228. 11

kenkenememti a name of the ape of Thoth, or of the moon **89.** 2

kent hatred (?) **255.** 3

kehabu to strike **55.** 6

keràut shrine **54.** 3

kerti two horns **296.** 10

kes, kesu , homage **41.** 9; **199.** 1; **301.** 9

kesem to turn away **81.** 4

Keś, Keśt , Kush (Ethiopia and Nubia) **38.** 11; **95.** 12; **180.** 11

kek darkness, night **202.** 3

kekui darkness **9.** 11; **287.** 12

kektu flower **89.** 3

ket another **80.** 7; **113.** 12; **187.** 4; **272.** 7; **252.** 2

ket-θà another **12.** 4; **13.** 8; **34.** 12; **285.** 4; **326.** 3

keteχet other things **15.** 5; **149.** 2, 10; **154.** 12; **155.** 7; **281.** 6

ket little **43.** 3

ketet little, small **241.** 6; **257.** 5

ketet an object **251.** 7

ketket to shake **34.** 7

Q.

qa natural disposition **117.** 8

qa to be high, exalted **58.** 8 ; height **80.** 5

qau height **301.** 71

qa ȧb to be haughty **261.** 5

qa he wept his loudest **16.** 5 ; a mighty defeat **193.** 5 ; **197.** 6 ; to lie at full length on their backs **180.** 10

qa ḥeťet exalted one of the white crown **296.** 12

qa śuti exalted one of the two plumes **296.** 11

qaȧ form, image, aspect, phase **21.** 11 ; **275.** 9, 13 ; **278.** 10 ; **285.** 12 ; **290.** 12

qai staircase **122.** 2

Qairθȧ-ānbu a city of Syria **281.** 11

Qaiqaśa name of a nation **175.** 6

qab to multiply **256.** 3

qanre dust, mud, ground **315.** 8

Qarbana a proper name **174.** 13

qarere boats, barges **159.** 4

qaḥaut windows **151.** 1

qaqa to look at, to see **147.** 9

Qaḳabut name of a scribe **40.** 3

qaťa a kind of shrub **285.** 2

Qaťairṭi an Assyrian prince **283.** 11

Qaťaθȧ Gaza **291.** 5

qāḥ, qāḥu shoulder **132.** 2; **254.** 9; **263.** 3; **264.** 11

quir boats, barges **150.** 7

qubu (?) shadow **180.** 4

qurt first-fruits **239.** 4

qeb , to double, to increase, company **43.** 9; **127.** 10; **147.** 3; **166.** 1; **184.** 3; **221.** 4; **243.** 6

qeb = ***qebḥ*** = to refresh oneself **126.** 9

qebat breast **117.** 7

qebeb to refresh oneself **128.** 13

qebeb lake, place of water **128.** 13; **199.** 4

qebḥ to pour out libations **85.** 12

qebḥ libation **112.** 3

qebḥ to refresh oneself, refreshings **264.** 8; **265.** 5

qebḥ cool water **17.** 12; **28.** 11; **95.** 7

qebḥ ȧb cool of heart, *i. e.*, appeased **221.** 1

Qebtit the city Coptos **178.** 2

qefn sacred bread or cake **240.** 4

qem , to find **5.** 5; **21.** 9; **209.** 3; to find a mouth, *i. e.*, to speak **293.** 13

qemi found **310.** 1; **311.** 9; **312.** 3; **313.** 2; **314.** 3; **315.** 4; **320.** 8

qemit a finding **179.** 3

qem, qemt , black stone **147.** 7; **149.** 12

qem to abide, to endure **190.** 7; **253.** 2; **272.** 5; period **45.** 8

qema, qemau , to create, to make **122.** 9; **144.** 13

qema maker, begetter **229.** 11

qema natural disposition **113.** 8

qemat product, products **120.** 1; **130.** 9

qemam to make, to form **295.** 4; **300.** 1

qemamu hammered on, inlaid **147.** 8; **150.** 2, 10; **153.** 2; **154.** 7

qemȧti image, statue, form **296.** 13

qemā

qemā, qemāu ,

qemāt

south **73.** 8; **120.** 12; **143.** 9; **160.** 6; **294.** 8; , , , South and North, *i. e.*, all Egypt **57.** 7; **89.** 7; **143.** 9; **144.** 11

qemāu | *qemātu* — southern 7. 3; 11. 3; 114. 3

qemāi | *qemāt* — ladies of the confraternity of Ȧmen-Rā at Thebes 239. 2, 5; 314. 12

Qem-ur a city in Lower Egypt 216. 2

qemi to remove 59. 3

qemḥ | *qemḥet* | *qemḥu* — to look, to see, to shew oneself 122. 8; 140. 9; 250. 3, 4; 299. 2

qemqem to pant, to breathe laboriously 292. 7

Qemt , the black land, Egypt 22. 10; 41. 3; 47. 10; 120. 5; 125. 8; 143. 11; 227. 8; 228. 11

qemtu mutilated condition 65. 12

qen strength, valour 190. 6

qen , warrior, soldier 191. 2; 195. 12; 202. 13

qen (?) read *seššau* skilled, eminent 121. 5

qen (?) refined (of metal) 125. 1; 154. 4

qenȧu to embrace 29. 9

qenȧu bosom, breast, body 287. 3, 10

qenu , many, great 226. 11; 227. 3

qenbet a class of high officials who stood near the king 43. 6; 107. 10; 113. 3; 251. 11; 263. 5

qennu many 3. 3; 39. 3; 144. 3; 147. 4; very many indeed 175. 2

qennu calamity 59. 10

qennu horses 189. 2

qennu to vanquish 62. 4

qenqen to beat, to hurt, to be beaten 9. 4; 319. 12; 9. 1

qenṭet to be angry, to rage 291. 9

qenṭtu angry, wrathful 7. 4

qerȧu bolts 176. 12

qerer burnt-offering 235. 11; 238. 12

qerḥ vase, vessel 168. 8

qeres to bury, burial 319. 3

qeres sarcophagus 97. 10

qeres burial chamber 312. 9

Qeheq name of a nation 172. 13; 180. 9

qeḥqeḥ to hammer, to cut with a hammer and chisel 154. 10; 155. 2, 8; 156. 3

qes body 245. 4

qesu[1] bones 65. 6

qesen, *qesenu*[2] bad, evil 55. 11; 72. 1; 201. 1; 261. 1; despair 228. 2; unpleasant, detestable 248. 5; 255. 9; 264. 9

qesert canon 268. 2

qesqeset curse, evil 246. 9

qek to strike (?) 253. 11

qeq to eat 223. 13; 224. 2

qeqet boat 45. 7

qeṭ to build 19. 6; 117. 11; 147. 11; 150. 13; to fashion a human being 20. 6; 147. 6

qeṭu builders 206. 11

qetȧu to build up 72. 9

qeṭ the like, manner of, form, quality 2. 2; 21. 7; 104. 4; 118. 8; 121. 10; 251. 2; 265. 8; 267. 4; 295. 11; 297. 13

qeṭ, *qeṭi*, *qeṭu* to go, to walk, to go round about 22. 2; 147. 11; 162. 7; 288. 11

qeṭ heavy sleep 277. 11

qeṭiṭi sleep 287. 8

Qeṭeś Kadesh on the Orontes 134. 7; 136. 4; 137. 10; 140. 3; 276. 5; 281. 9

1. On pp. 221. 11; 277. 10 for *ḳesu* and *ḳesen* read *qesu*.
2. In a few places this word has been wrongly transliterated *ḳesen*.

qeṭet weights 221. 4

Qeṭet name of a district 177. 6

qeṭet 266. 11

qeṭet, *qeṭtut* sailors 159. 7; 177. 1; 319. 4; 320. 10; 321. 6; 324. 9

Qeṭeti name of a district 137. 7

qeṭeter dirty, filthy 9. 1

K̦.

ḳa to remove, to be empty 53. 6; 197. 12

ḳaȧubeχ . . . = τὰ Κικήλλια 238. 9

ḳauatennu to mend 285. 13

ḳautet mountain pass, a defile, road 284. 1; 285. 11

ḳai vessel 28. 10; 29. 9

ḳaire pet a kind of pigeon 168. 6

ḳairepu to hammer together, to bolt 289. 2

ḳabui dreary, wretched 277. 13

ḳanen to faint, to drop with exhaustion 29. 4; 283. 7

ḳaḥu rest 88. 7

ḳaḥsi a species of gazelle (?) 149. 5 ; 167. 8

ḳasa mourning, grief 18. 11

ḳat poverty 264. 2

ḳu to destroy 60. 7

ḳua to besiege 186. 3 ; 187. 4 ; 188. 2 ; 197. 7 ; 208. 8

Ḳutut name of a city 175. 2

ḳebḳebet dead bodies 141. 7

ḳep flood, storm 195. 9 ; 209. 9 ; 210. 11

ḳemḥu a stone object connected with a shrine (?) 98. 2

ḳen, **ḳennu** to abuse, to harass 256. 5, 9

ḳenen to faint 16. 2 ; 51. 3

ḳenχapet (?) a kind of bird (?) 300. 8

ḳant time 232. 3, 4, 10 ; 233. 10 ; always 226. 12 ; plur. 233. 13 ; times of old 233. 13

ḳer, ḳert , but, moreover 106. 9 ; 112. 11 ; 232. 2 ; 272. 4 ; 273. 4

ḳer fraud, deceit, treachery 14. 11 ; 36. 4 ; 269. 1

ḳer, ḳeru to have, to hold, to possess, to take possession of **4.** 1; **19.** 8; **136.** 3; **175.** 13; **258.** 12; property **253.** 1

ḳer = possessor **251.** 10

ḳert possession **263.** 3; fittings of a place **315.** 9

ḳer to be or to keep silent **128.** 13; **186.** 12; **242.** 12; silence **263.** 3

ḳeru silence **241.** 2

ḳerḥ night **28.** 13; **188.** 5; **195.** 3; **277.** 13; **278.** 4; to pass the night **250.** 11

ḳerḳ to dig (?) **119.** 2

ḳes side, half, part **109.** 7; **115.** 3; **120.** 13; **124.** 11; **201.** 4; **285.** 6; **311.** 2; two sides (?) **99.** 12

ḳesu (?) a class of men, artisans (?) **100.** 8; **201.** 4

ḳesa to be troubled **263.** 11

ḳeśȧ a dagger or knife **15.** 12

T.

t , thou, thee **9.** 13; **21.** 6

t = ṭemt all **207.** 1

ta the **3.** 7; **5.** 5; **129.** 11; **307.** 1, 8; **309.** 2; = thou **36.** 3

ta land, earth, country **2.** 2; **67.** 9

taui the two lands, *i. e.*, Upper and Lower Egypt **40.** 9; **56.** 8; **182.** 10; **210.** 10; **226.** 4; **229.** 6; **232.** 6; the whole empire of Egypt **66.** 3; **82.** 8

taiu all lands, the world **70.** 9; **83.** 11; **125.** 9; **171.** 7

tauu (?) lands, districts **192.** 6; **215.** 3

taiu the people of a land **227.** 12

ta meḥt land of the north **99.** 12; **191.** 2, 8; **192.** 8; **193.** 5; **195.** 3; **197.** 5

taui meḥt the two lands of the North **195.** 6

Ta-merȧ the lands of the Inundation **155.** 4; **165.** 6; **172.** 10; **180.** 5; **283.** 10

Ta-mert Egypt **225.** 4; **226.** 12; **228.** 5; **229.** 8; **232.** 3; **233.** 9

Ta-netert "the divine land", *i. e.*, Egypt **229.** 2

Ta-ser[1]
Ta-sert[2]
Ta-sertet[3] "the holy land", *i. e.*, Egypt **60.** 8; **130.** 5; **142.** 6

1. Or *t'eser.* 2. Or *t'esert.* 3. Or *t'esertet.*

Ta-qebḥ		a proper name (?) **213.** 1
Ta-θām		name of a country **100.** 3
ta, tau		bread, cakes, food, meat **85.** 13; **112.** 3; **127.** 2, 5; **132.** 4, 5; **221.** 9; **241.** 6; **249.** 7; **266.** 7
ta àb		to be of a fiery disposition **261.** 9
tau		to burn **59.** 1
Ta-àn		name of a city **218.** 4
Taā-Rā (?)		a proper name **218.** 5
Tau-āa		a king of the XVIIth dynasty **313.** 6
Tau-āa-āa		a king of the XVIIth dynasty **313.** 9
Tauḥibit		a city near Memphis **211.** 11
tauśet		boundaries, confines **282.** 2
tai		this **24.** 2; **31.** 8; **138.** 9; **321.** 9
tai-à		my **5.** 13; **141.** 9; **181.** 13
tai-u		their **324.** 12
Taiuṫait		a city in Upper Egypt (?) **186.** 2
tai-f		his **2.** 11; **8.** 1
tai-sen		their **279.** 4
tai-k		thy **274.** 8

Tait name of a goddess **91.** 5

Tafneχtθ a proper name **185.** 5; **186.** 13; **192.** 9; **196.** 3; **204.** 1; **220.** 6

Taruṭ a proper name **84.** 11

ta ḥet' to dawn **3.** 1

Ta-χaā-āā a proper name **79.** 1

taś boundary **109.** 11; **110.** 3; **114.** 9; **115.** 1; **175.** 9; plur. **173.** 2

Ta-śere a proper name **76.** 7

Ta-qāḥti name of a city **153.** 1

tat āat the great council, chief governors of a town (?) **329.** 4, 8; **330.** 13

Ta-tenen an ancient god **75.** 1; **172.** 7; **182.** 11

Ta-tehen a fortress near Memphis **195.** 11

tȧa, tȧat emanation **82.** 13; **83.** 2; **119.** 10; **184.** 9

tȧt hieroglyphics (?) **116.** 3

tām to put on **239.** 3

tu thou, thee **51.** 5; **80.** 3; **250.** 8; **251.** 2; **263.** 4

tu one **31.** 9; **326.** 10

tu their (?) **170.** 8; **174.** 3, 4

tu sign of the passive 10. 2

tu-ȧ , I, me 6. 10; 17. 3; 21. 7; 291. 10; 325. 12

tui that 64. 11

tut thou 7. 7; 36. 5

tup a species of cattle 167. 2

Tubaχet a district in Syria 276. 5

tun we 136. 11

Tunep a city in Northern Syria 135. 7

turpu a species of goose 167. 13

tut to assemble 226. 7; to establish 161. 12; to form 59. 11; customary 235. 13; doubly established 125. 6; to look fixedly 65. 1

tut , image, statue, form, likeness 40. 8; 54. 6; 83. 9; 202. 8; 215. 11; 300. 2; 310. 7; plur. , images, statues 112. 1; 149. 10; 153. 4; 154. 7

tutu , one 30. 6; 315. 9; likewise, moreover 138. 7; 230. 11

tebui sandals 183. 4

tebha name of a fiend 51. 12; 52. 5

tebt brick, ingot 179. 7

tepȧ breathing 131. 12

tepḥet cavern, hole 130. 10

tef divine emanation, watery abyss, essence (?) 63. 10; 67. 5, 6; 83. 5

tef , father 42. 7; 107. 1; 124. 2; 134. 8; 140. 10

teftef to be profuse with 260. 12

tem, temiθ , ; ***temtu, temθ*** , all, whole, the whole, entire 54. 1; 65. 3; 71. 6; 72. 7; 125. 3

tem , , ; ***temt*** not, without 9. 8; 10. 6, 10; 20. 7; 66. 1; 135. 12; 139. 5; 247. 6; 265. 10; 293. 7

temit so that not 5. 12; the non-existent, *i. e.*, the dead 173. 8

temu to come to an end 245. 3

temu mortals 305. 4

temt the base of a statue, sledge 237. 6

Tem , name of a god 40. 8; 111. 8; 141. 12; 171. 2; 184. 10; 214. 3

Temu name of a god 297. 13

Temu-Ḥeru-χuti Tmu-Harmachis 301. 2

Temu-χeperȧ Tmu-Kheperȧ 214. 9; 305. 5

ten this 50. 3; 103. 12

ten you, your 43. 7

ten , to distinguish, to be distinguished 297. 13; to tarry 47. 11; where (?) 137. 1

tenȧ maturity **244.** 9

tenemem , to turn back, to tread, to depart **59.** 4 ; **60.** 2 ; **121.** 10

Tenen name of a god **50.** 10 ; **51.** 2

ten abundant in **295.** 11

tennu , great, how great!, how many **50.** 12 ; **53.** 11 ; **193.** 3 ; **196.** 2 ; **279.** 7 ; **280.** 7, 10 ; **281.** 4 ; very great one **54.** 12 ; very numerous **55.** 2

tennu perfect **256.** 1 ; **270.** 9 ; **273.** 6

tennu , of every sort and kind **216.** 5 ; each, every **2.** 7 ; **232.** 13

tennu weakness, failure **245.** 8

Tennu name of a nation **293.** 10

teni each **153.** 10 ; **154.** 5

tenten strength **66.** 2

tenťat throne **172.** 8

trȧ , time, season **3.** 12 ; **32.** 7 ; **58.** 3 ; **64.** 2 ; **127.** 2 ; **221.** 5 ; **222.** 1 ; **321.** 1 ; at the time, when **241.** 1 ; *trȧiu* (?) the two seasons or times, *i. e.*, the rising and setting of the sun **51.** 9 ; plur. **131.** 11 ; **234.** 6 ; festival times **157.** 11

trȧ neb always **227.** 1

trȧ en ruha eventide **8.** 5

trȧt toe, claw 284. 3

teh
teha
teha } to attack, to invade, to transgress, invasion, invader 17. 13; 146. 12; 173.3; 180.6; 222.11; 241. 4; to transgress an ordinance 253. 10

tehai to break into 309. 13; 312. 4; 314. 9; 315. 5; 324. 2

tehet transgression 246. 9

tehan to appoint to a rank or dignity 25. 11

tehem to drive cattle 3. 4

teheni to dedicate 161. 11

Teḥuti the god Thoth 40. 7; 81. 10; 303. 11

Teḥutit festival of Thoth 131. 8

Teḥuti-em-ḥeb a proper name 43. 10

teχu to be filled with drink 180. 13

teχu a wine-bibber, a heavy drinker 242. 5

teχenui two obelisks 120. 12; 122. 10; 124. 1

teχteχ confused chatterings 292. 5

teχteχ to be hard or difficult (?) 293. 3

Tes Aphroditopolis 257. 5

teś to depart 50. 8

teken — to enter into, to walk 257. 2; 264. 13; 265. 9; 266. 10; goer in 163. 12; a going in 265. 3

tekeni

tet (or *tut*) likewise 233. 3

Tetȧ a king of the VIth dynasty 96. 9

Ṭ

ṭaȧr restraint, to be held in check 241. 7; 247. 7; 264. 12

Ṭaȧnȧuna name of a nation 173. 4

ṭaāu bread 101. 2

ṭab fig tree 101. 12

ṭȧbi wolves 276. 10

ṭā, ṭāu , , to give, to let, to allow, to cause, to hand over, to permit, to put, to place 5. 7; 49. 3; 108. 6

ṭā ānχ ṭeṭ usr giver of life, stability, and power 114. 6. As examples of used as an auxiliary compare 7. 13; 8. 10; 10. 10; 11. 3; 11. 8; 13. 4; 135. 12; 194. 10

ṭāṭā , see , 118. 8; 121. 9; 127. 6; 187. 8; 197. 5; 262. 5

ṭāt to give, to allow, giver, act of giving, gift 3. 3; 10. 10; 36. 5; 87. 10; 262. 12

ṭāi, ṭāit gift **17**. 9; **47**. 9; act of giving or making **5**. 10

ṭāṭāt to give, act of giving, gifts **130**. 9; **249**. 13

ṭāṭ-em-àb to set in the mind **235**. 3

ṭā met to correct **234**. 8

ṭā-nif to spare the life of any one **332**. 7

ṭāt reχ to inform **191**. 8

ṭā-sa to give the back, *i. e.*, to yield **189**. 10

ṭu, ***ṭut*** mountain, quarry **65**. 9; **109**. 7; **124**. 8; **147**. 5; **176**. 8; **276**. 12; stone **123**. 4; plur. **149**. 7

Ṭut-Ḥeru-nub "Mountain of the golden Horus" **107**. 7

Ṭut-en-χer-āba name of a place **212**. 11

ṭu, ***ṭut*** evil, harm, calamity, accident, sorry plight **51**. 6; **55**. 9; **82**. 9; **177**. 8; **257**. 11; evil one **55**. 9

ṭua ⋆ five **6**. 7; **45**. 7; **232**. 1

ṭua ḥeru renpit the festival of the five epagomenal days **112**. 9

ṭua, ***ṭuau*** to praise, praise, to sing hymns to **70**. 11; **128**. 9; **142**. 9; **294**. 8

ṭua compliment **258**. 8

ṭua to rise early, to watch **128**. 9

ṭua, **ṭuau, ṭuaut** — dawn, daybreak, sunrise, morning 4. 5; 64. 6; 153. 10; 193. 1; to-morrow 259. 11

ṭuat, ṭuȧt, **ṭuaut** — the underworld 62. 4; 67. 4; 83. 9; 132. 11; 133. 9; 142. 7; 203. 2; 159. 1

ṭun — to slay, to sacrifice 215. 9

ṭun (?) — to employ oneself 250. 11

ṭuni — to lift, to ascend 288. 1

ṭi — to wait, to stand still, to remain 13. 12; 20. 1; 48. 4; 54. 4; 55. 3; 195. 7

ṭi meḥ — to stand full of 207. 7

Ṭiauasa — the month Dios 226. 4; 230. 8

Ṭeb — name of a city in Upper Egypt 84. 13

ṭebu — leather workers 288. 12

ṭebu — to equip, to provide with 172. 9; 222. 4

ṭebu — payment, reward 96. 7; 229. 1

ṭebui — wooden sarcophagus 315. 7

ṭebiut — wheels 289. 3

ṭeben — to revolve 69. 13

ṭebḥ — to pray, to beseech, prayer 42. 2; 288. 6

ṭebḥeṭet prayer 118. 6

ṭep (?) measure 157. 2

Ṭep a sacred lake at Thebes 189. 6

ṭep , to taste, taste 195. 6

ṭep taste, the sense of taste 245. 5; 277. 6; 286. 10

ṭep , head 45. 3; 51. 7; 73. 11; 74. 9; plur. 90. 13; as one man 183. 11; heads of a book, chapters 279. 12

ṭep , , , beginning, at the beginning 82. 12; 110. 13; 131. 10; first [born] 77. 1; first 42. 8; 78. 2; 107. 7; 118. 4; 121. 5; 128. 2; the best, the finest 121. 11; 189. 2; finest (horses) of the stable 215. 12; the best of every thing 217. 7; the chief or best wife 71. 11; of the highest consideration 254. 7; the very finest speech that can be imagined 246. 7; the very best (metal) 120. 13

ṭep the best things 217. 13; prime, fine (trees) 35. 1

ṭep , chief, governor 34. 4; 206. 13; 264. 2; captive chiefs 227. 10; chief in command 272. 1

ṭep-ā of old 58. 1

ṭepāu

ṭepu-āu

ṭepu-ā

} ancestors, those who lived in olden time 116. 5; 184. 9; 274. 5

ṭepu-ā ancestral dwellings 118. 11

ṭep per first month of the *pert* season 225. 3

ṭep renpit festival of the beginning of the year 112. 6 = τὰ γενέθλια birthday festival 226. 4

ṭep ṭuaut the earliest time of day 178. 10

ṭep upon 120. 8; *ṭepu* those upon 129. 4

ṭep ta he that is on the earth, *i. e.*, the living 112. 10

ṭep ṭu he that is on the mountain, *i. e.*, the dead 112. 11

ṭep ṭu-f he on his mountain, *i. e.*, Anubis 126. 8

Ṭep-àḥet name of a city (Aphroditopolis) 71. 13; 91. 1

ṭep-re
ṭepi-re
ṭept-re
ṭept reṭ
rule, law, decree, ordinance, manner of acting 75. 1; 108. 13; 113. 5; 121. 9; 183. 11; 208. 6; 249. 7; 290. 13; 293. 12; 300. 4

Ṭepur a city in Syria 281. 9

ṭepḥut cavern, hole, chamber 83. 4

ṭept boat 123. 11

ṭefa overflowing, benevolent 242. 10

ṭem to declare, to proclaim 132. 1

ṭemamu a class of men 163. 9

ṭemau choirs of singing men and women 239. 6

ṭemȧ
ṭemȧit
ṭemȧt
} town, city, village, homestead 5. 4; 8. 11; 30. 11; 31. 11; 46. 5; 134. 10; 196. 10; plur. , 174. 11; 281. 6

ṭemȧu to join, to unite 183. 3

ṭemu to slaughter, to massacre 175. 10

ṭemseb (?) 239. 9

ṭemt slaughter 20. 13

ṭemtu to sharpen a knife 11. 3

ṭemṭ total 114. 13

ṭemṭ
ṭemṭi
} all, entire 165. 4; 171. 8; 185. 9; 192. 6

ṭenȧ a share 231. 8

ṭenȧ basket 225. 9

ṭenȧt festival of the first and last quarter of the moon 299. 1

ṭennu each and every, number, many 175. 13; 177. 1

ṭennu division 124. 5

ṭenḥ wing 174. 5; 175. 11

ṭensmen heavy, weighty 286. 2; 292. 11

ṭeneset weight (?), to burden oneself 324. 6

ṭer to harvest 251. 8

ṭer to be injured, thrown down 310. 6

ṭer to beat into shape 296. 8; to destroy 80. 13; 94. 2; to lay waste a country 102. 6, 12; subduer 40. 9; conqueror, destroyer 126. 4; 130. 2

ṭerp , to make an offering 206. 4; to pour out a libation 211. 2

ṭehan to salute 38. 10

ṭehen to praise 113. 4

ṭeheni to dedicate, to inscribe 171. 6

ṭeḥȧ cringing 261. 6

ṭeḥer fear, terror 221. 11

ṭeχut rough stones 283. 3; 284. 13

ṭeχen tambourines 94. 9

ṭes a vessel full of drink 127. 12

ṭes stone knife 304. 4; plur. 241. 3

ṭes self 187. 3; 194. 9; 214. 4

ṭeś fiends 55. 8

ṭeś to pierce (?) 275. 5

ṭeśert the red crown 123. 8

ṭeśert the red, sandy desert 41. 3; 125. 8

ṭeḳa to plant **160.** 11; to be planted with trees **148.** 1; to overlay with gold, inlaid **156.** 12; **158.** 7; **161.** 2

ṭeḳa plants **150.** 12; **153.** 18; **158.** 1; fruit, branches **162.** 2; blossoms, grapes **164.** 5

Ṭeḳar a city in Syria **280.** 12

Ṭeḳareȧaire a city in Syria **280.** 12

ṭeḳas to pass through **276.** 7; **279.** 5; **290.** 4

ṭeḳu to be hidden **246.** 13

ṭet **114.** 10

ṭet hand **9.** 9; **230.** 3; plur. **300.** 1

ṭet , chariot pole, axle (?) **285.** 8, 11; **289.** 2, 4

ṭeṭ hand **217.** 3

ṭeṭ to give **100.** 12; **103.** 13;

ṭeṭ, ṭeṭu , to be firm, stable, stability **78.** 10; **108.** 6; **116.** 12

Ṭeṭ the stable one, name of a god **74.** 12

ṭeṭṭeṭ to be established **40.** 8; established **93.** 6

Ṭeṭṭu, Ṭeṭṭet , *Ṭeṭṭeṭ* a name given to the cities Busiris and Mendes **75.** 7; **83.** 13; **84.** 2; the celestial Tattu **93.** 6

ṭeṭem seedlings **162.** 4

TH (θ)

θ thou, thee 46. 4; 50. 7; 68. 5

θȧireȧa door 34. 11; 35. 5

θȧire-qaire a city in Syria 282. 7

θȧmenti a city in Syria 281. 9

θȧχisa a city in Syria 281. 8

θȧs to sit 54. 6

θāu to run 12. 11

θu to declare 39. 9

θu to mount 141. 1

θufi papyrus plants 162. 4

θut unśȧu a species of plant 285. 2

θireȧa door 147. 7; plur. 151. 7; 152. 5

θiθi to dispute 323. 6

θebut, *θebt* sandals 101. 1; 103. 8

θebt sandal-bearer 103. 4

θef to move about excitedly 278. 3

θen course 231. 13; 233. 11

θen ye, you, your 43. 8; 123. 3; 129. 9, 10; 189. 4

θen this 234. 12

θenu each 101. 7; 102. 7

θennu each 41. 8

θen
θennu to distinguish, to be distinguished 108. 1; 113. 1; 114. 4; 117. 9

θennu how great! 191. 4

θenre to work diligently 6. 10; mighty deeds 142. 9; 144. 3; 156. 10; 292. 7

θen-tu weight, quantity 125. 3

θent-remu name of a city 218. 4

θent-reti a proper name 78. 10

θent-ḥetrȧ cavalry 25. 5; 188. 9

θenθen to flee, to run 286. 3

θer conqueror 189. 8; 224. 10

θereri mounds thrown up round a city 197. 8

θerθer earthworks 208. 13

θeḥen to meet 19. 9

θeḥen, θeḥin yellow-coloured, crystal (?) 52. 12; 86. 13

θeḥennu name of a nation 188. 12

θeḥeḥut divine beings who rejoice 90. 12

θeḥent yellow-coloured 126. 4; 130. 2

θes to be exalted, to mount up, to ascend, to climb, high 69. 13; 196. 12; 202. 12; 213. 11; 229. 1; 276. 12

θes to lift up, to pardon 201. 6; 222. 2

θesi ascent 277. 4

θesu statements 292. 4; proverbs, precepts 246. 4; 268. 1

θesu canals (?) 105. 13

θes to tie, to tie on, to bind 72. 6; 96. 8; 154. 4; 213. 9; 289. 8

θes to set in battle array 187. 12

θes captain 187. 10, 11; 190. 8

θest companies of men, soldiers, troops 97. 12; 100. 8; 101. 7; 102. 2, 7; 191. 1; 210. 8

θes χas of a disgusting nature 257. 7

θesu to come, to arrive 254. 12

θesemu dog 310. 9; plur. 185. 10

θesem

θesemet towers on a wall, bastions 176. 10; 207. 5; 208. 4

θeset — a country in or beyond Nubia **102.** 13

θesti — teeth **73.** 9

θek — , thee, thou **182.** 4; **215.** 7

θekanś — a city near Oxyrhynchus **185.** 13

θet — writing, book **43.** 5

θet — to remove, to omit a word **272.** 6

θet per ānχ — scribes or authors of books **239.** 8

θet en ḥrȧ — to carry on in front (?) **186.** 13

θetu — leather sandals **27.** 2

θetet (?) — ,

θetetu (?)

θeteθ — to plunder **101.** 2; to carry off, to take possession of **82.** 3; **299.** 12; something stolen **109.** 10; to undertake to do something **266.** 1; vanquisher **41.** 4

θettaa — to reverse **106.** 11

θet-taui — name of a district **185.** 8; **205.** 5

θeθḥeḥtu — rejoicings **70.** 2

TCH.

t́a — governor, mayor of a city **215.** 2

t́a — phallus, male, male child, son **51.** 2; **53.** 1; **68.** 7; begetter, to impregnate with seed **67.** 10; **75.** 11; plur. males, men **239.** 7; male horses

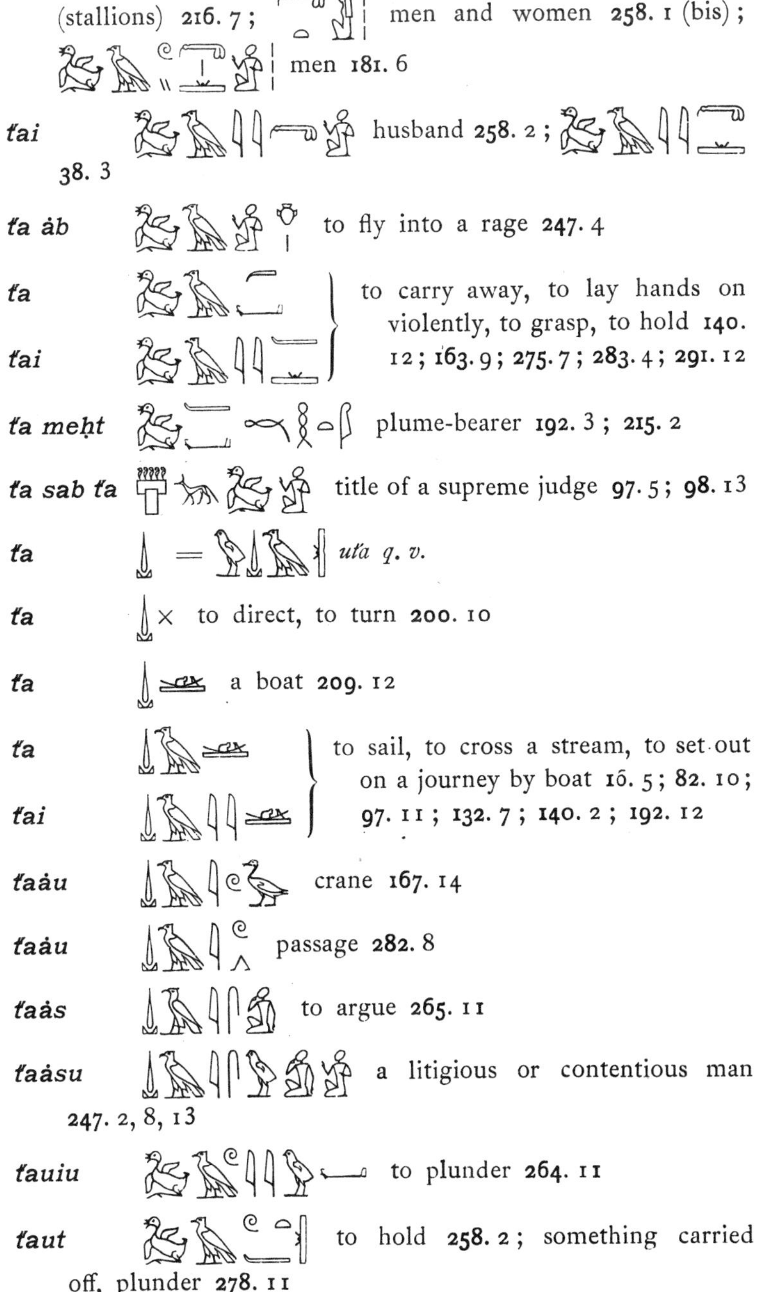

(stallions) 216. 7 ; men and women 258. 1 (bis) ; men 181. 6

ťai husband 258. 2 ; 38. 3

ťa àb to fly into a rage 247. 4

ťa / **ťai** to carry away, to lay hands on violently, to grasp, to hold 140. 12 ; 163. 9 ; 275. 7 ; 283. 4 ; 291. 12

ťa meḥt plume-bearer 192. 3 ; 215. 2

ťa sab ťa title of a supreme judge 97. 5 ; 98. 13

ťa = *uťa q. v.*

ťa to direct, to turn 200. 10

ťa a boat 209. 12

ťa / **ťai** to sail, to cross a stream, to set out on a journey by boat 16. 5 ; 82. 10 ; 97. 11 ; 132. 7 ; 140. 2 ; 192. 12

ťaàu crane 167. 14

ťaàu passage 282. 8

ťaàs to argue 265. 11

ťaàsu a litigious or contentious man 247. 2, 8, 13

ťauiu to plunder 264. 11

ťaut to hold 258. 2 ; something carried off, plunder 278. 11

t̕aut to be engraved **147.** 10

t̕aut wrong **260.** 7

t̕aut twenty **39.** 12; twenty-two **42.** 6; **49.** 6; twenty-six **44.** 4; **49.** 6

t̕ait iniquity **249.** 1

t̕ai to traverse **277.** 4

t̕aire guide **284.** 6

T̕aire Tyre **279.** 9

T̕aireāu a city in Syria **279.** 13

T̕airepuθȧ Sarepta **279.** 6

t̕aba soldiers **284.** 6; **289.** 12

t̕am foreskin **117.** 5

t̕am sceptre **266.** 11; sceptre of the North and South **103.** 4

T̕am name of a country **100.** 1

t̕am, *t̕amu* young men, young people, raw soldiers **1 8.** 10; **152.** 7; **172.** 10; **173.** 11; **189.** 13; **243.** 1

t̕amaāu papyrus **166.** 8

t̕an = governor **244.** 4

t̓anna despair 284. 11

t̓ar abomination, horribleness 221. 3

T̓are Tyre 276. 1

t̓arei mason 330. 9

t̓areinat lance (?) 140. 12

t̓art to be strong 65. 7

t̓akaire shutters, lattices 147. 12

T̓akire name of a nation 173. 5

T̓ah, T̓aha , a country in Syria 134. 5; 148. 8; 164. 10

t̓at , captain, officer, governor 139. 7; 243. 4; 246. 6; 306. 7; 307. 2; 308. 8; 309. 8; 316. 2; 318. 2

t̓at sound, firm 248. 11

t̓at passage, course 254. 3

t̓at̓a head, the top 17. 6; 18. 7; 19. 3; 21. 8; 284. 11

t̓at̓at divine chiefs 211. 2

t̓at̓aui walled places, walls 176. 9

t̓at̓at suburb, district 161. 7; plur. 165. 6, 12

t̓ā breath, air 259. 5

t̓āu whirlwind, storm 275. 5

t̓ār to seek out, to seek after 265. 8

Tiṭuna Sidon 279. 6

Tiṭipuθȧ a city of Syria 281. 13

t́ebā fingers 43. 9; 195. 6

t́ebā ten thousand 157. 2; plur. , 99. 10; 102. 3; 148. 10; 173. 1

t́ebāt sealed 214. 3

t́ebu boards of a chariot 289. 6

t́ebt name of a chamber 96. 10

t́ef drops 34. 9

t́efa to feed 262. 11; fed 255. 1

t́efau food 63. 7; 132. 2; 145. 12; 296. 7; 305. 2

t́efet́ pupil of the eye 75. 13

t́en round about, near 279. 8

t́er from, since, whilst, when 52. 10; 54. 8; 58. 11; 68. 10; 80. 4; 138. 7; 159. 4; 221. 10; 231. 2; 243. 6; 263. 12; when 10. 2

t́er , all 2. 2; 49. 7; 243. 12

t́erȧu wholly, thoroughly, completely 318. 9; 319. 8; 325. 5

t́er-ā at once, instantly 50. 6; 61. 4; 79. 7; 179. 2

ṫer-baḥ from olden time 99. 6; 103. 12; 55. 4

ṫer-enti because 232. 10

ṫer-entet because 223. 12; 224. 2; 232. 10

ṫer, ṫeru , limit, boundary, bar 68. 3; 246. 12

ṫeru , } limits, borders, boundaries 125. 11; 173. 2; 208. 12; 215. 11

ṫeruu

ṫeru outside (of a building) 311. 3

ṫeru grains 166. 8

ṫerti ancestors, a name given to Isis and Nephthys 32. 8; 49. 4; 306. 11; 315. 2

ṫes own, self 252. 8; 254. 12; for my own self 249. 2; my own name 117. 13; themselves 249. 13; , himself, itself 72. 12; 88. 9; 109. 9; 122. 4; 248. 3

ṫeser (or *ser*) , } to venerate, to make holy, holy 82. 13; 86. 8; 145. 6; 154. 6; 214. 2

ṫeseri, ṫesert ,

Ṫesert the "holy land", *i. e.*, cemetery 314. 5

ṫet body 55. 1; 56. 9; the shaft of an obelisk 124. 11; plur. , 125. 10; 223. 6

ṫetta , ever, eternity 49. 3; 106. 12; 306. 5

t̔eṭ, ***t̔eṭtu*** to speak, to say 3. 6; 7. 6; 93. 10; having spoken 12. 5; to speak unanimousyl 19. 12; to make a report 24. 12; 25. 2; , 79. 1; 84. 11; 229. 13; 232. 7

t̔eṭ word, speech 3. 7; 247. 5; plur. , 50. 4, 5; 53. 9; 58. 7; 62. 12

t̔eṭeṭet something said 270. 7; plur. 182. 6

Ṭeṭ-Ȧmen-ȧf-ānχ a proper name 191. 11

Ṭeṭ-Ȧmen-ȧf-ānχ-ȧ a proper name 218. 4

t̔eṭfet reptiles 83. 3; 300. 10

t̔eṭbu torch 280. 1

t̔eṭna a kind of cloth (?) 287. 6

t̔eṭḥu to imprison, prison, restraint 316. 13

Ṭeṭχiȧu a proper name 219. 4

t̔eṭtu olive trees 162. 6

Words of unknown reading.

89. 7; 99. 11; 101. 6; 101. 7; 102. 10; 103. 6; 105. 2; 105. 2: 245. 12; 296. 8; 298. 11

ERRATA.

On p. 57, l. 18, p. 58, l. 15, p. 59, l. 19, etc., for *māšem* read *šem;* p. 58, l. 12 for read *uat;* p. 80, l. 17 for *kert* read *ket er;* p. 98, l. 2 for read ; p. 102, l. 16 for *ermaā* read *er maā;* p. 107, l. 16 for *nu neḥeḥ* read *en nuḥeḥ;* p. 112, l. 3 for read ; p. 118, l. 20 for *ubut* read *ābut* or *ḥemut;* p. 123, l. 1 for read *reχit;* p. 123, l. 19 for *mutui* read *muti;* p. 124, l. 16 for *fa* read *kat;* p. 125, l. 14 for *χa nem* read *χa-nȧ em sa* (?); p. 125, l. 17 for *em āu* read *em ȧsu;* p. 129, l. 16 for *ḥentui* read *ḥenti;* p. 133, l. 8 for read ; p. 135, l. 14 for *emnai-n* read *em nai-n;* p. 148, l. 18 for *seχeperu* read *seχeperu-ȧ;* p. 165, l. 14 for *setu* read *Sati* or *Satiu;* p. 176, l. 19 for *seqḥu* read *sāqḥu;* p. 191, l. 19 for *Śaśānq* read *Śaśanq;* p. 207, l. 13 for read ; p. 210, l. 4 for read ; p. 242, l. 4 for *trȧ-s χem-nef* read *trȧ seχem-nef;* p. 244, l. 15 for *Ṭuait* read *Sbait;* p. 258, l. 14 for *t'ait* (?) read *t'ait ḥemt* (?), in both places; p. 267, l. 15 for *s-a* read *sba*; p. 278, l. 10 for read ; p. 292, l. 11 for read ; p. 295, l. 19 for *maqeṭ-f* read *mȧ qeṭ-f;* p. 296, l. 6 for read .

A CATALOG OF SELECTED

DOVER BOOKS

IN ALL FIELDS OF INTEREST

A CATALOG OF SELECTED DOVER BOOKS IN ALL FIELDS OF INTEREST

CONCERNING THE SPIRITUAL IN ART, Wassily Kandinsky. Pioneering work by father of abstract art. Thoughts on color theory, nature of art. Analysis of earlier masters. 12 illustrations. 80pp. of text. 5⅜ x 8½. 23411-8 Pa. $3.95

ANIMALS: 1,419 Copyright-Free Illustrations of Mammals, Birds, Fish, Insects, etc., Jim Harter (ed.). Clear wood engravings present, in extremely lifelike poses, over 1,000 species of animals. One of the most extensive pictorial sourcebooks of its kind. Captions. Index. 284pp. 9 x 12. 23766-4 Pa. $12.95

CELTIC ART: The Methods of Construction, George Bain. Simple geometric techniques for making Celtic interlacements, spirals, Kells-type initials, animals, humans, etc. Over 500 illustrations. 160pp. 9 x 12. (USO) 22923-8 Pa. $9.95

AN ATLAS OF ANATOMY FOR ARTISTS, Fritz Schider. Most thorough reference work on art anatomy in the world. Hundreds of illustrations, including selections from works by Vesalius, Leonardo, Goya, Ingres, Michelangelo, others. 593 illustrations. 192pp. 7⅛ x 10¼. 20241-0 Pa. $9 95

CELTIC HAND STROKE-BY-STROKE (Irish Half-Uncial from "The Book of Kells"): An Arthur Baker Calligraphy Manual, Arthur Baker. Complete guide to creating each letter of the alphabet in distinctive Celtic manner. Covers hand position, strokes, pens, inks, paper, more. Illustrated. 48pp. 8¼ x 11. 24336-2 Pa. $3.95

EASY ORIGAMI, John Montroll. Charming collection of 32 projects (hat, cup, pelican, piano, swan, many more) specially designed for the novice origami hobbyist. Clearly illustrated easy-to-follow instructions insure that even beginning papercrafters will achieve successful results. 48pp. 8¼ x 11. 27298-2 Pa. $2.95

THE COMPLETE BOOK OF BIRDHOUSE CONSTRUCTION FOR WOODWORKERS, Scott D. Campbell. Detailed instructions, illustrations, tables. Also data on bird habitat and instinct patterns. Bibliography. 3 tables. 63 illustrations in 15 figures. 48pp. 5¼ x 8½. 24407-5 Pa. $2.50

BLOOMINGDALE'S ILLUSTRATED 1886 CATALOG: Fashions, Dry Goods and Housewares, Bloomingdale Brothers. Famed merchants' extremely rare catalog depicting about 1,700 products: clothing, housewares, firearms, dry goods, jewelry, more. Invaluable for dating, identifying vintage items. Also, copyright-free graphics for artists, designers. Co-published with Henry Ford Museum & Greenfield Village. 160pp. 8¼ x 11. 25780-0 Pa. $9.95

HISTORIC COSTUME IN PICTURES, Braun & Schneider. Over 1,450 costumed figures in clearly detailed engravings–from dawn of civilization to end of 19th century. Captions. Many folk costumes. 256pp. 8⅜ x 11¾. 23150-X Pa. $12.95